# ILLUSTRATIONS

TO THE

# ARMORIAL GÉNÉRAL

V & VI

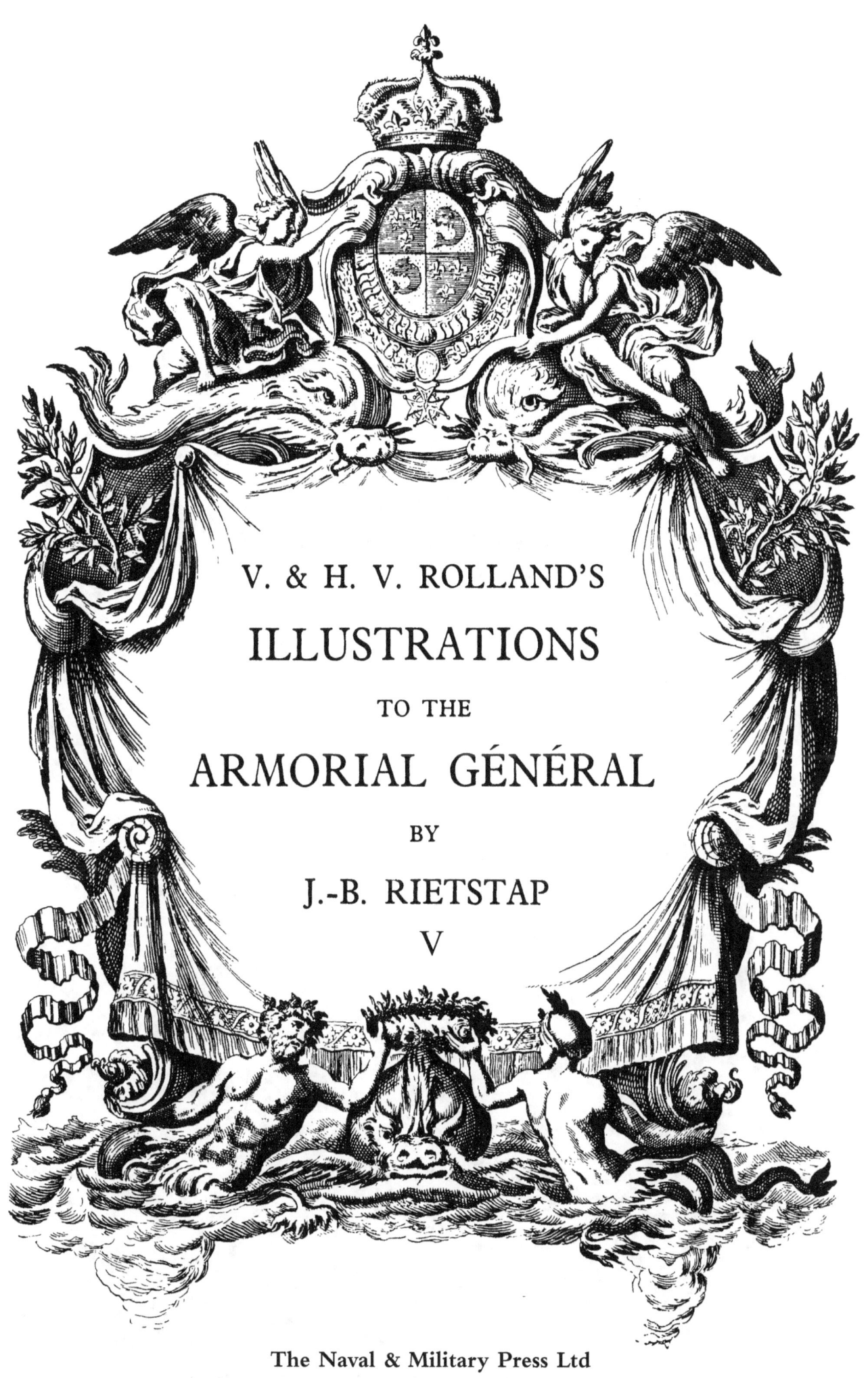

# V. & H. V. ROLLAND'S ILLUSTRATIONS TO THE ARMORIAL GÉNÉRAL BY J.-B. RIETSTAP

V

The Naval & Military Press Ltd

*Published by*

**The Naval & Military Press Ltd**
Unit 10 Ridgewood Industrial Park,
Uckfield, East Sussex,
TN22 5QE England

Tel: +44 (0) 1825 749494
Fax: +44 (0) 1825 765701

www.naval-military-press.com
www.nmarchive.com

*In reprinting in facsimile from the original, any imperfections are inevitably reproduced and the quality may fall short of modern type and cartographic standards.*

Pl. I

| Paal Bav | Paar Aut | Paats Rotterdam | Paats Leyde | Paats van Santhorst Leyde | Paauw Amsterdam | Pabor Silésie |
|---|---|---|---|---|---|---|
| Paborch (va) Brab. | Pabsdorf Saxe | Pabst la Haye | Pabst Prov. rhen | Pabst Nuremberg | Pabst Allem | Pabst (van) van Bingerden Gueldre |
| Pabst d'Erstein & de Bolsenheim Alsace | Pabst d'Ohain Saxe, Prusse | Pabst de Rotersdorf Alsace | Pabst de Staffelfelden Alsace | Pac Lithuani | Pac (au) de Badens la Bastide, Monsac & Lang | Pacaroni Paccaroni Rome, Poitou |
| Paccassy Aut | Paccassy Aut | Paccoton Yverdon | Pace Trevise | Pace Vicence | Pace (ael) Florence | Pace-Dardi (ael) Florence |
| Pace Friedensberg Aut | Pach de Hansenheim Tyrol | Pach de Zellhofen Aut | Pachaly Prusse | Pache Morges (P.de Vaud) | Pache Moudon (Vaud) | Pacheco Castille |
| Pacheco Castille | Pachelbl-Gehag Prusse | Pacheleb d'Ober Walterstorf Aut | Pacher Aut | Pachhamer Bav | Pachi Dalmatie | Pachich Dalmatie |

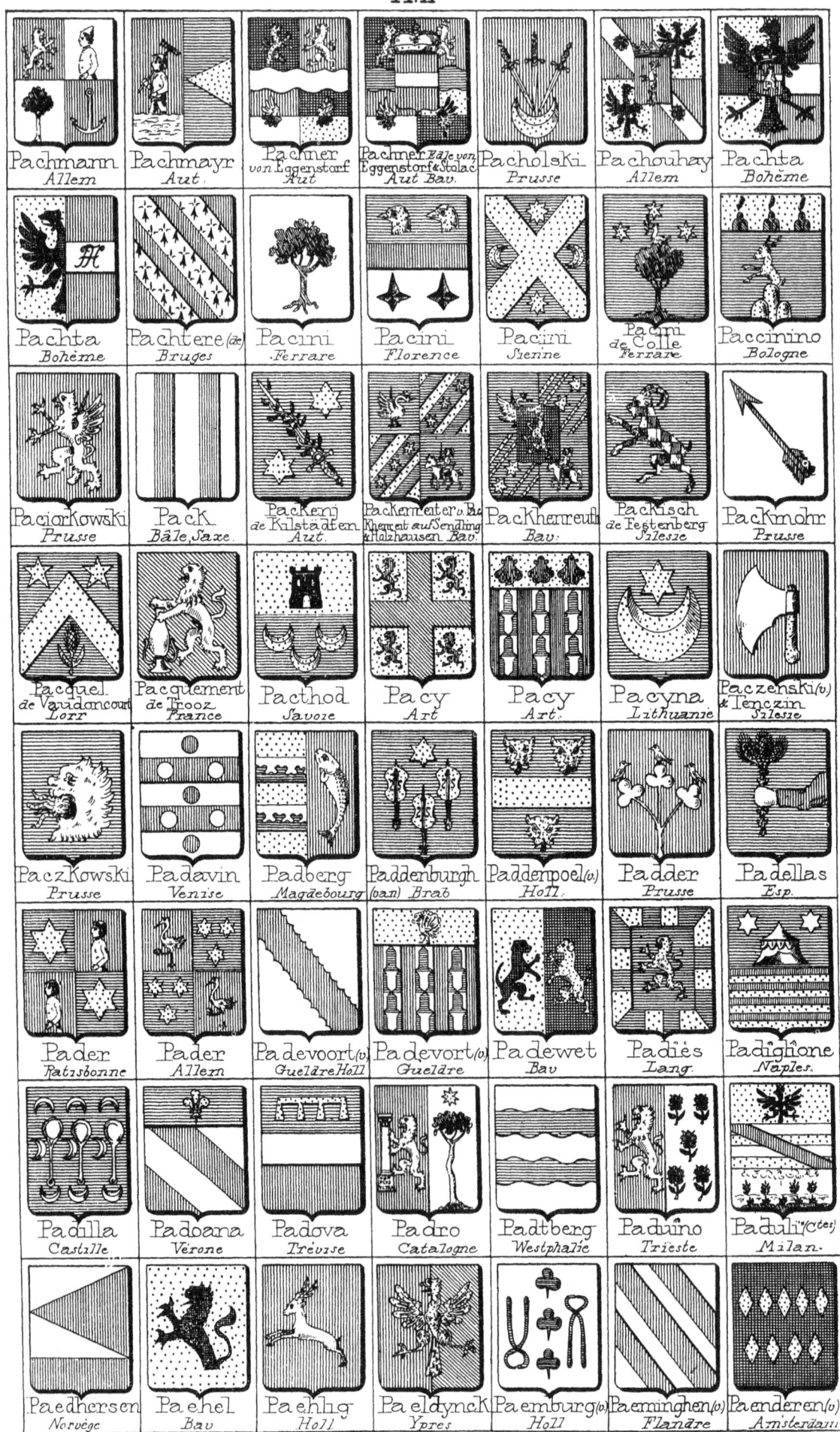

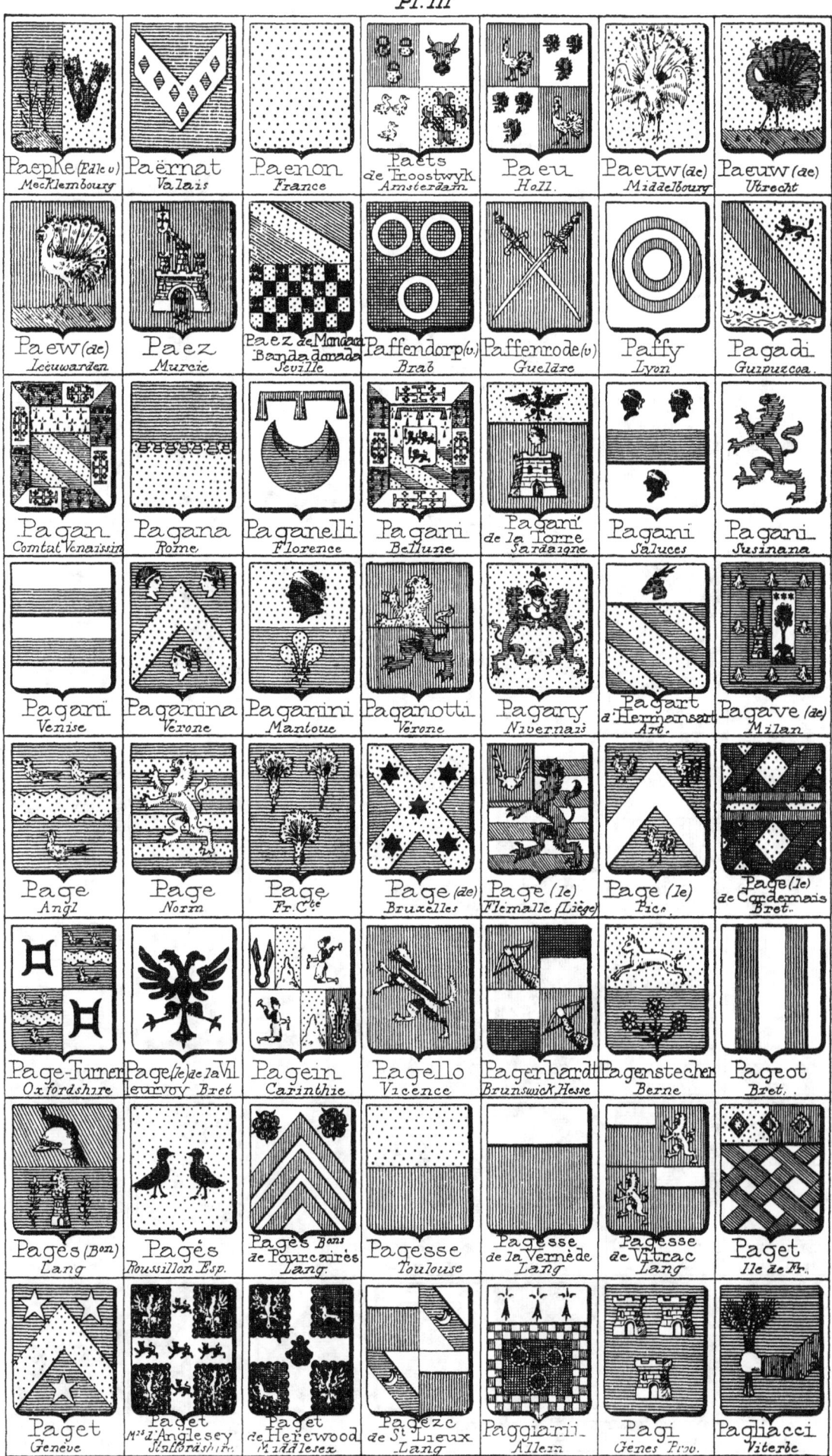

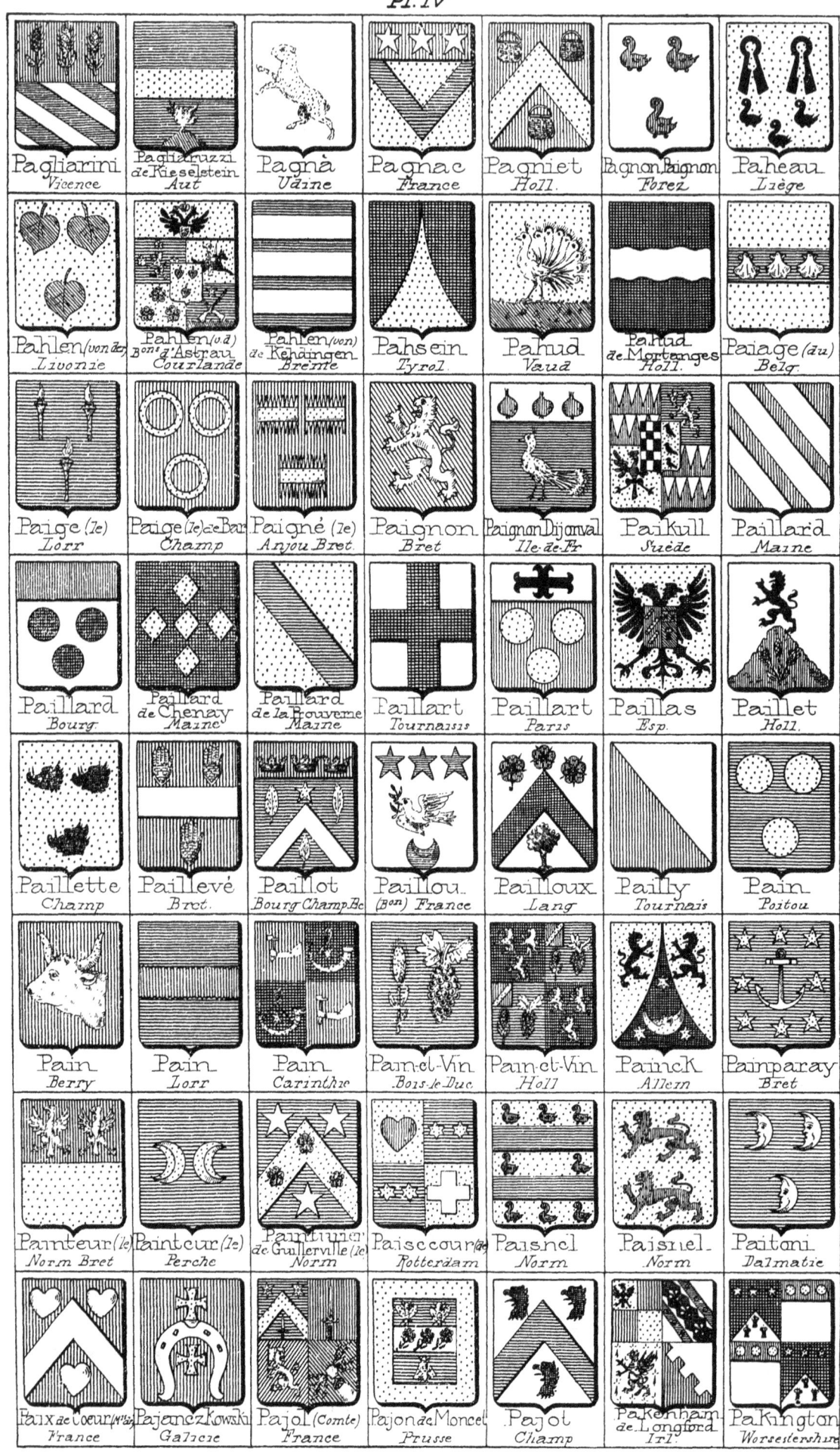

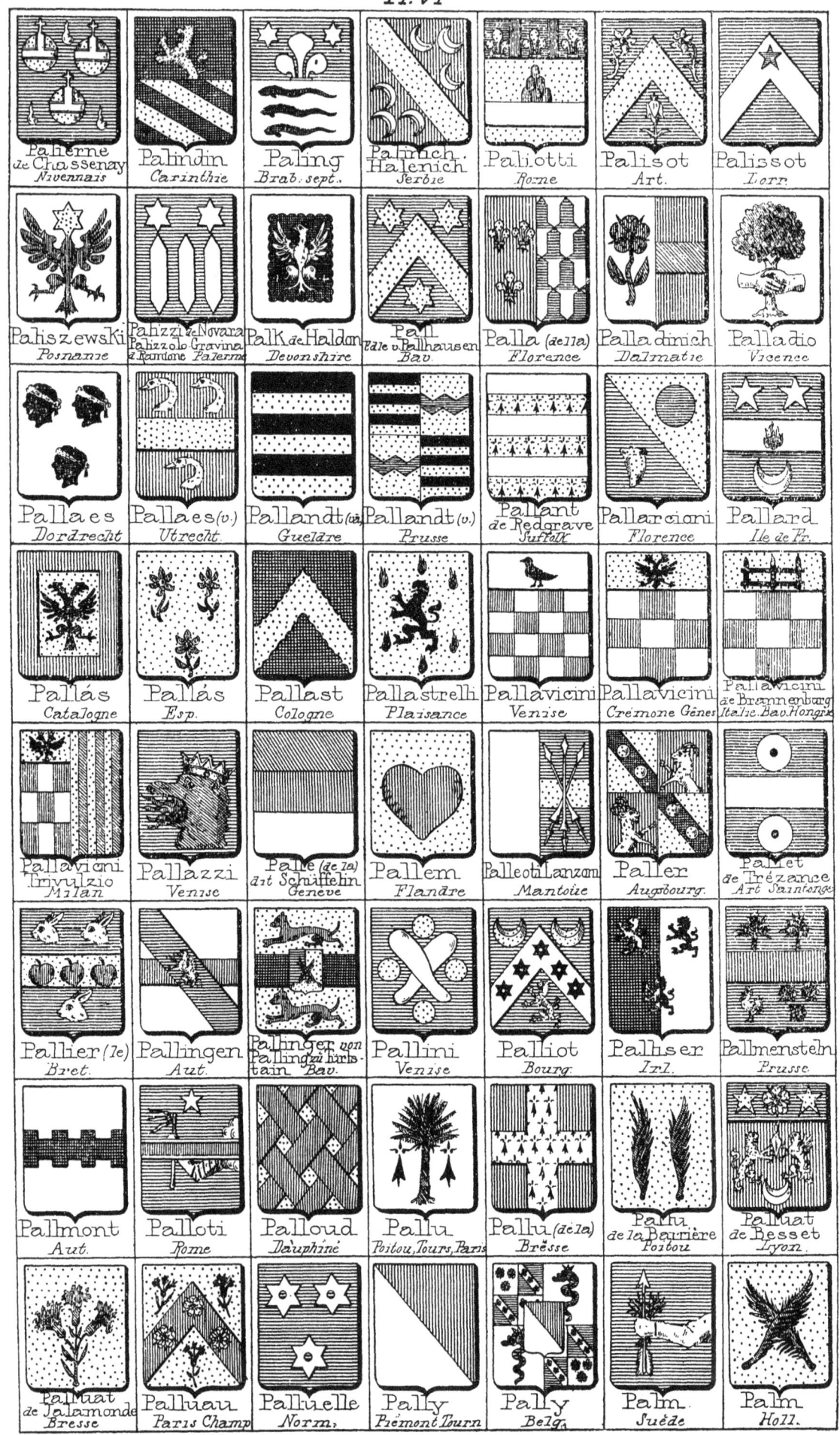

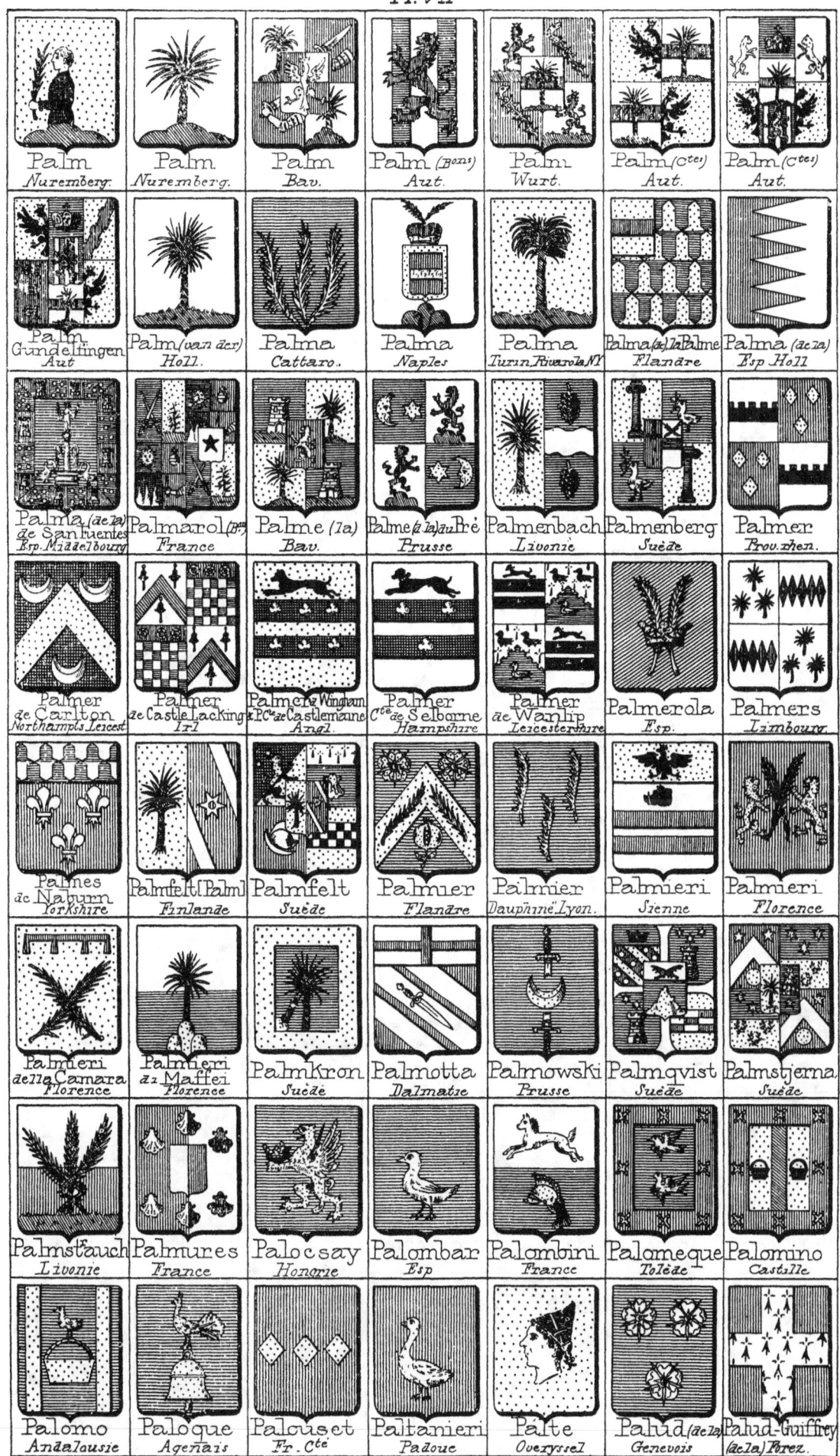

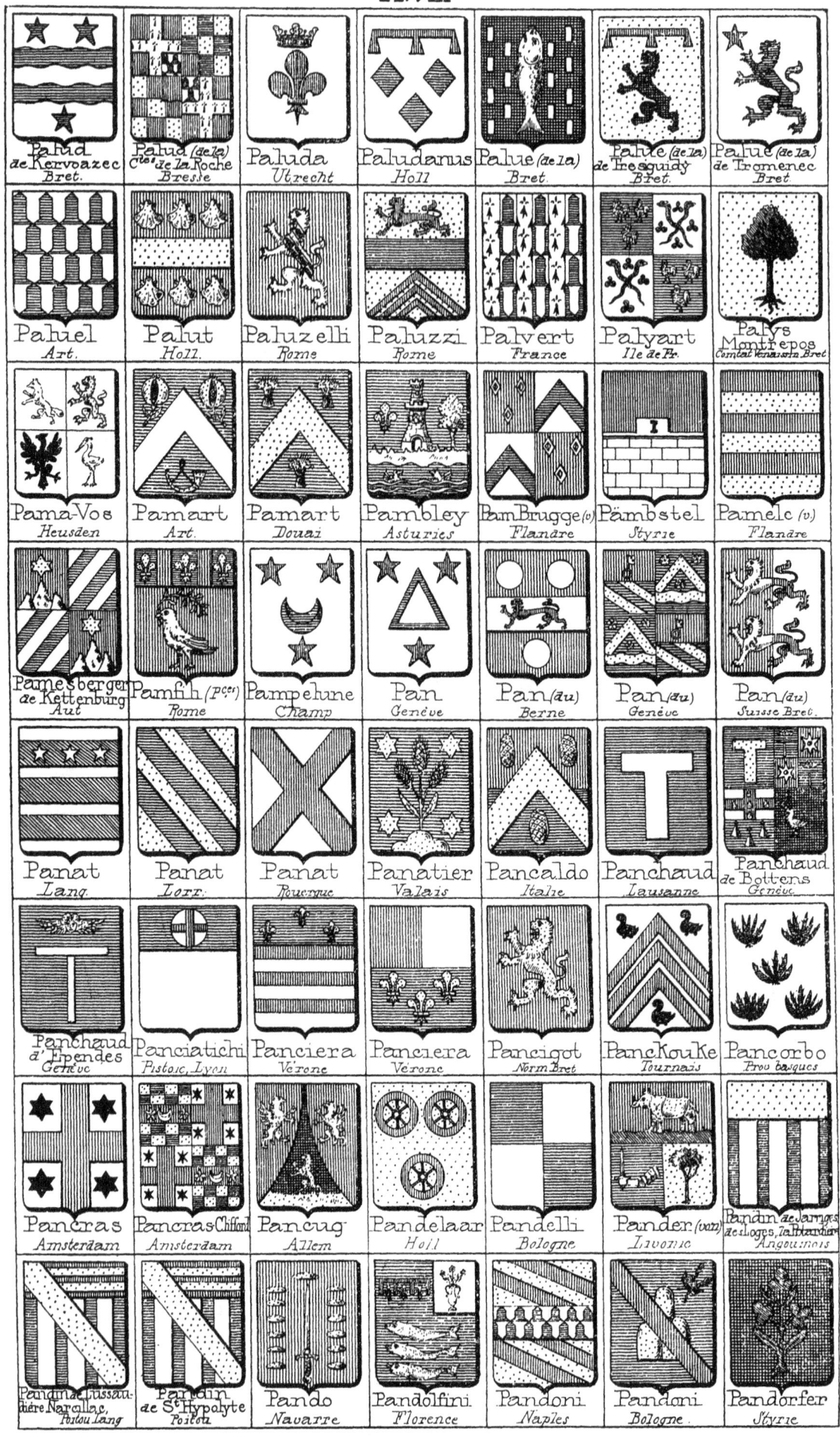

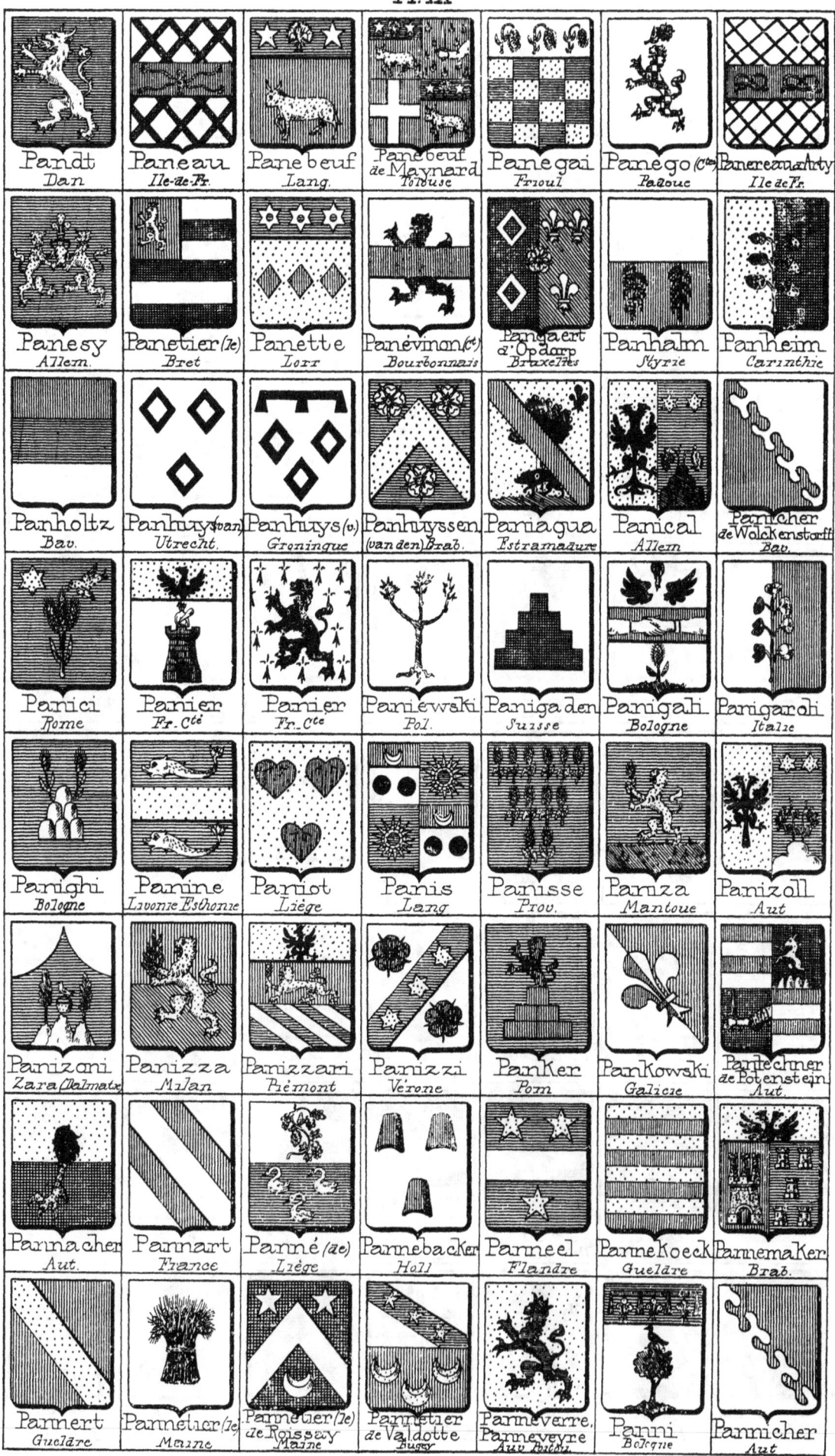

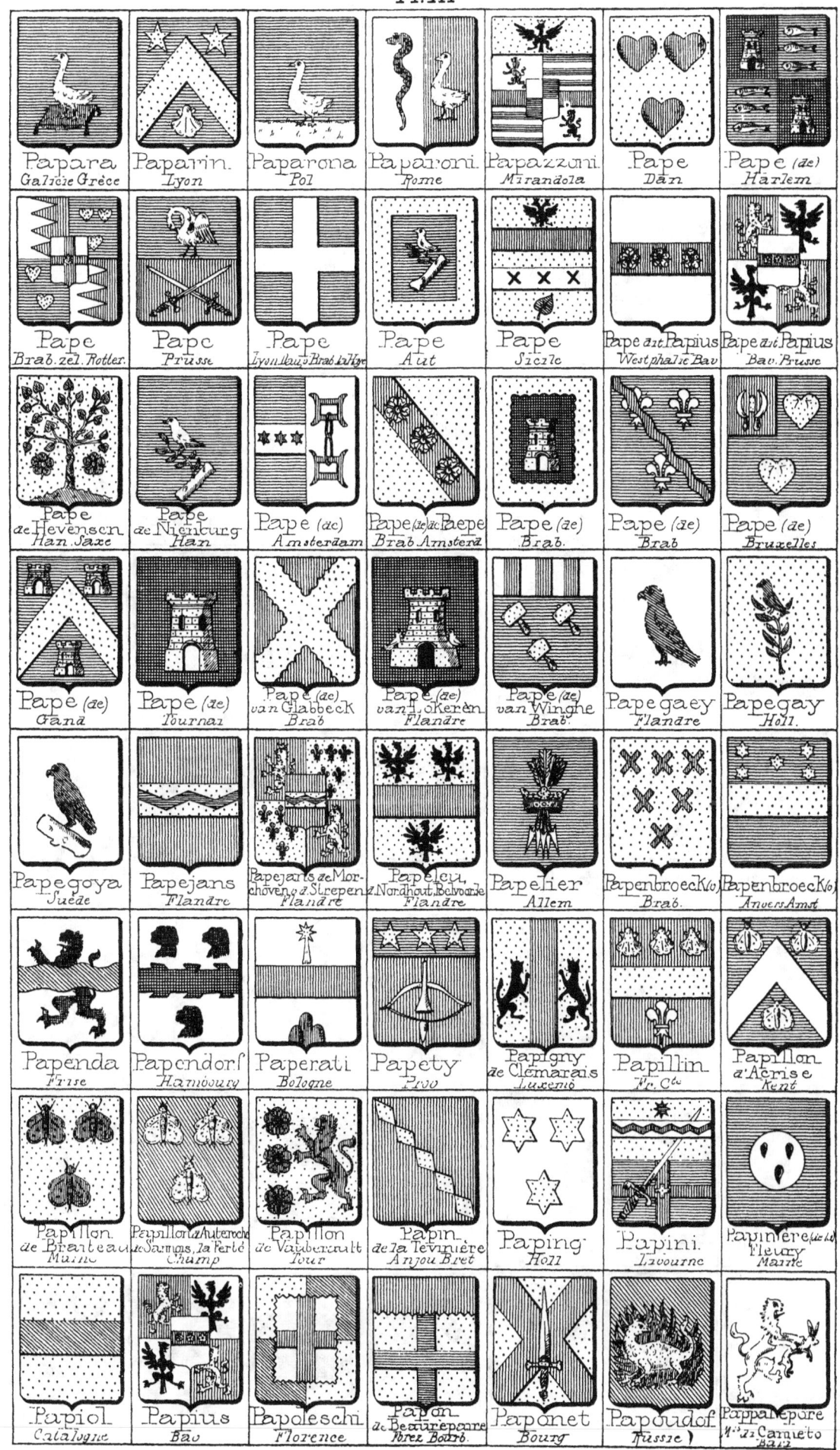

Pl. XIII

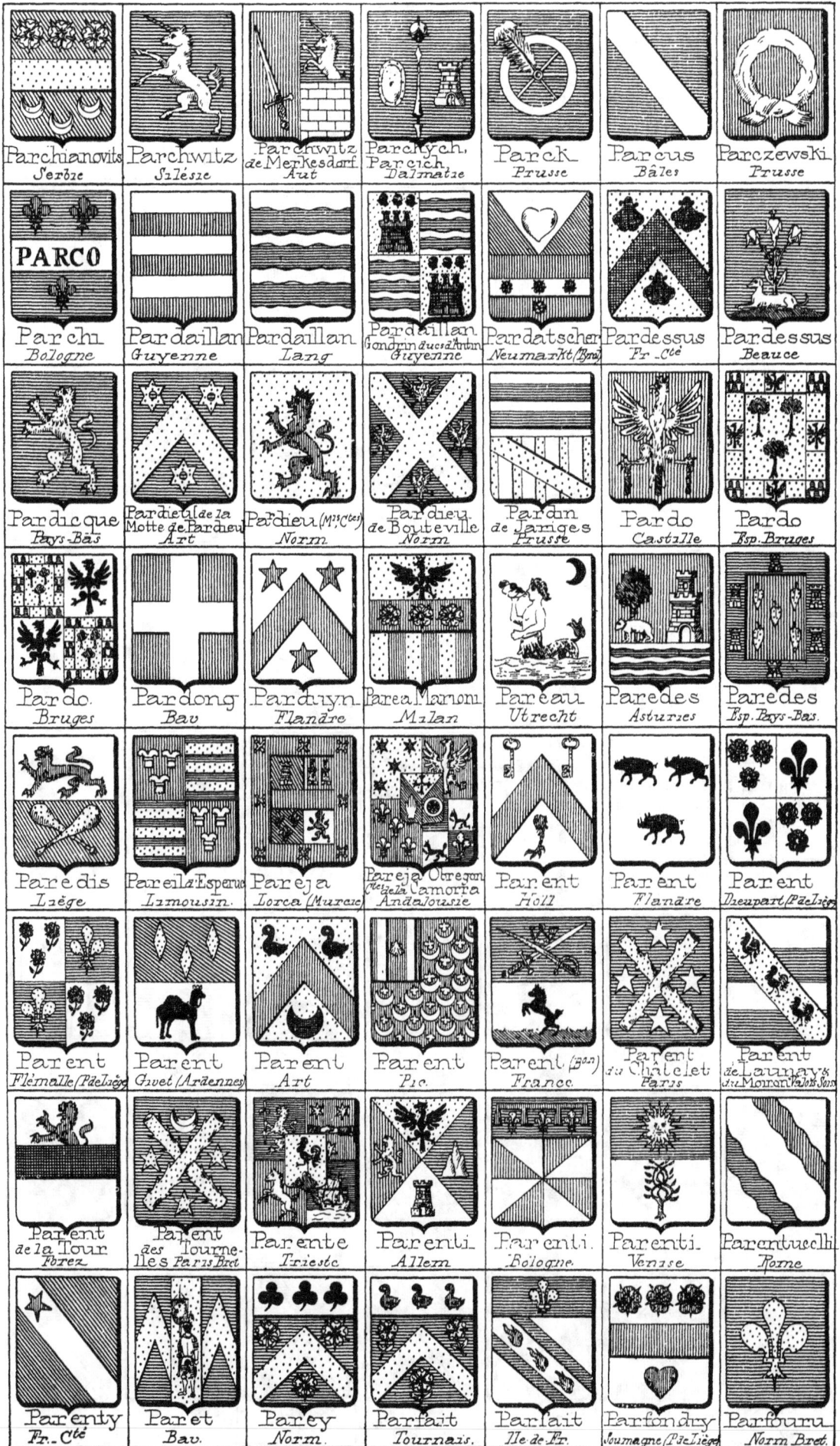

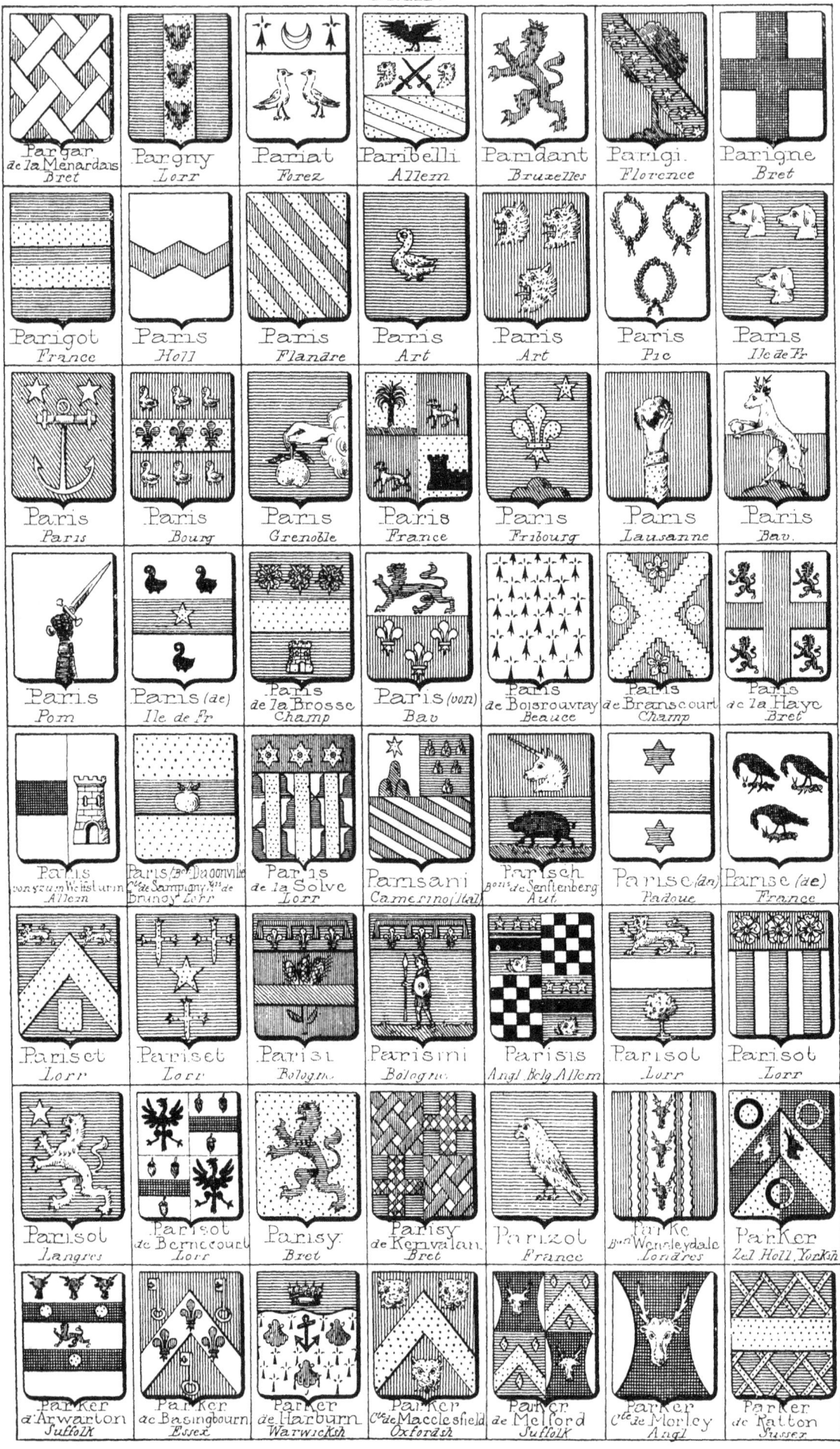

Pl. XV

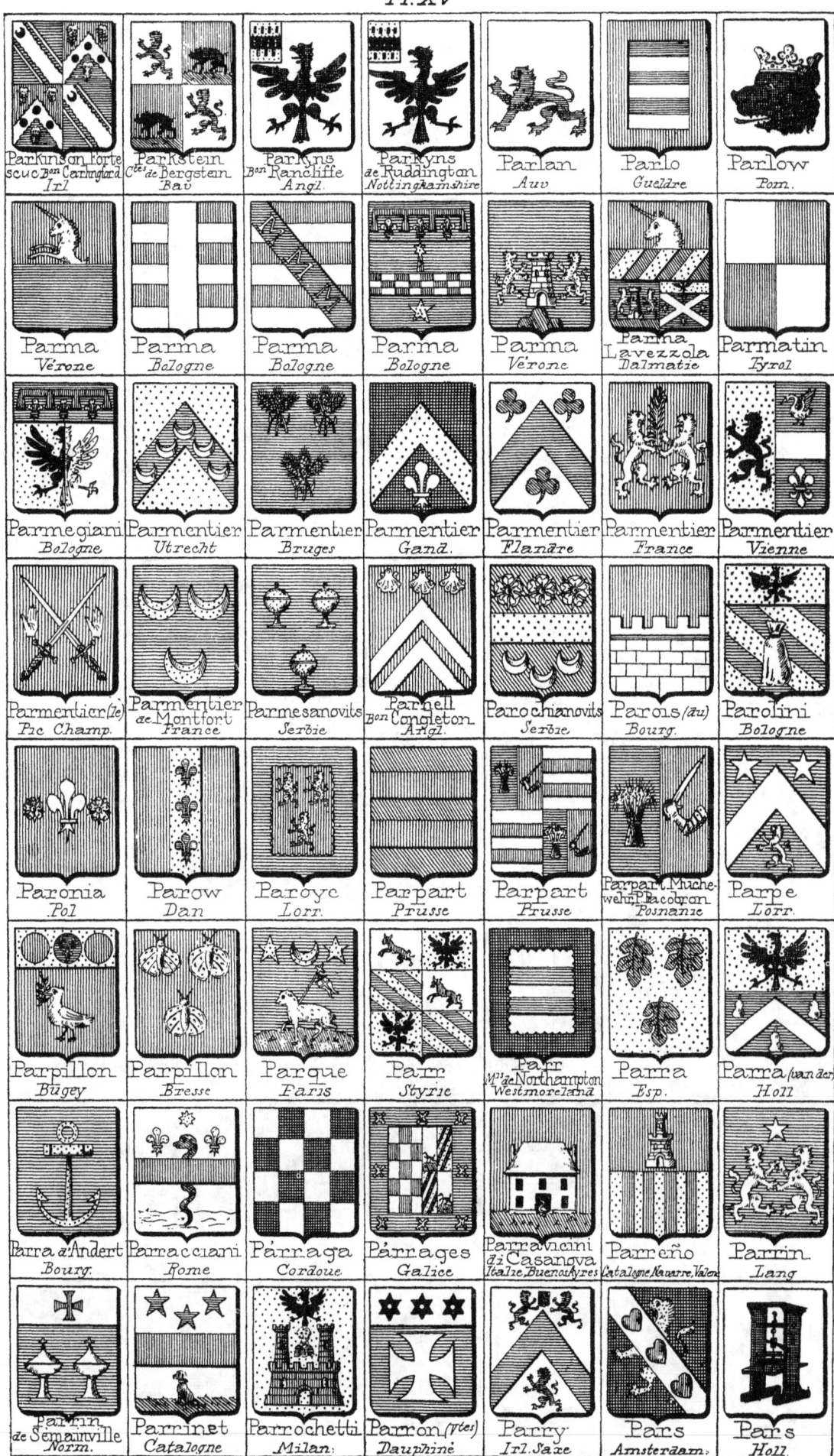

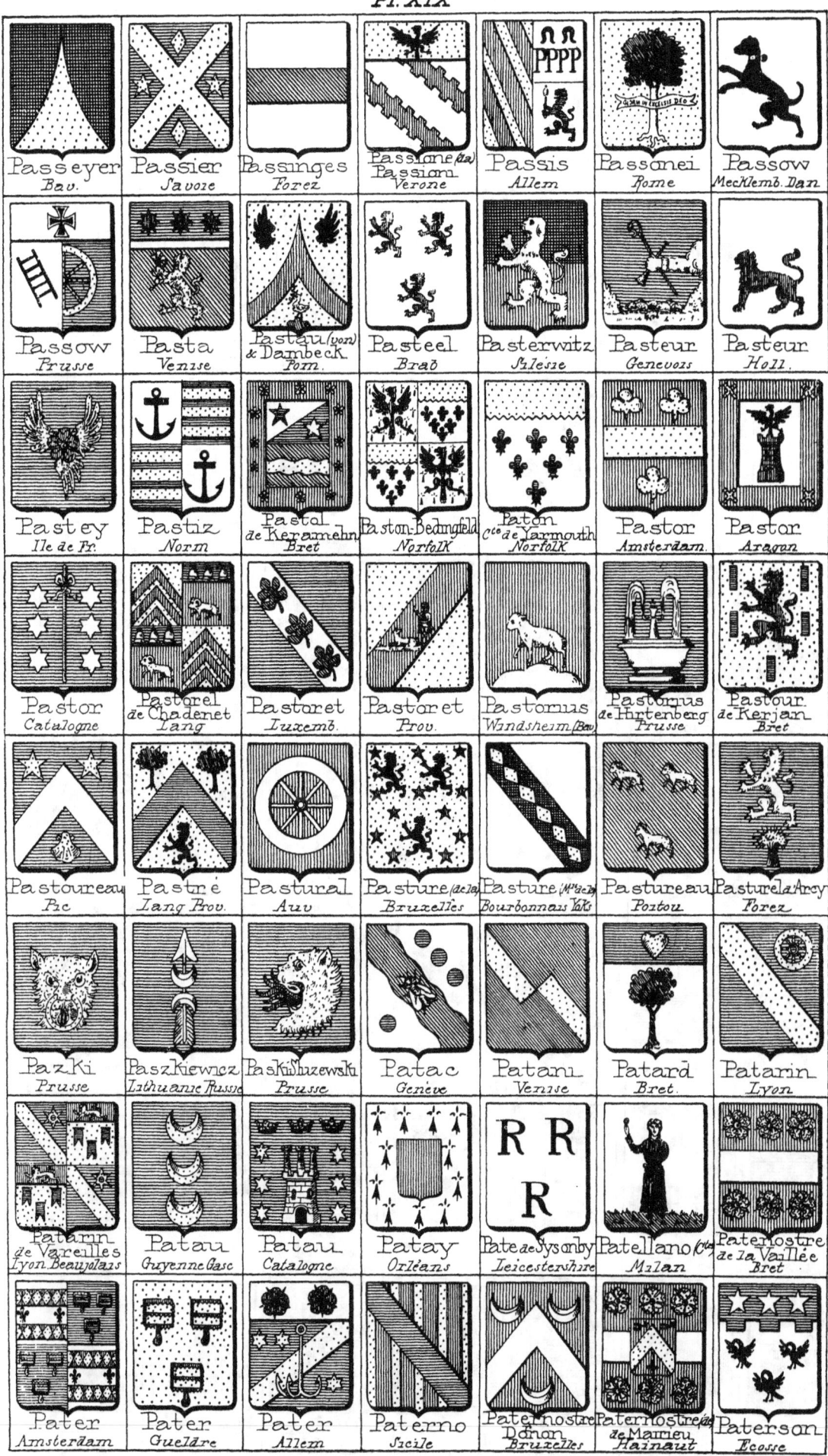

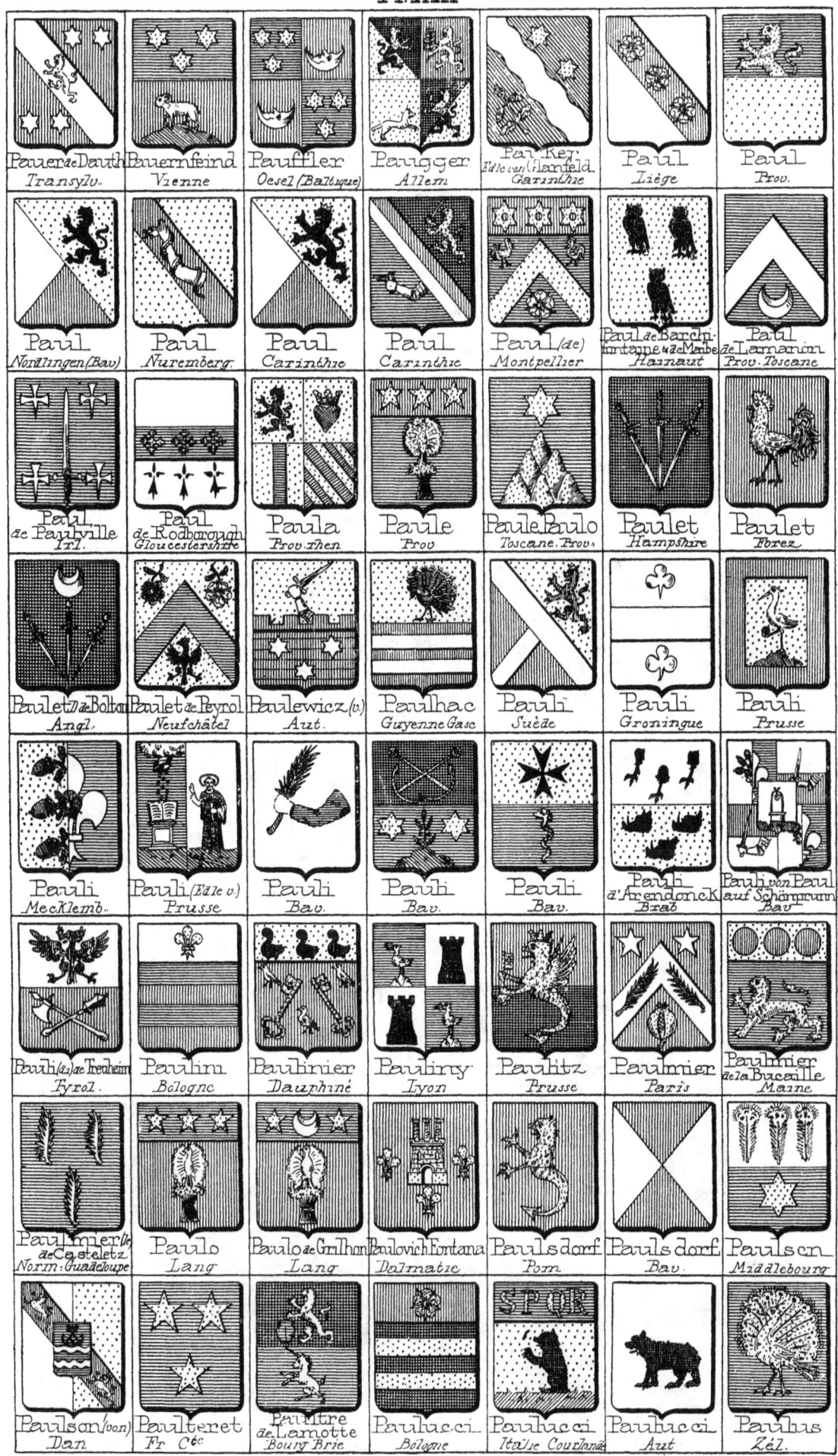

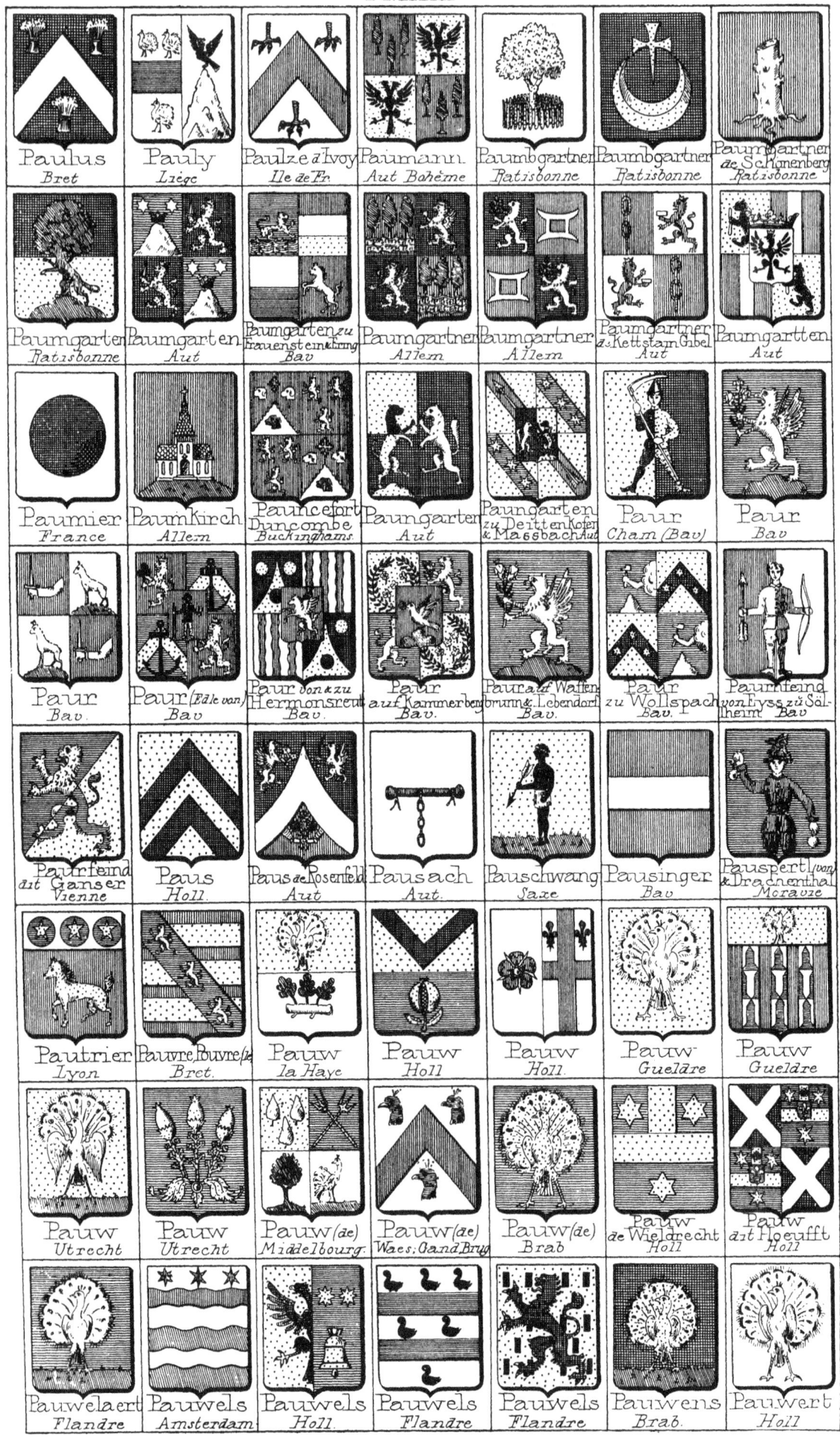

Pl. XXIII

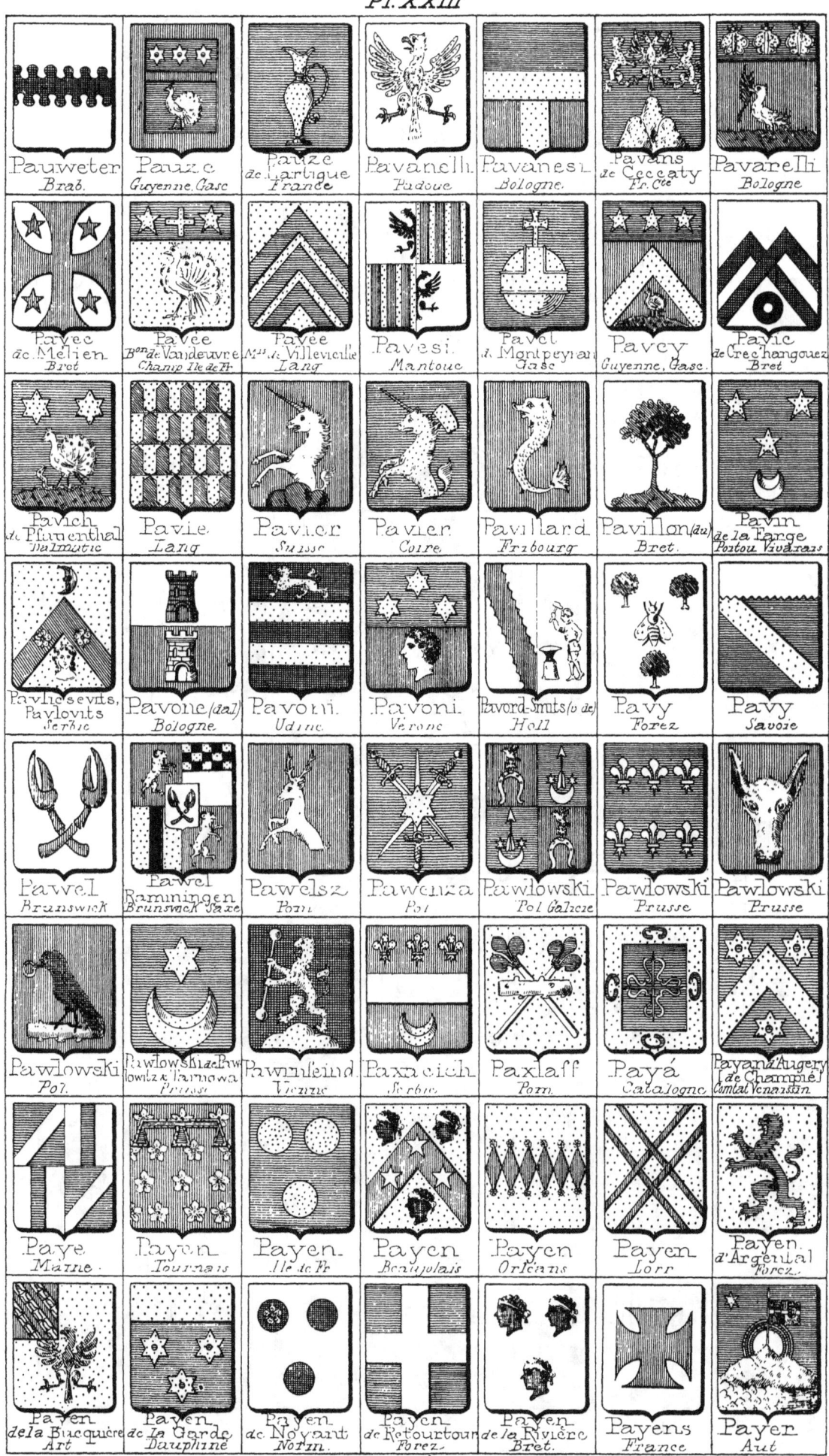

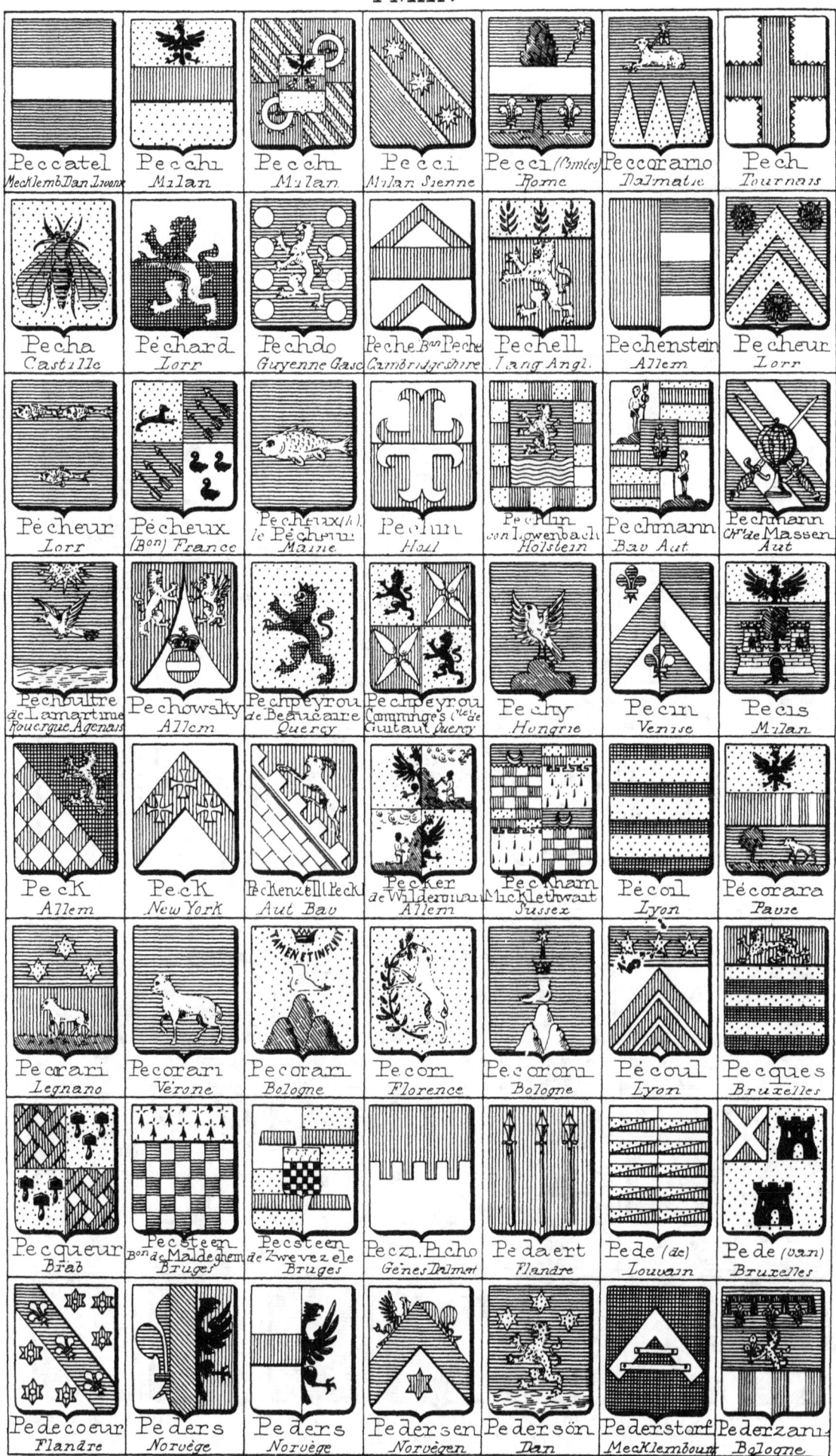

Pl. XXVI

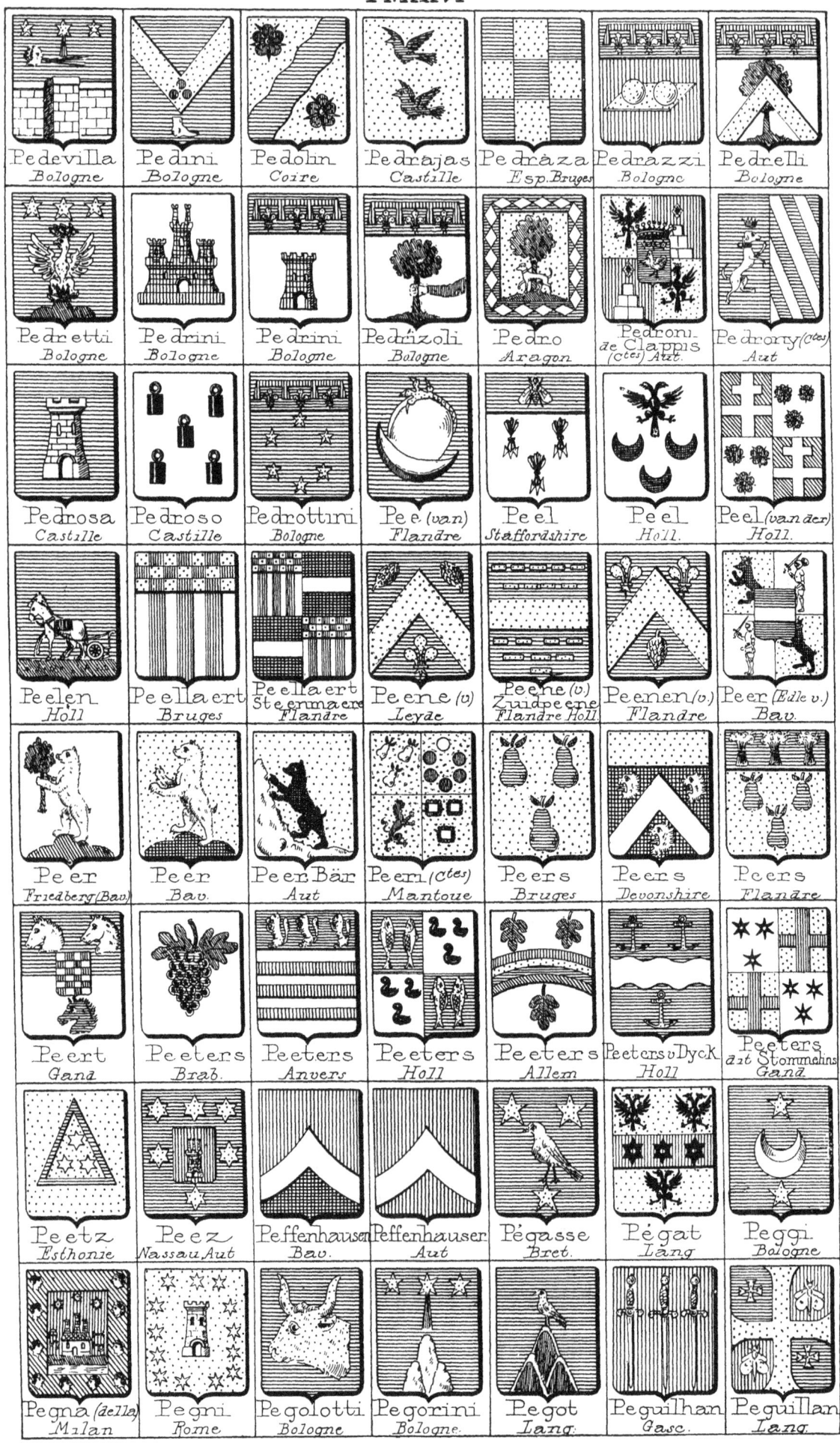

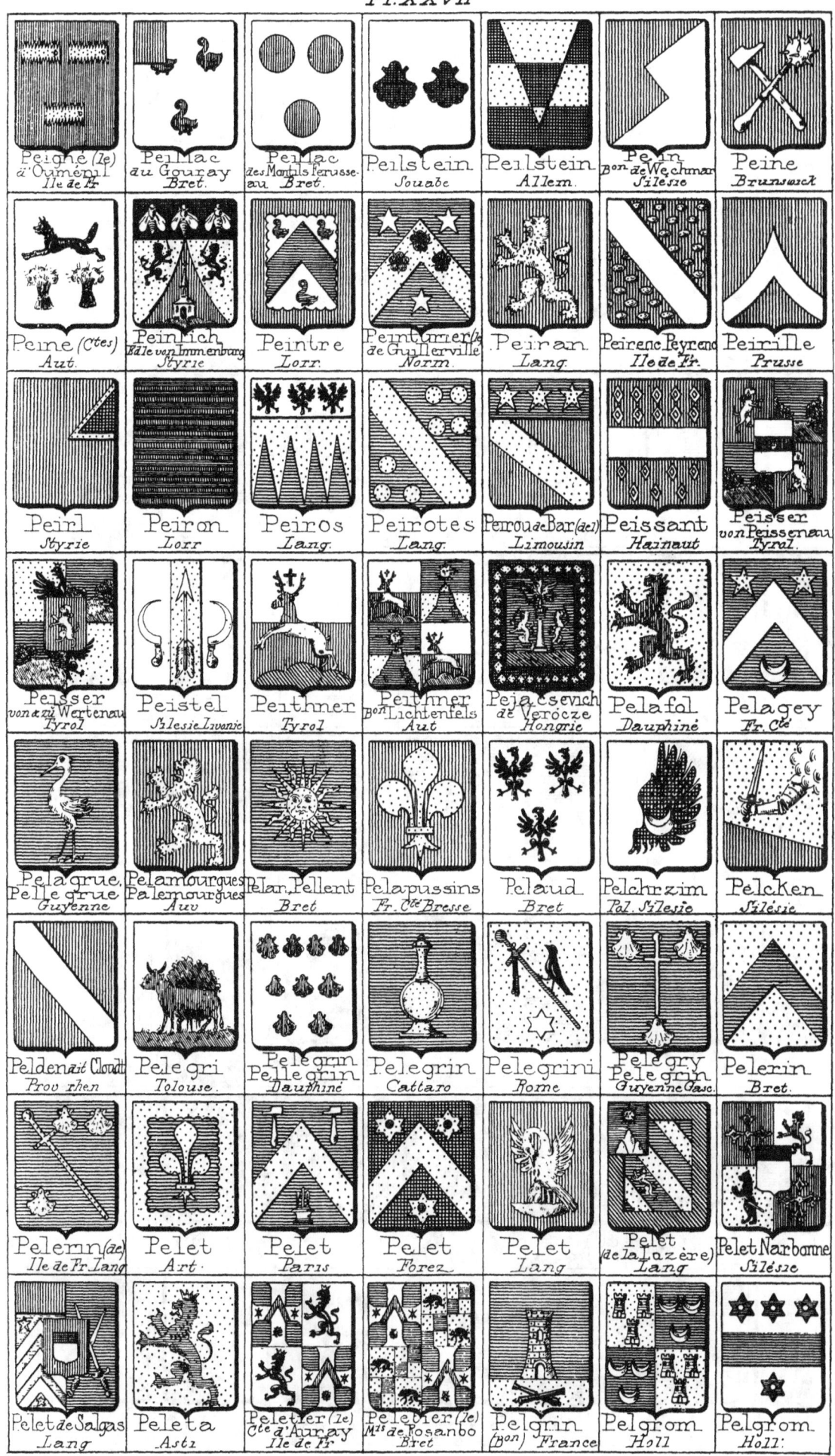
Pl. XXVII

Pl. XXIX

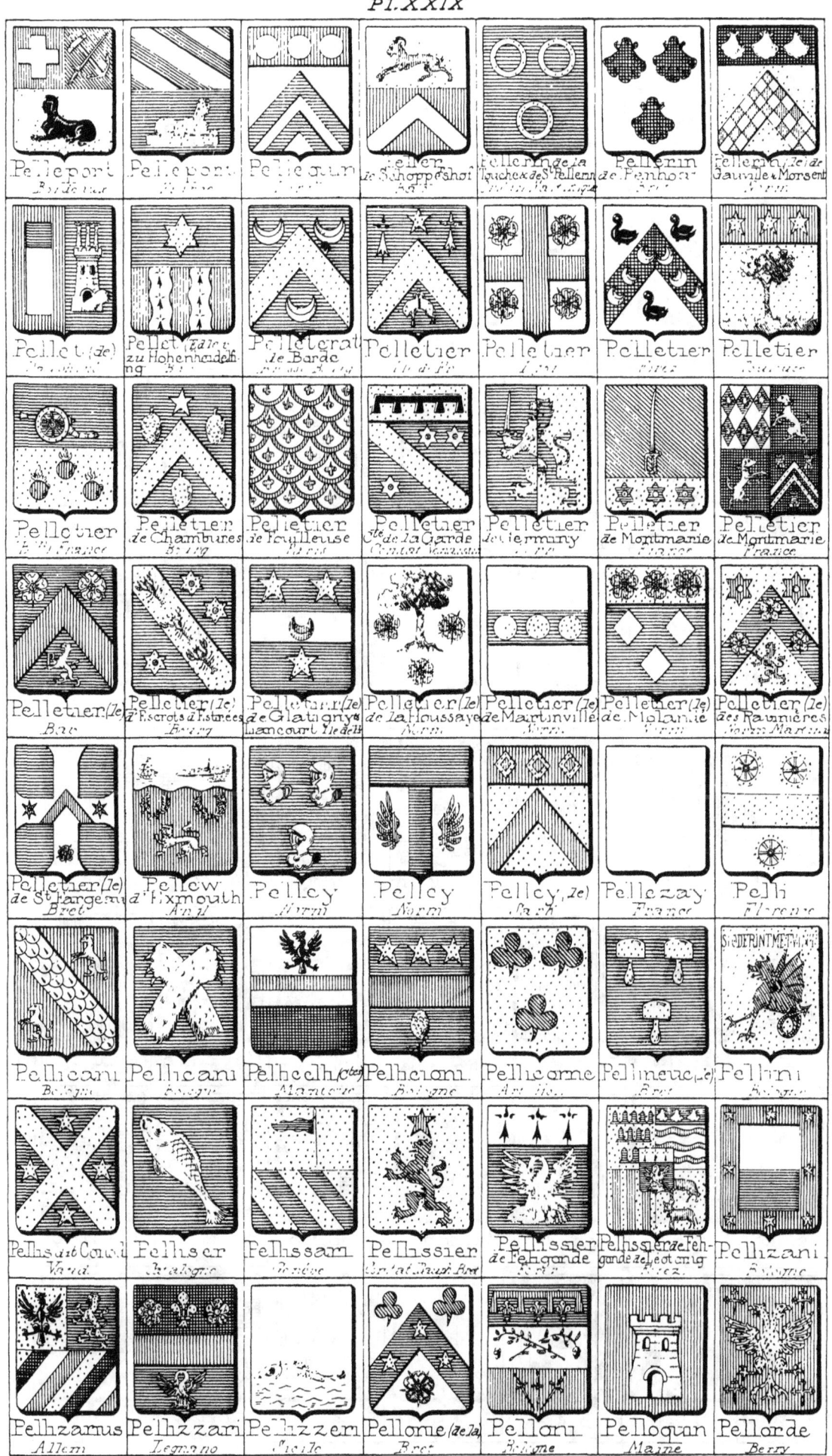

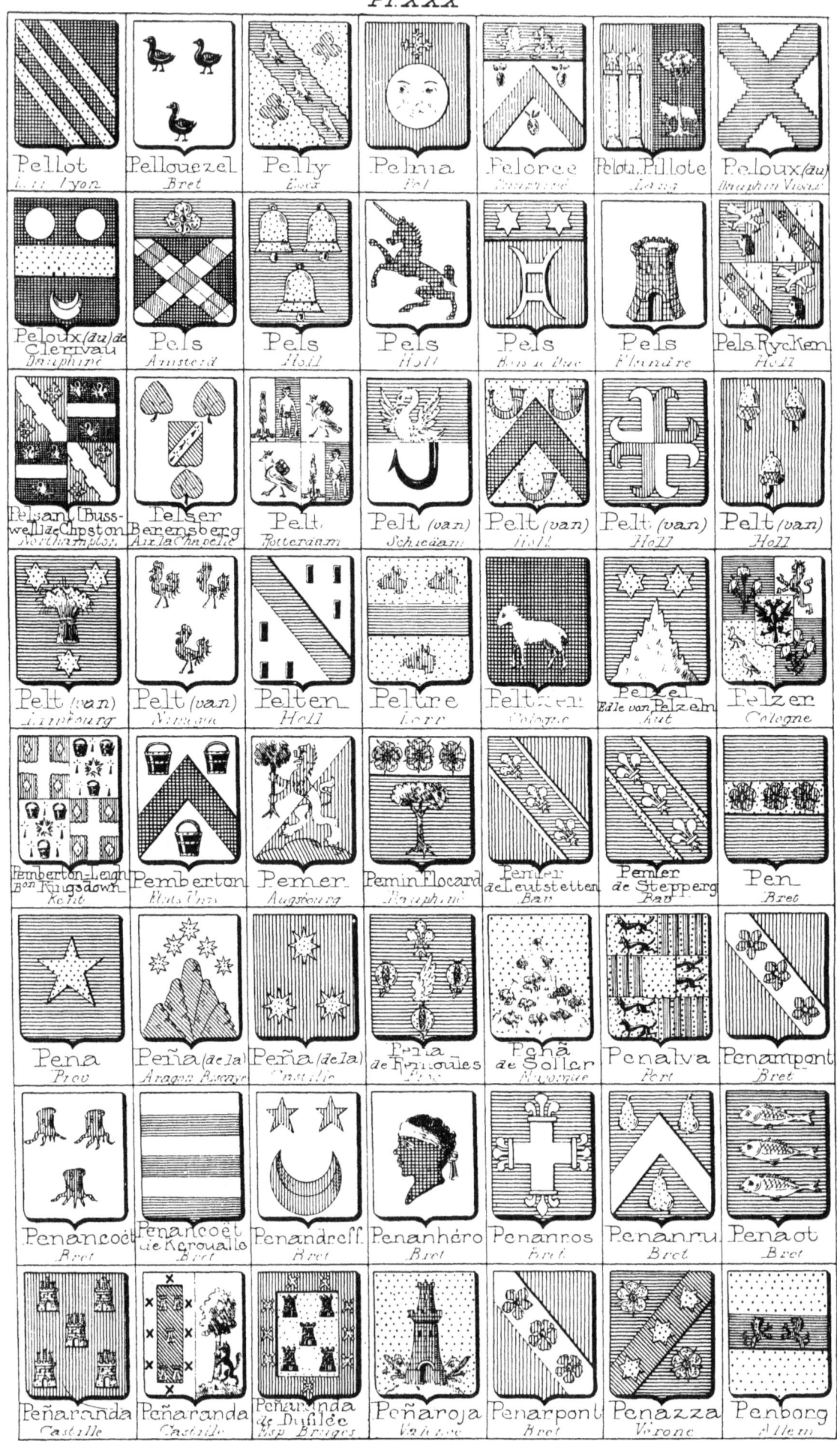
Pl. XXX

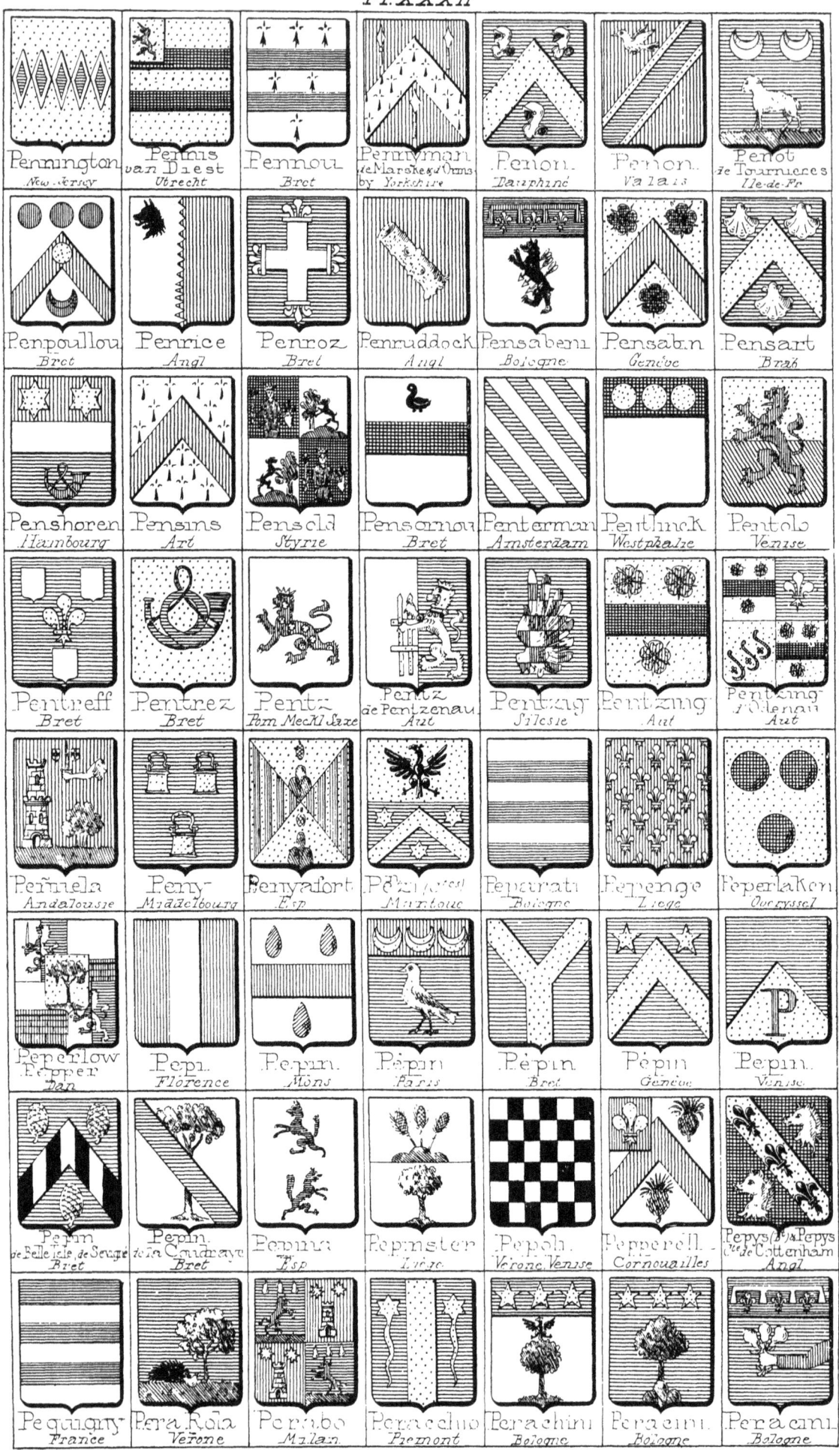

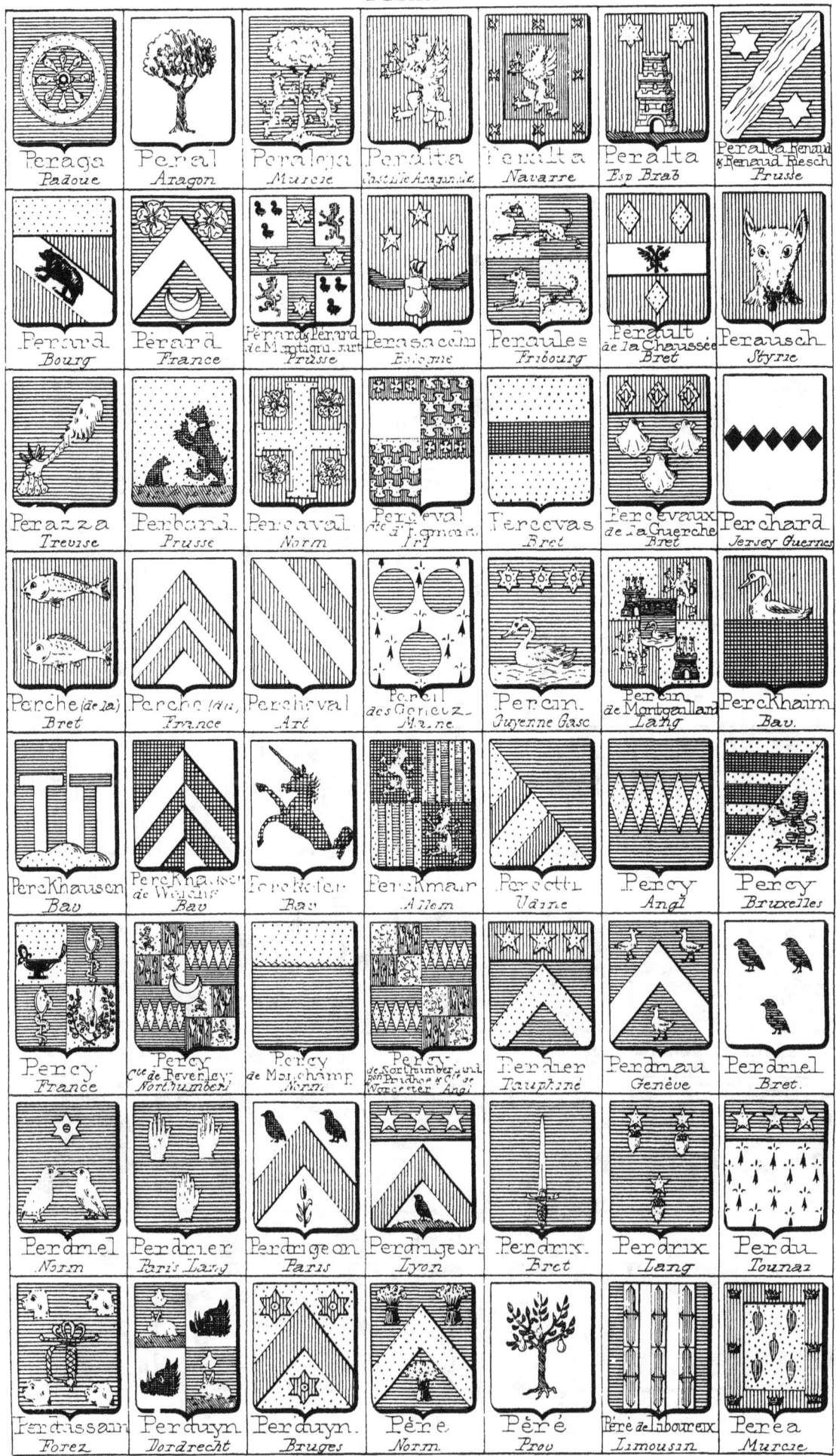

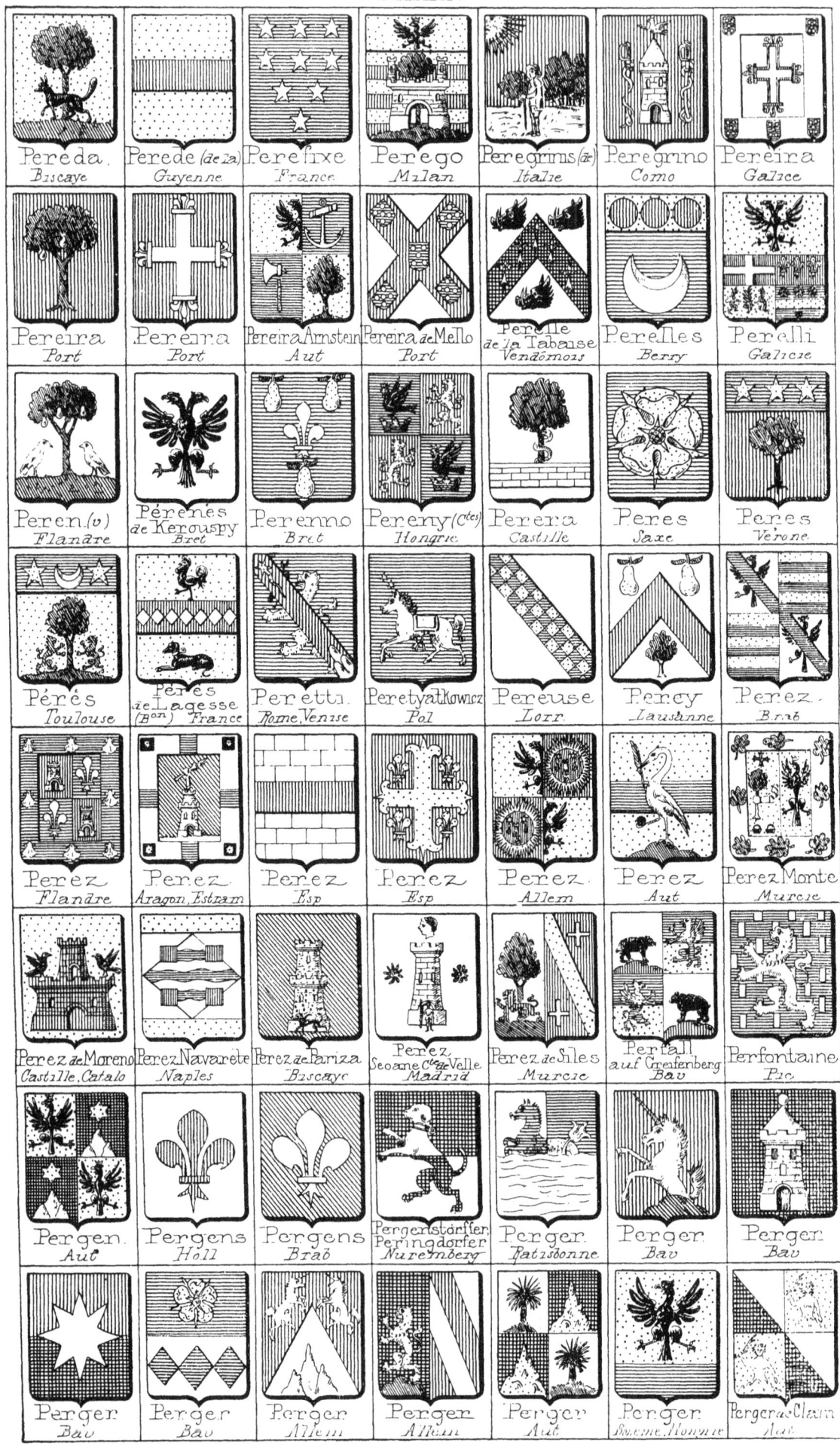

Pl. XXXV

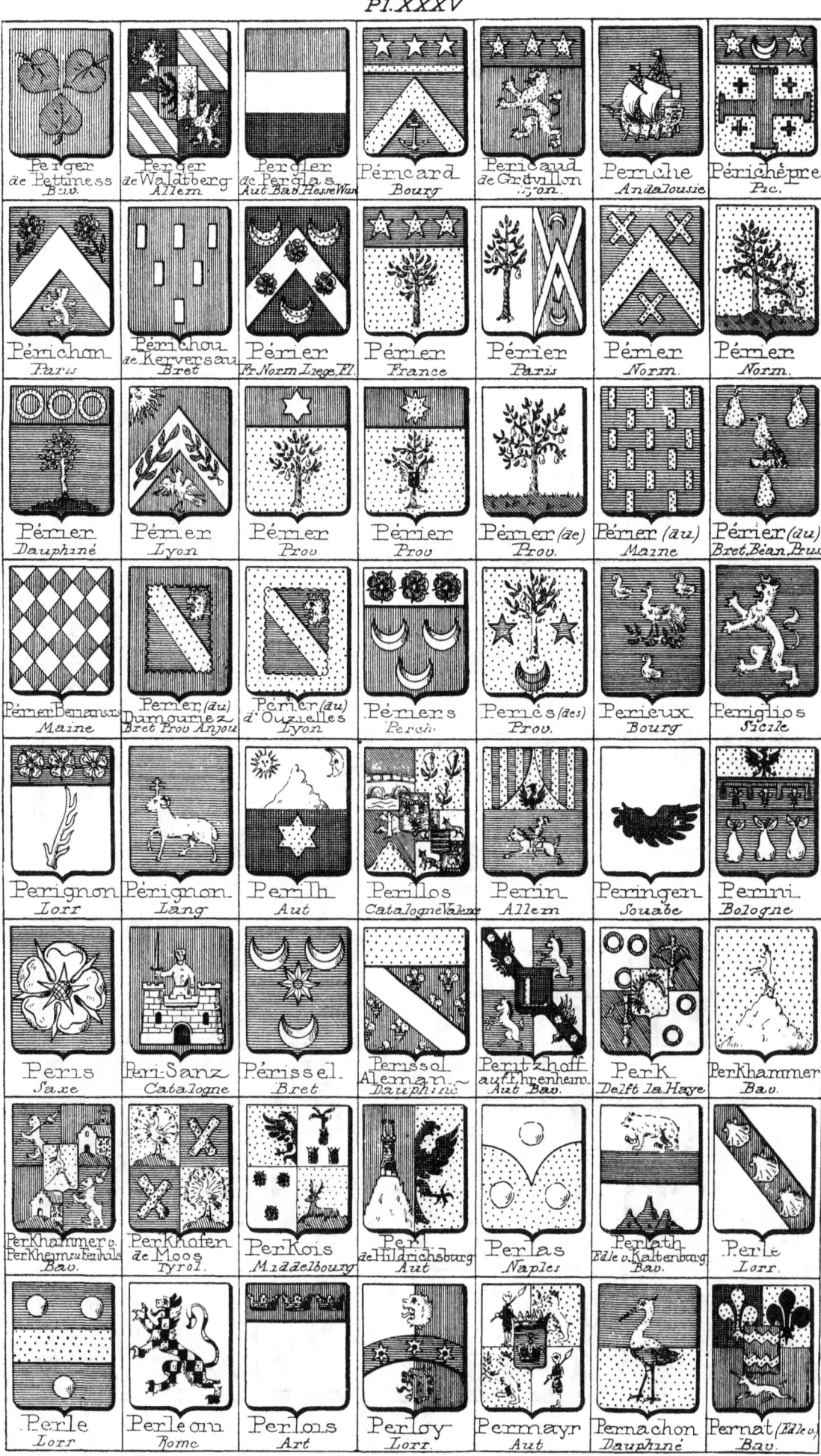

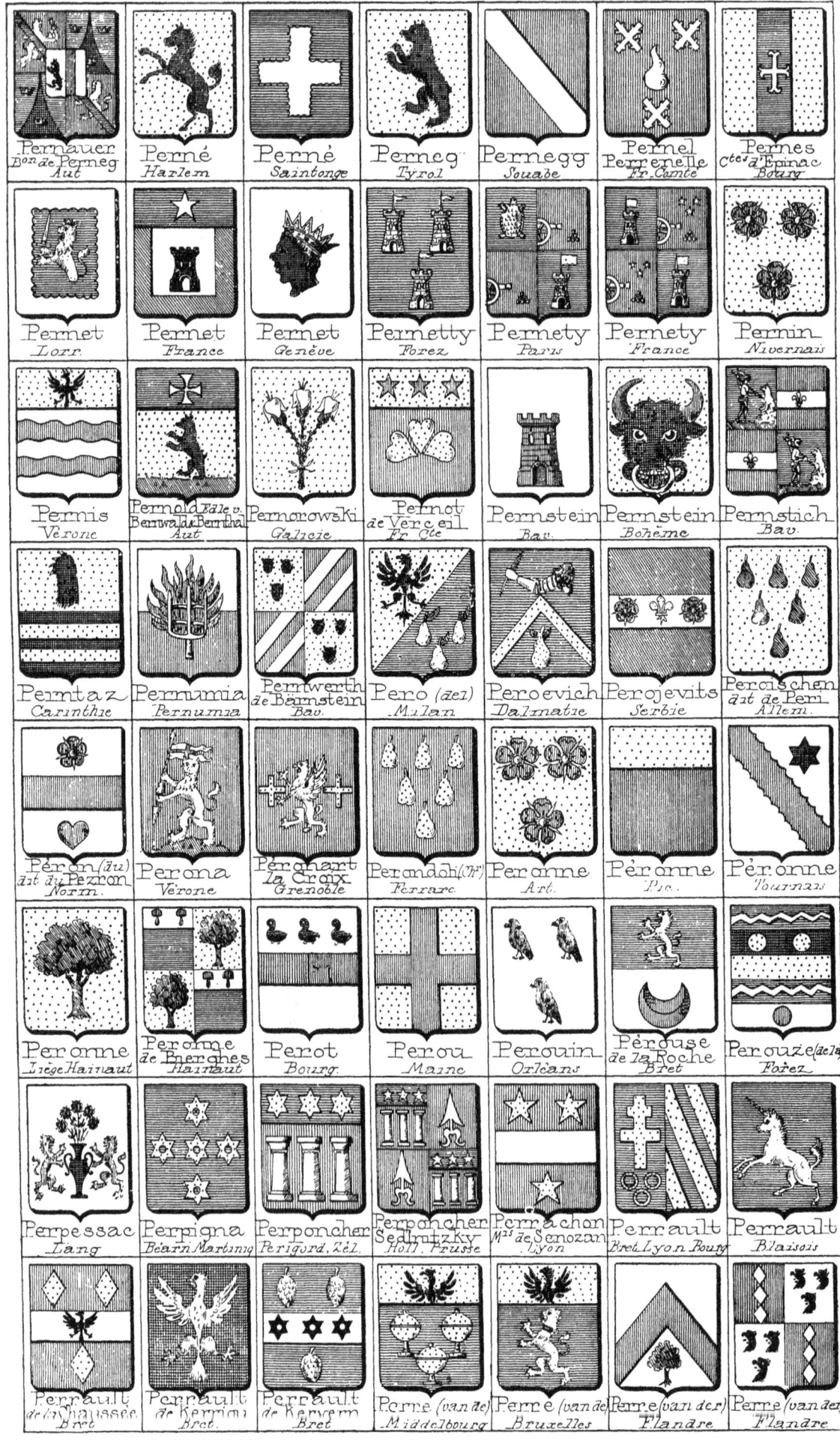

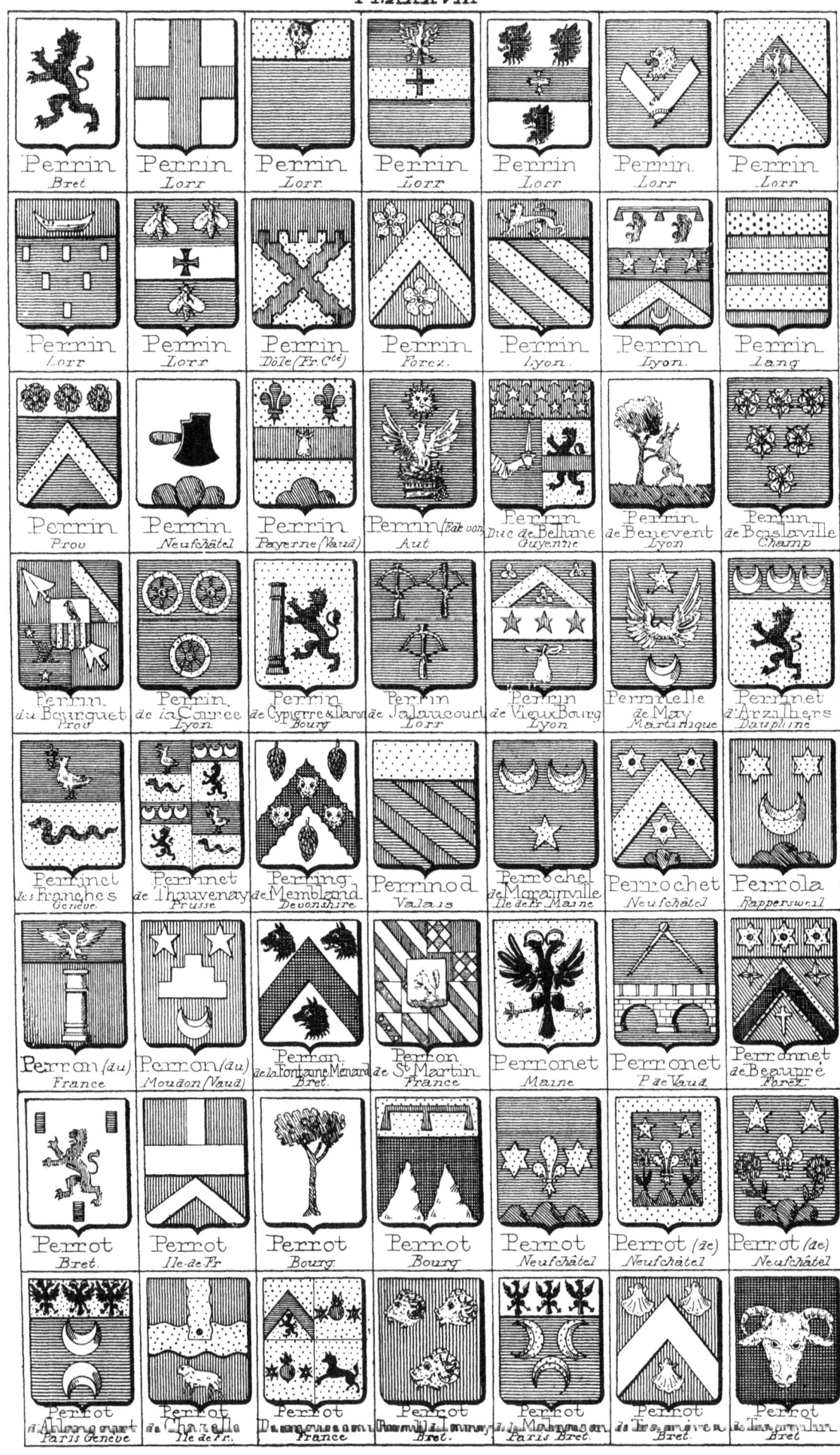

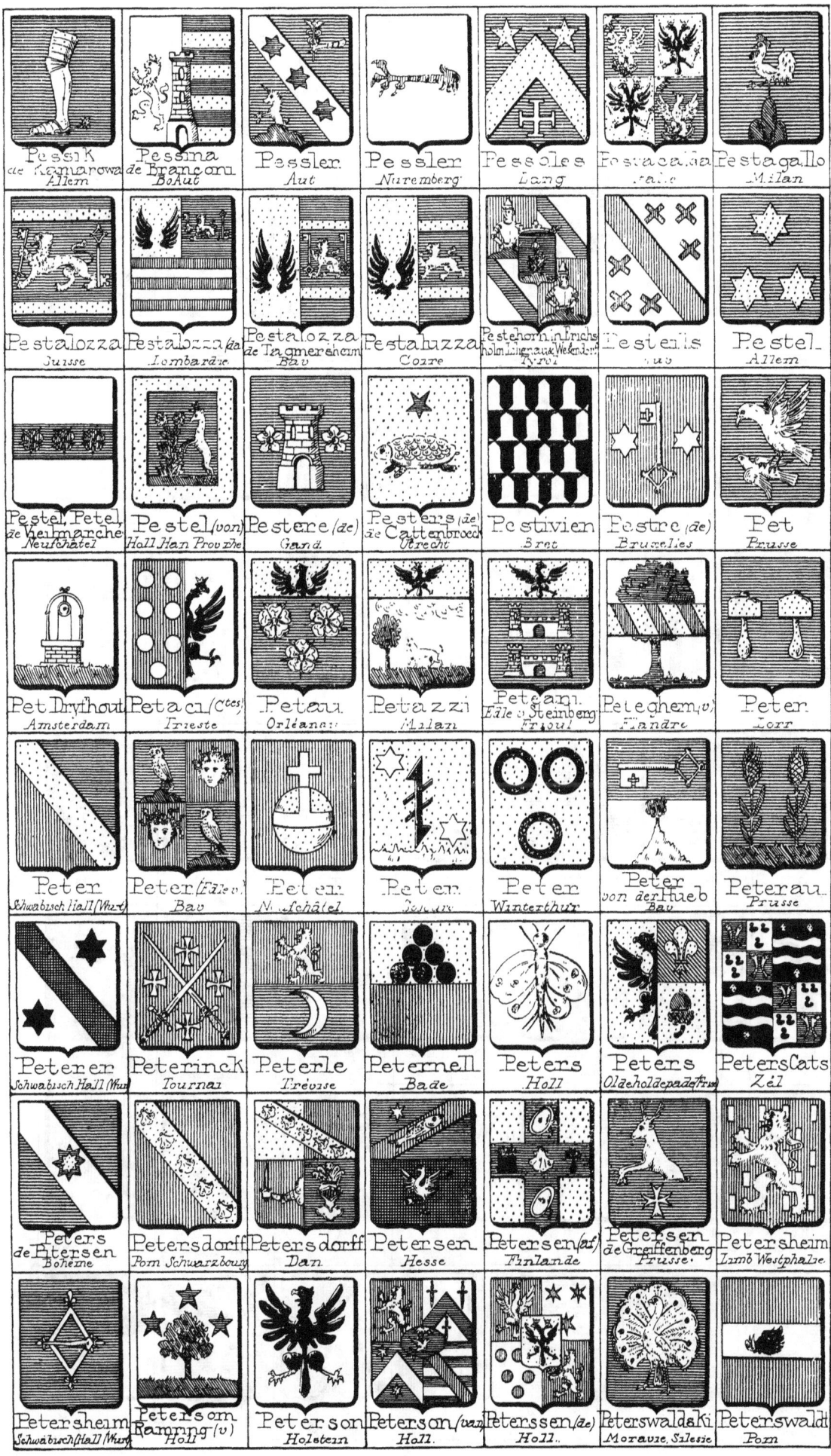

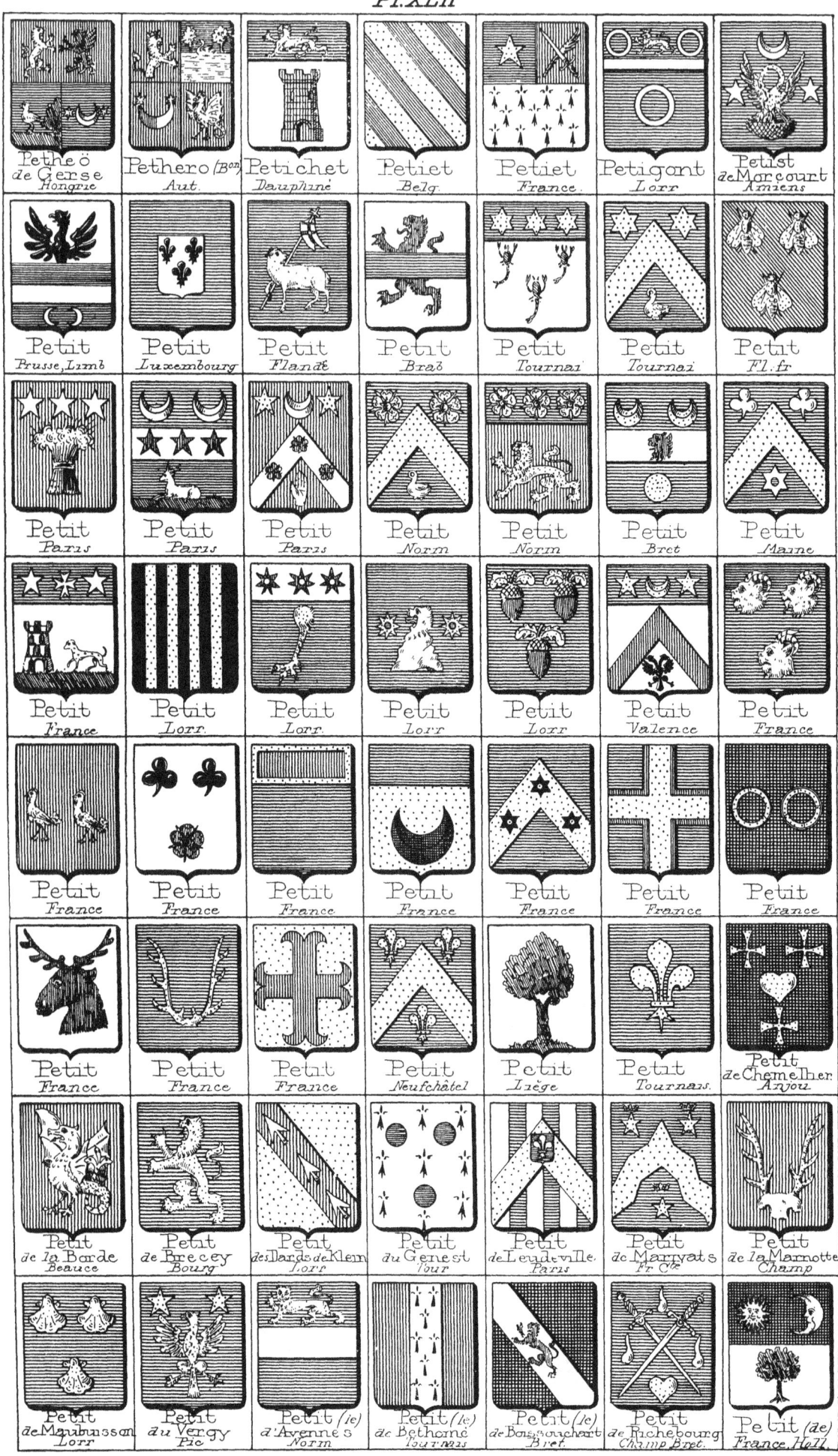

Pl.XLIII

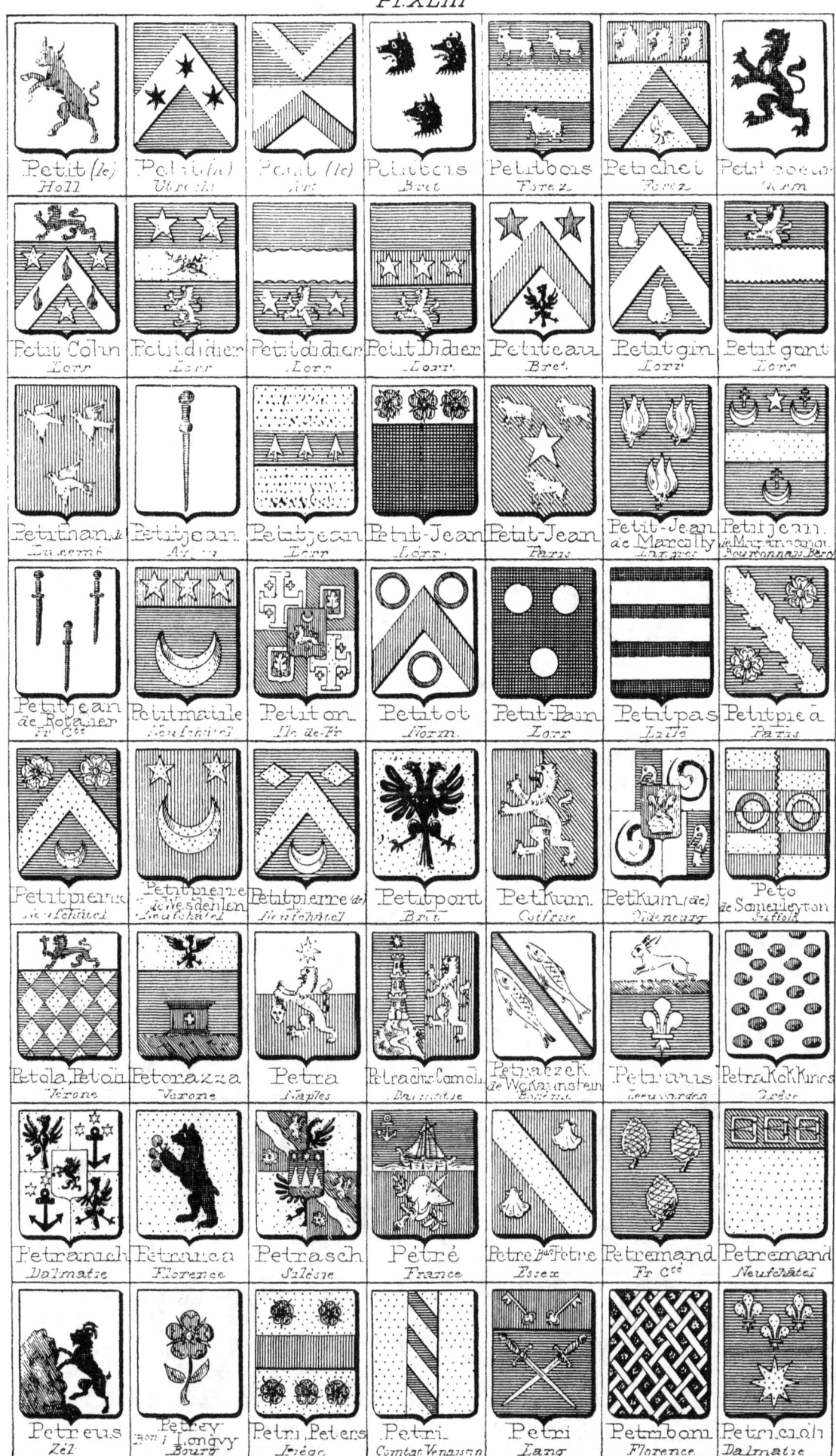

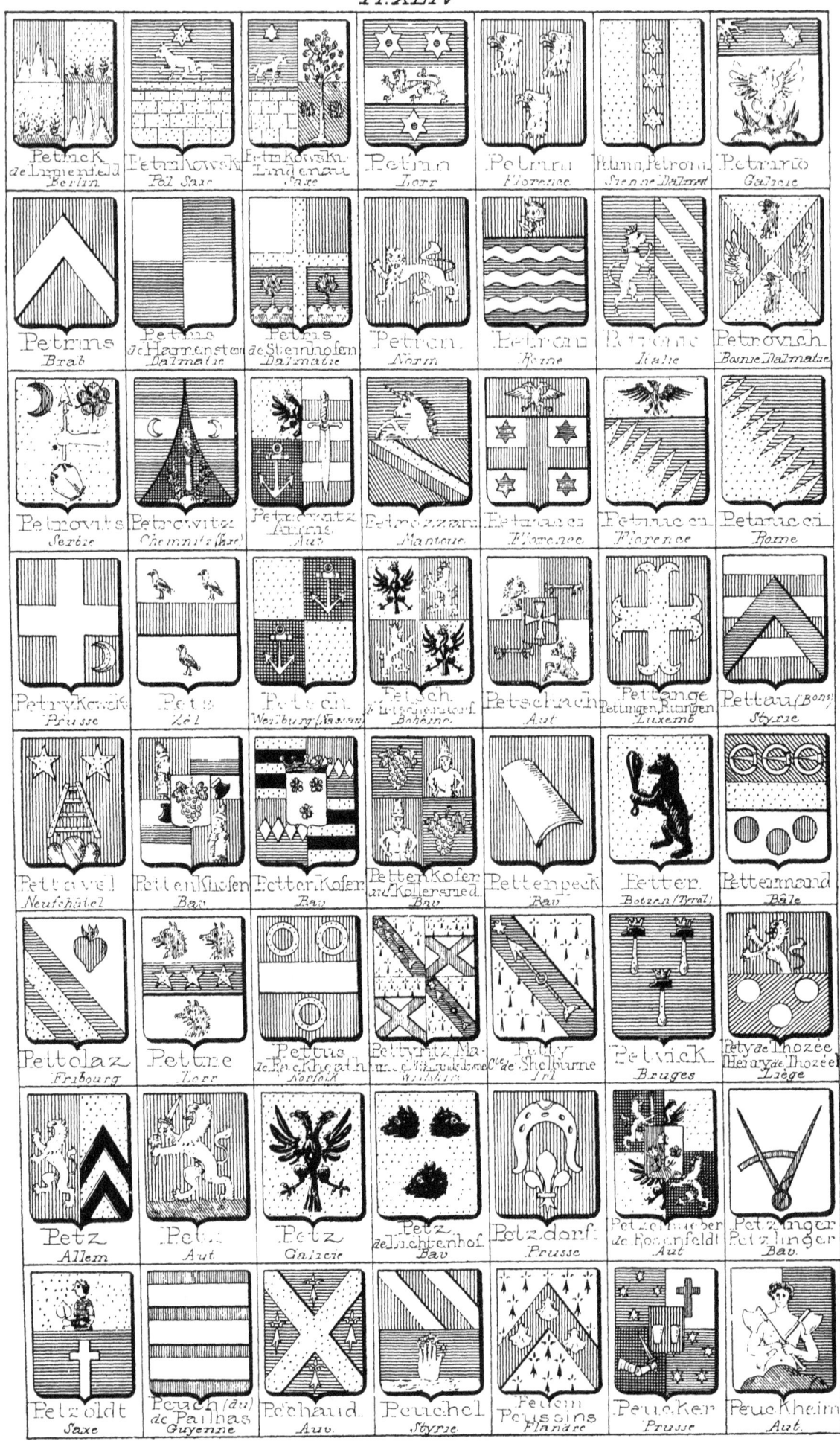
Pl. XLIV

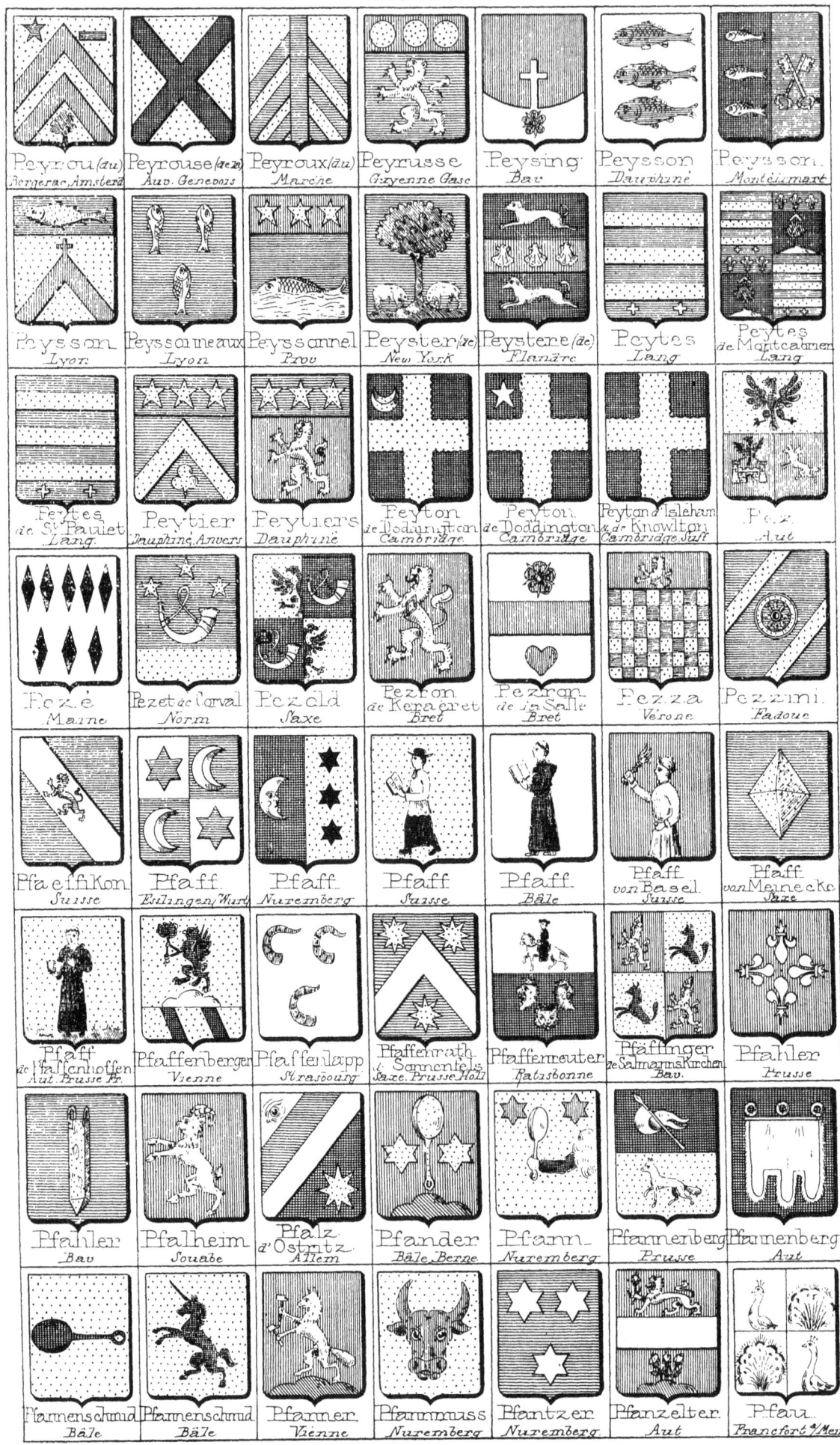

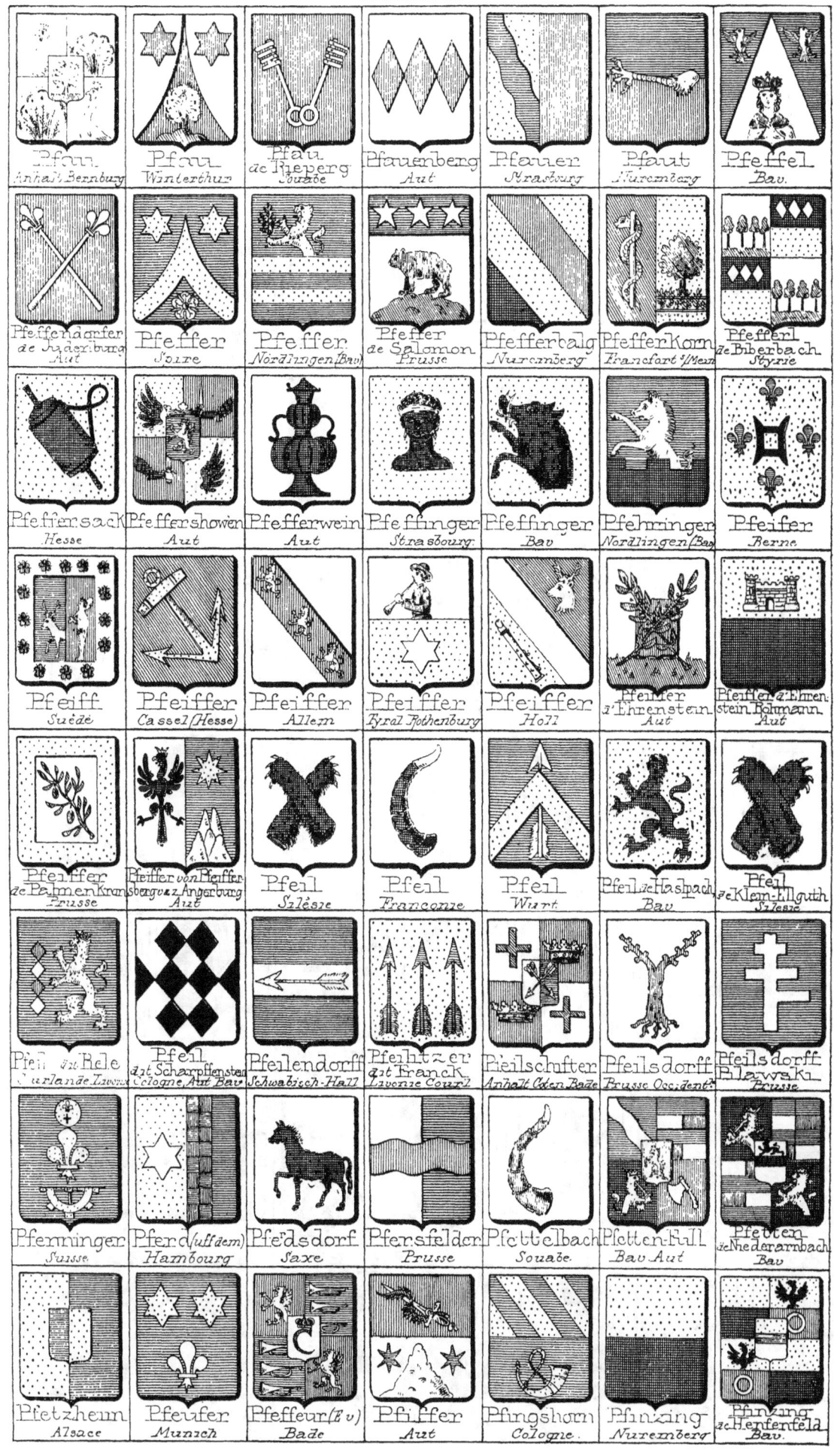
Pl. XLVII

Pl. II.

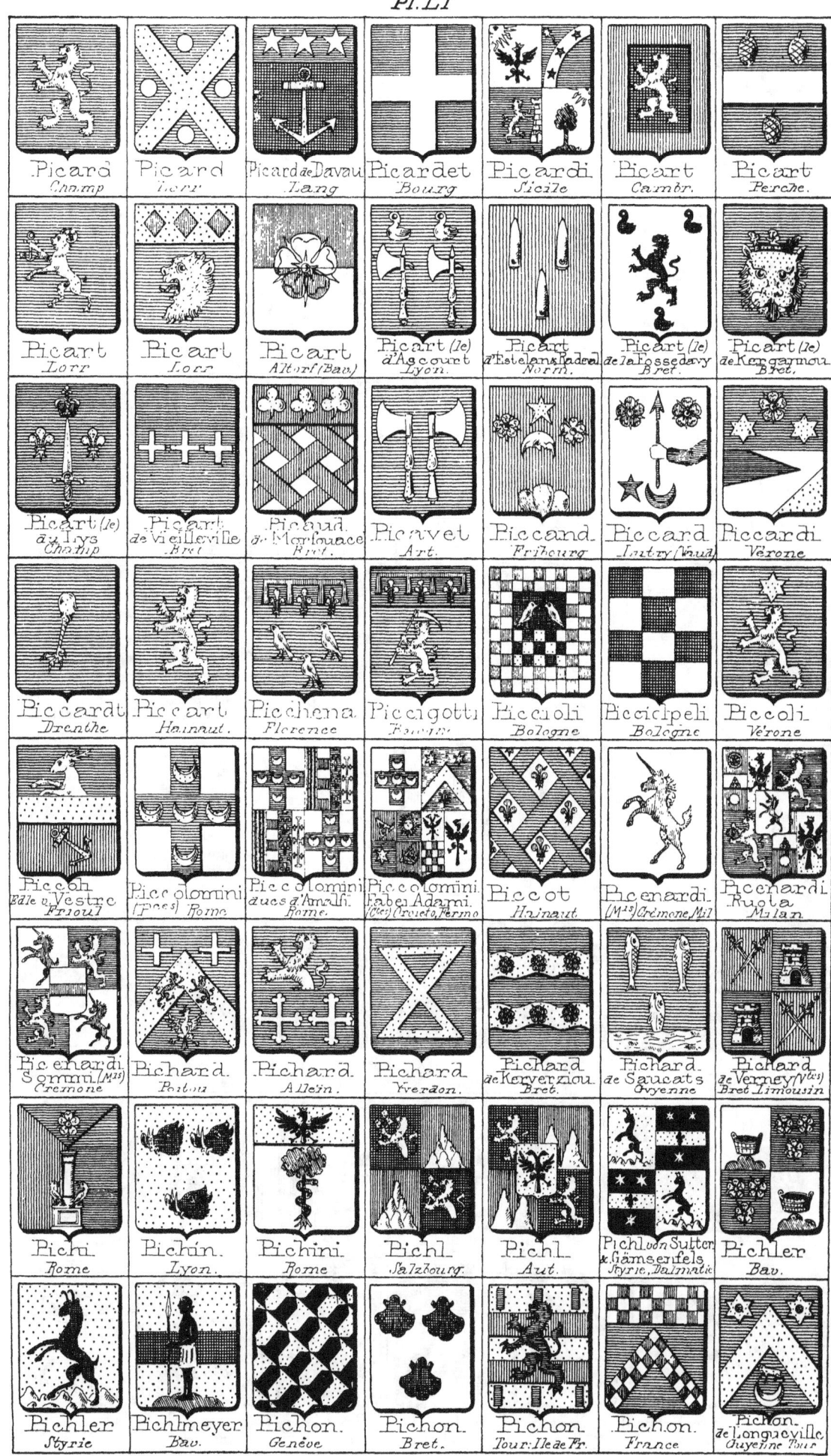

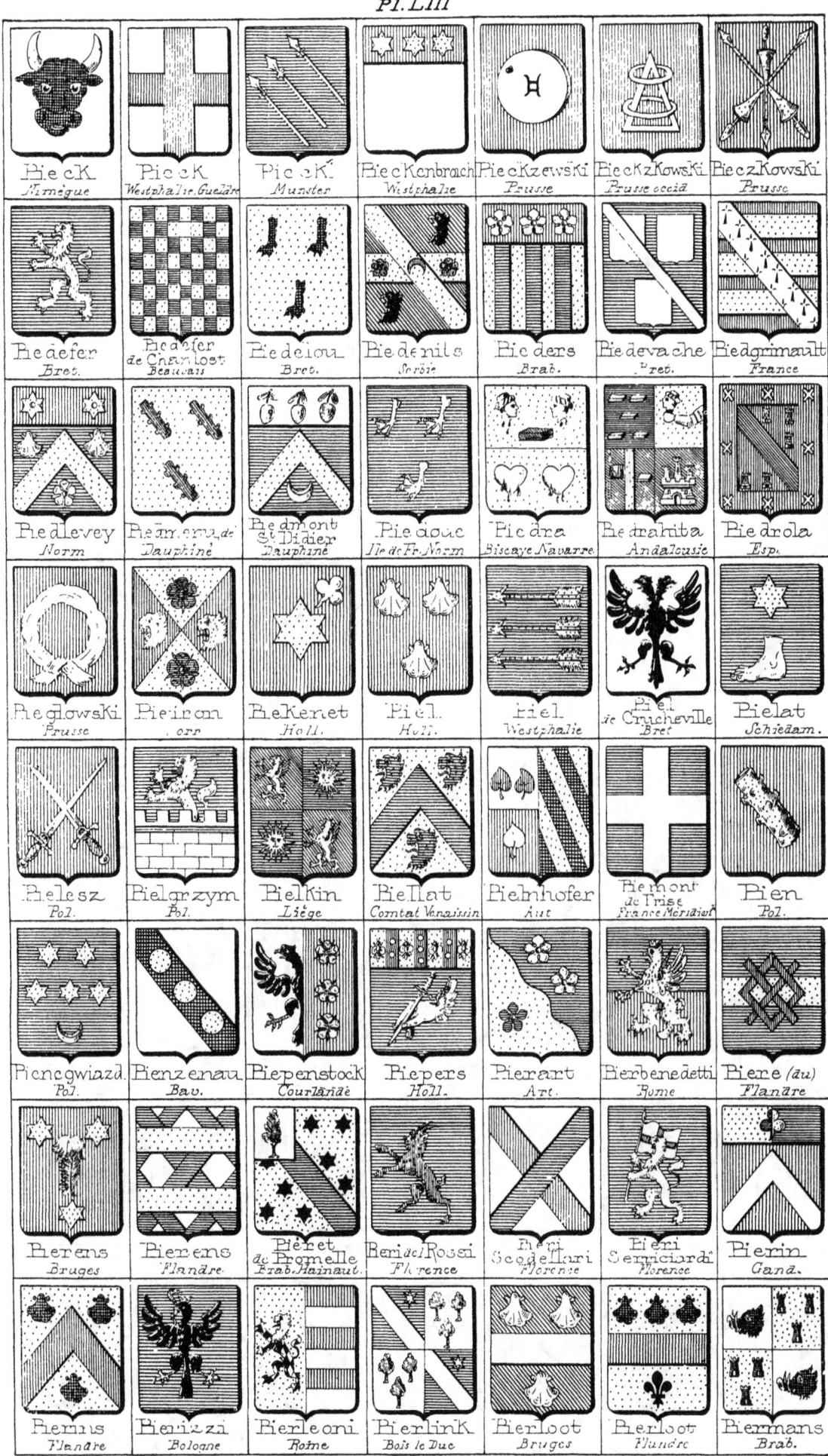

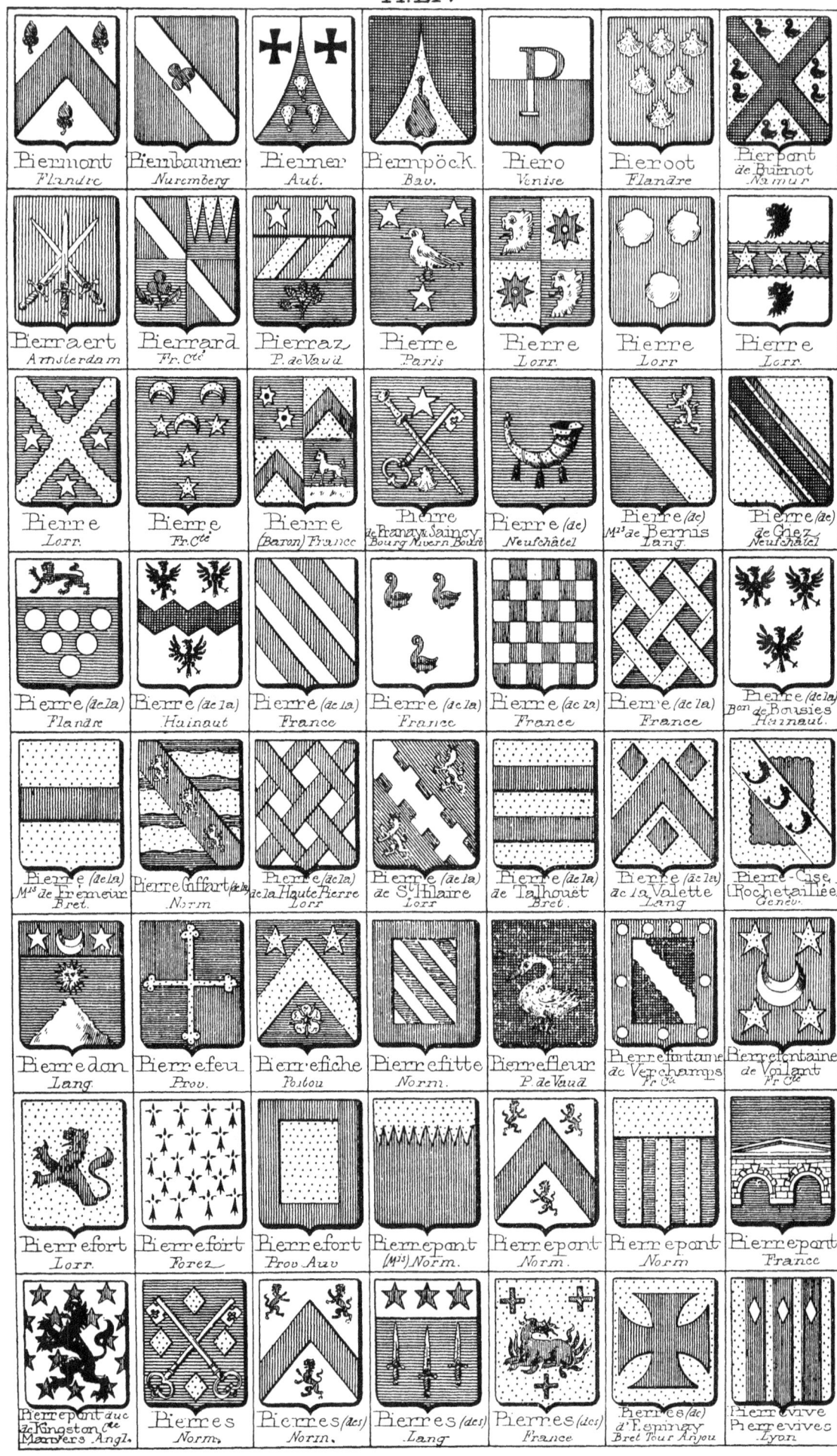

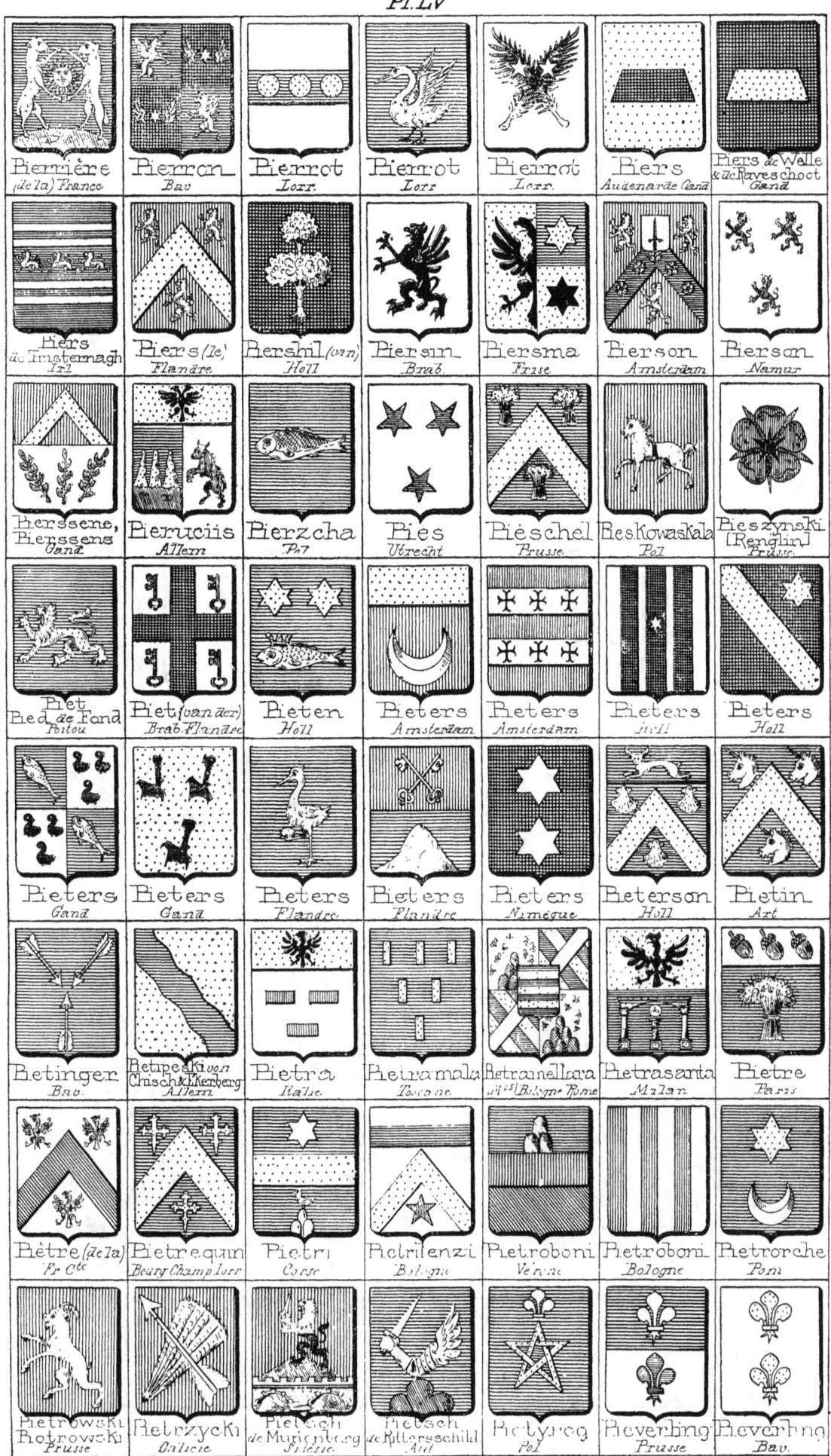

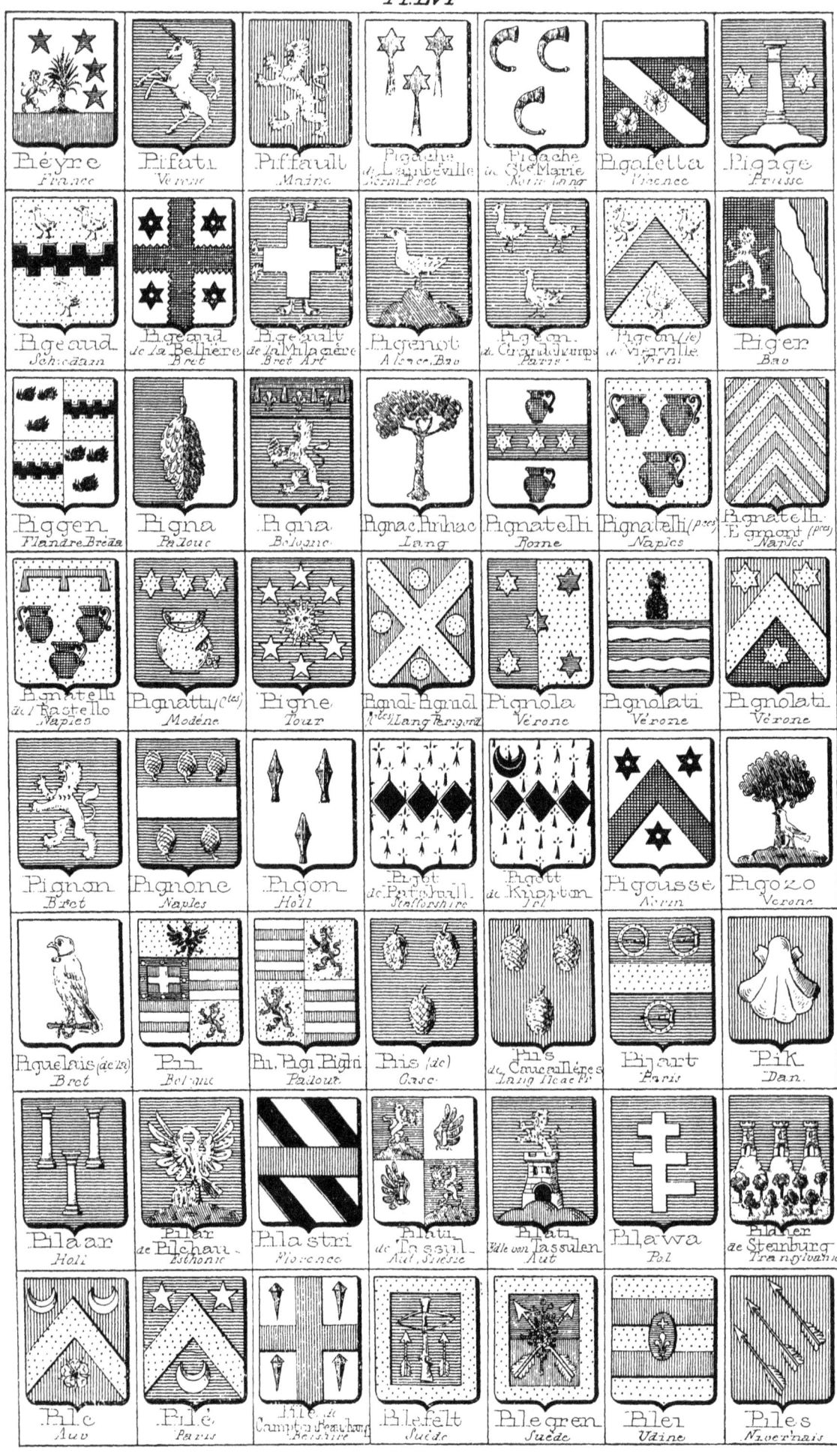

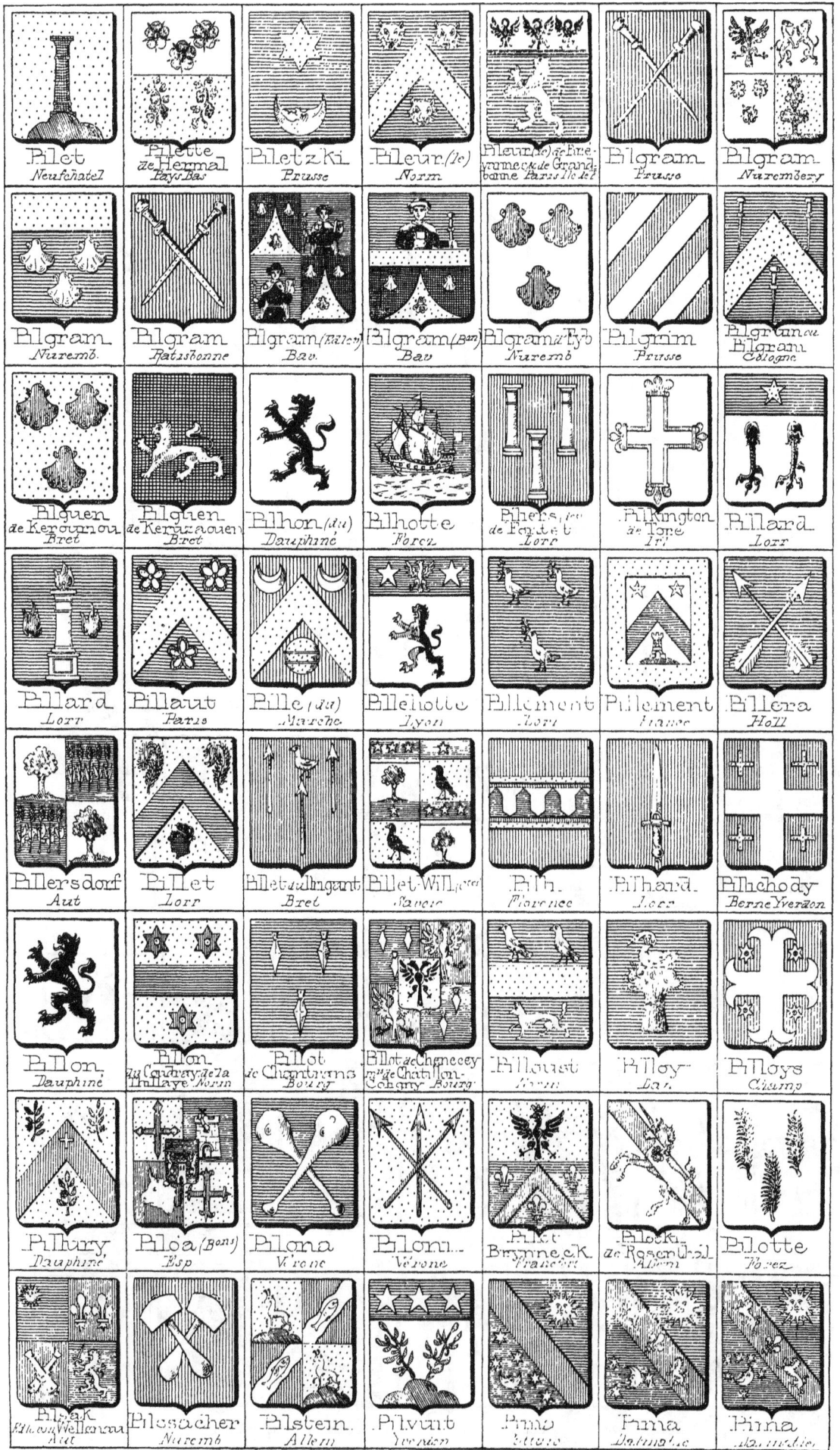

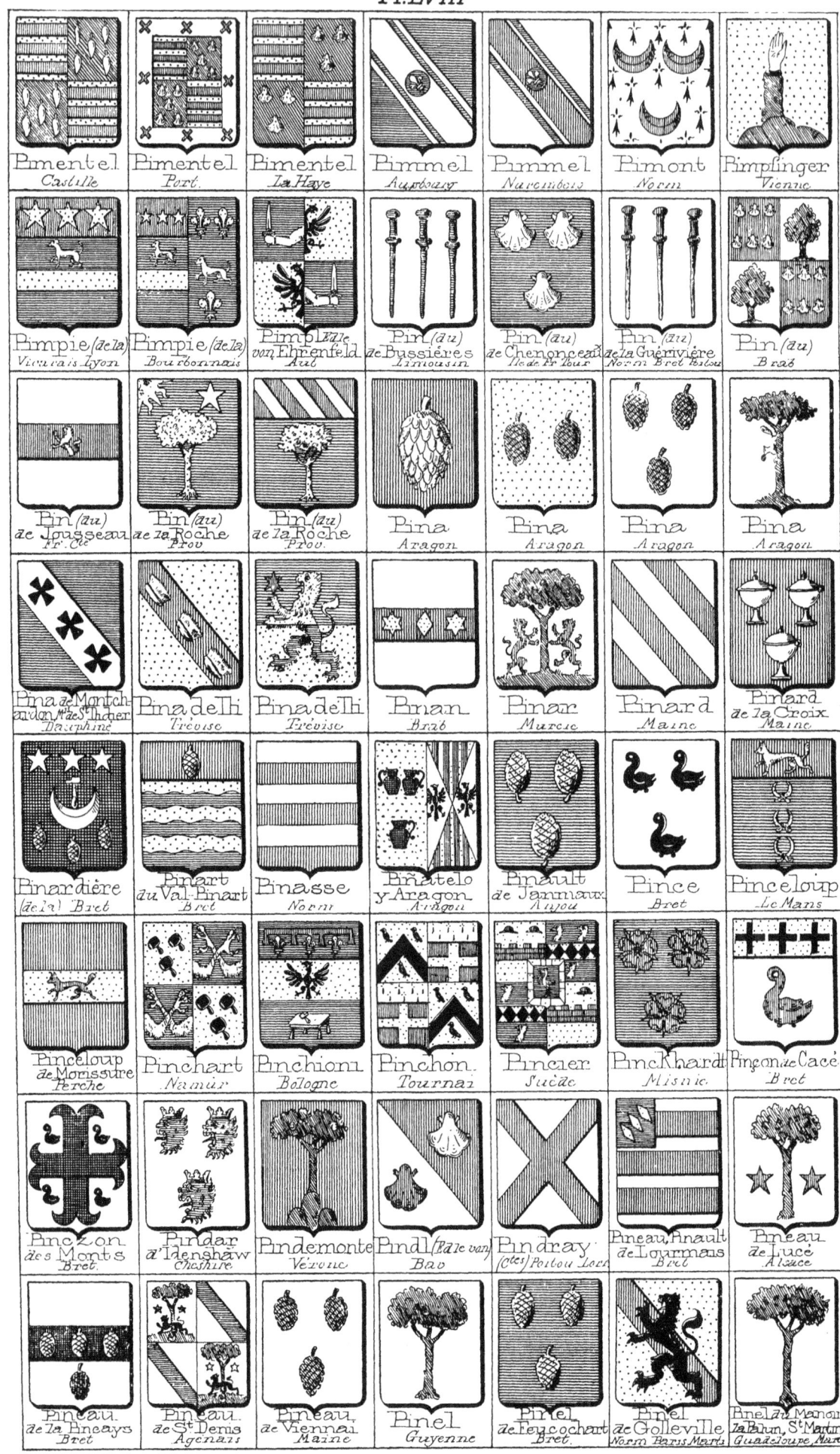

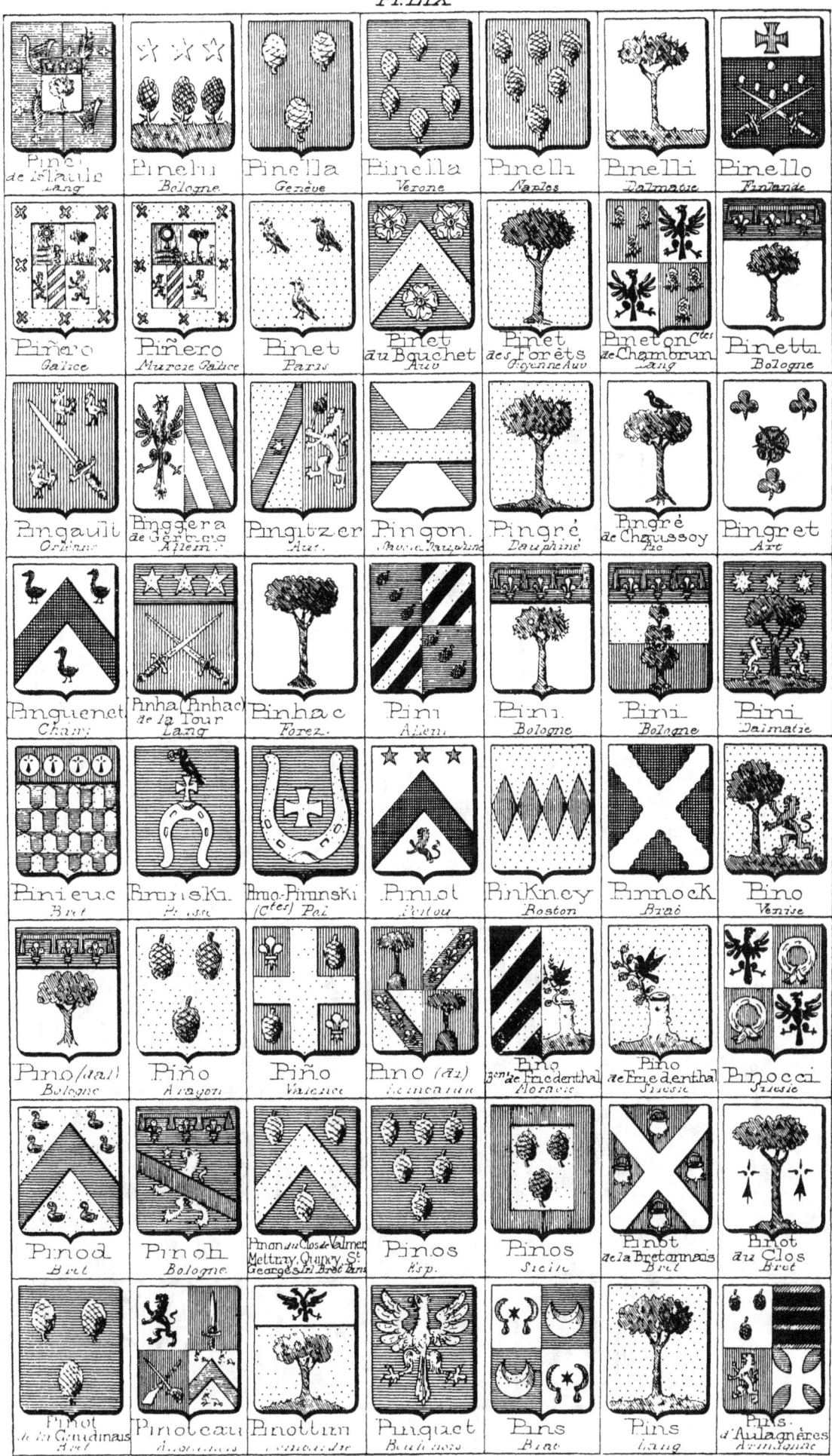

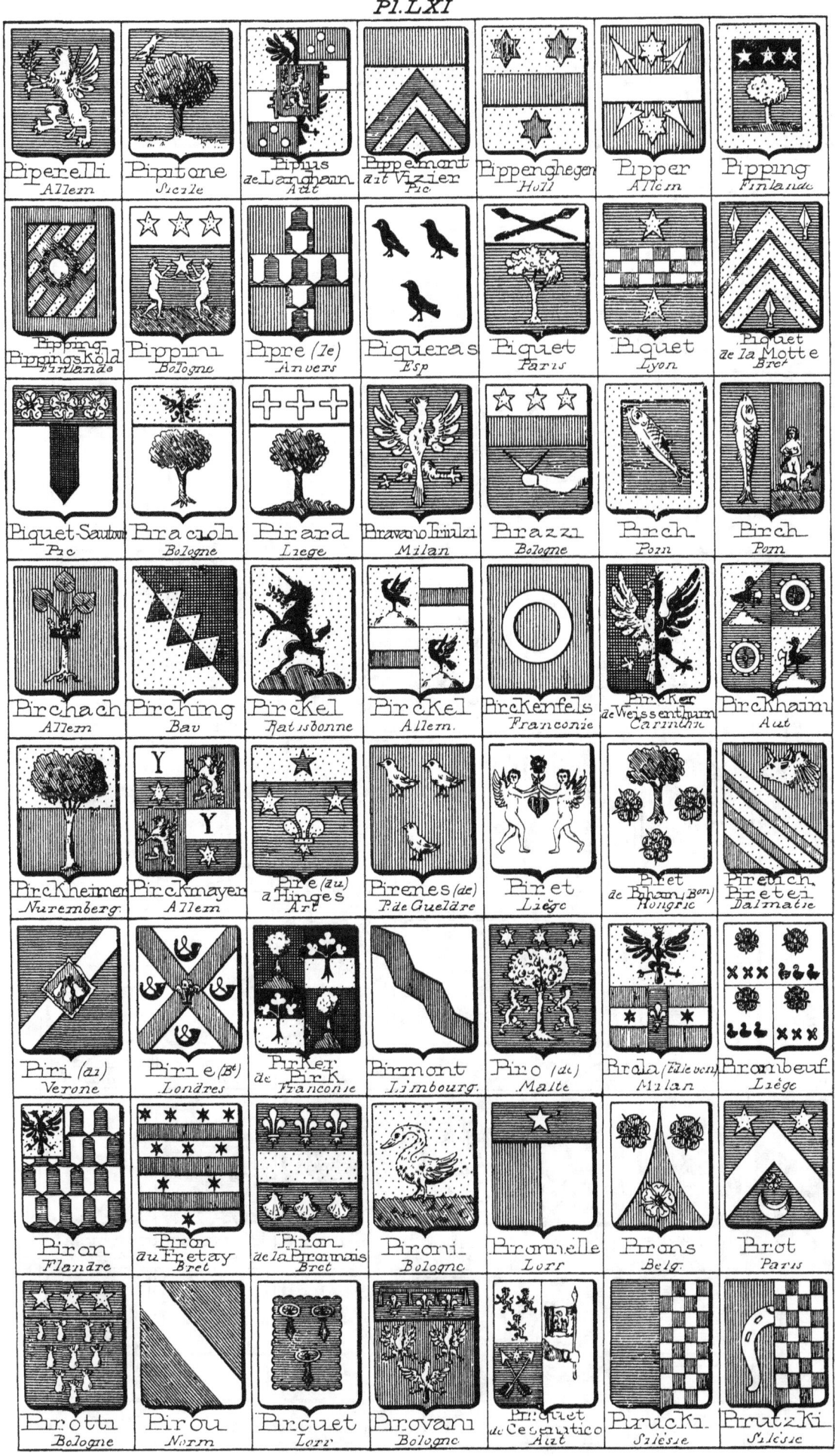

Pl. LXII

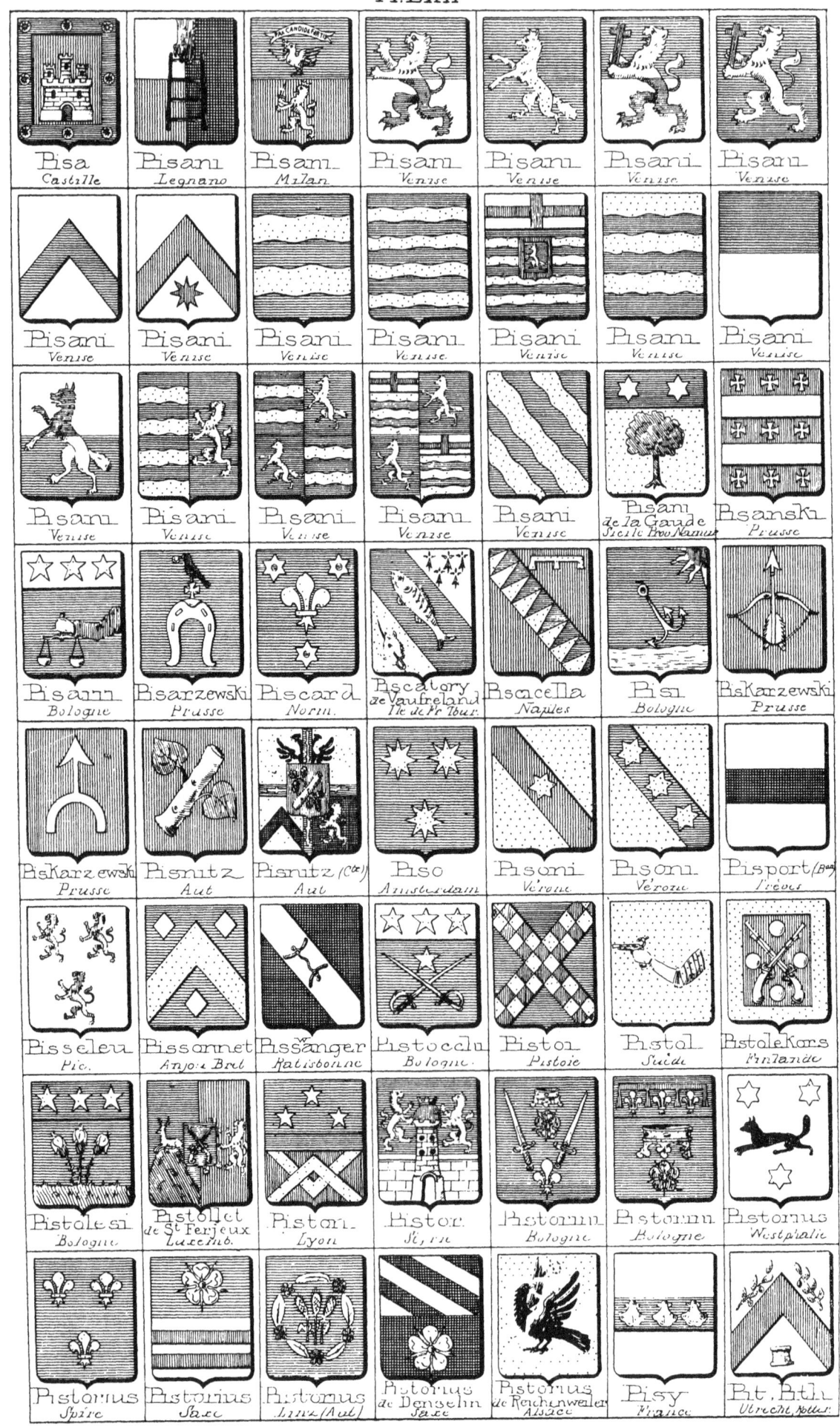

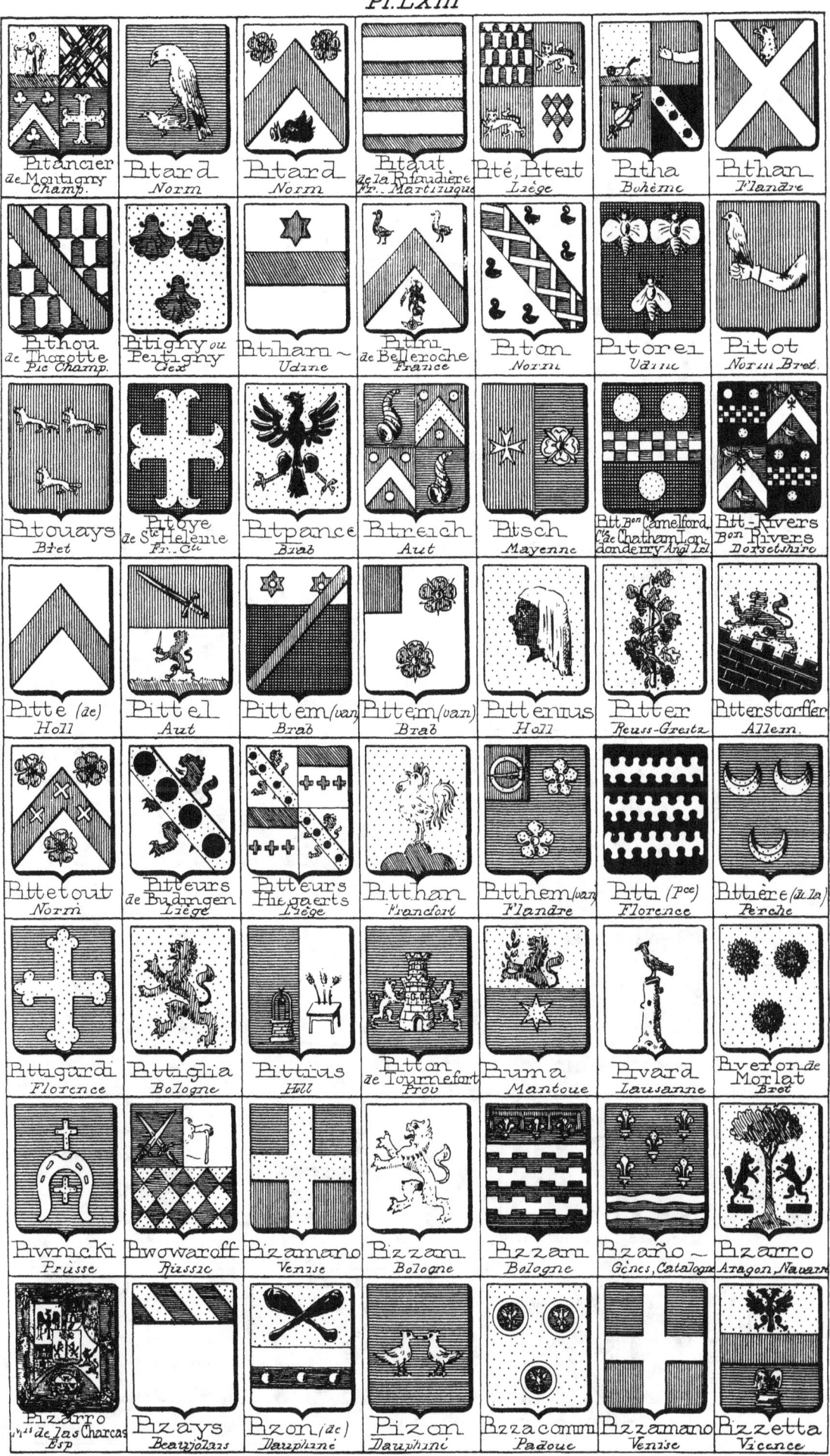

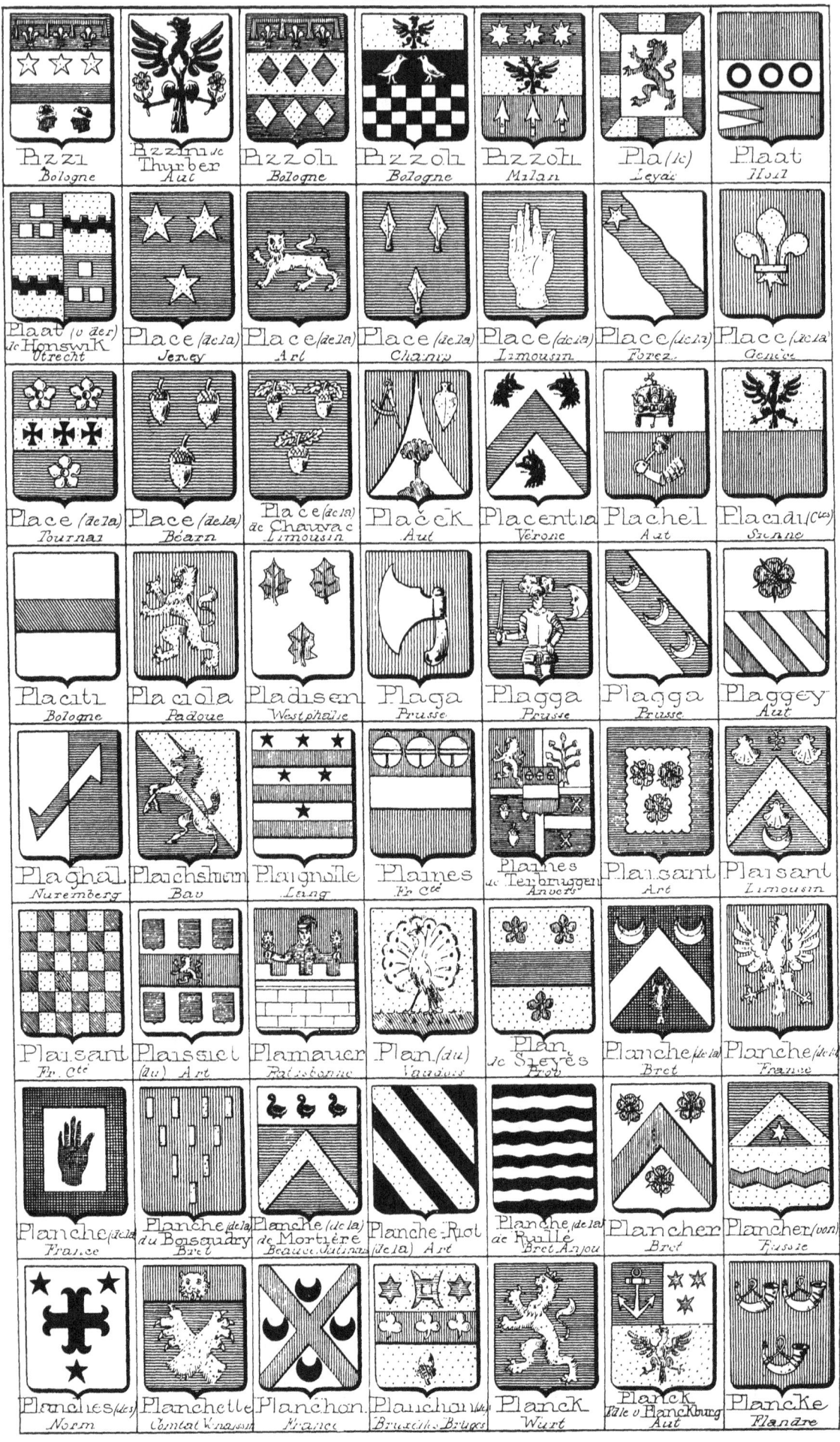

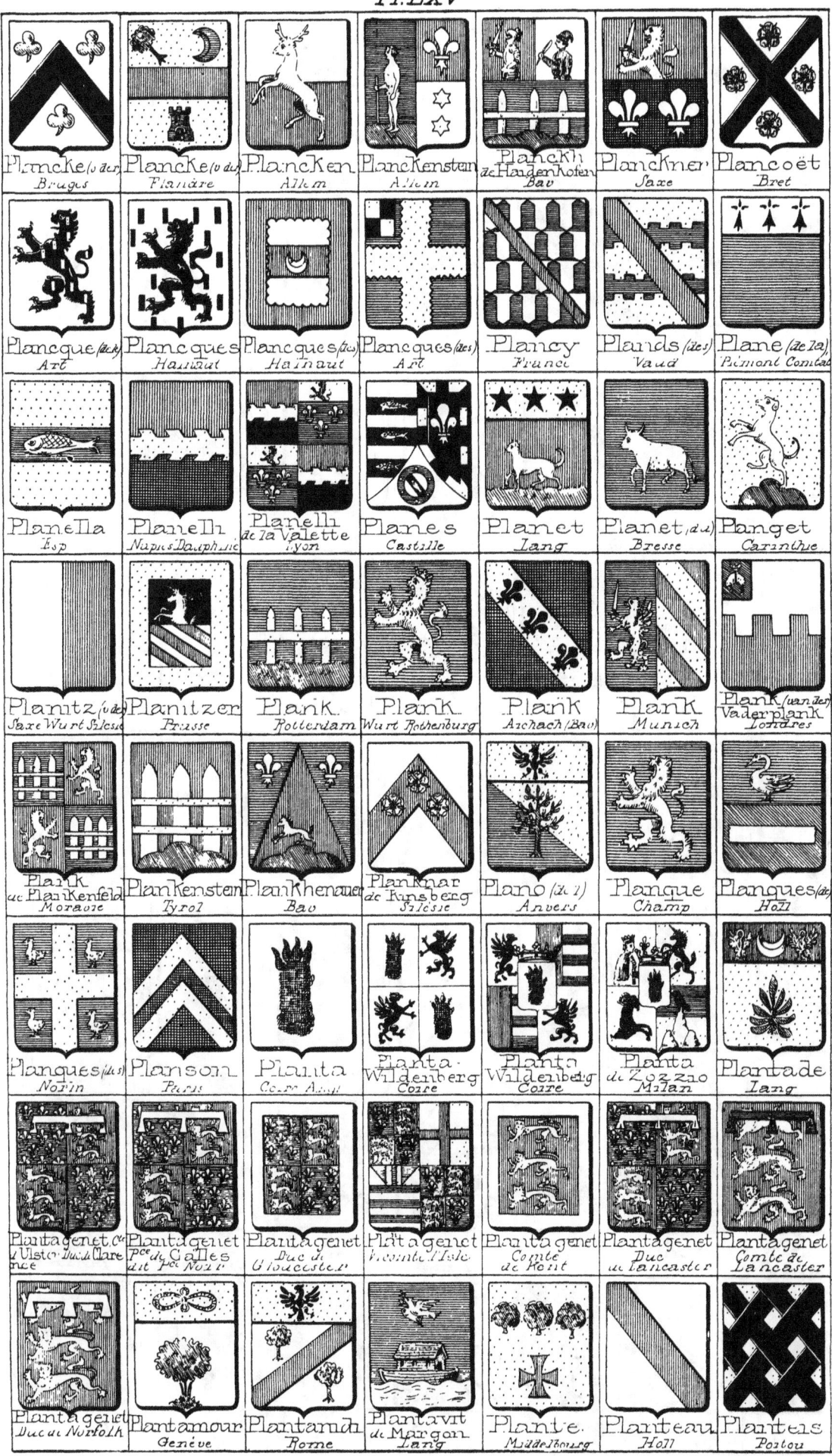

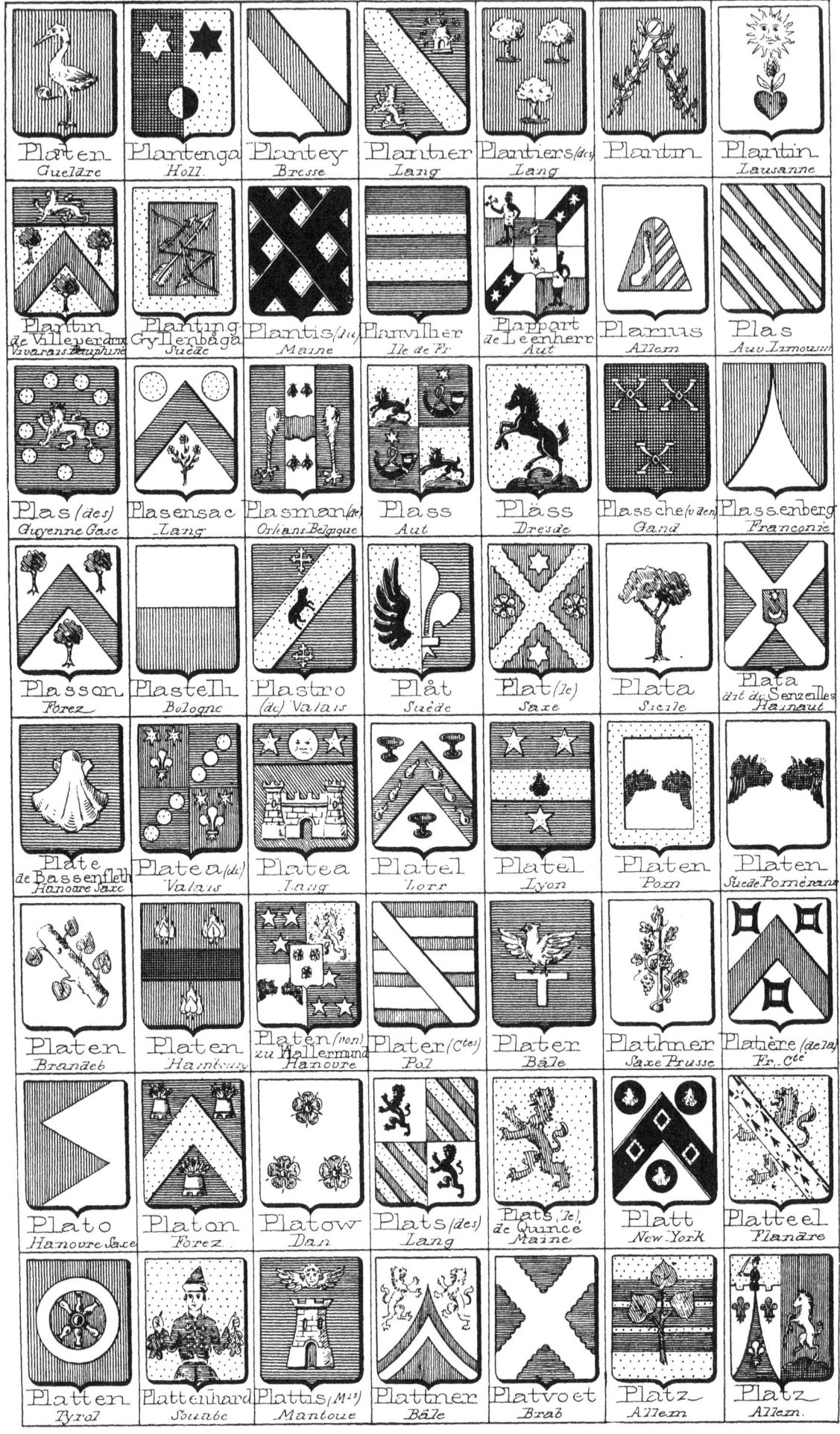

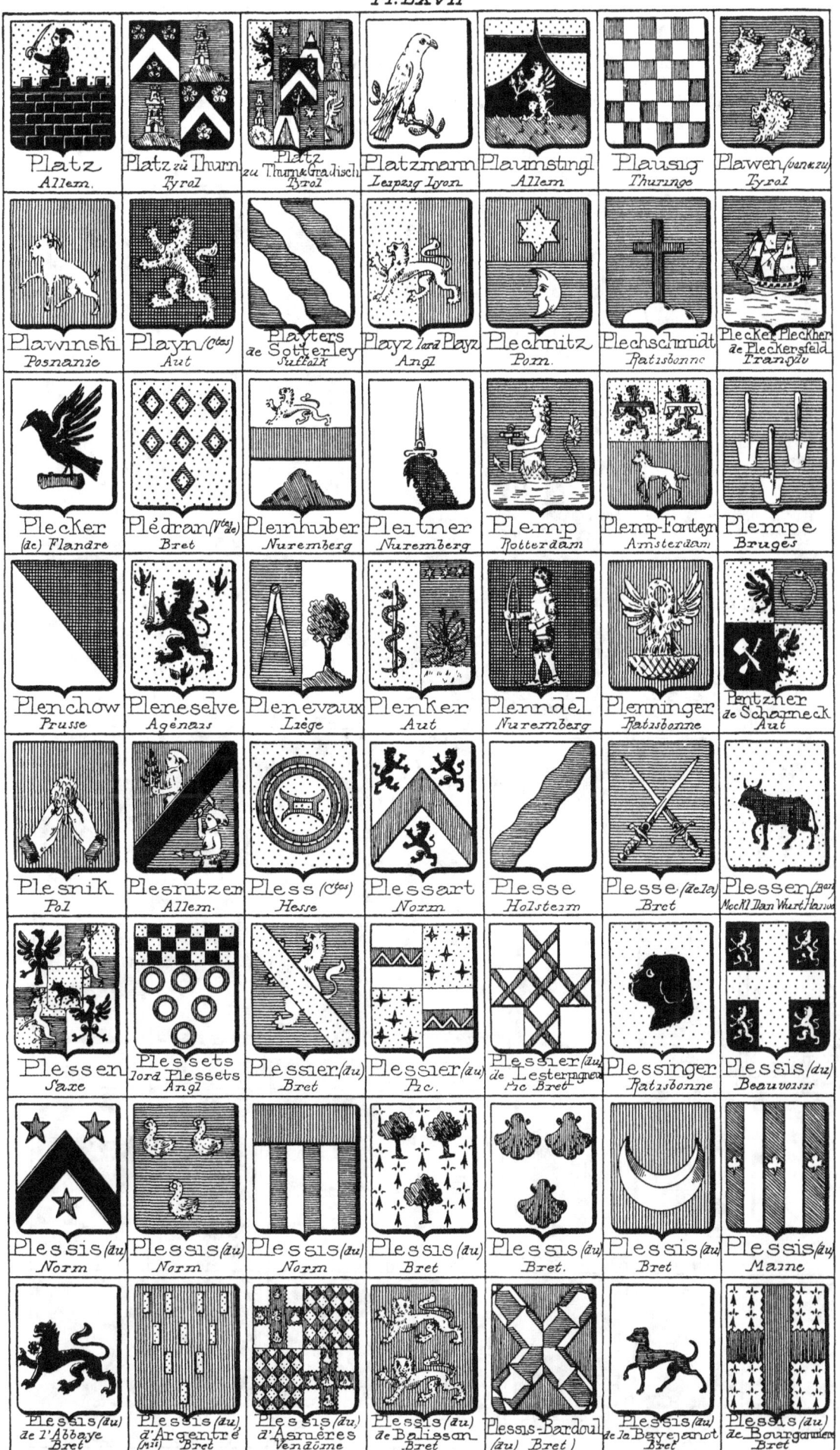

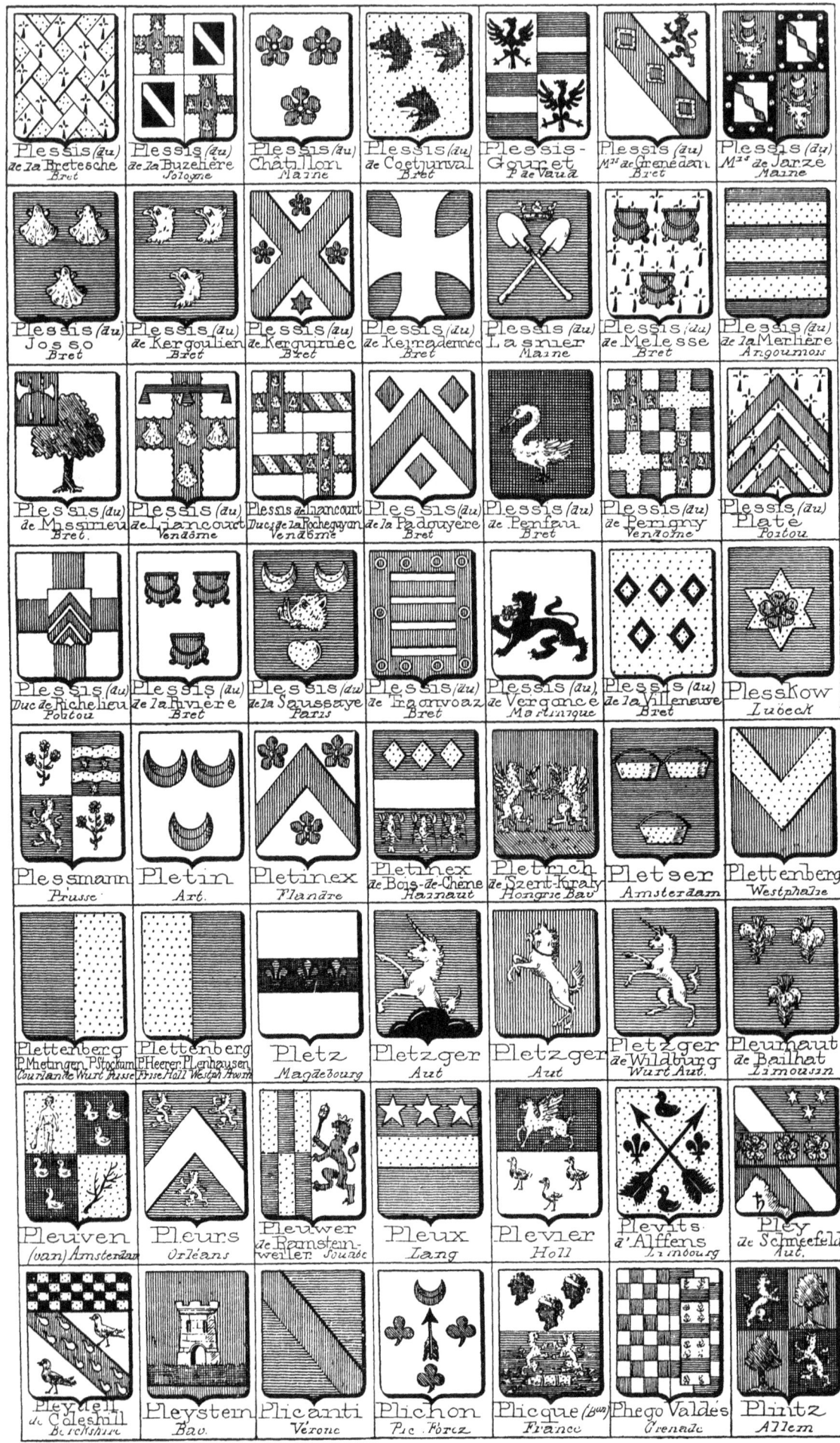

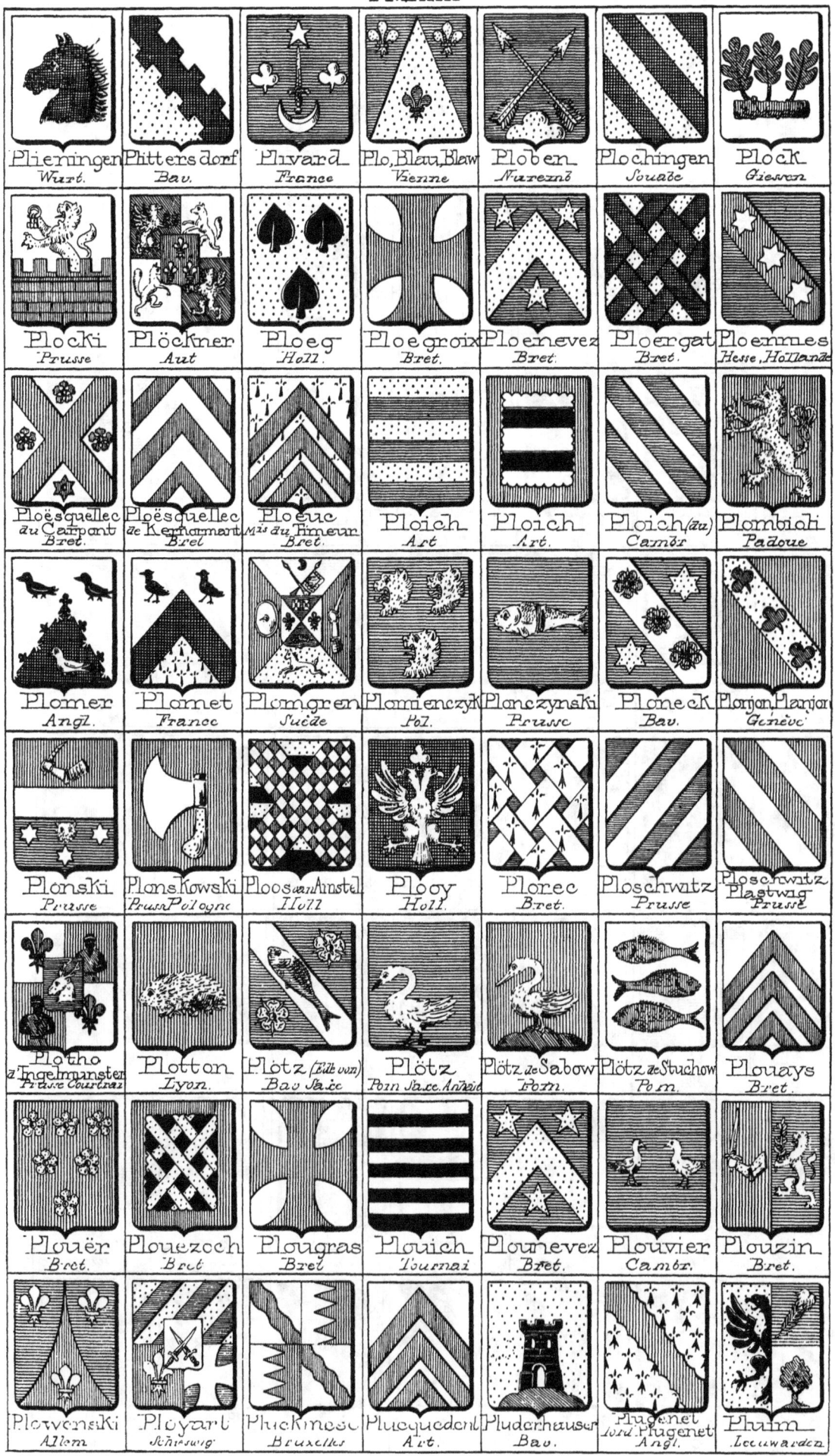

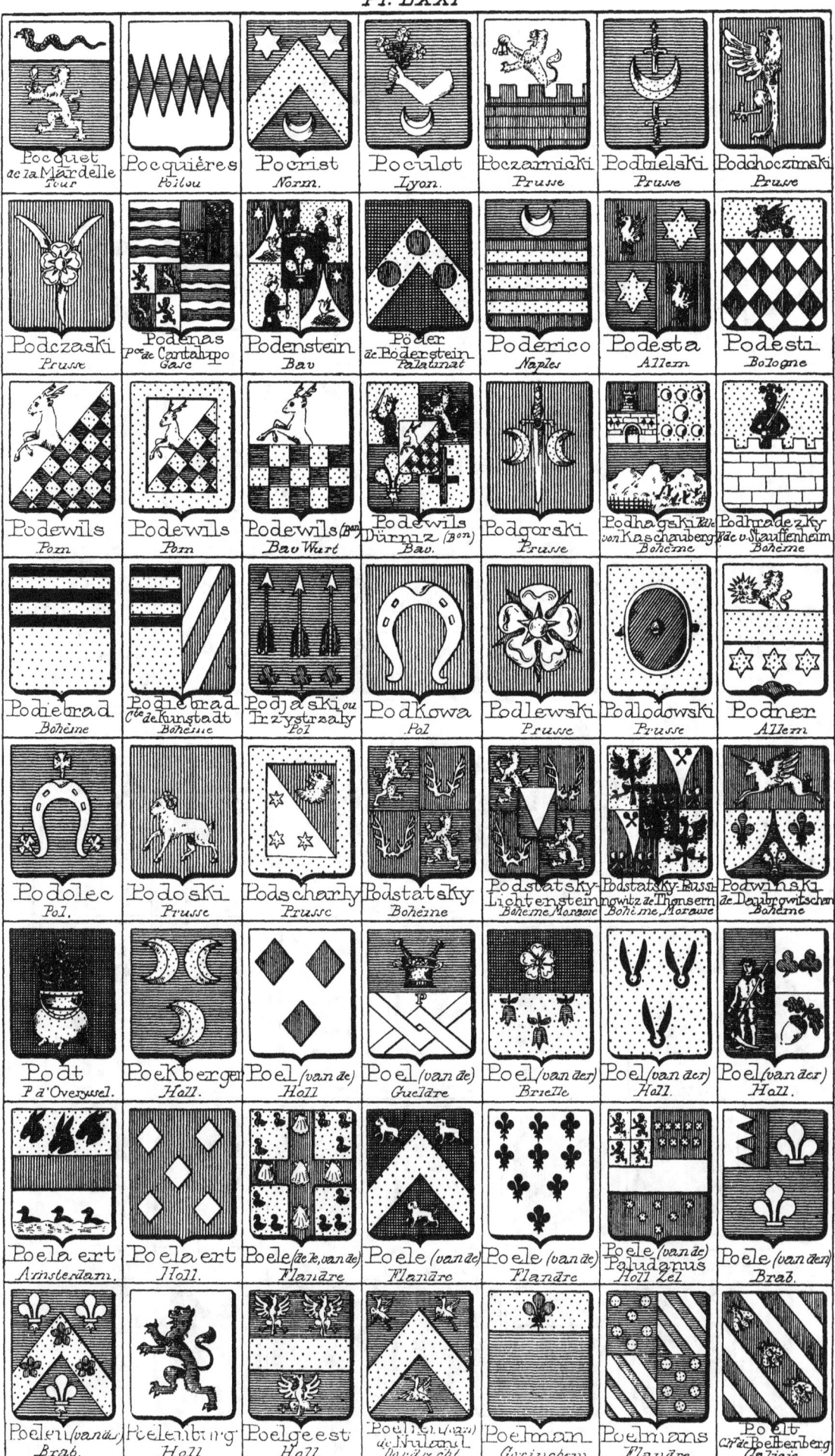

Pl. LXXIII

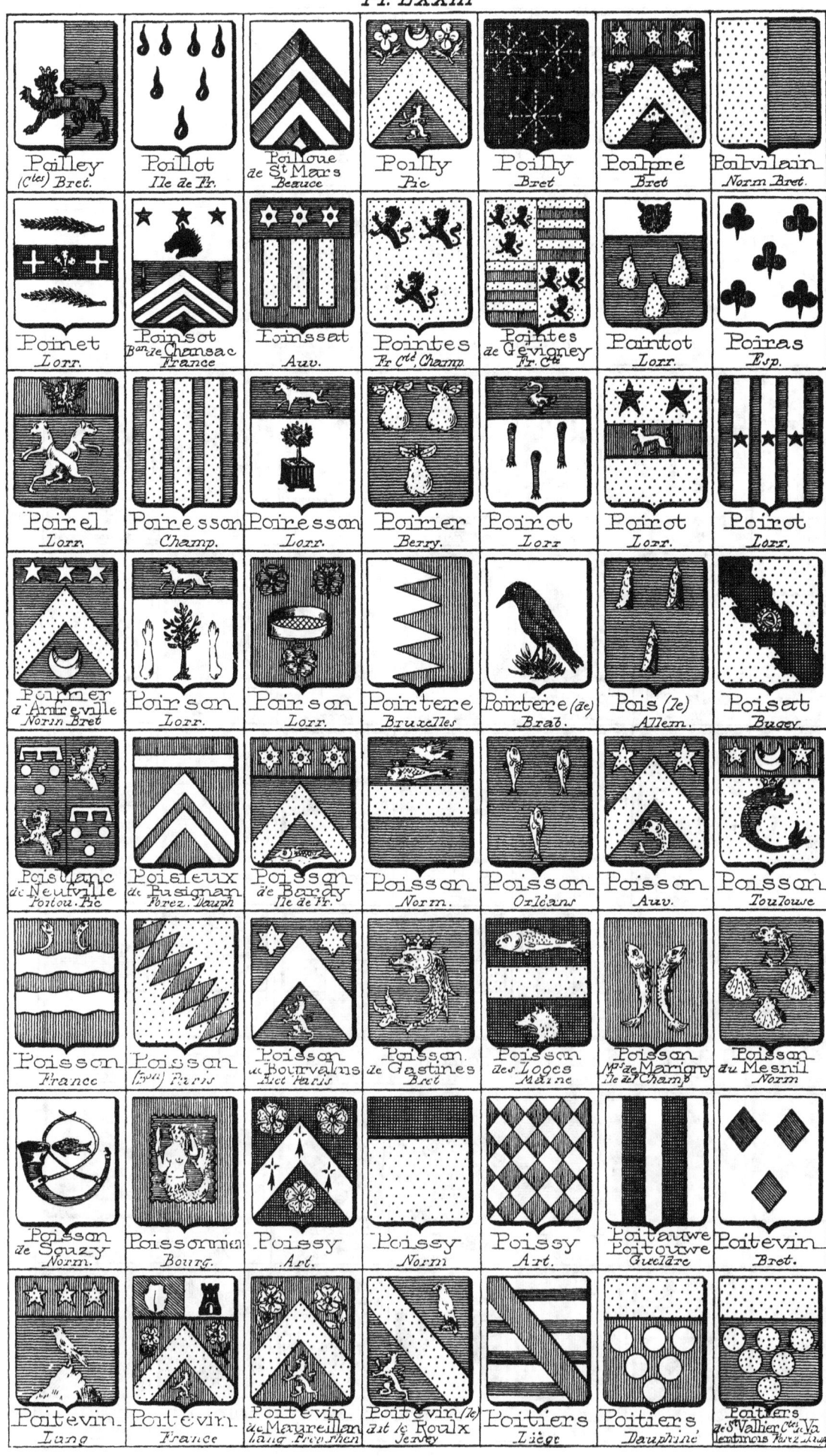

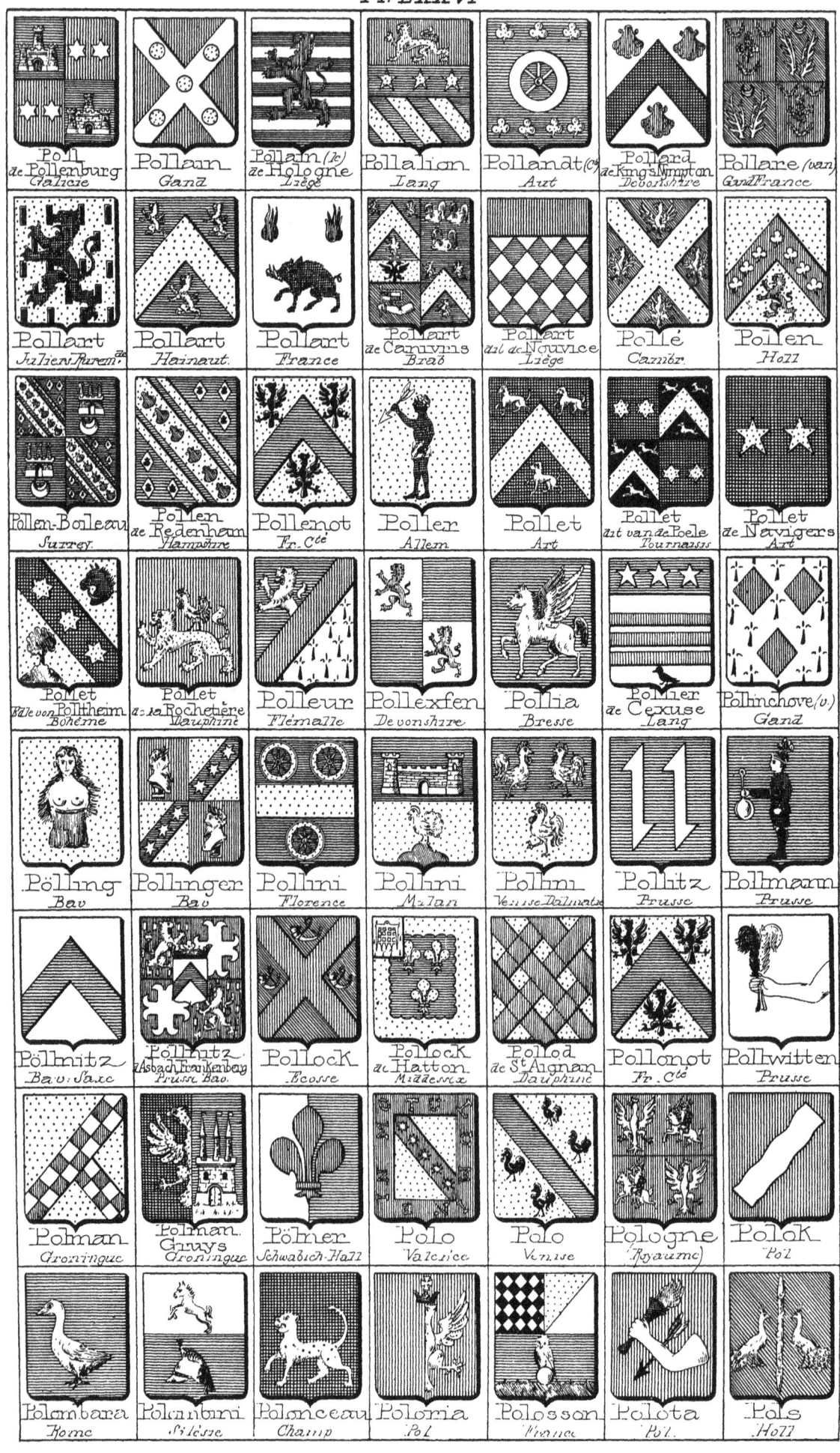

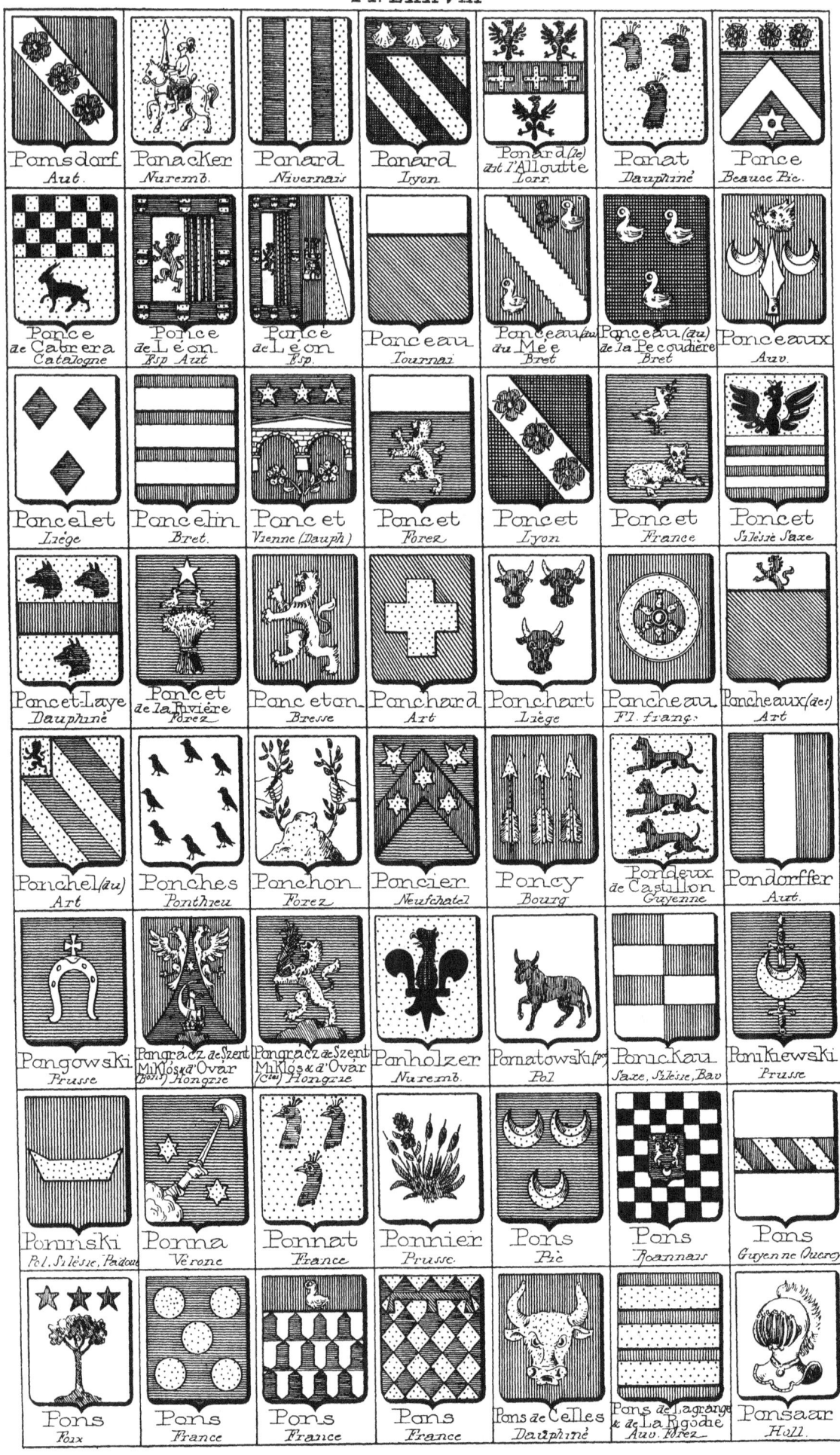

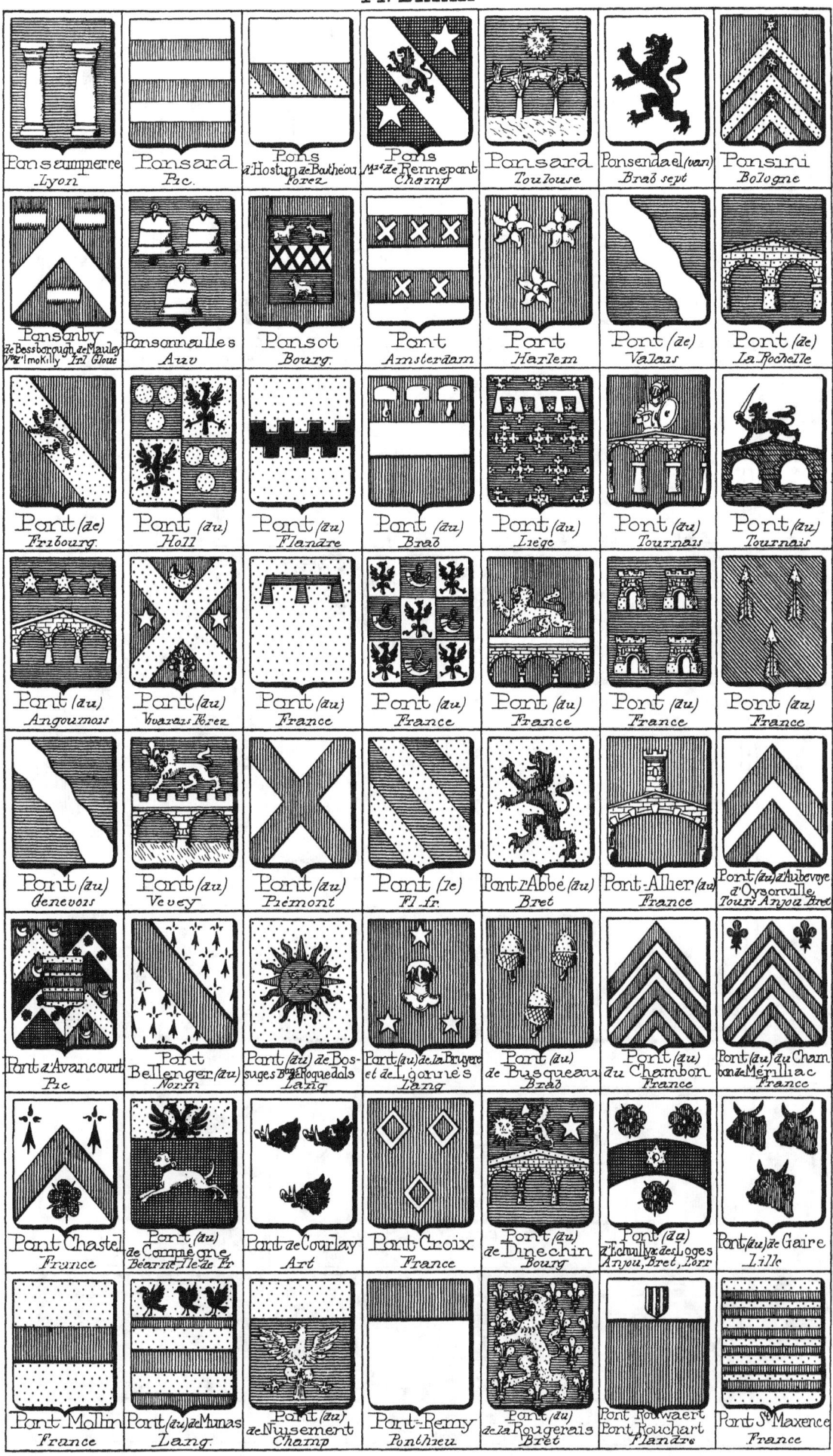

Pl. LXXX

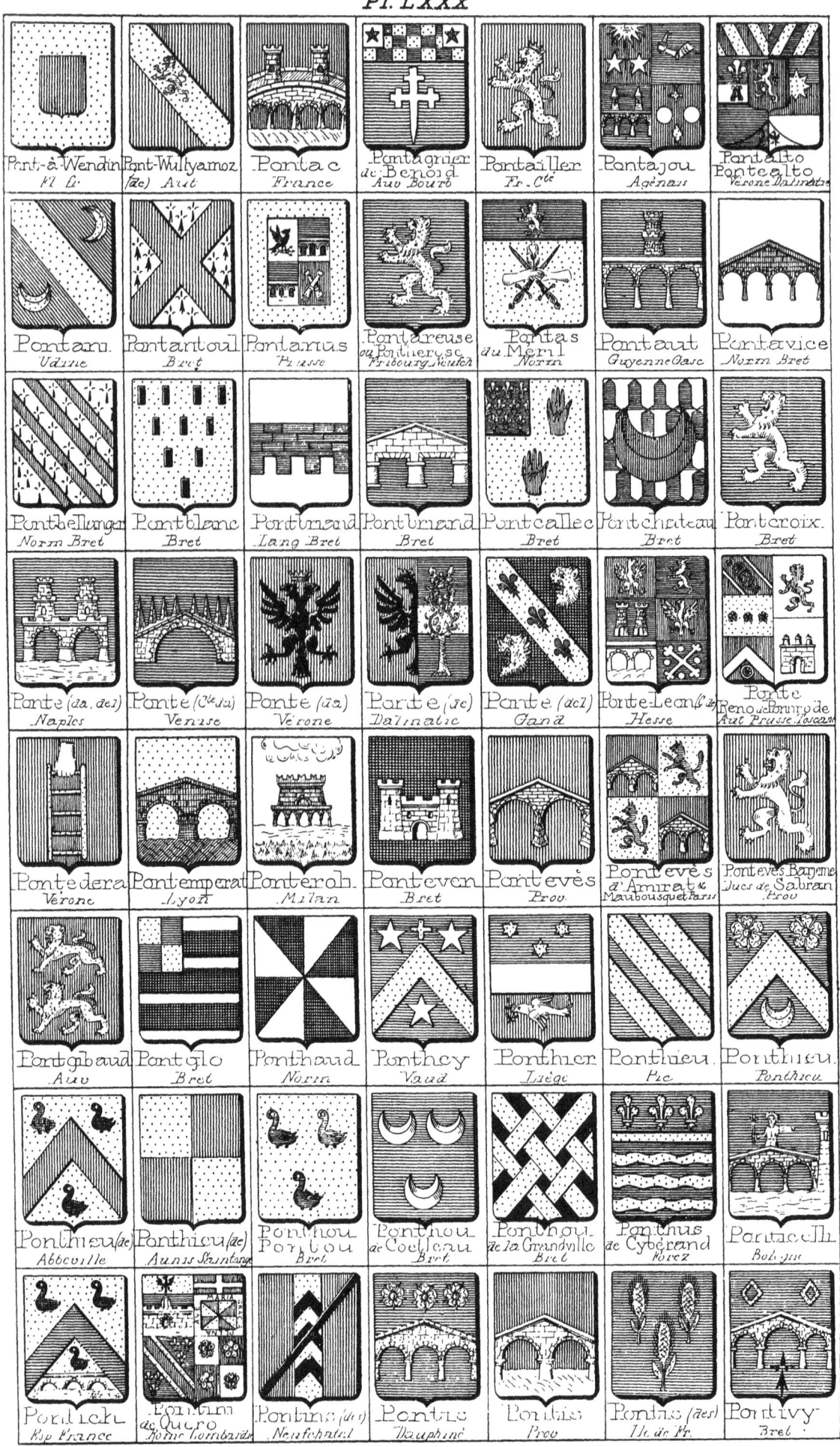

Pl. LXXXI

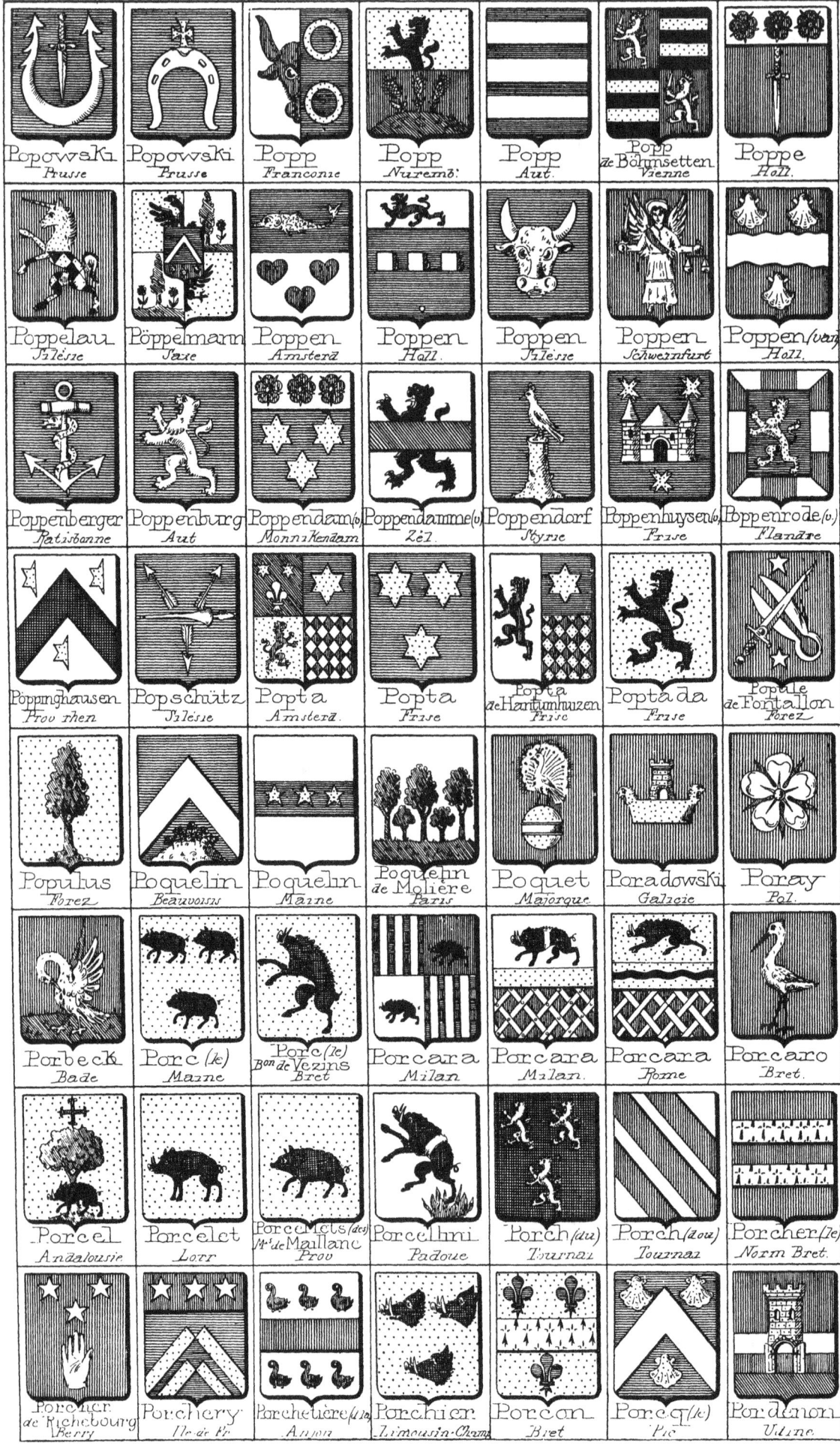

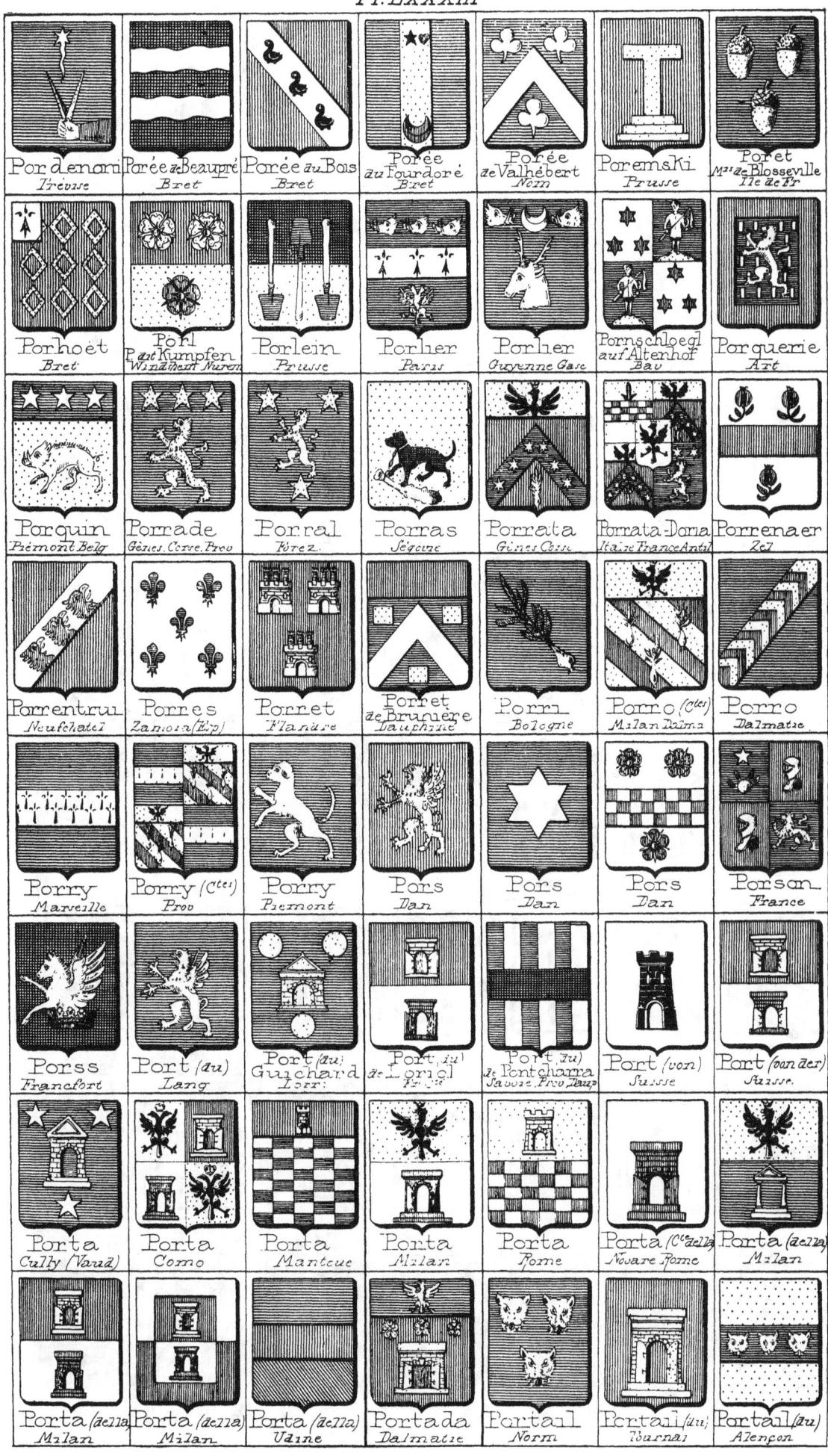

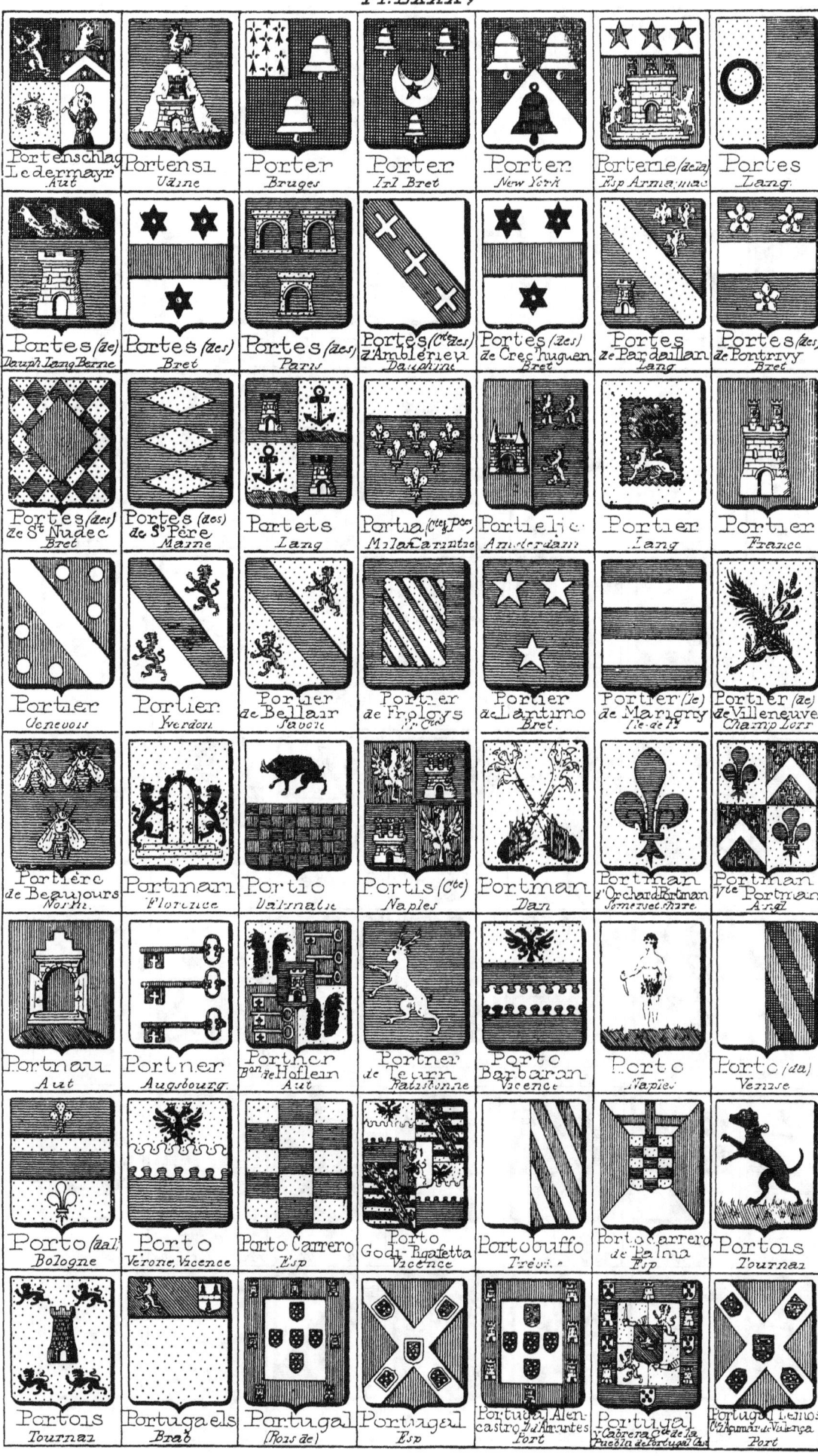

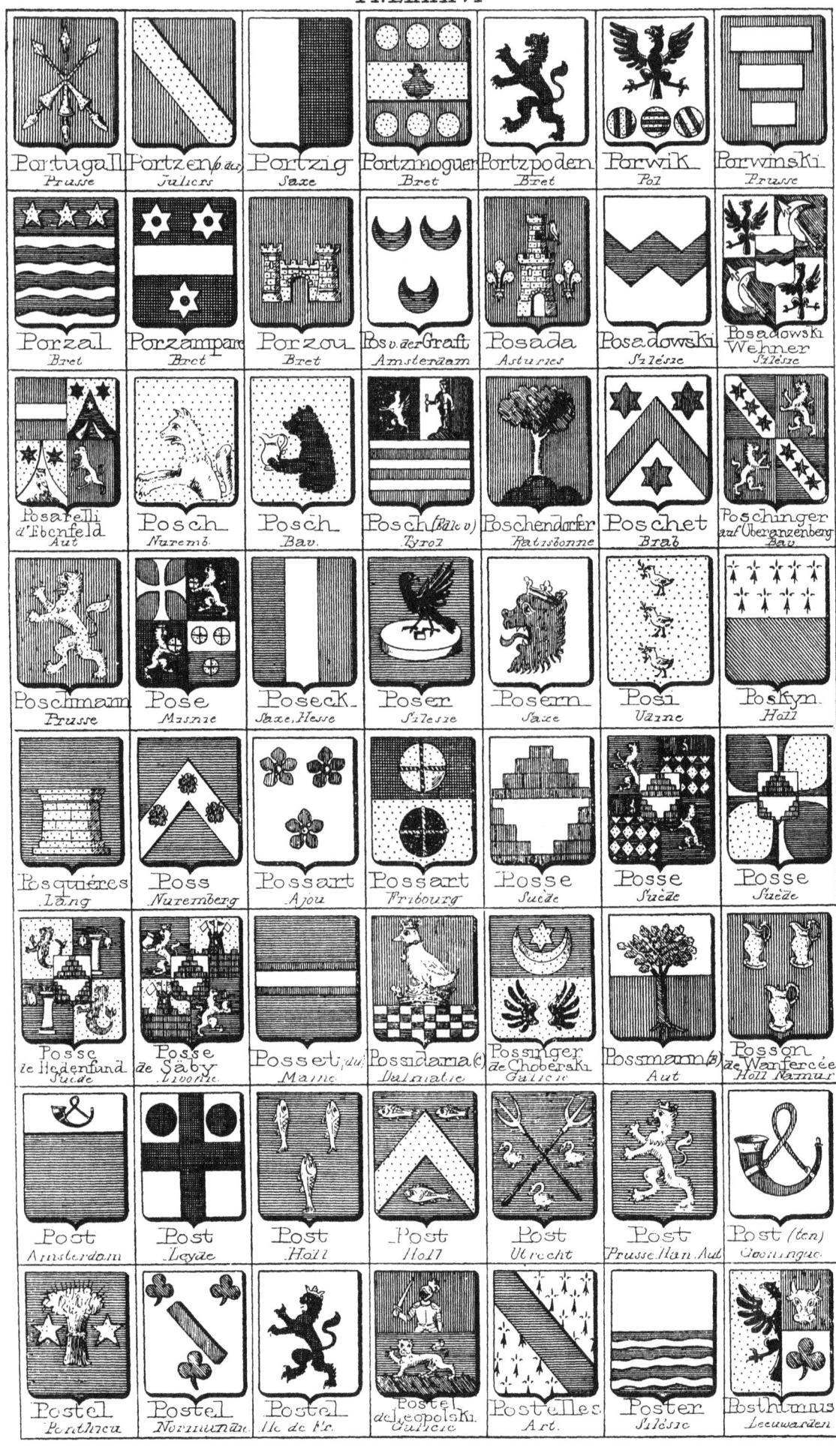

Pl. LXXXVI

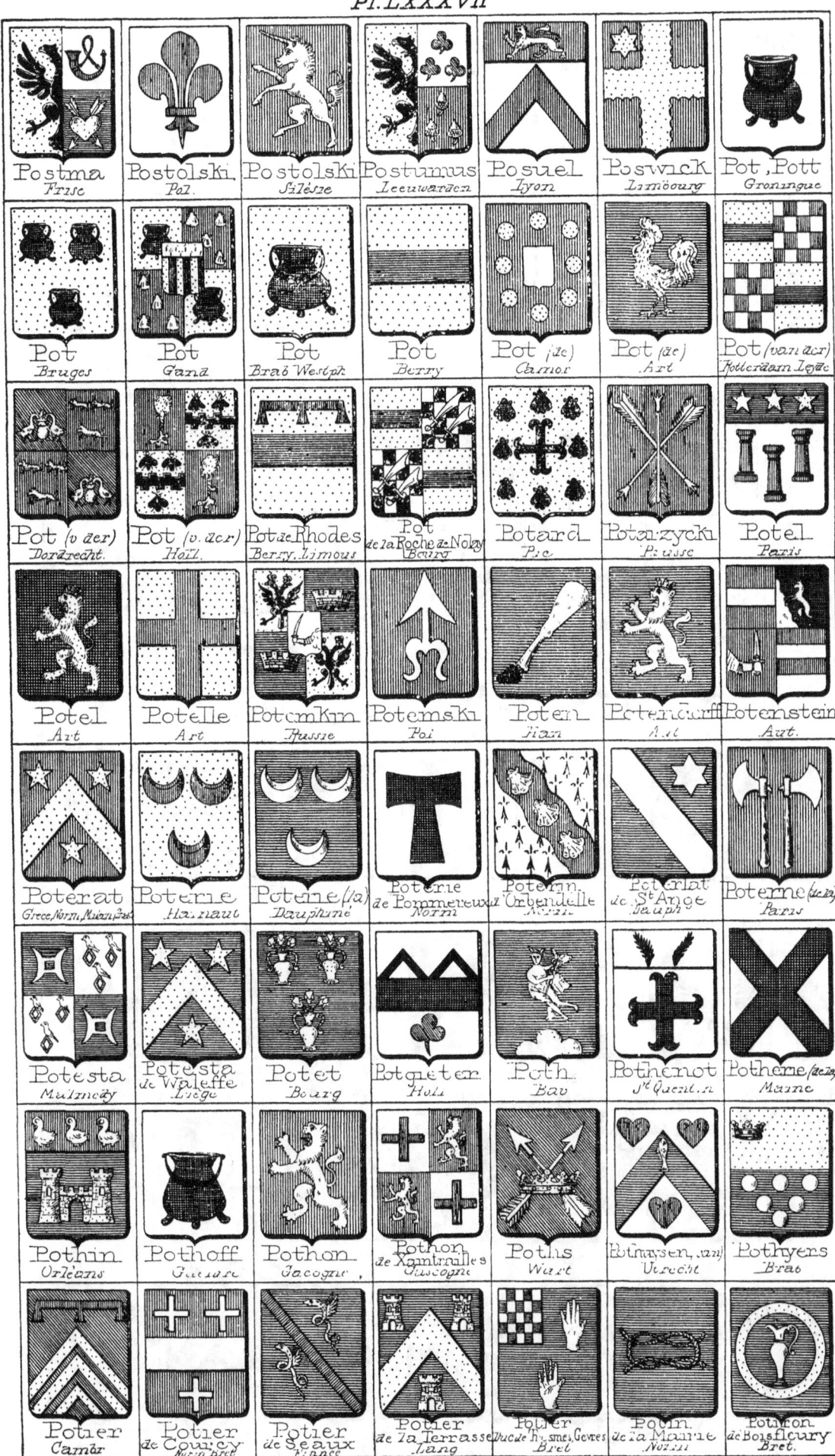

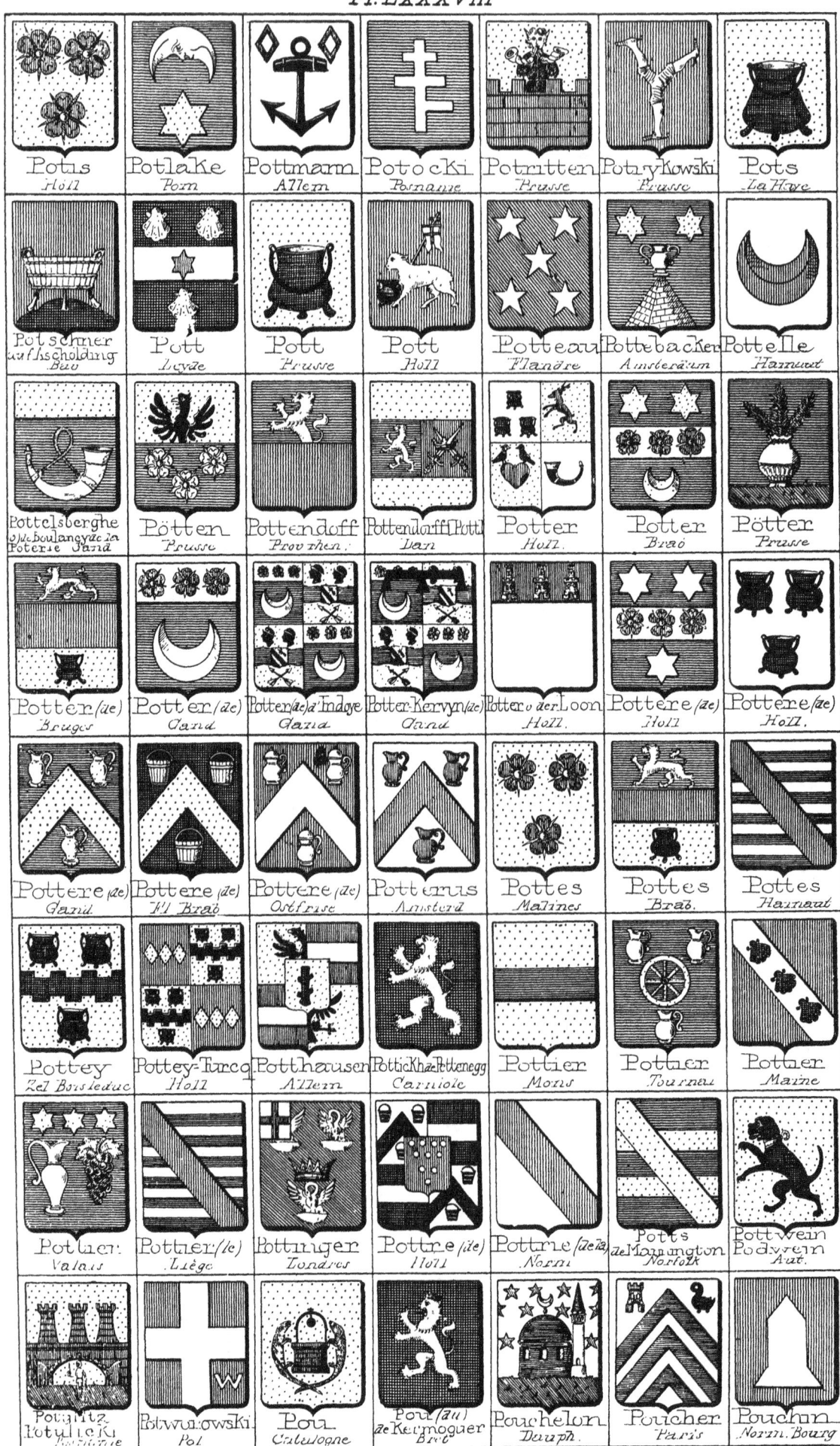

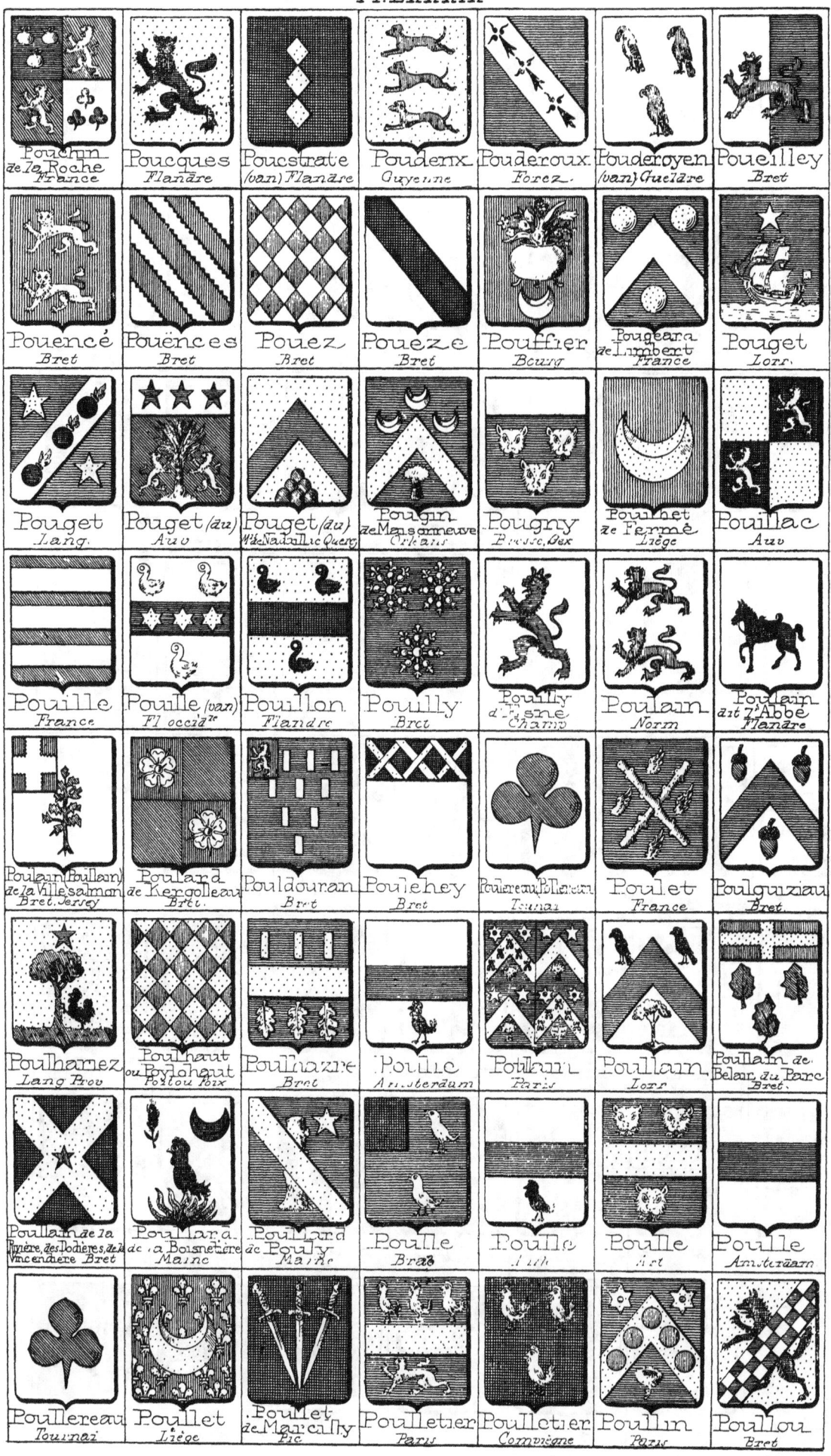

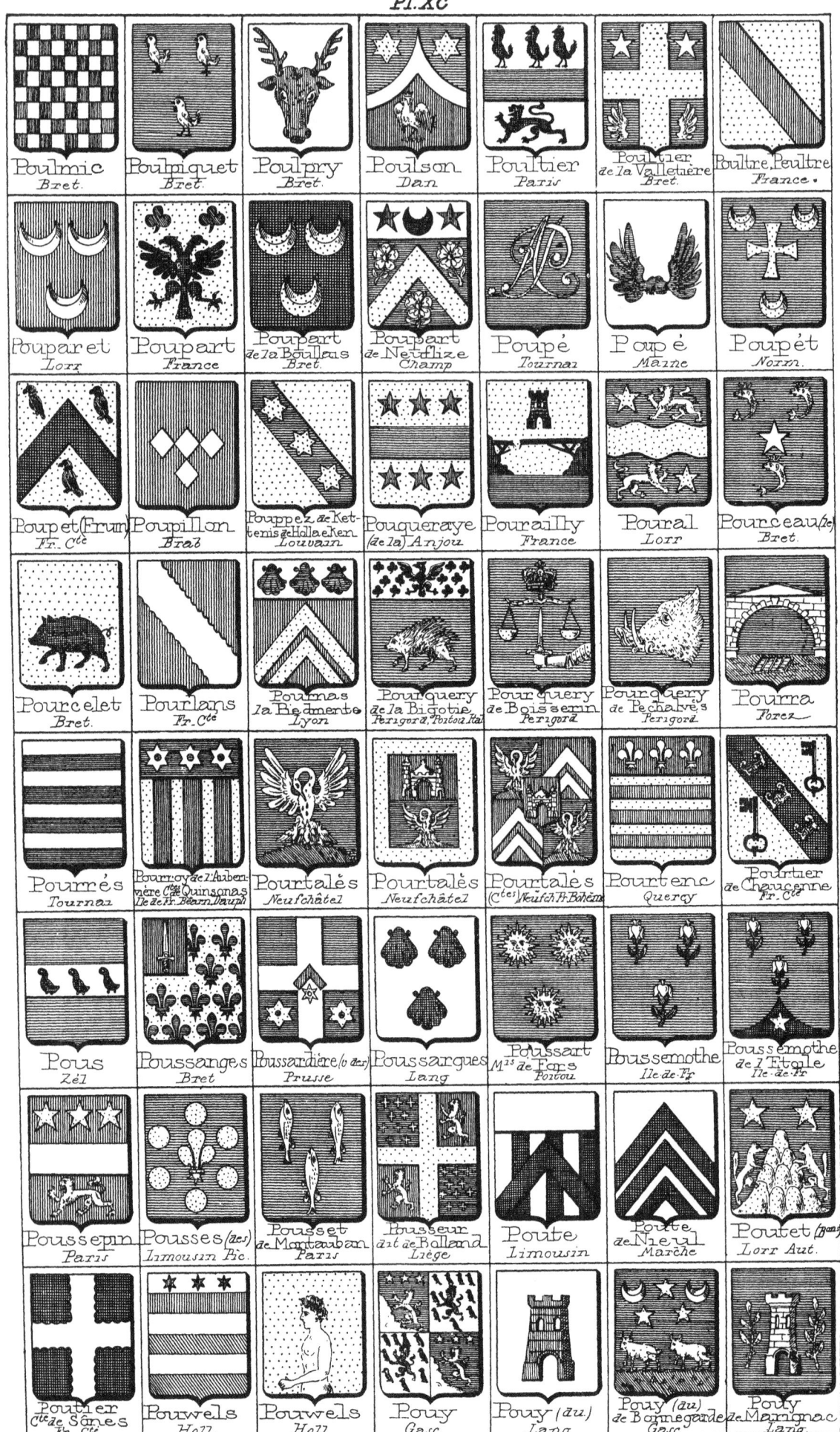

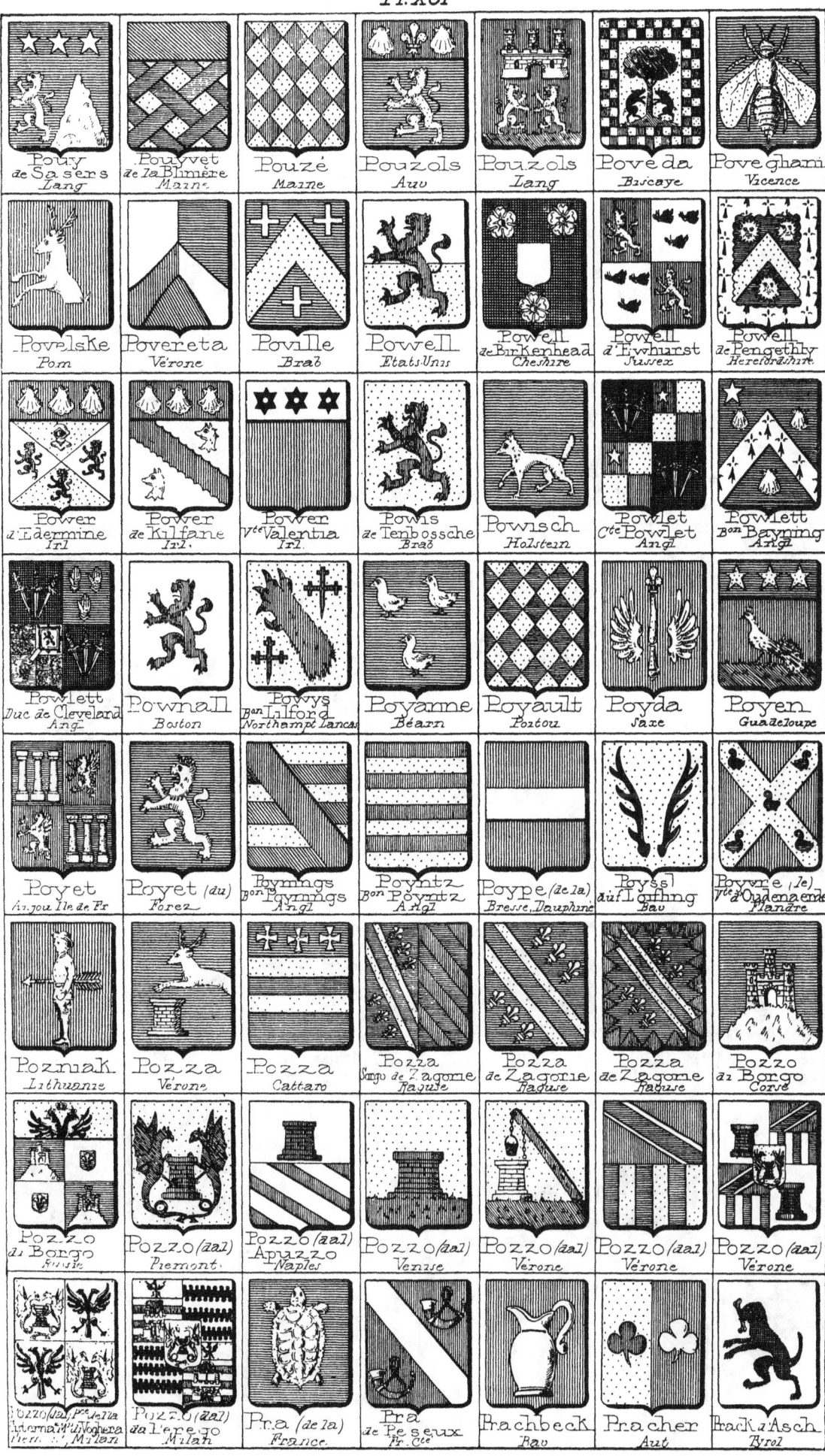
Pl. XCI

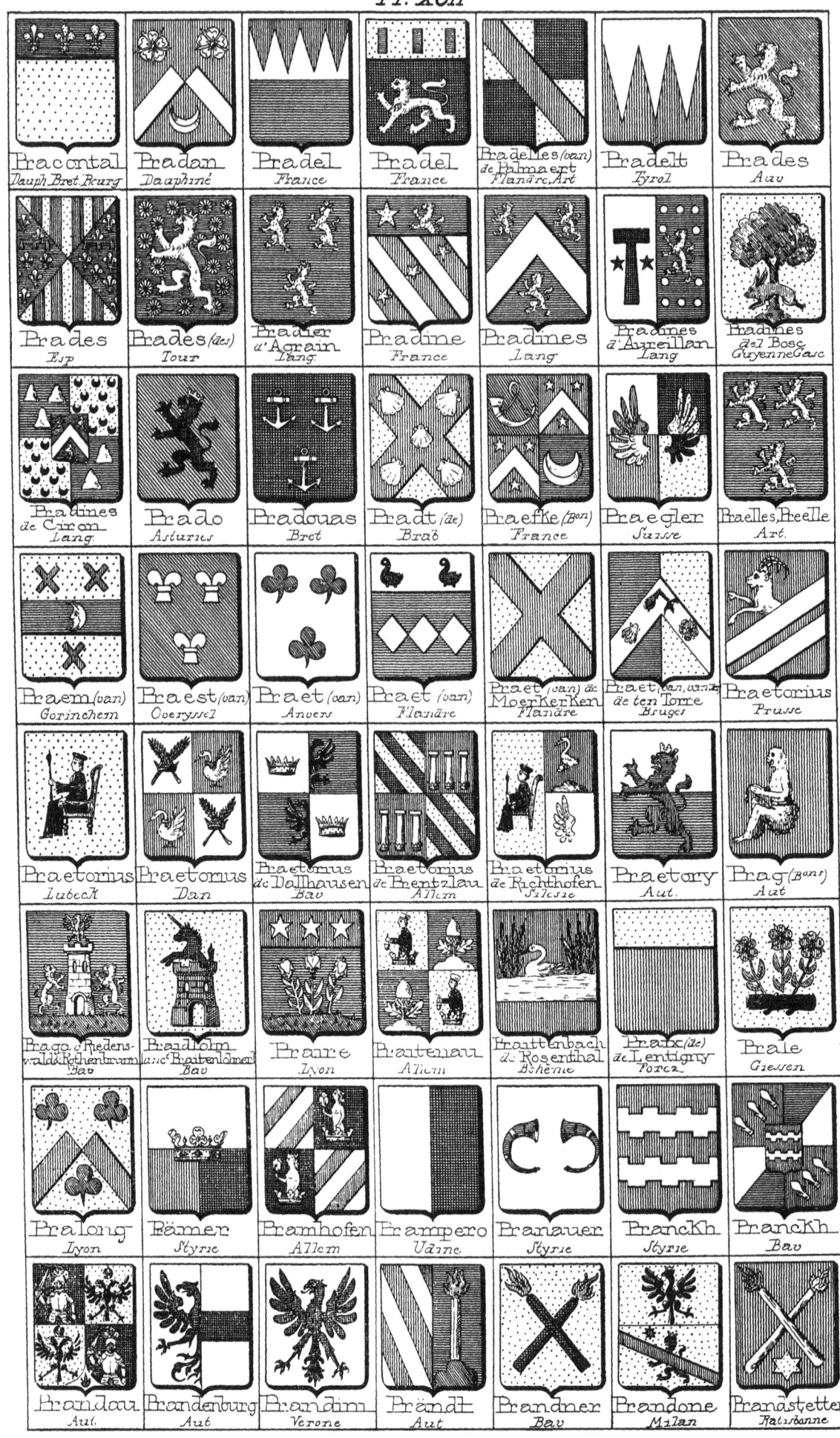

Pl. XCIII

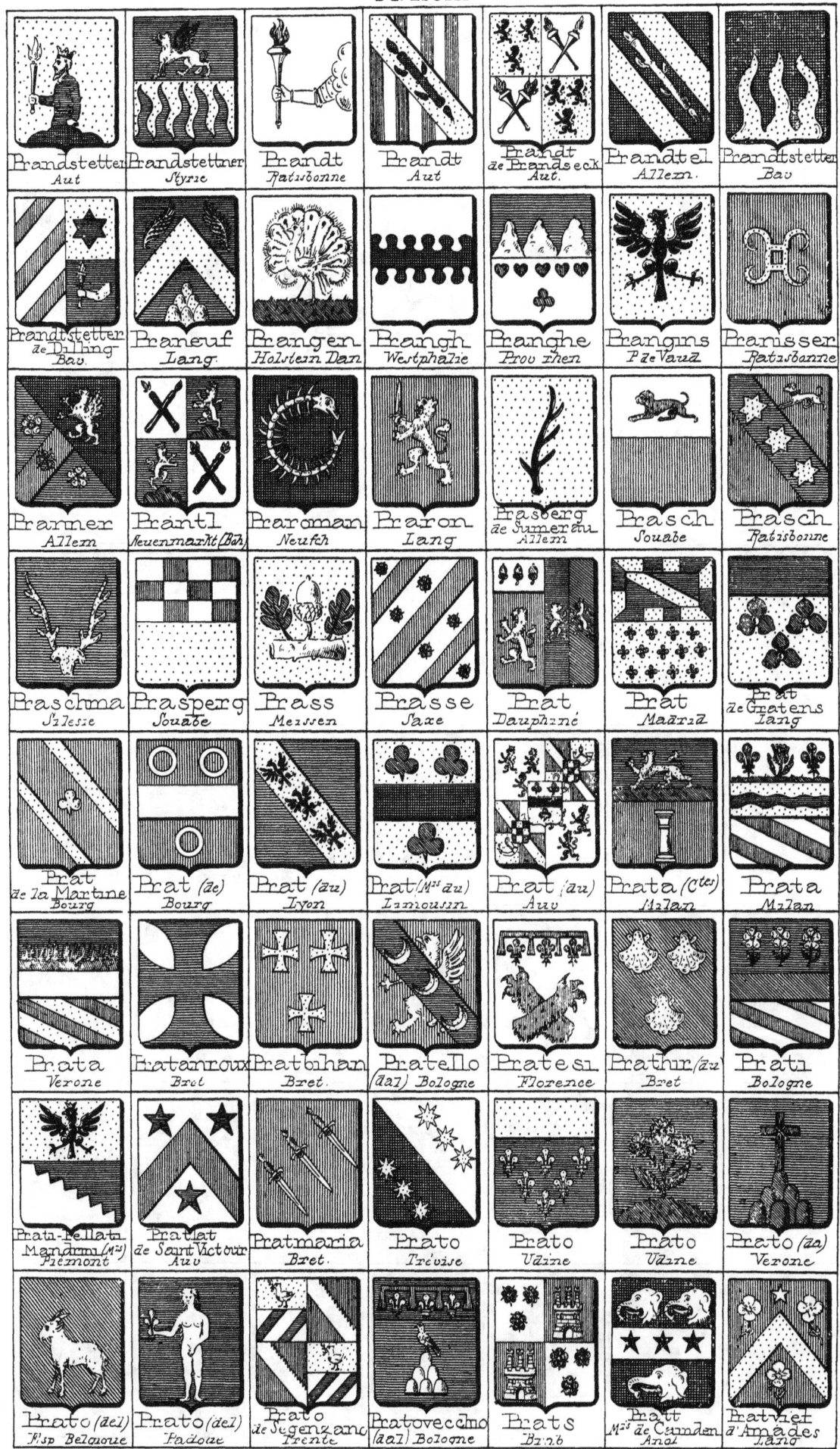

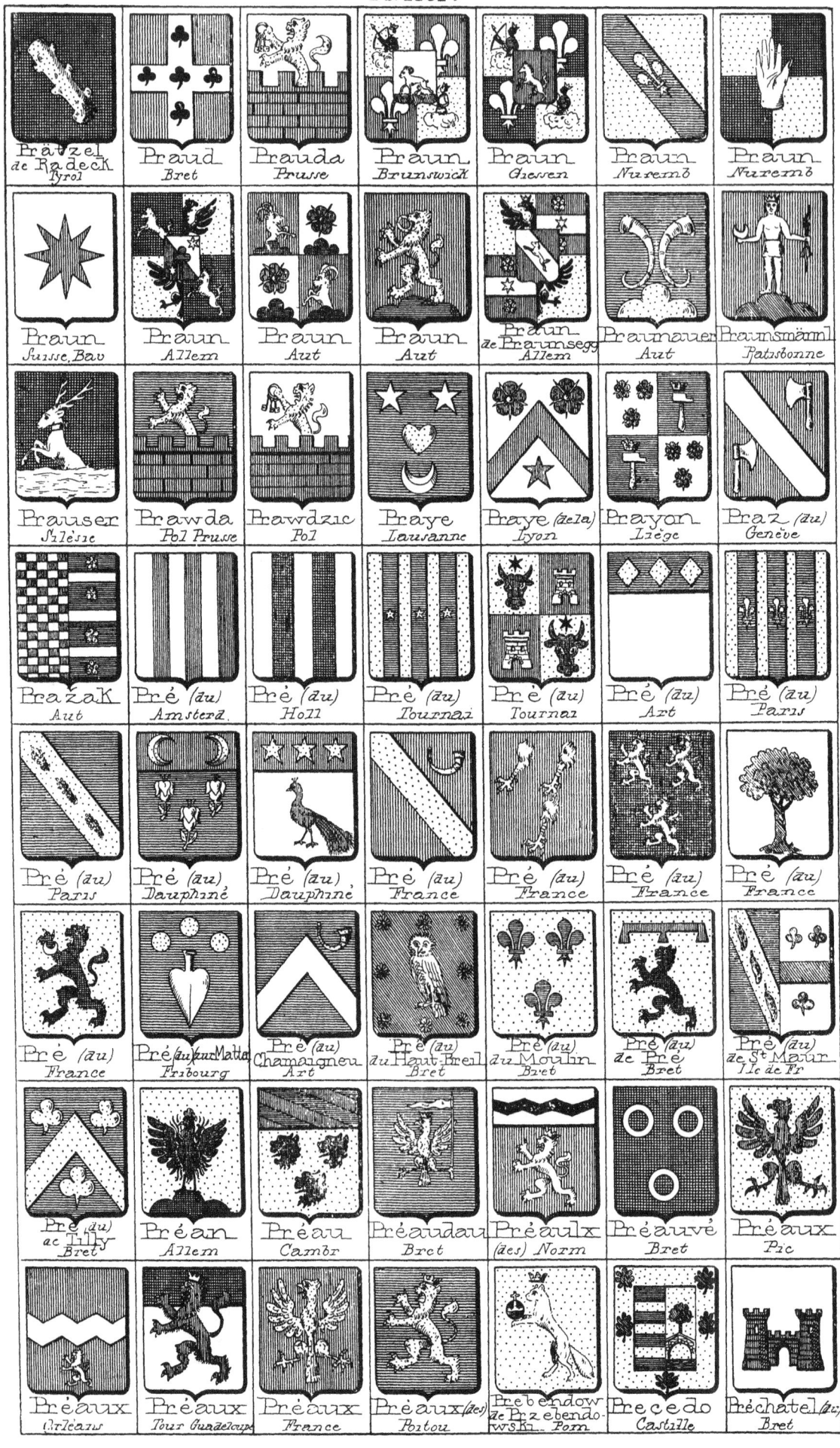

Pl. XCIV

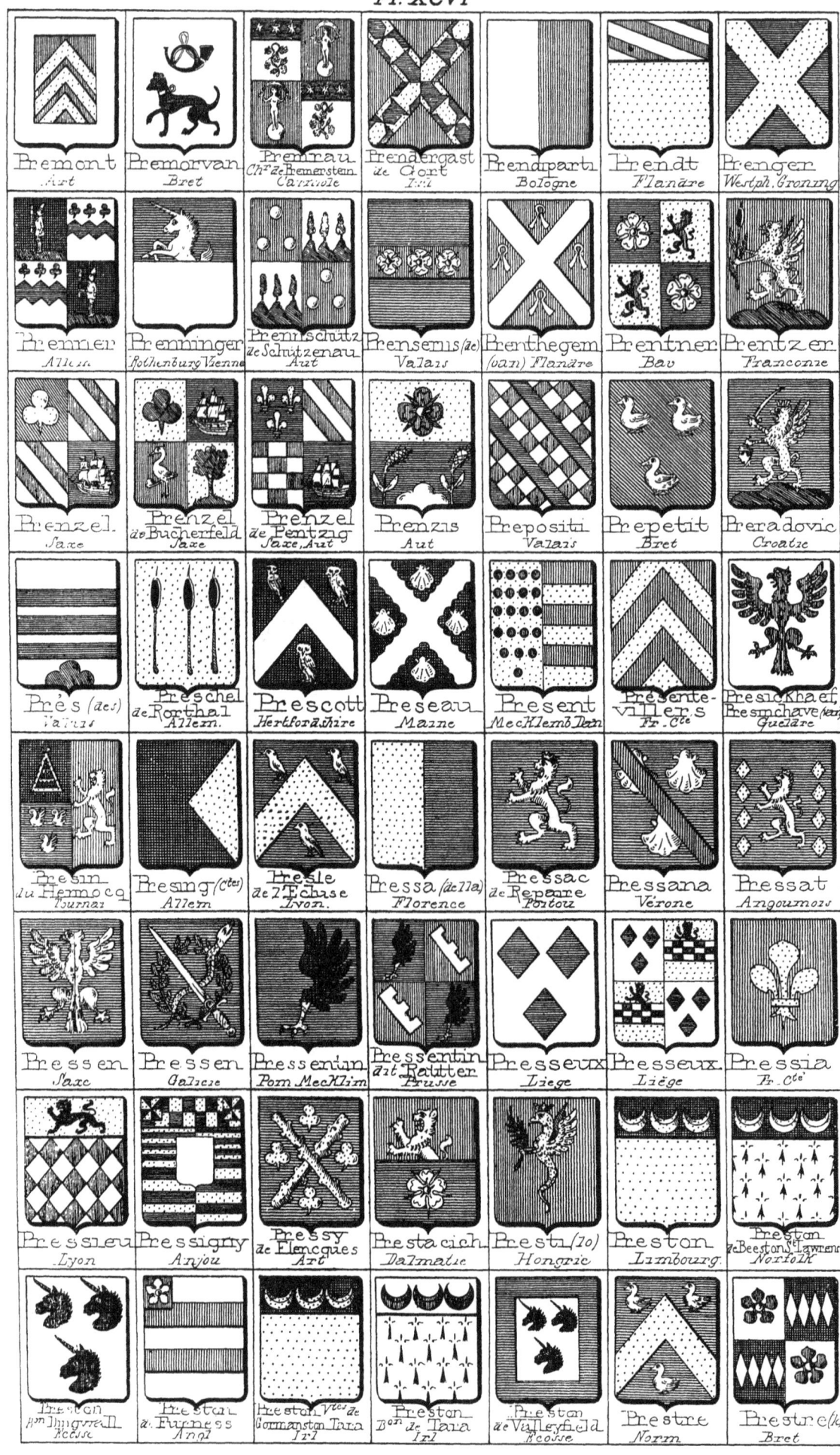

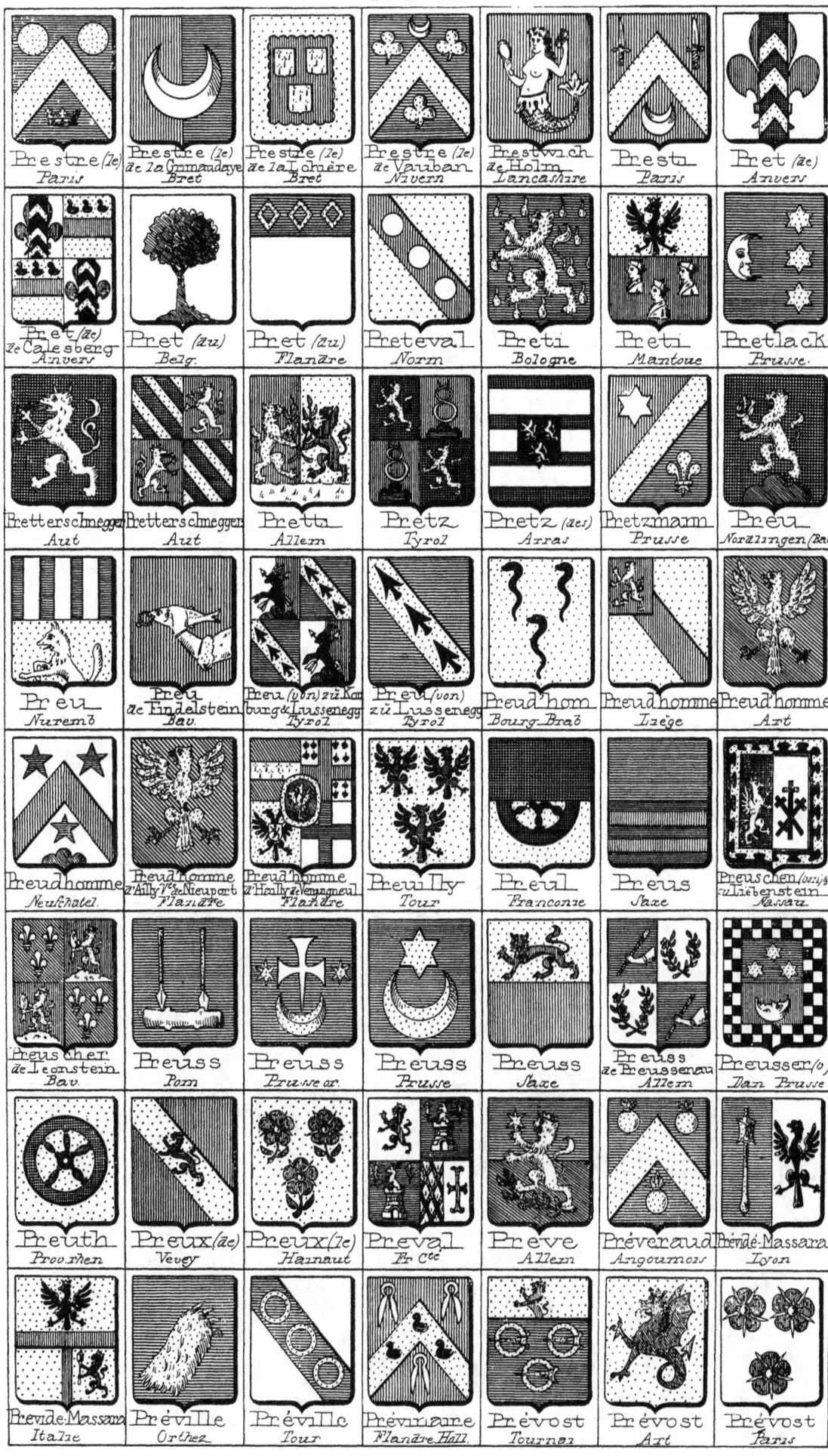

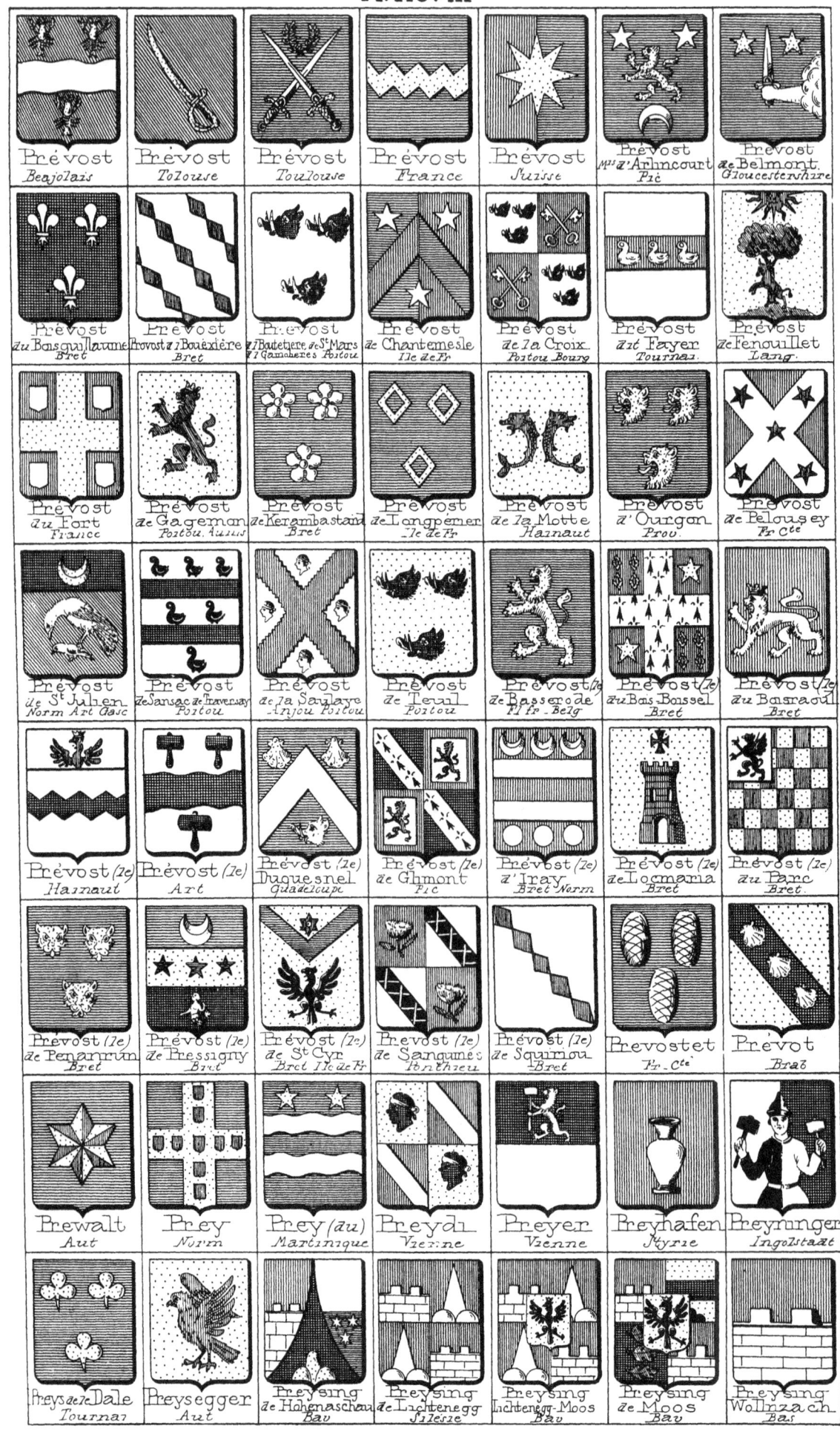

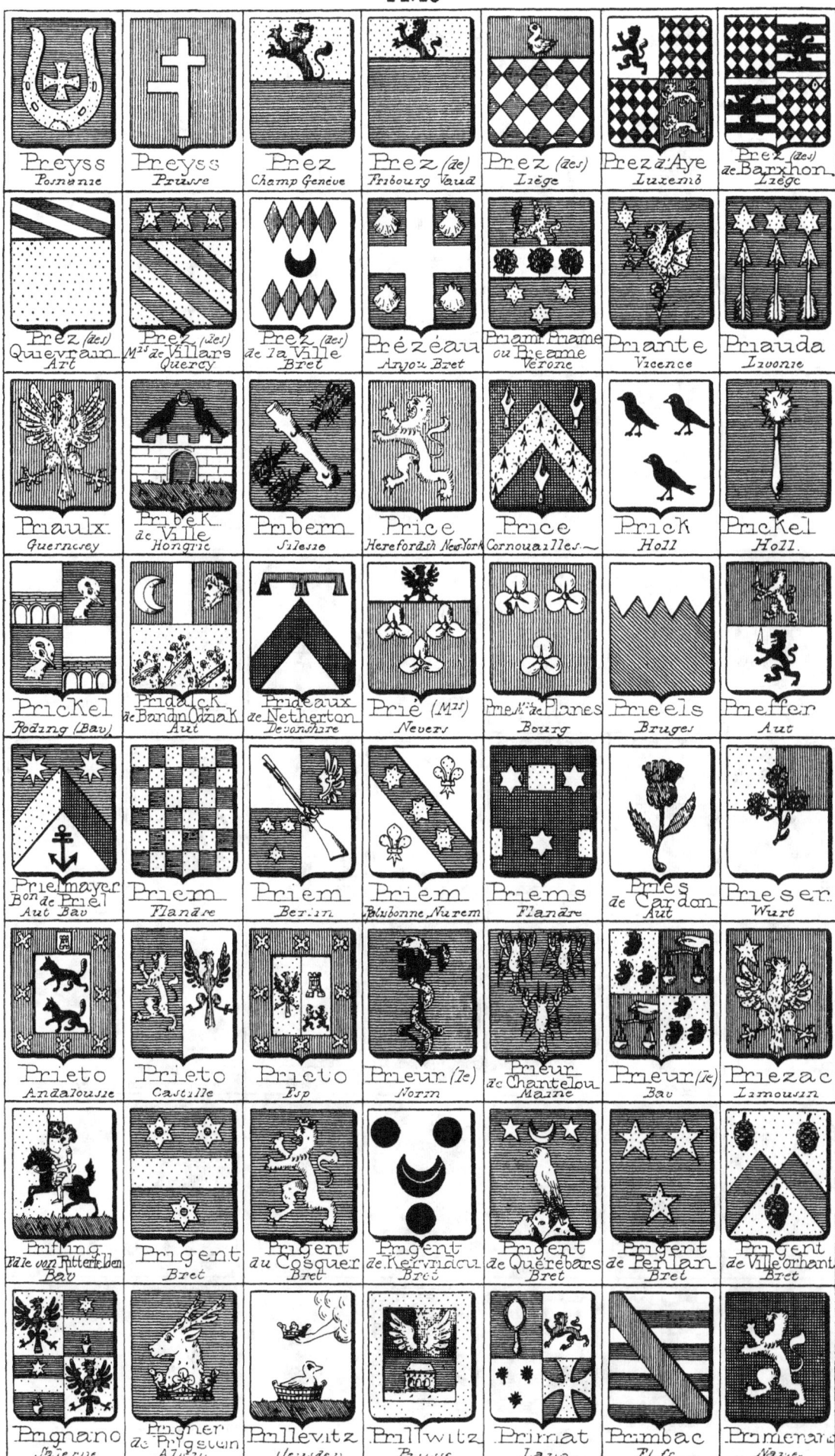

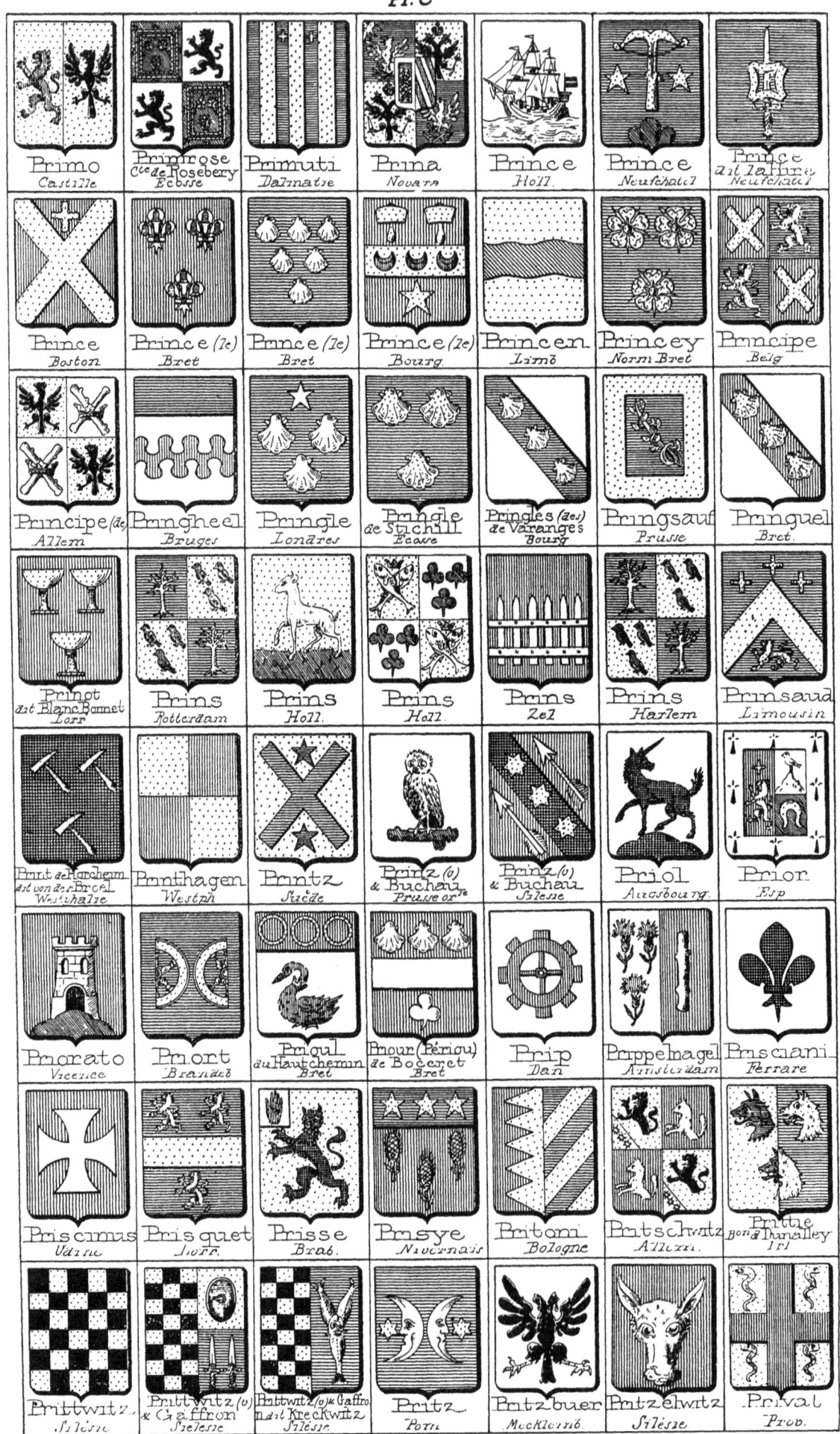

Pl. CI

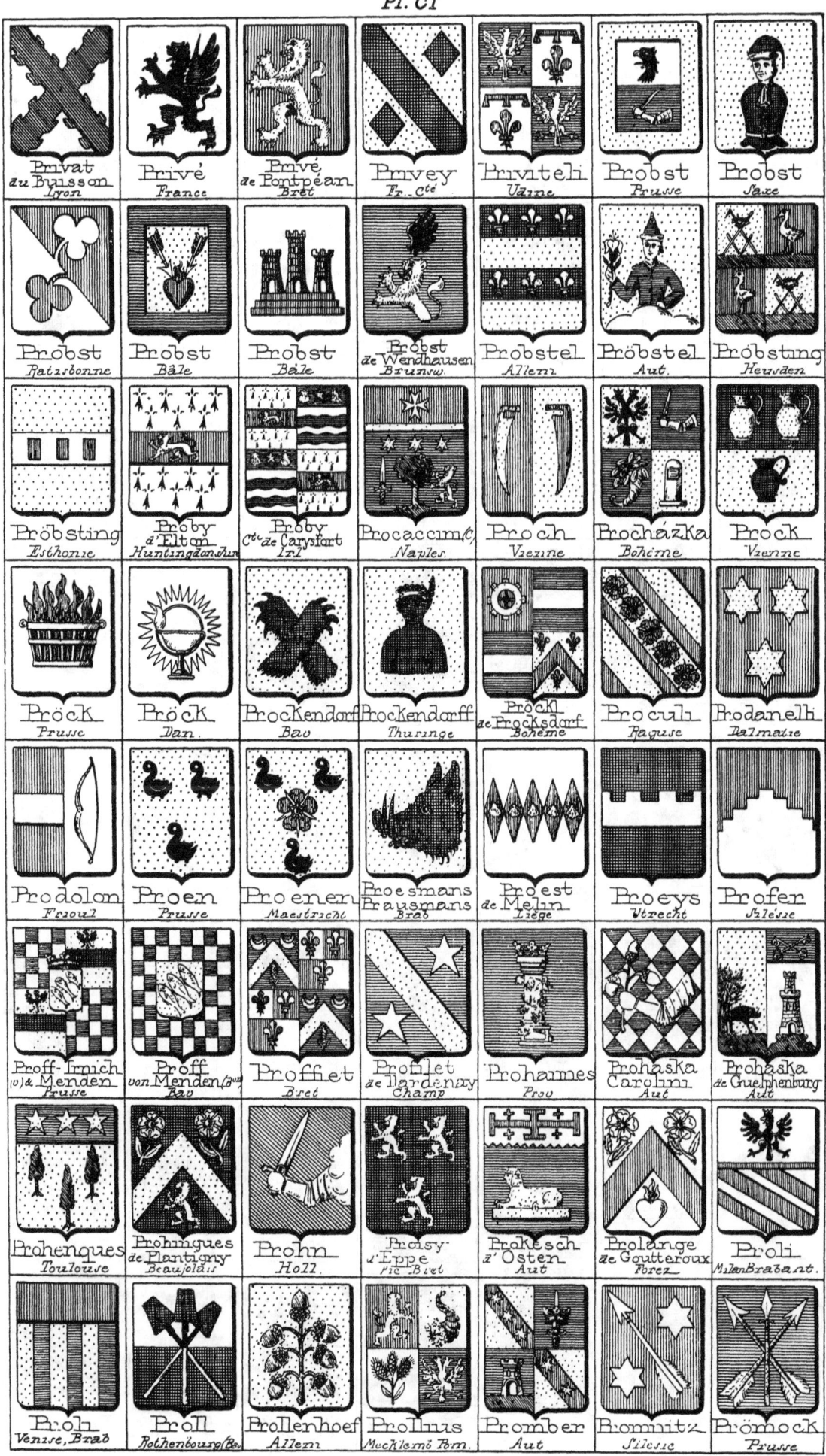

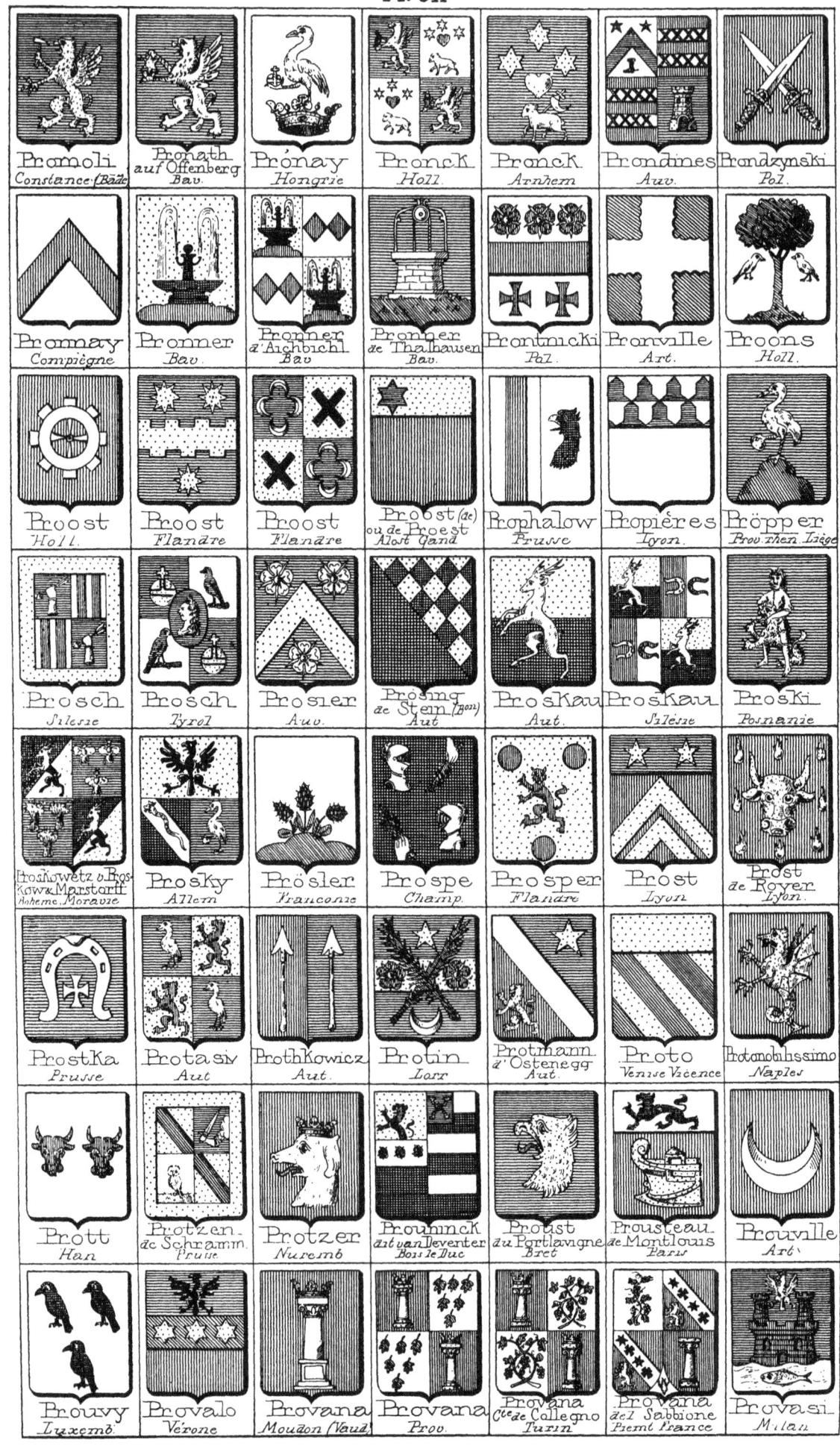

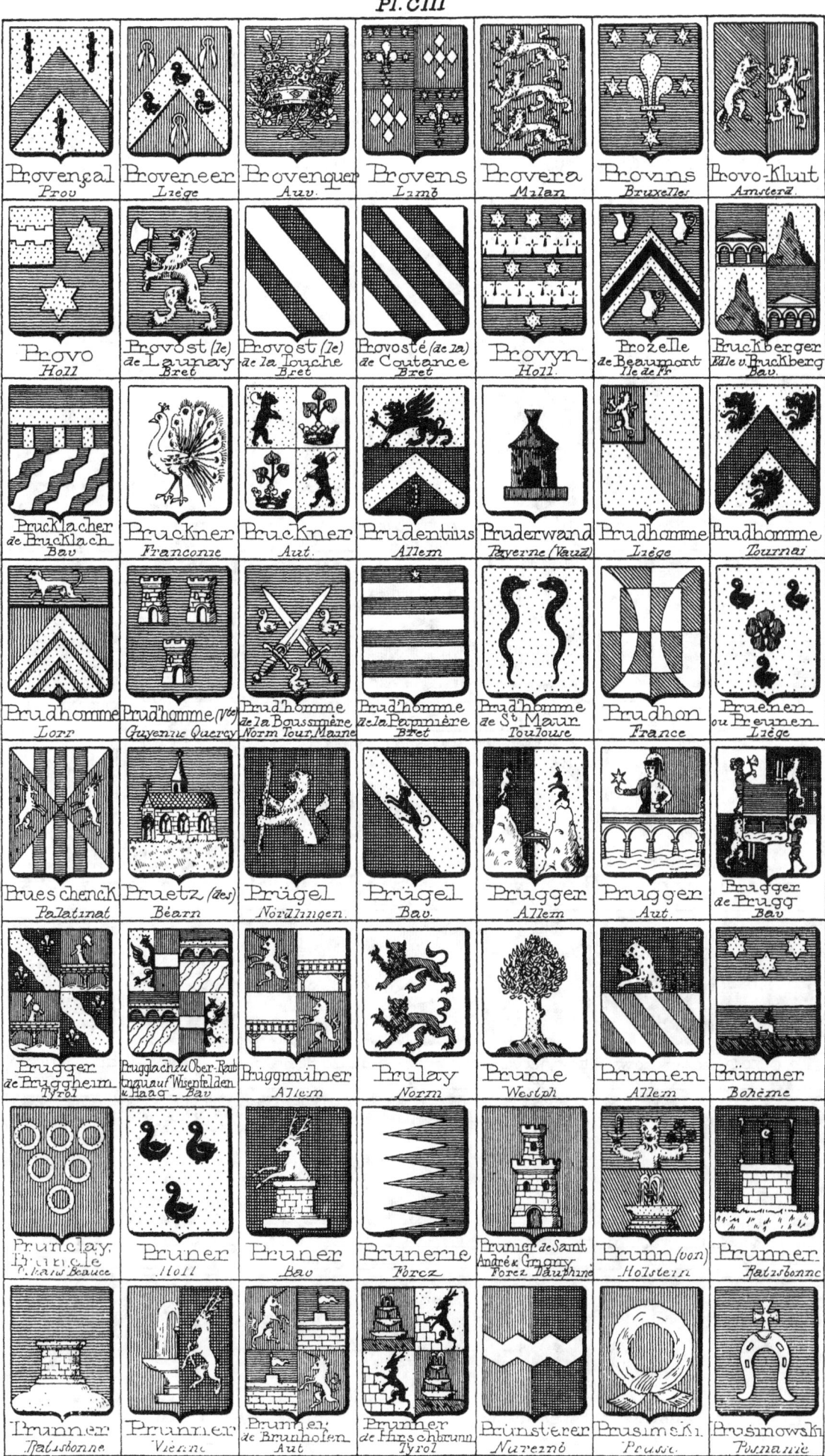

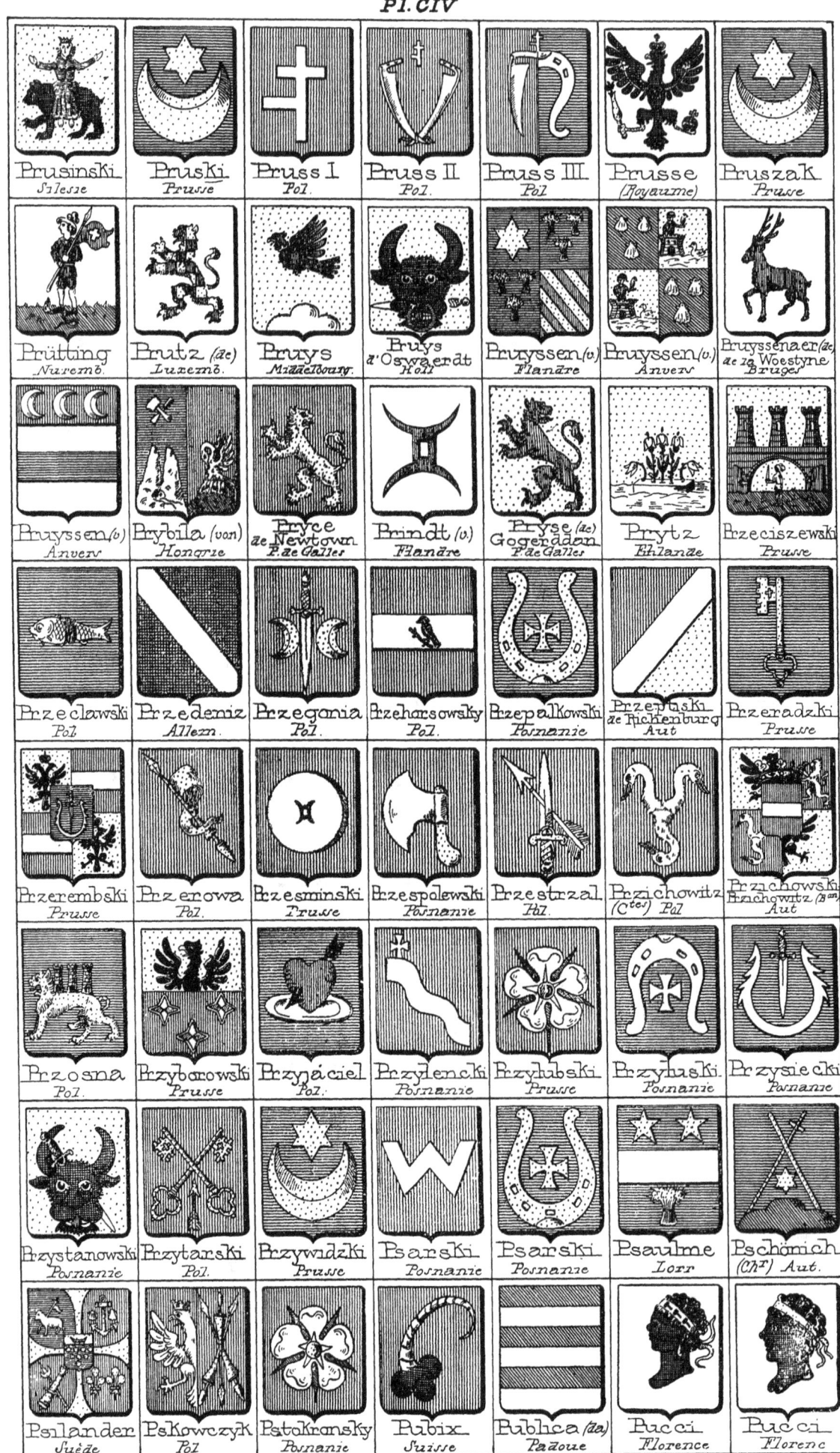

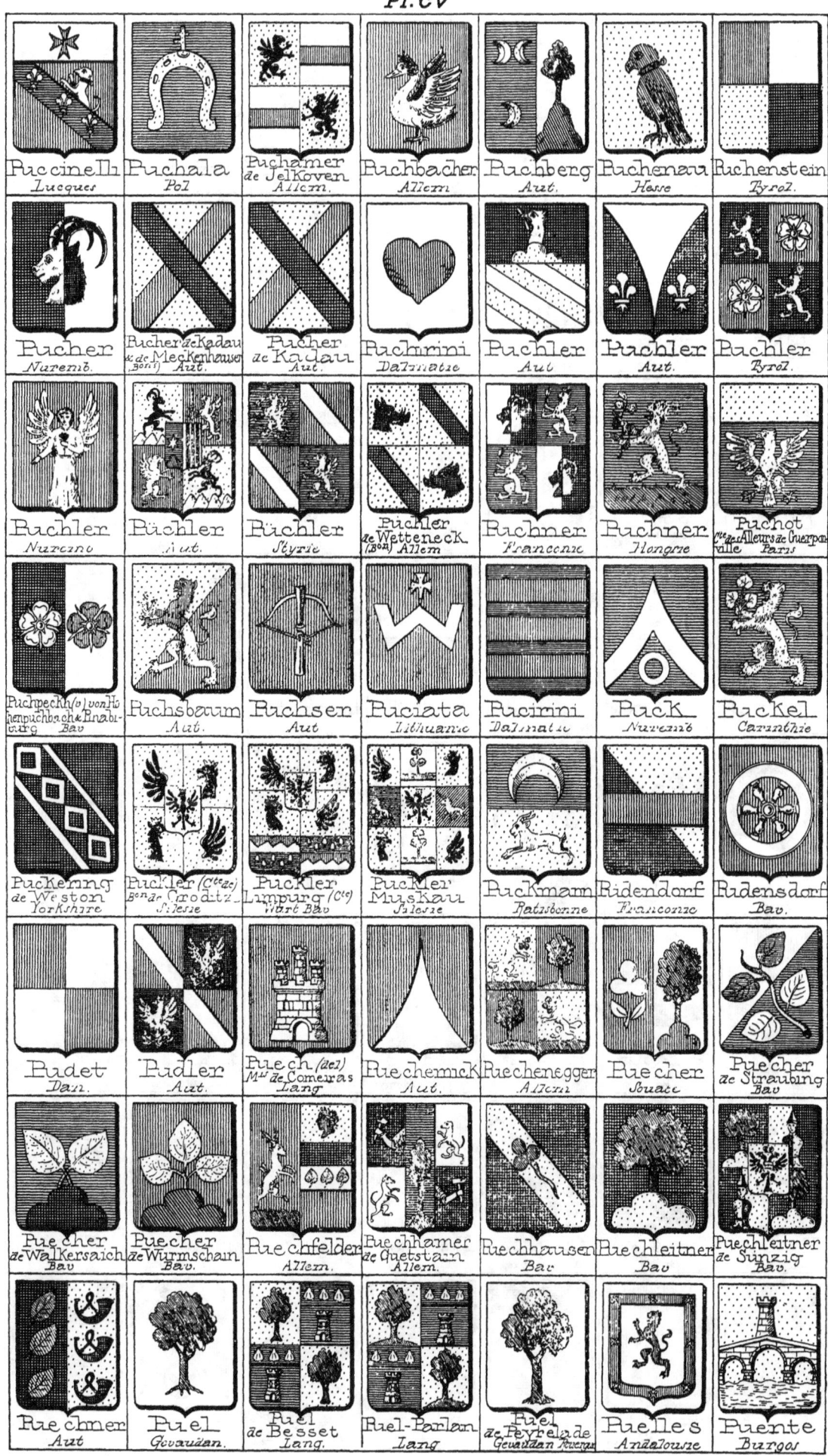

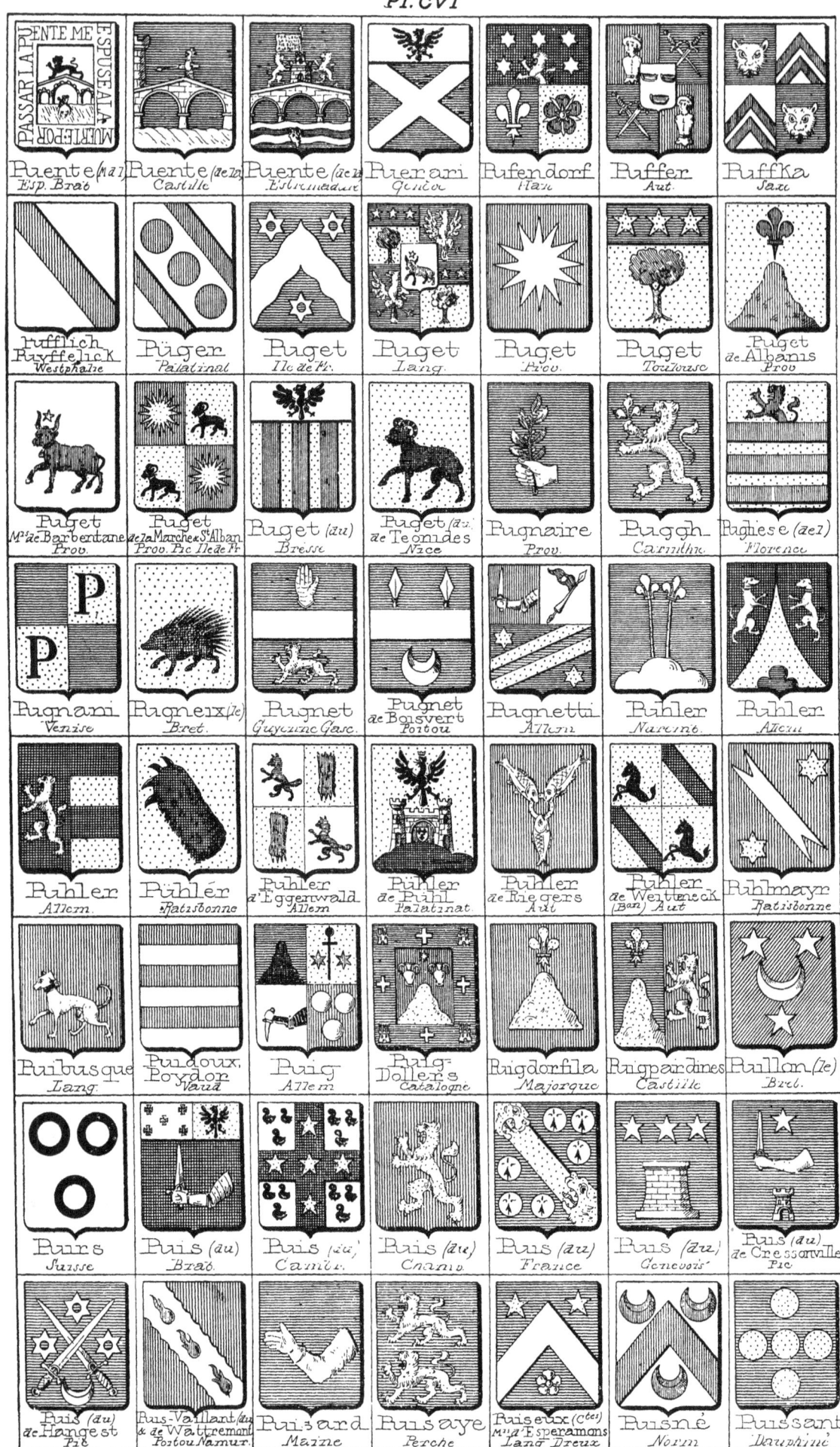

Pl. CVII

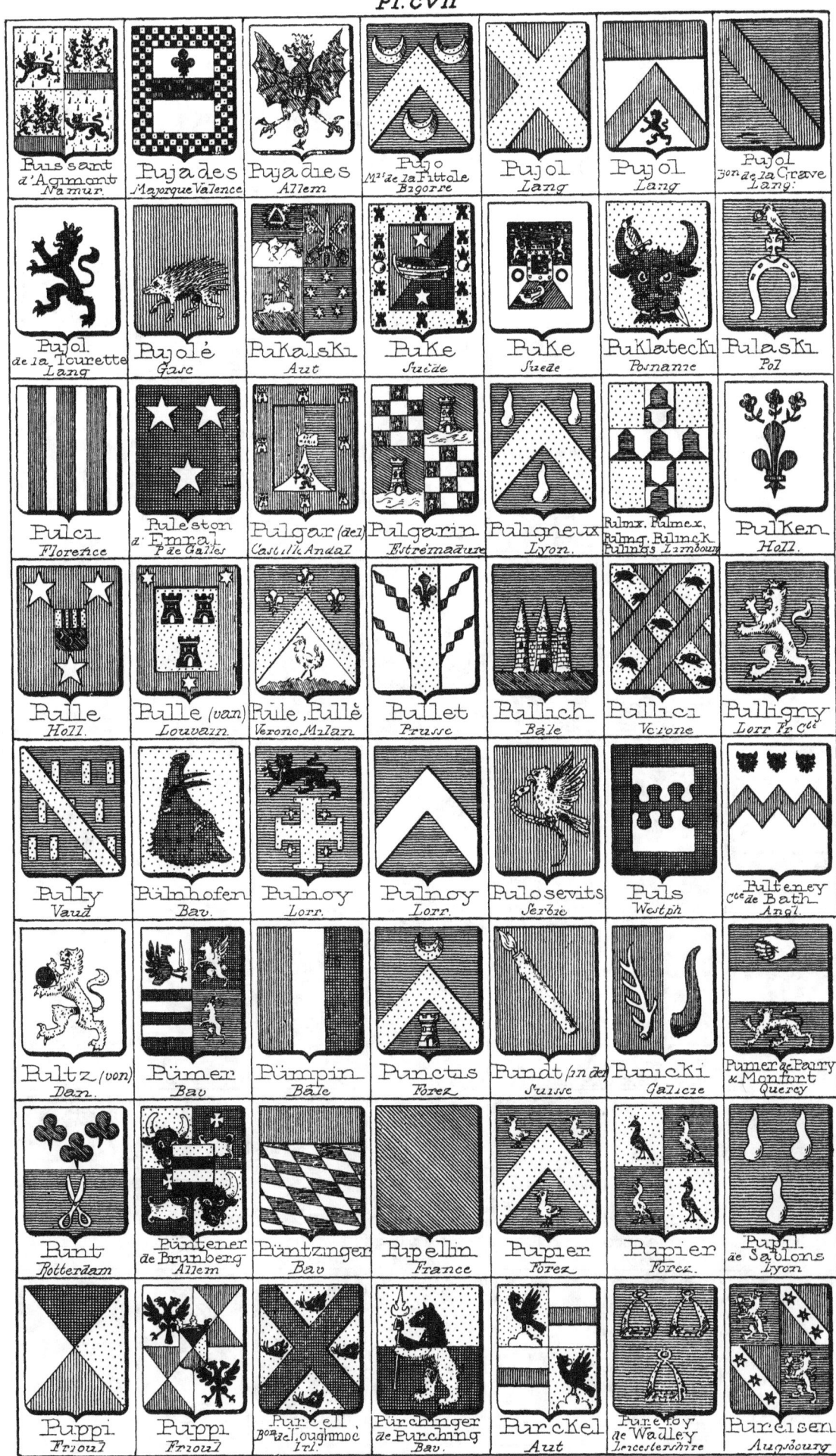

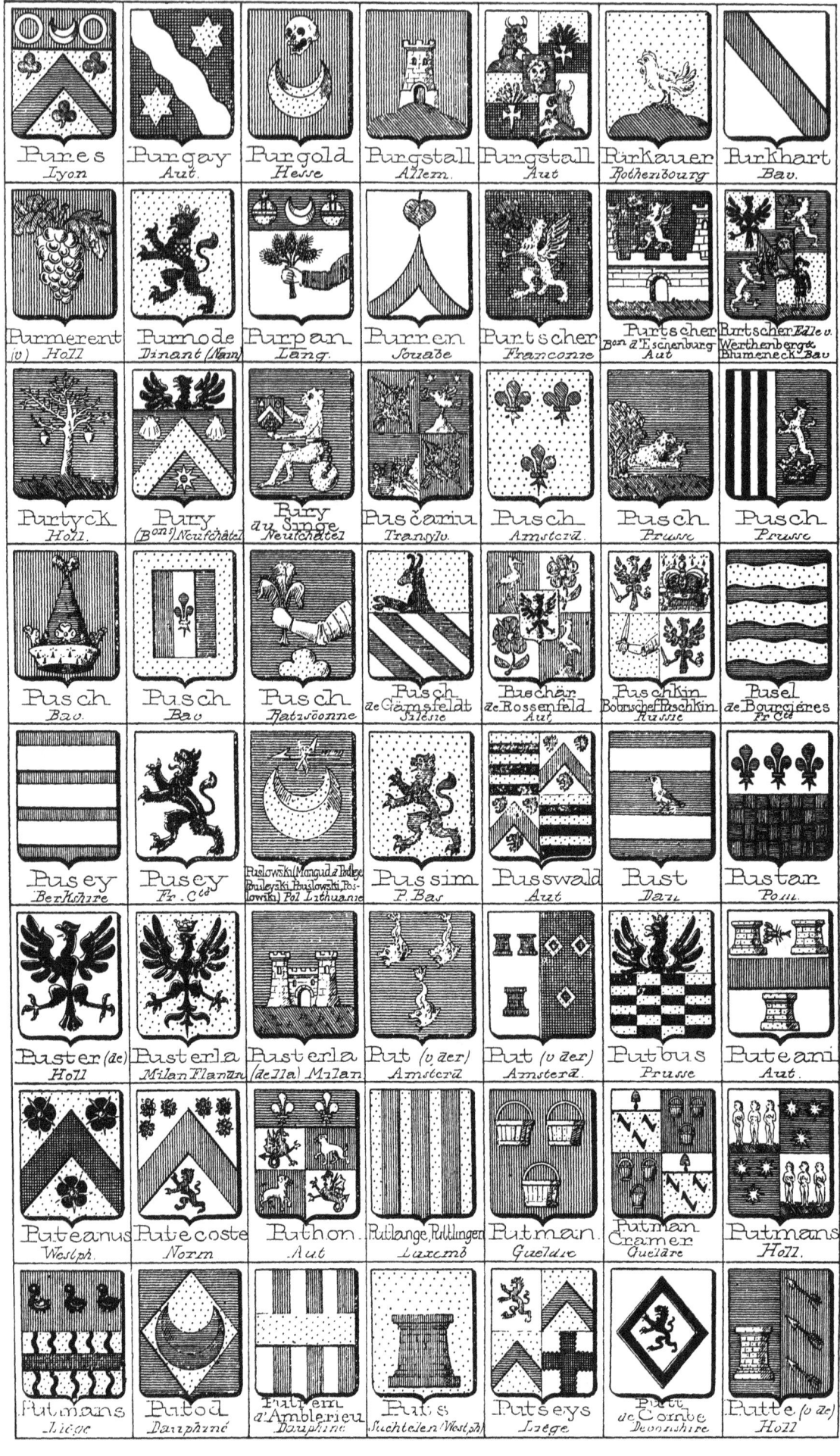

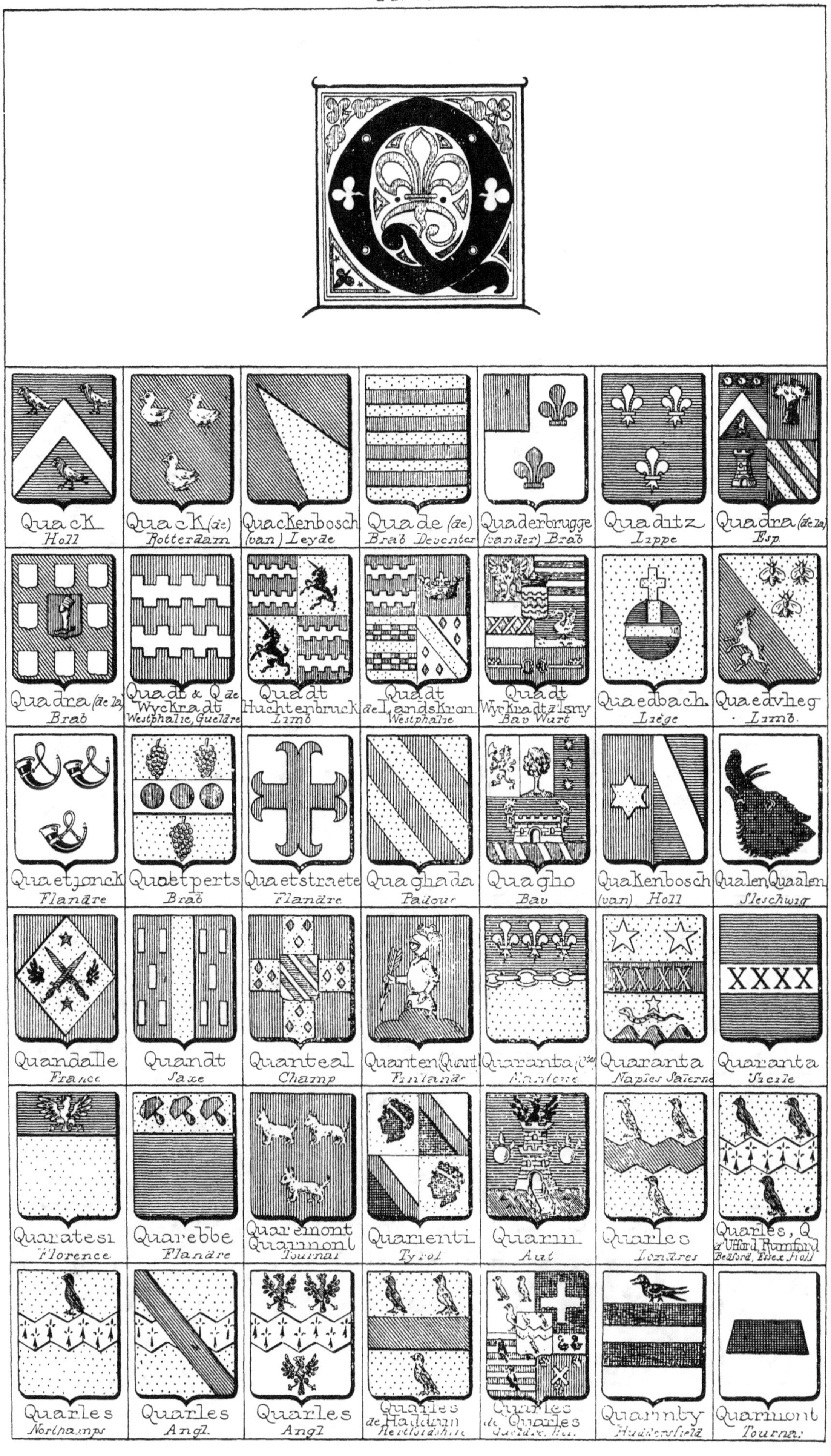

Pl. CXI

| Quack | Quack (de) | Quackenbosch | Quade (de) | Quaderbrugge | Quaditz | Quadra (de la) |
|---|---|---|---|---|---|---|
| Holl. | Rotterdam | (van) Leyde | Brab. Deventer | (vander) Brab. | Lippe | Esp. |
| Quadra (de la) | Quadt & Q. de Wyckradt | Quadt Huchtenbruck | Quadt de Landskron | Quadt Wyckradt zu Isny | Quaedbach | Quaedvheg |
| Brab. | Westphalie, Gueldre | Limb. | Westphalie | Bav. Wurt. | Liège | Limb. |
| Quaetjonck | Quaetperts | Quaetstraete | Quaghada | Quagho | Quakenbosch | Qualen Quaalen |
| Flandre | Brab. | Flandre | Padoue | Bav. | (van) Holl. | Sleschwig |
| Quandalle | Quandt | Quanteal | Quanten Quart. | Quaranta C.te | Quaranta | Quaranta |
| France | Saxe | Champ. | Finlande | Mantoue | Naples Salerne | Sicile |
| Quaratesi | Quarebbe | Quaremont Quarmont | Quarienti | Quarin | Quarles | Quarles, Q. d'Ufford Rumford Bedford, Essex Holl |
| Florence | Flandre | Tournai | Tyrol | Aut. | Londres | |
| Quarles | Quarles | Quarles | Quarles de Haddon Hertfordshire | Quarles de Quarles Gueldre Holl | Quarmby | Quarmont |
| Northamps | Angl. | Angl. | | | Huddersfield | Tournai |

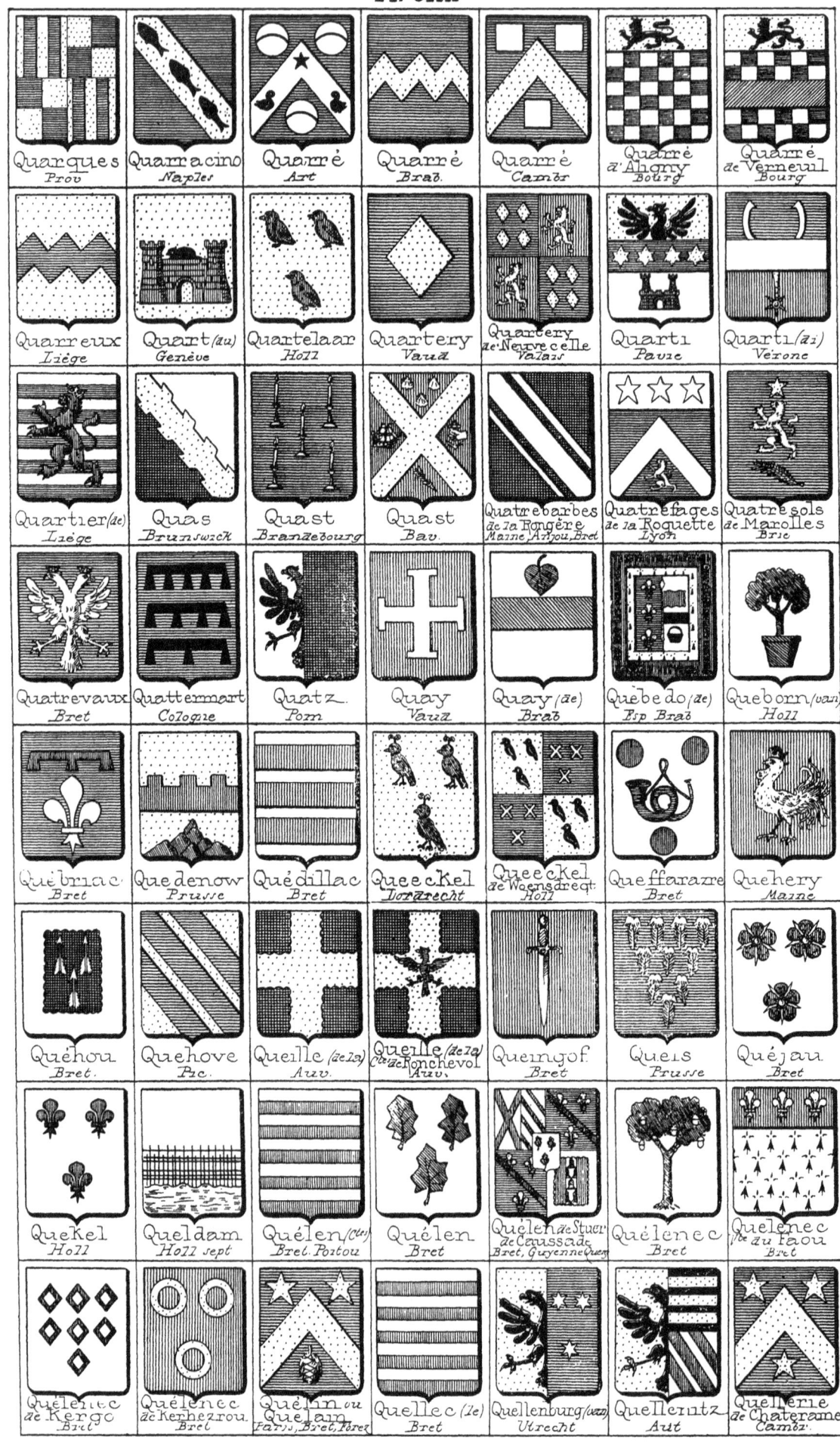

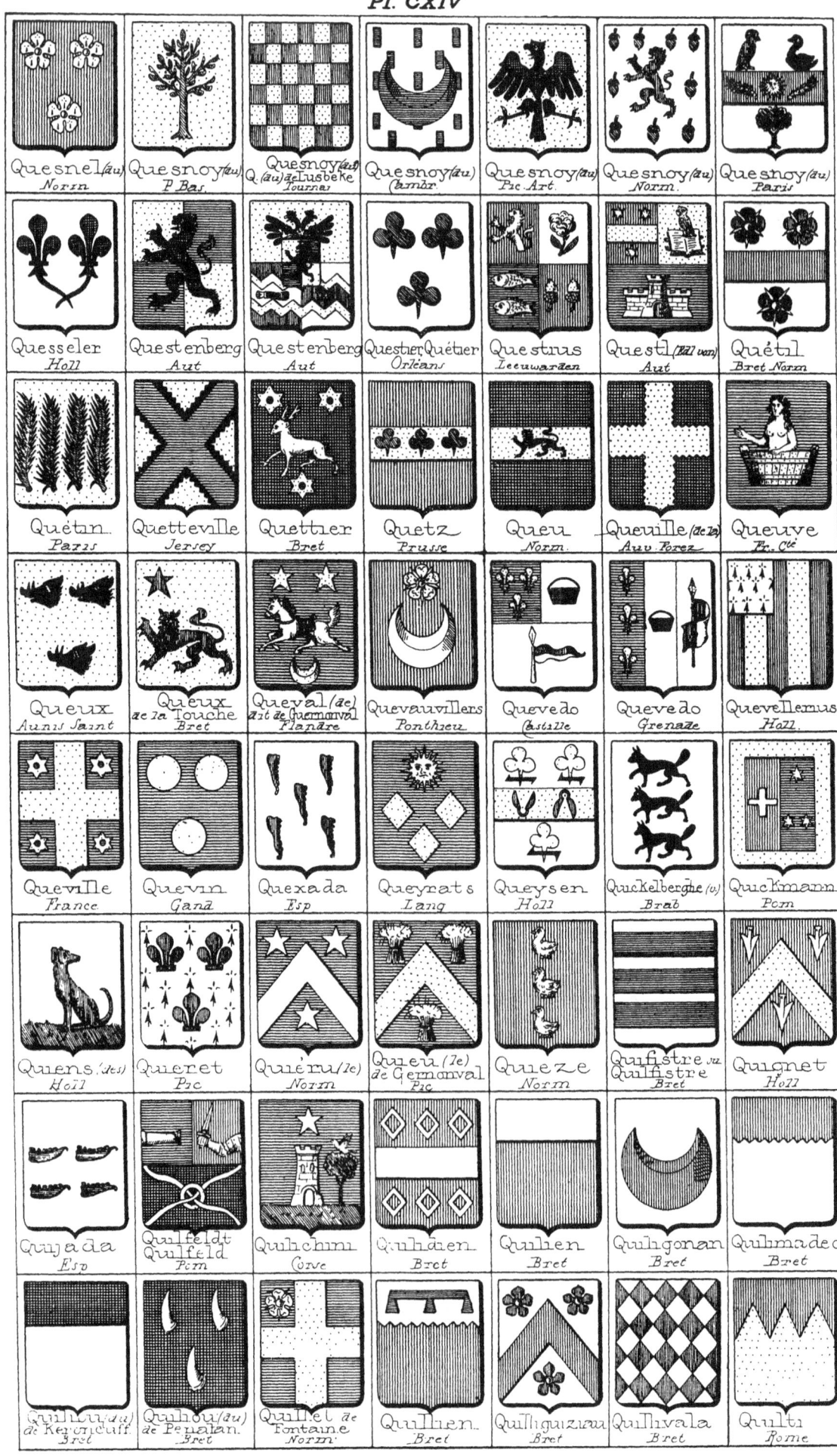

Pl. CXVI

|  |  | 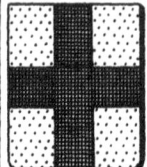 |  |  | 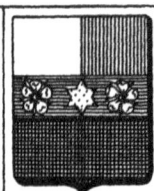 |  |
|---|---|---|---|---|---|---|
| Quistinit *Bret* | Quistorp *Pom. Mecklemb* | Quistorp *Han. Pom.* | Quityer *Bret* | Quitzow *Brandb. Meckl.* | Qumana *Vérone* | Quona *Florence* |
|  |  | 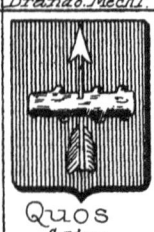 | | | | |
| Quoquette *Belg* | Quorcki *Allem* | Quos *Silésie* | | | | |

Pl. CXVII

| Raab Suède | Raab Prusse | Raab Saxe | Raab Ansbach (Bav) | Raab Rothenburg (Bav) | Raab Aut | Raab Carinthie |
|---|---|---|---|---|---|---|
| Raab de Carstein (Rave de Papenheim) Westphalie, Holl | Raab de Freiwalden Aut | Raab de Ravenheim Aut | Raab von der Aa Thilen Curlande | Raabl von Blankenwaffen Moravie | Raad Holl | Raadenraa Dan |
| Raadt (de) Holl | Raadt (de) Groningue | Raadt (de) Allem | Rääf Suède | Rââf Finlande | Raamsdonck (v.) Brab. | Raap, Raep Amsterdam |
| Raaphorst (v) Holl | Raaphorst (v) Utrecht | Raas Holl | Raasted Dan | Raasvelt Leeuwarden | Raat (de) Holl. | Raat (de) Bois-le-Duc |
| Rabaine Saintonge | Raban Franc | Rabar Saintonge, Guyenne | Rabaschiero Esp | Rabasse Prov | Rabasse Prov Dauphiné | Rabasté Anjou Bret |
| Rabastens Lang | Rabatta Aut | Rabatta (aa) Florence | Rabatta (aa) Florence | Rabatto (Cte) Aut | Rabaud de la Rabaudière Bret | Rabaudy Lang |

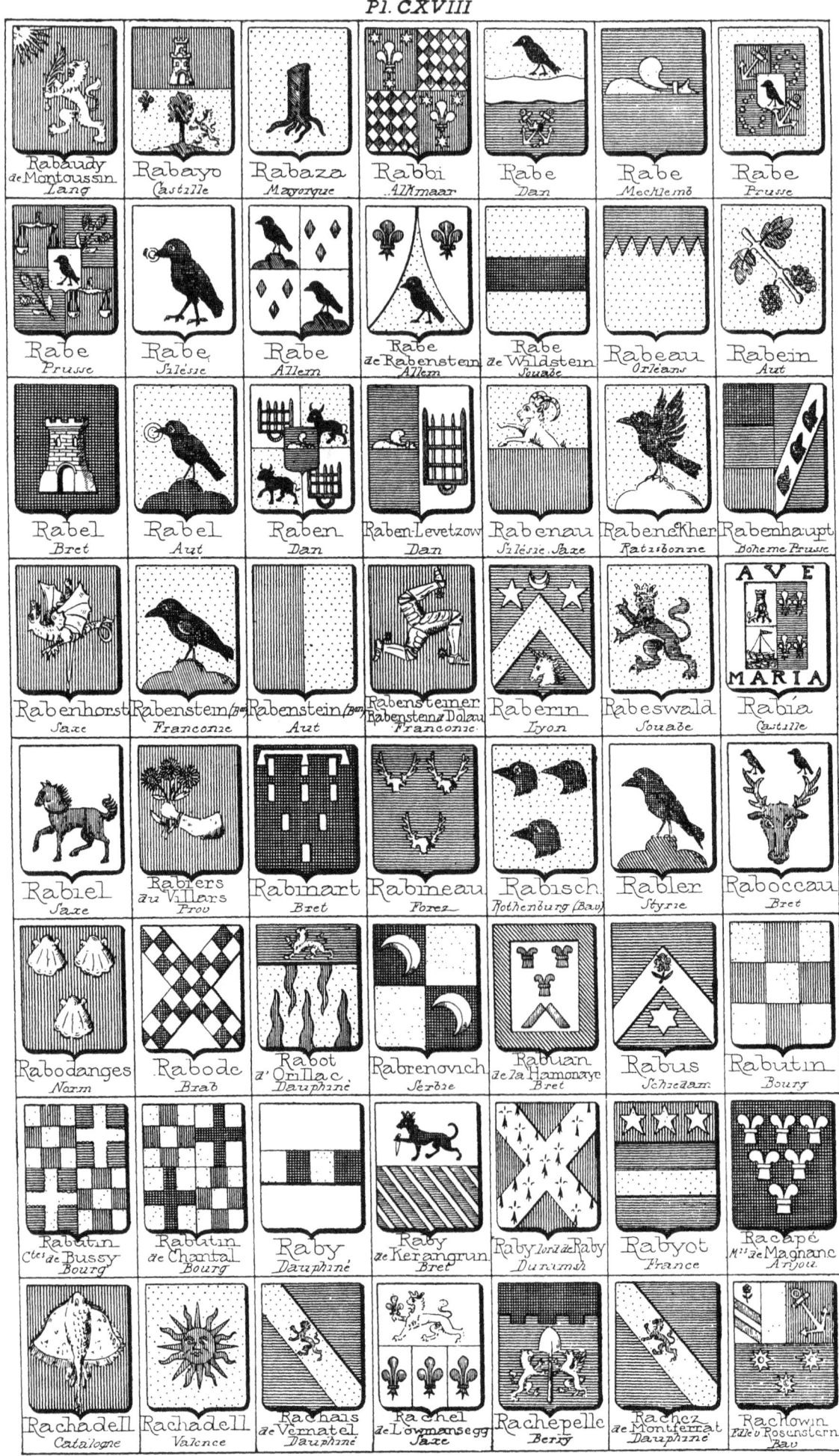

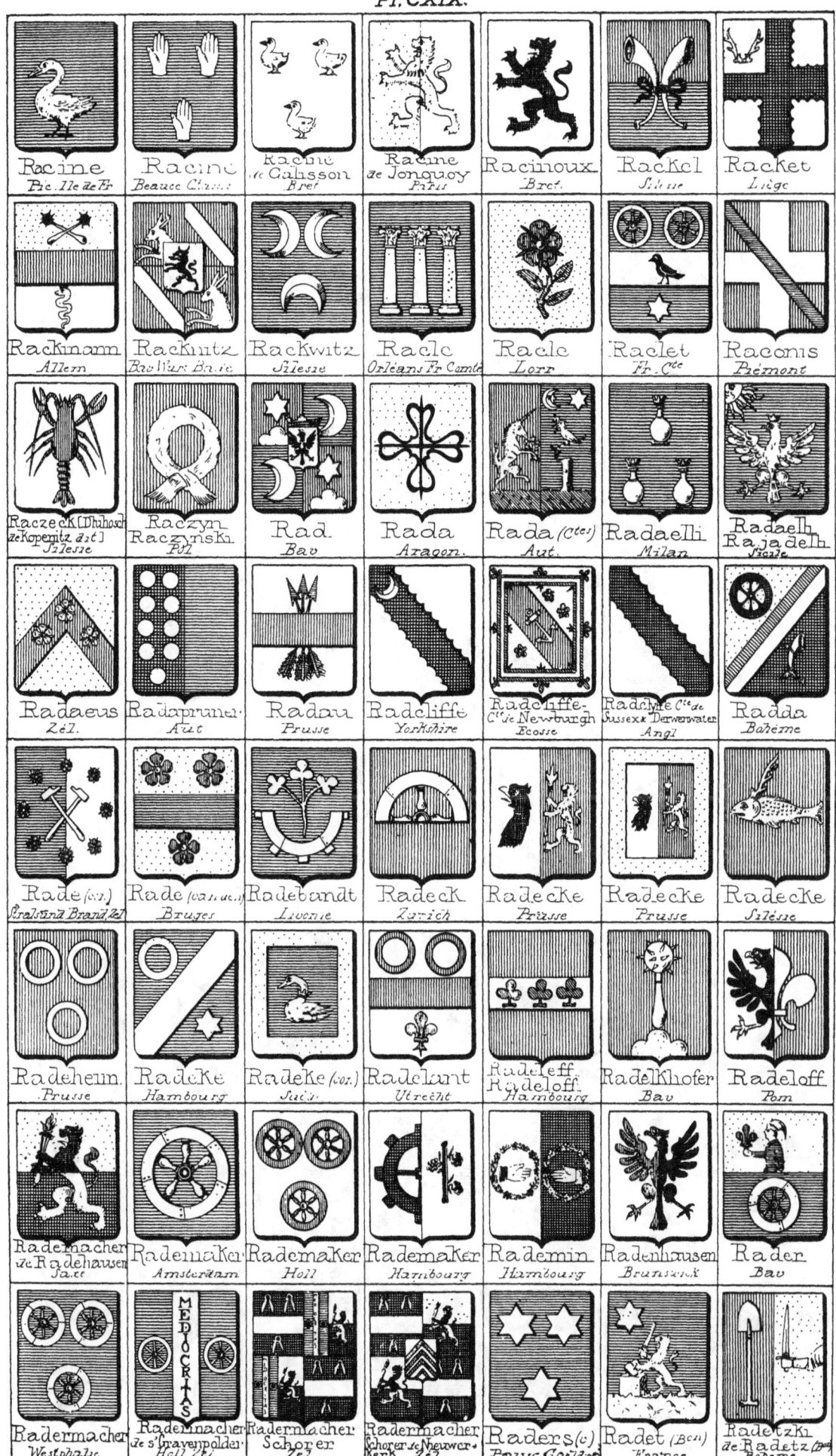

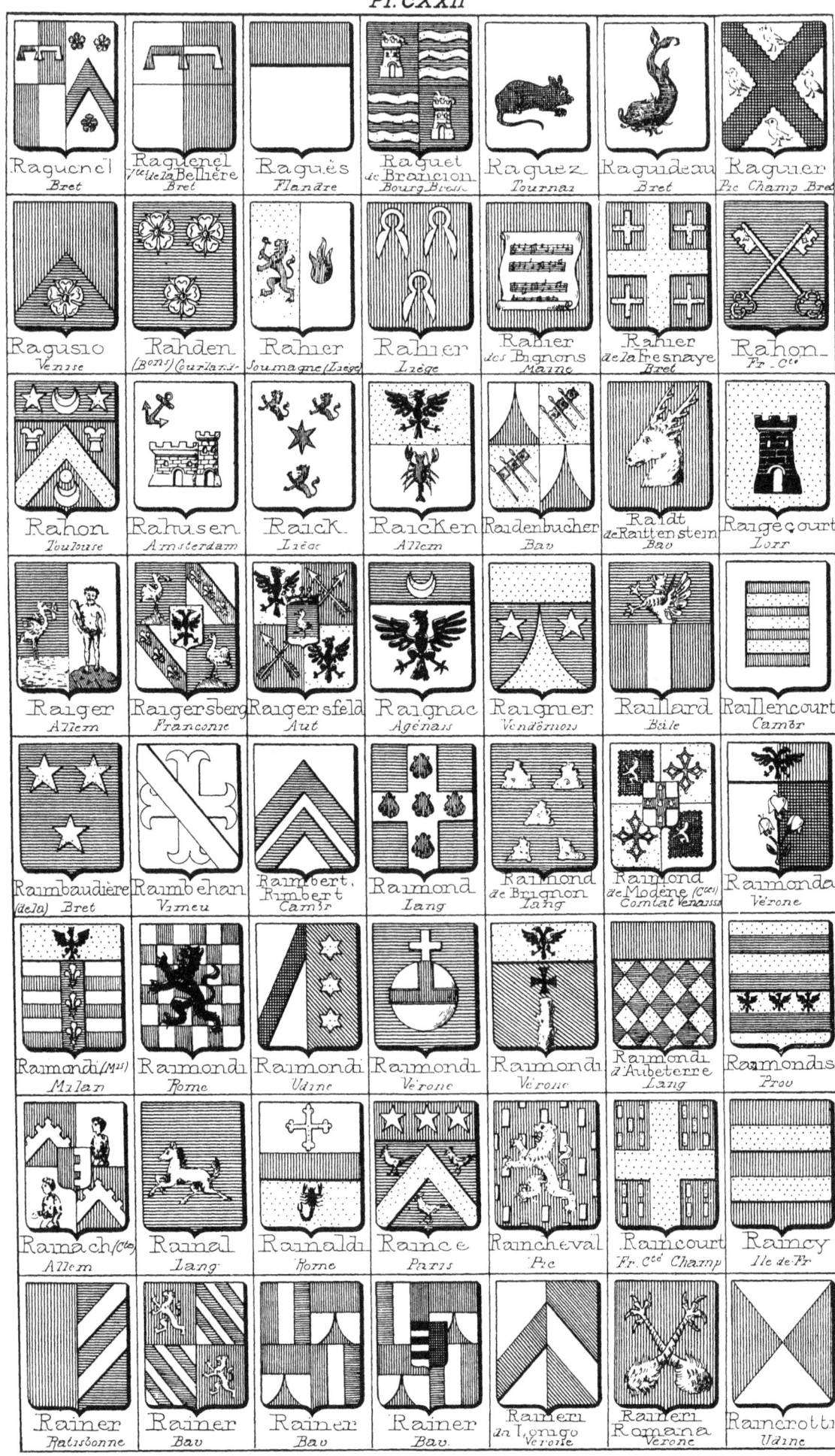

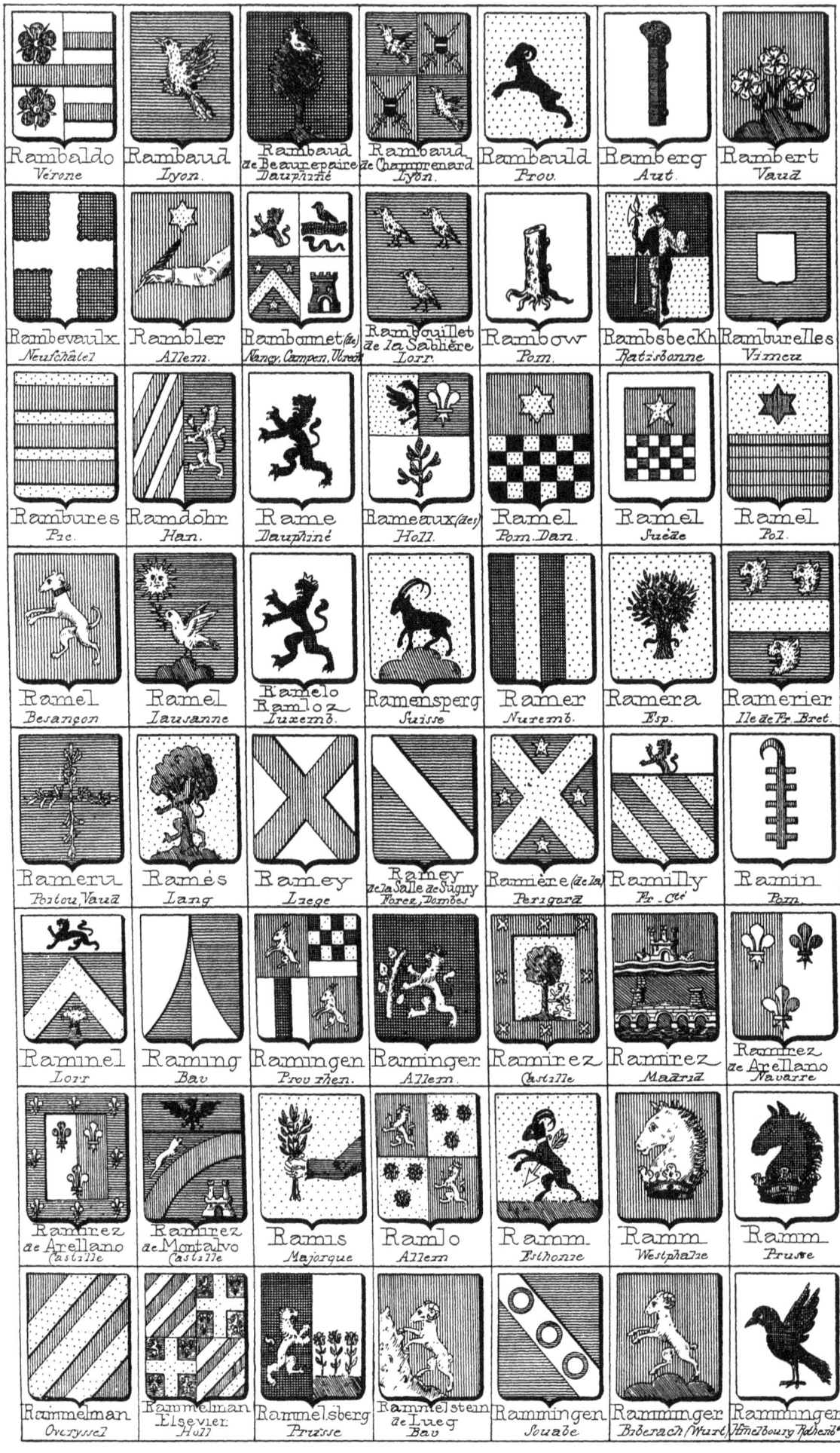

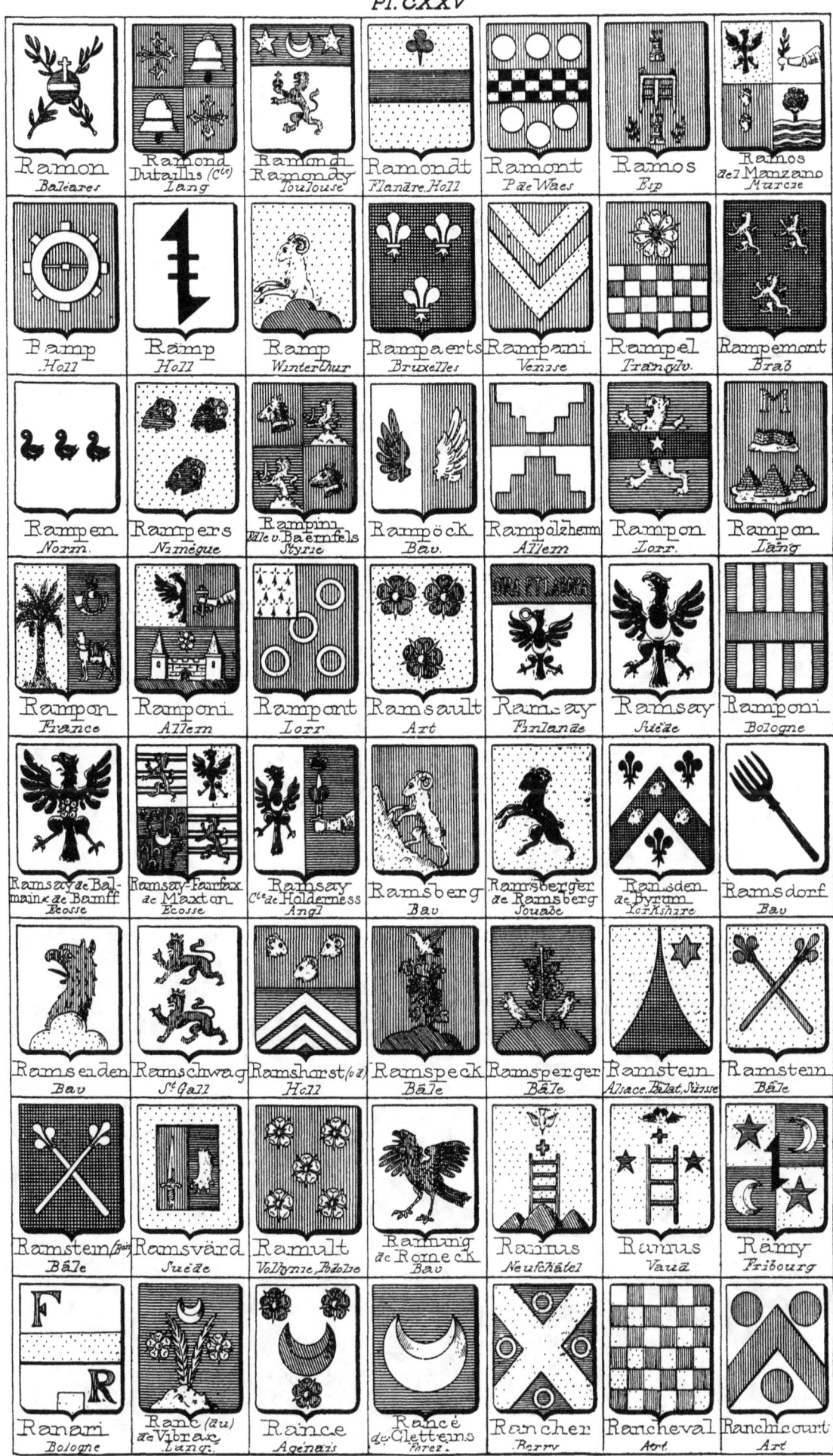

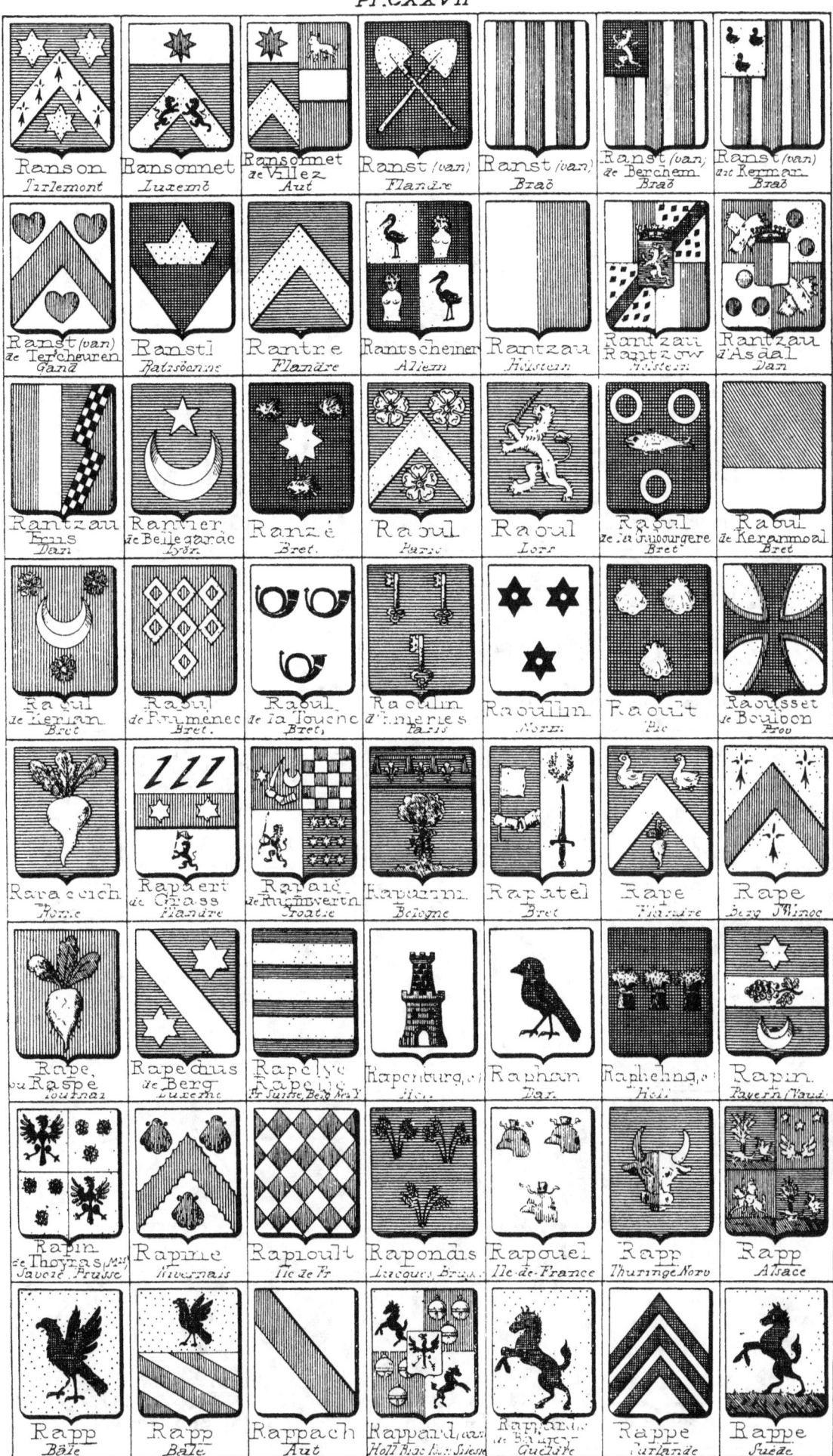

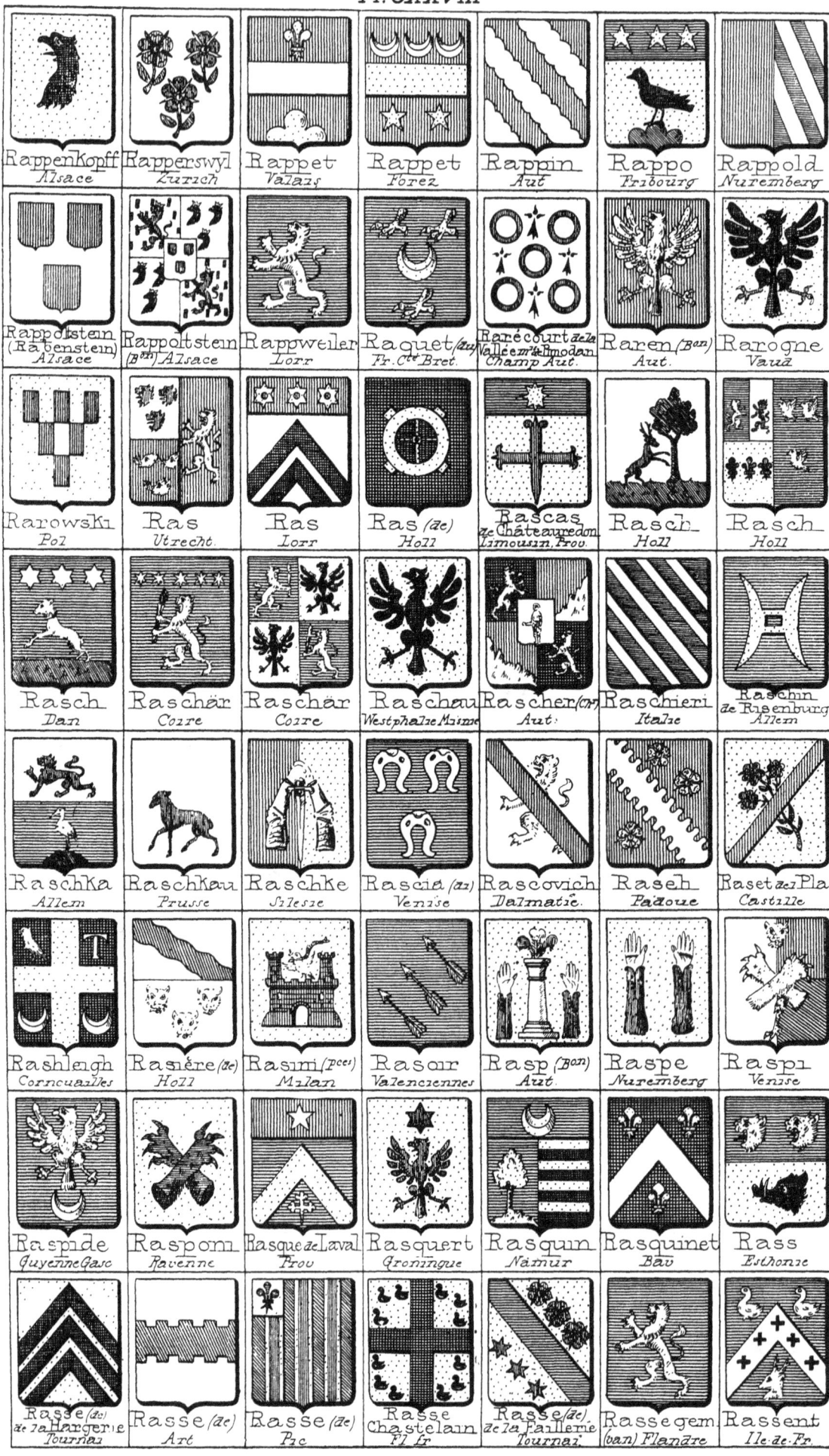

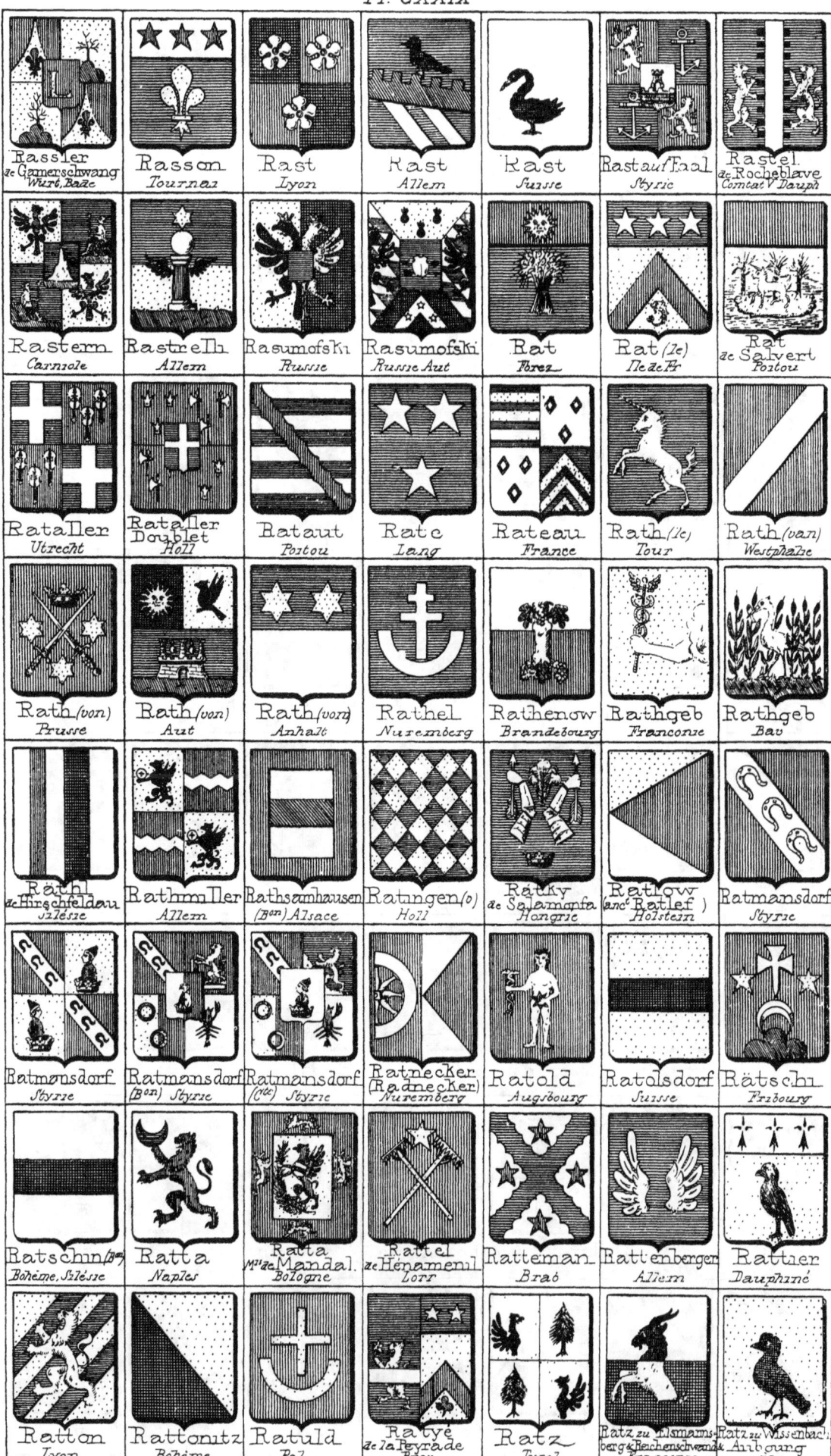

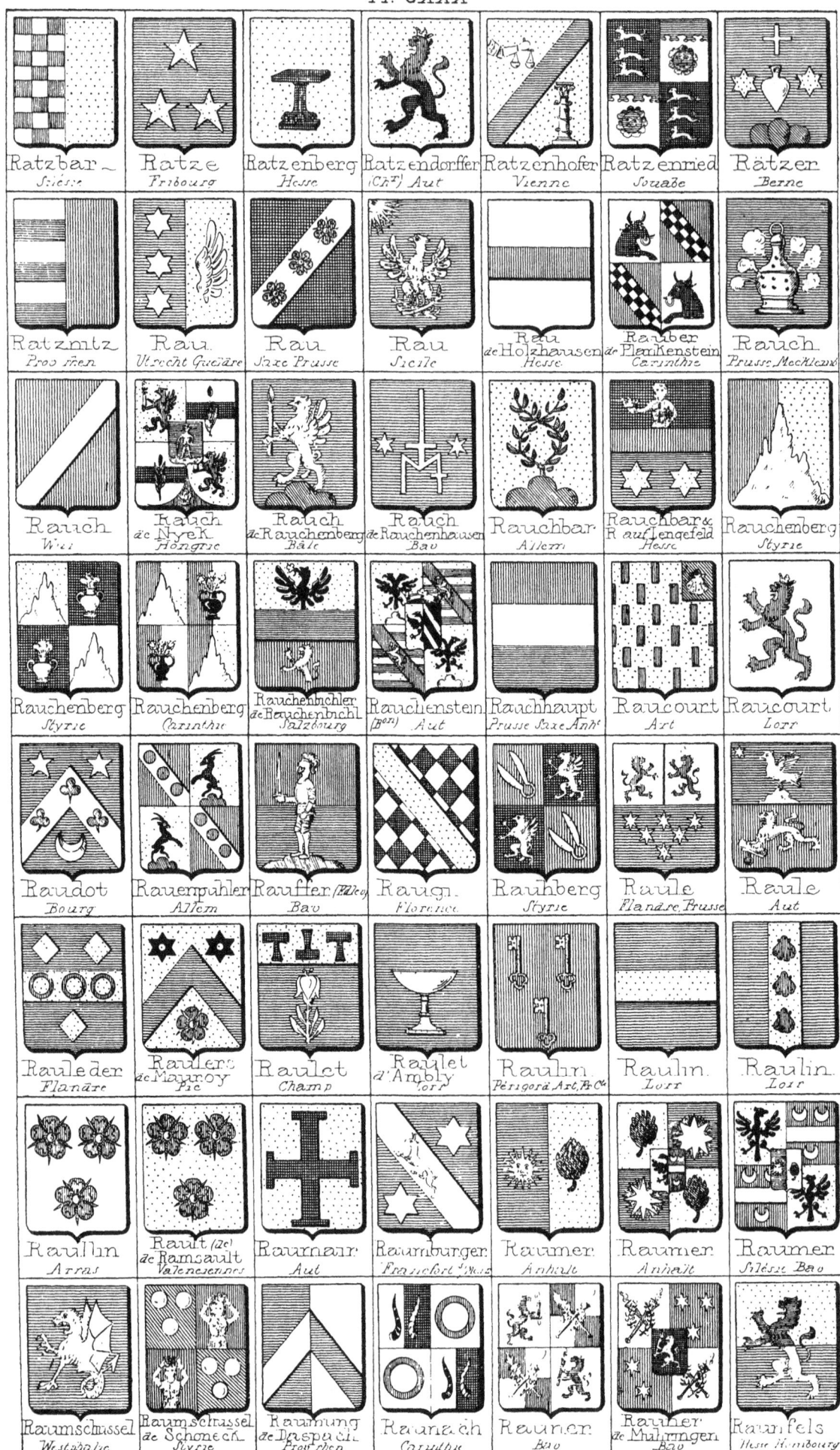

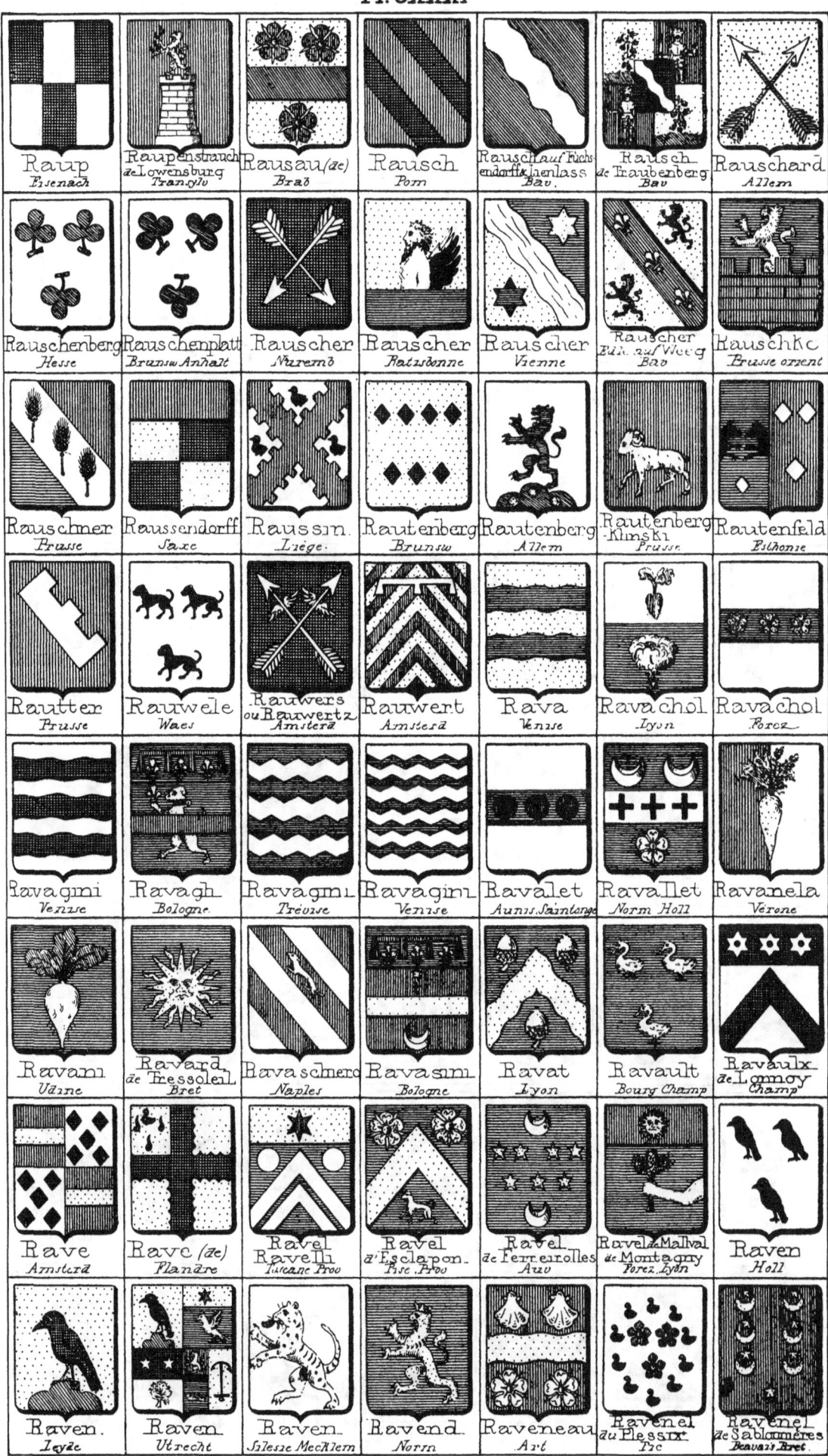

Pl. CXXXI

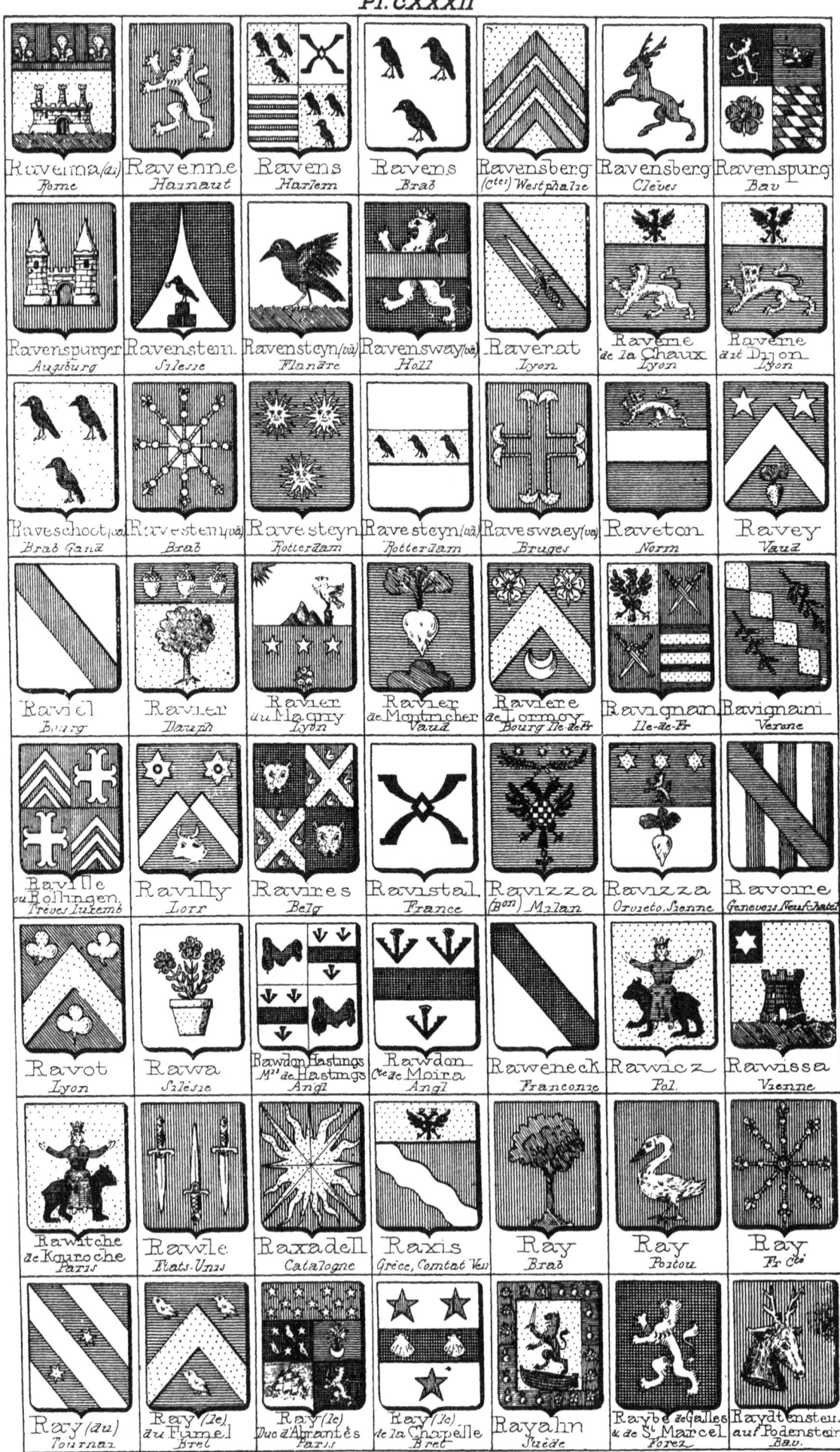

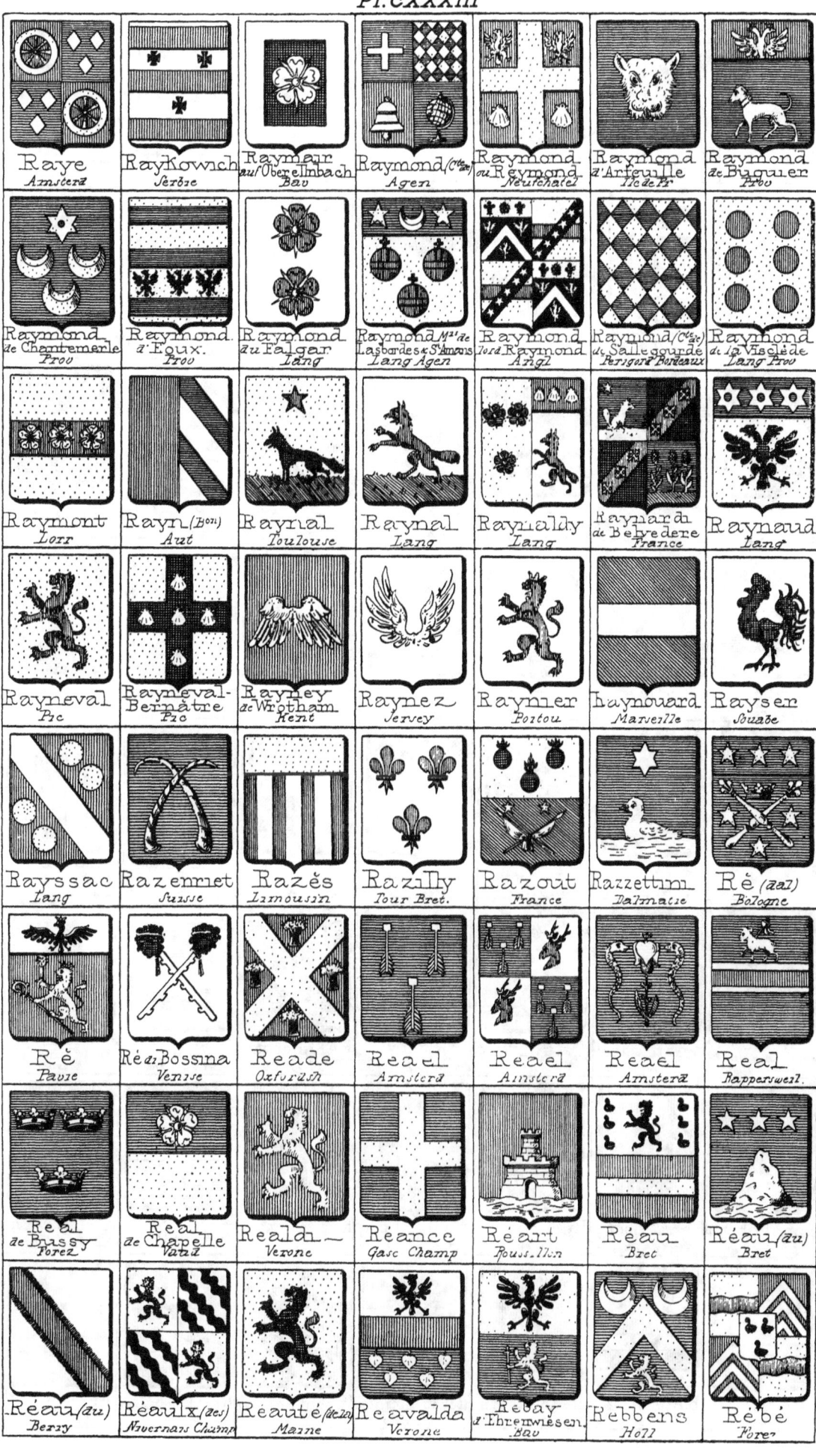

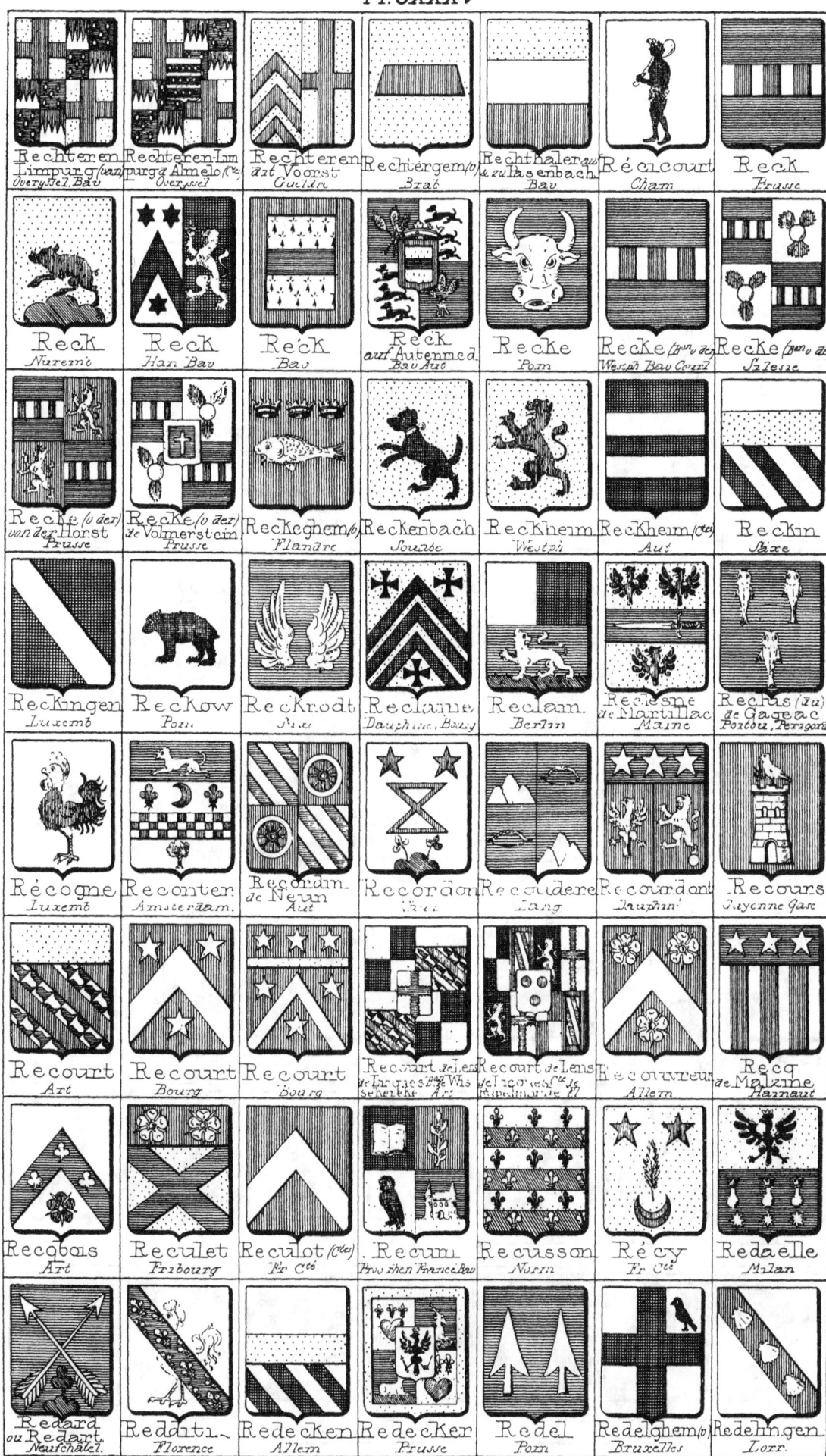

Pl. CXXXV

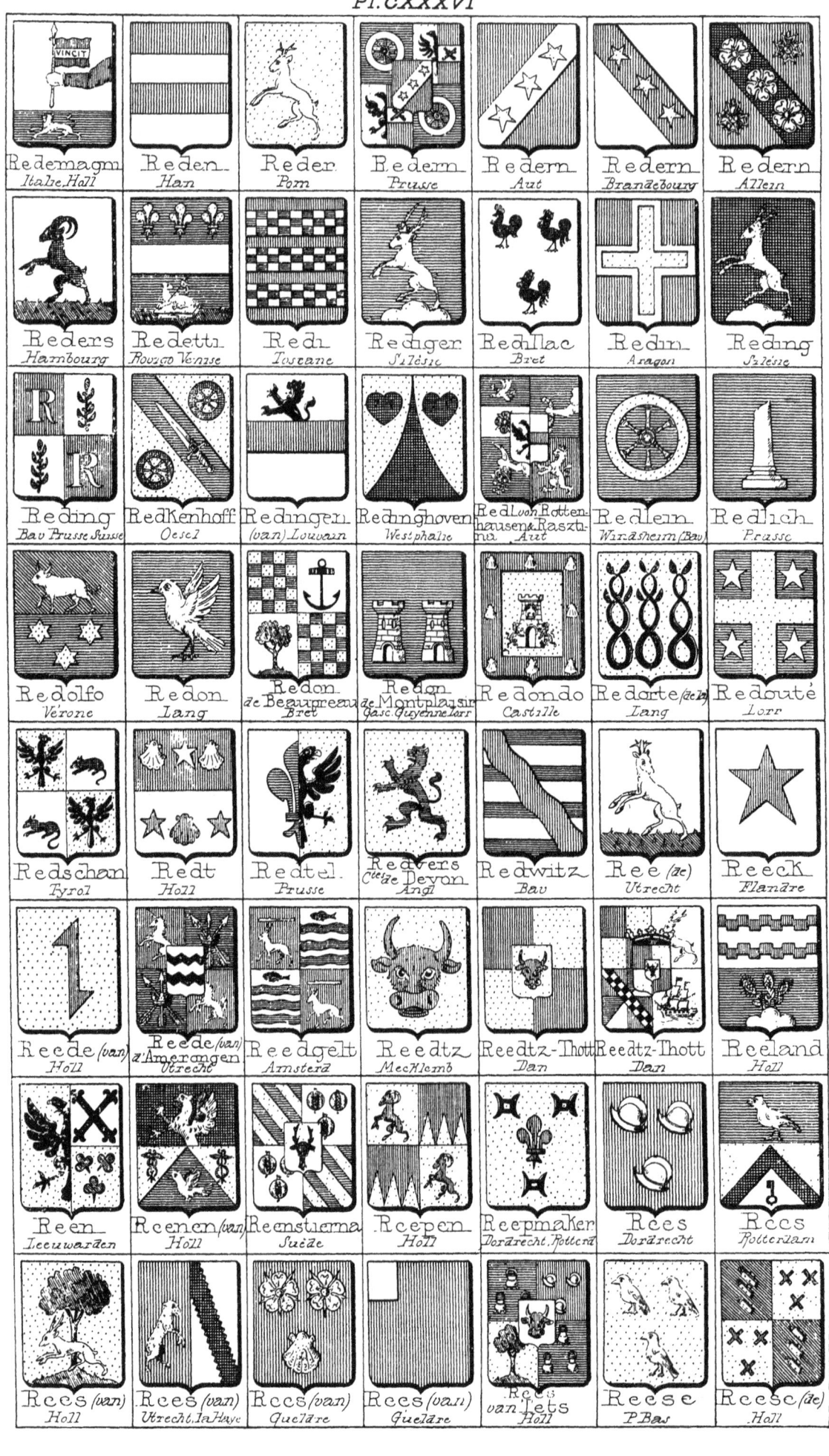

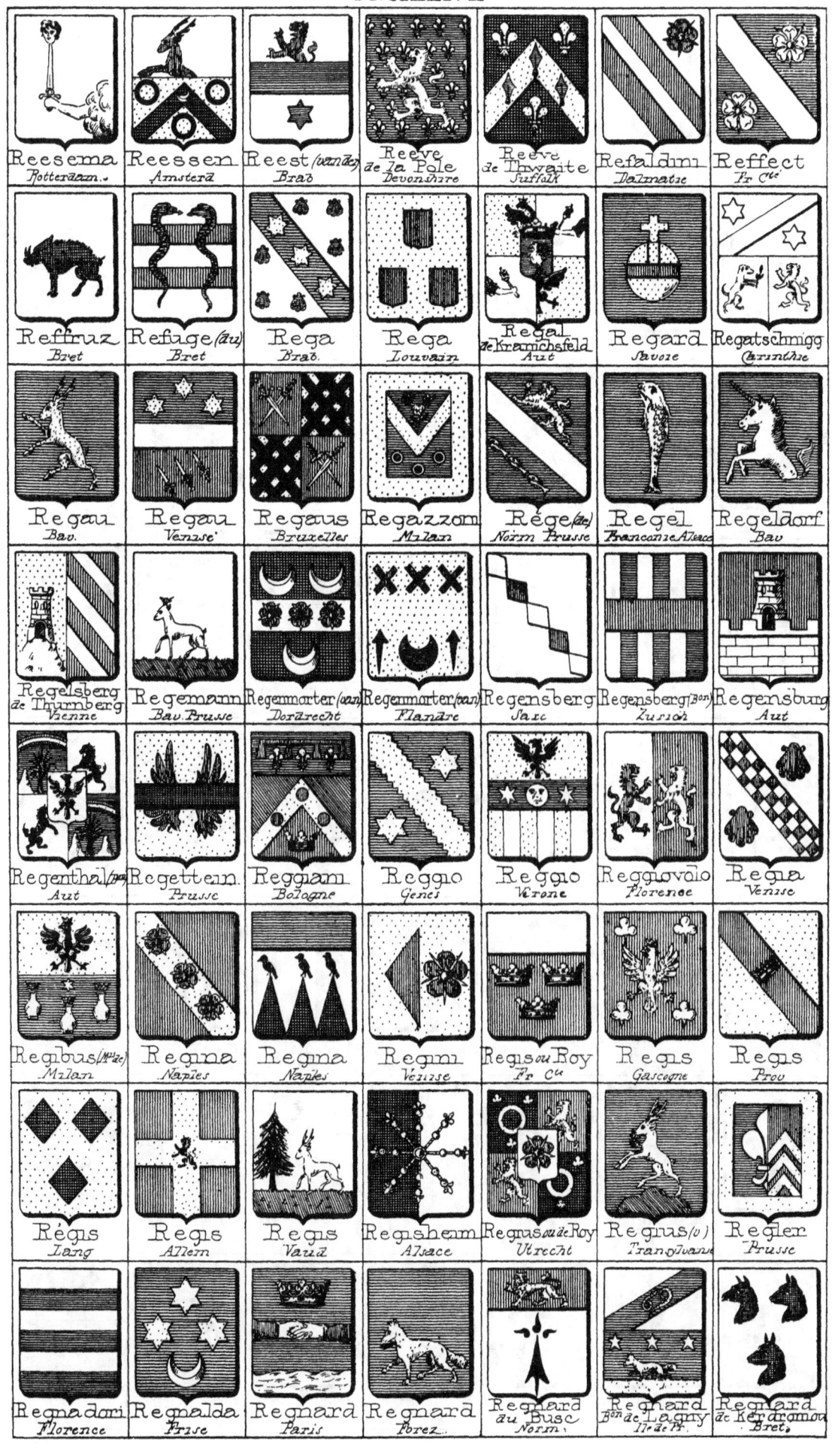

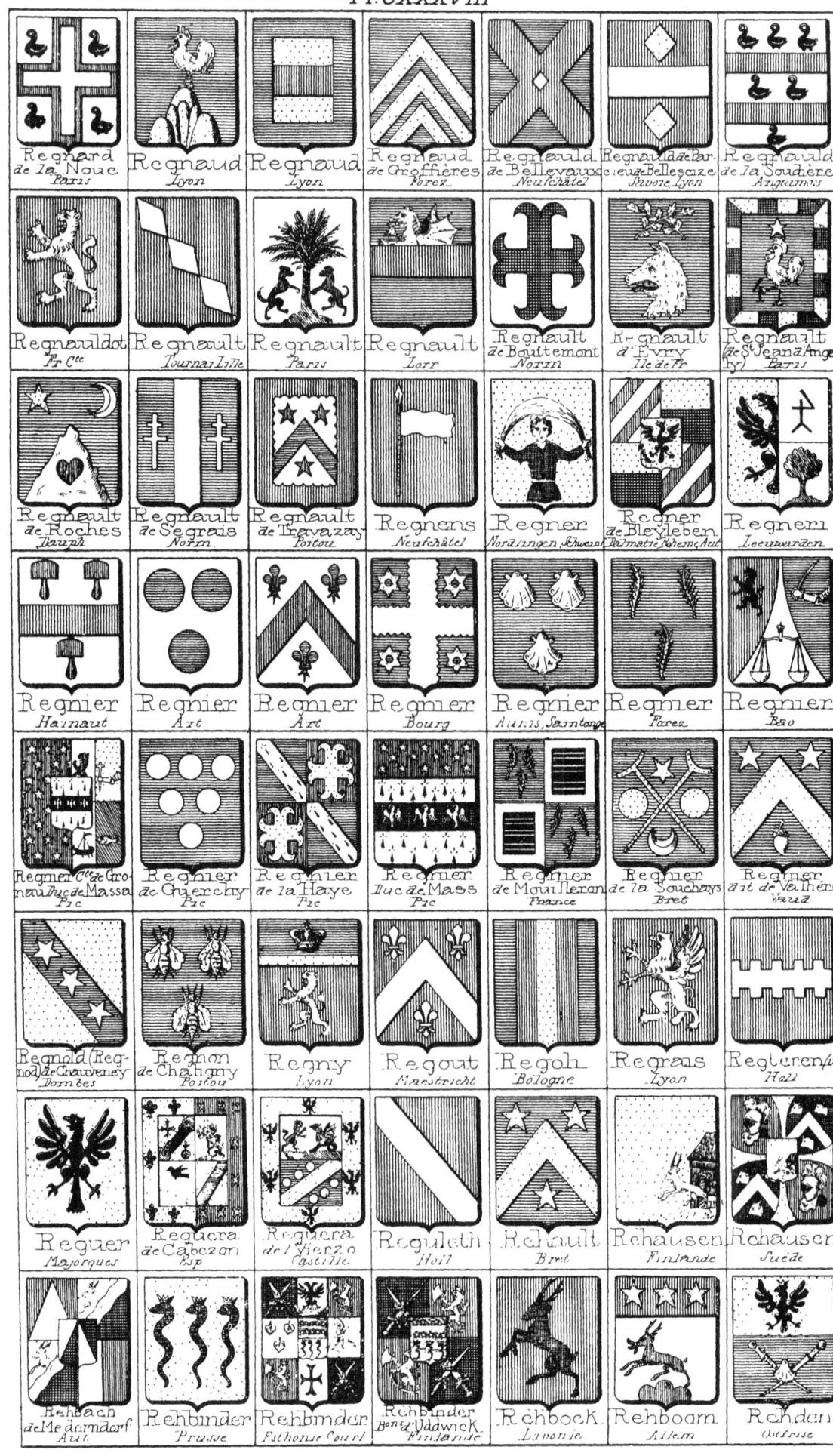

Pl. CXXXIX

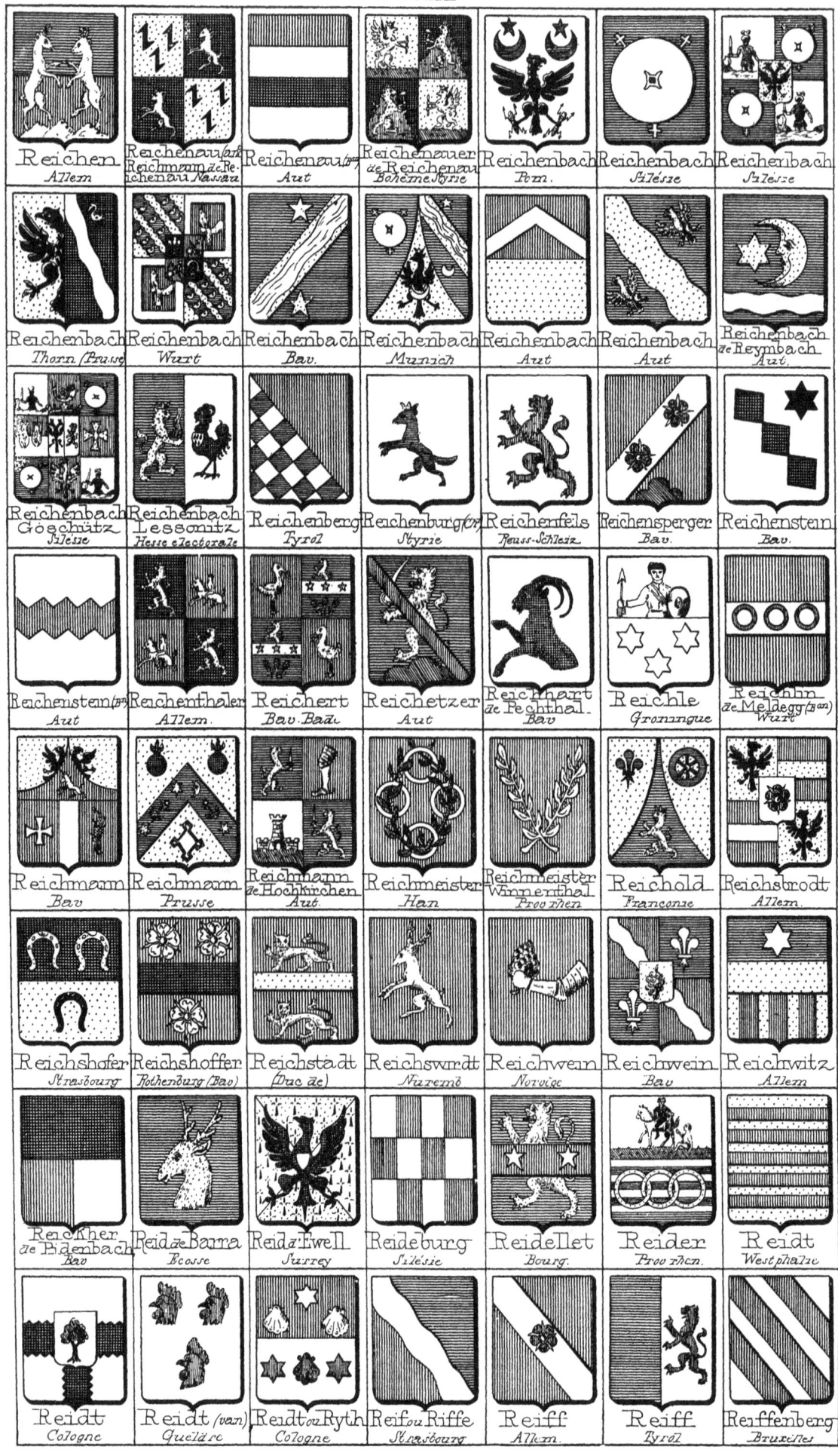

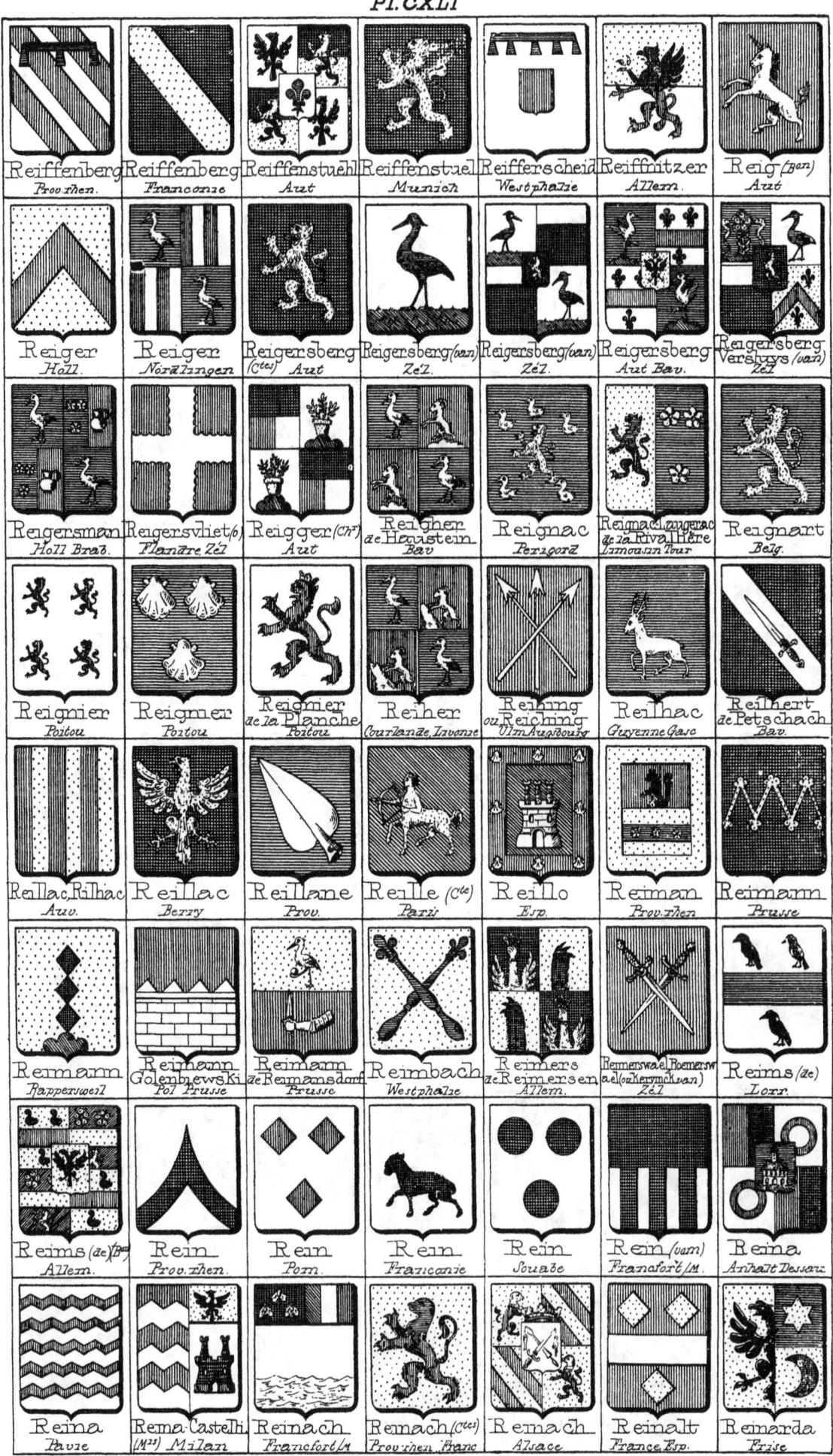

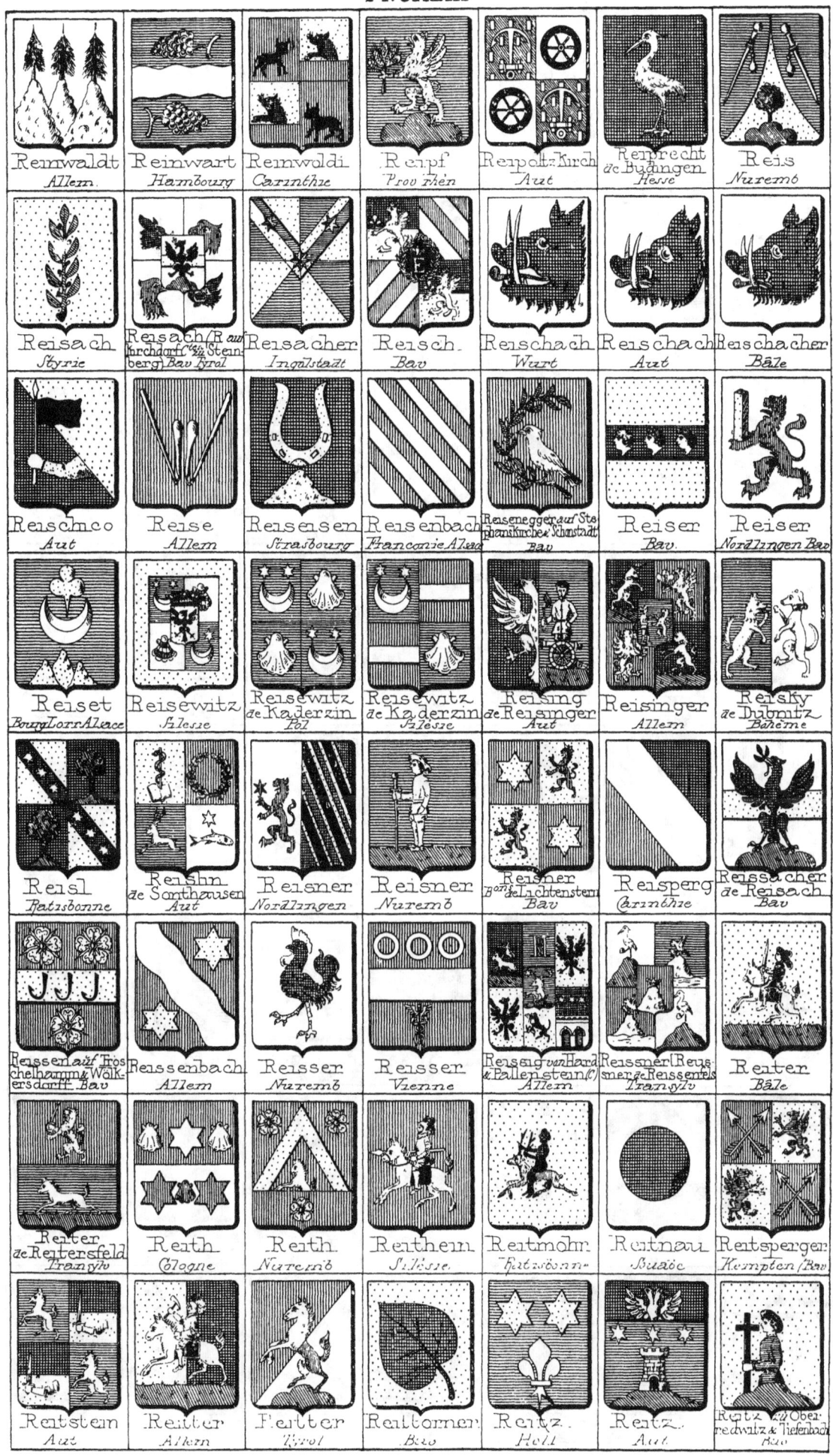
Pl. CXLIII

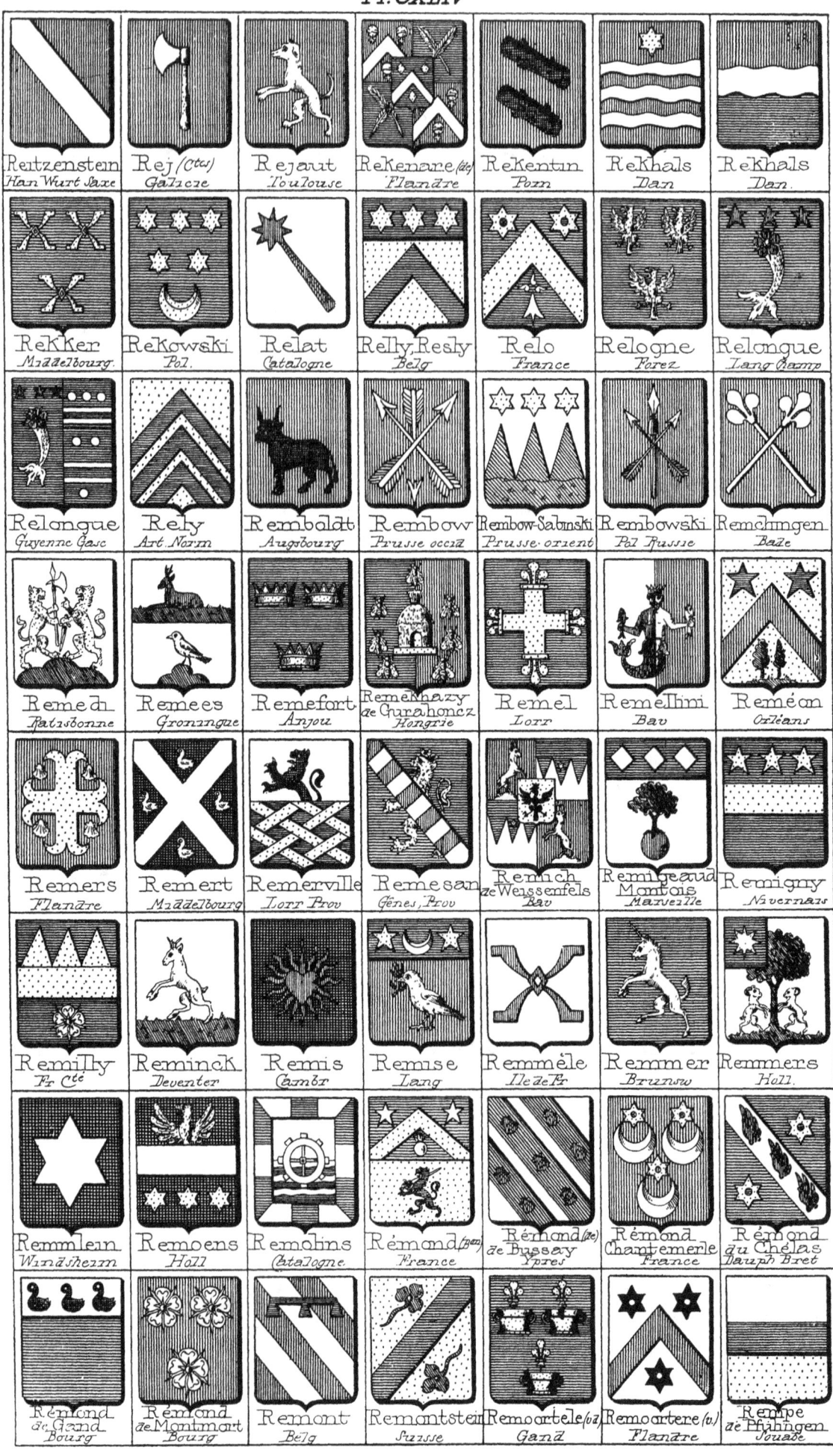

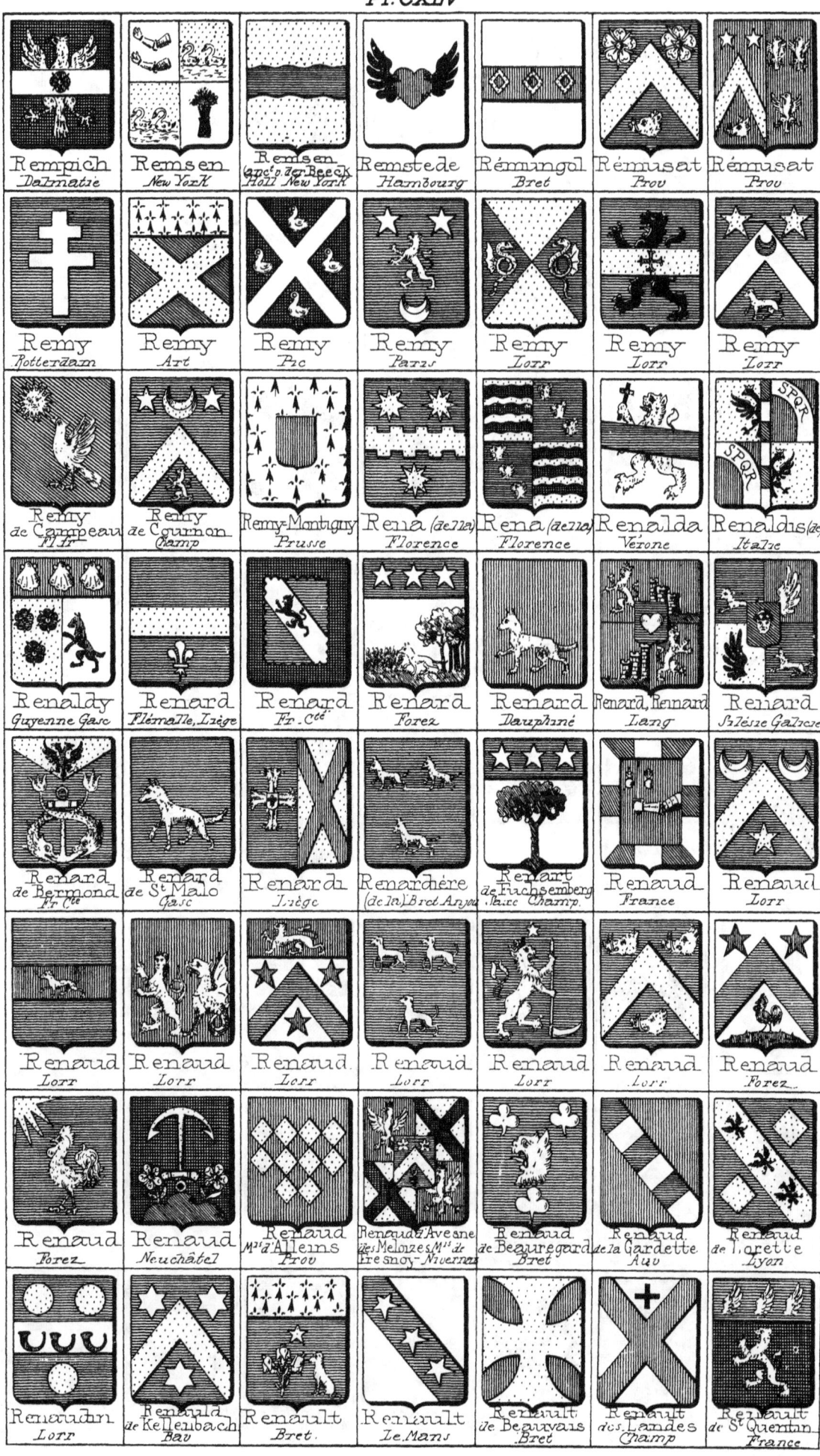

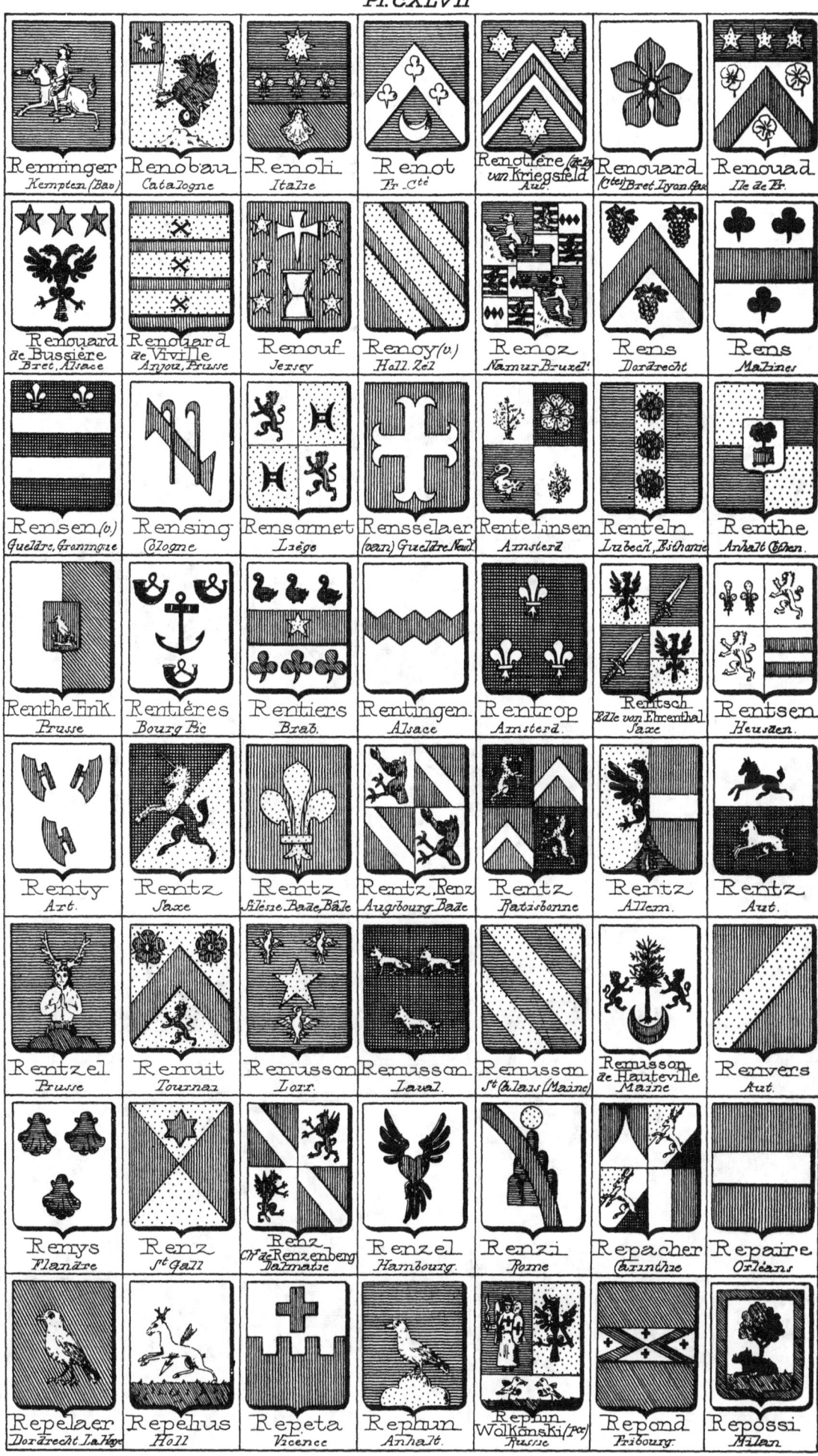

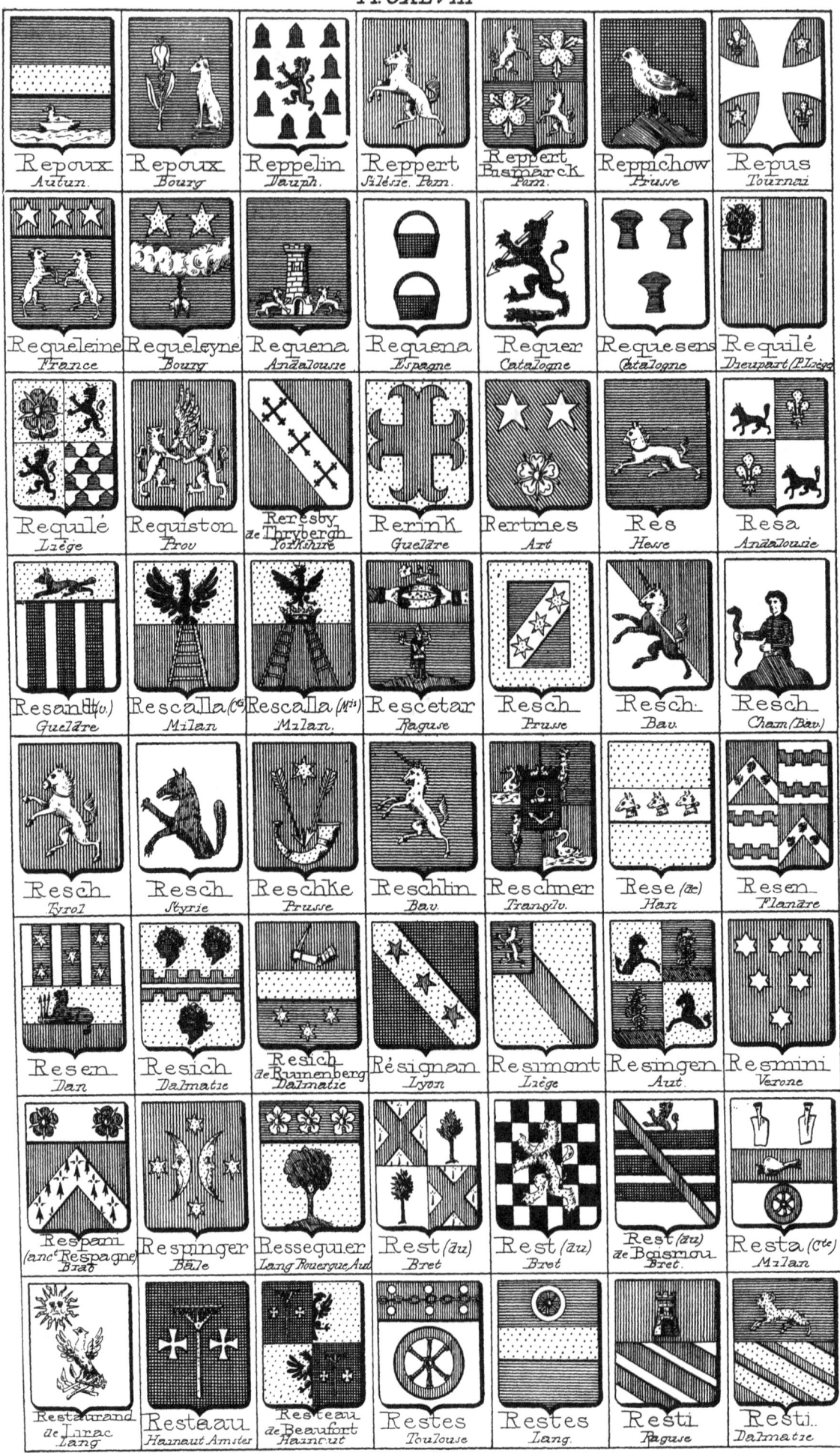

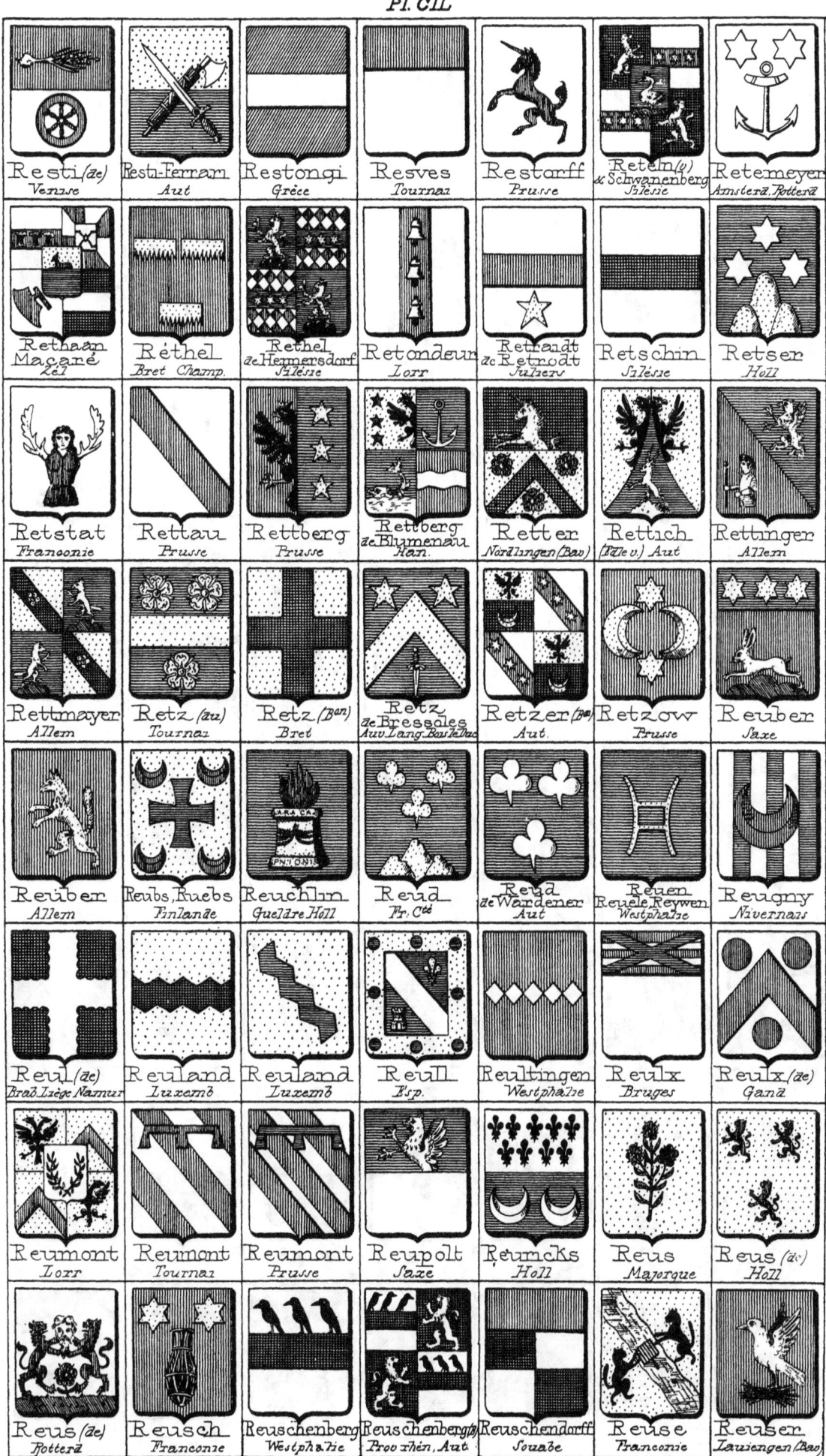

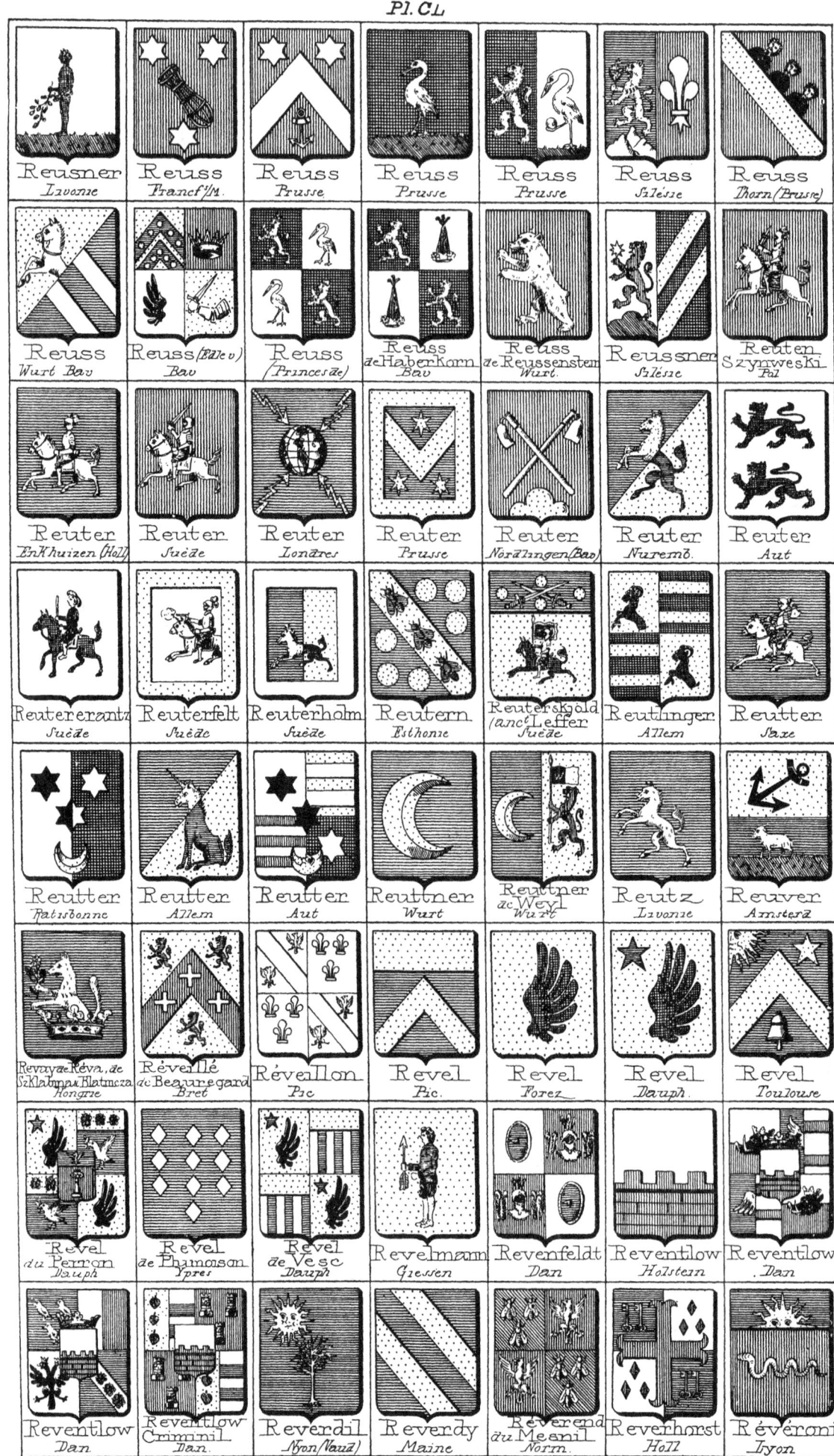

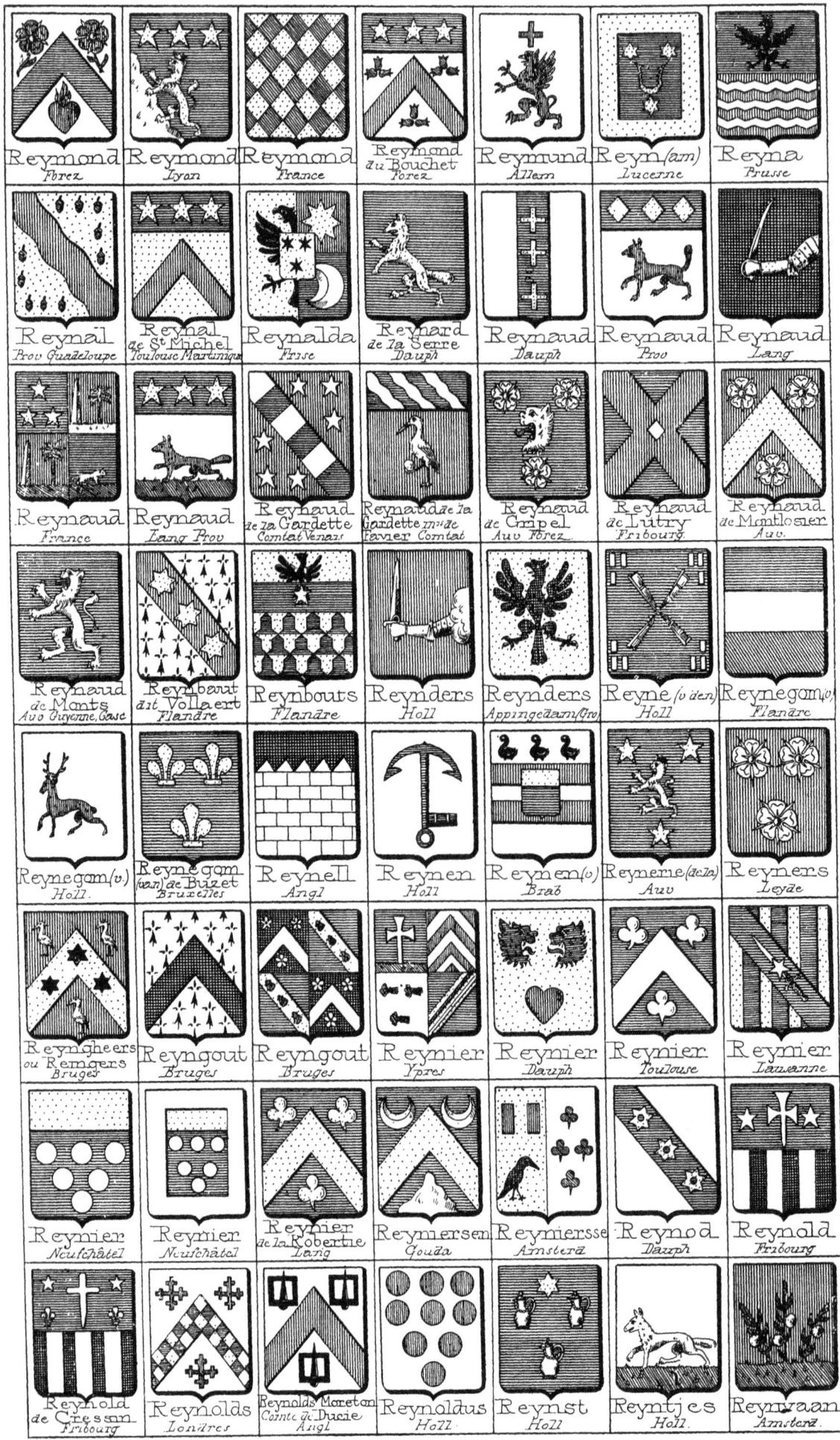

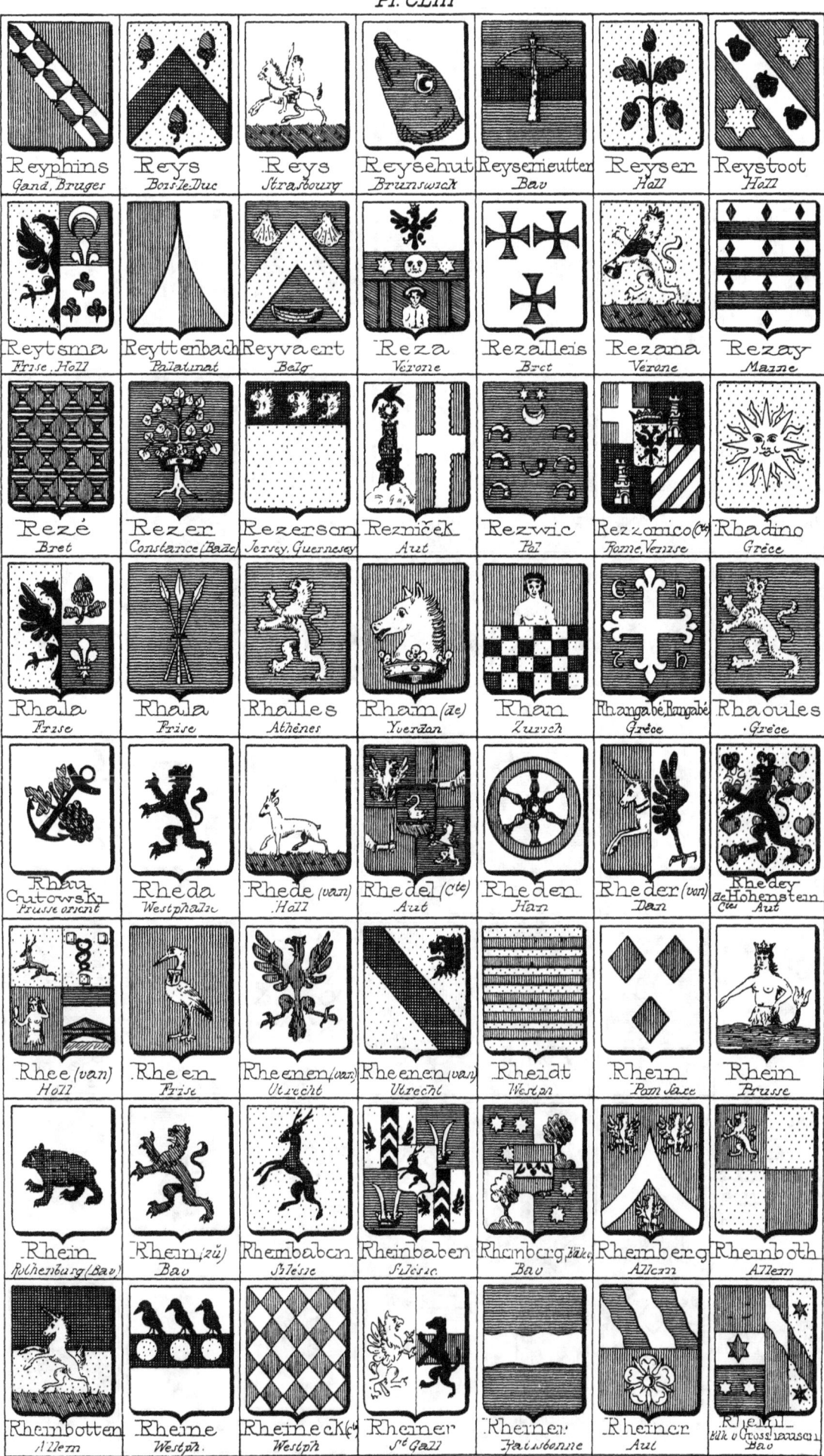

Pl. CLVII

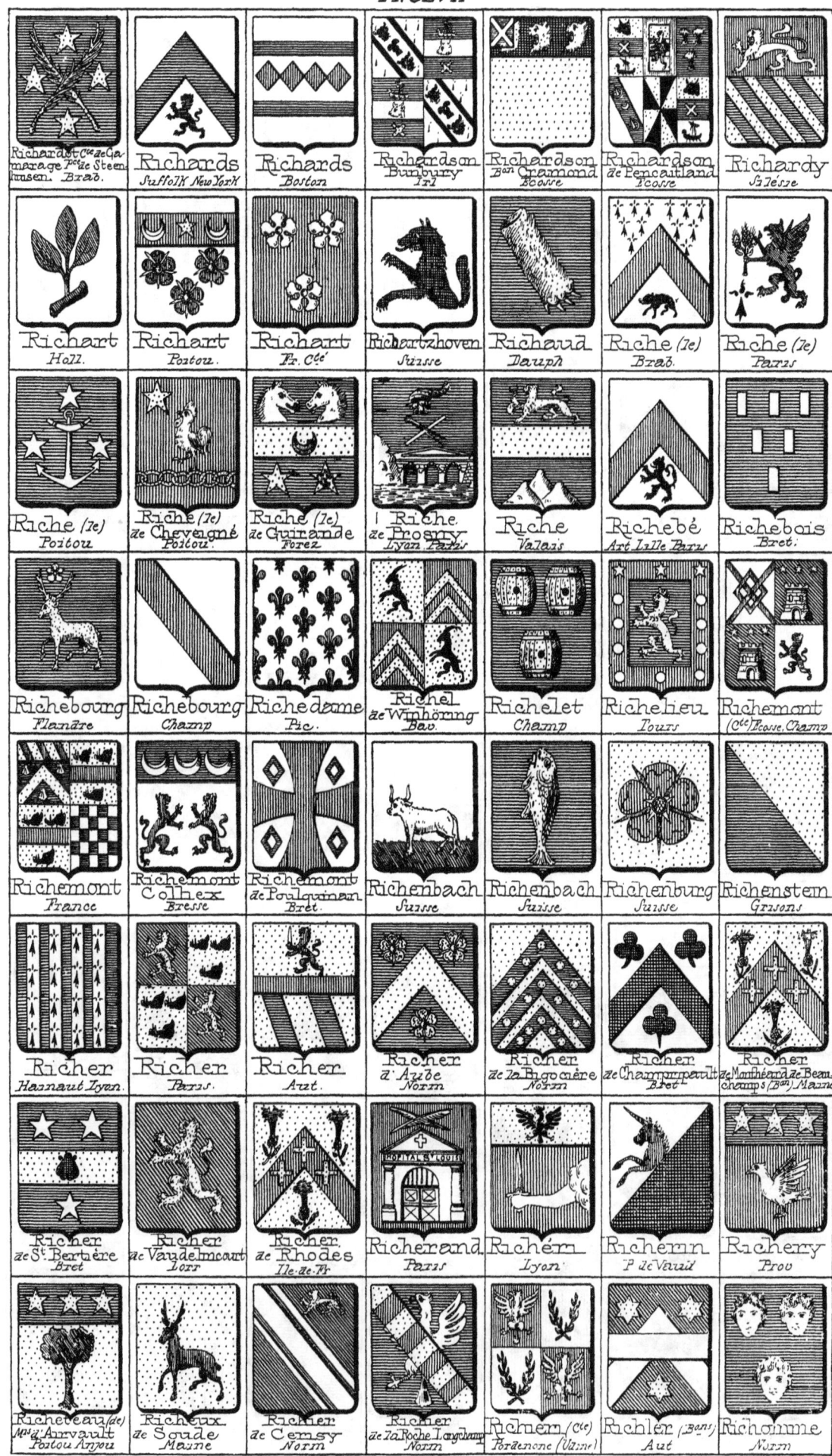

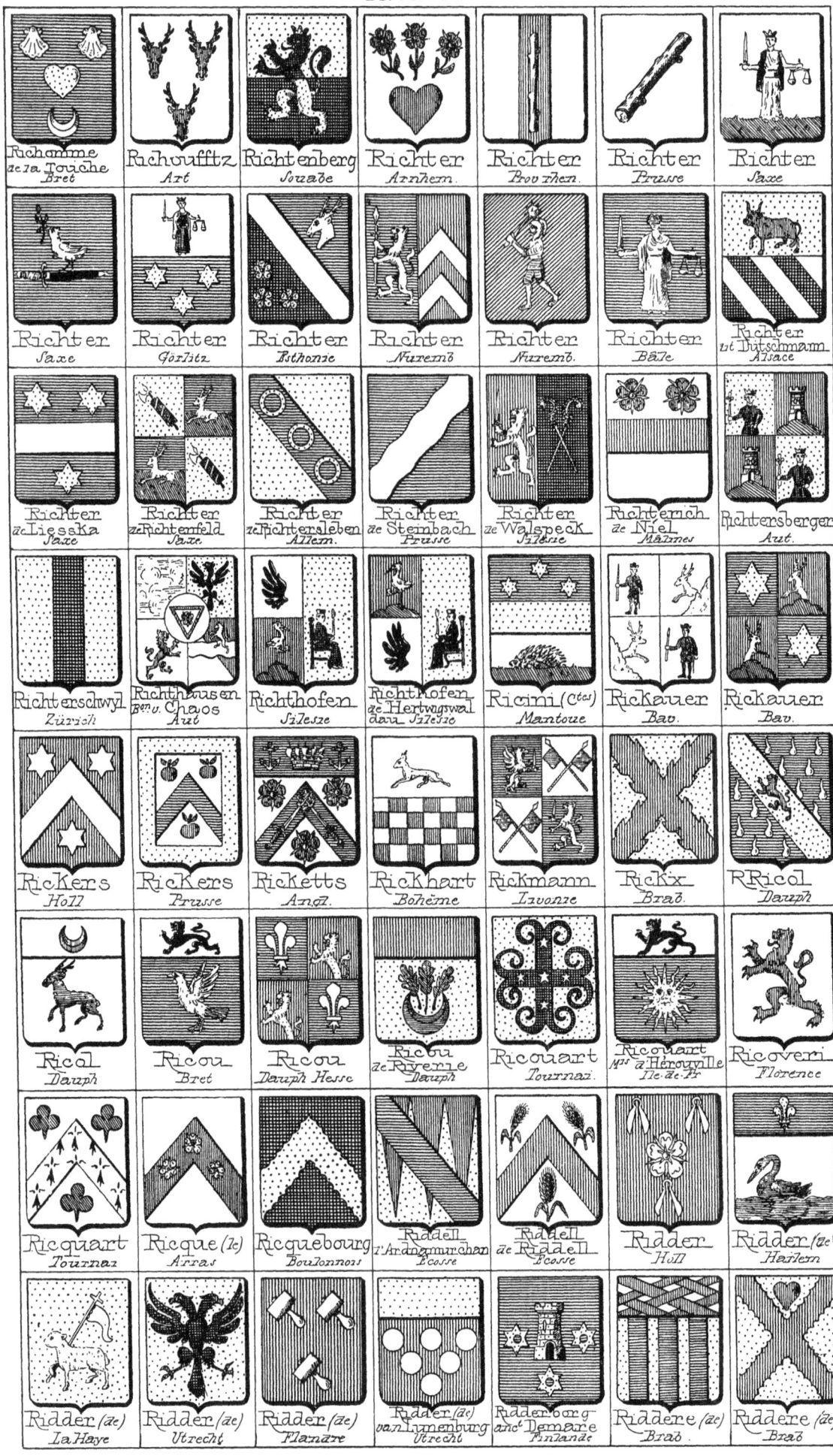

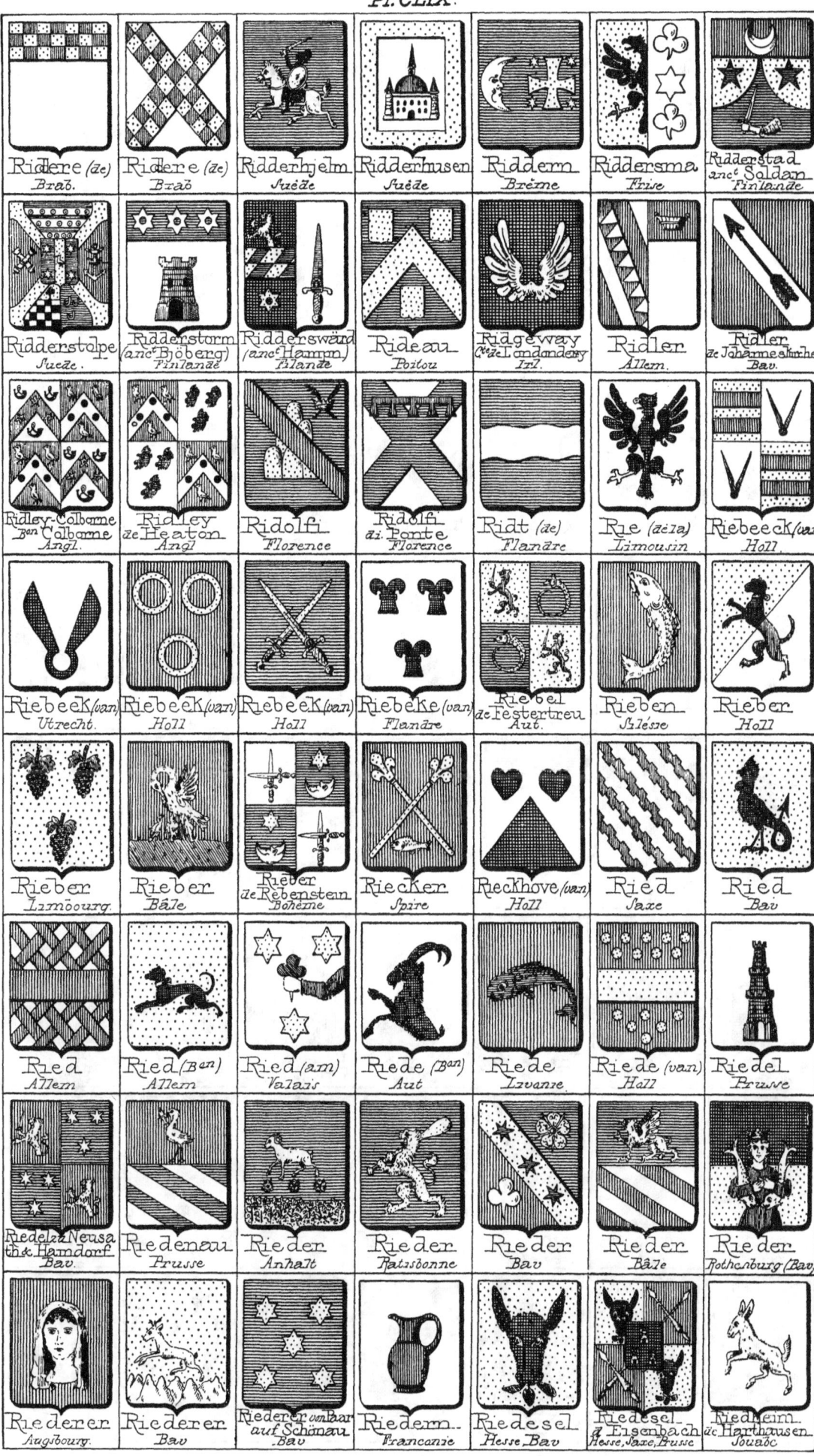

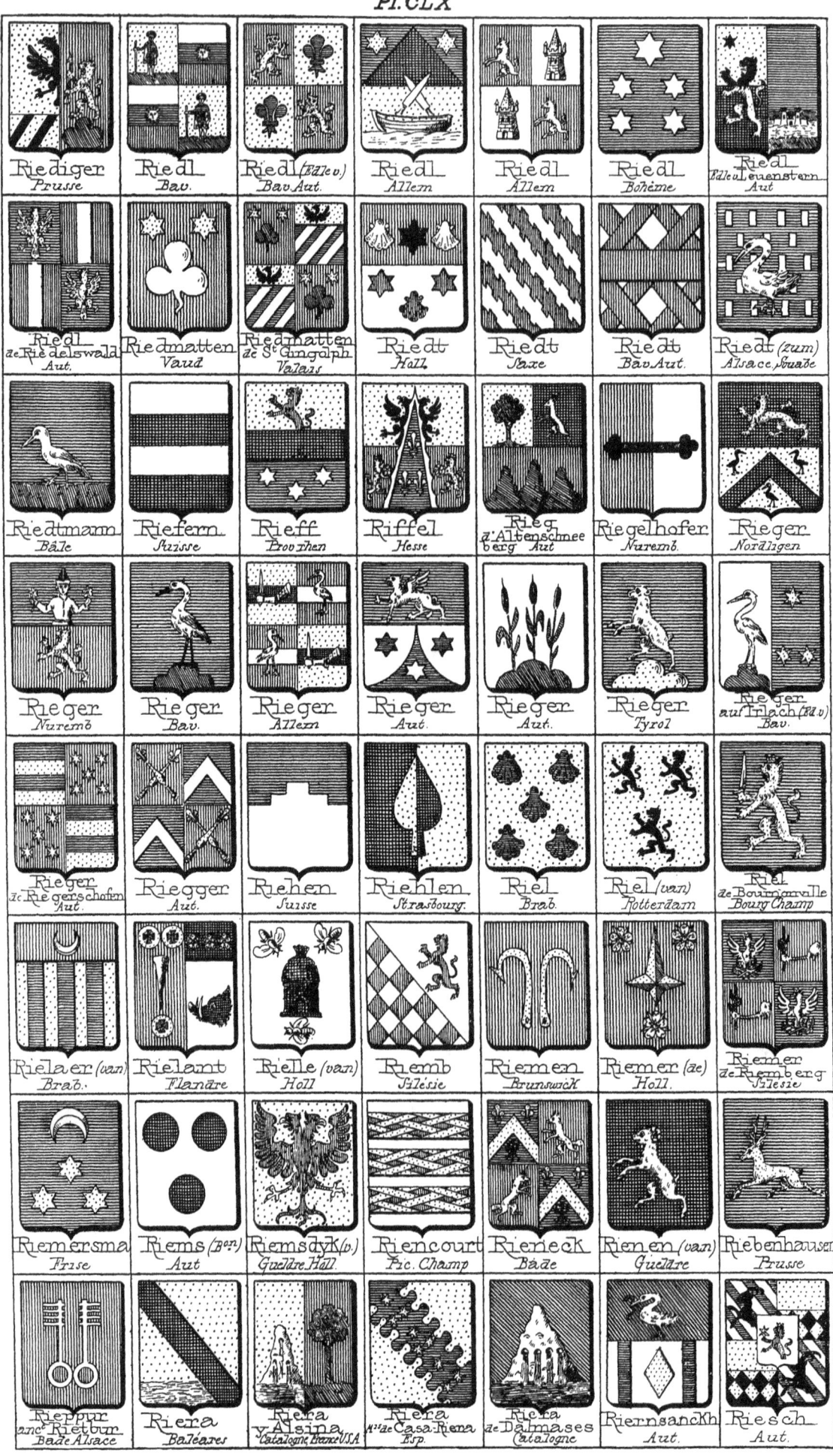

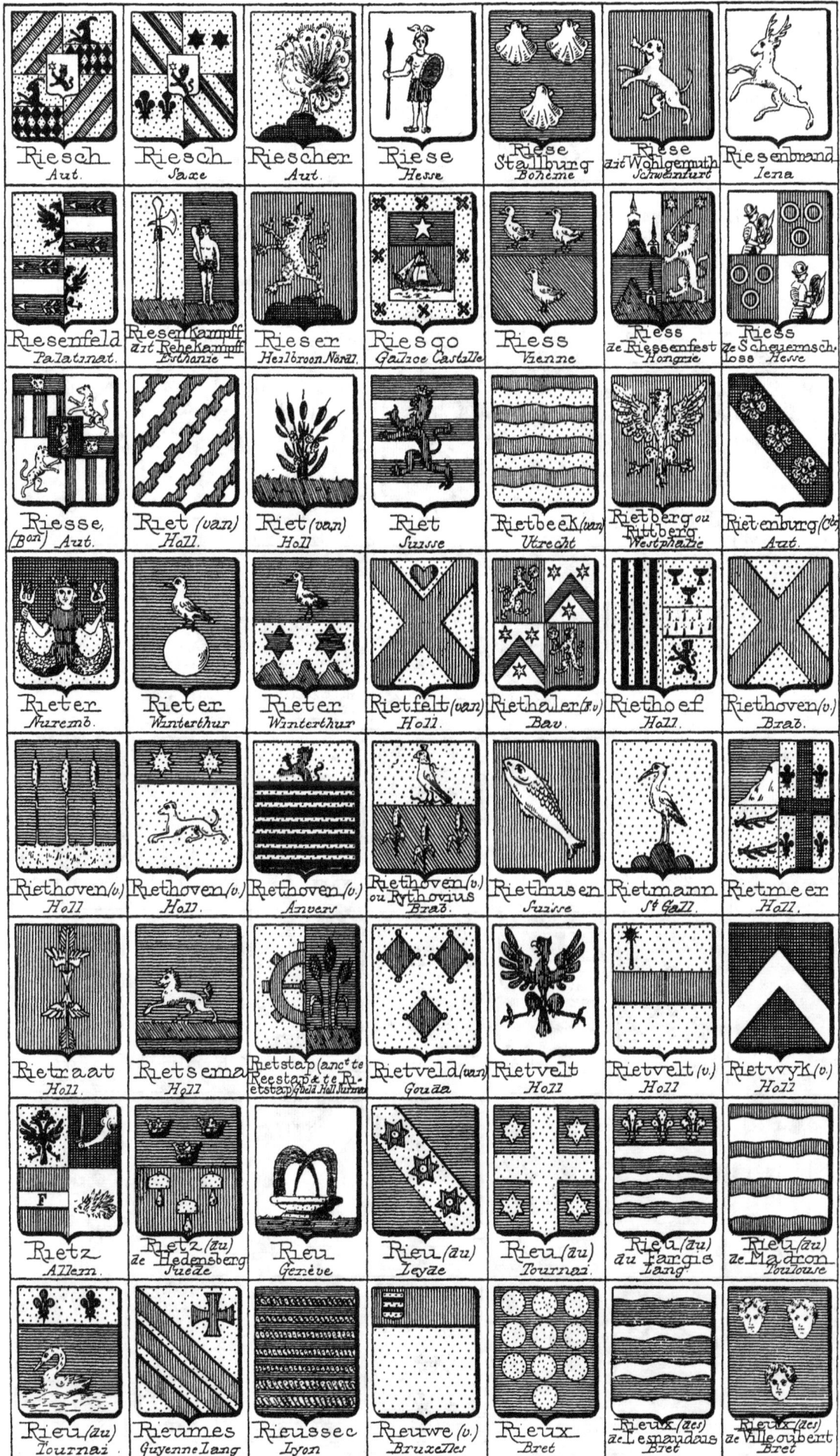

Pl. CLXII

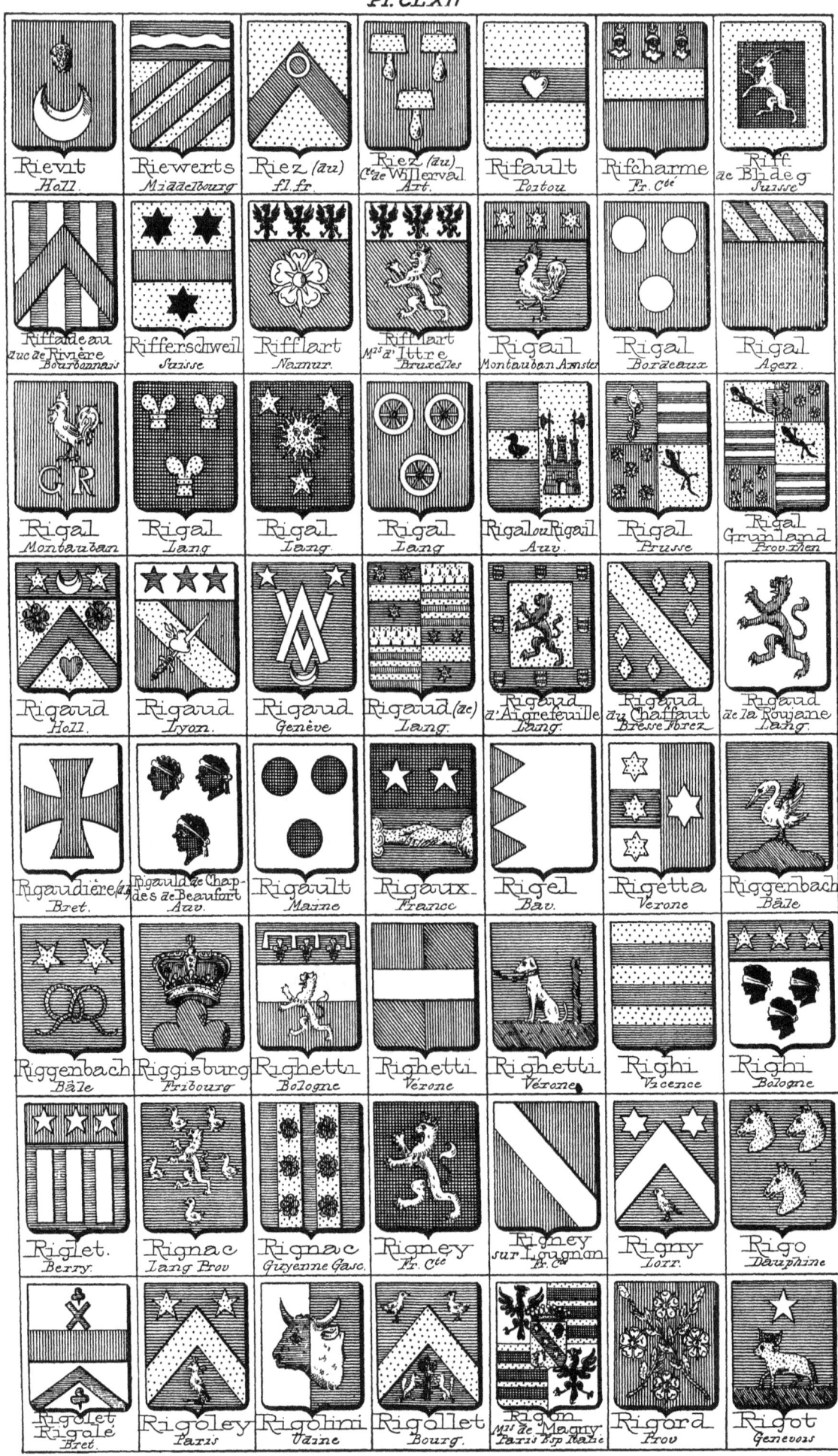

Pl. CLXV

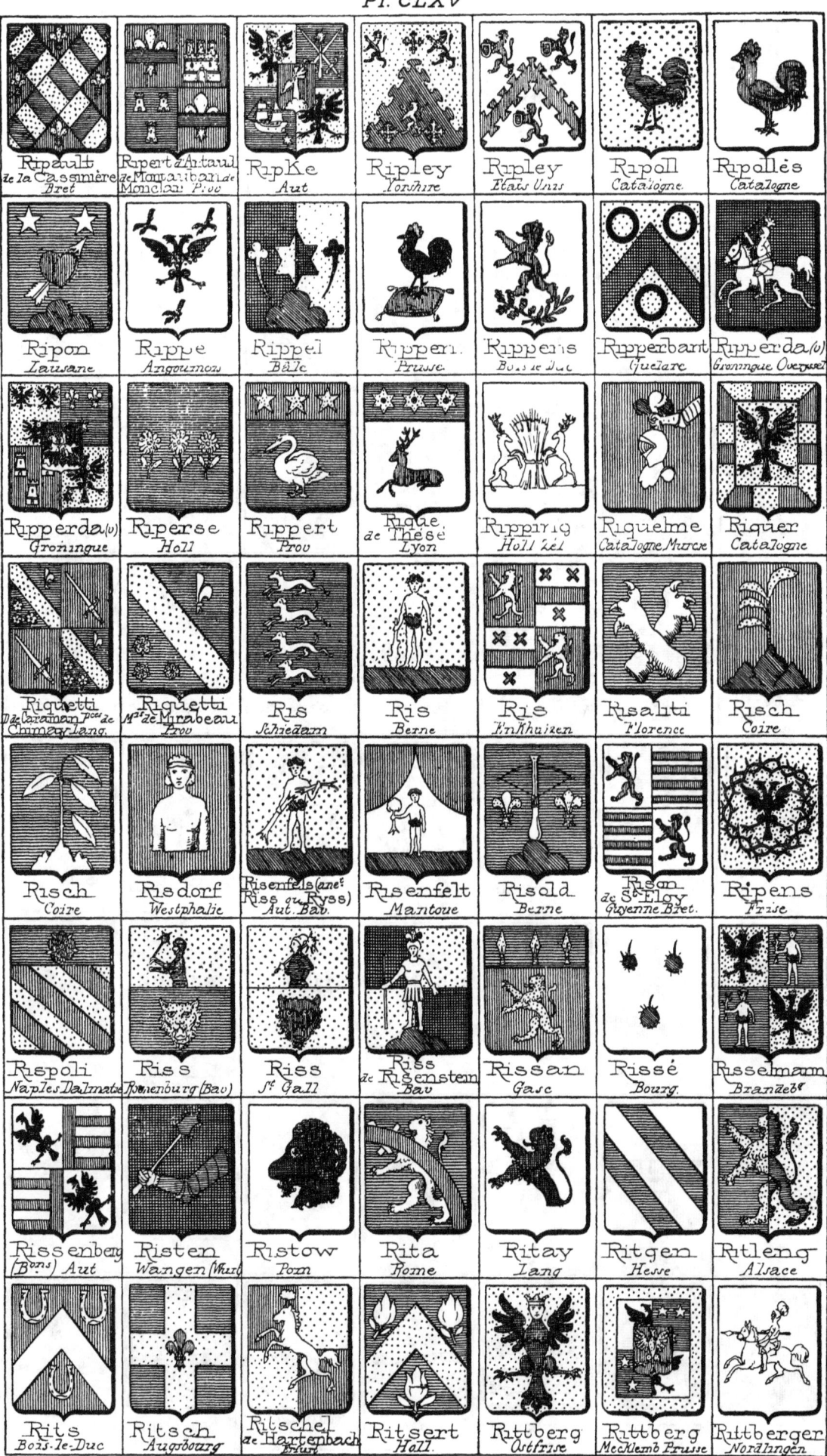

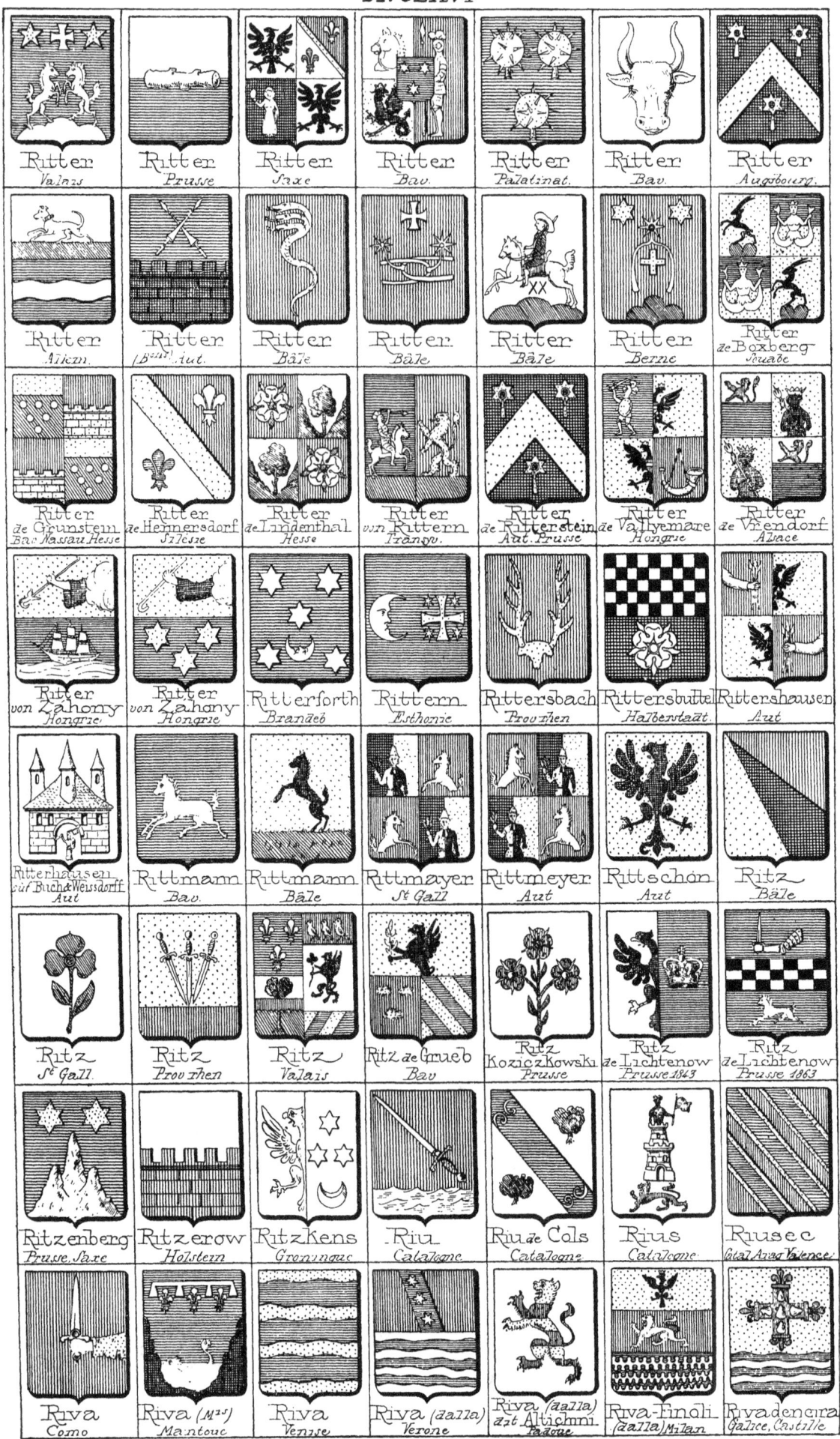

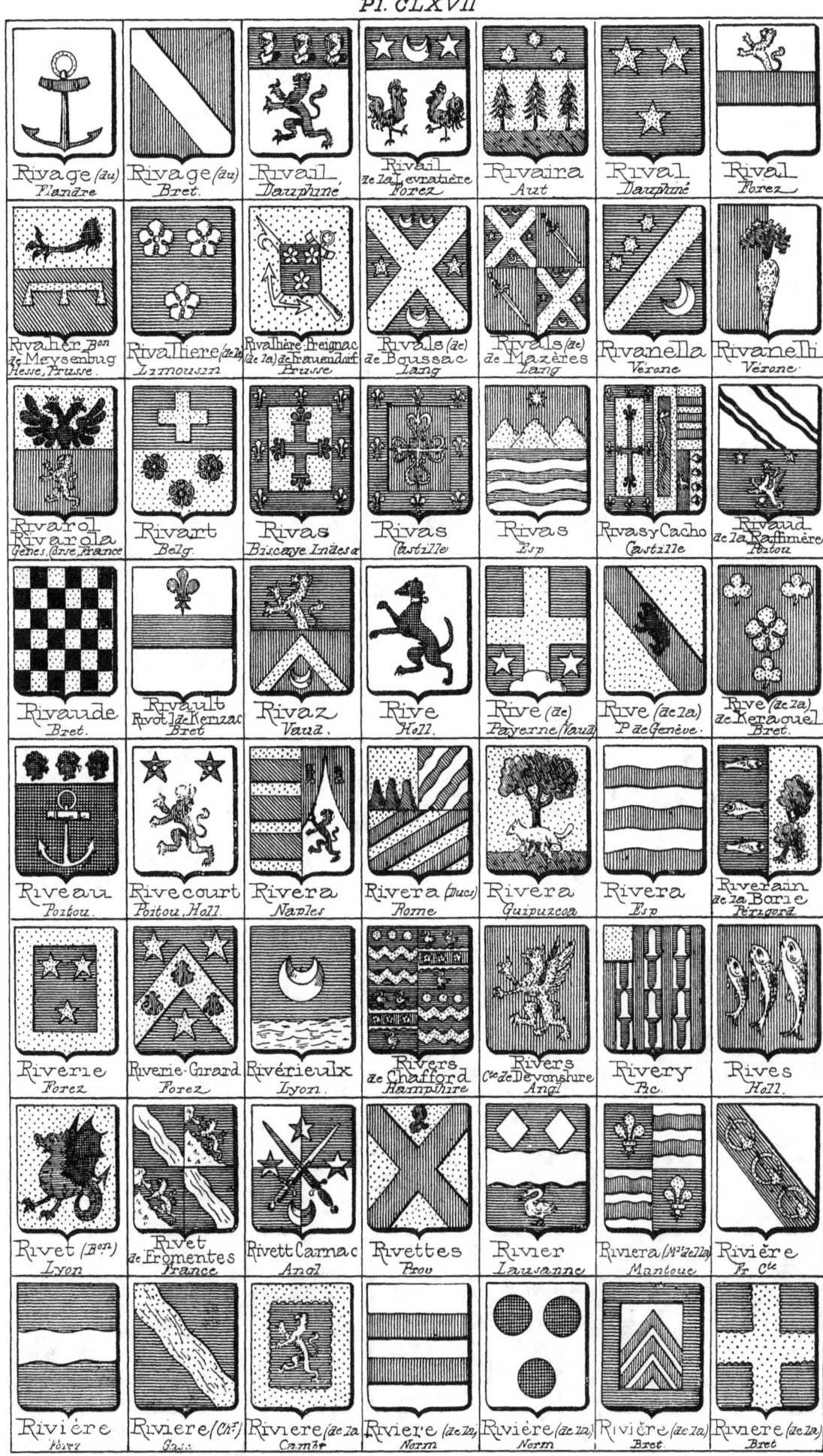

Pl. CLXVIII

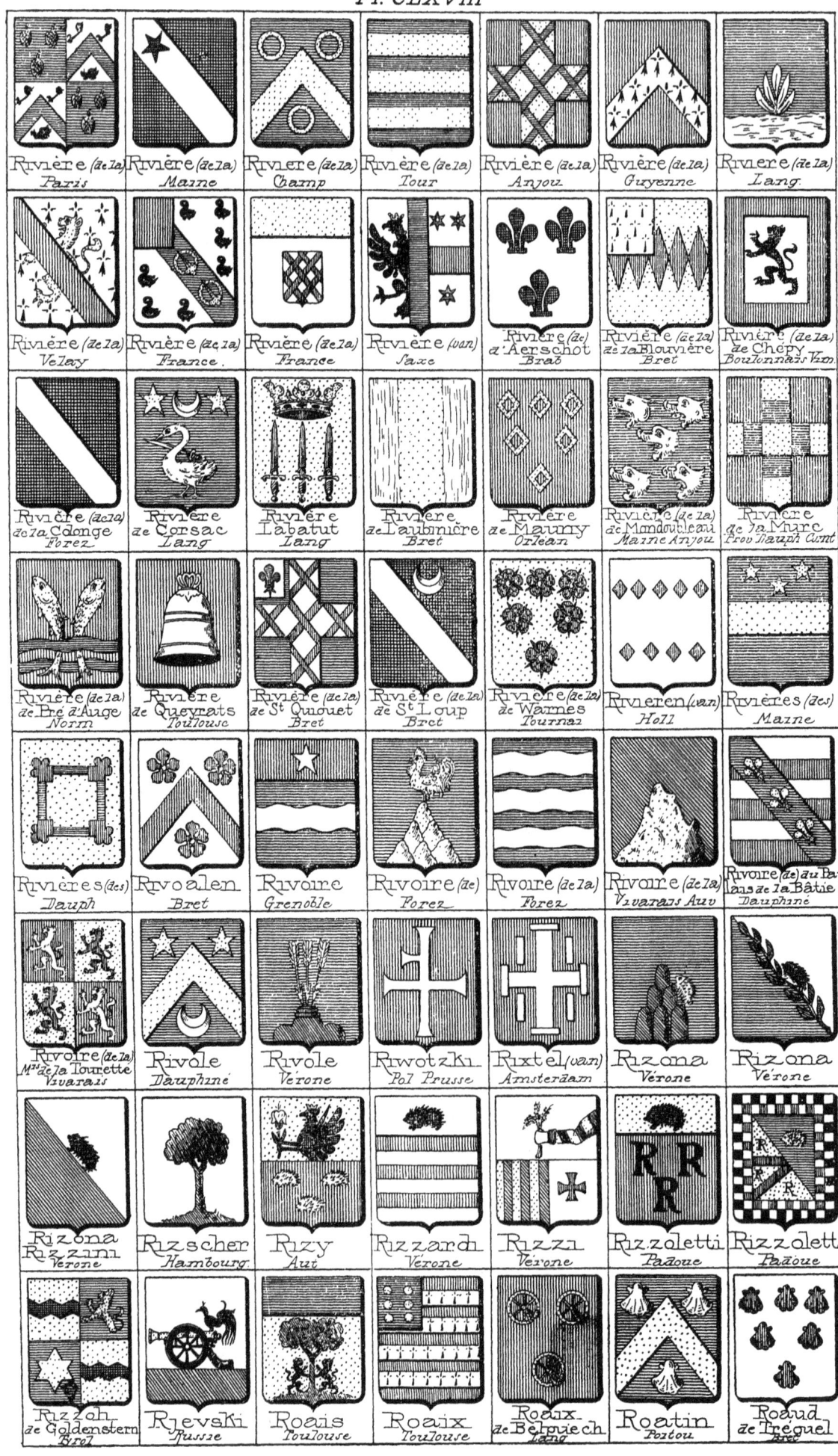

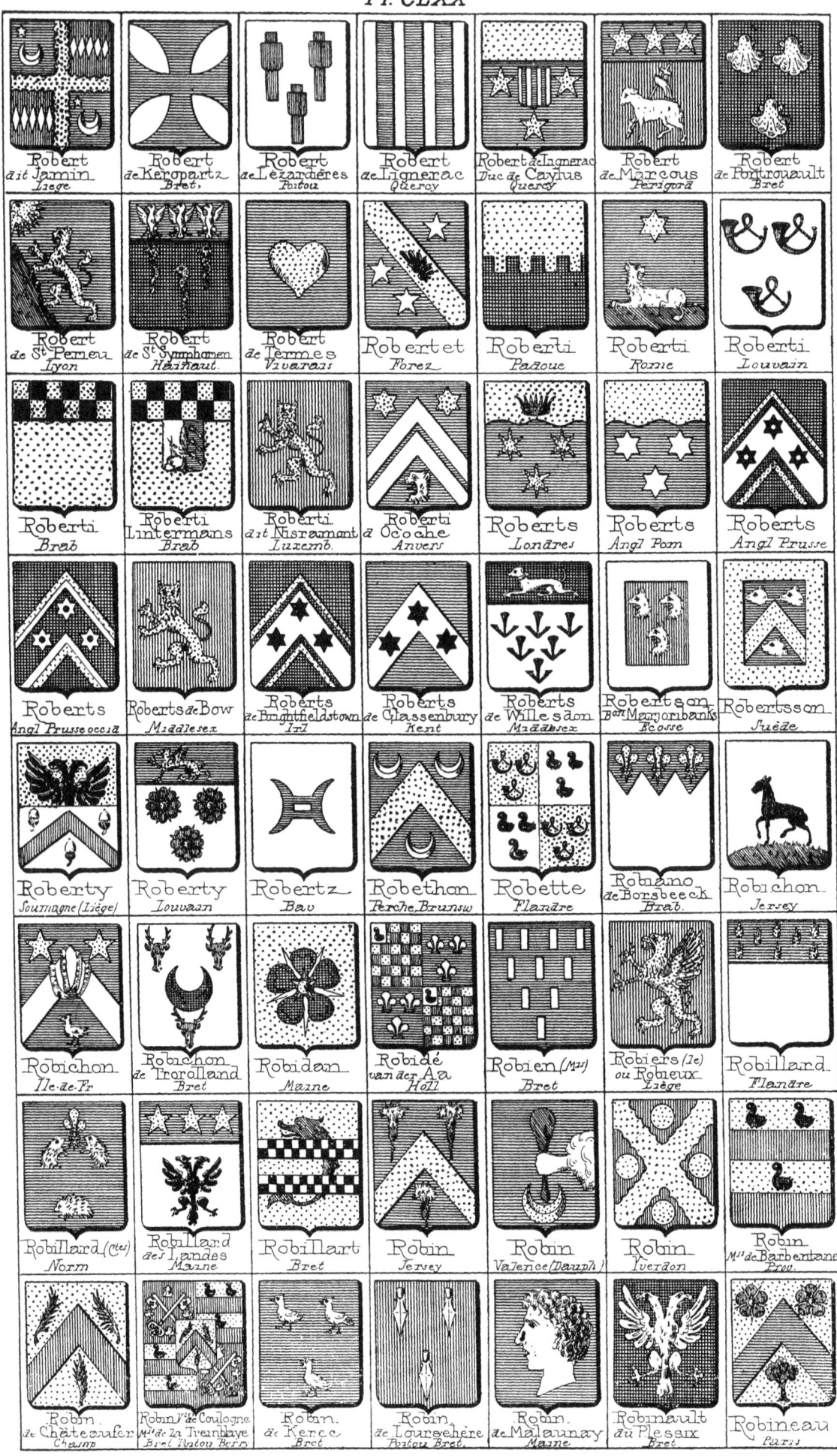

Pl. CLXXI

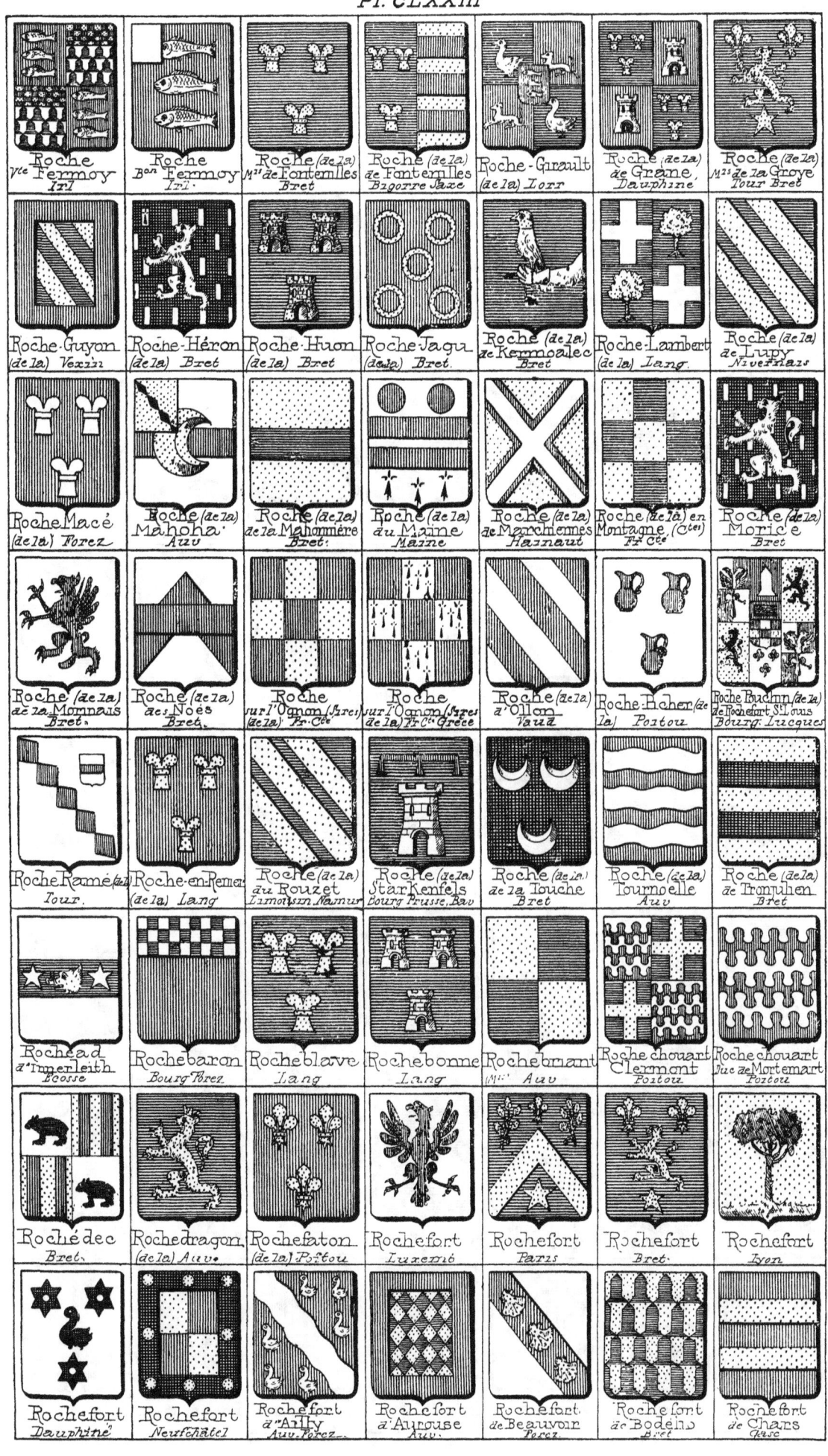

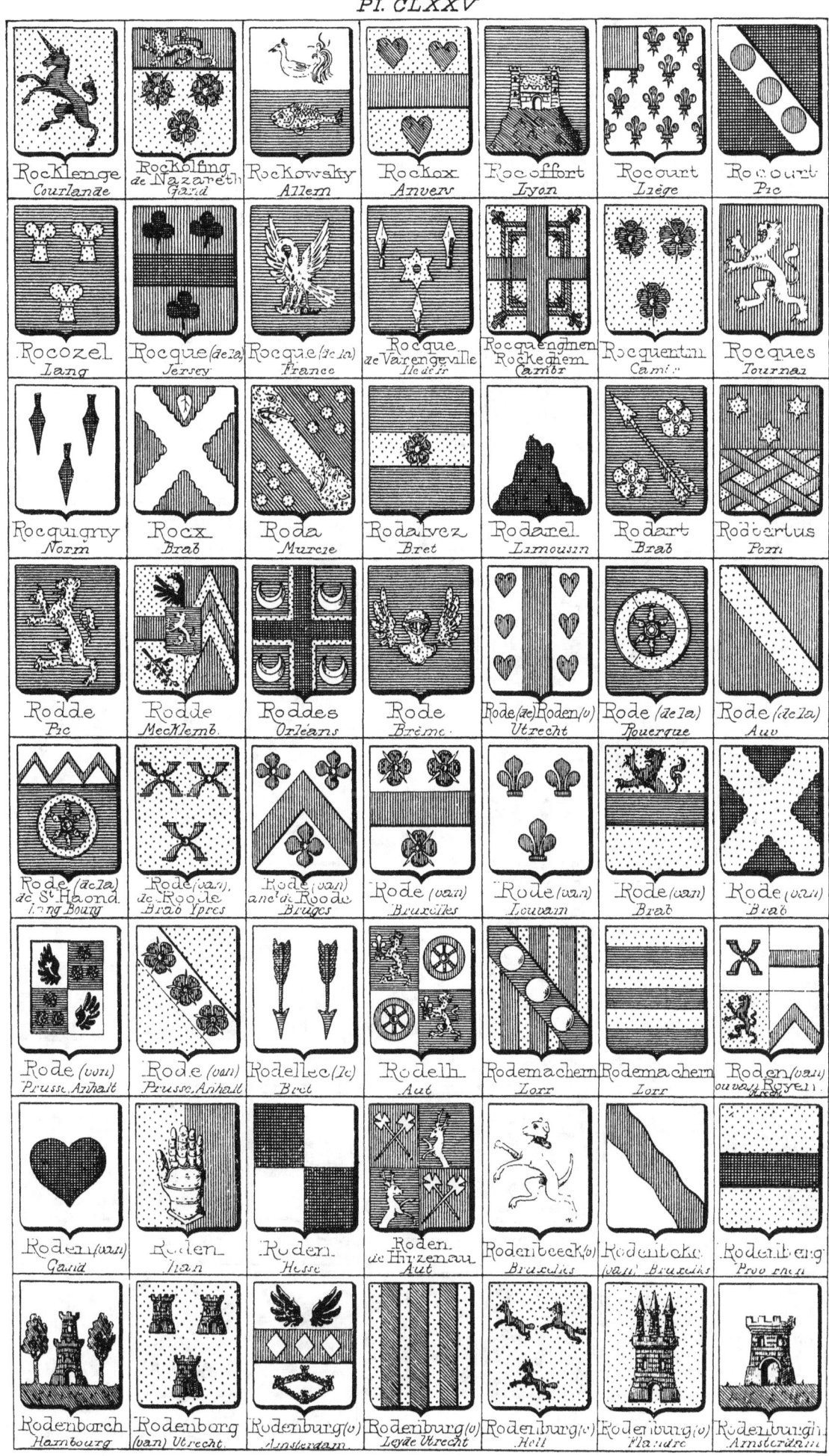

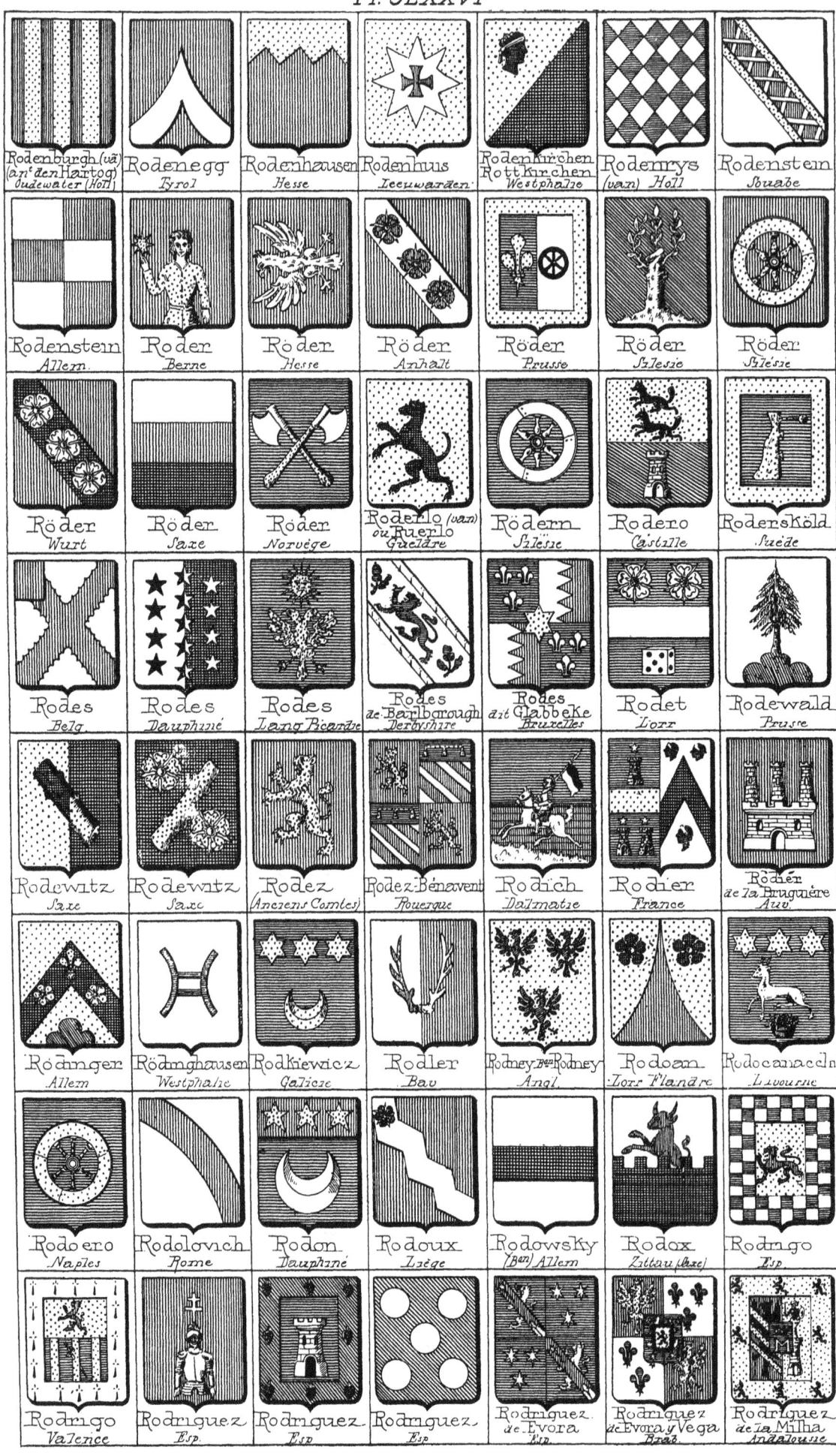

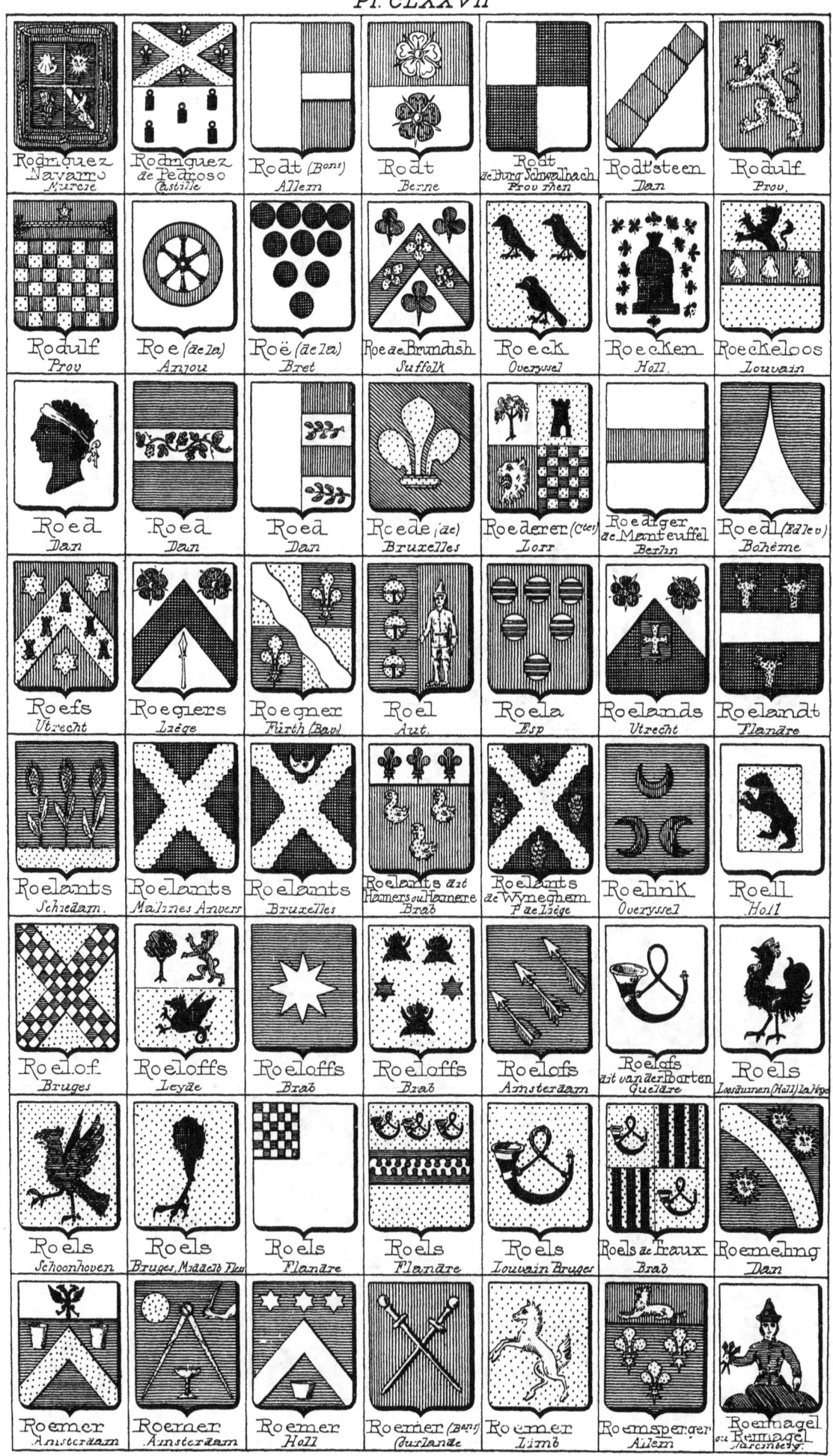
Pl. CLXXVII

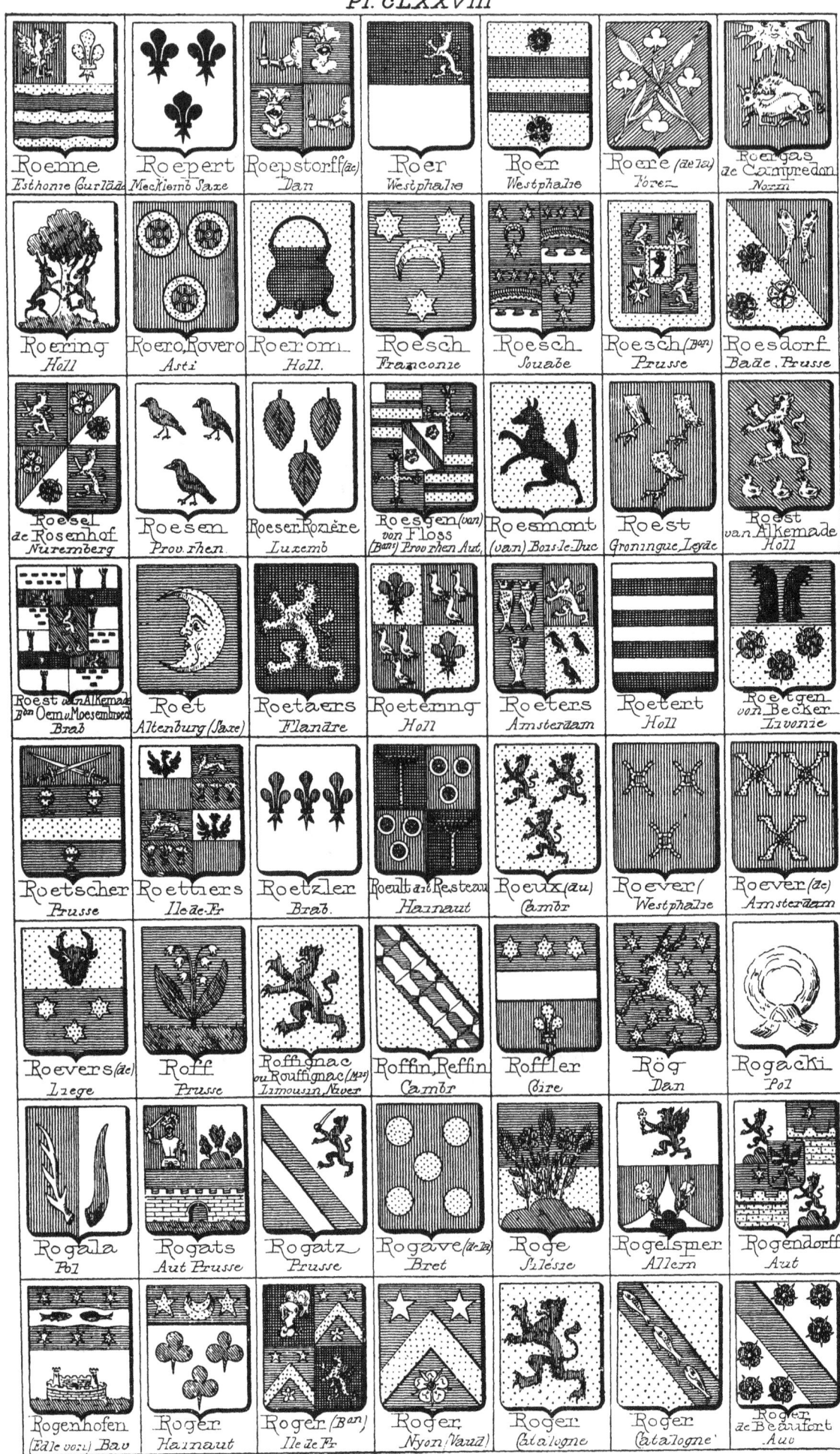

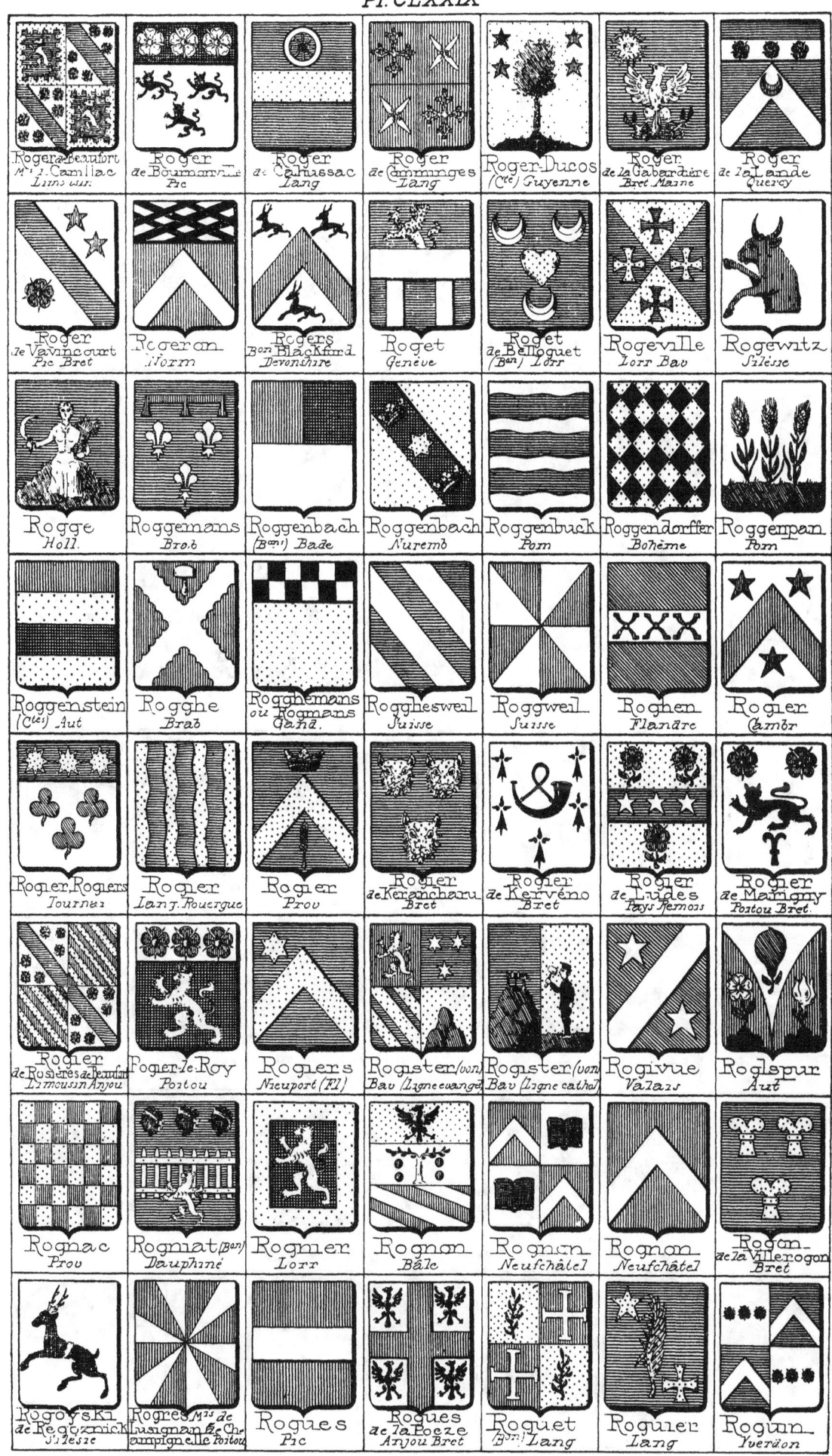

Pl. CLXXX

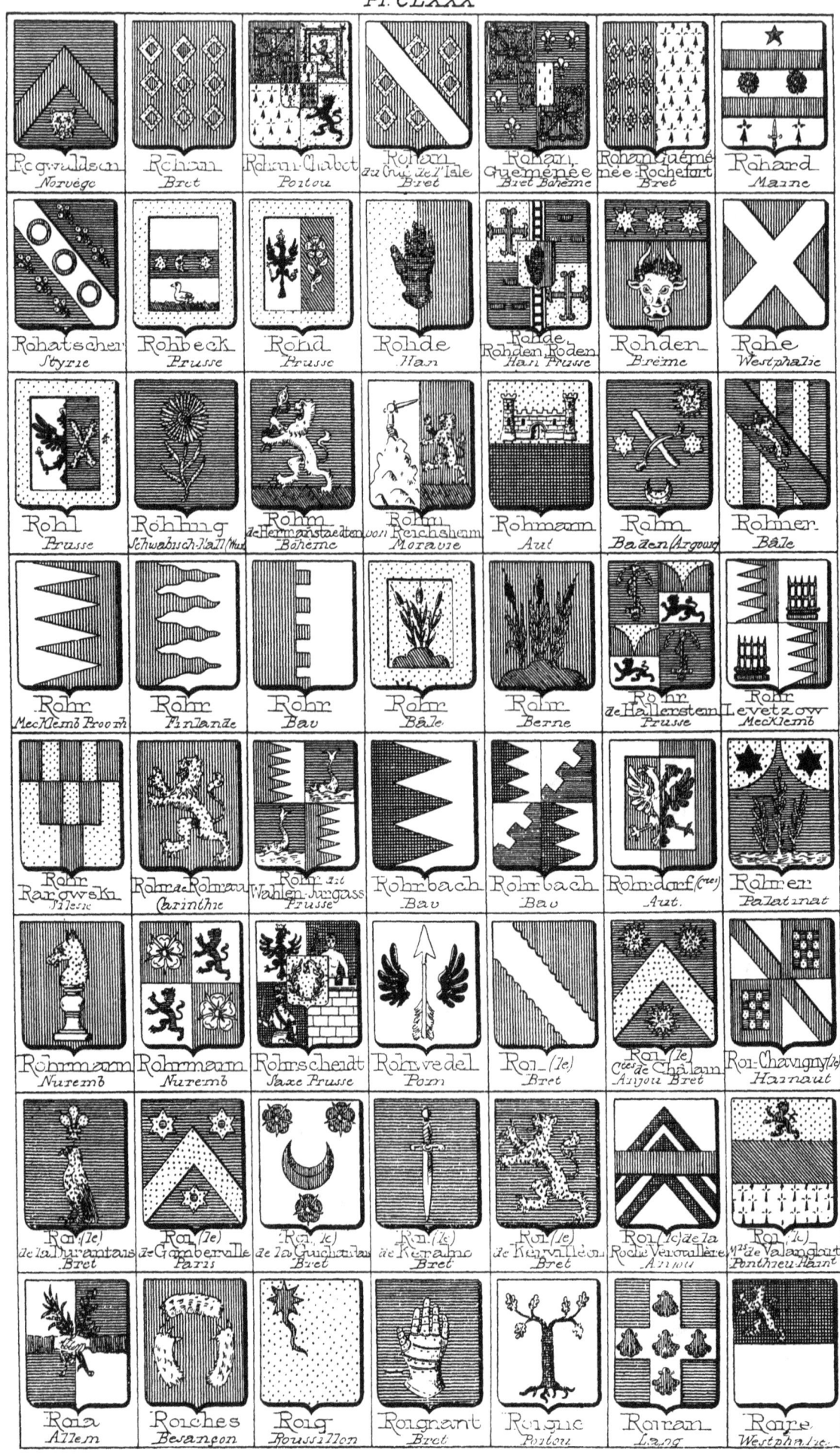

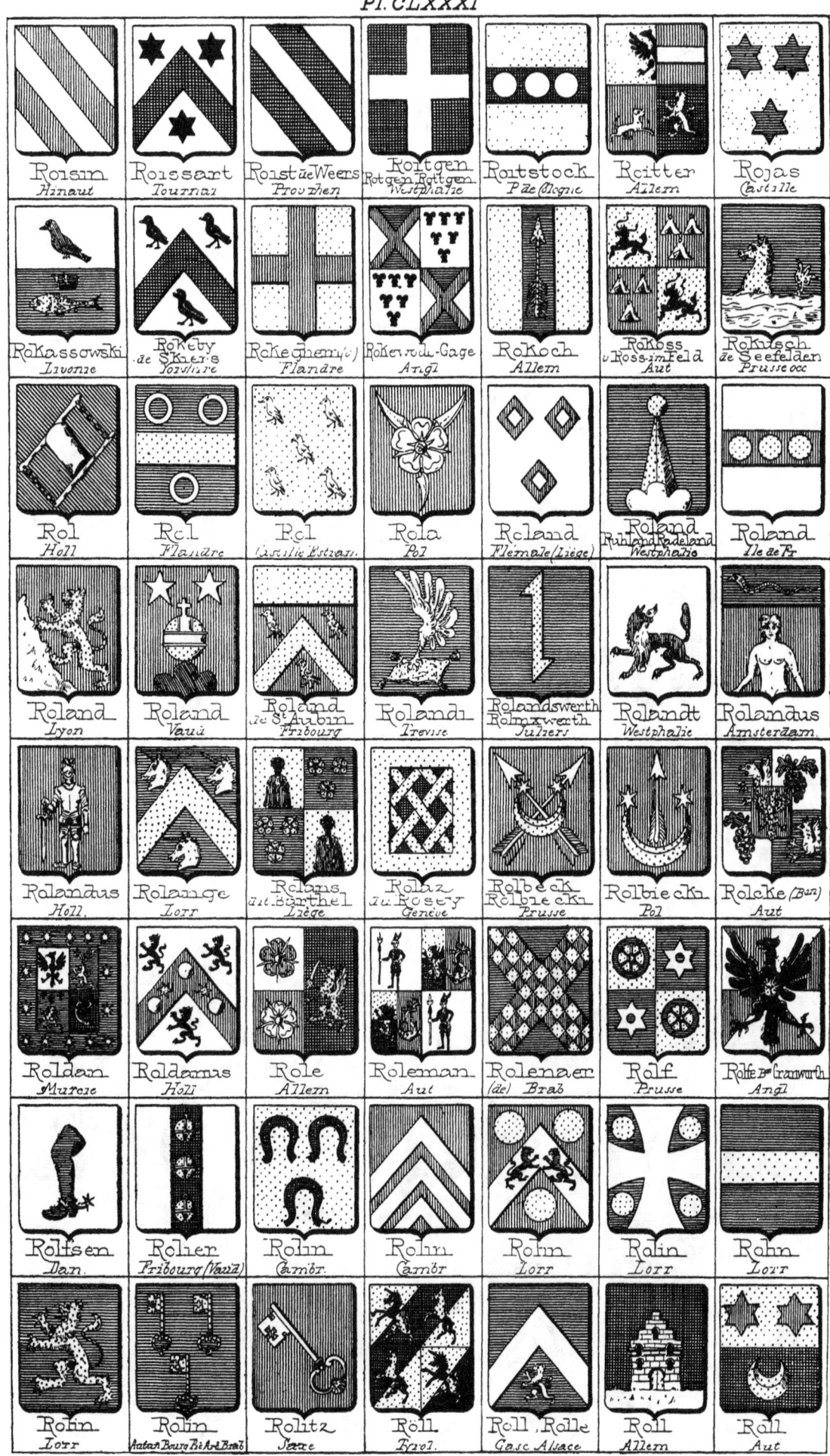

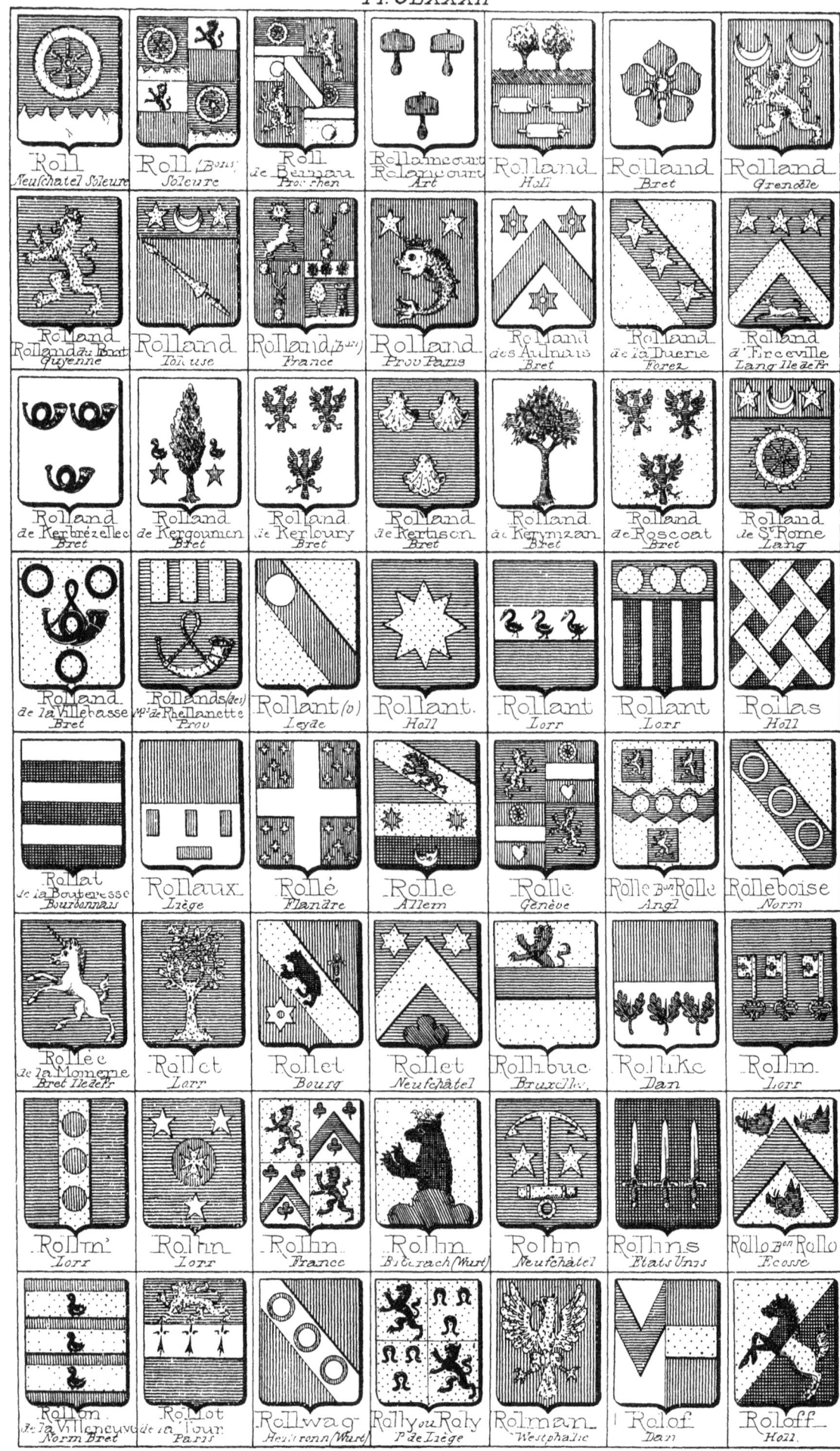

Pl. CLXXXIII

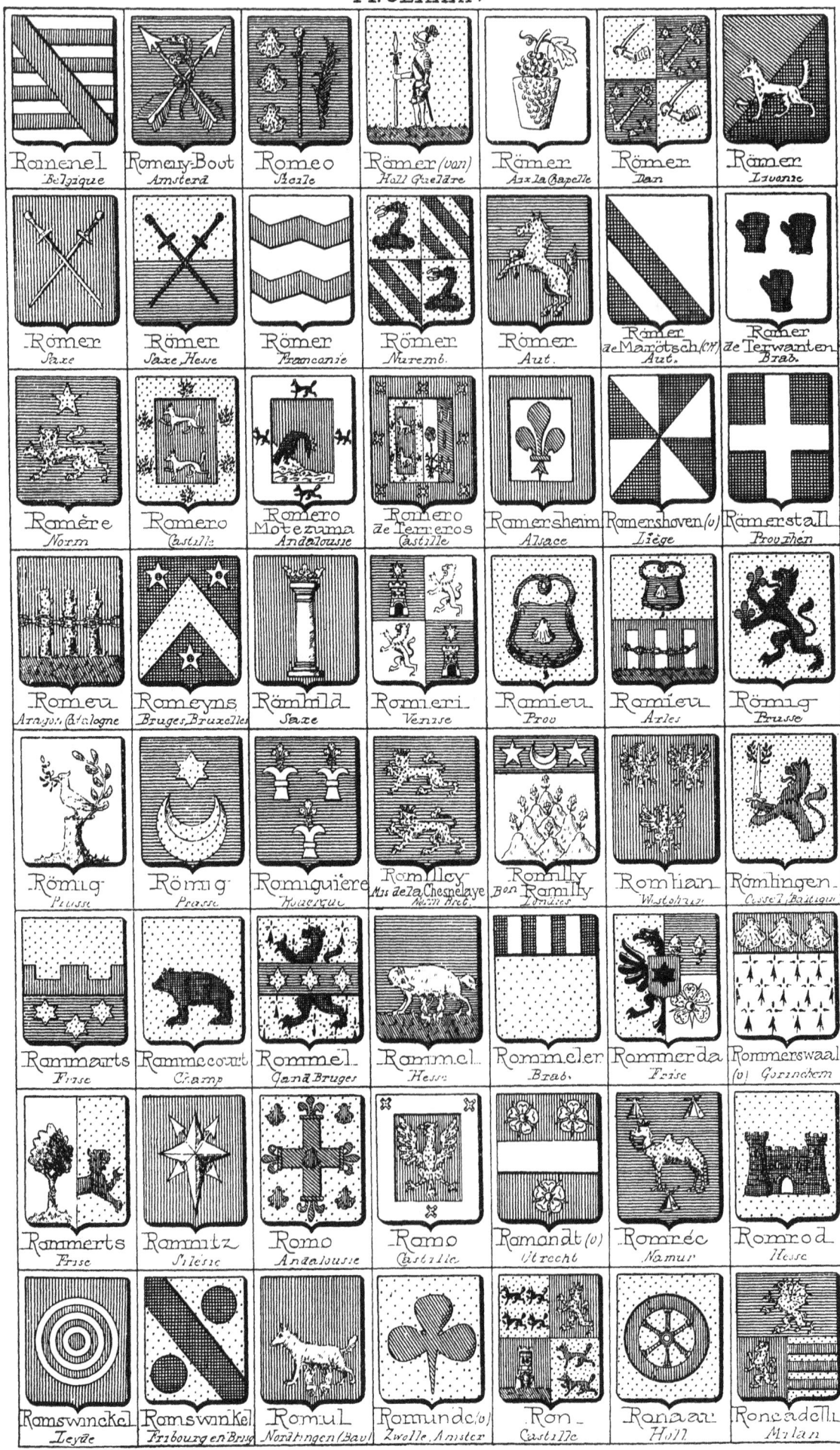

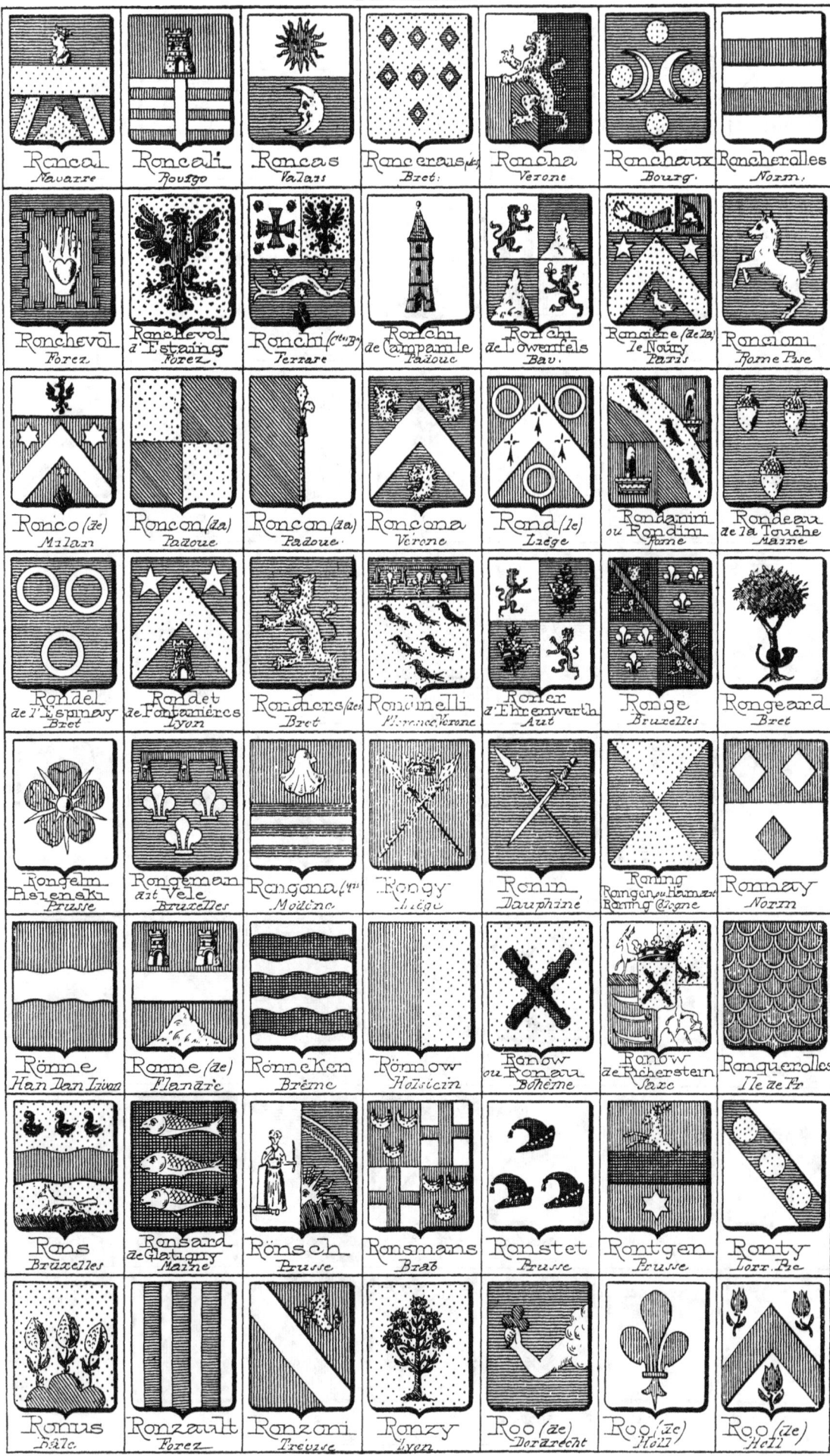

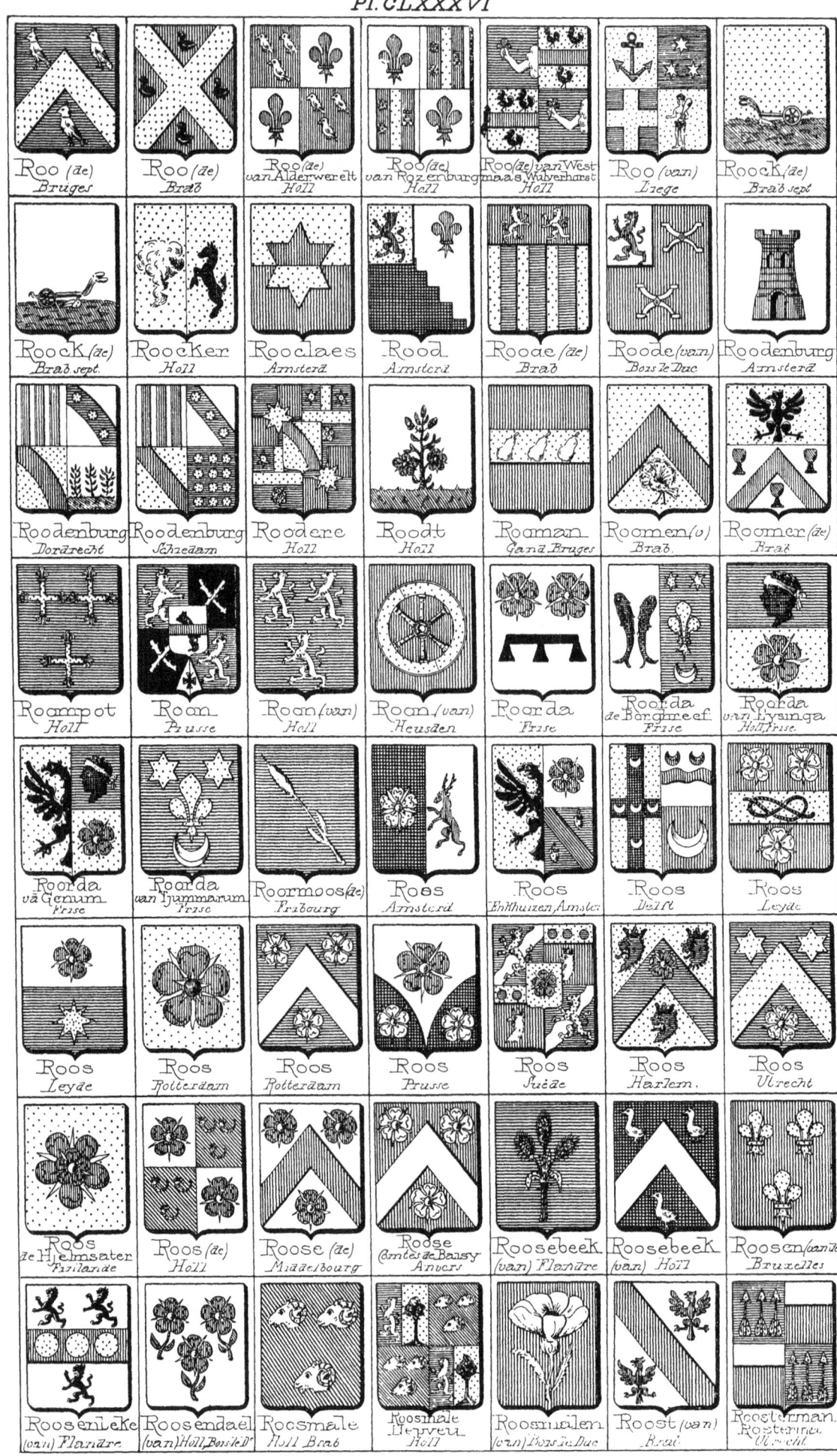

Pl. CLXXXVII

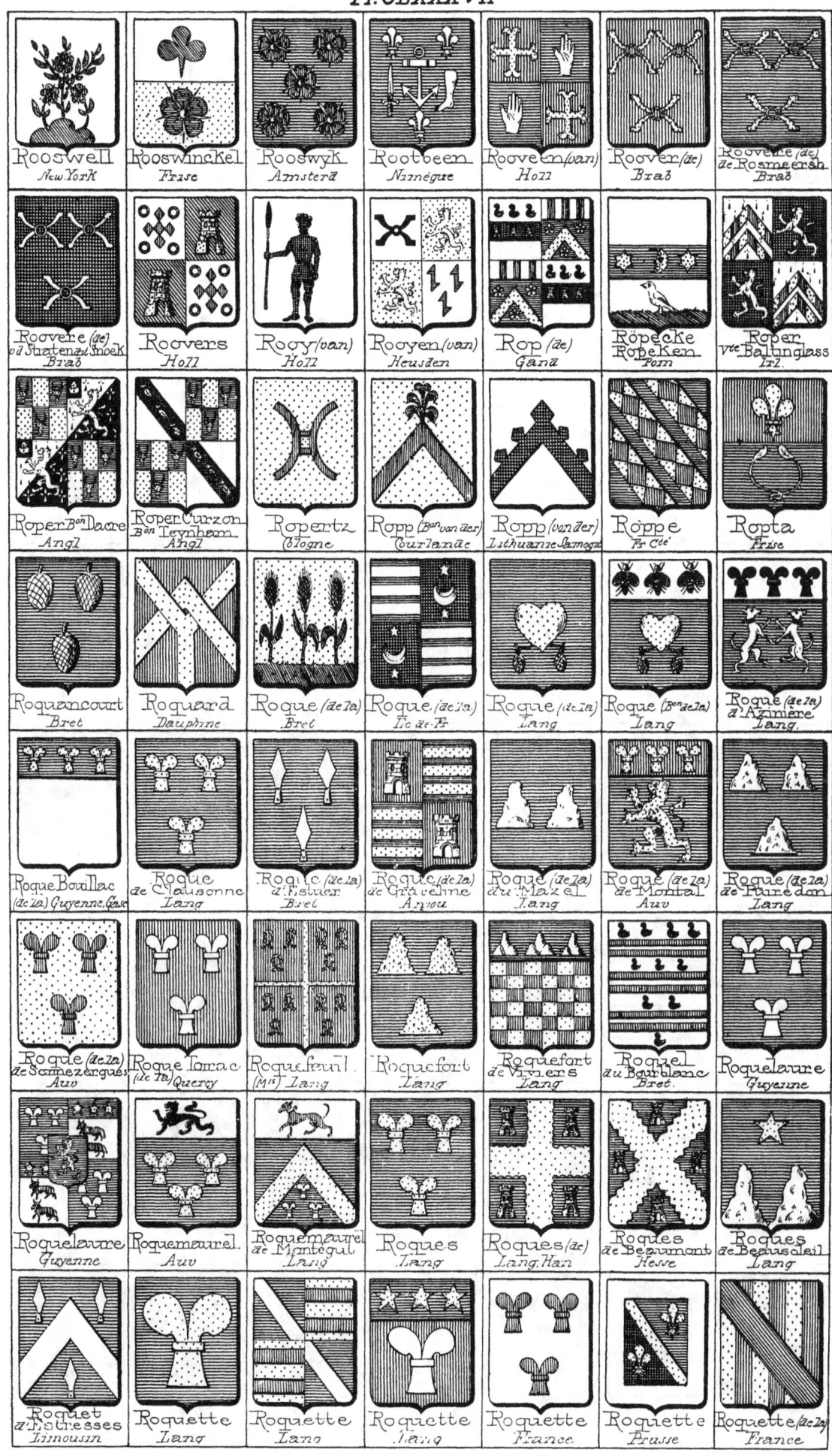

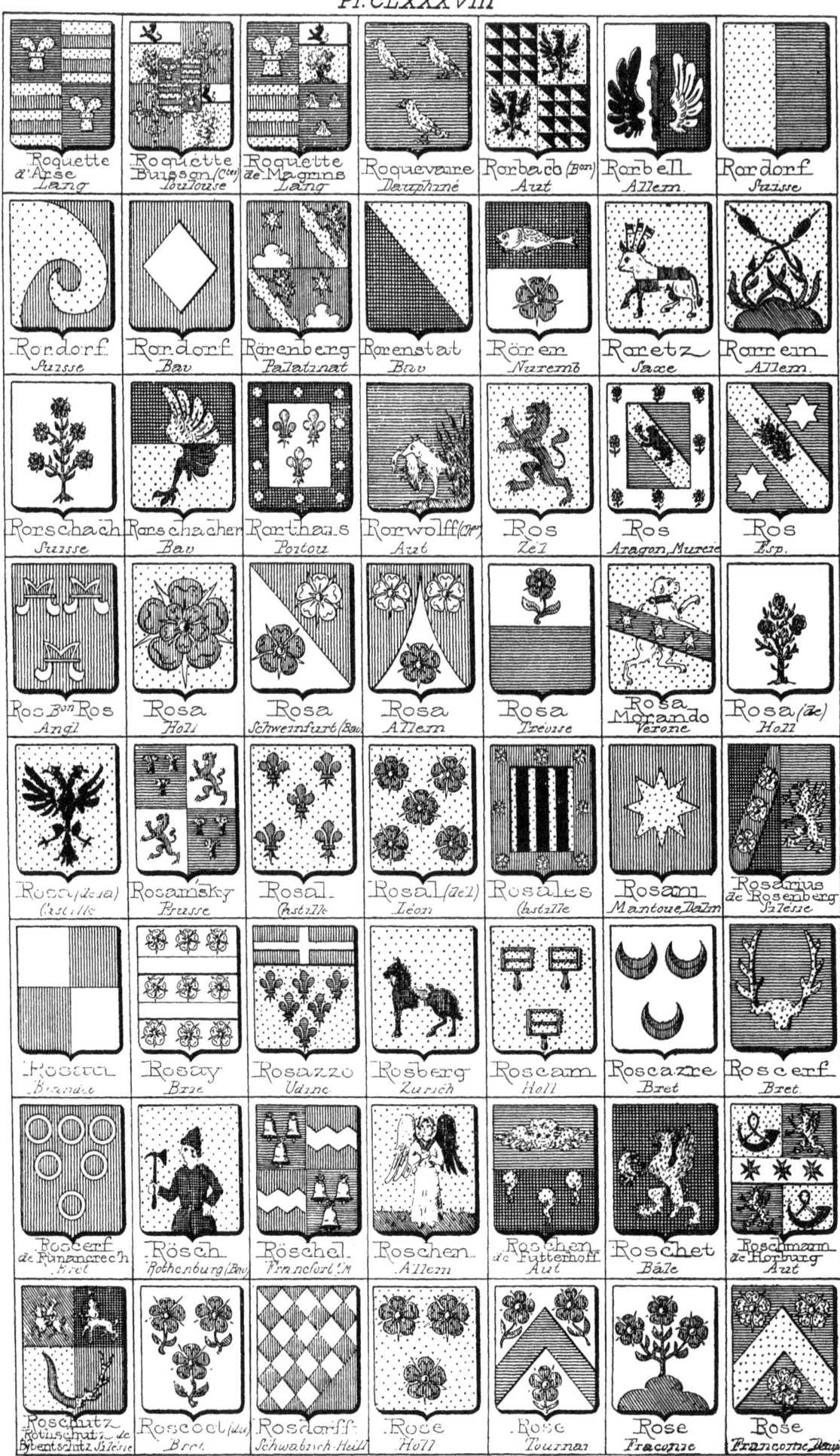

Pl. CLXXXIX

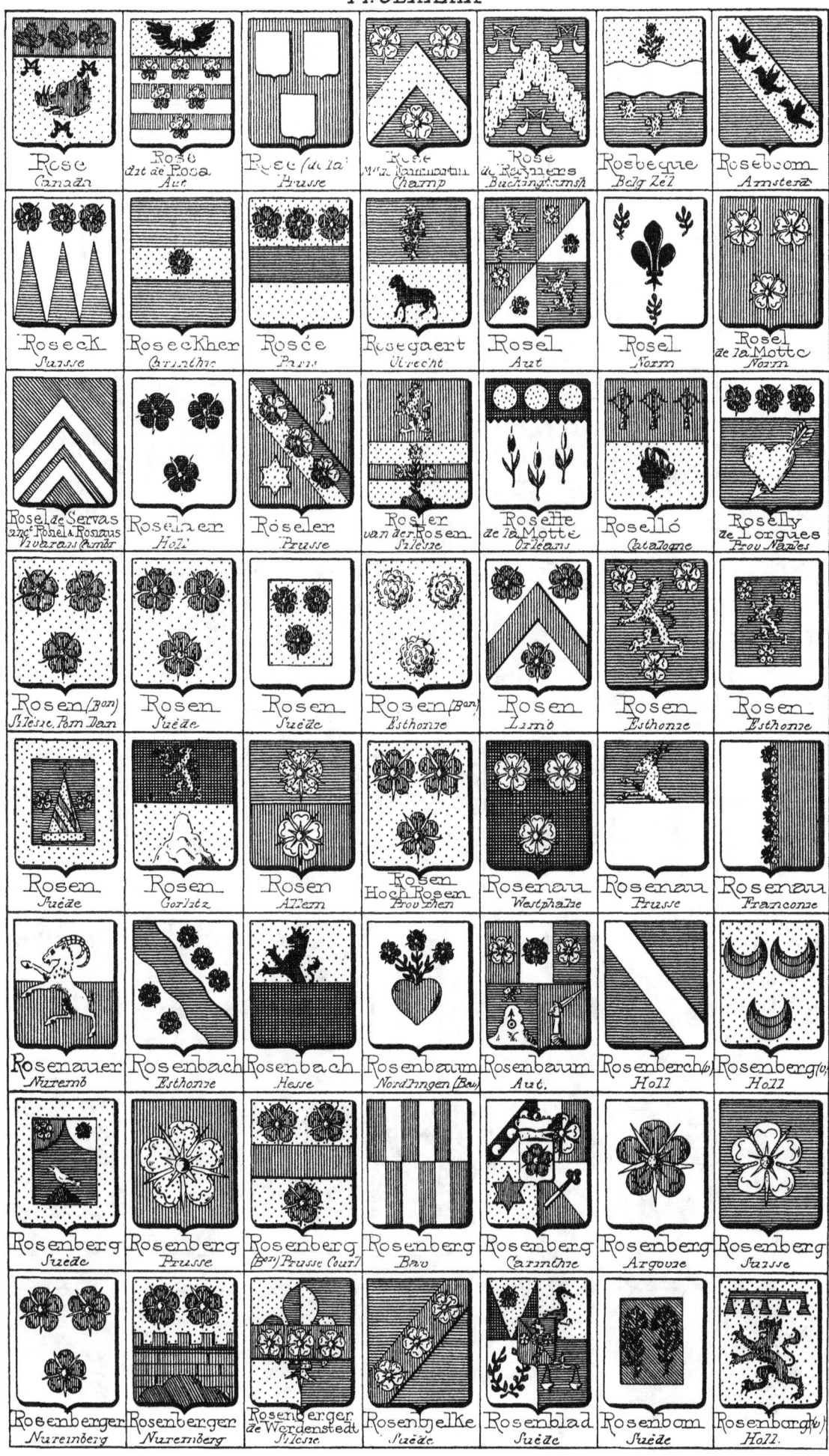

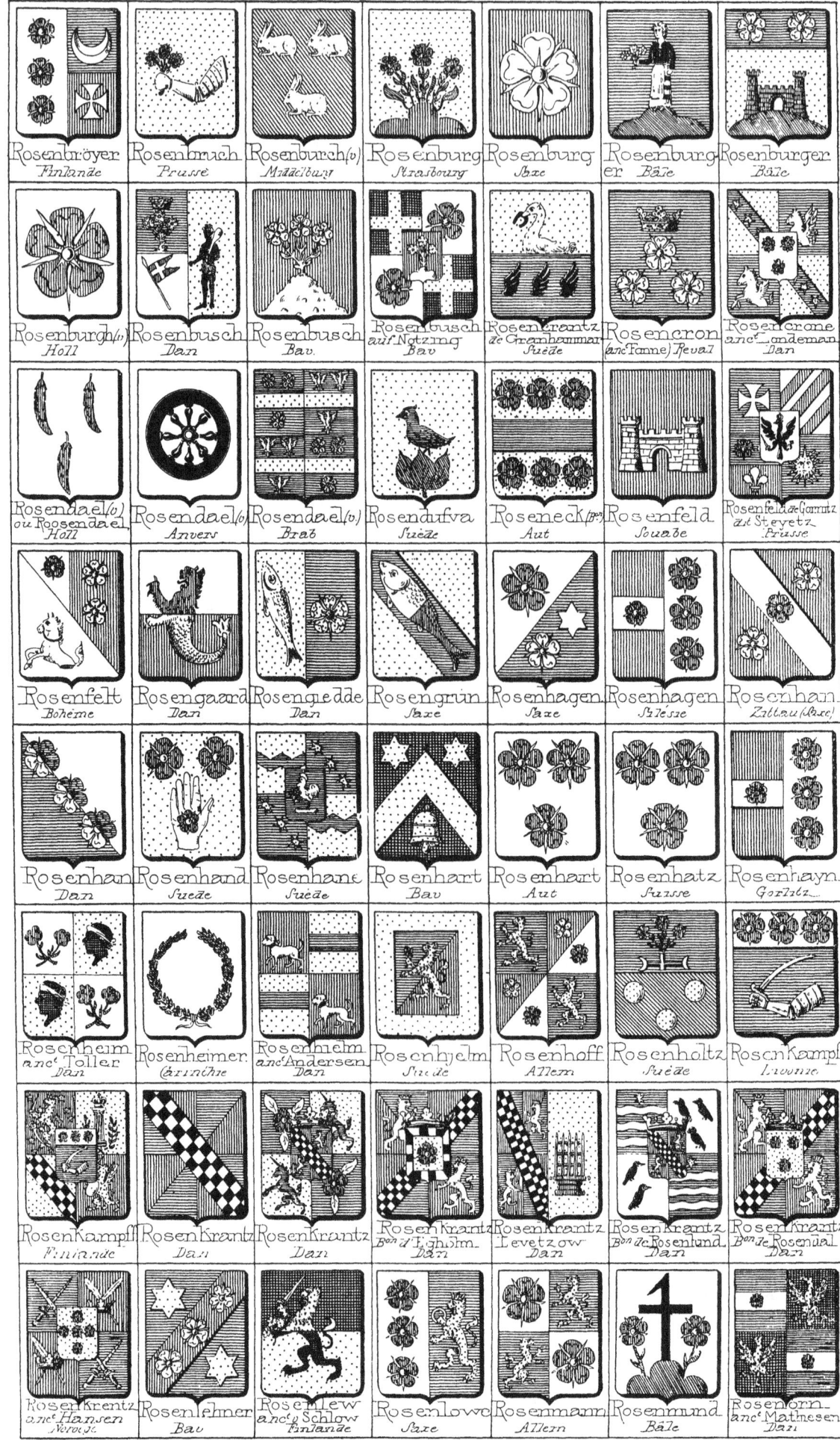

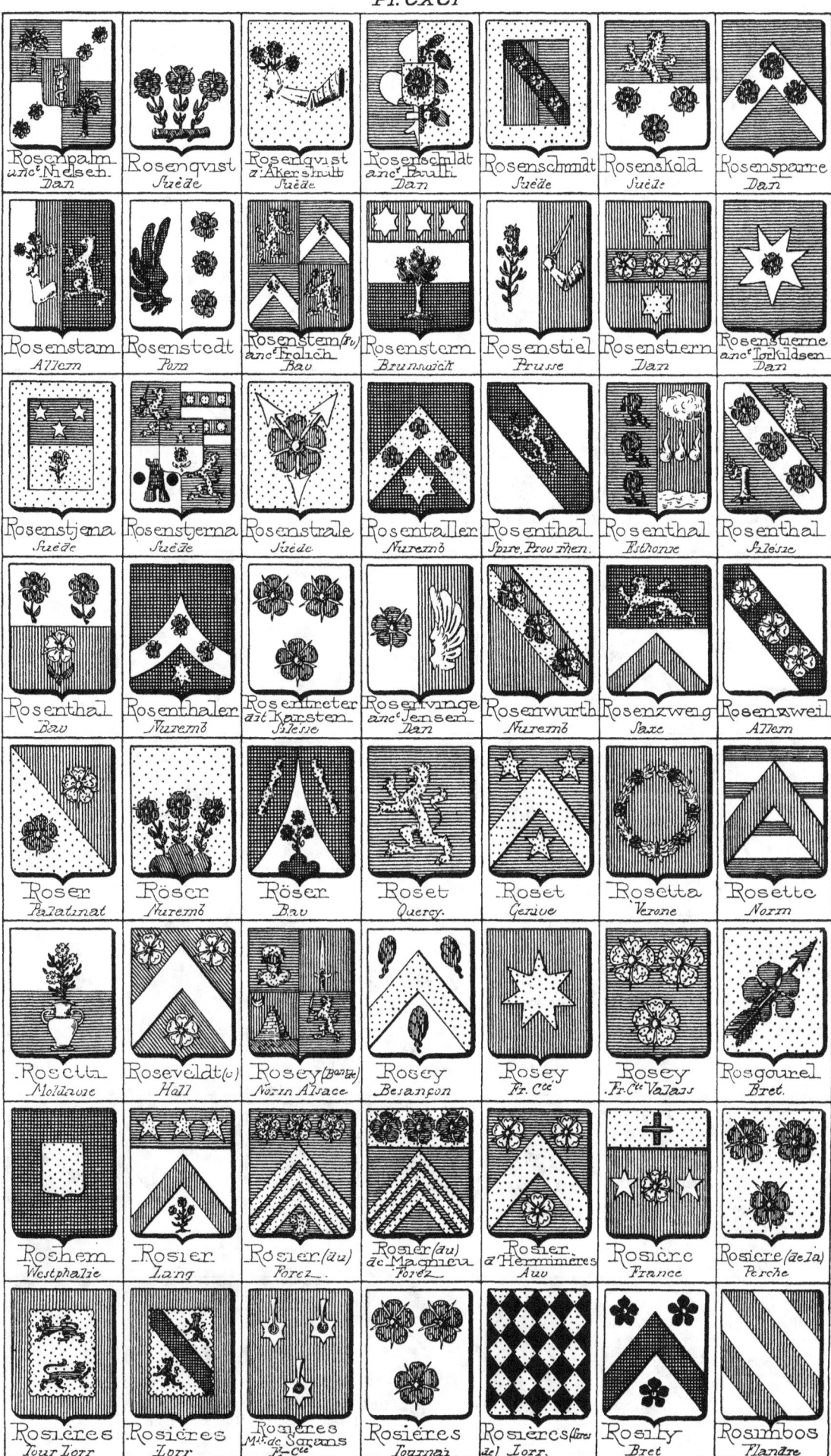

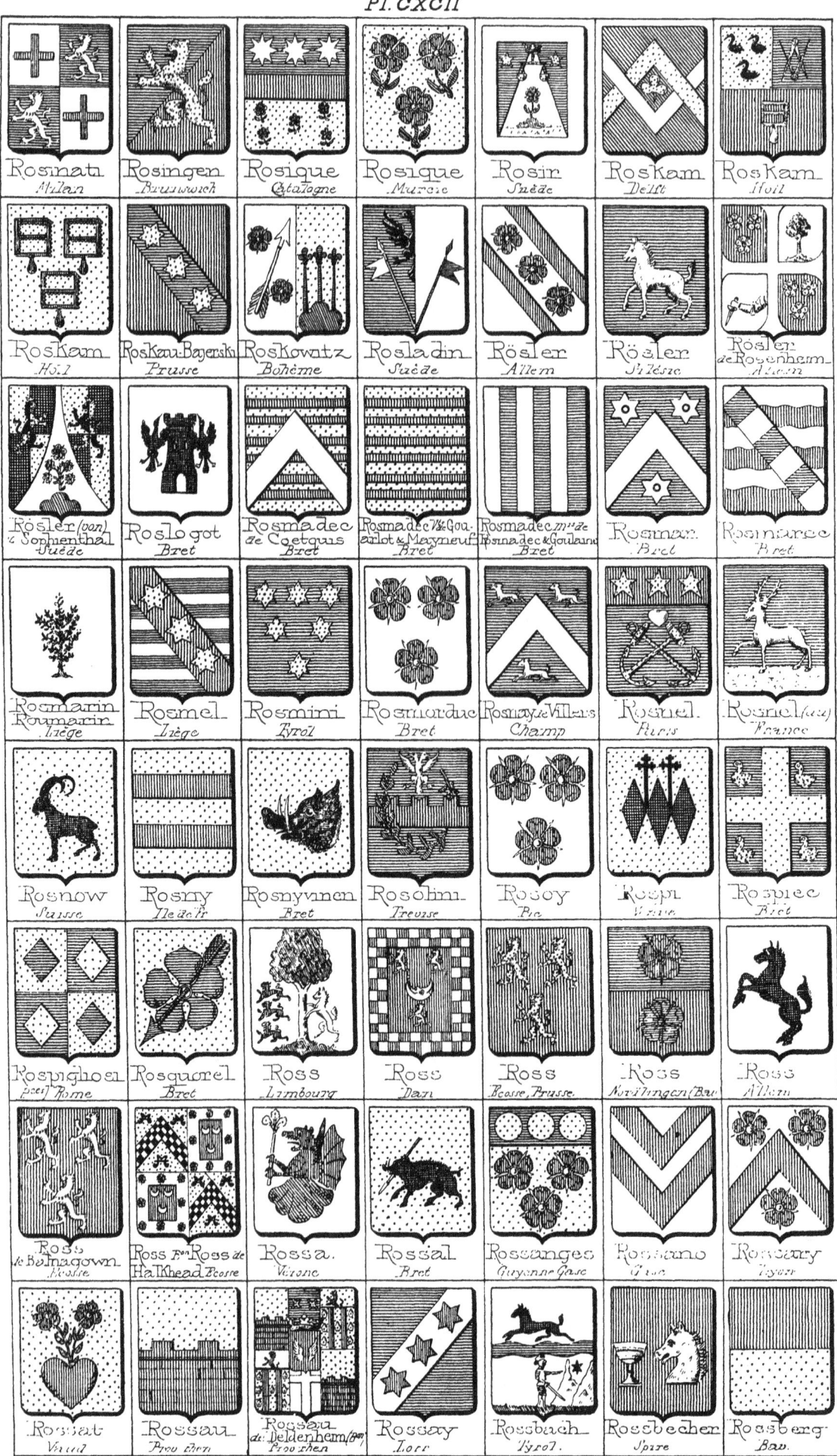

Pl. CXCIII

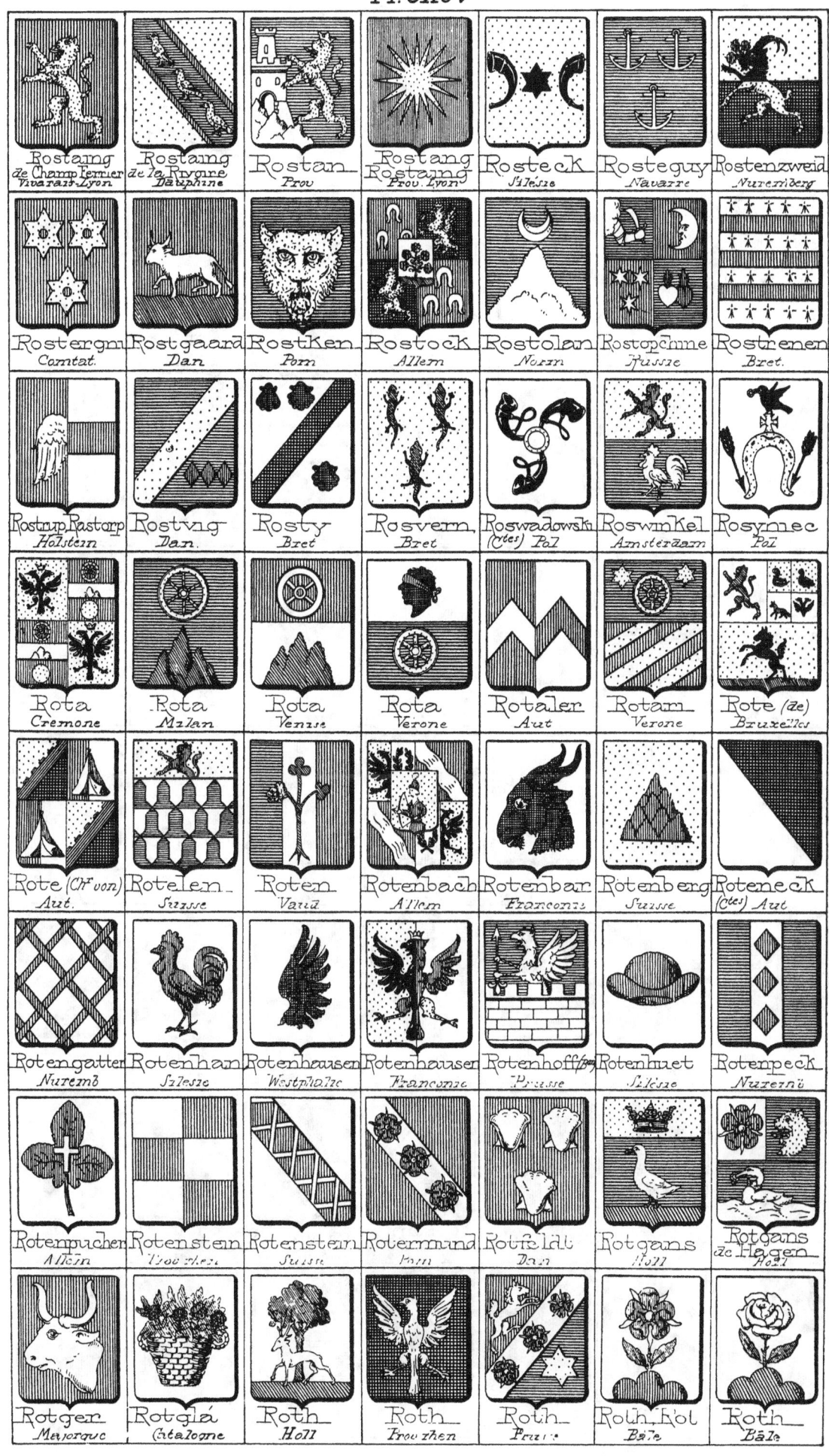

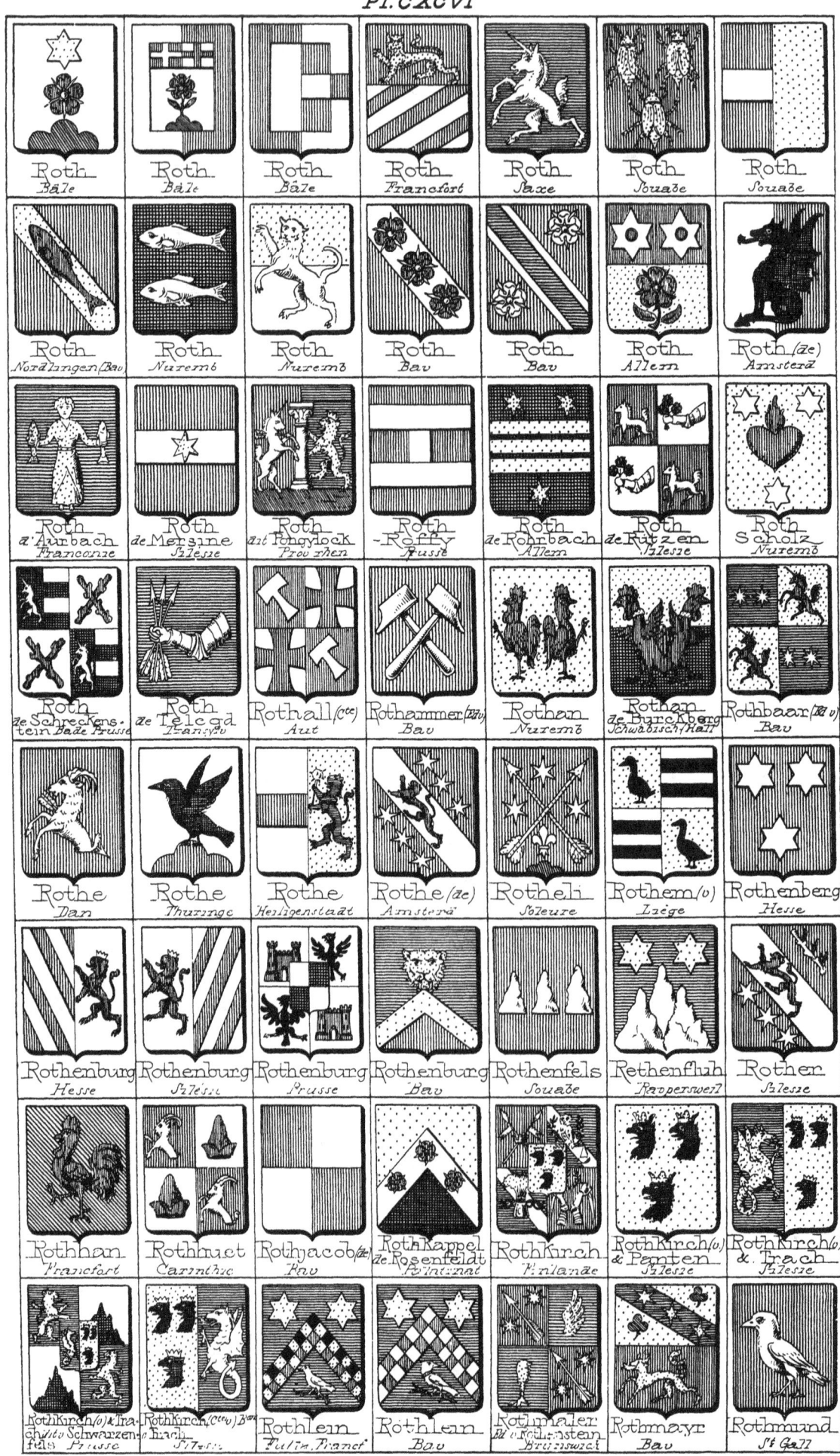
Pl. CXCVI

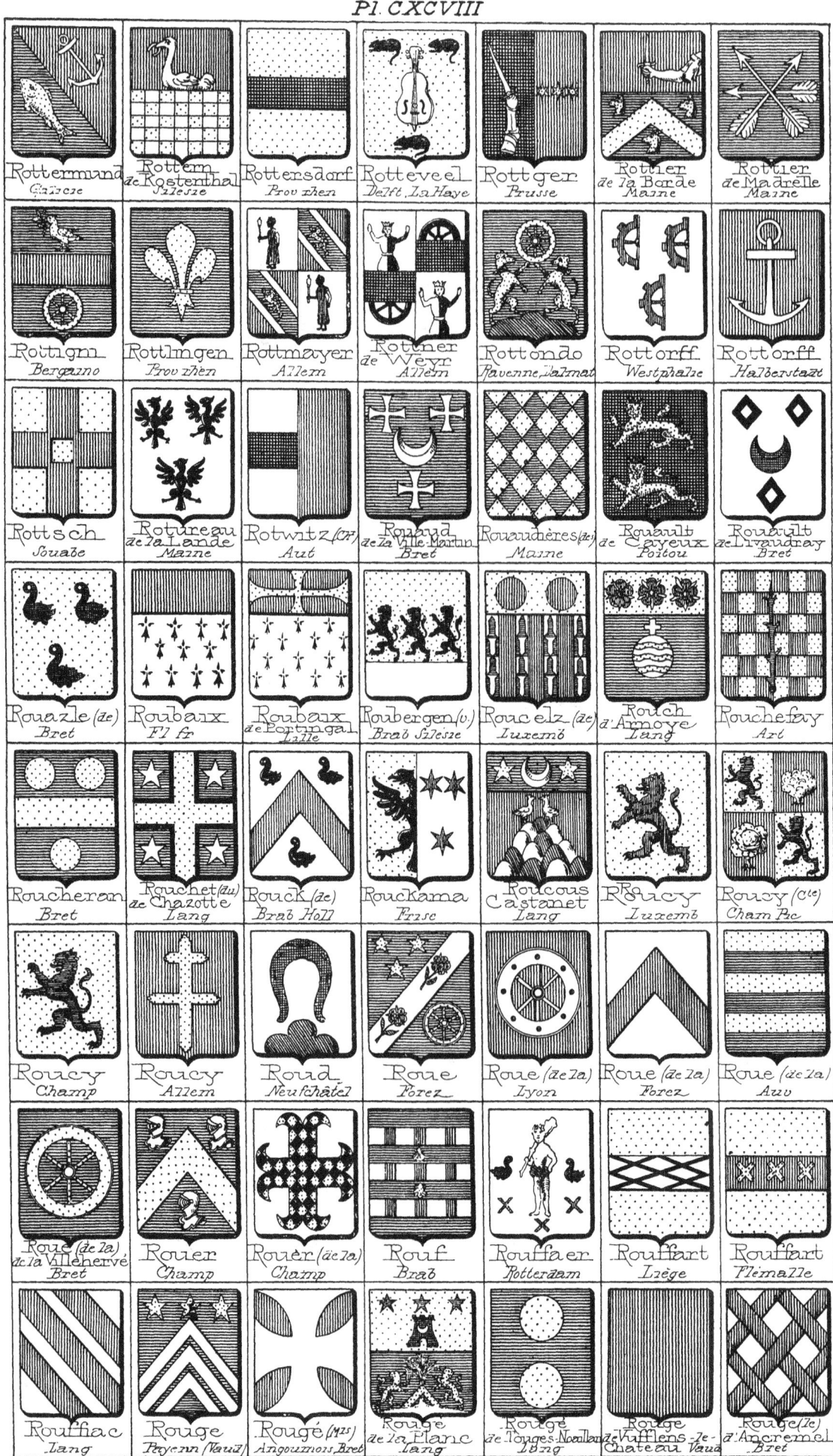

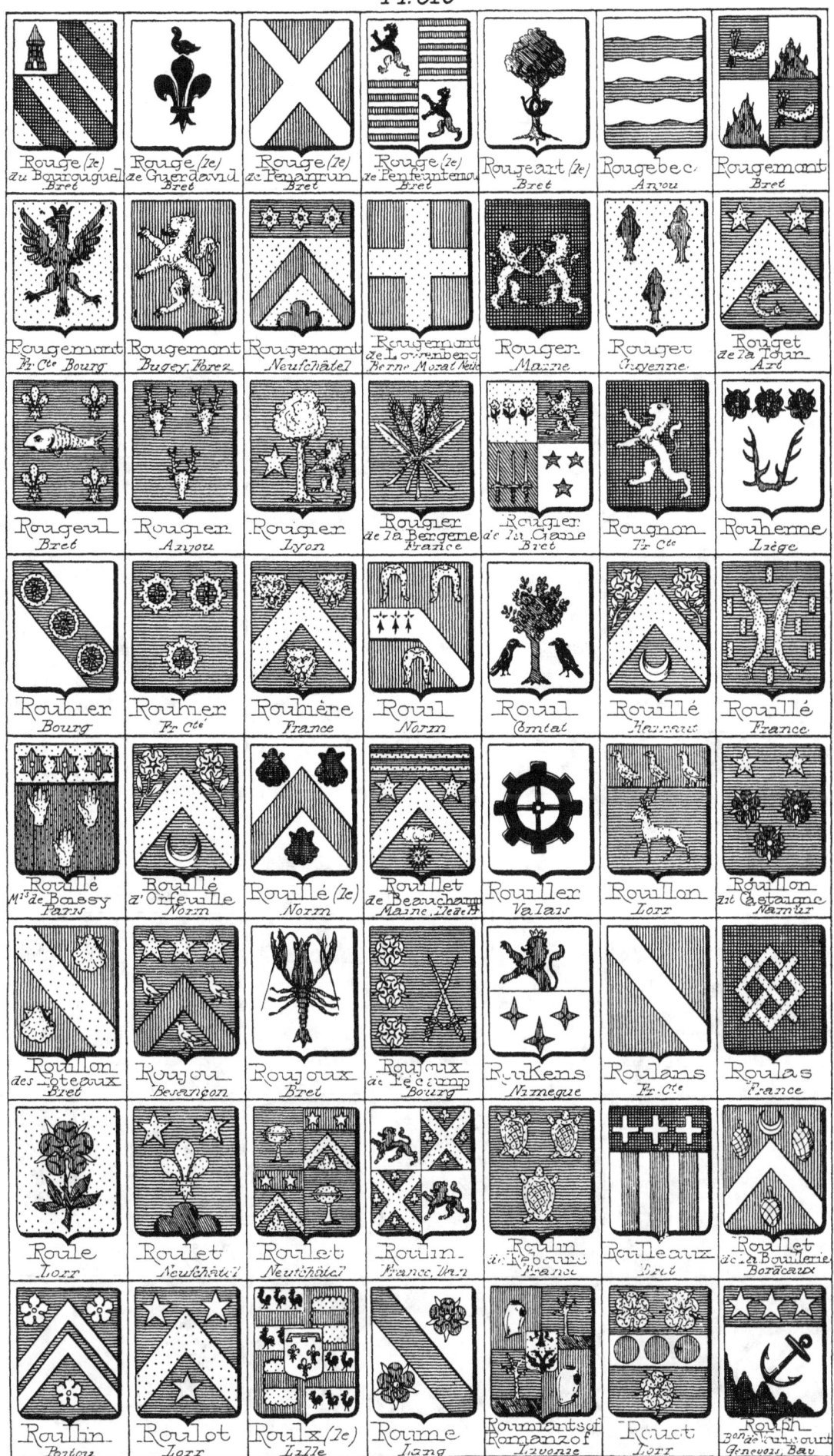

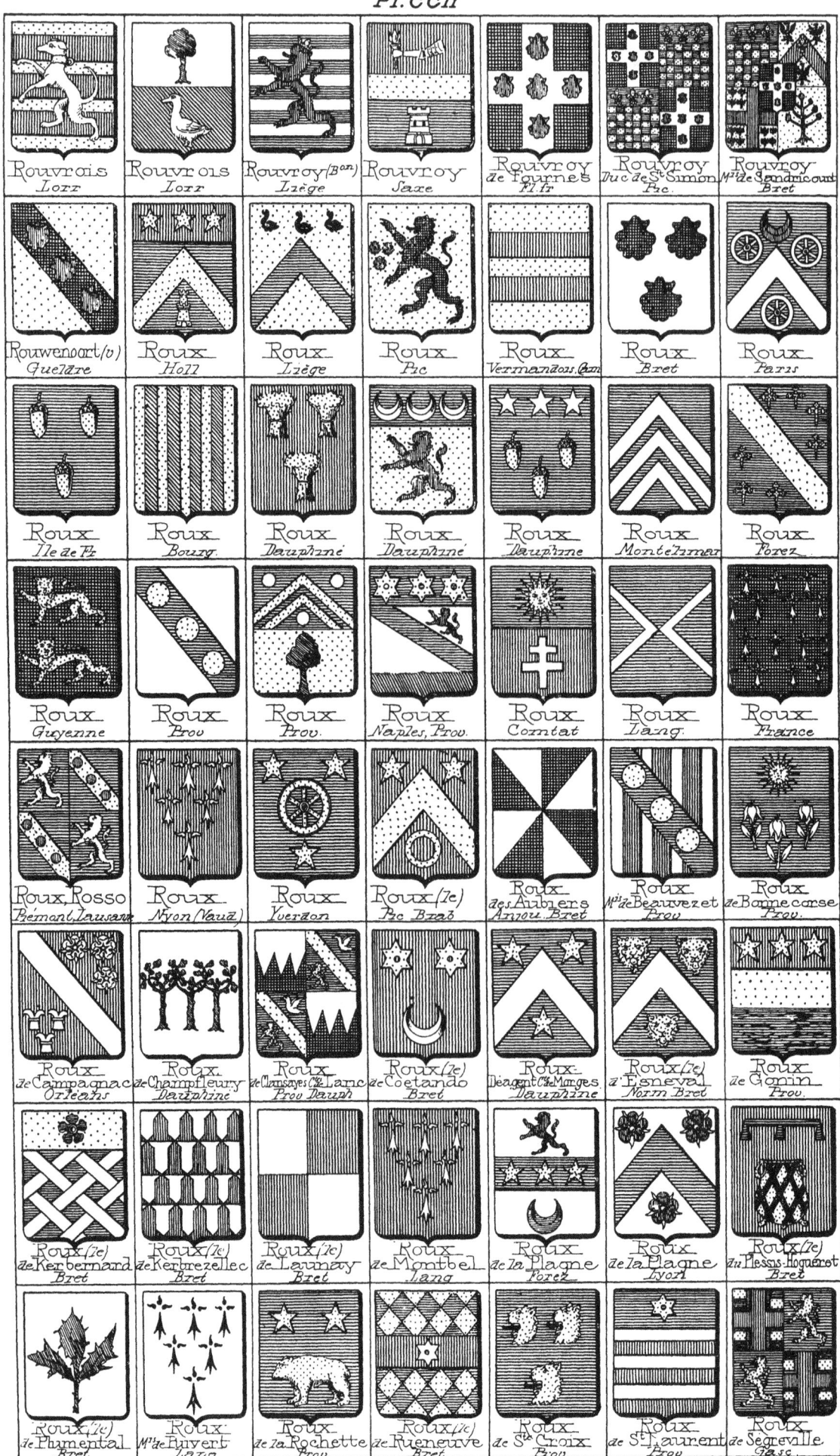

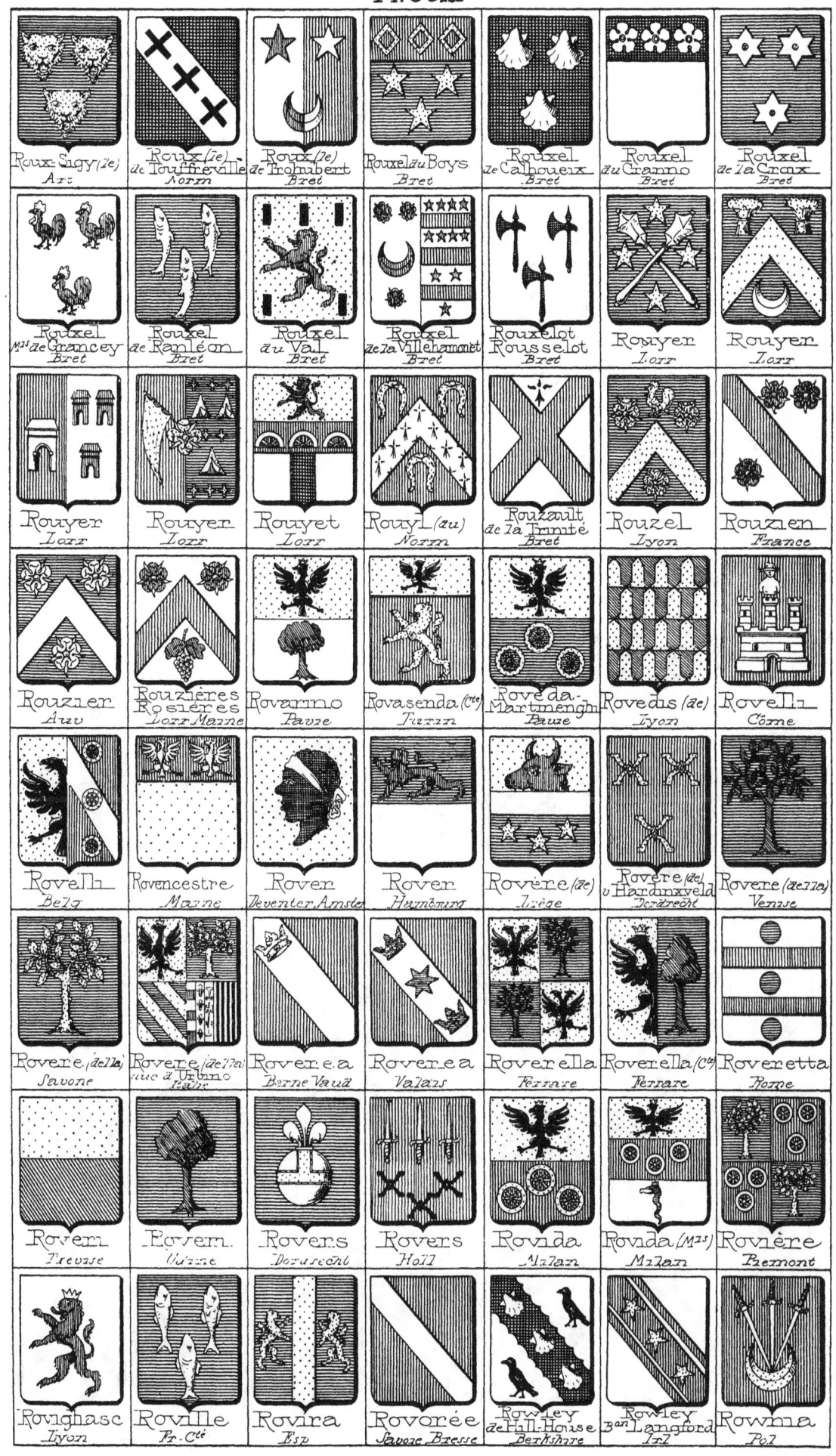

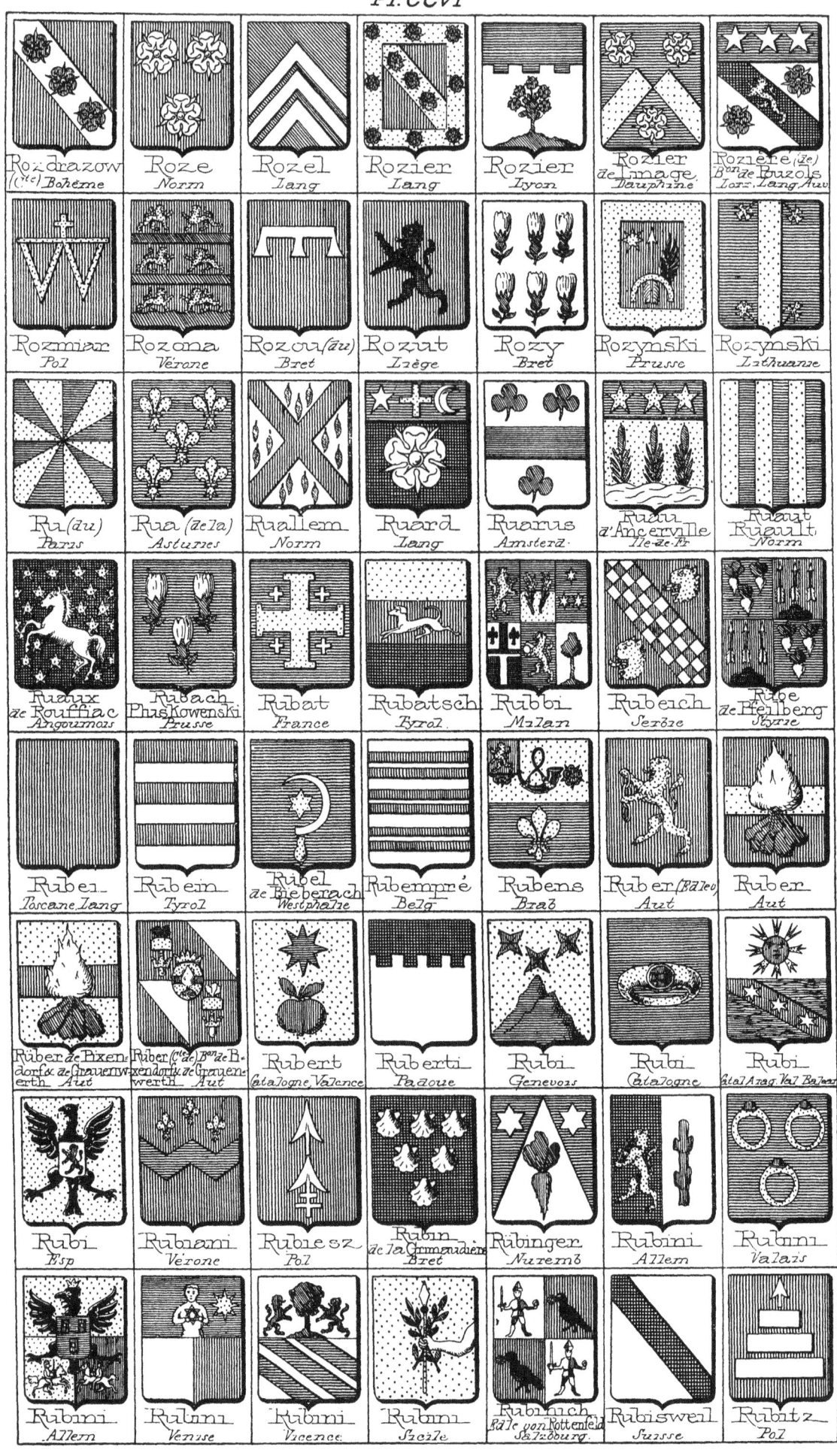

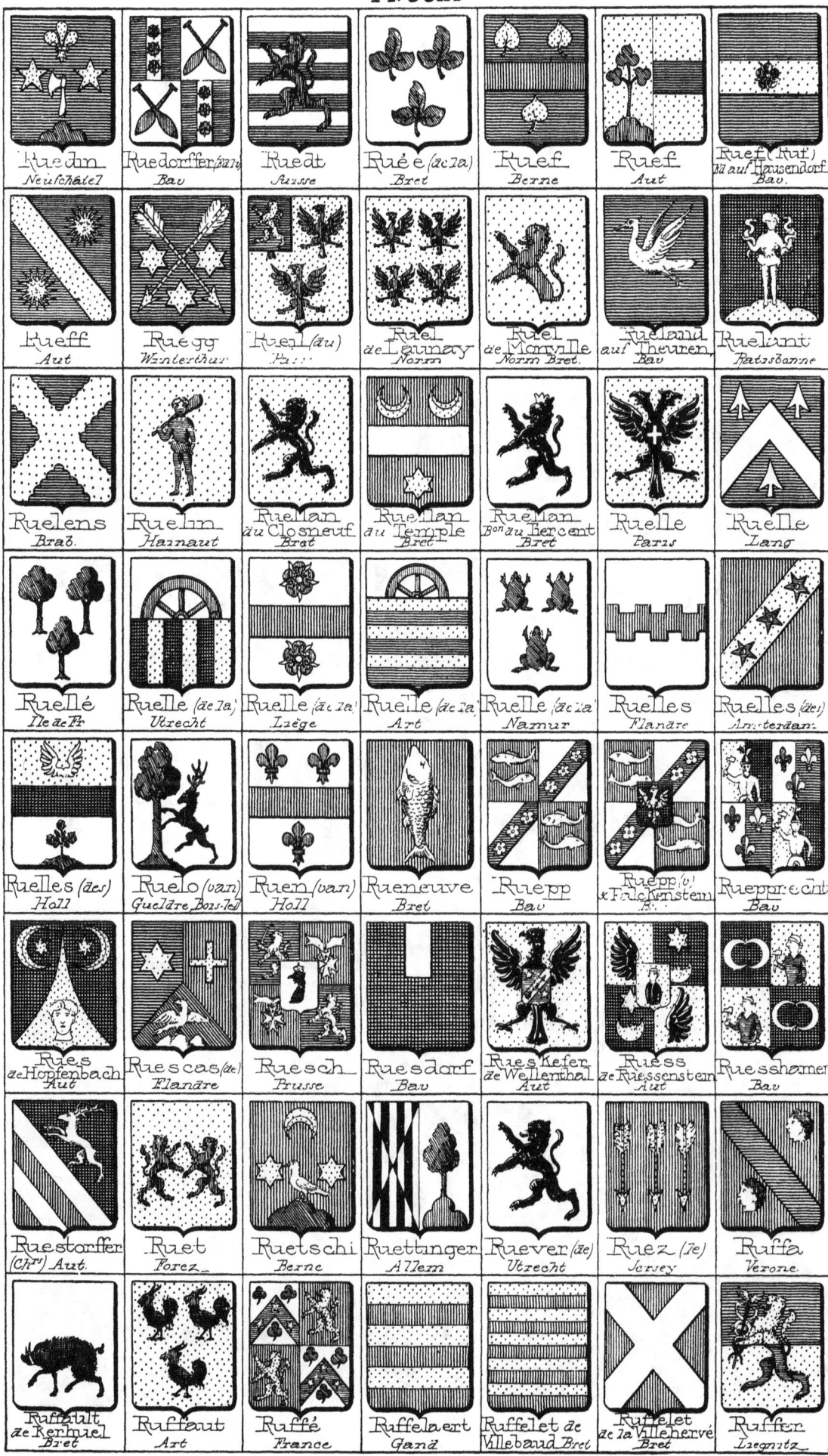

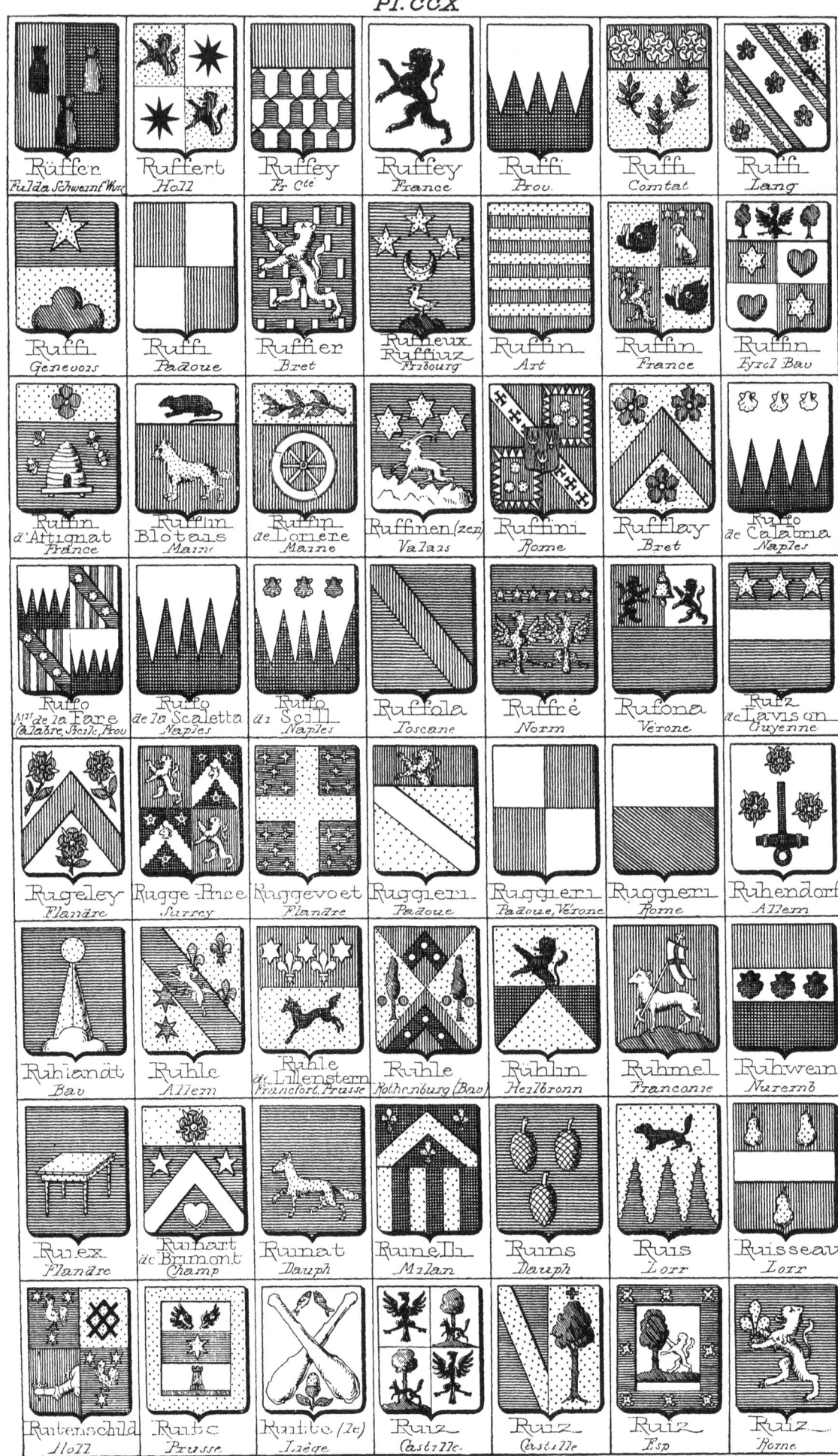

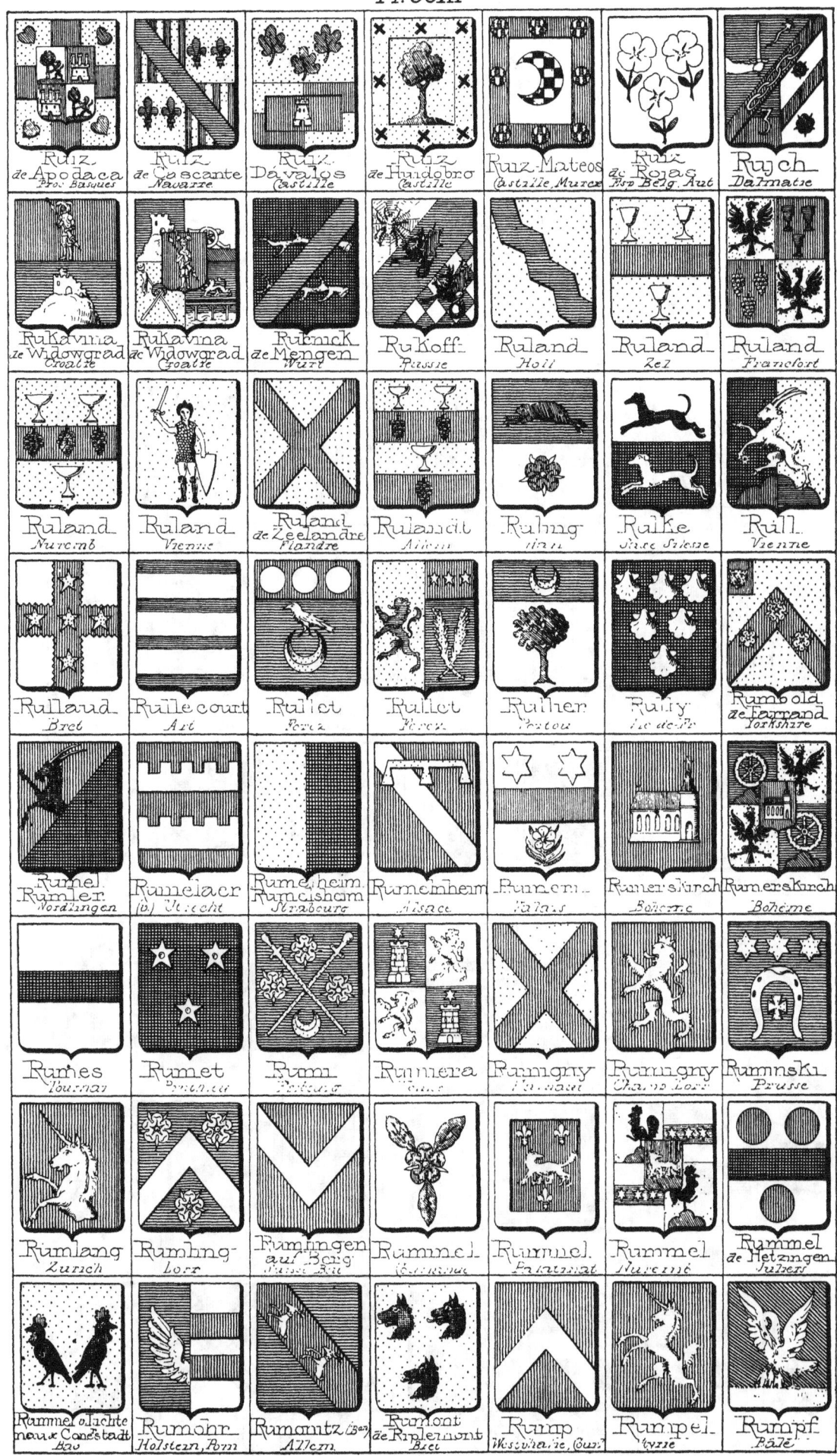

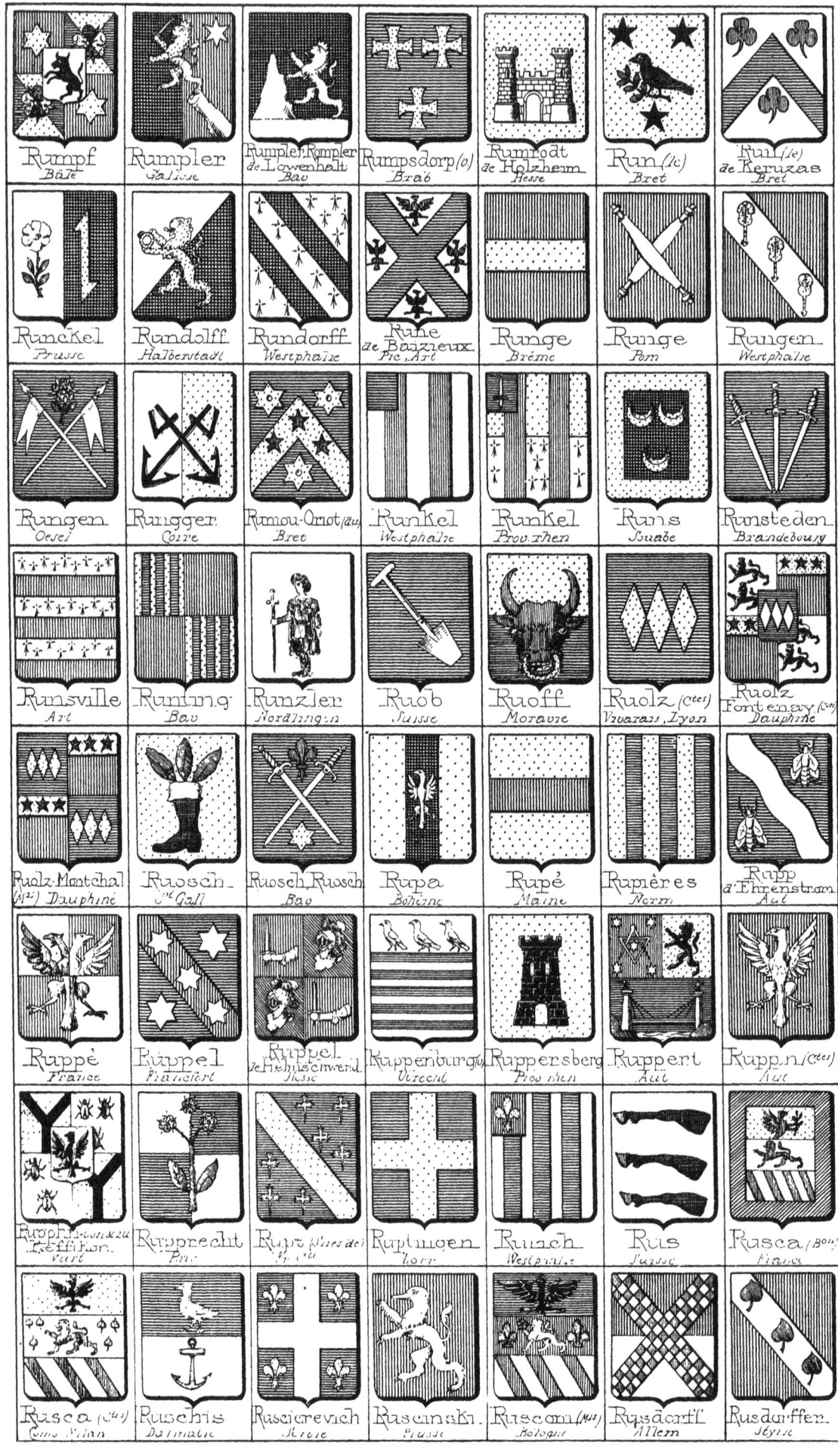

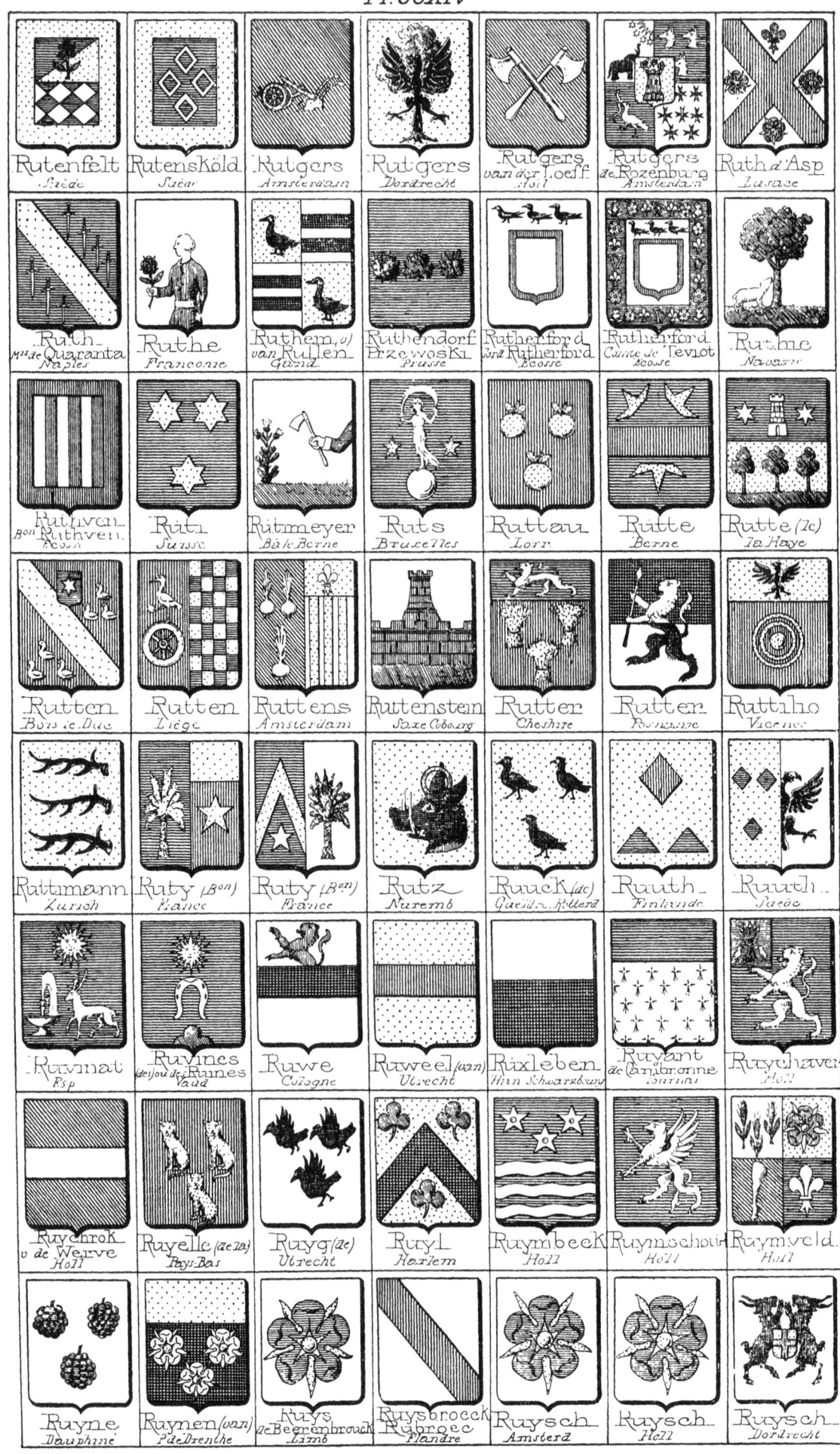

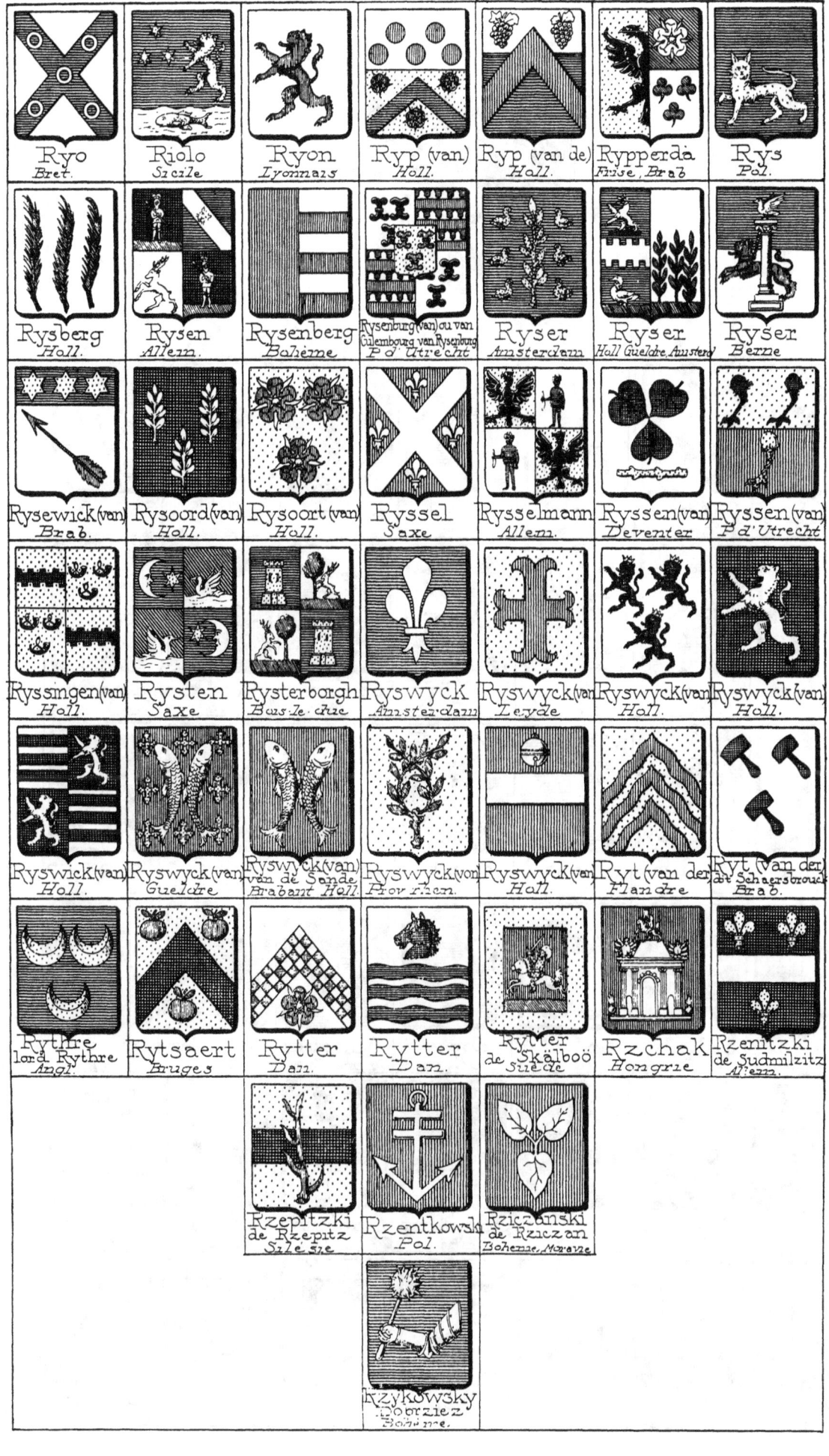

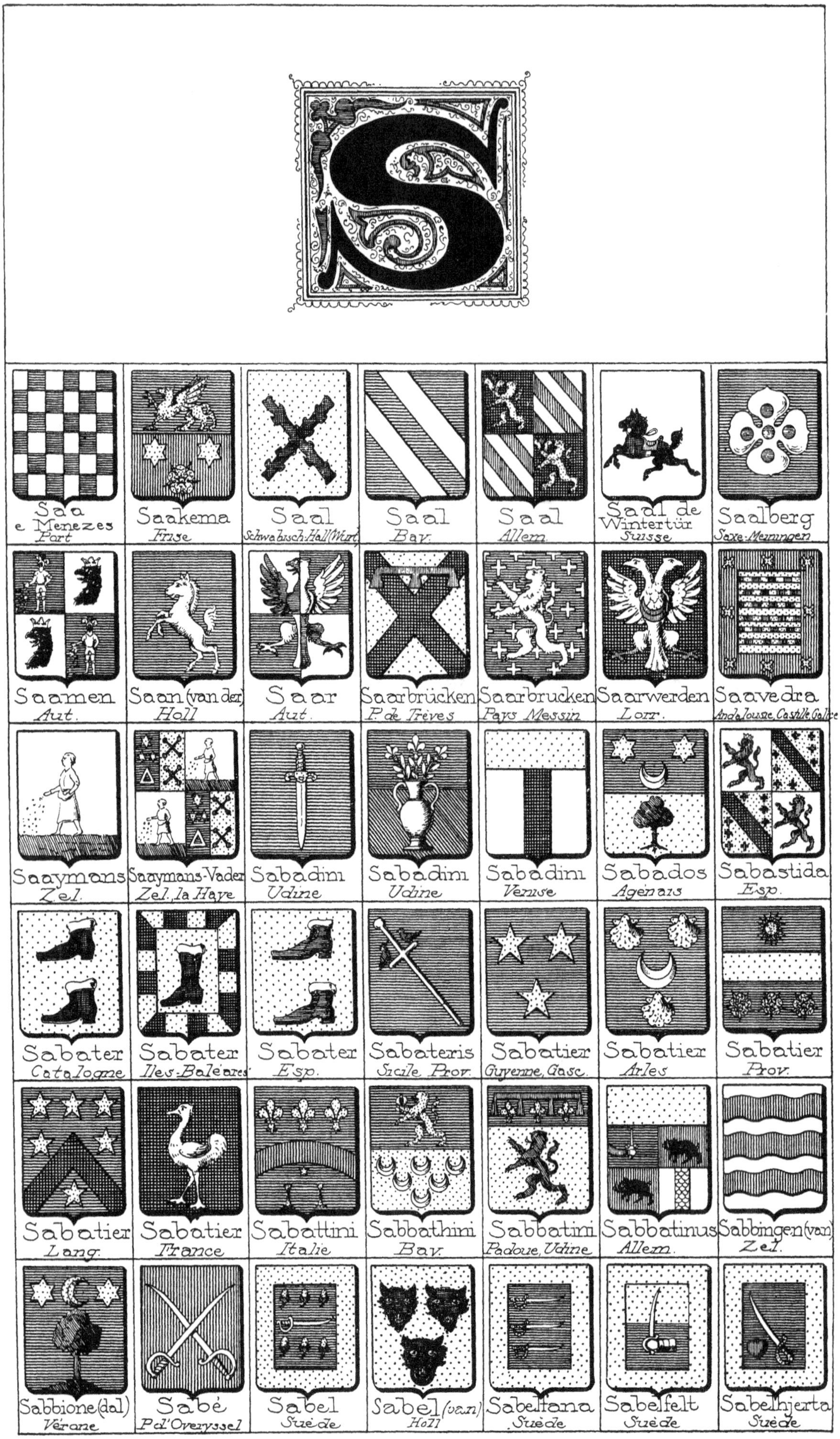

Pl. CCXVIII

| | | | | | | |
|---|---|---|---|---|---|---|
| Saa e Menezes Port. | Saakema Frise | Saal Schwabisch-Hall (Wurt.) | Saal Bav. | Saal Allem. | Saal de Wintertür Suisse | Saalberg Saxe-Meiningen |
| Saamen Aut. | Saan (van der) Holl. | Saar Aut. | Saarbrücken P. de Trèves | Saarbrucken Pays Messin | Saarwerden Lorr. | Saavedra And.e Tousse, Castille Galice |
| Saaymans Zel. | Saaymans-Vader Zel., la Haye | Sabadini Udine | Sabadini Udine | Sabadini Venise | Sabados Agenais | Sabastida Esp. |
| Sabater Catalogne | Sabater Iles-Baléares | Sabater Esp. | Sabateris Sicile, Prov. | Sabatier Guyenne, Gasc. | Sabatier Arles | Sabatier Prov. |
| Sabatier Lang. | Sabatier France | Sabattini Italie | Sabbathini Bav. | Sabbatini Padoue, Udine | Sabbatinus Allem. | Sabbingen (van) Zel. |
| Sabbione (dal) Vérone | Sabé P.d'Overyssel | Sabel Suède | Sabel (van) Holl. | Sabeltana Suède | Sabelfelt Suède | Sabelhjerta Suède |

Pl. CCXIX

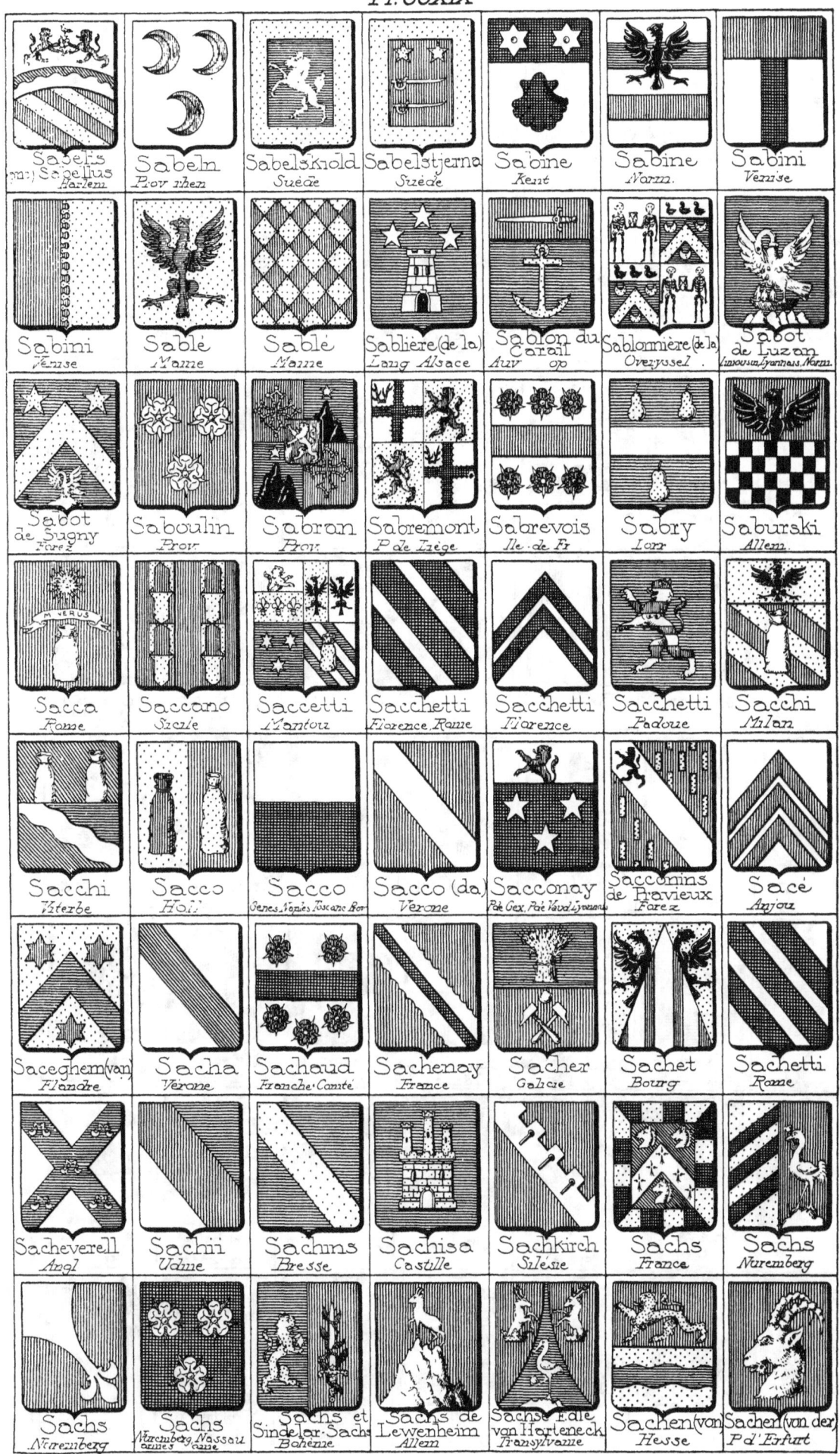

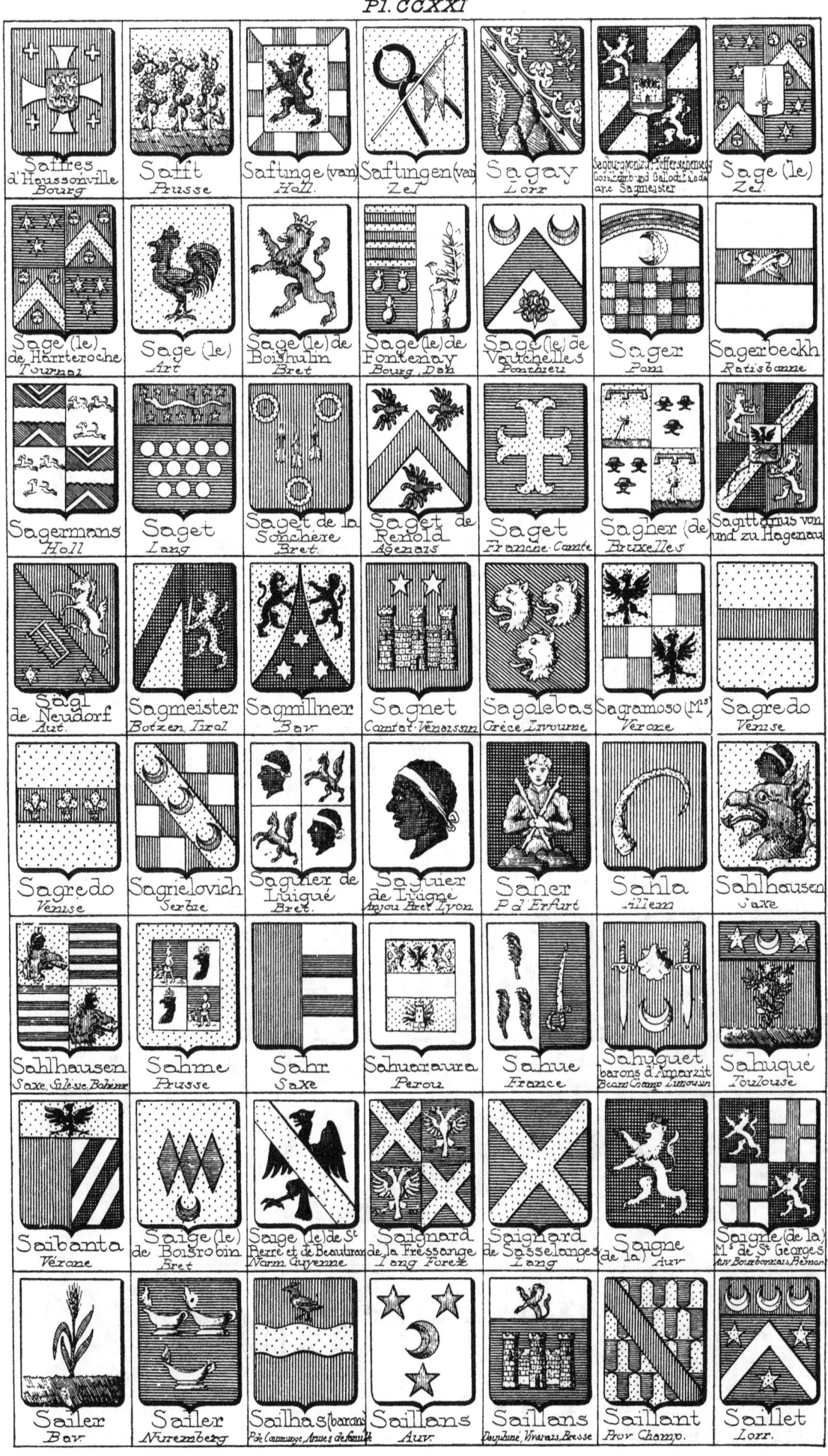

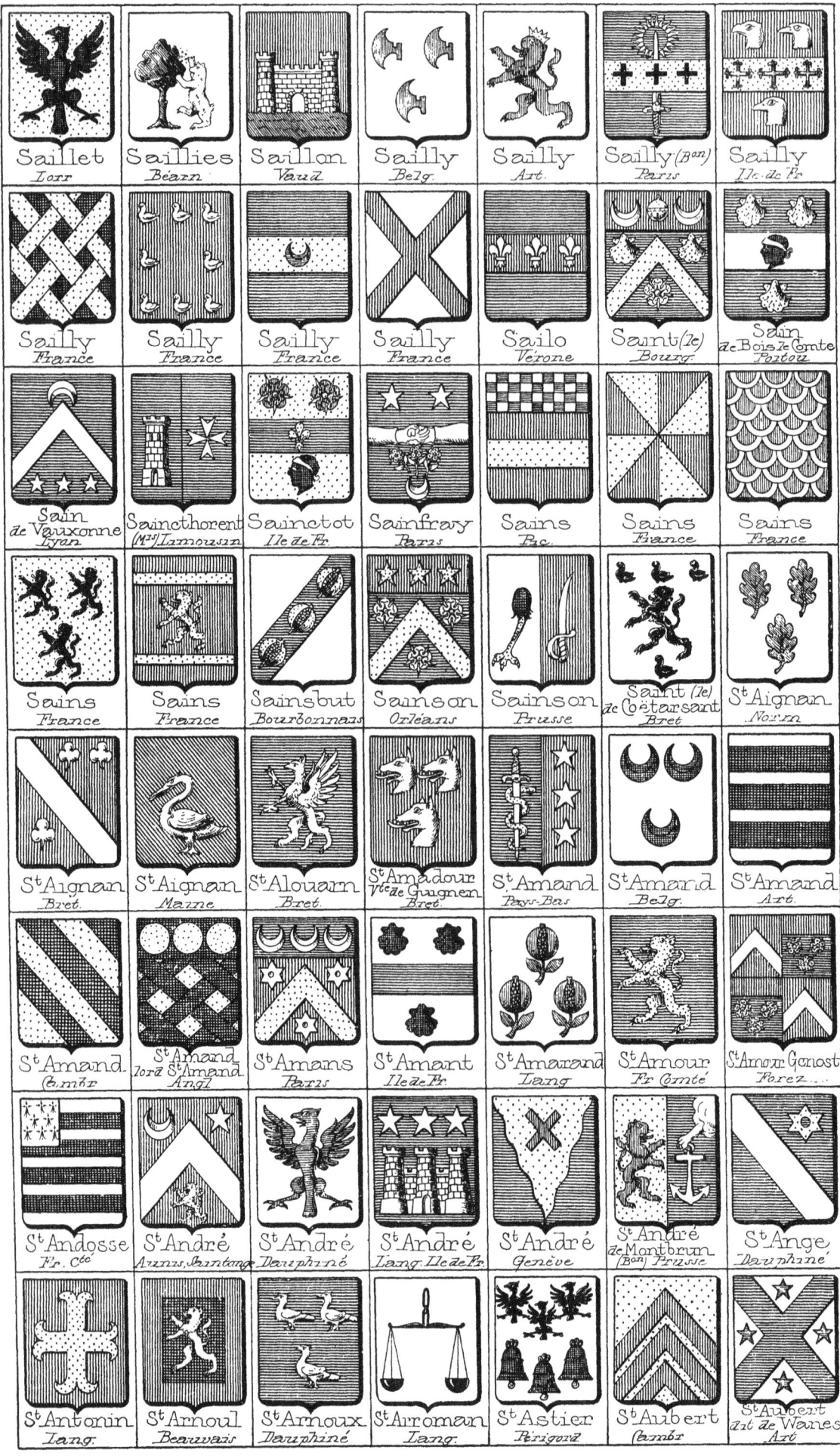

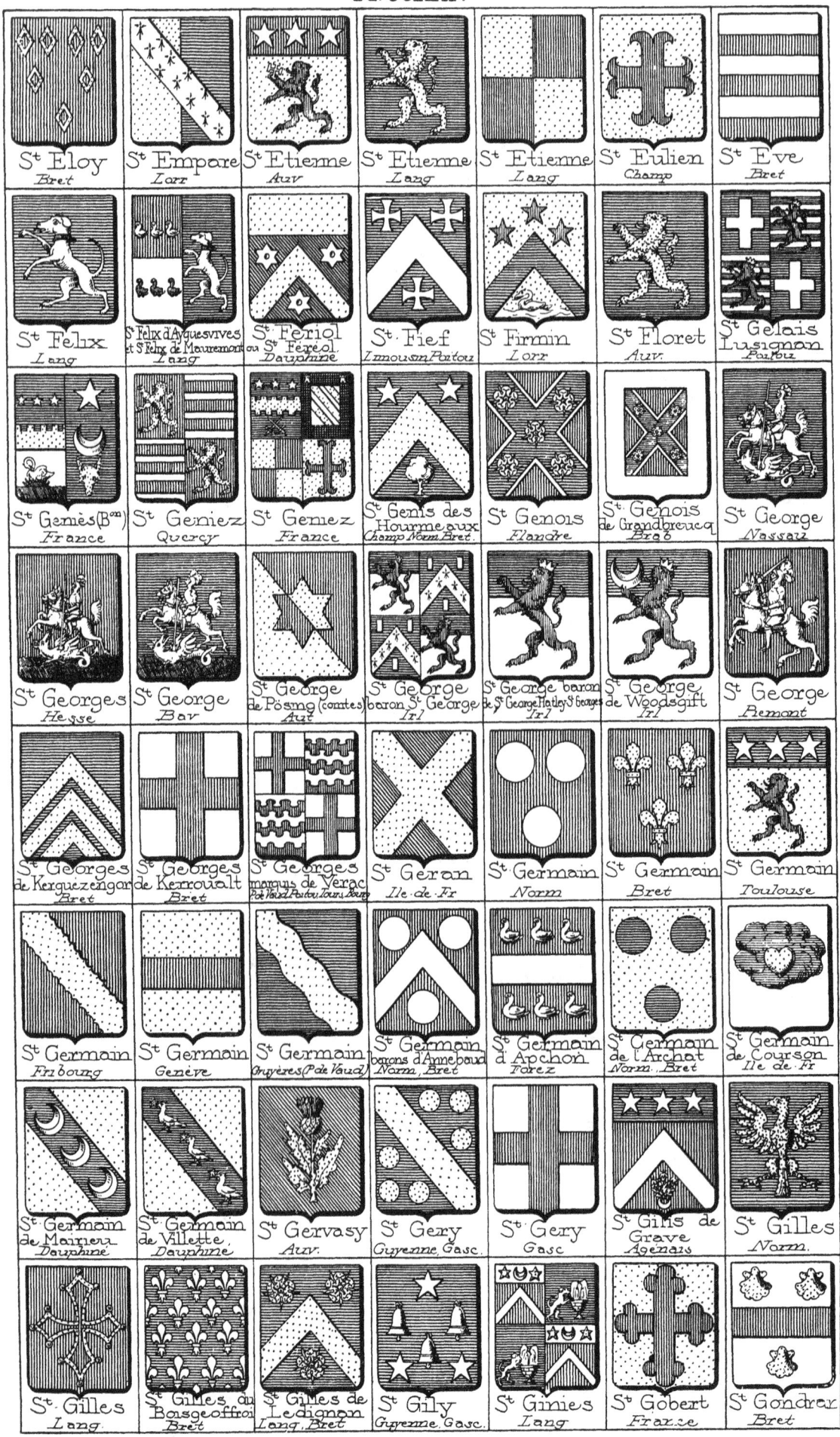

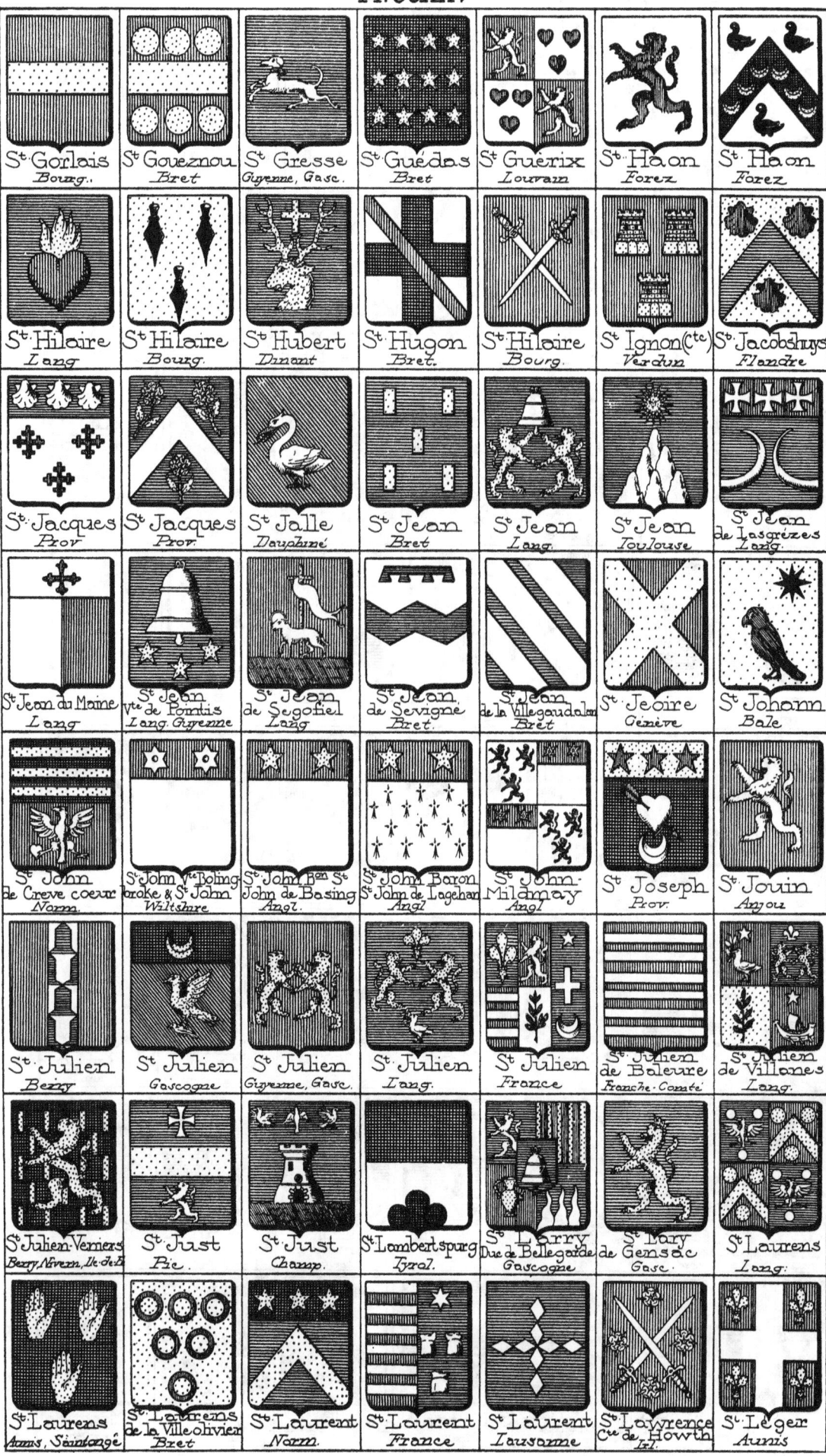

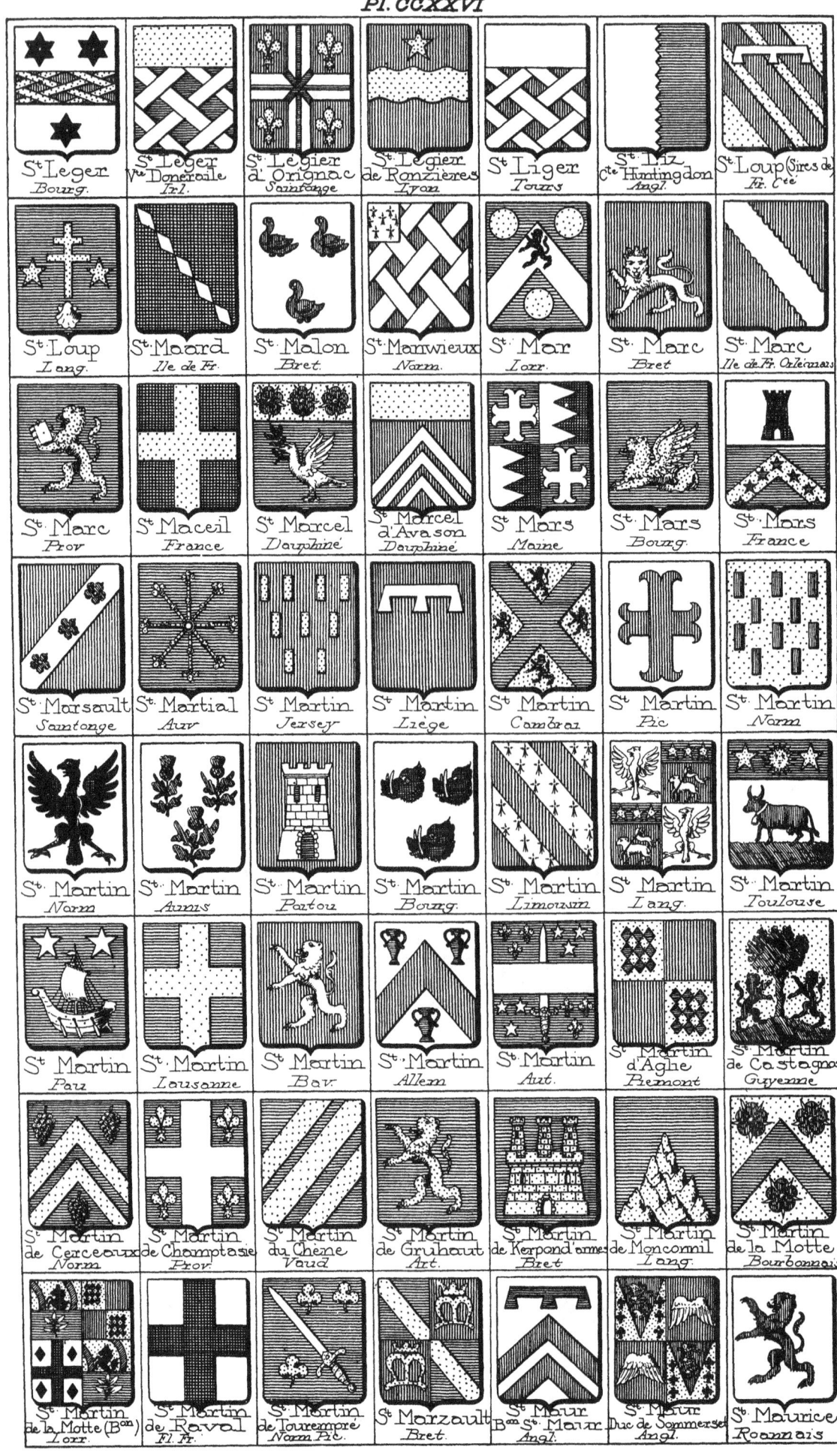
Pl. CCXXVI

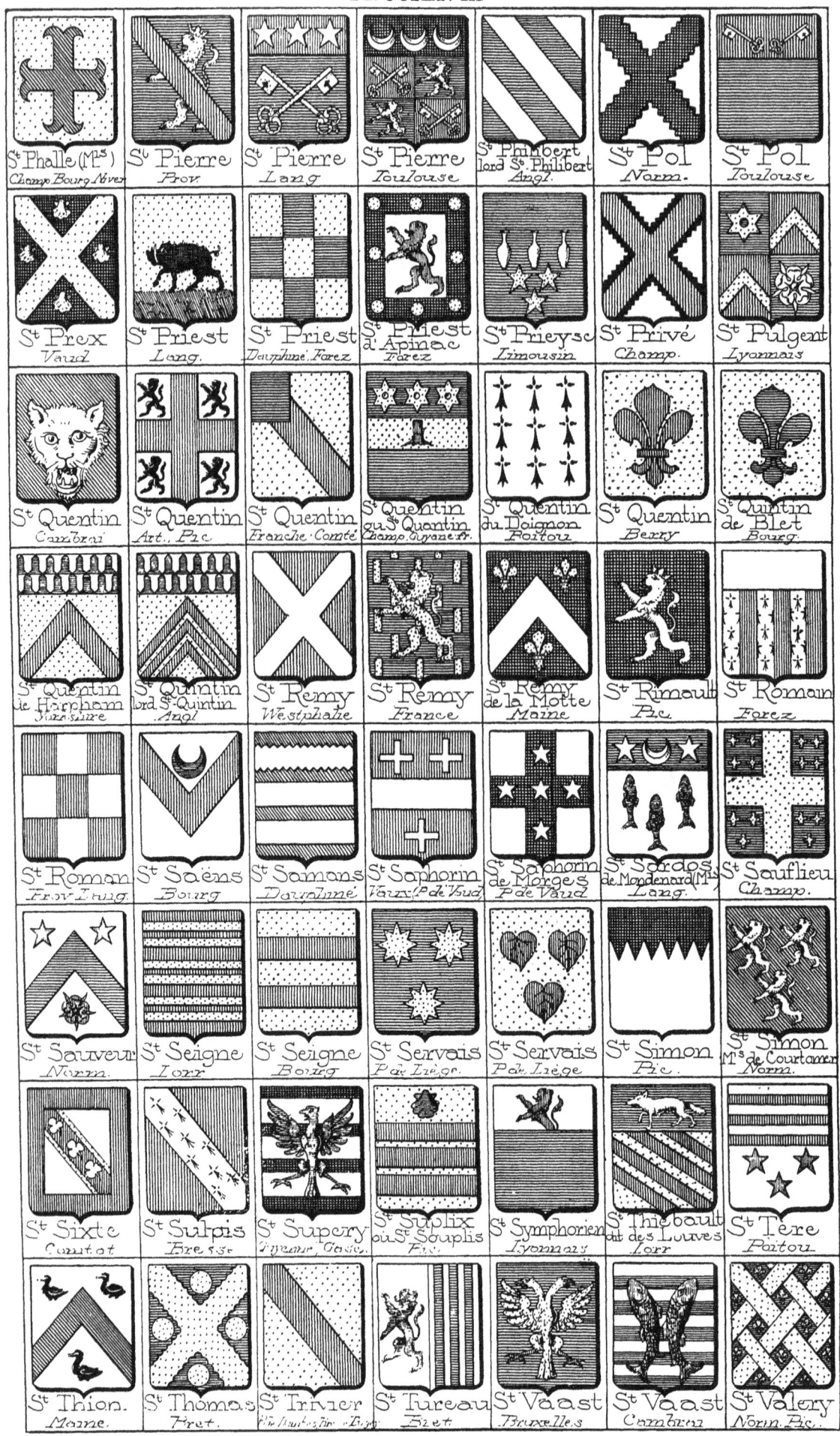

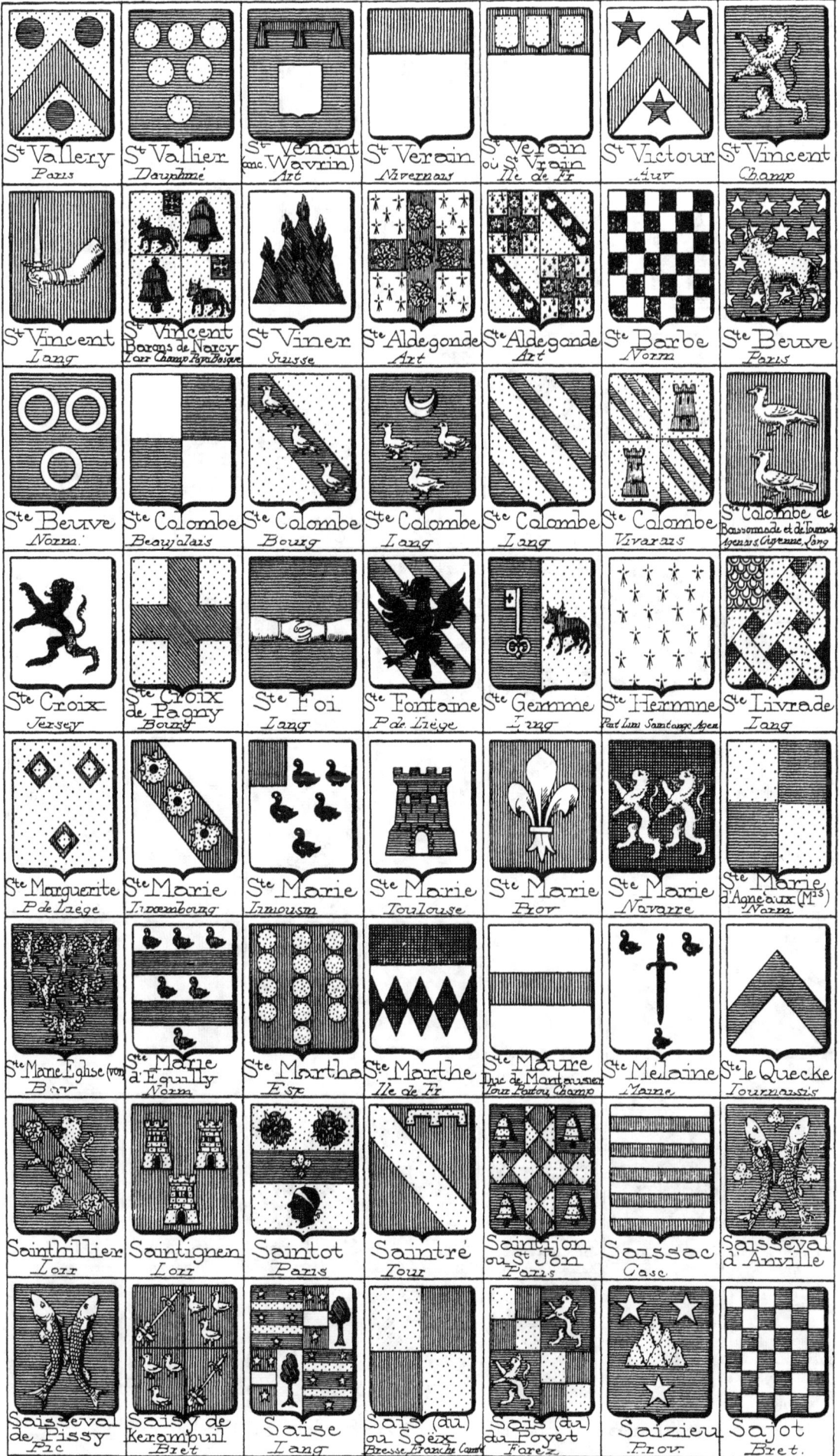

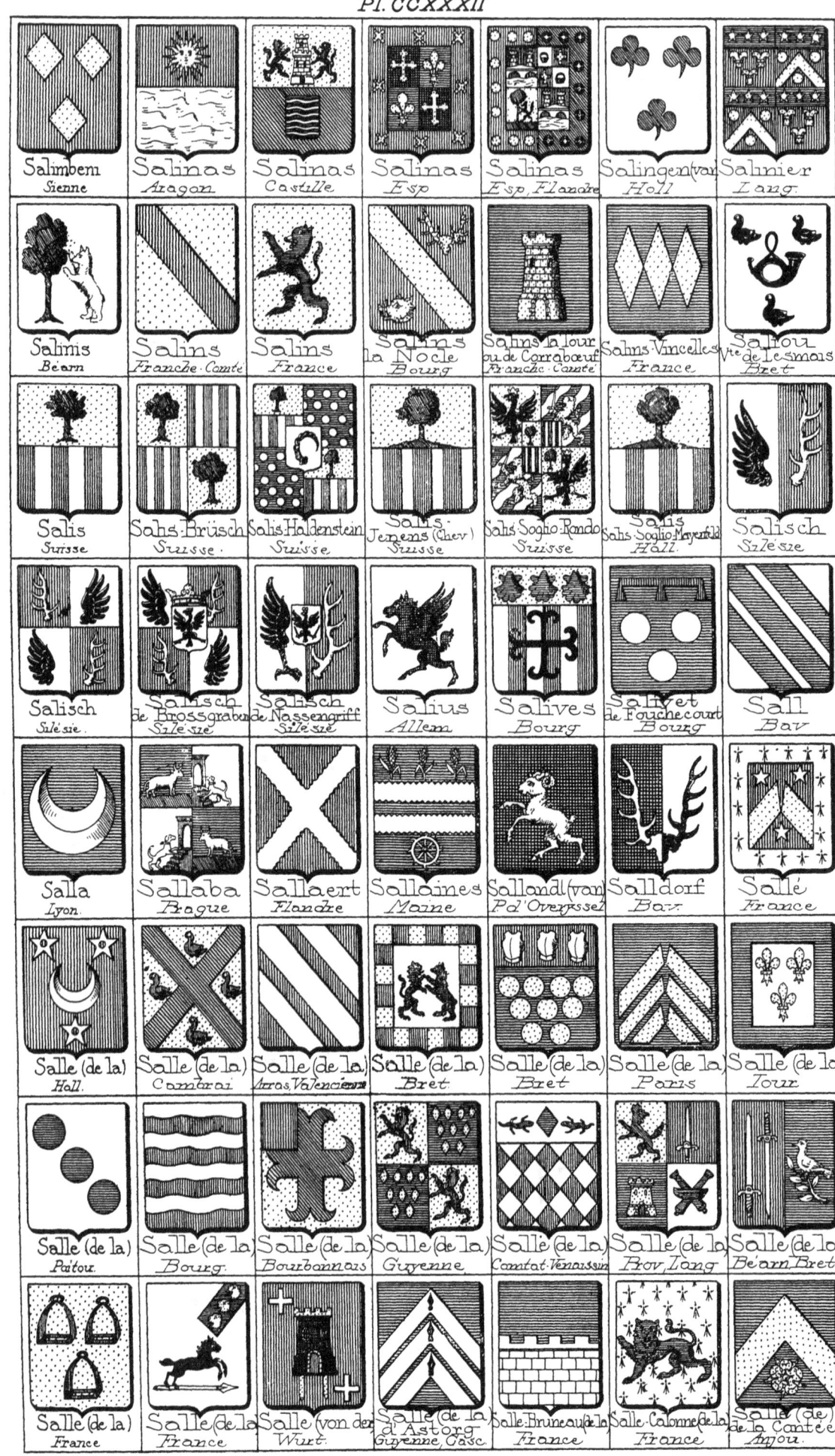

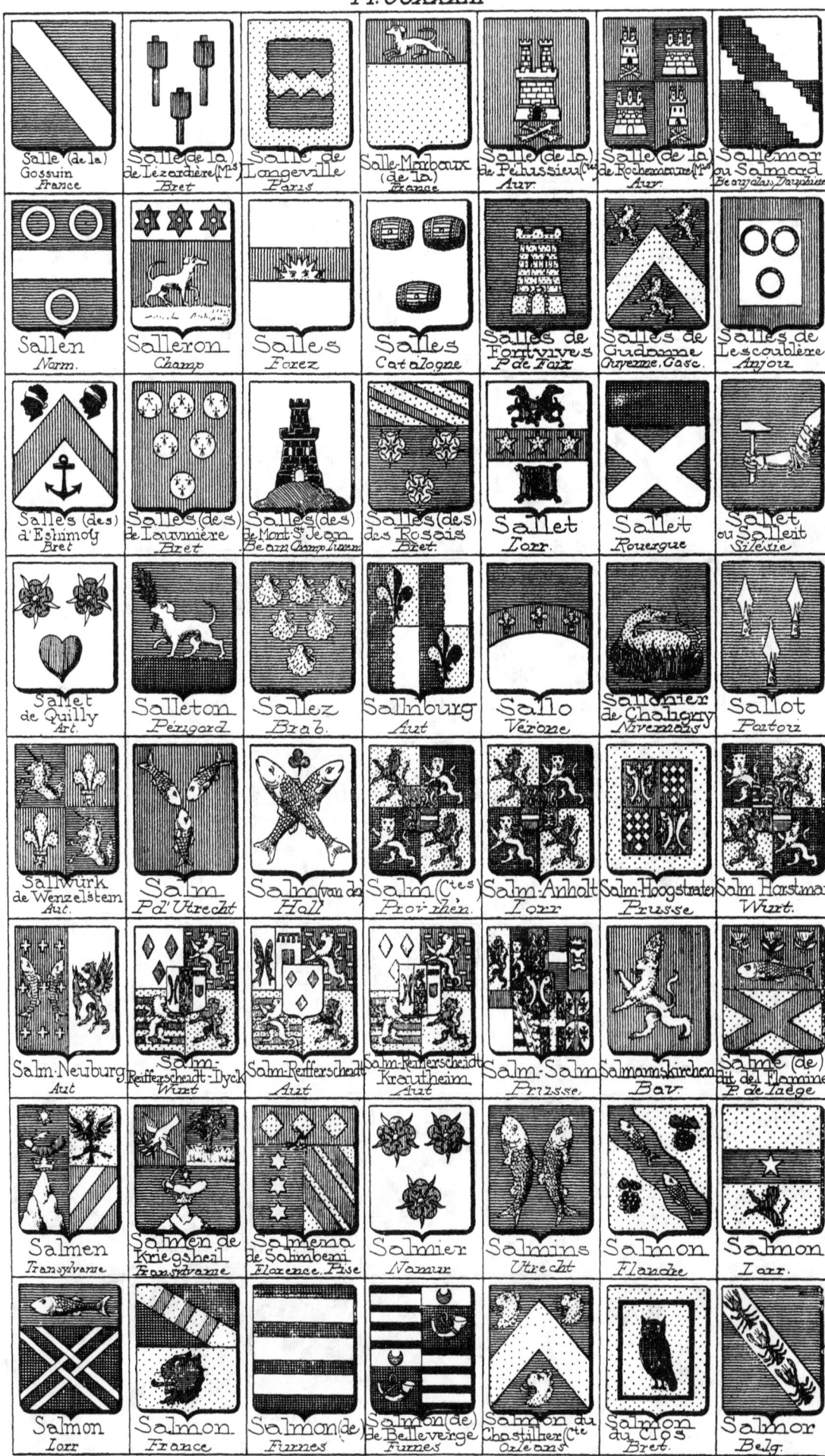

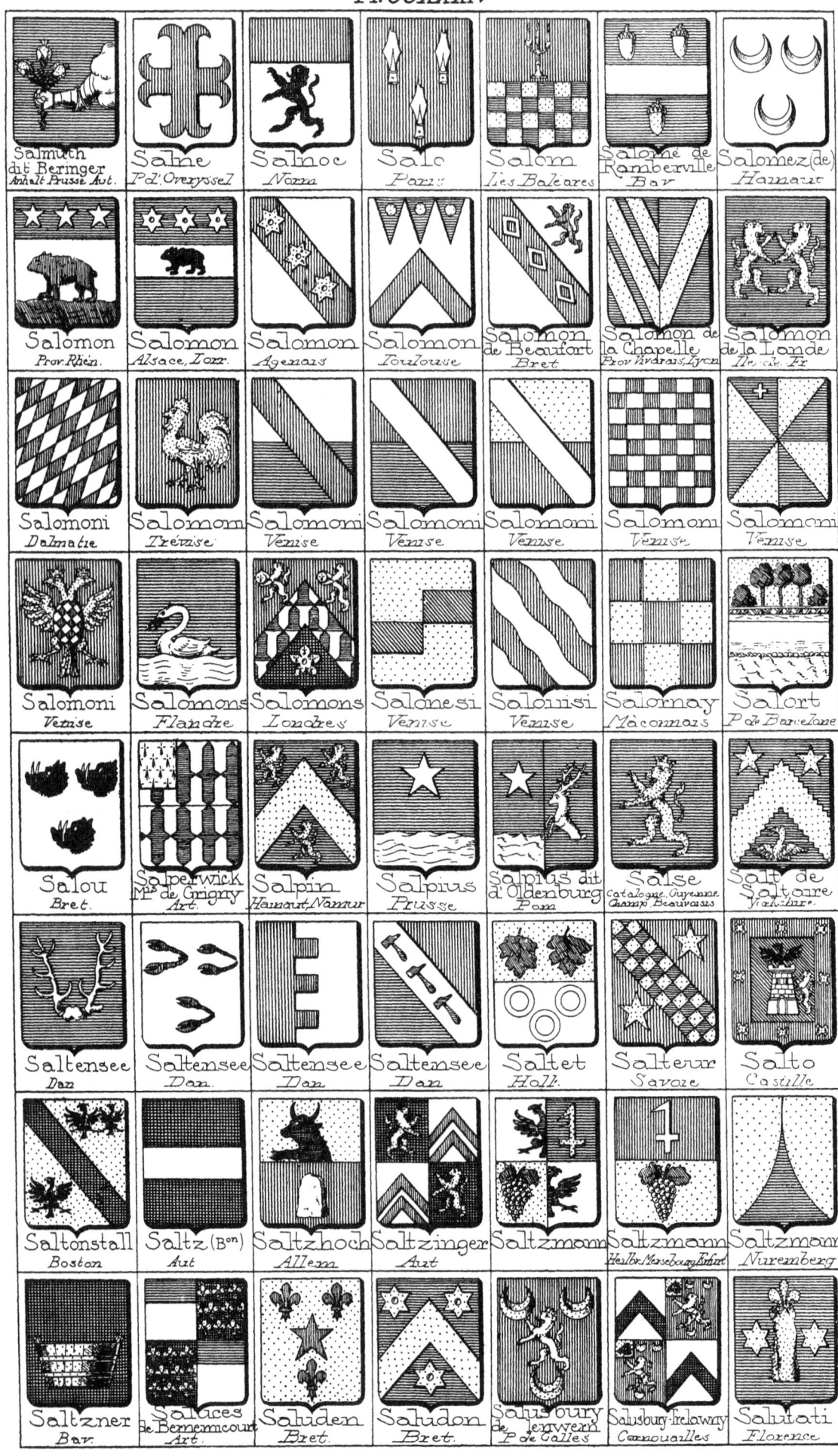

Pl. CCXXXIV

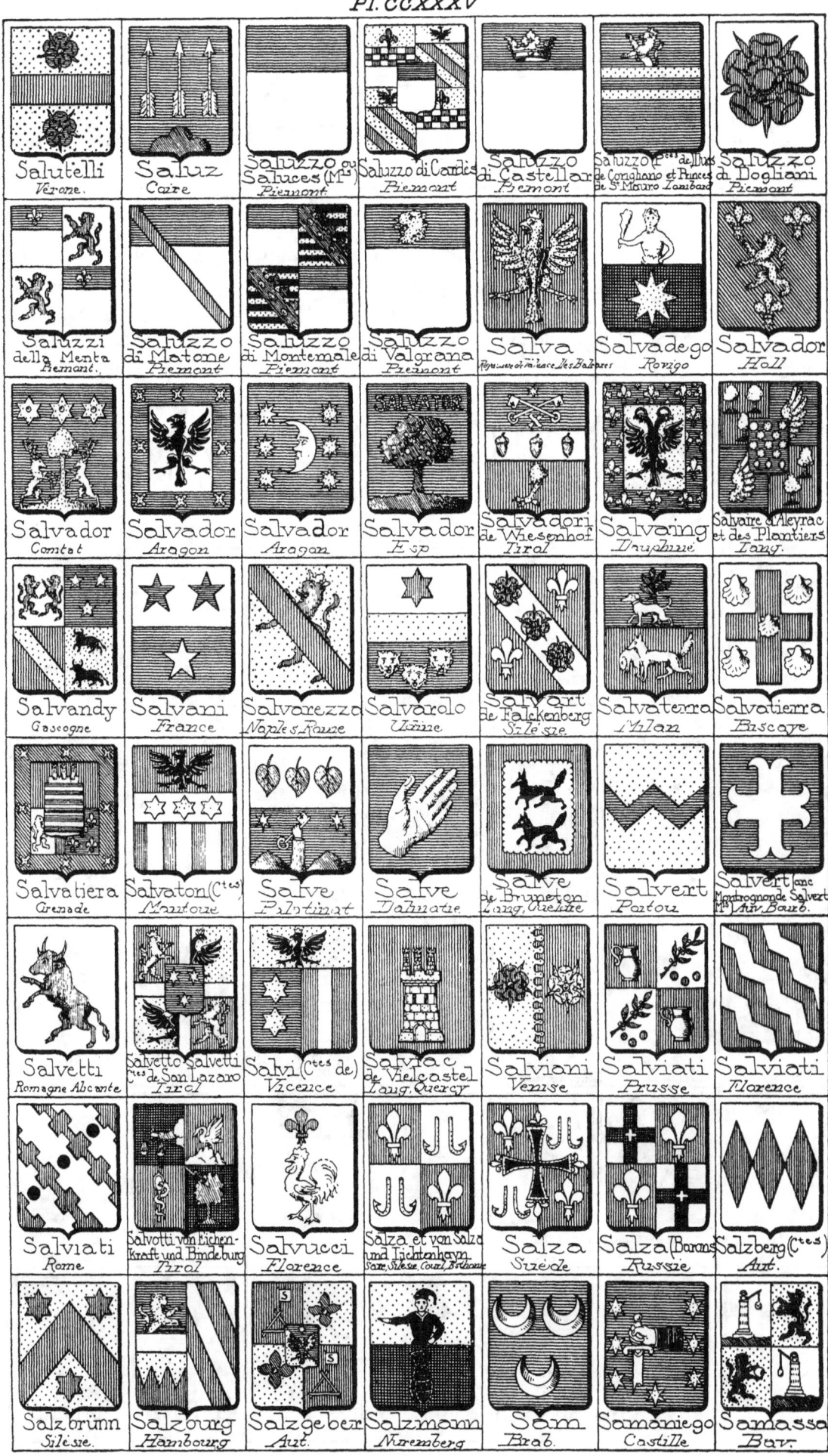

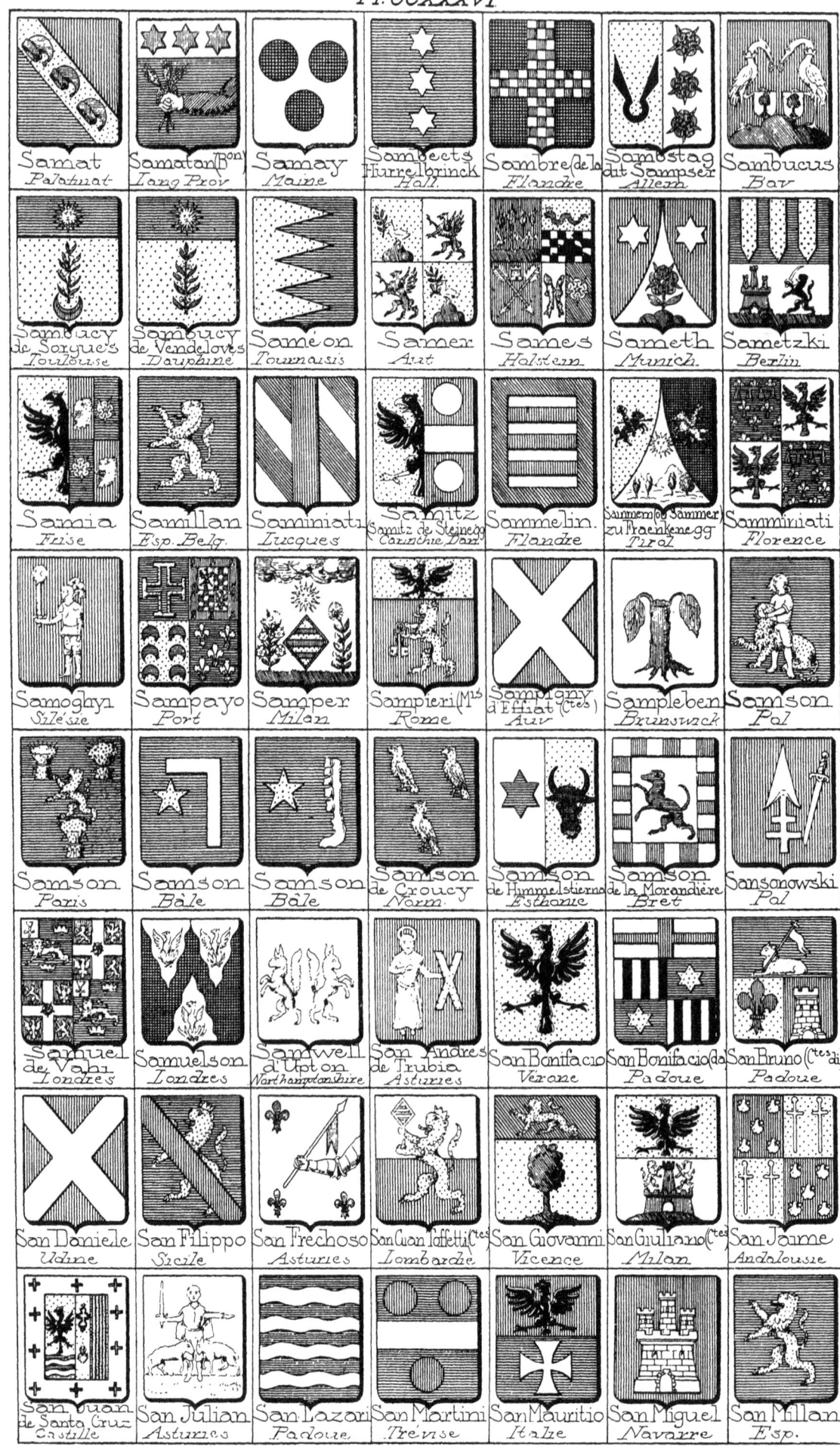

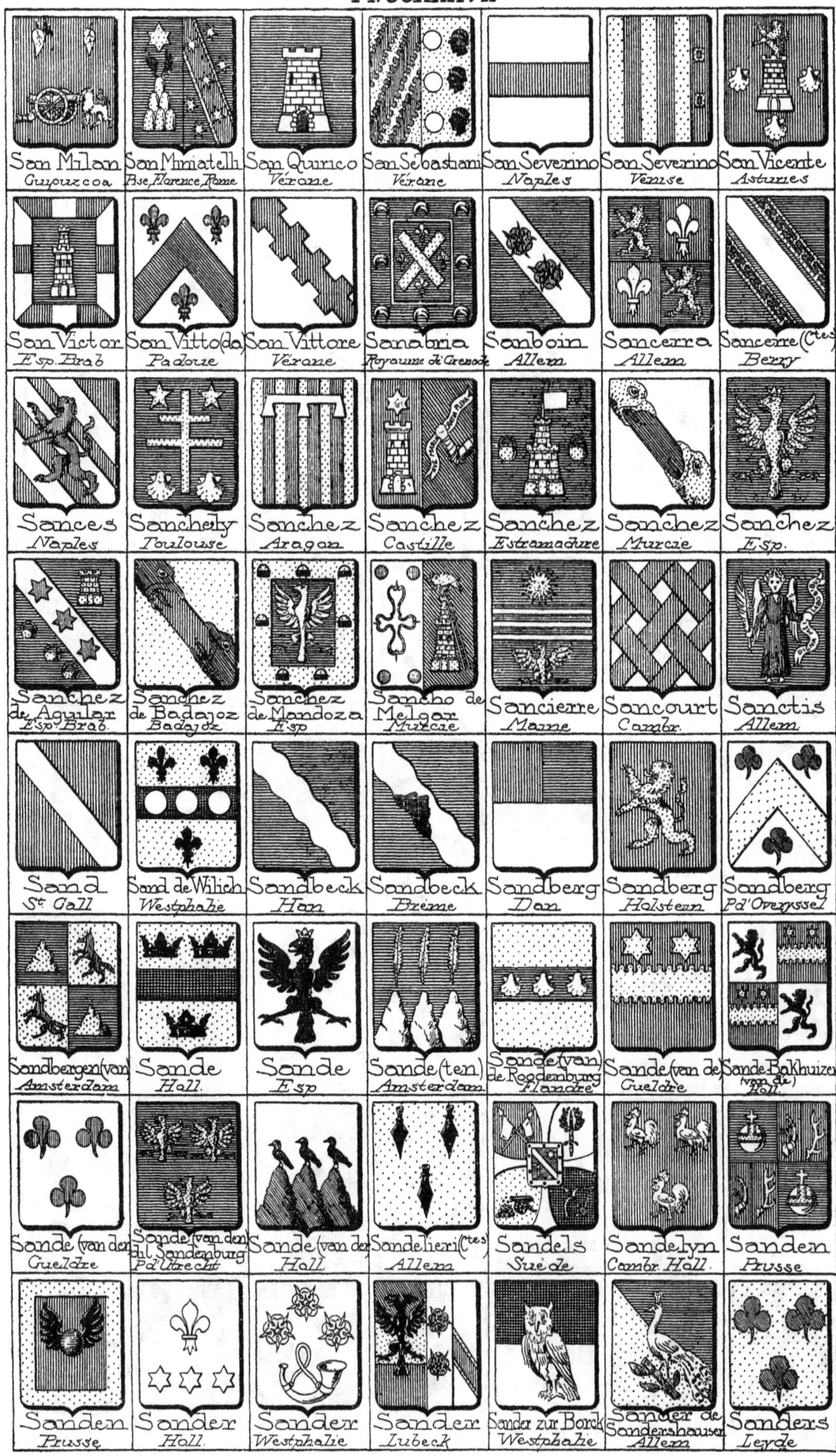

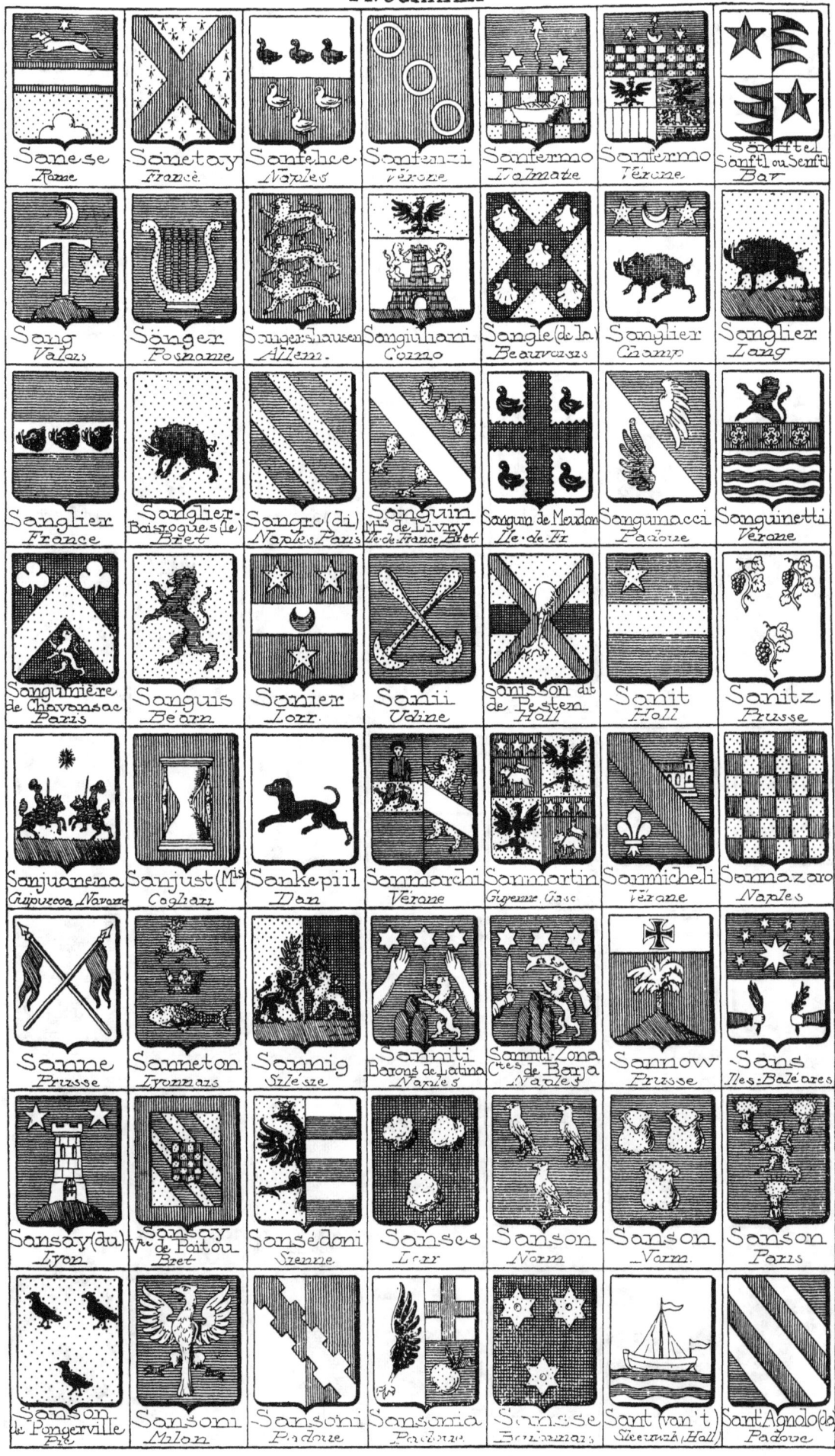

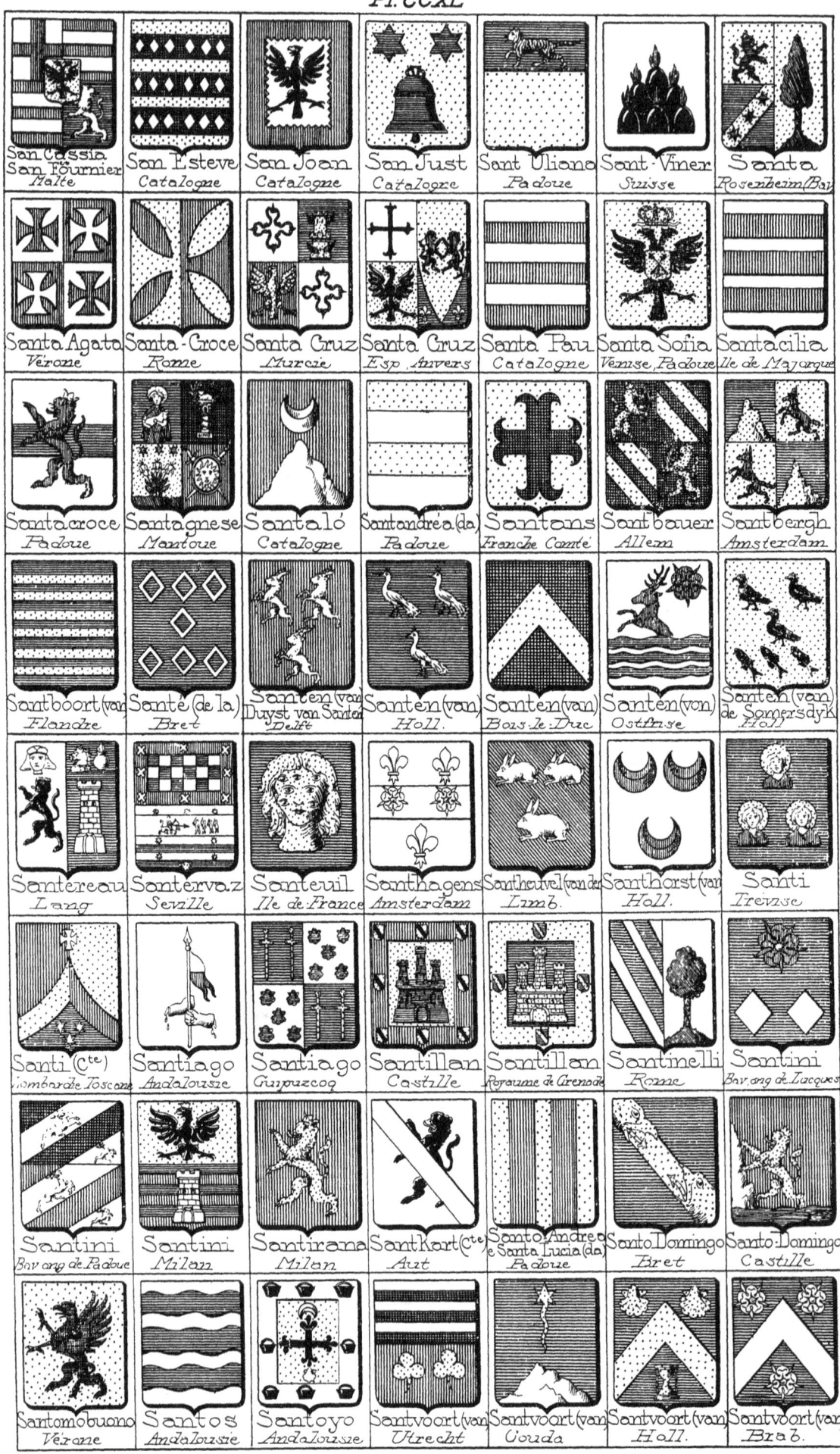

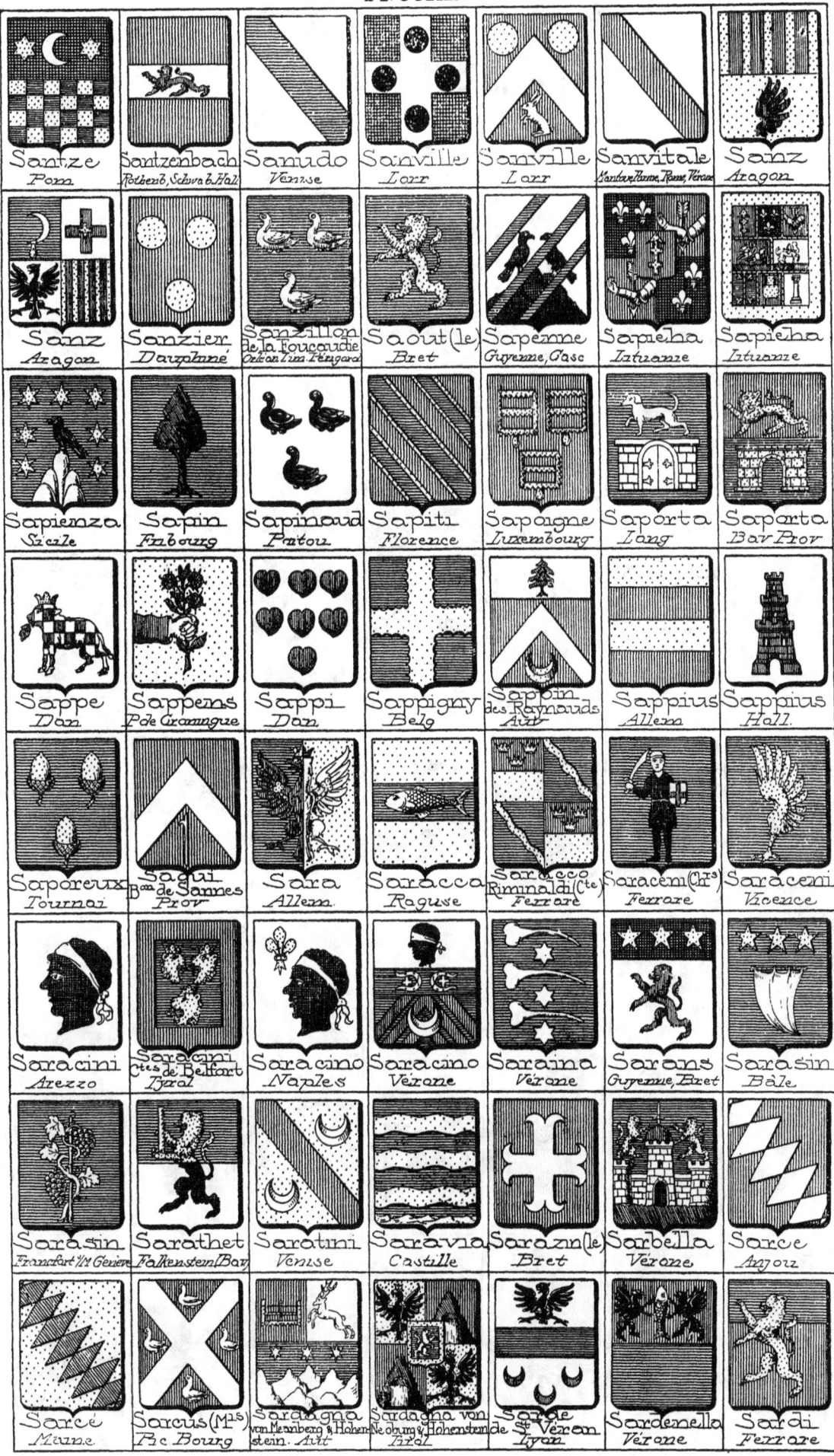

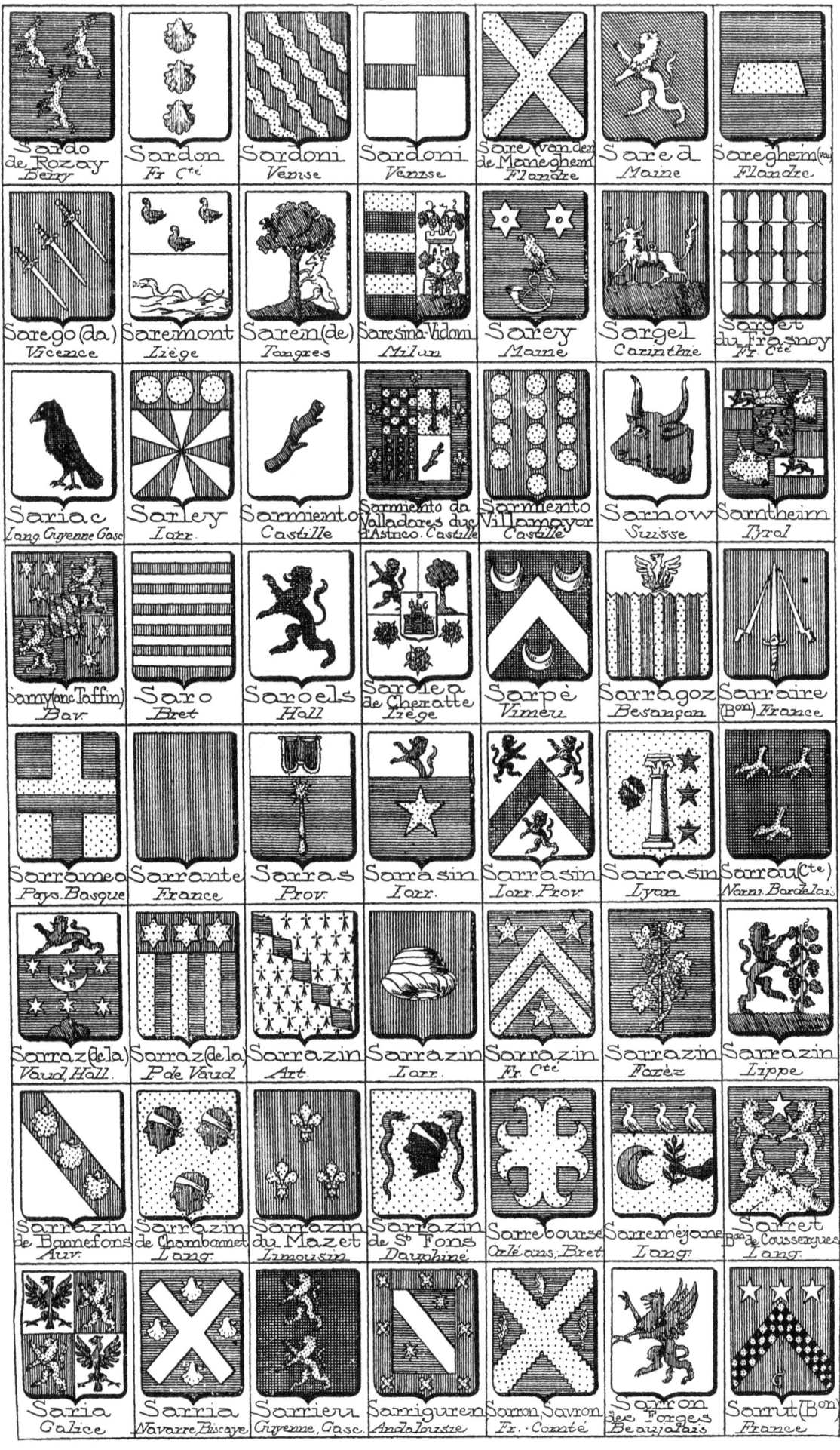

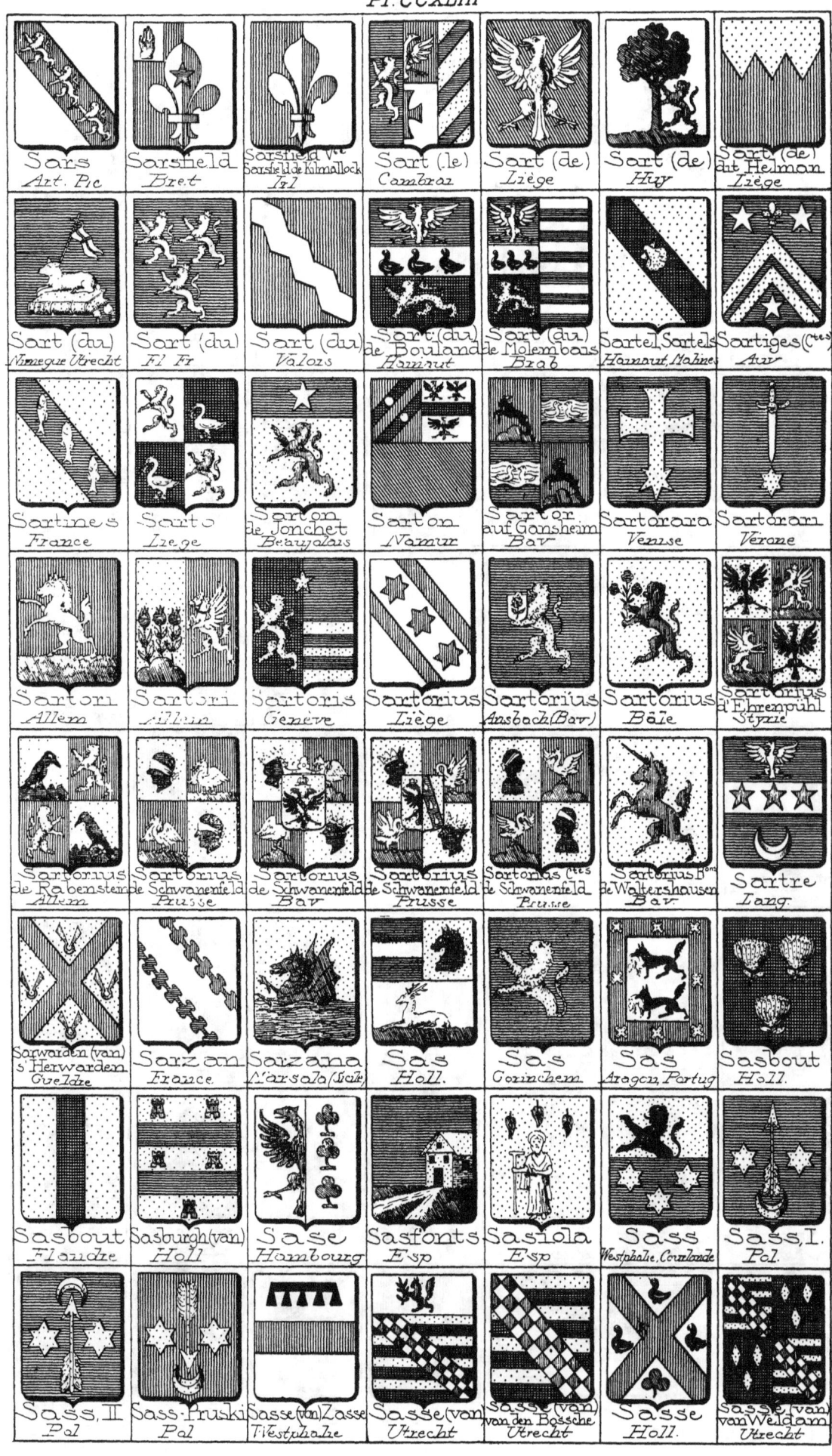

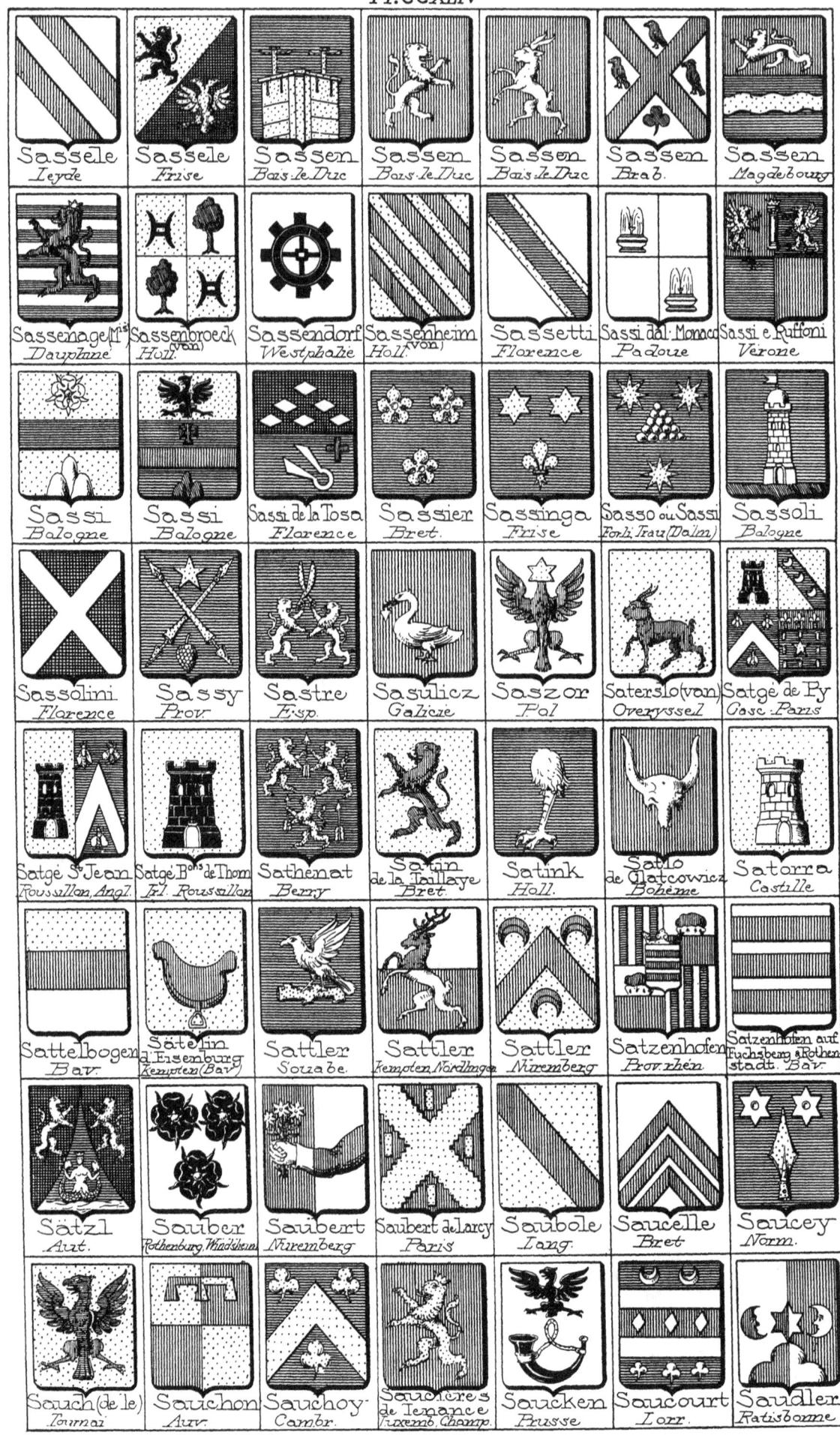

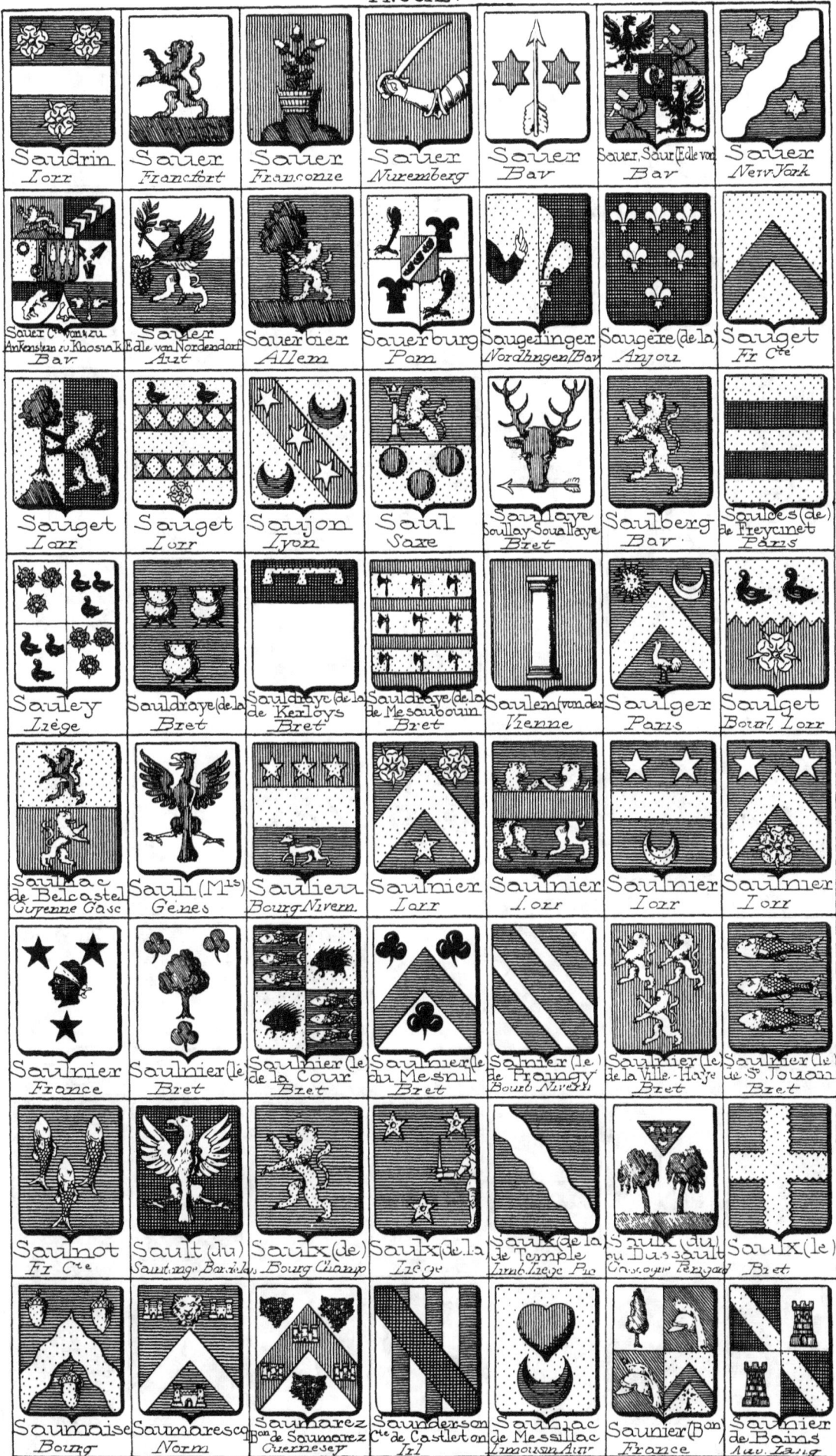

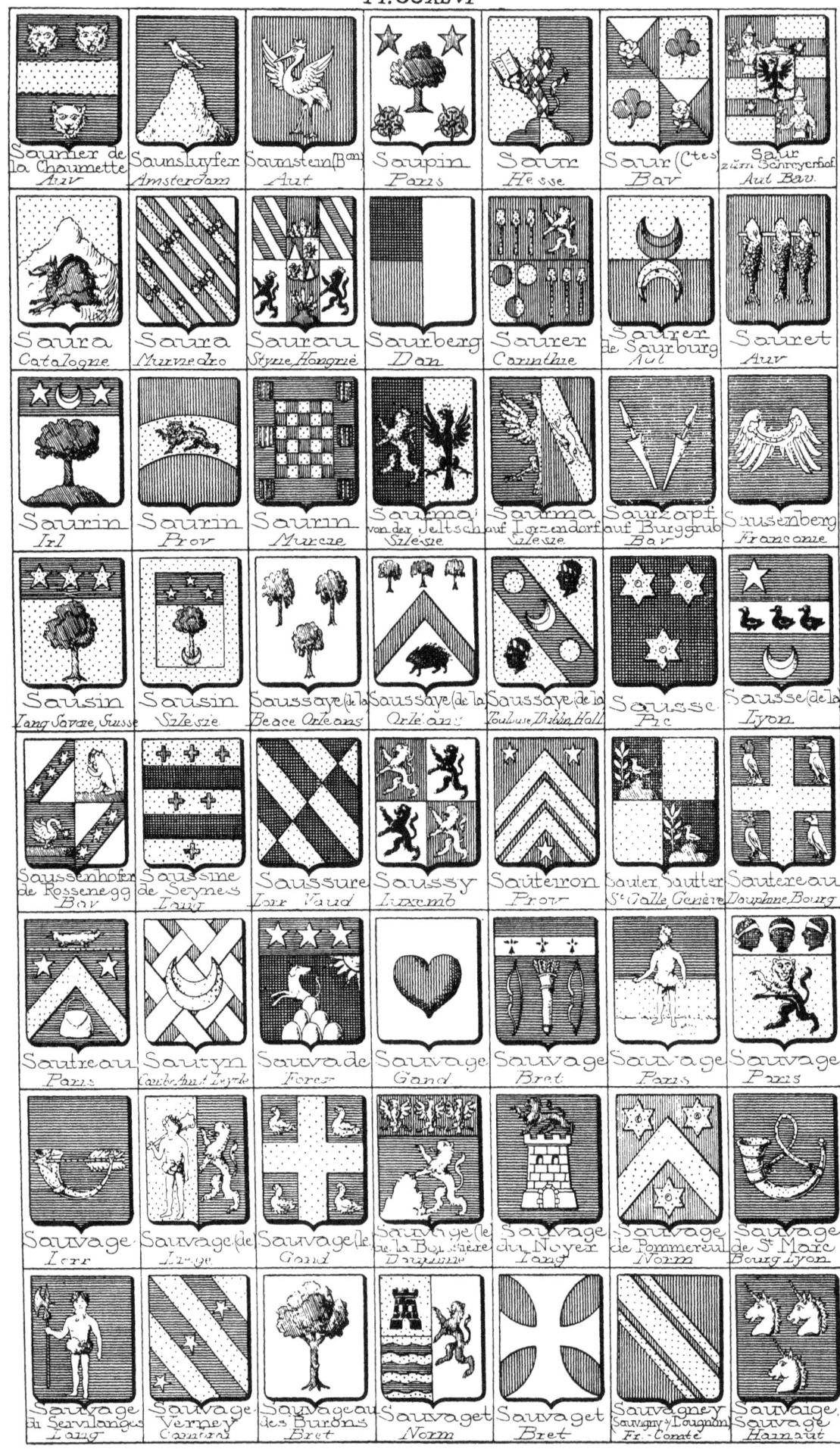

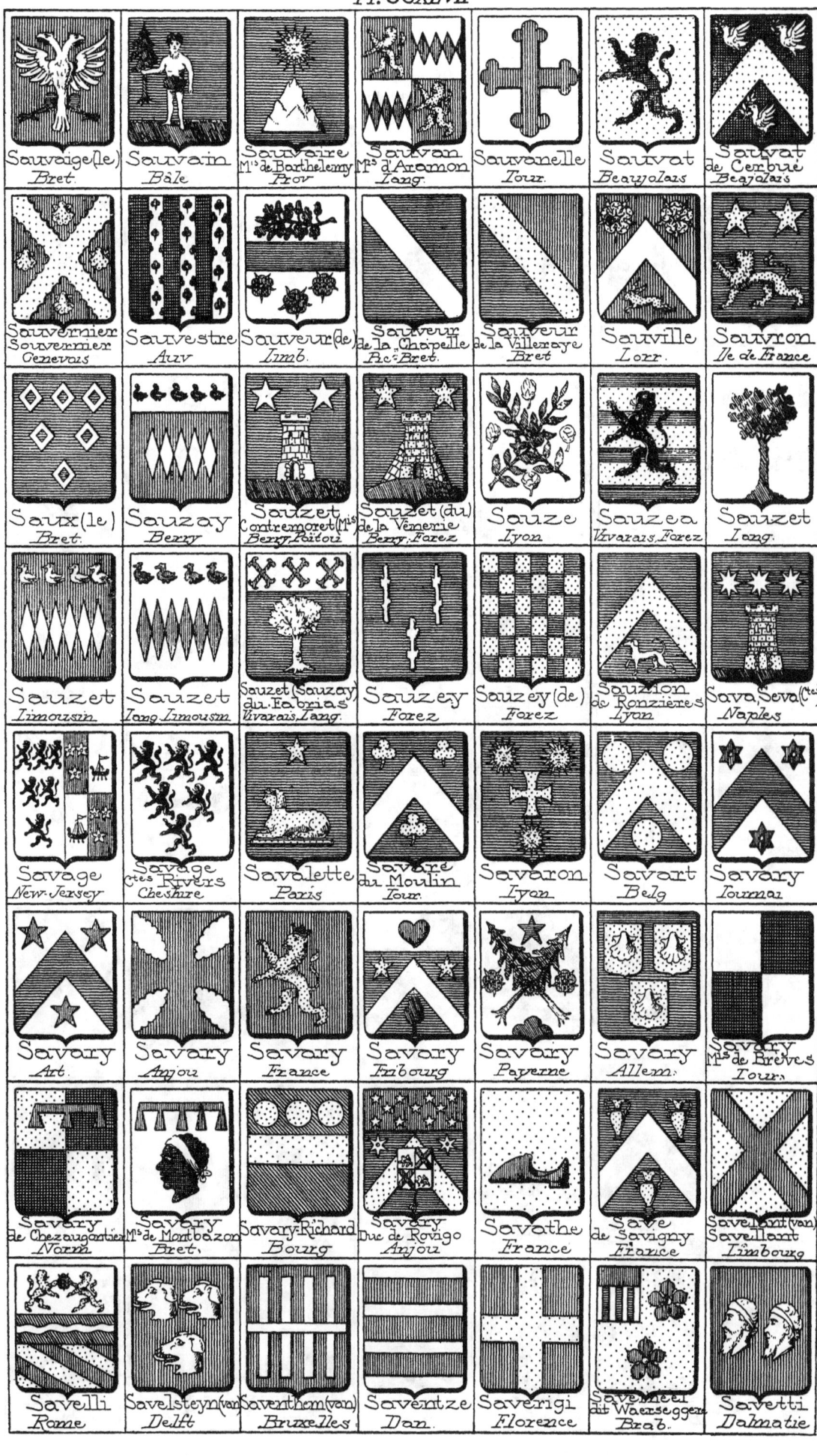

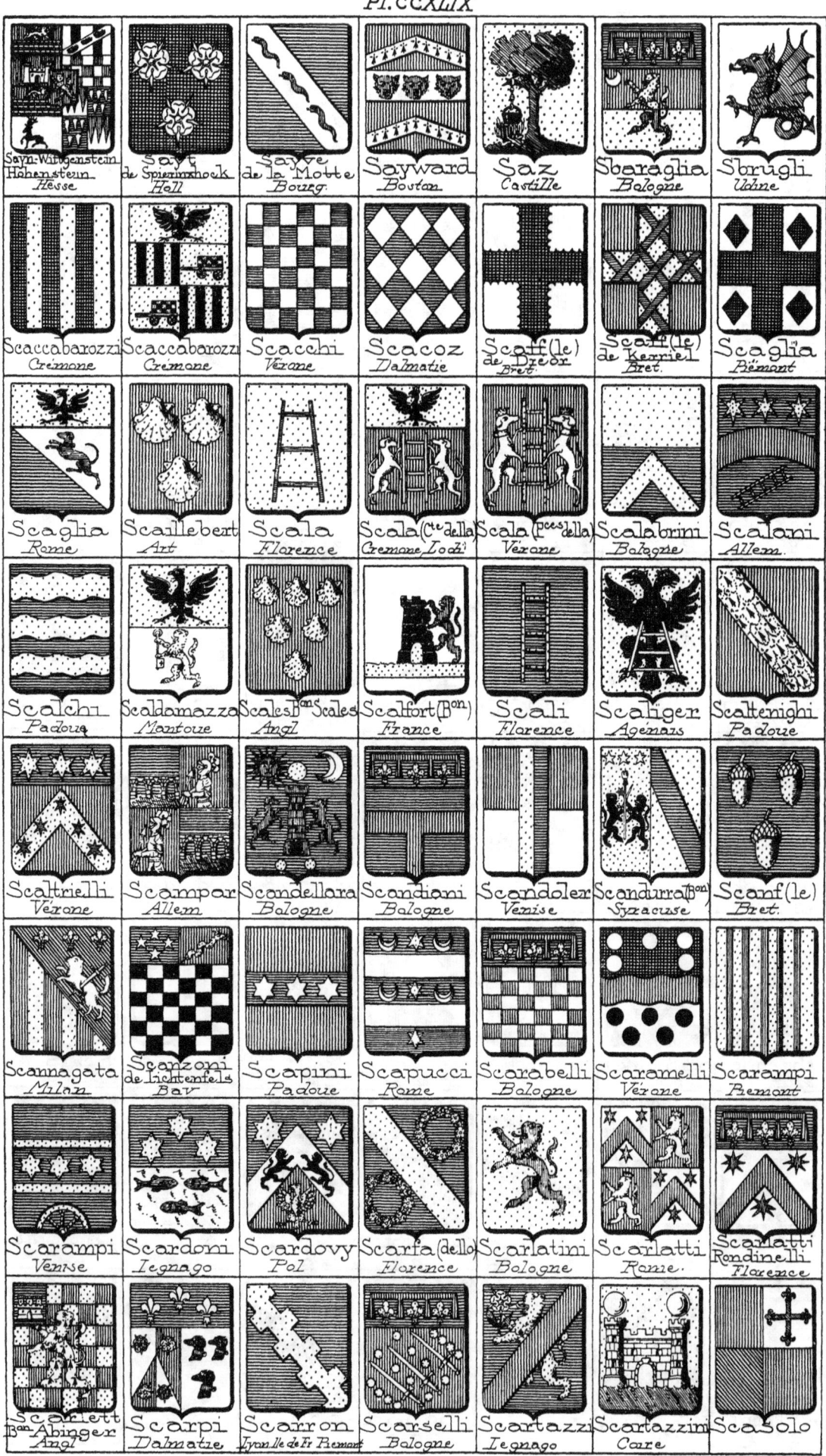

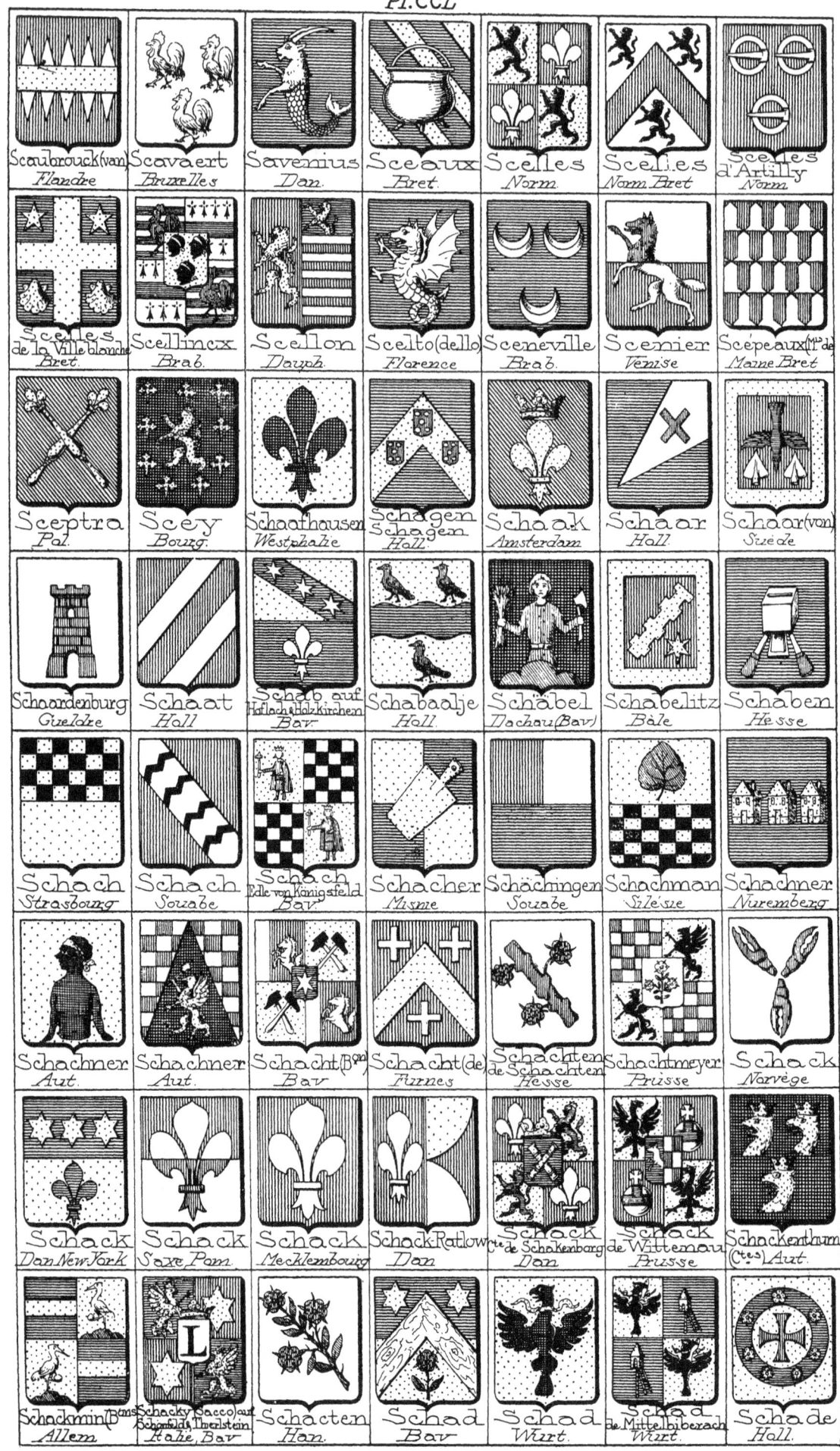

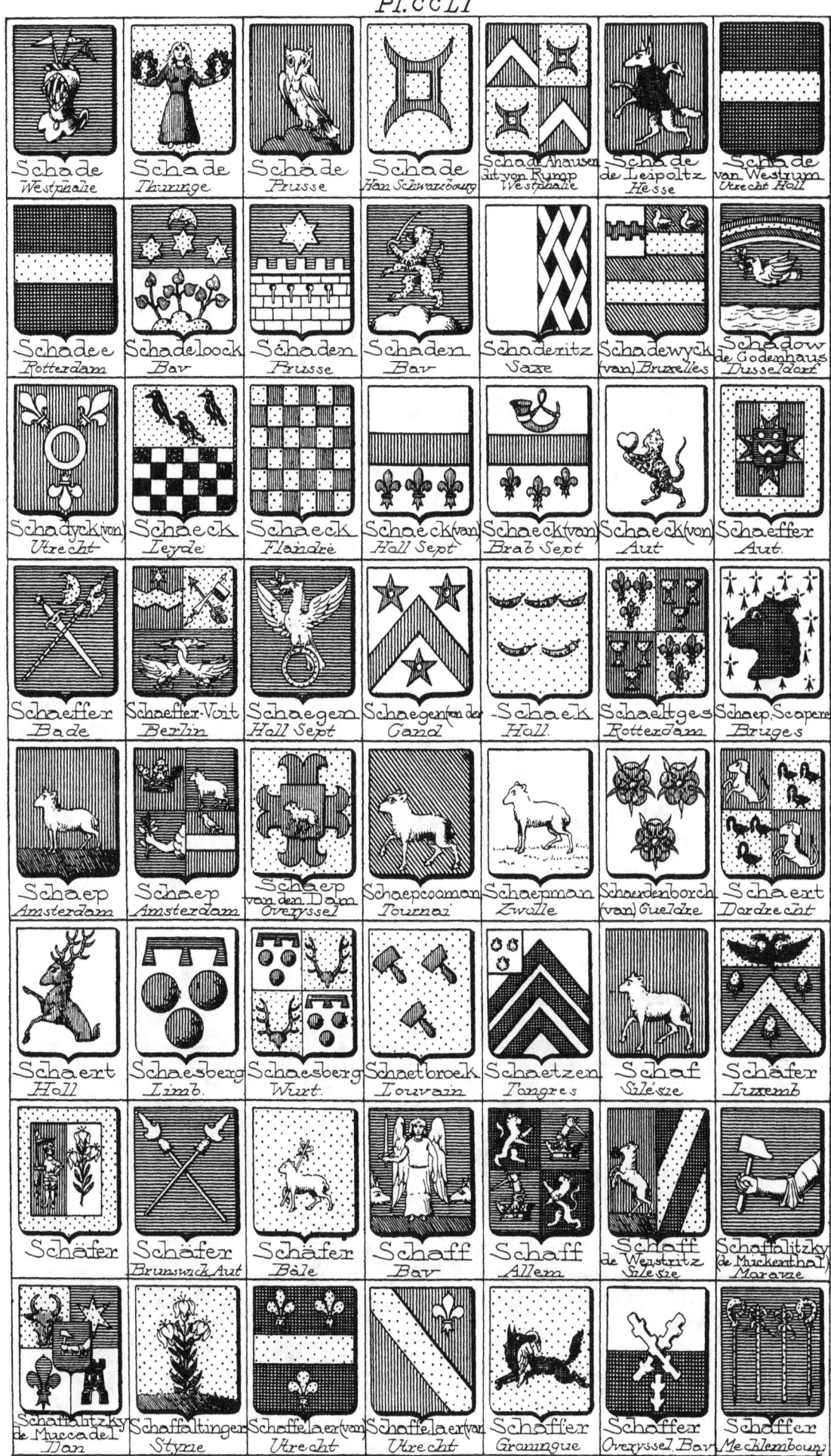

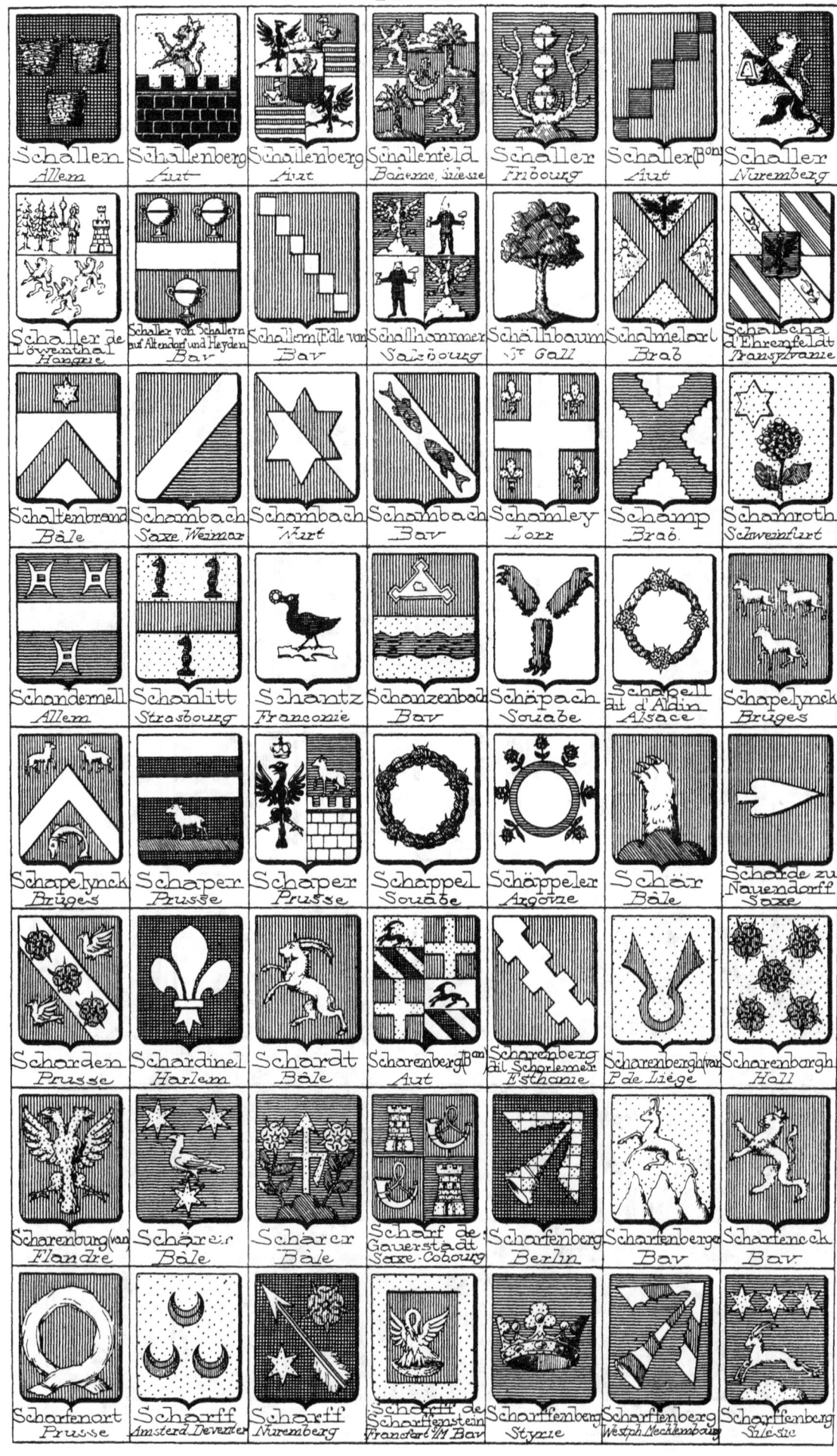

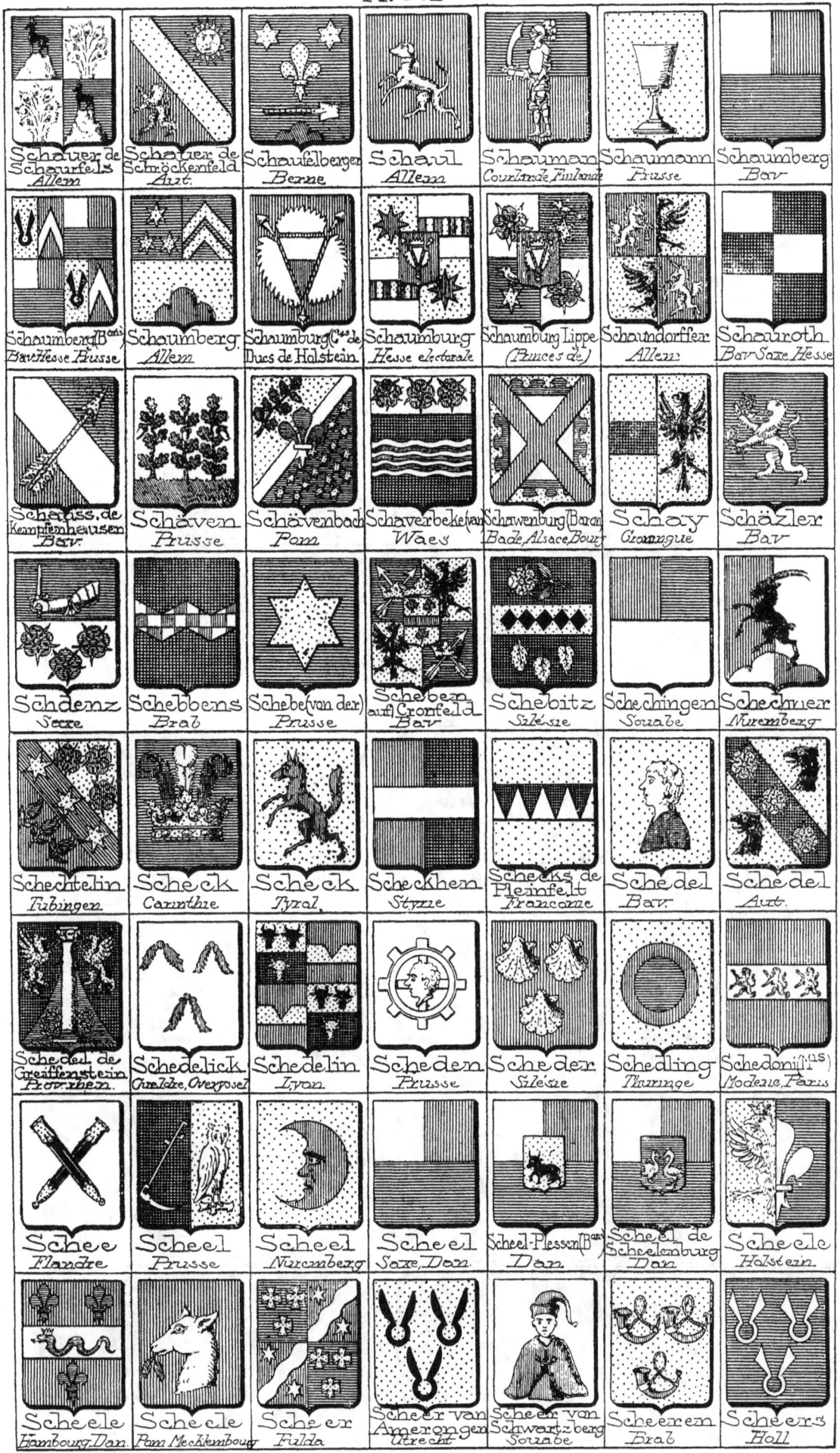

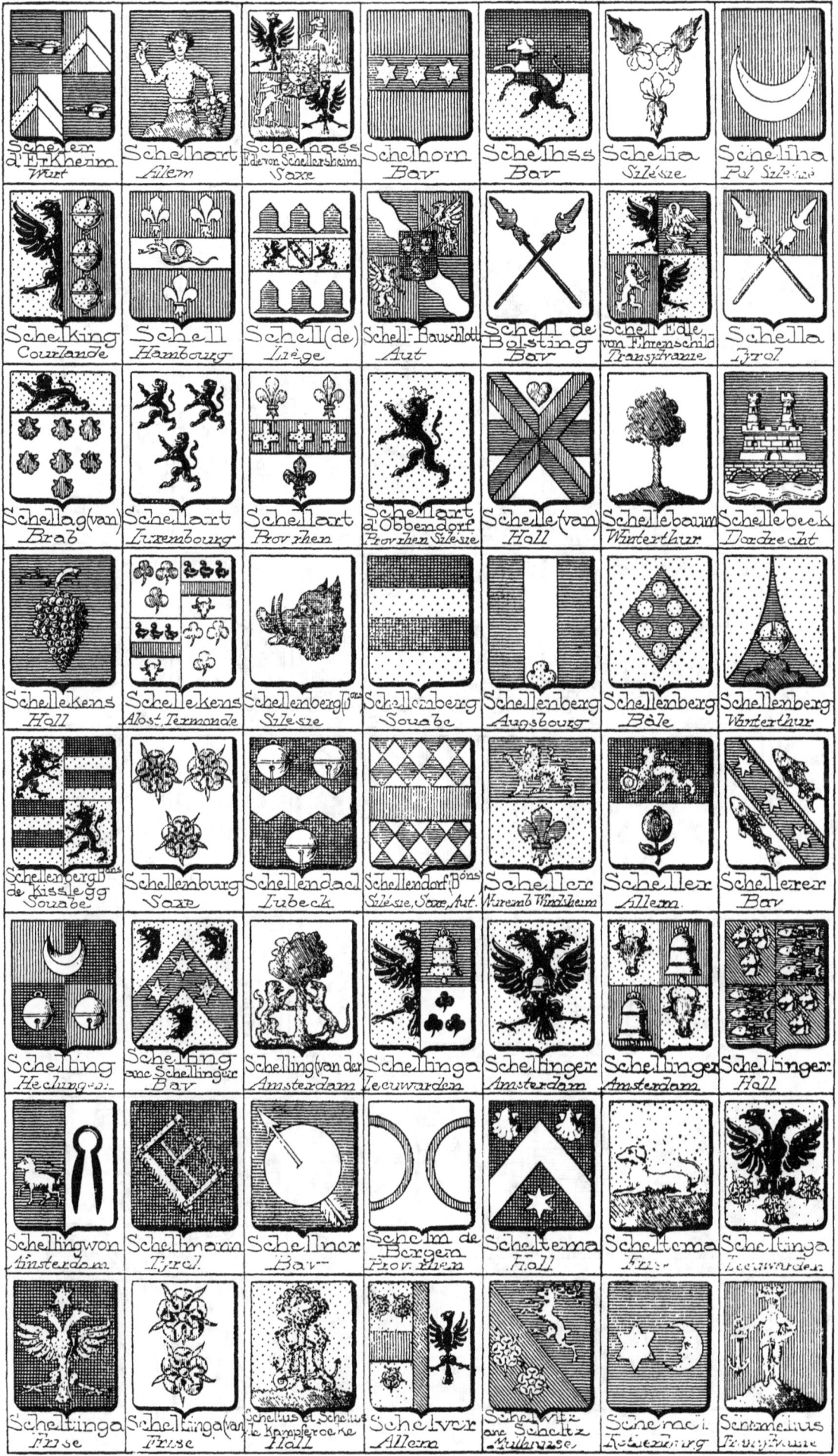

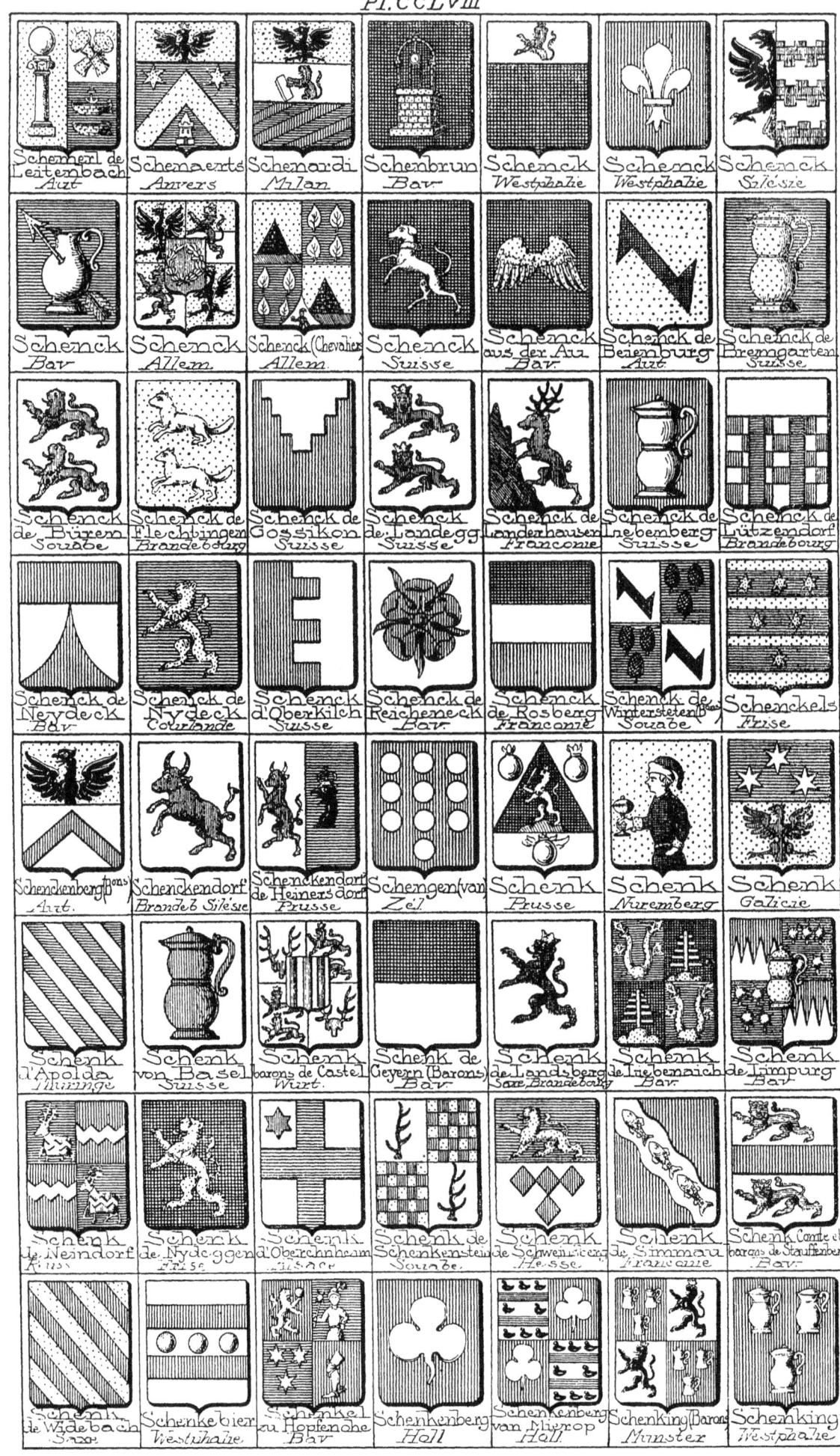

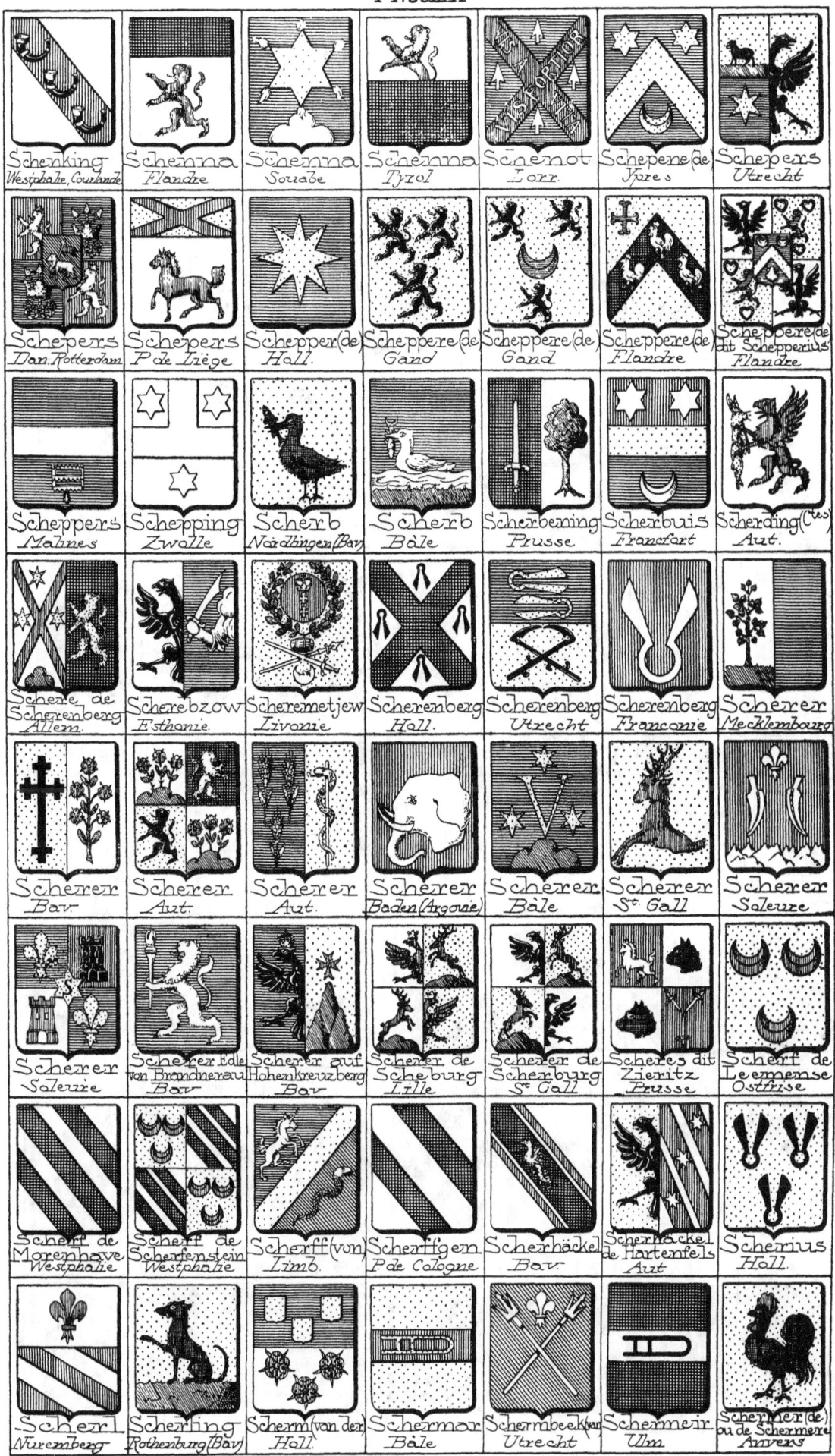

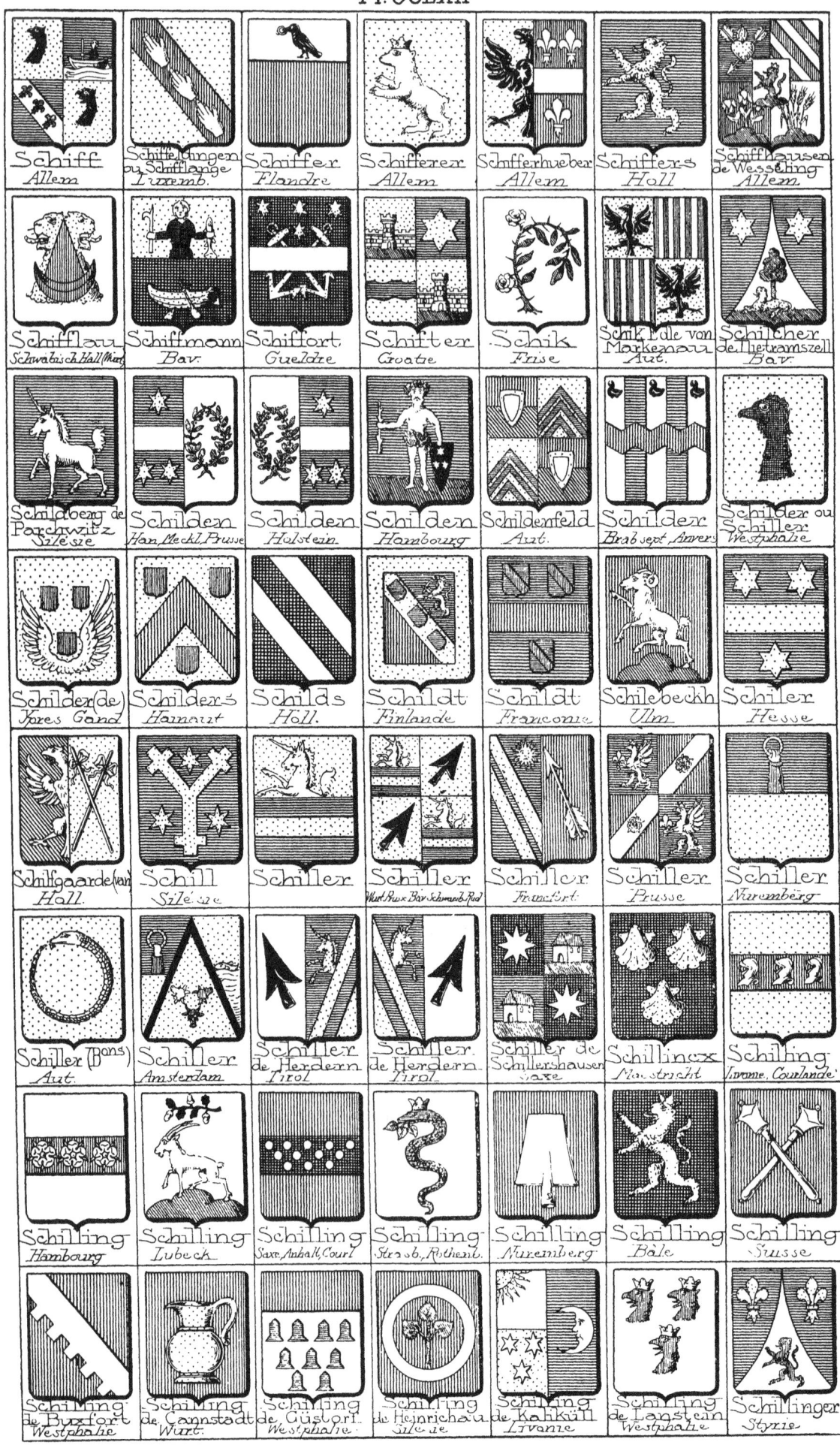

Pl. CCLXIII

Pl. CCLXV

Pl. CCLXVI

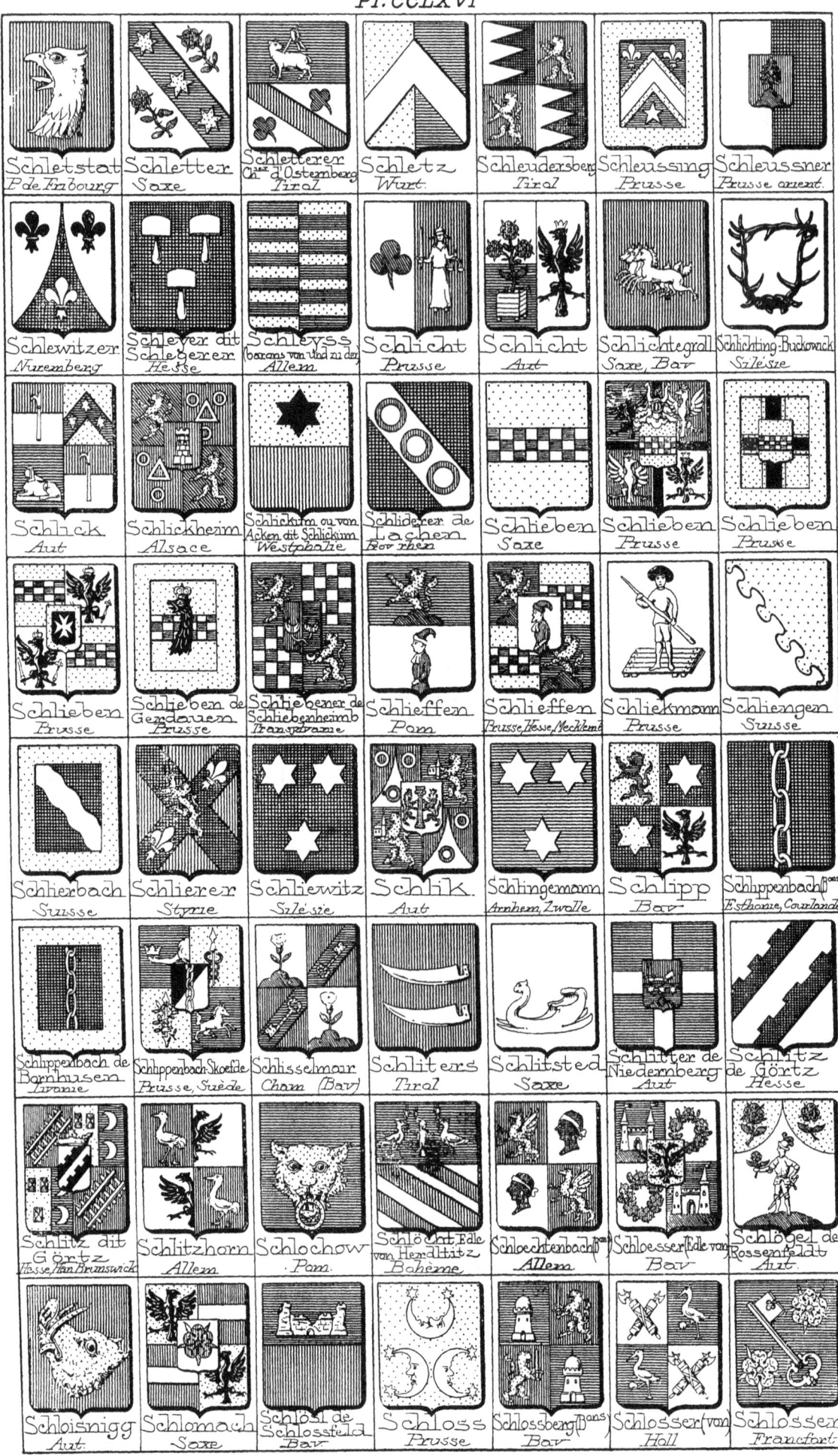

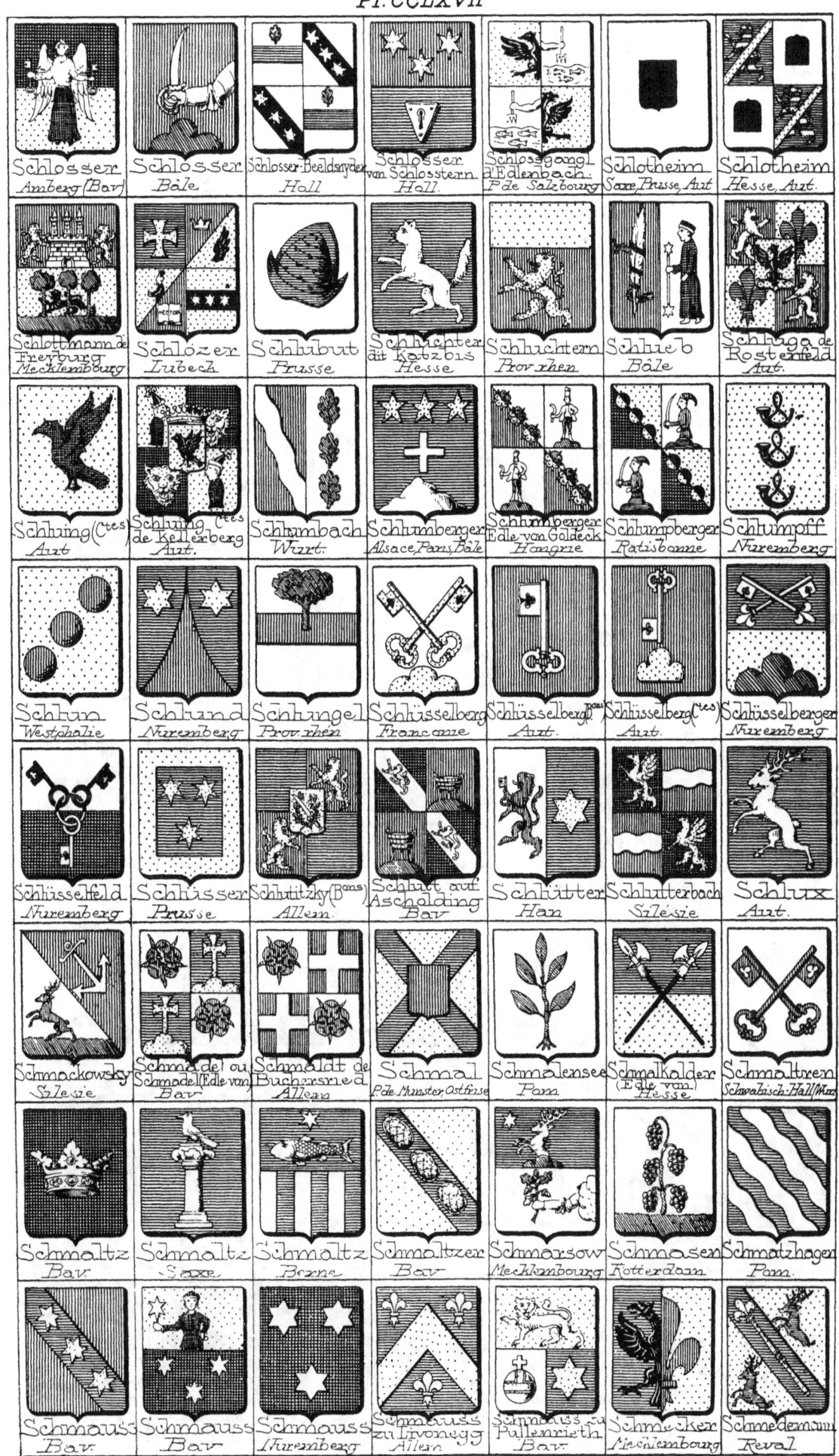

Pl. CCLXIX

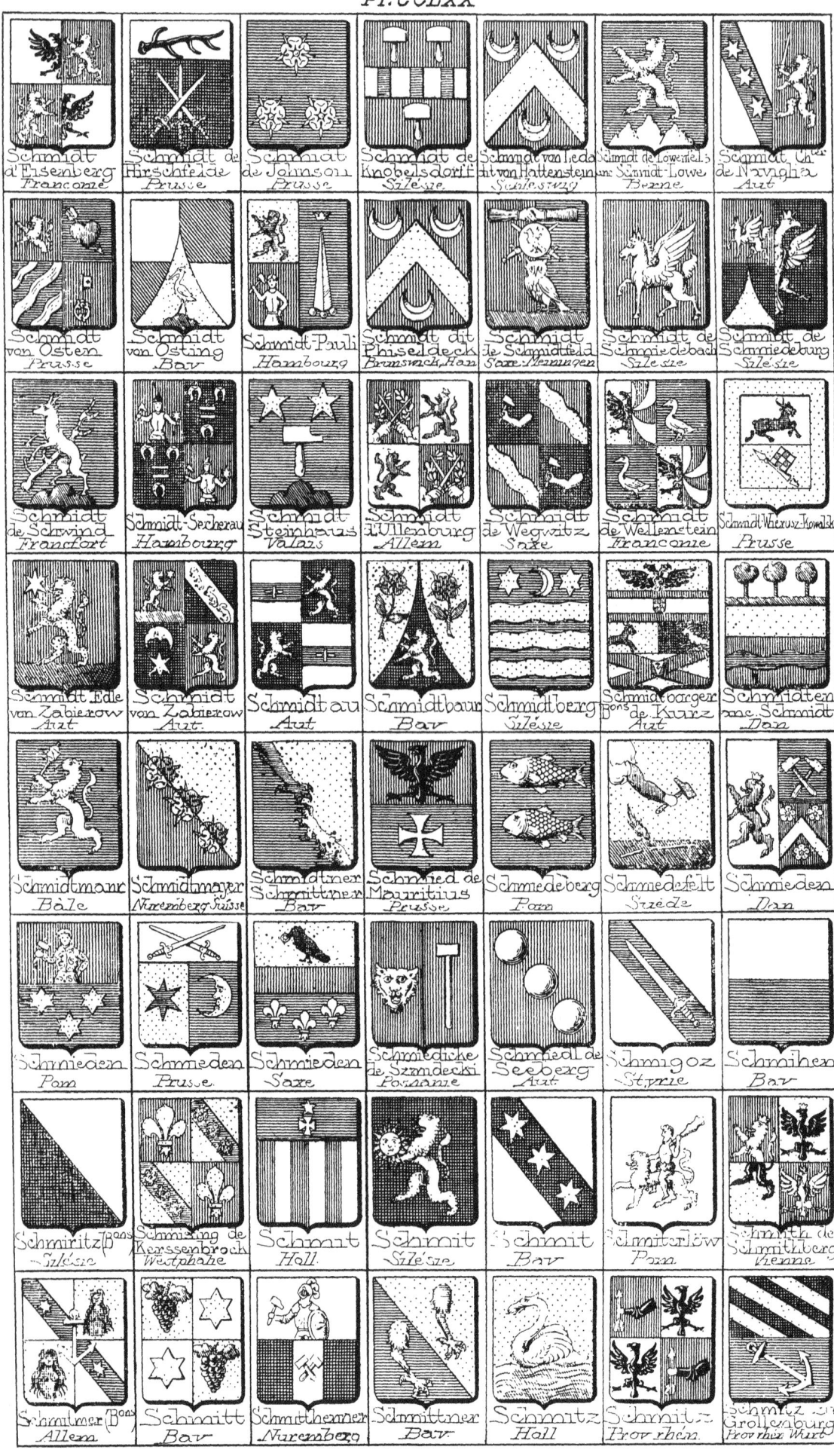

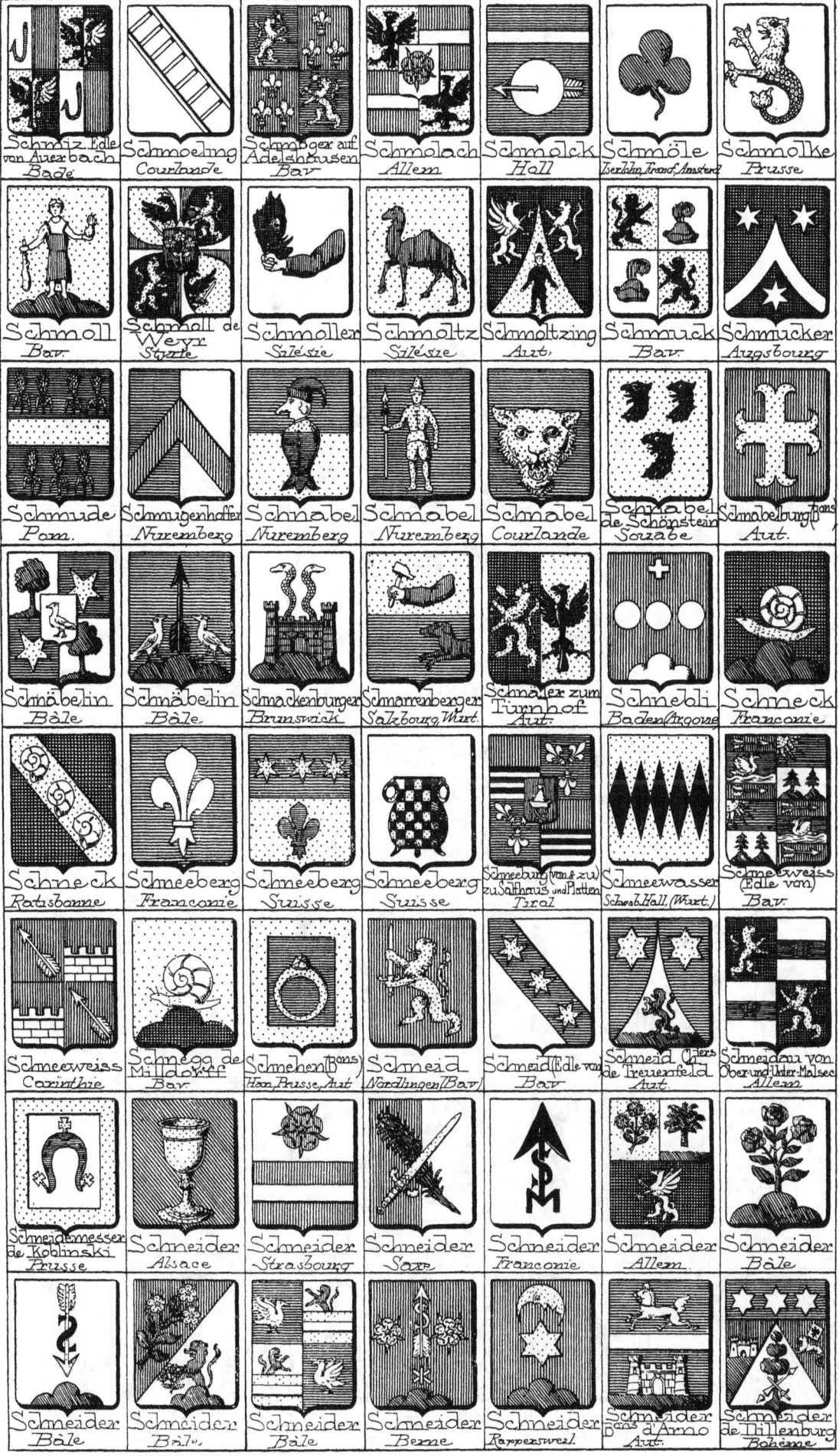

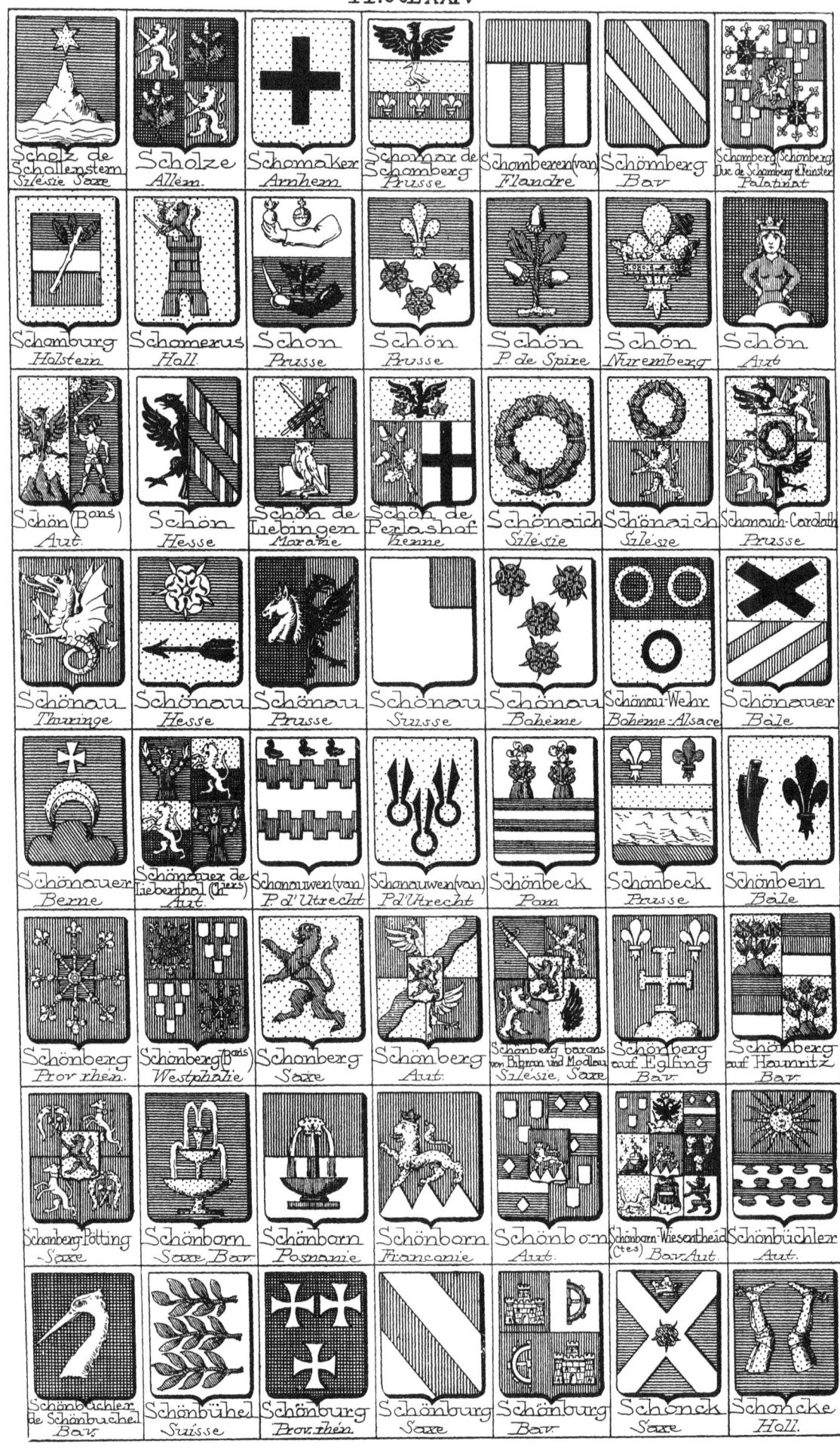

Pl. CCLXXVI

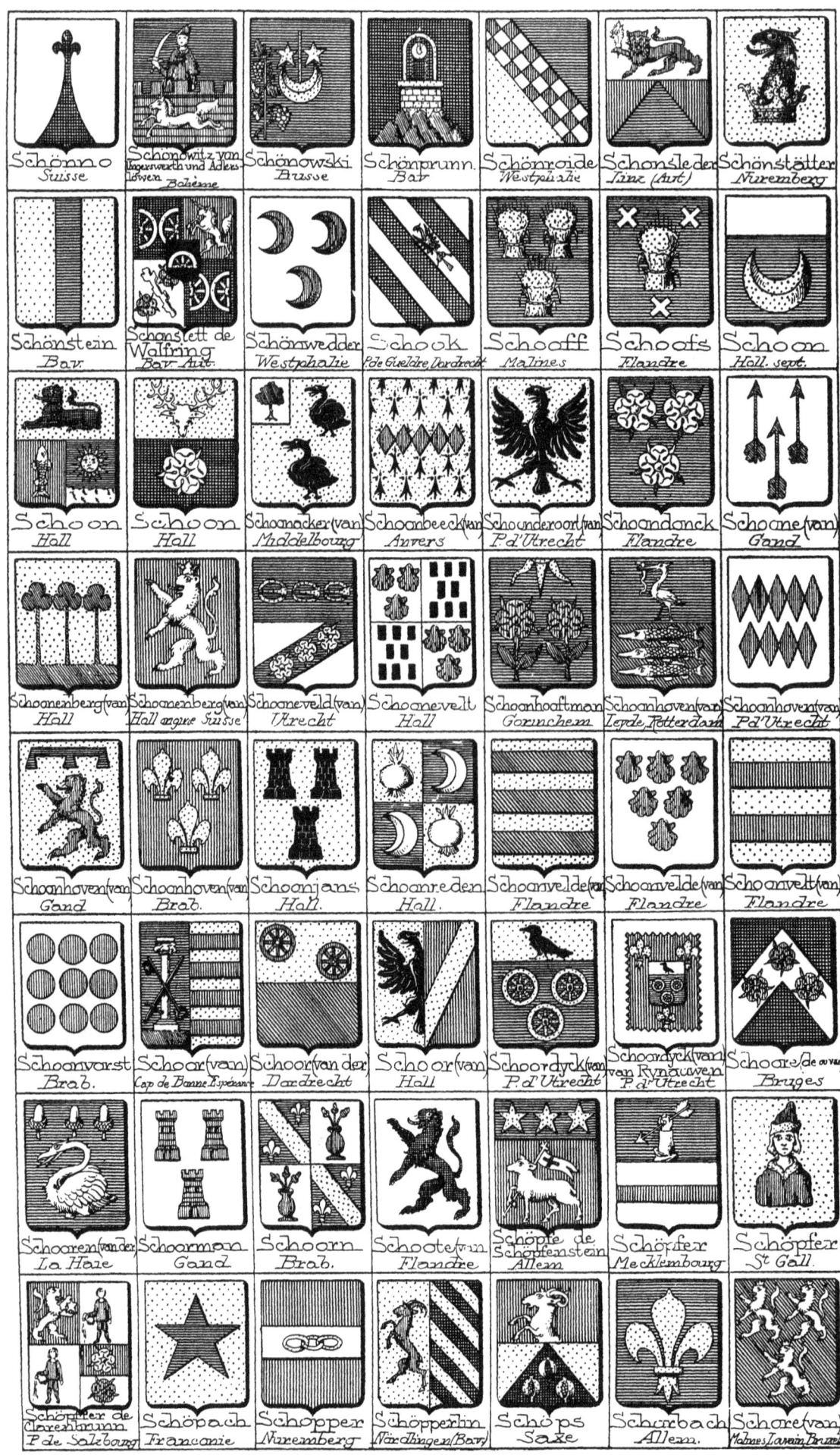

Pl. CCLXXVII

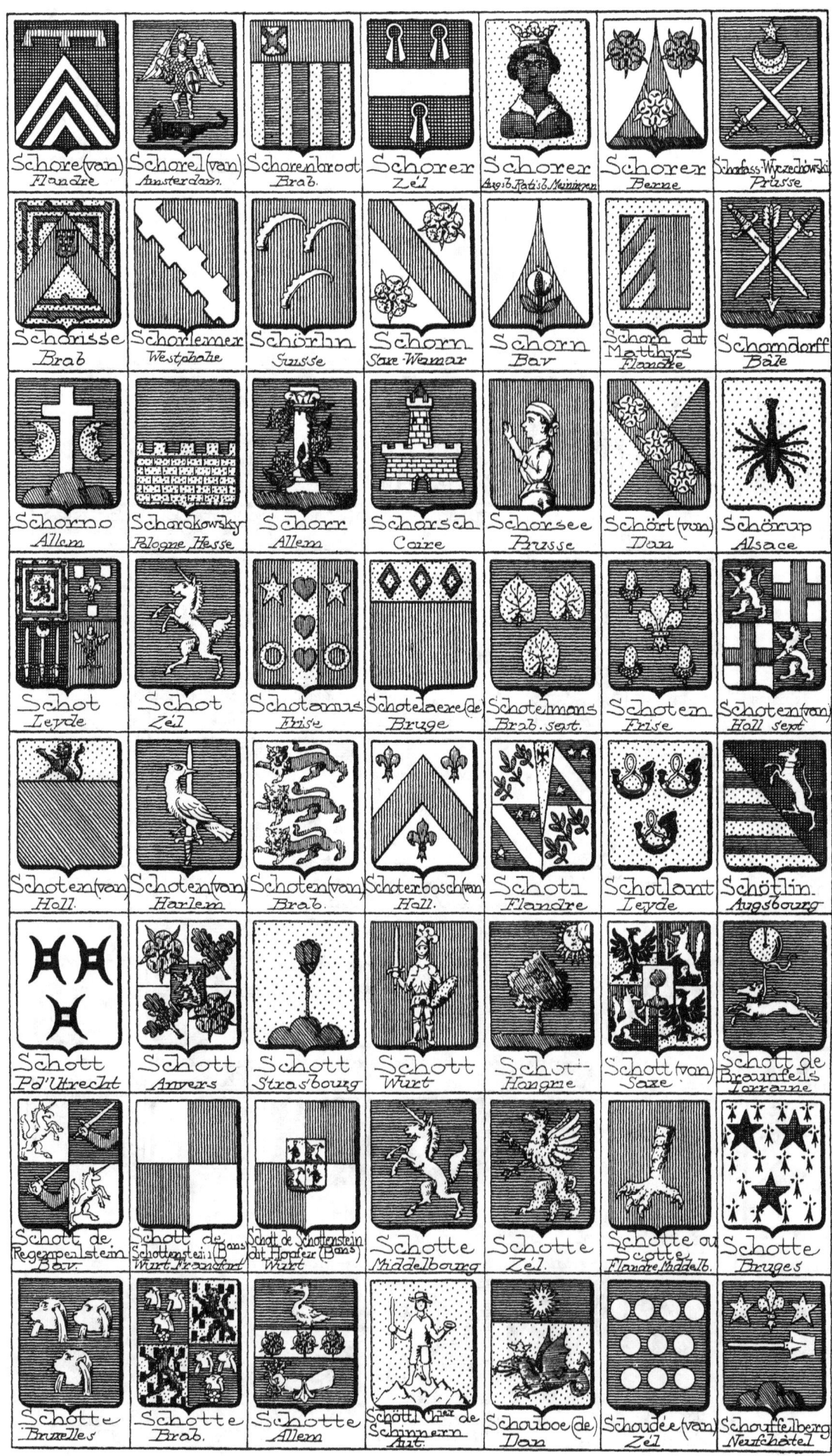

Pl. CCLXXIX

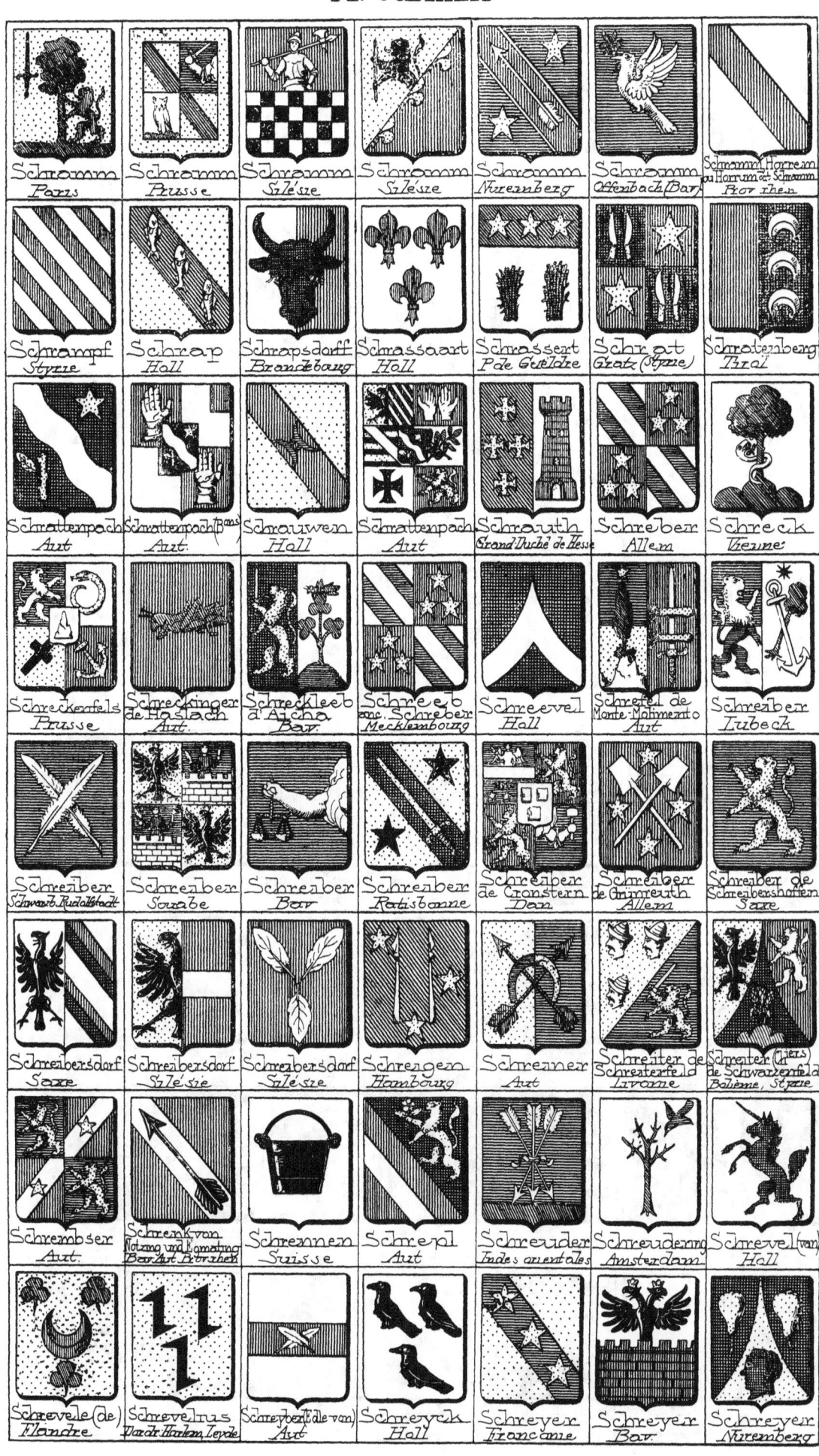

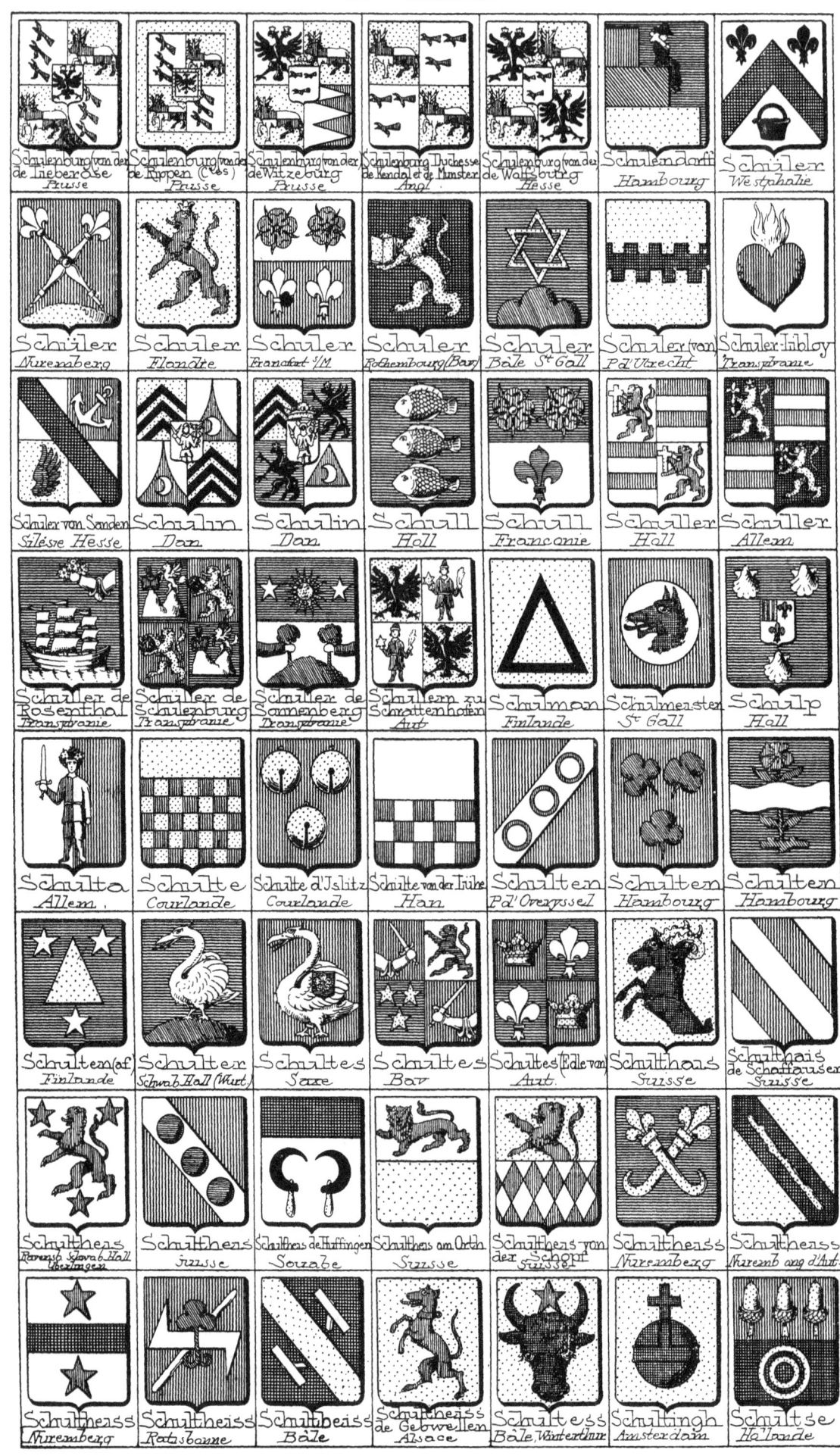

Pl. CCLXXXIII

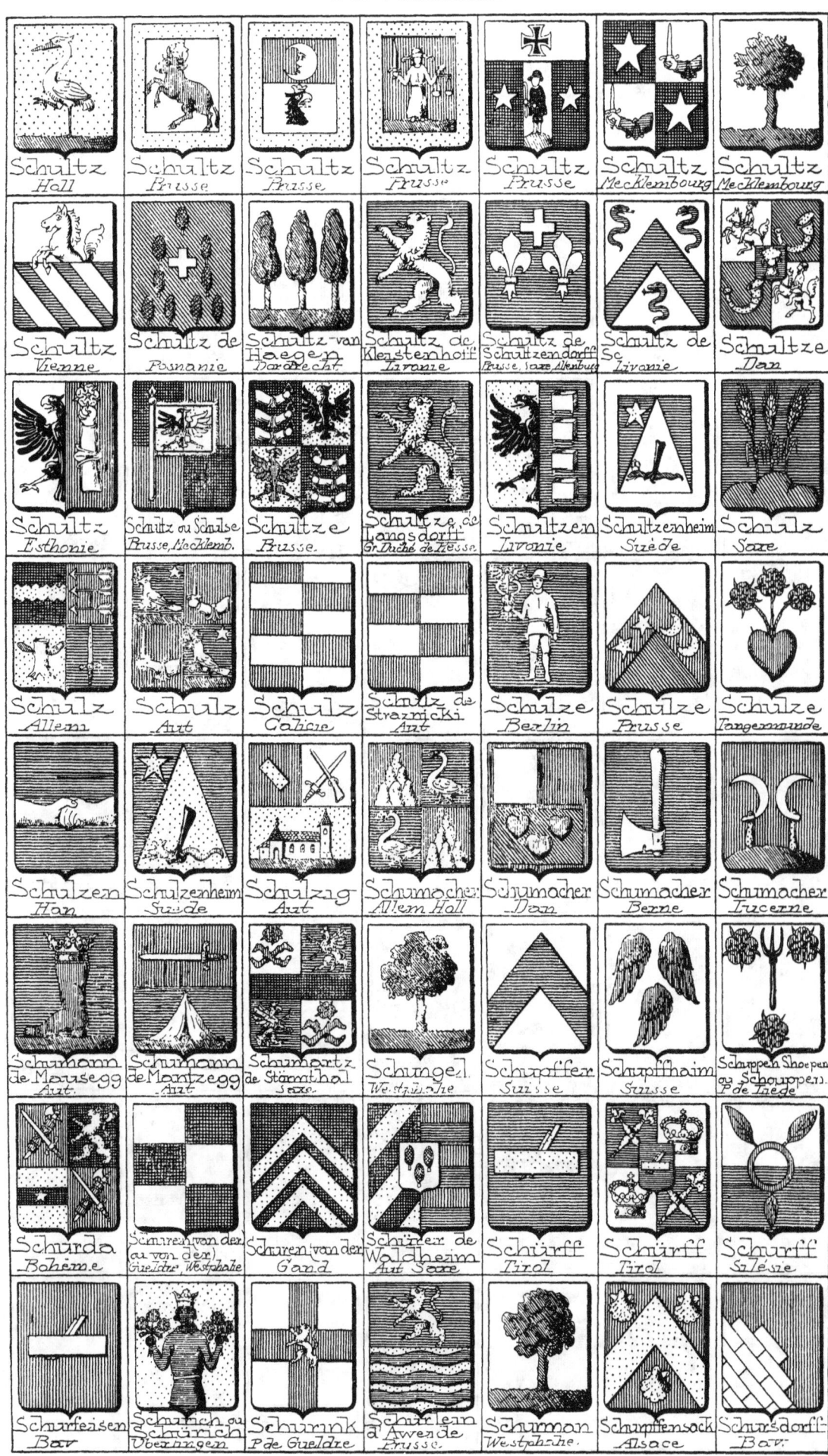

Pl. CCLXXXV

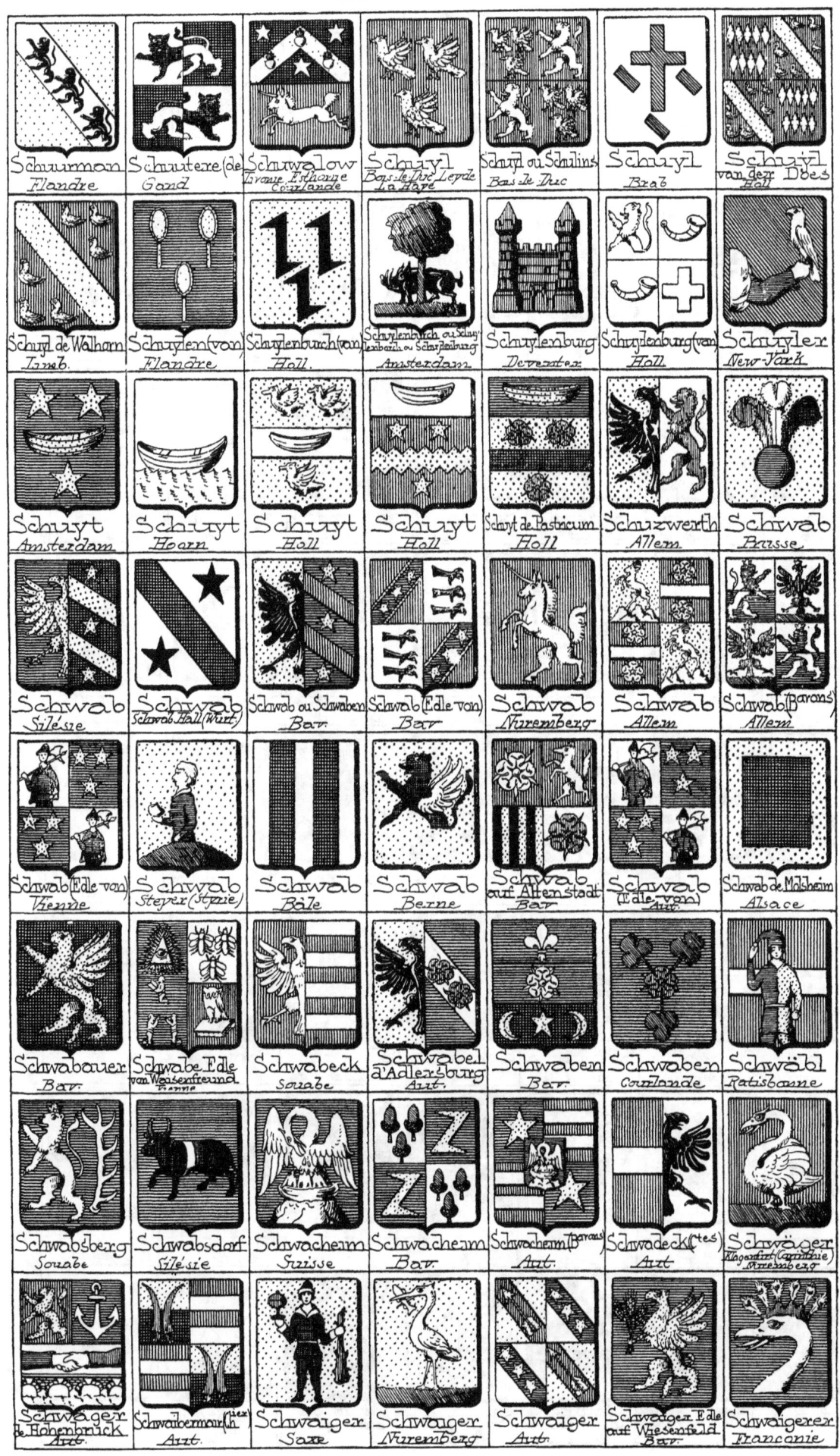

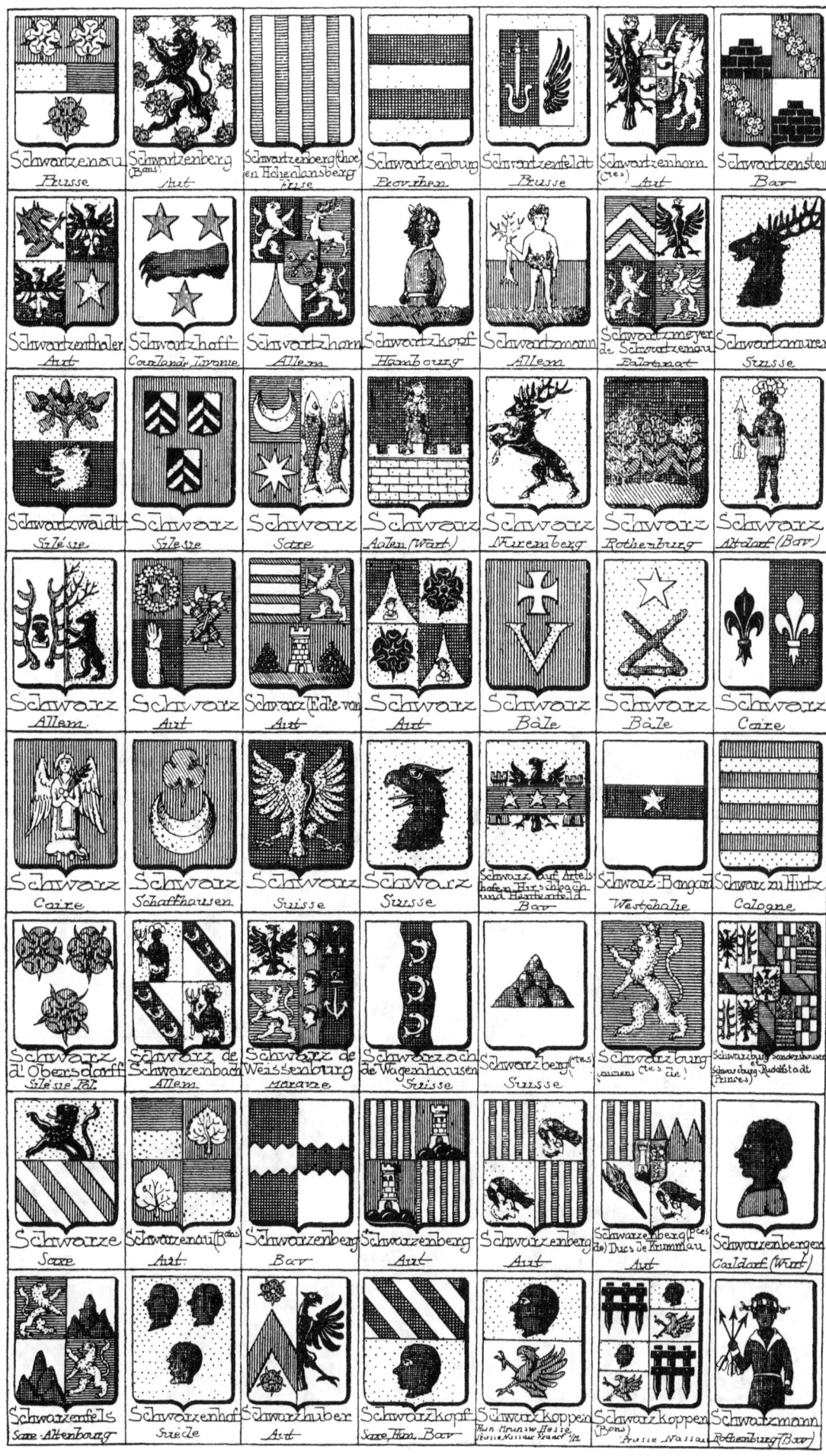

Pl. CCLXXXVIII

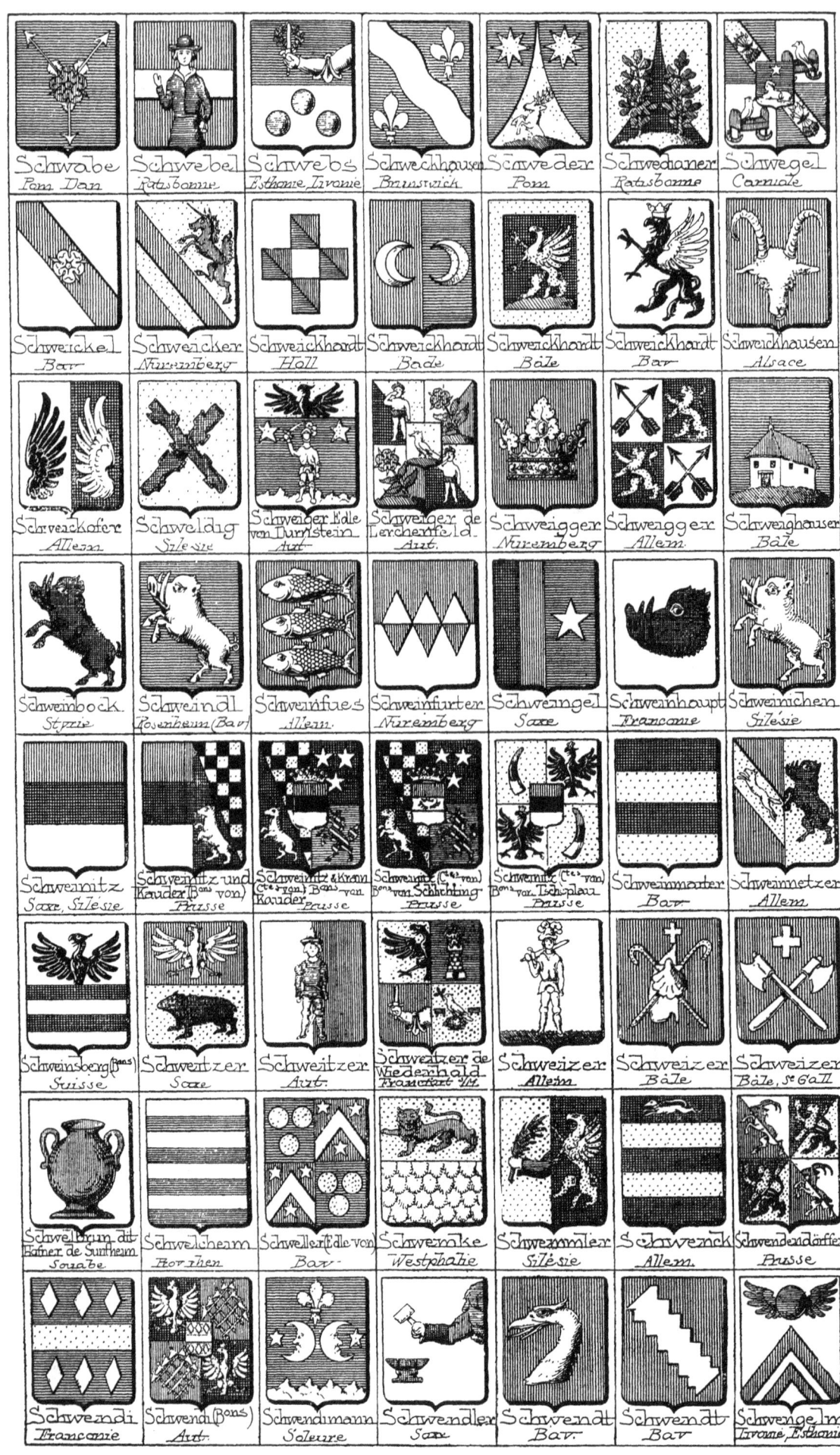

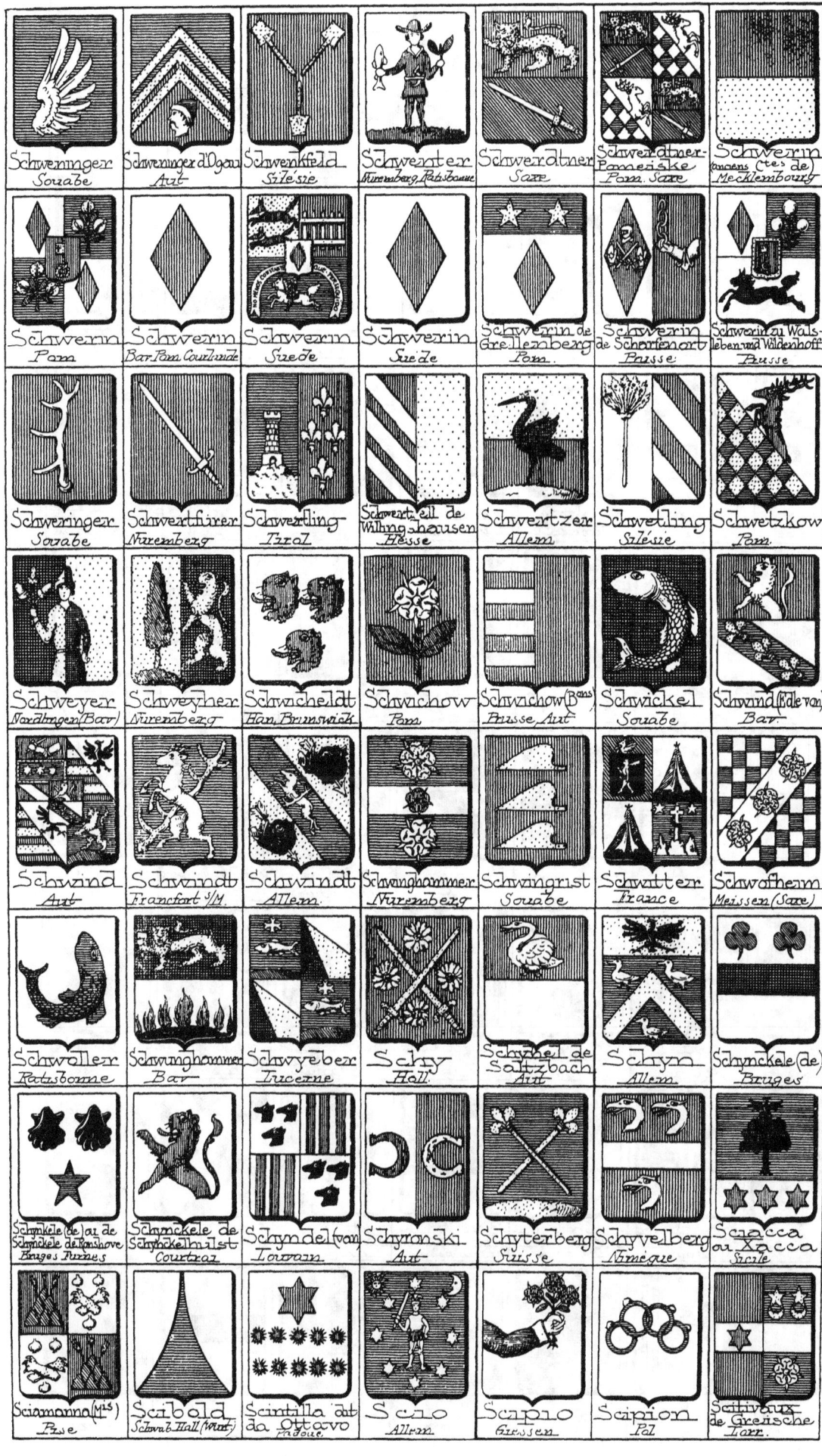

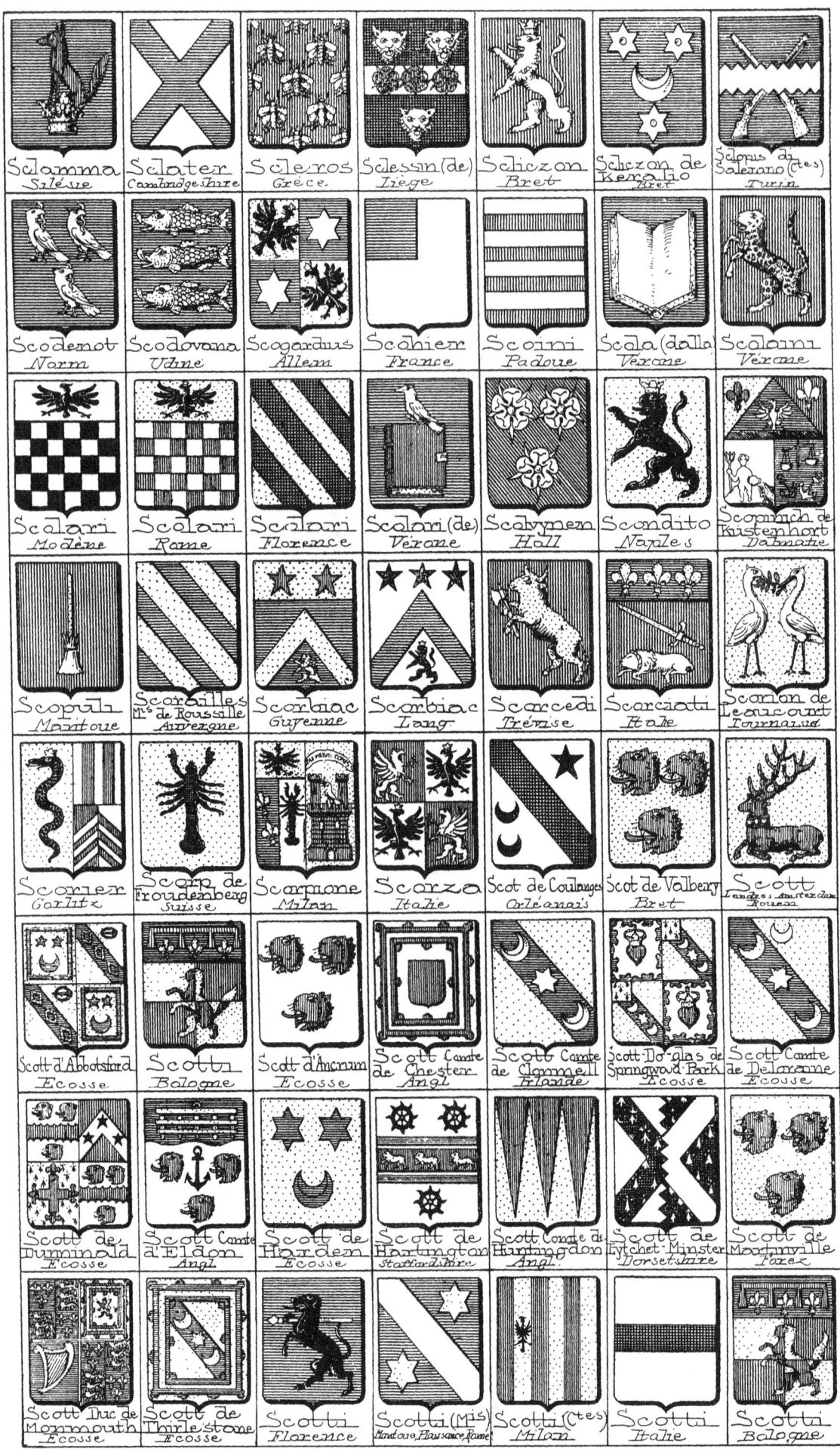

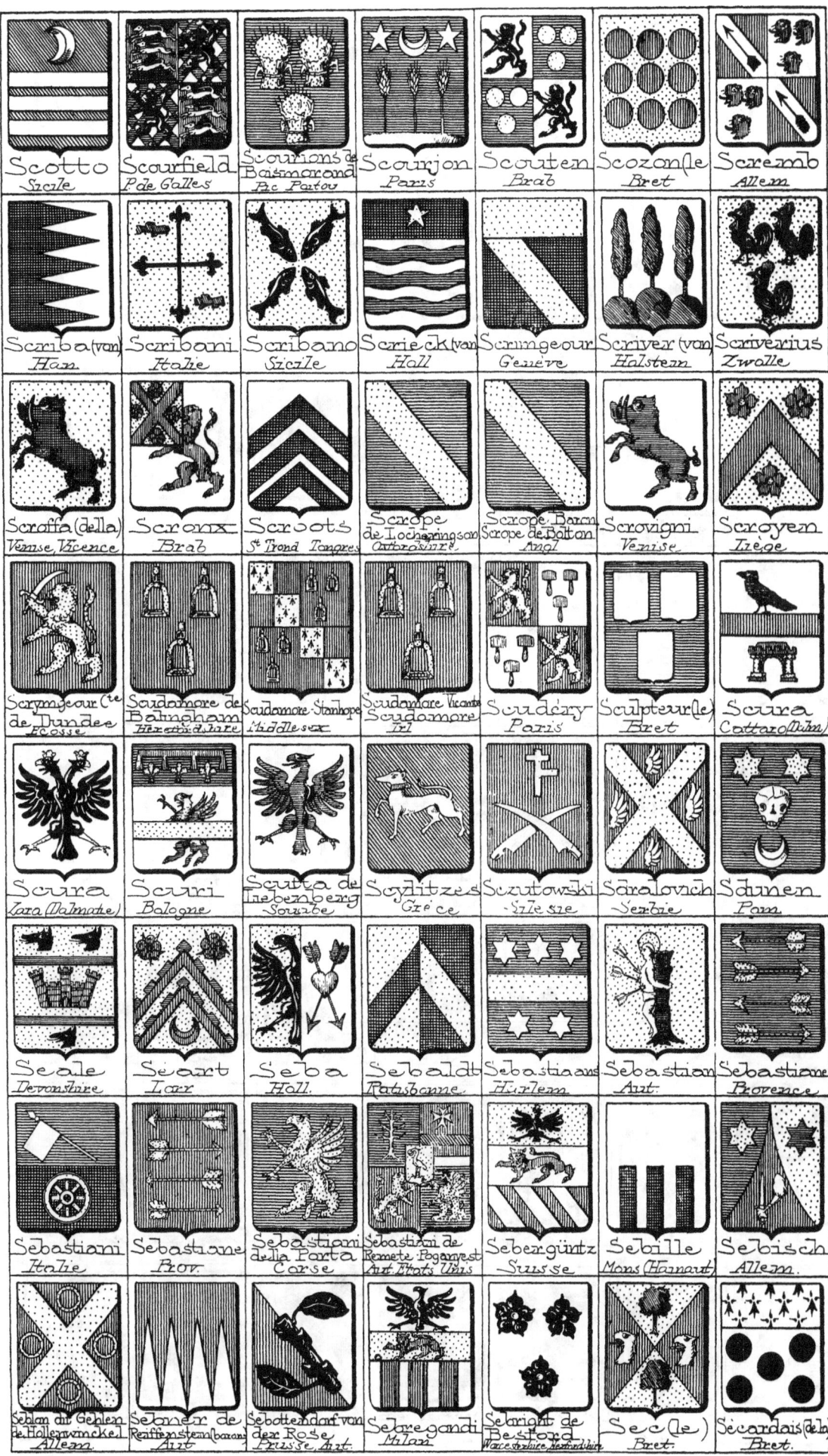

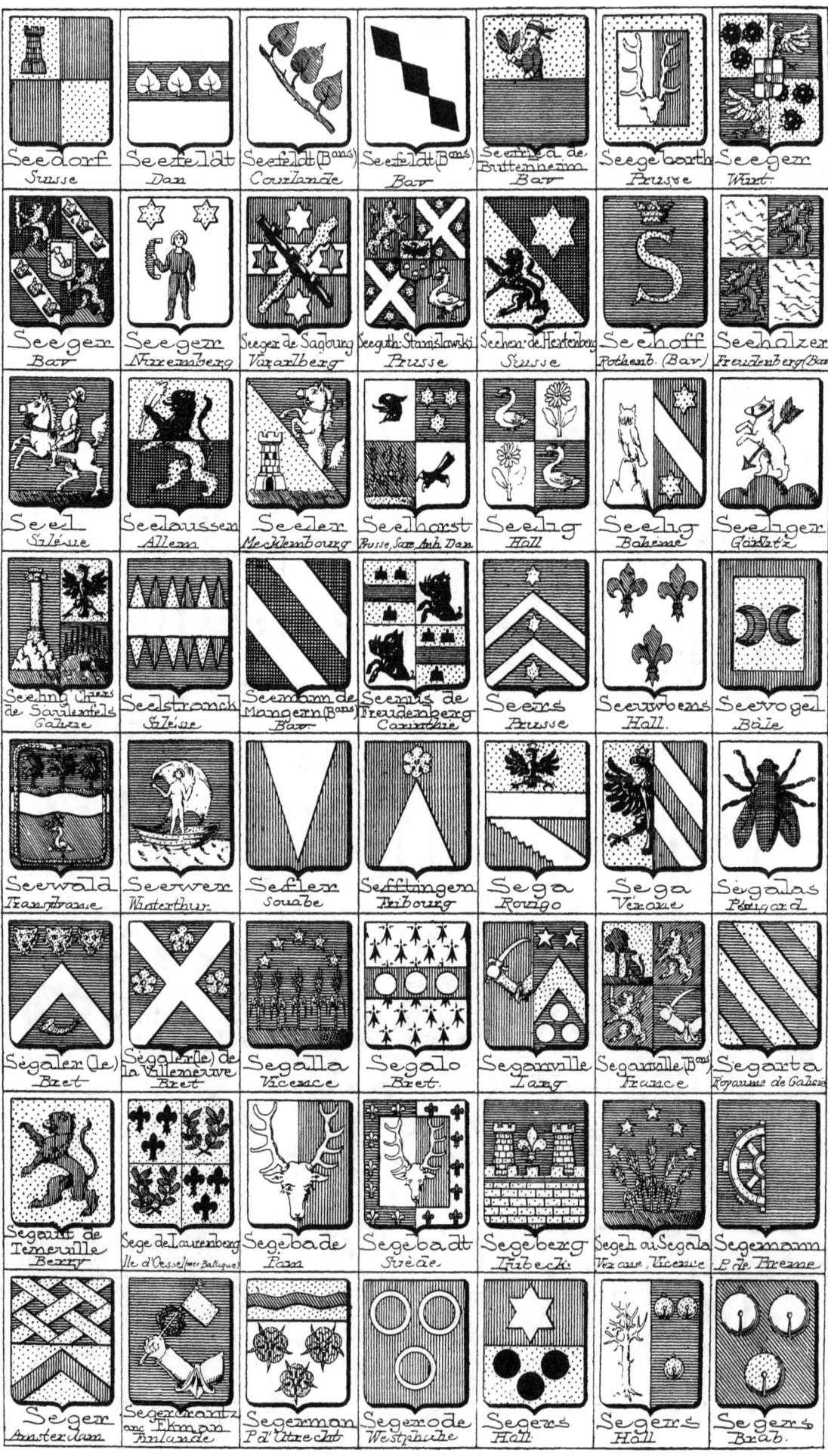

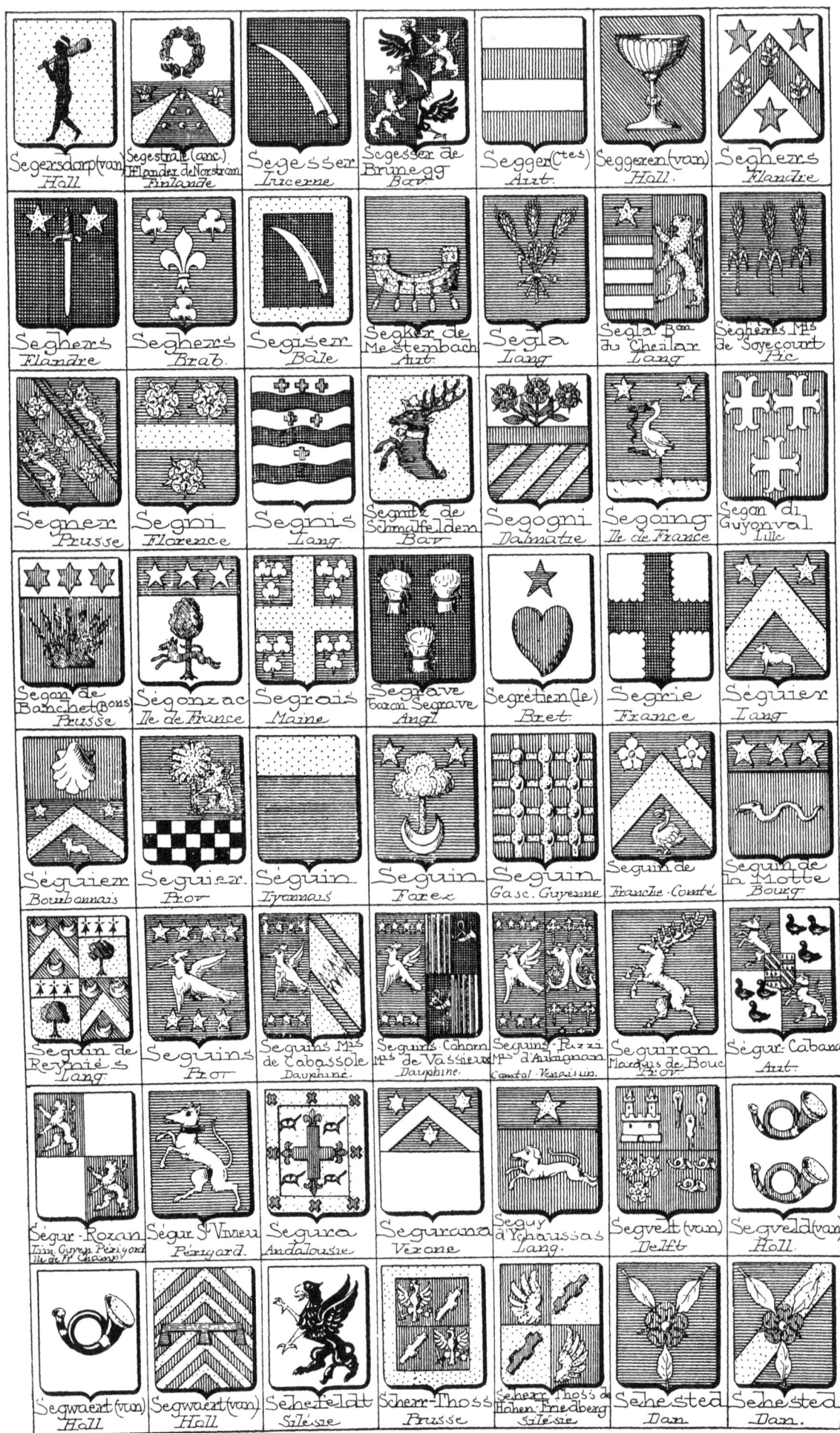

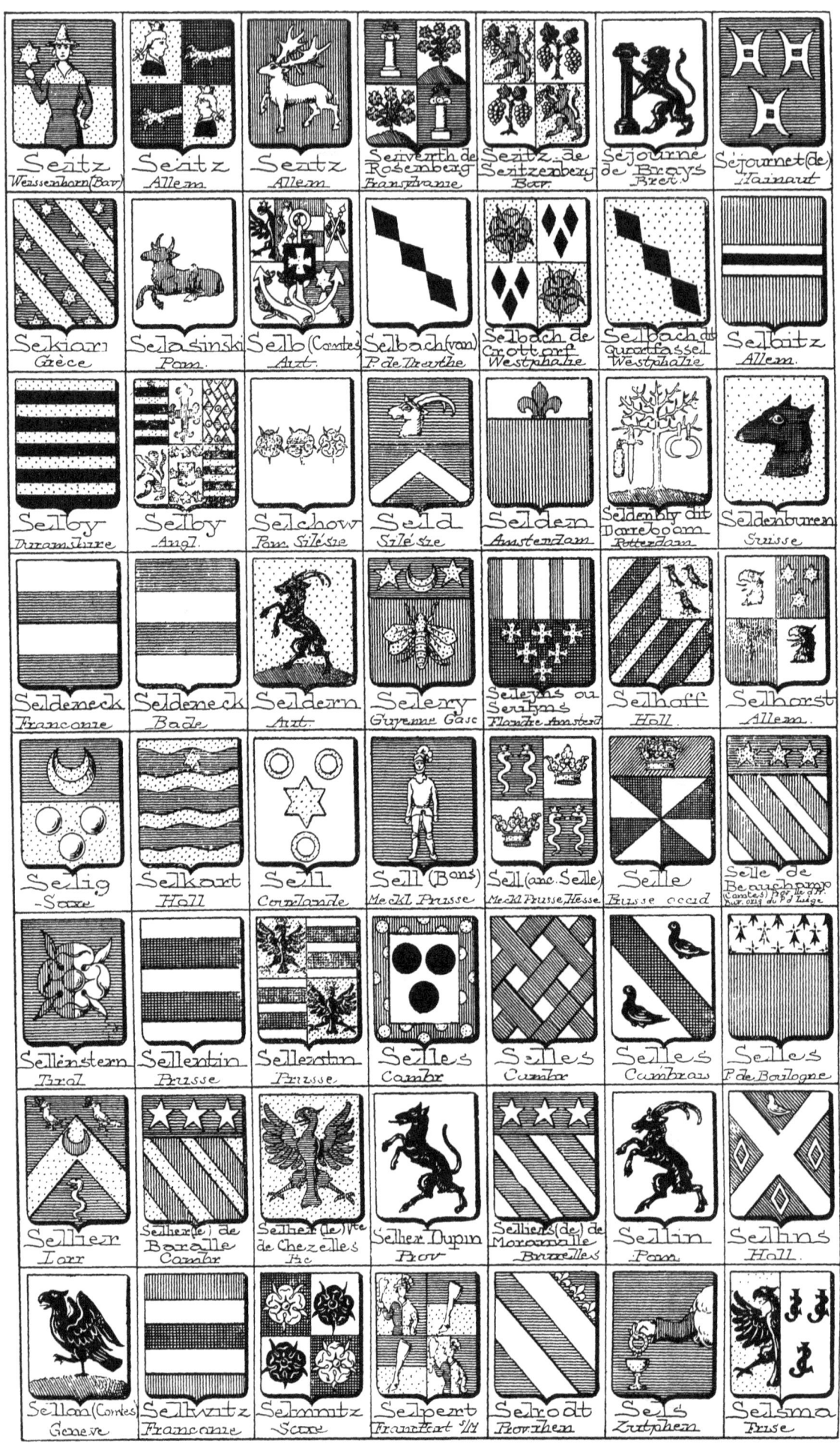

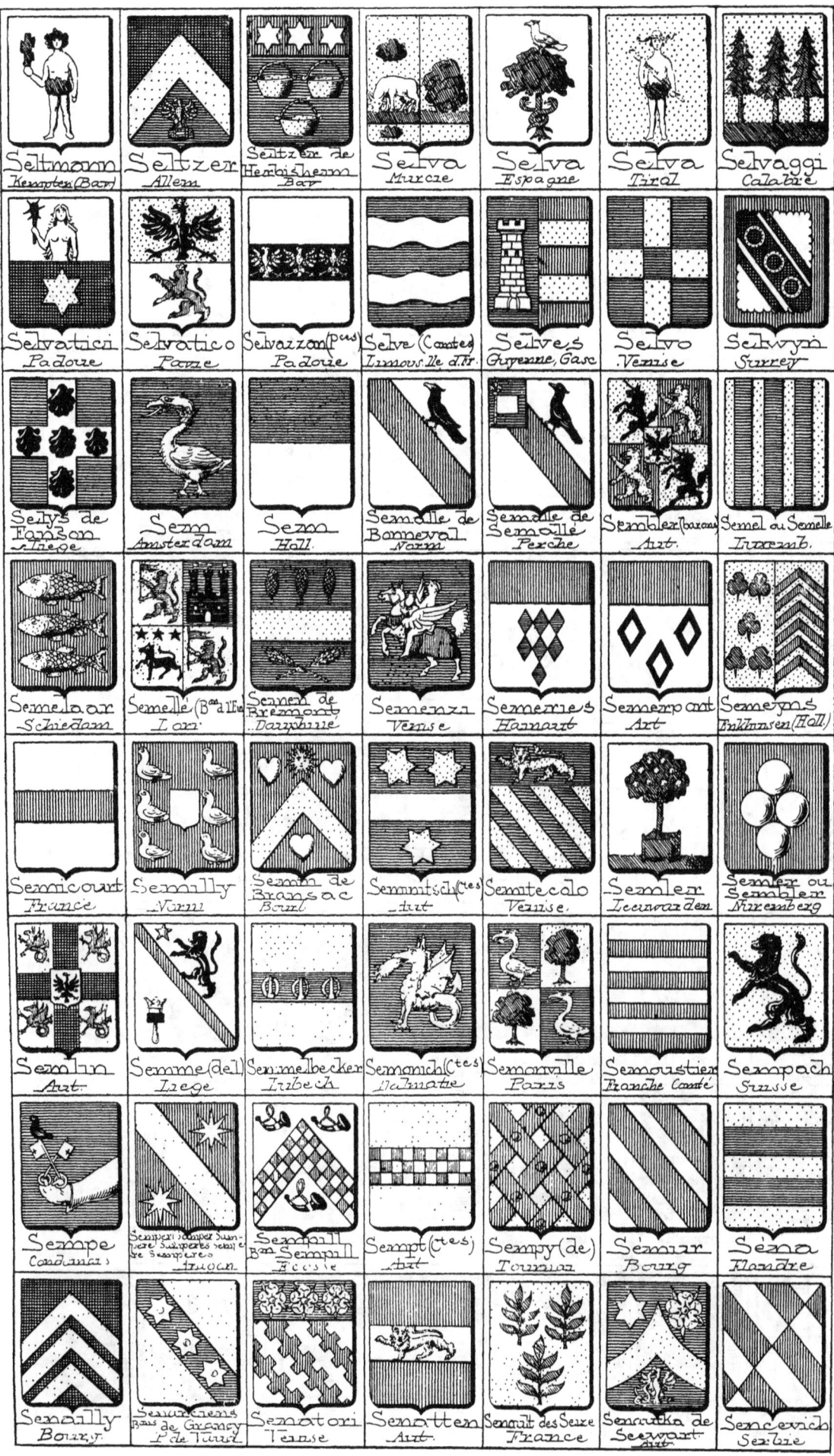

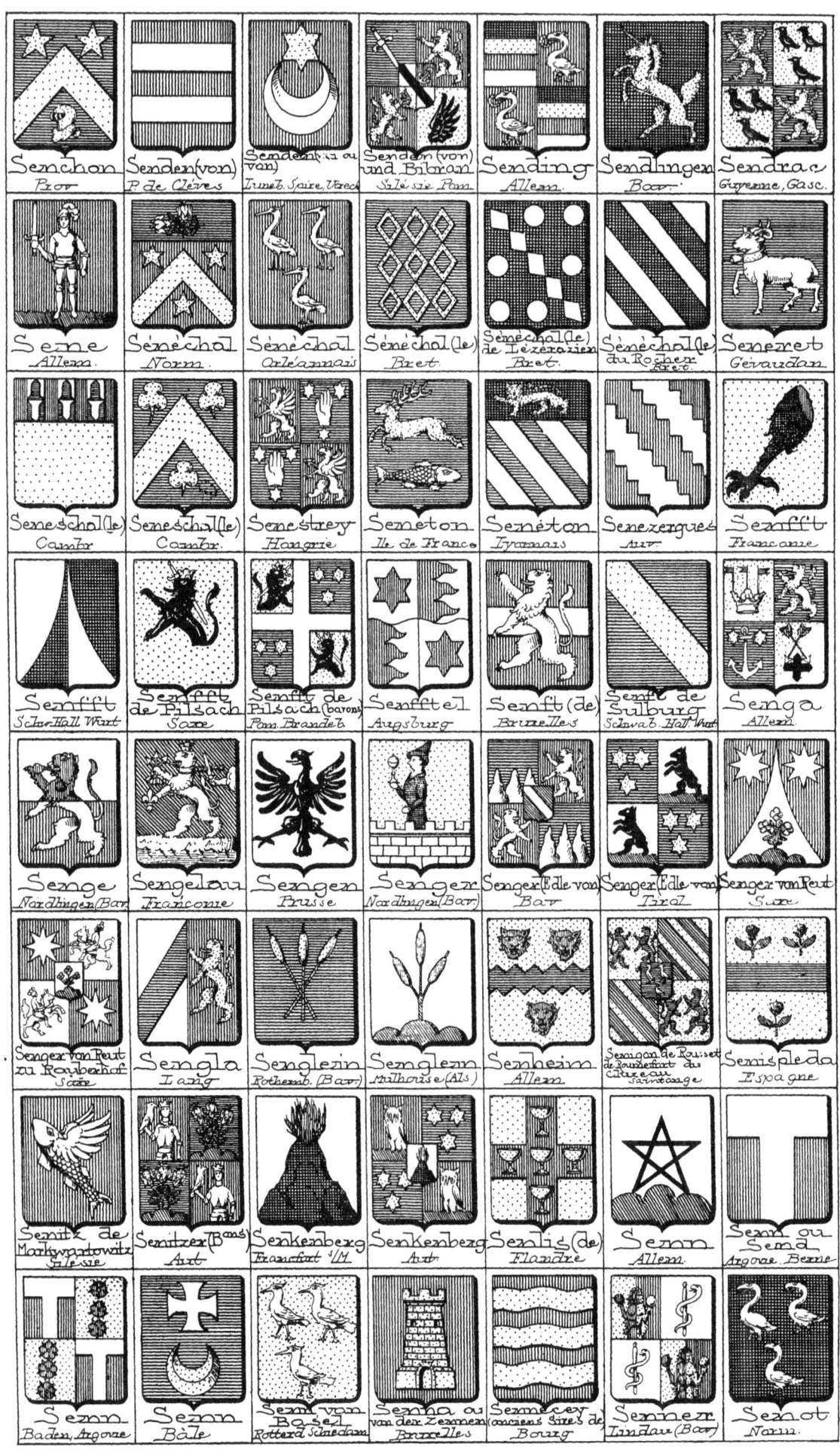

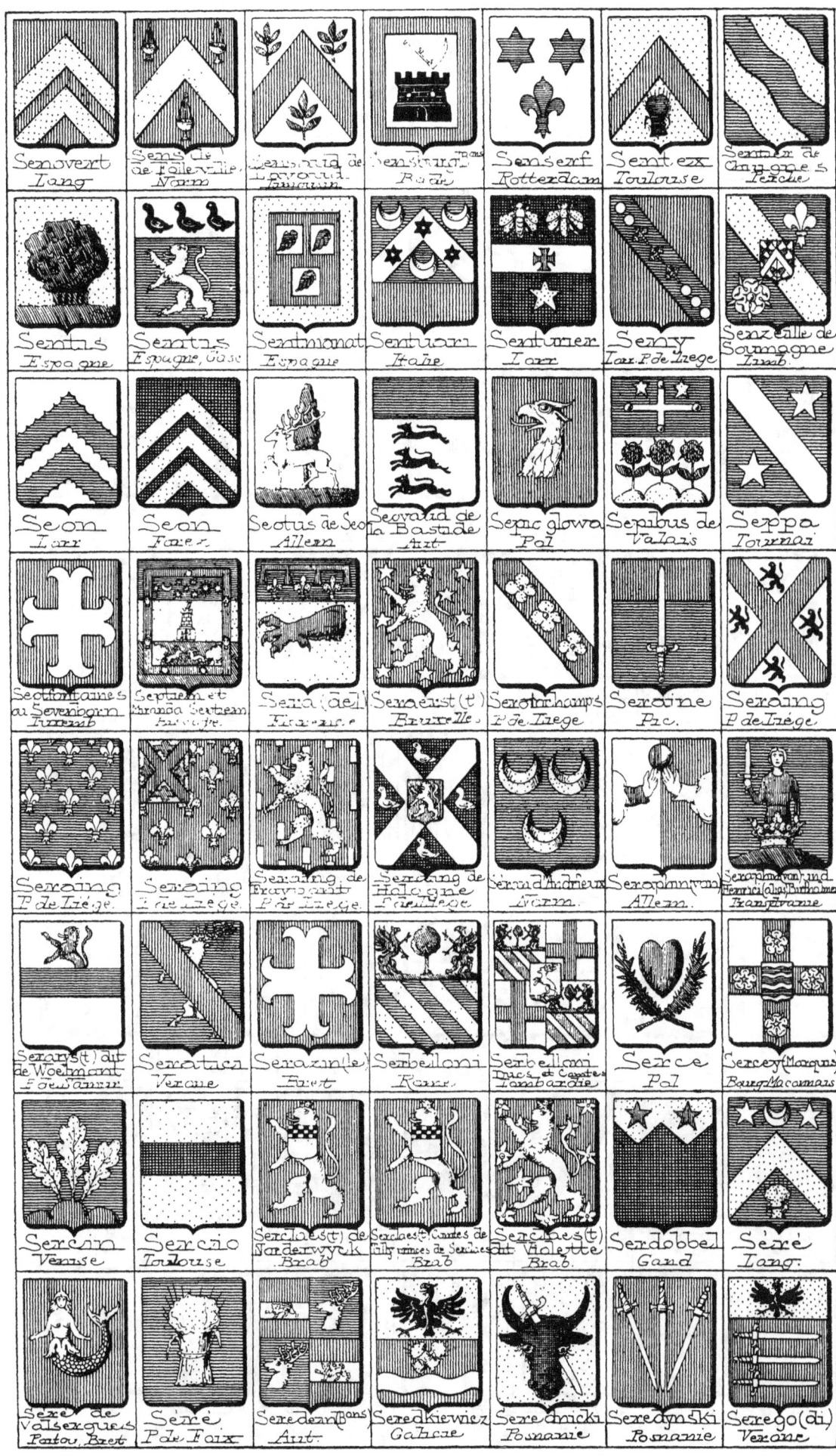

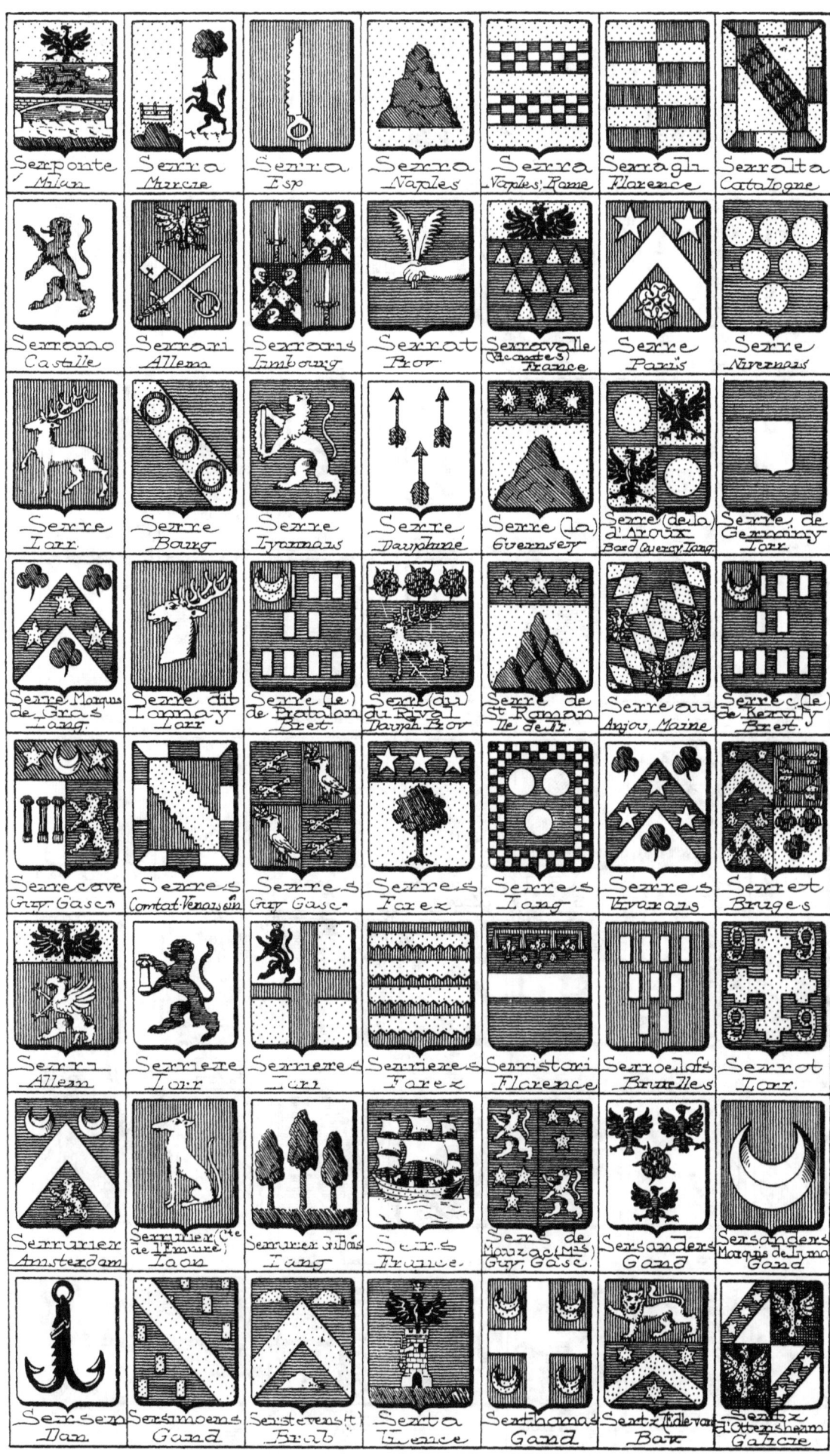

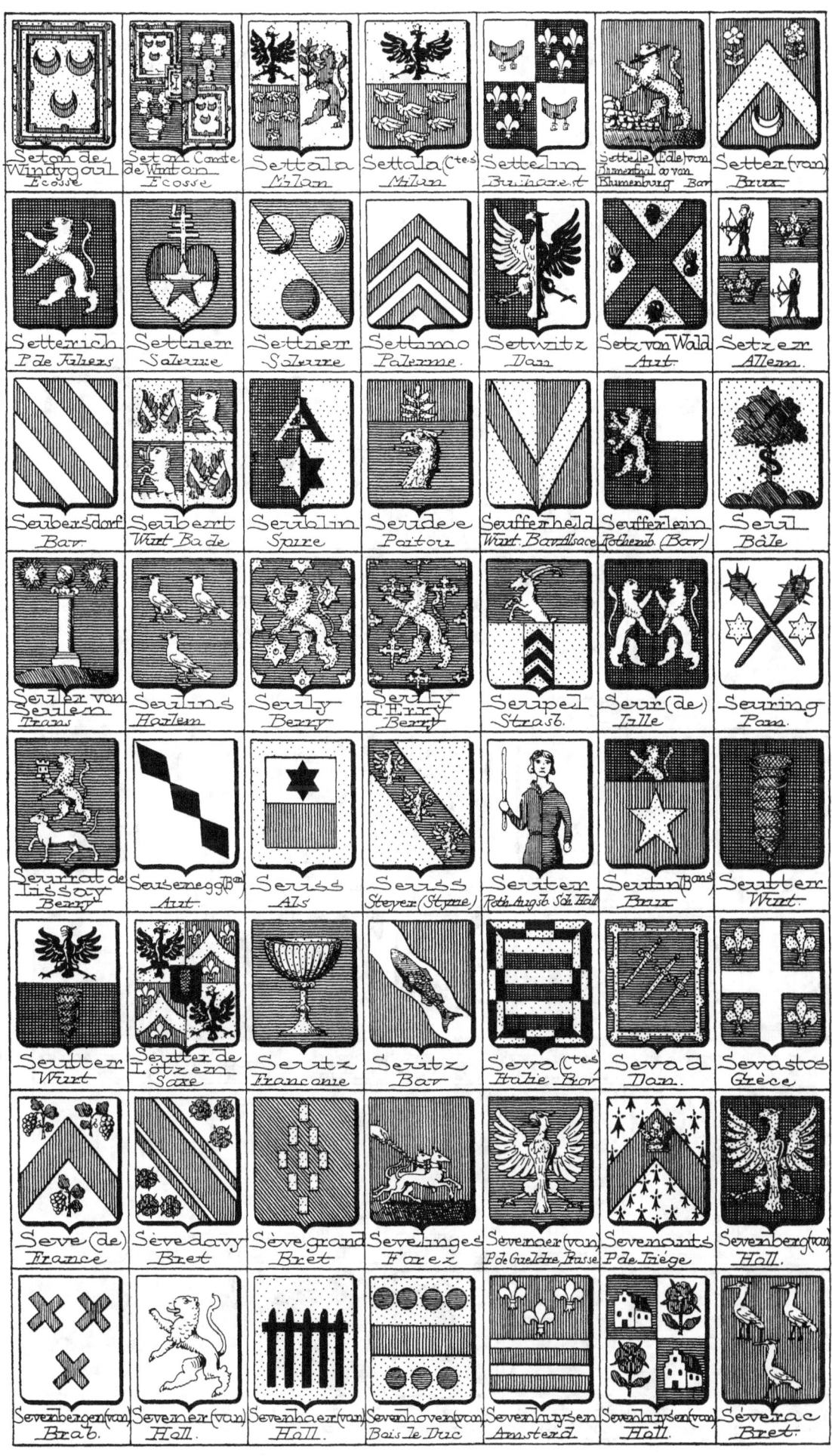

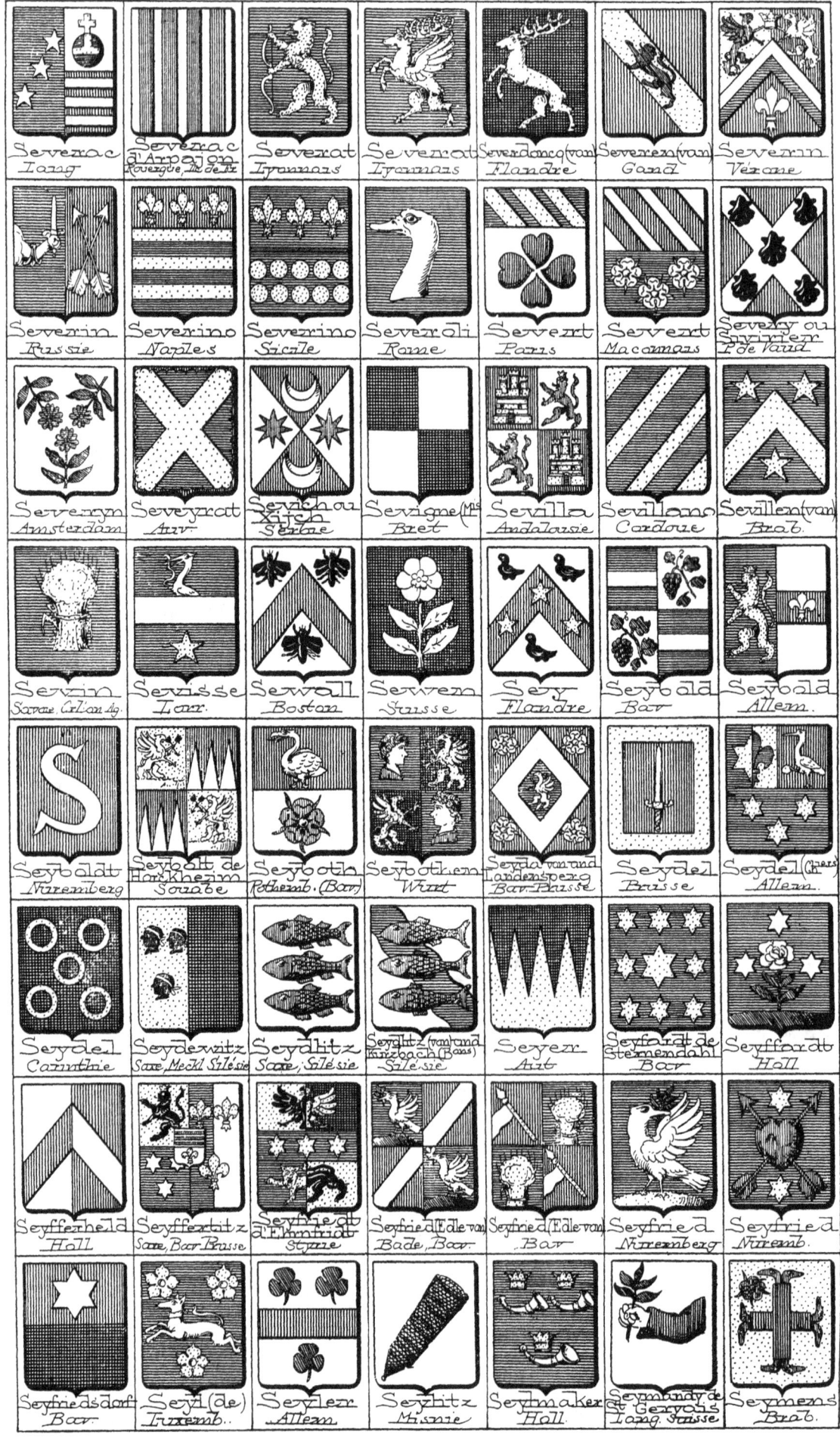

PL. CCCV

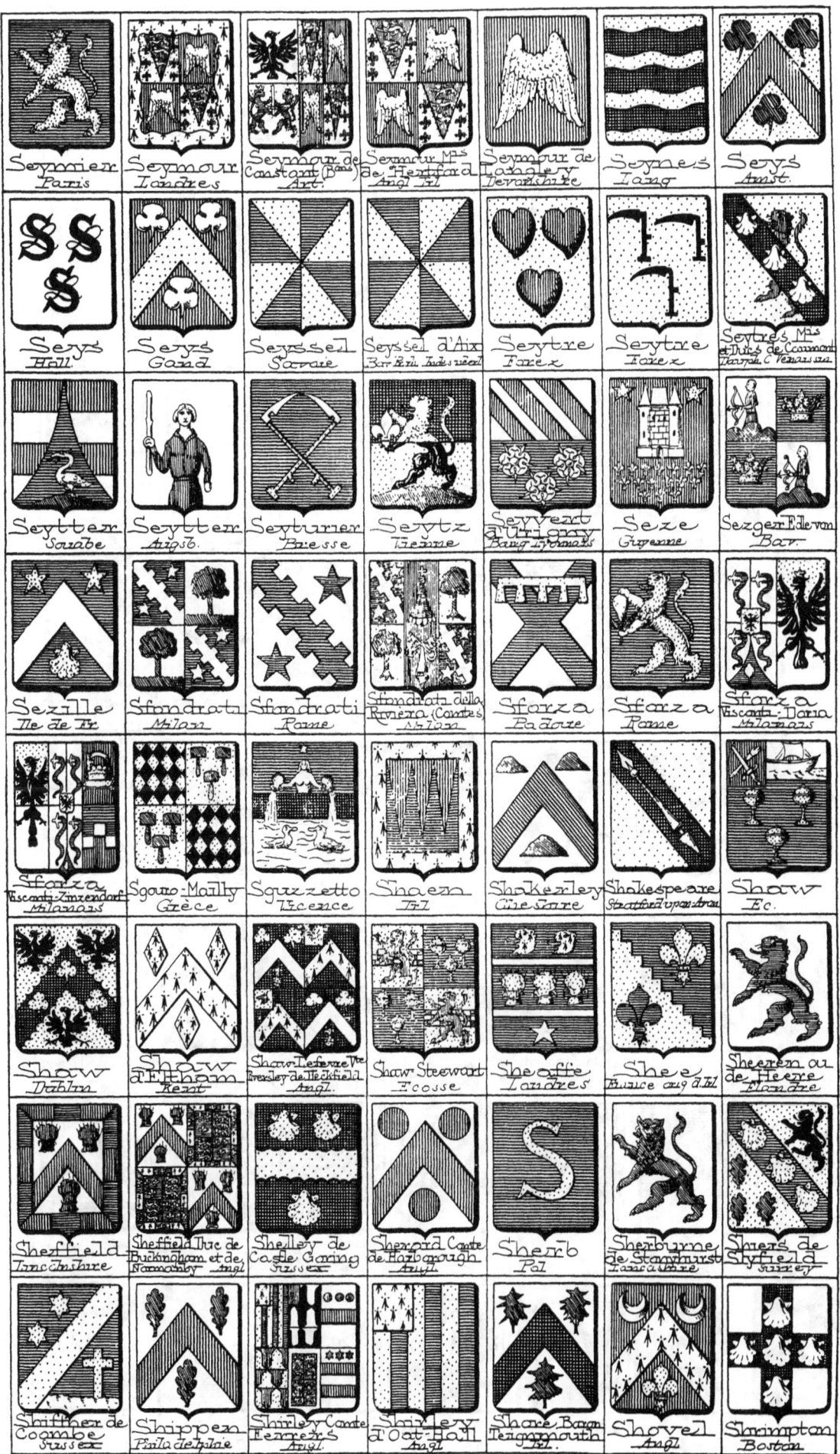

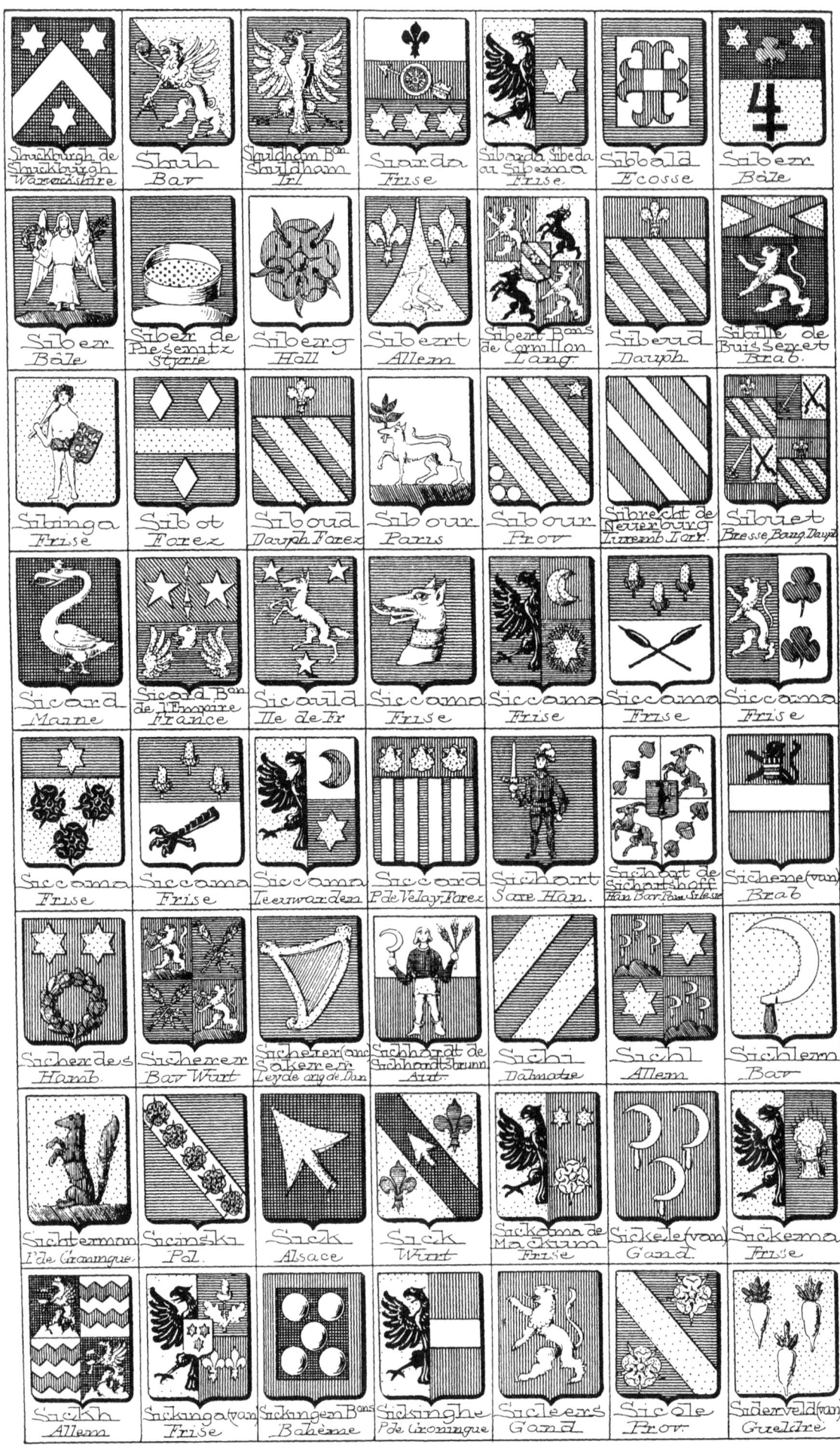

PL. CCCVII

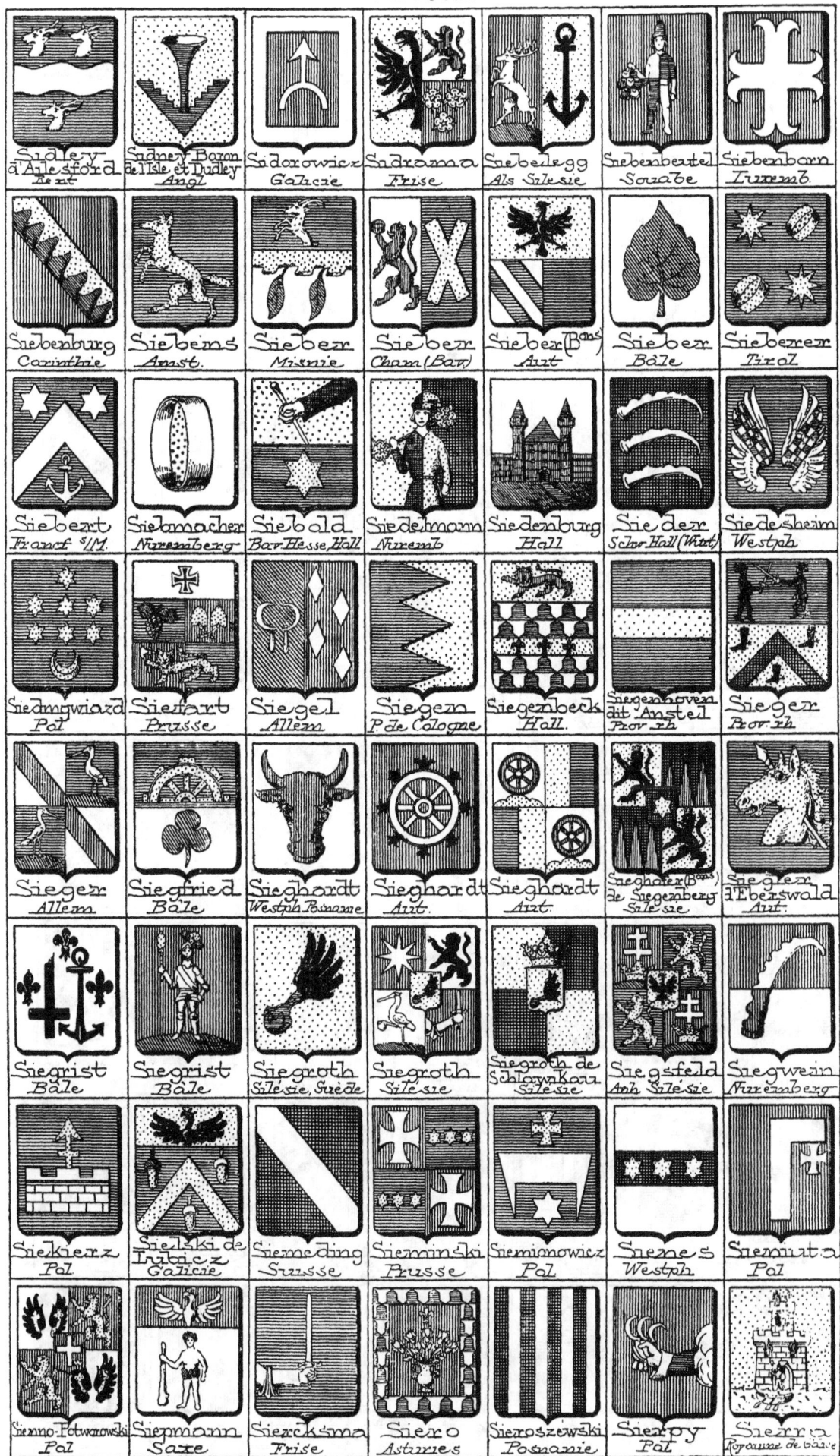

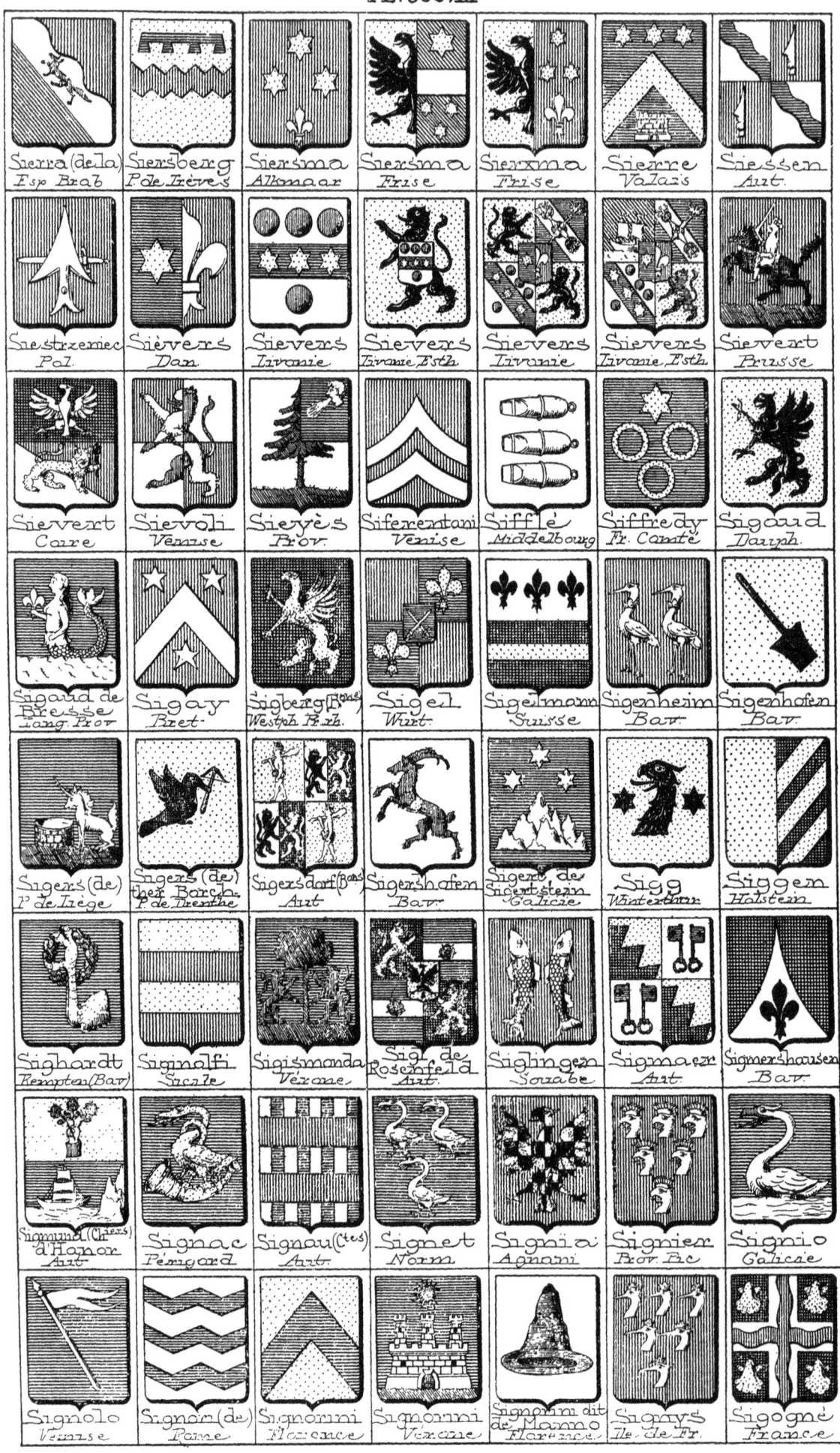

PL. CCCX

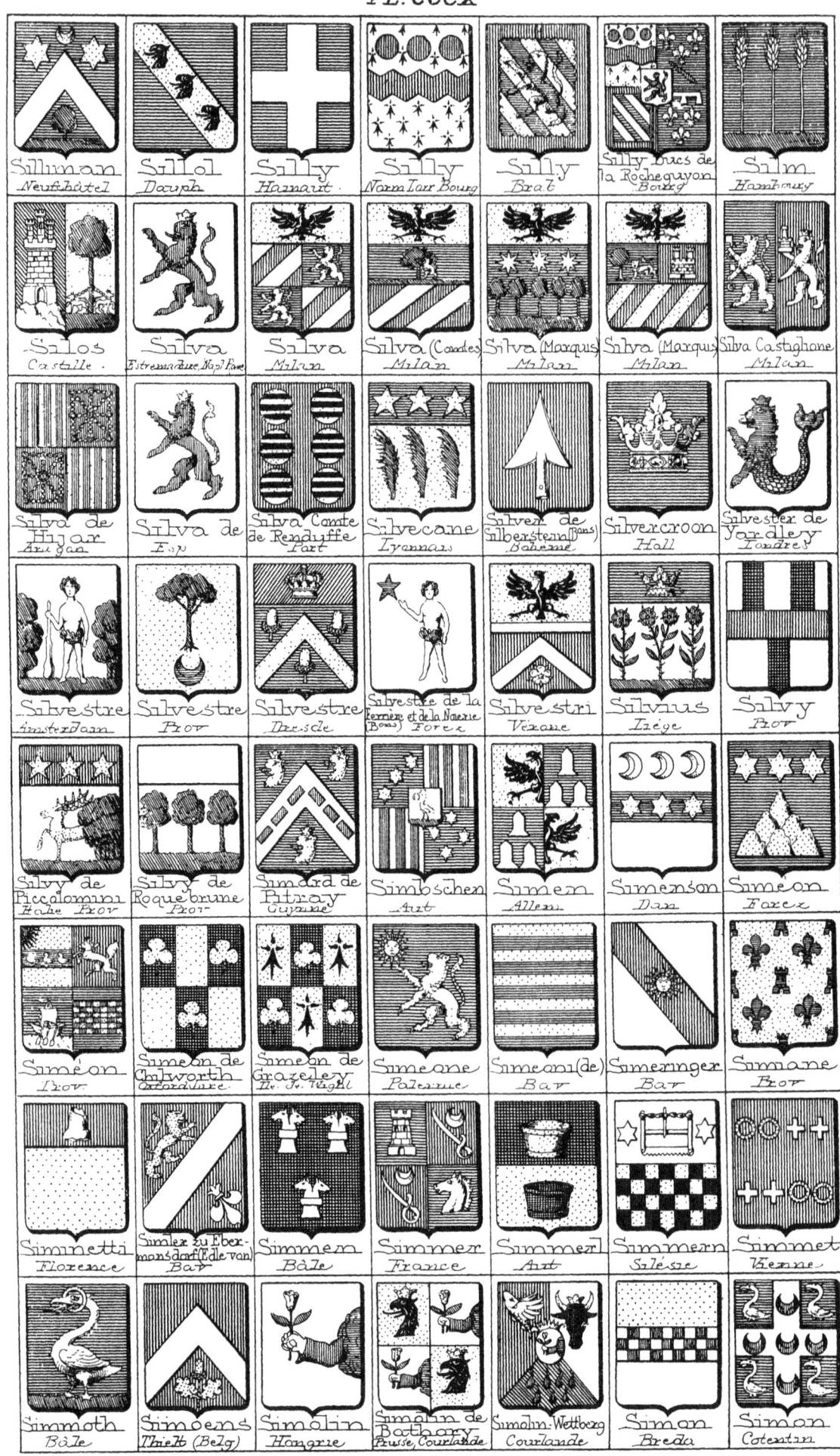

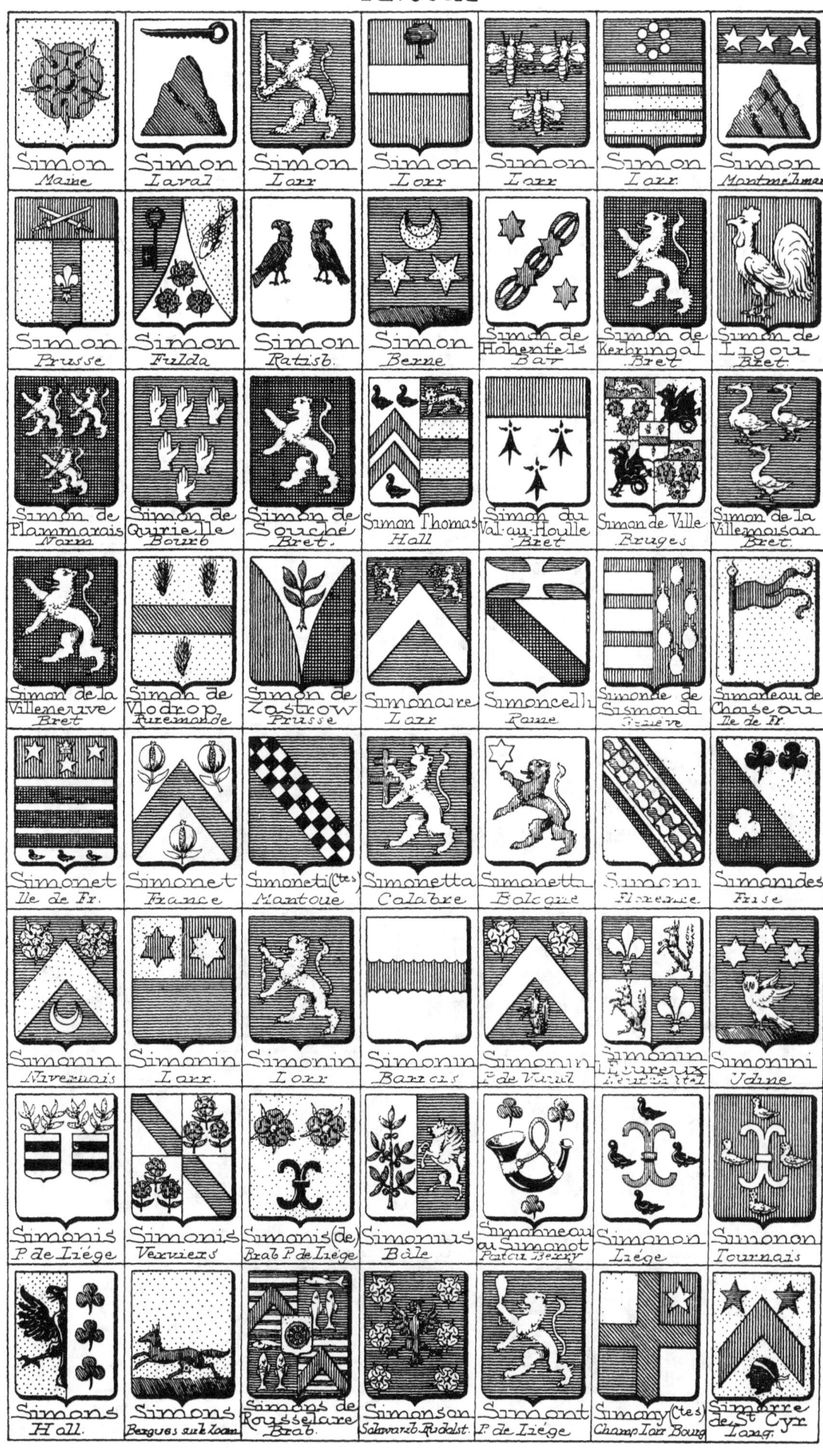

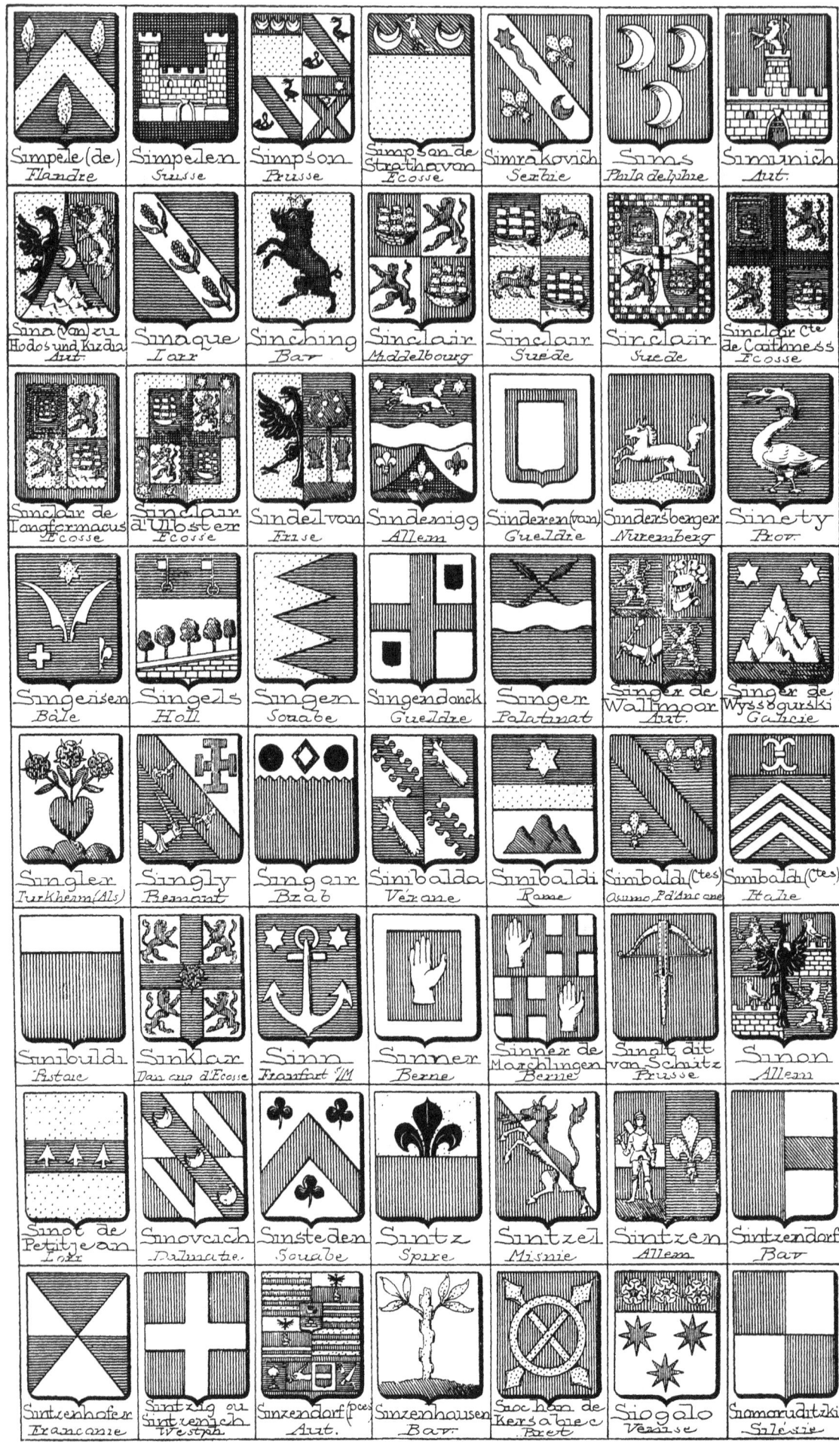

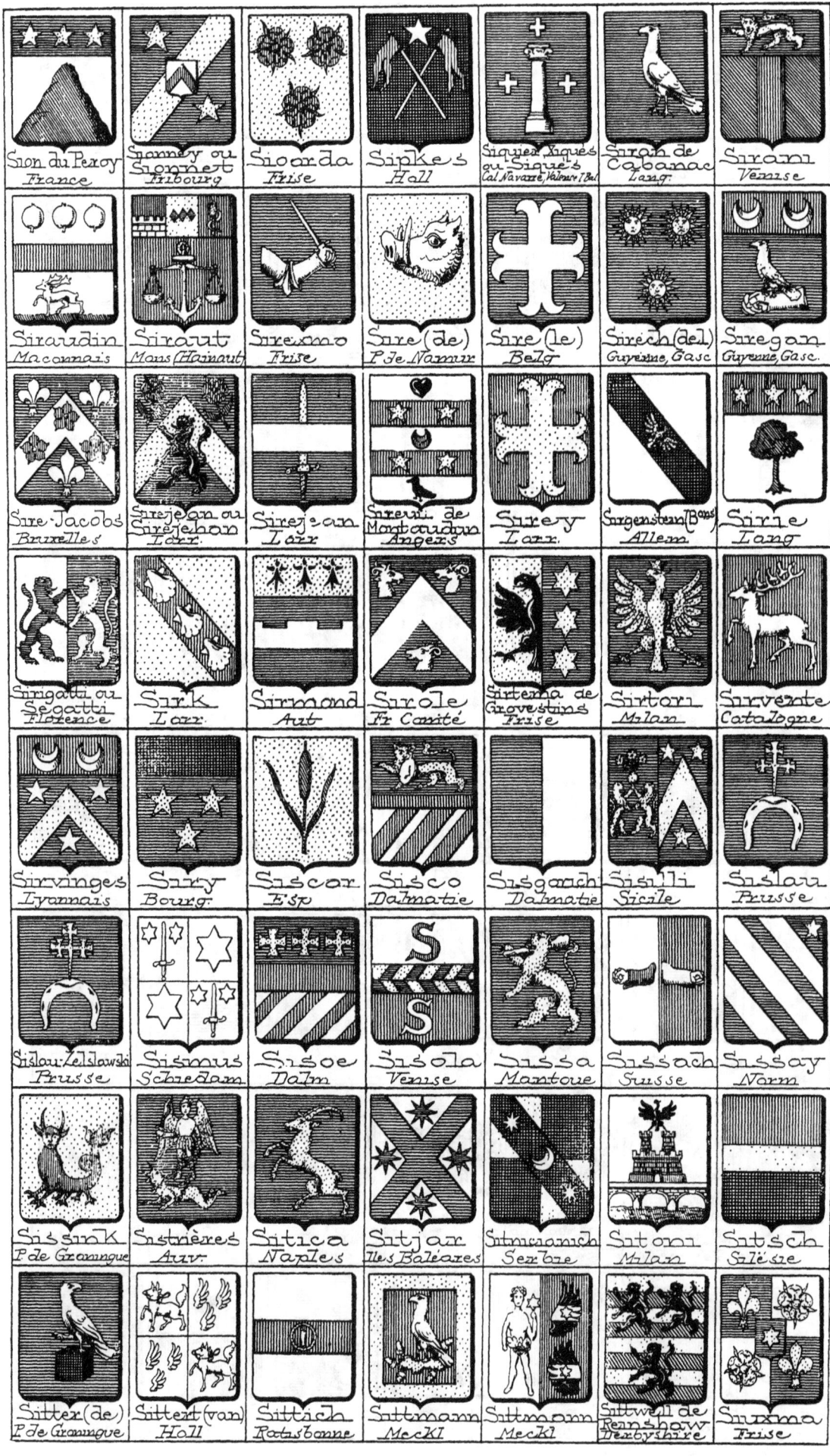

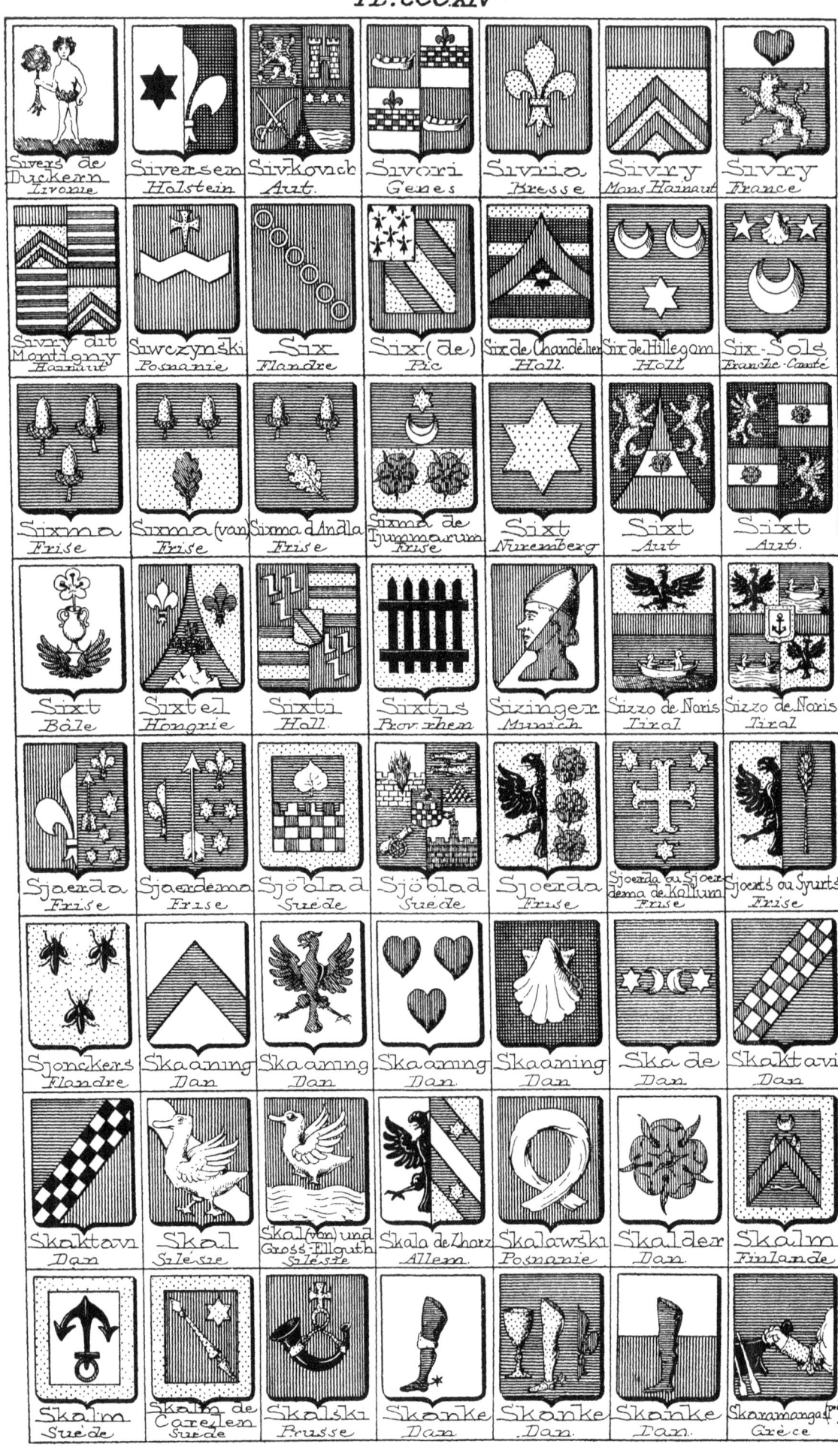

PL. CCCXV

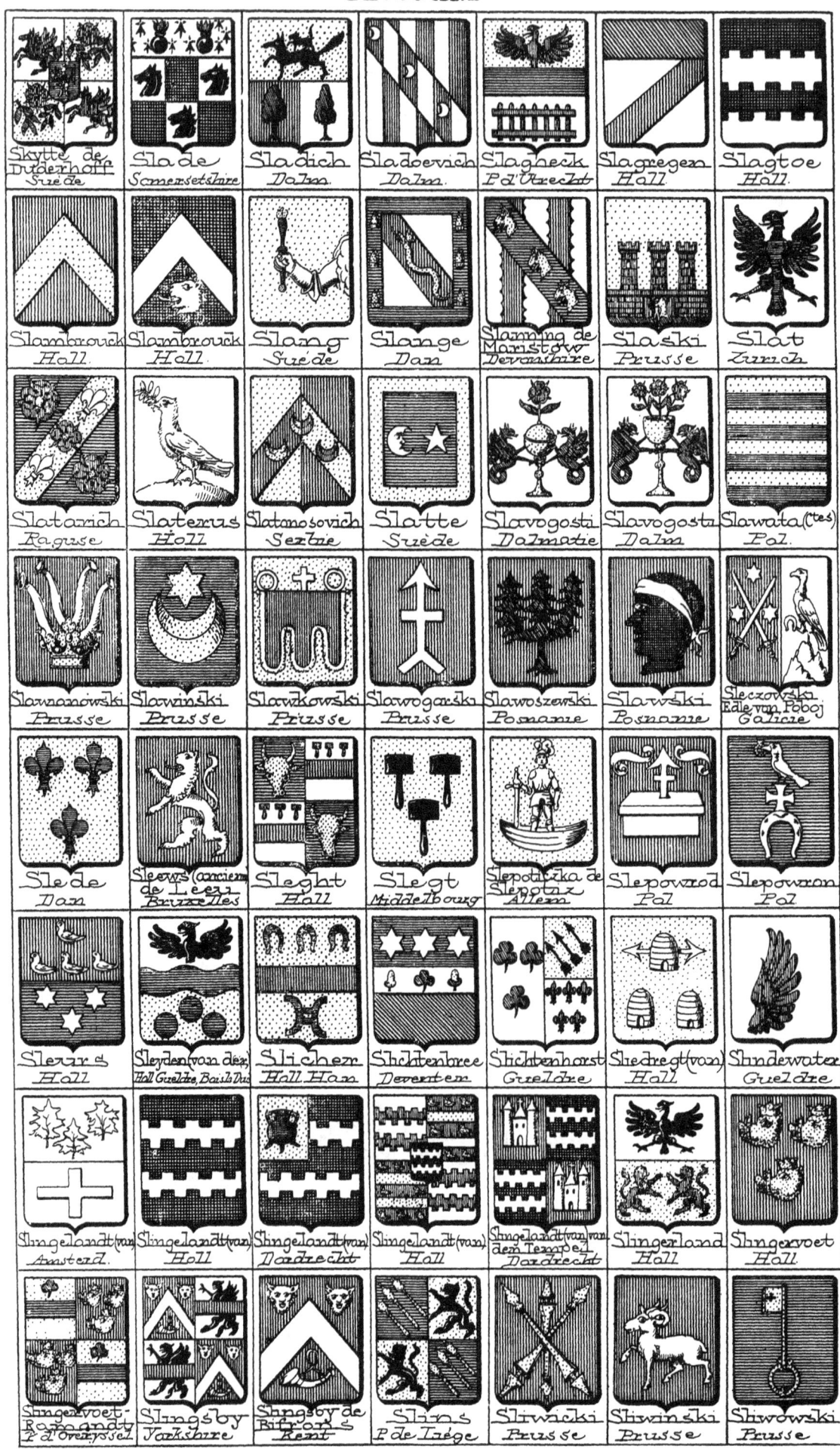

PL. CCCXVII

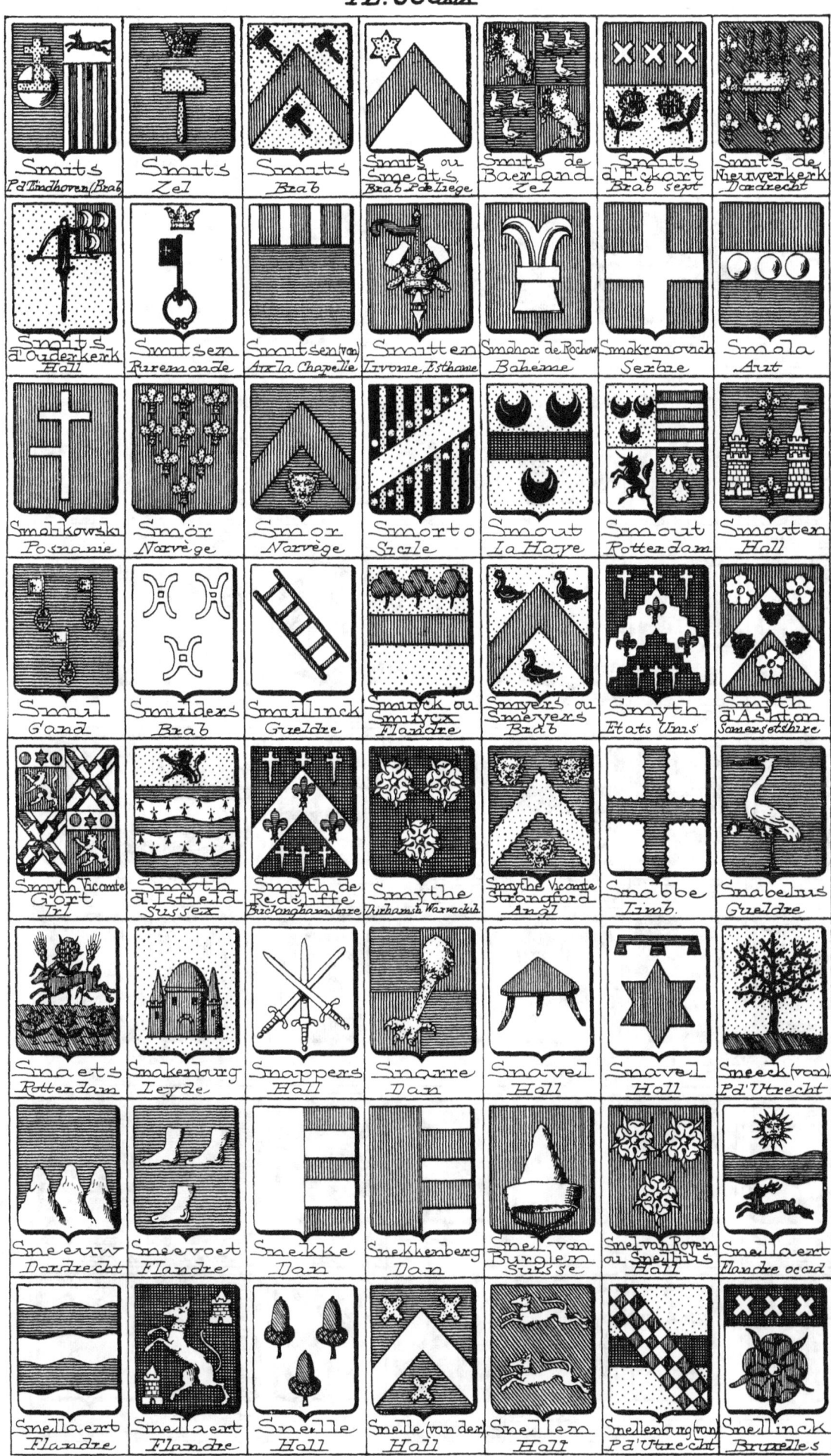

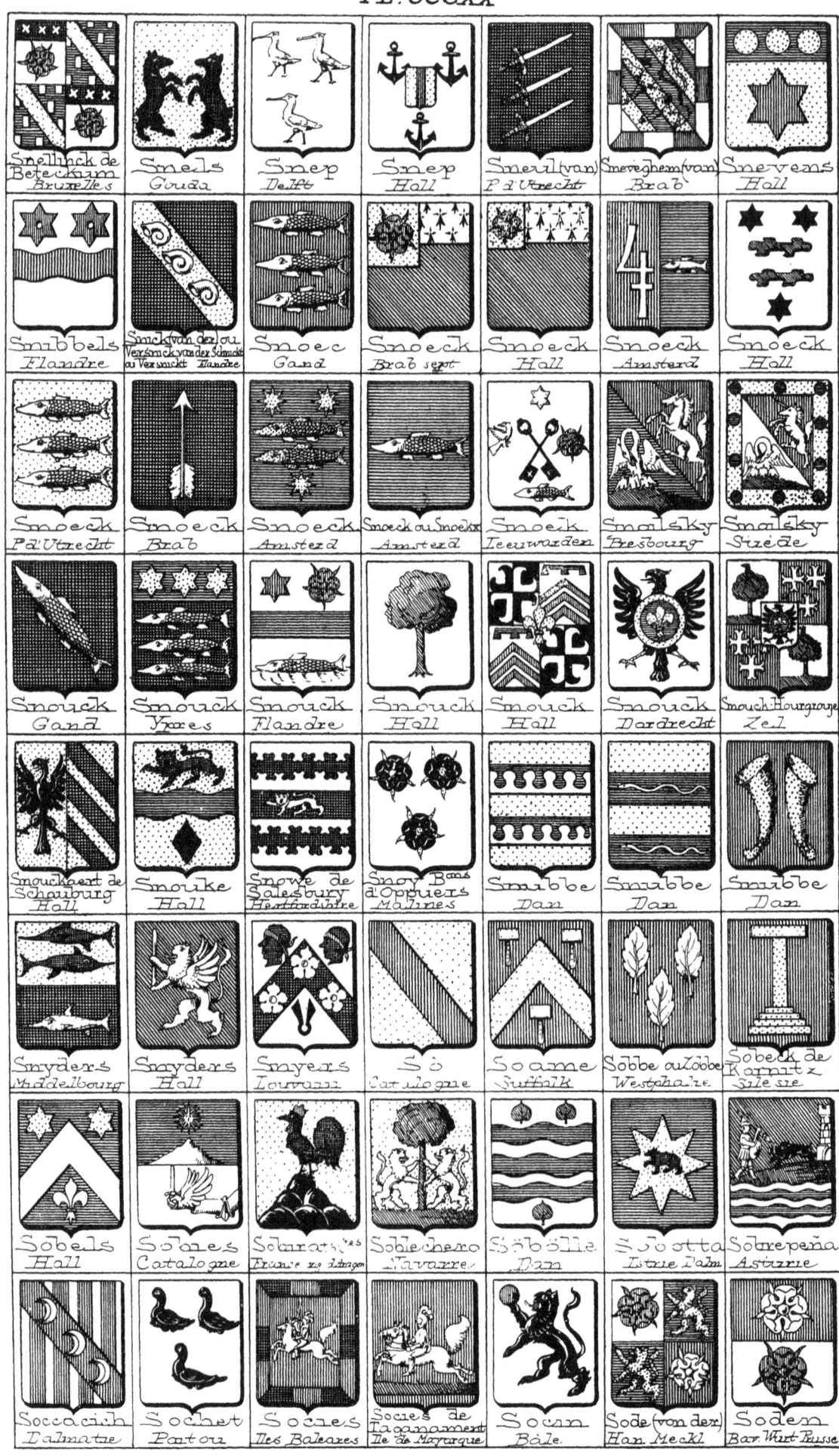

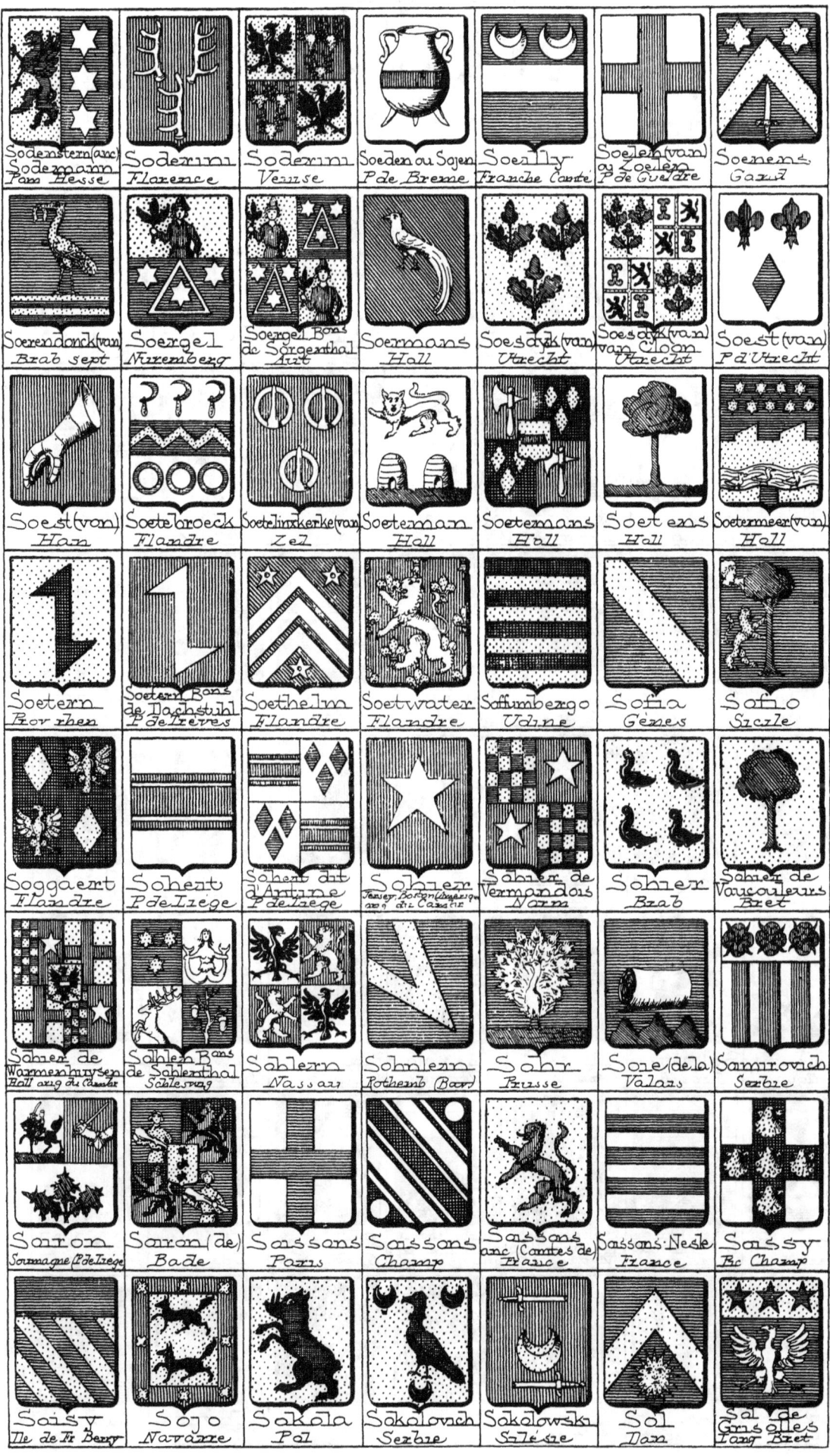

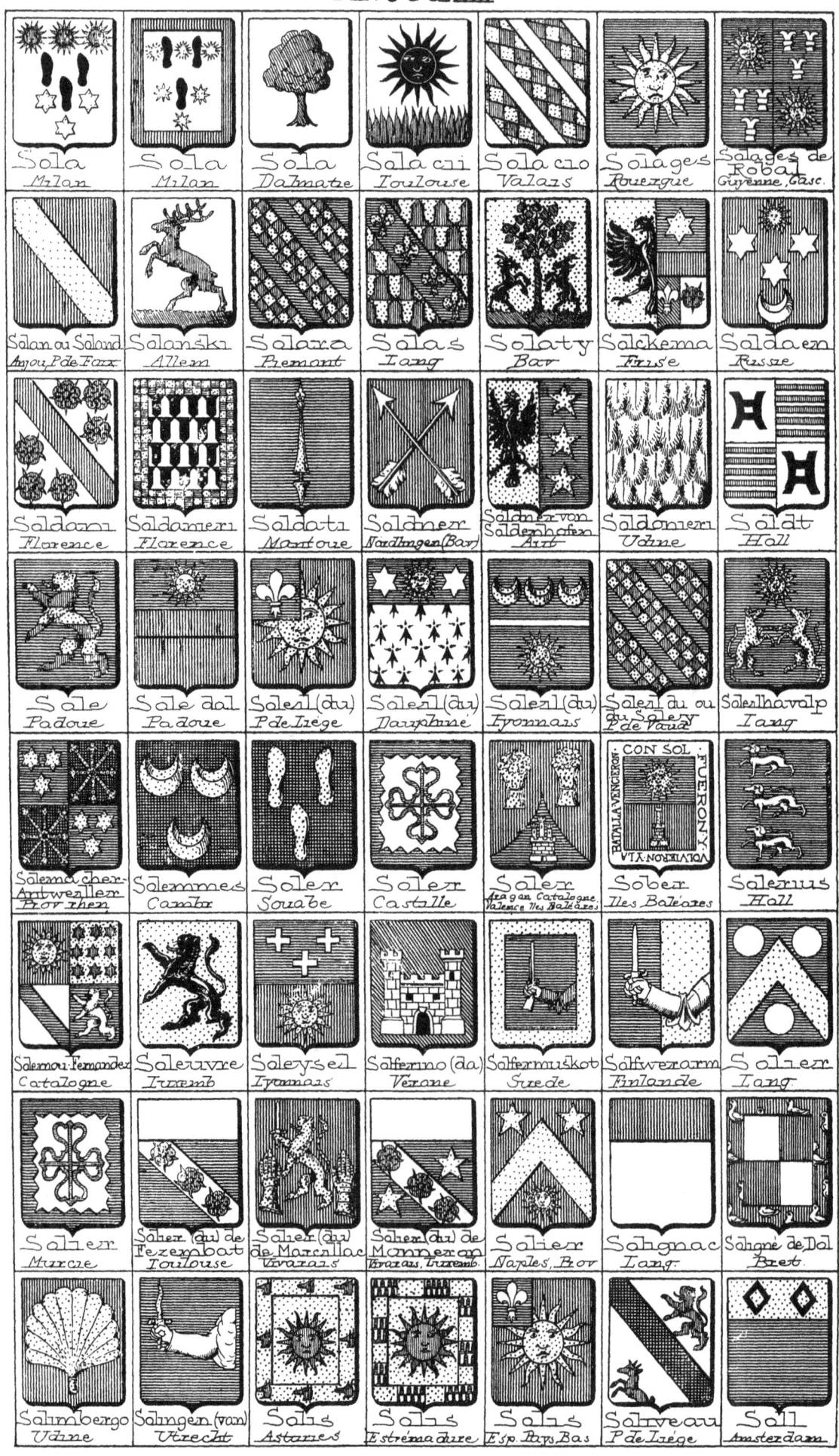

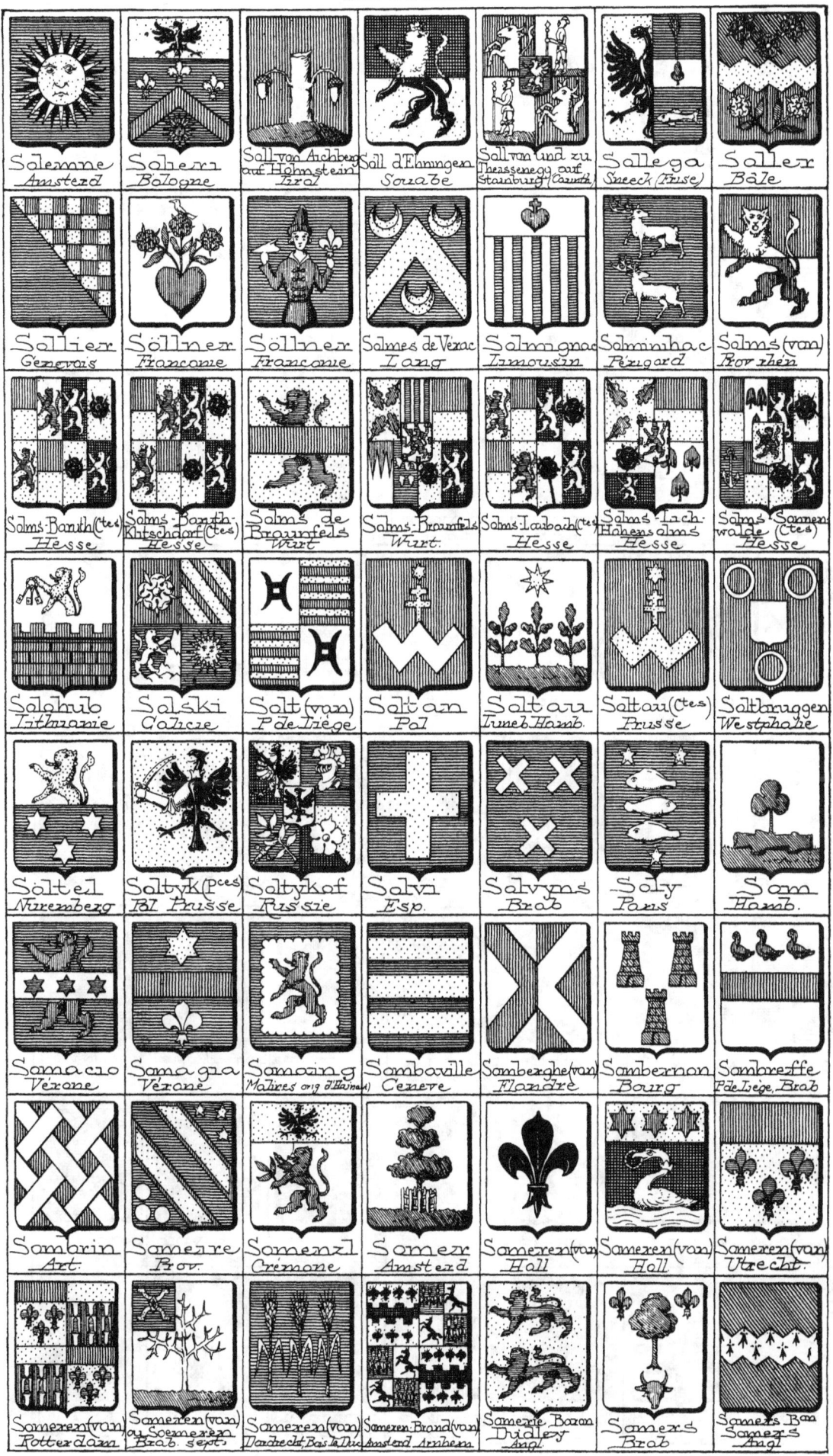

PL. CCCXXIII

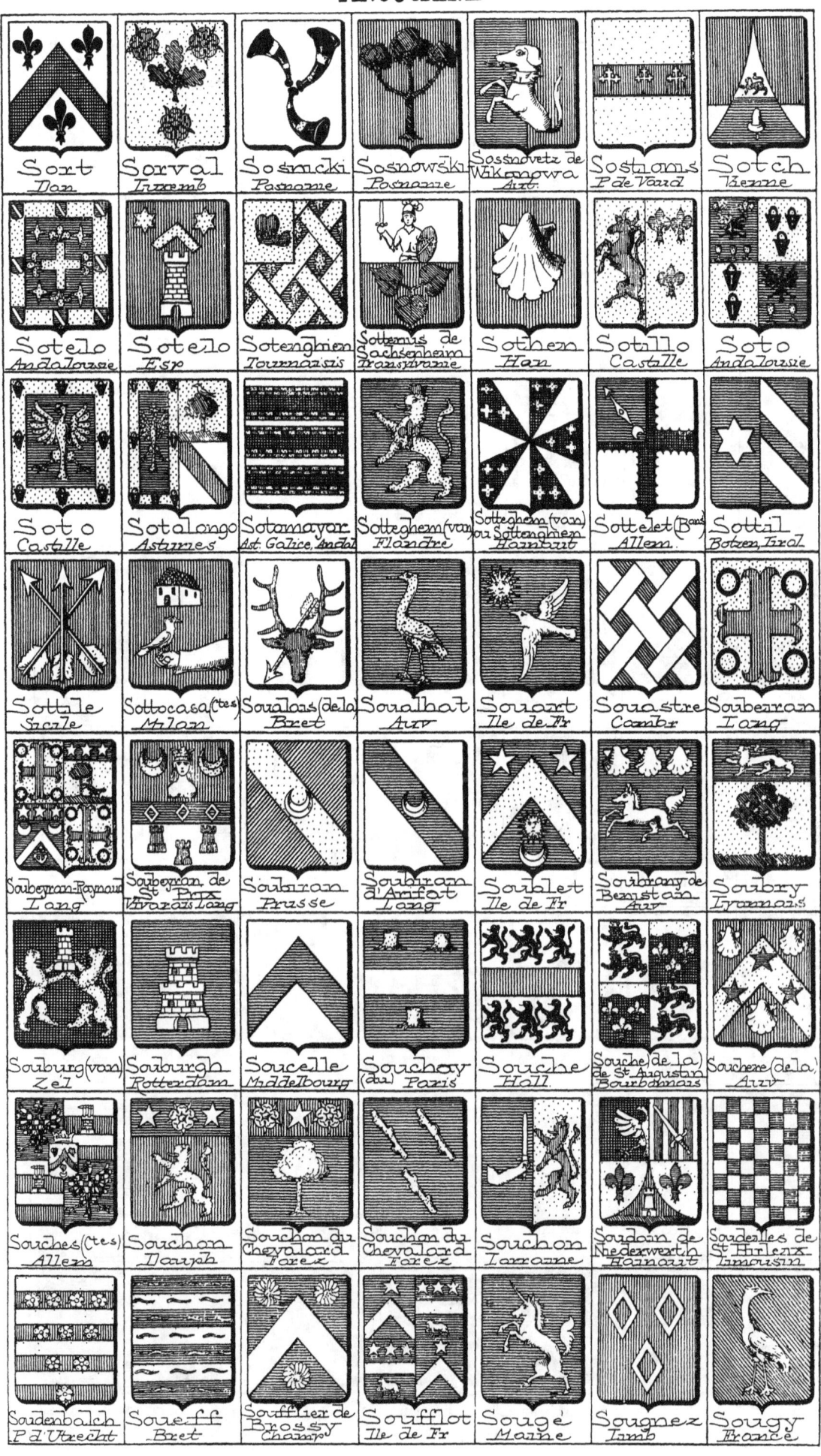

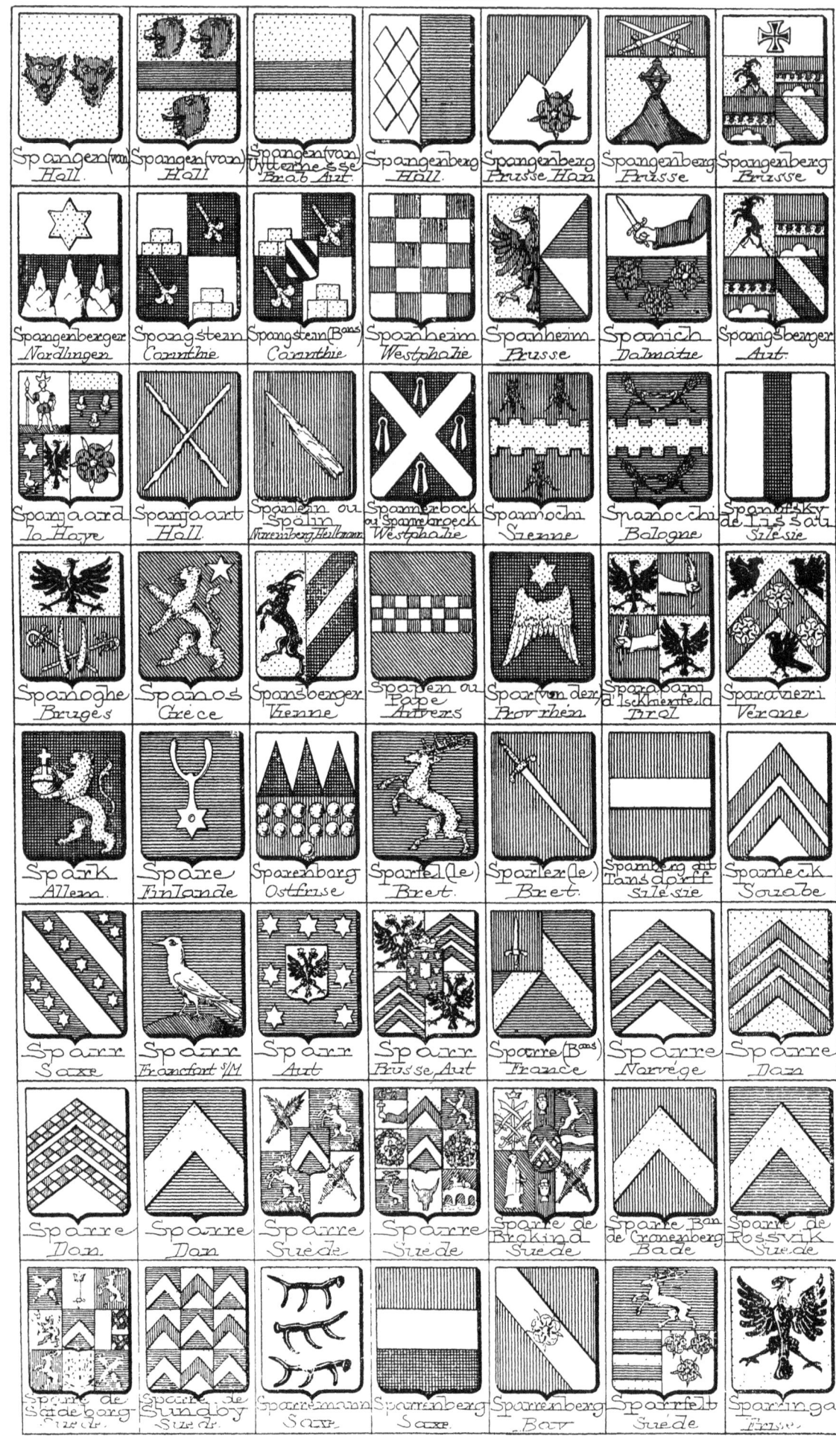

PL. CCCXXXI

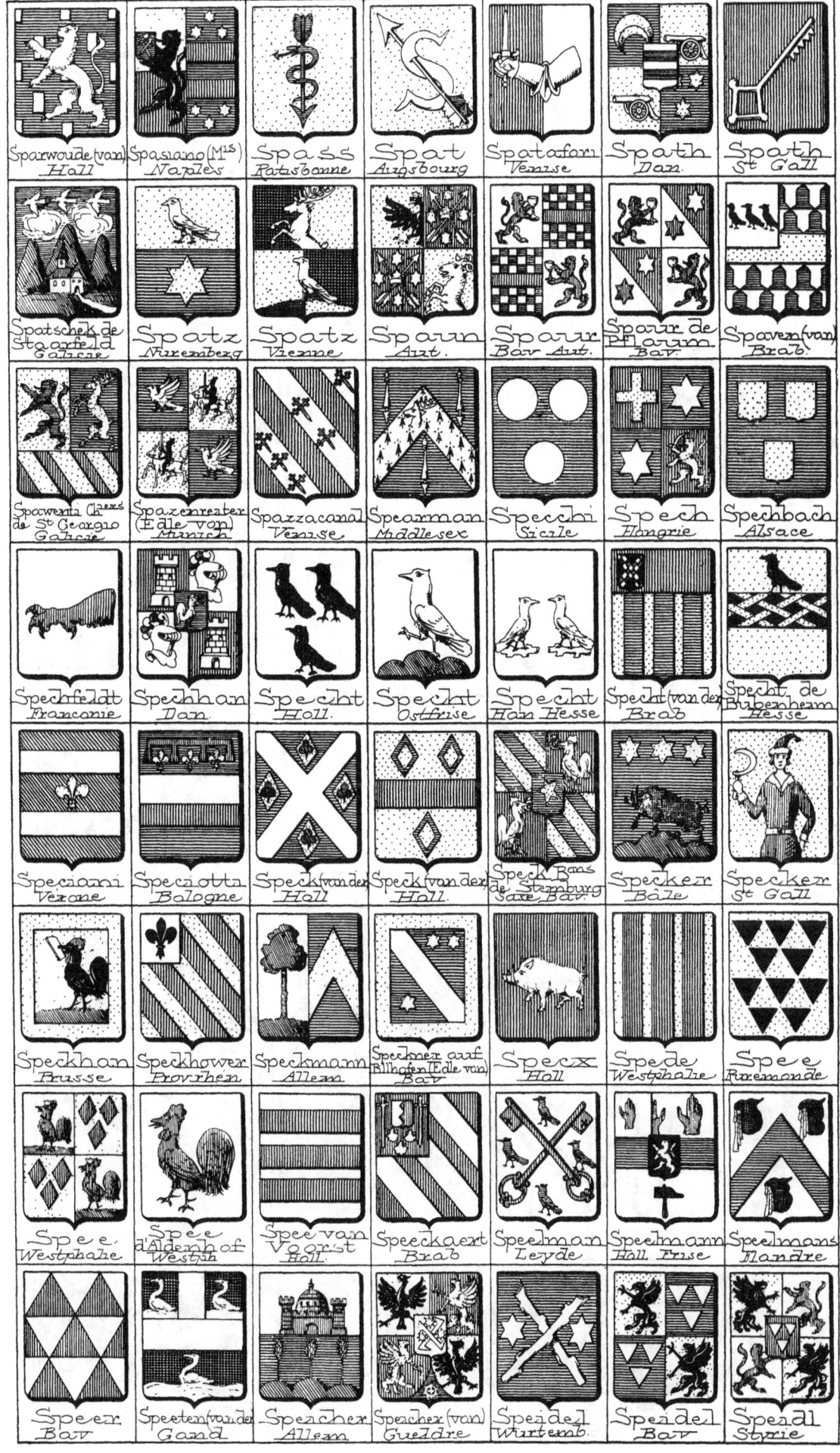

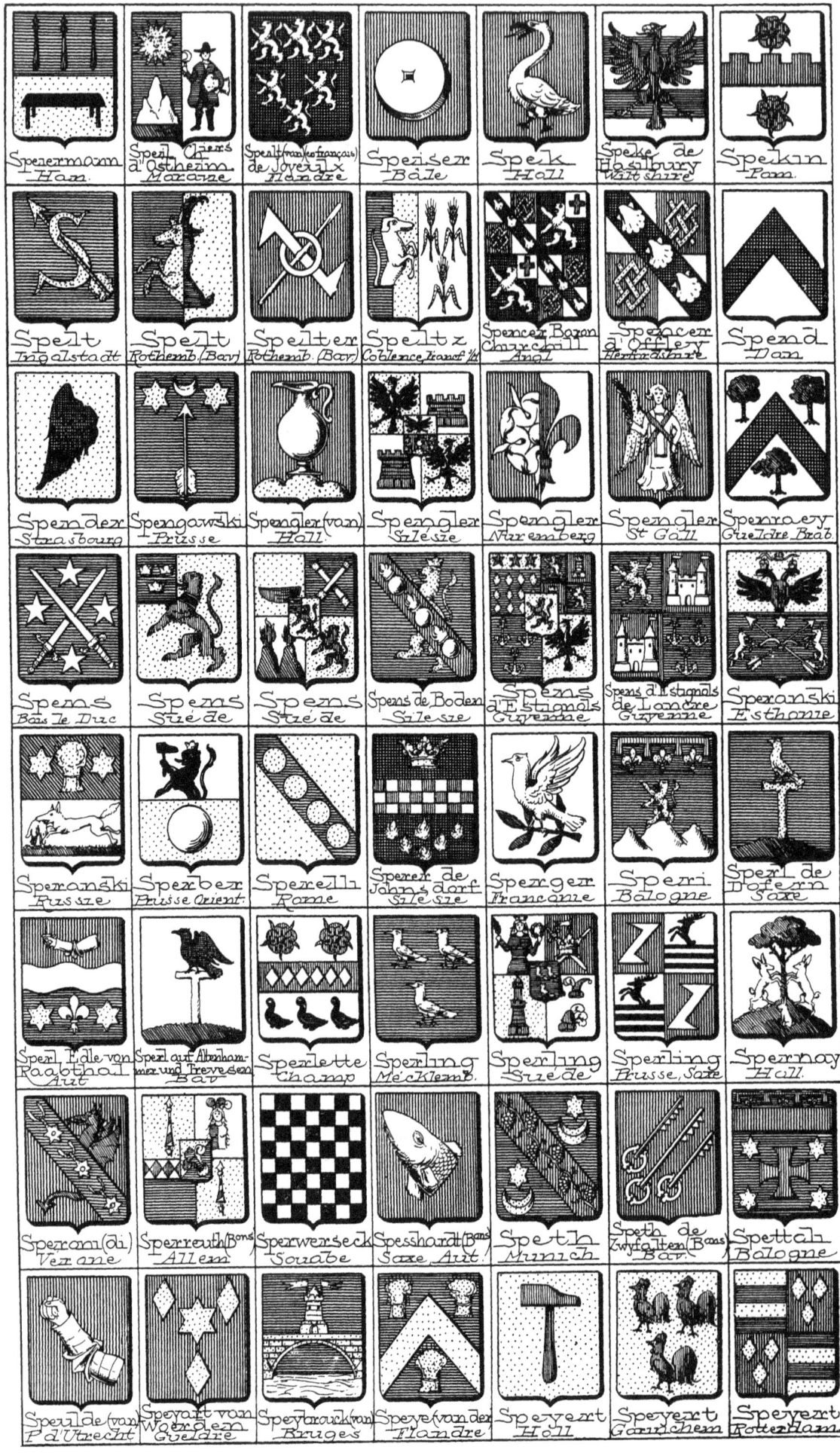

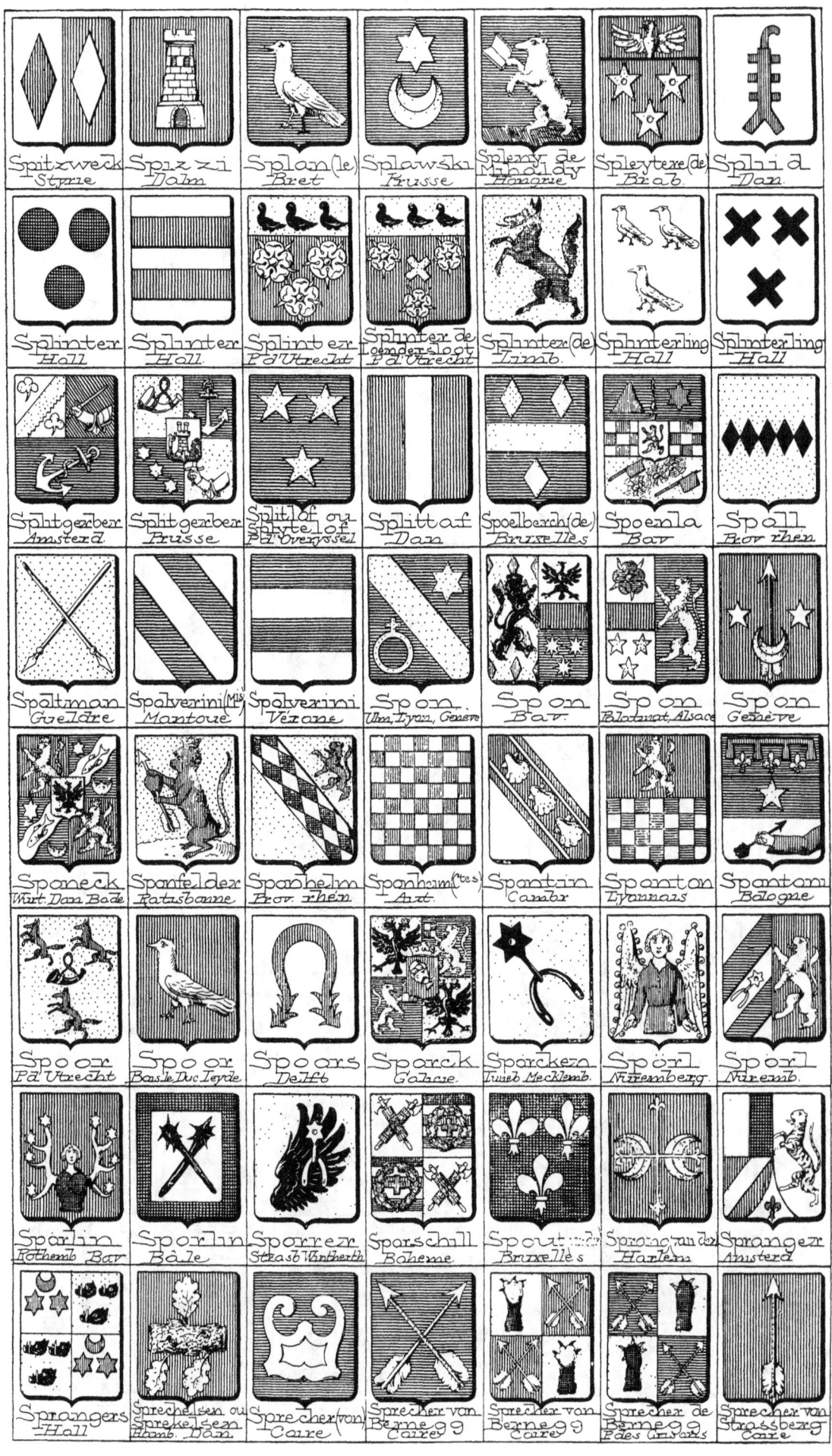

PL. CCCXXXVI

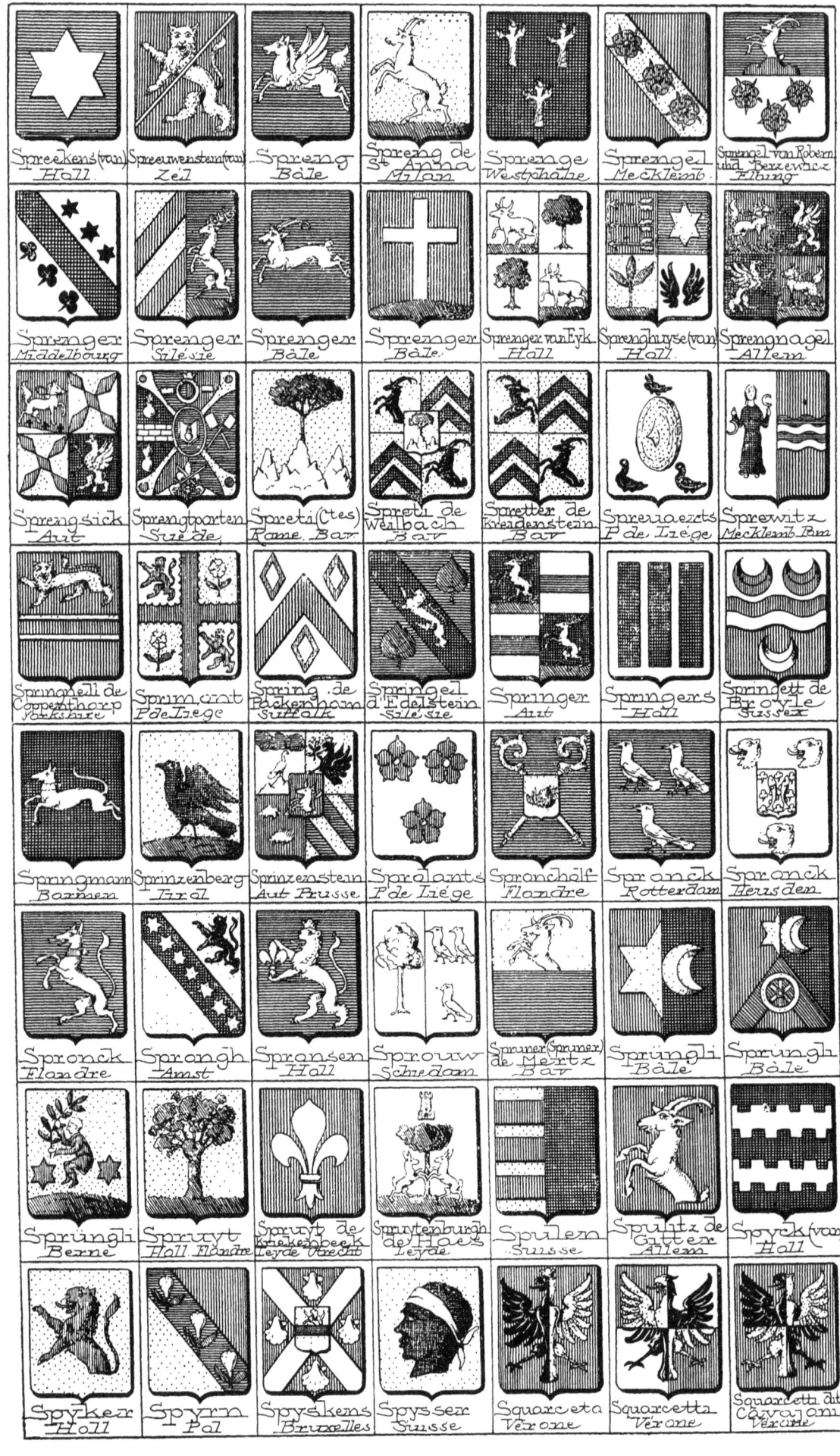

PL. CCCXXXVII

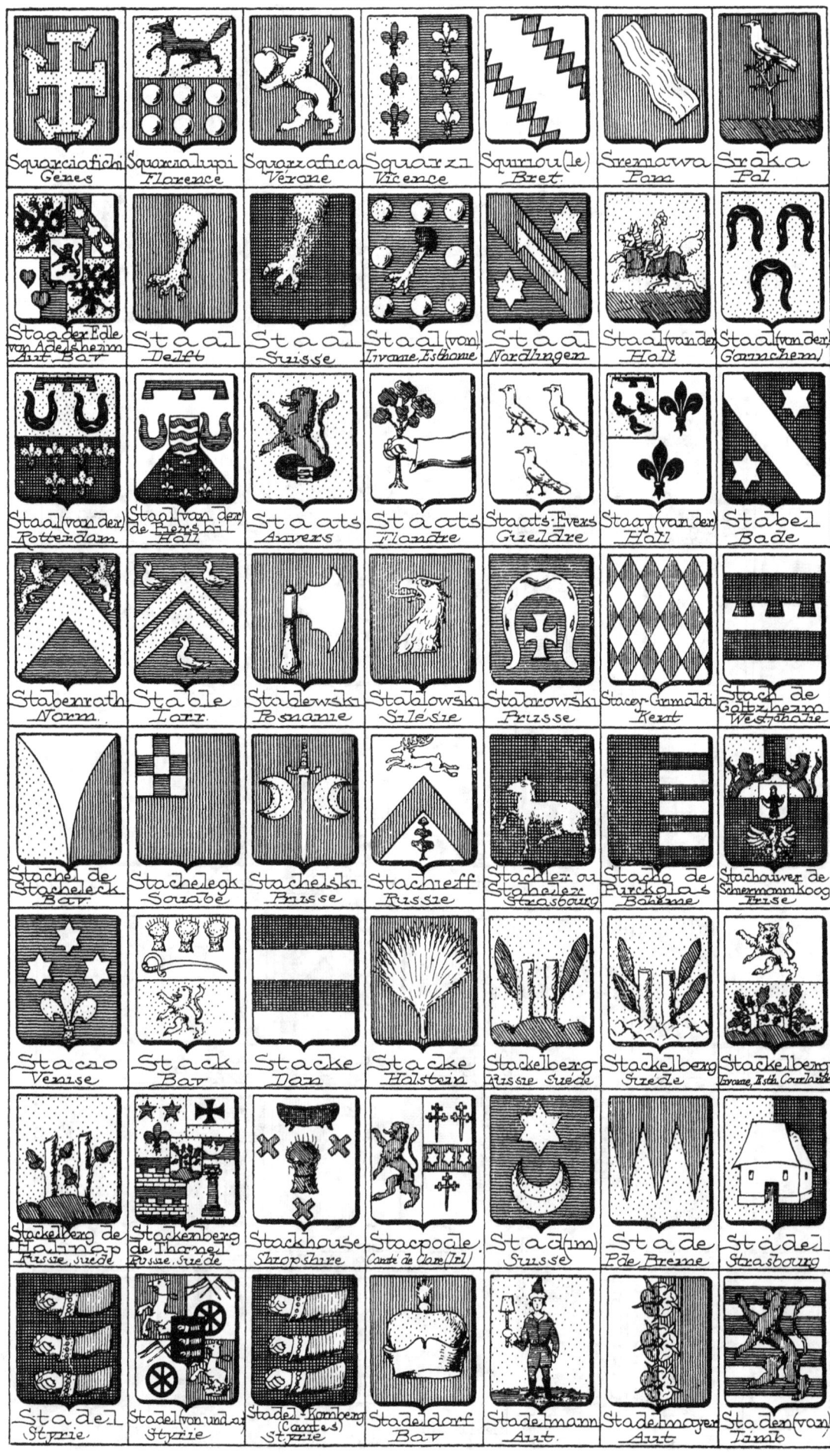

PL. CCCXXXVIII

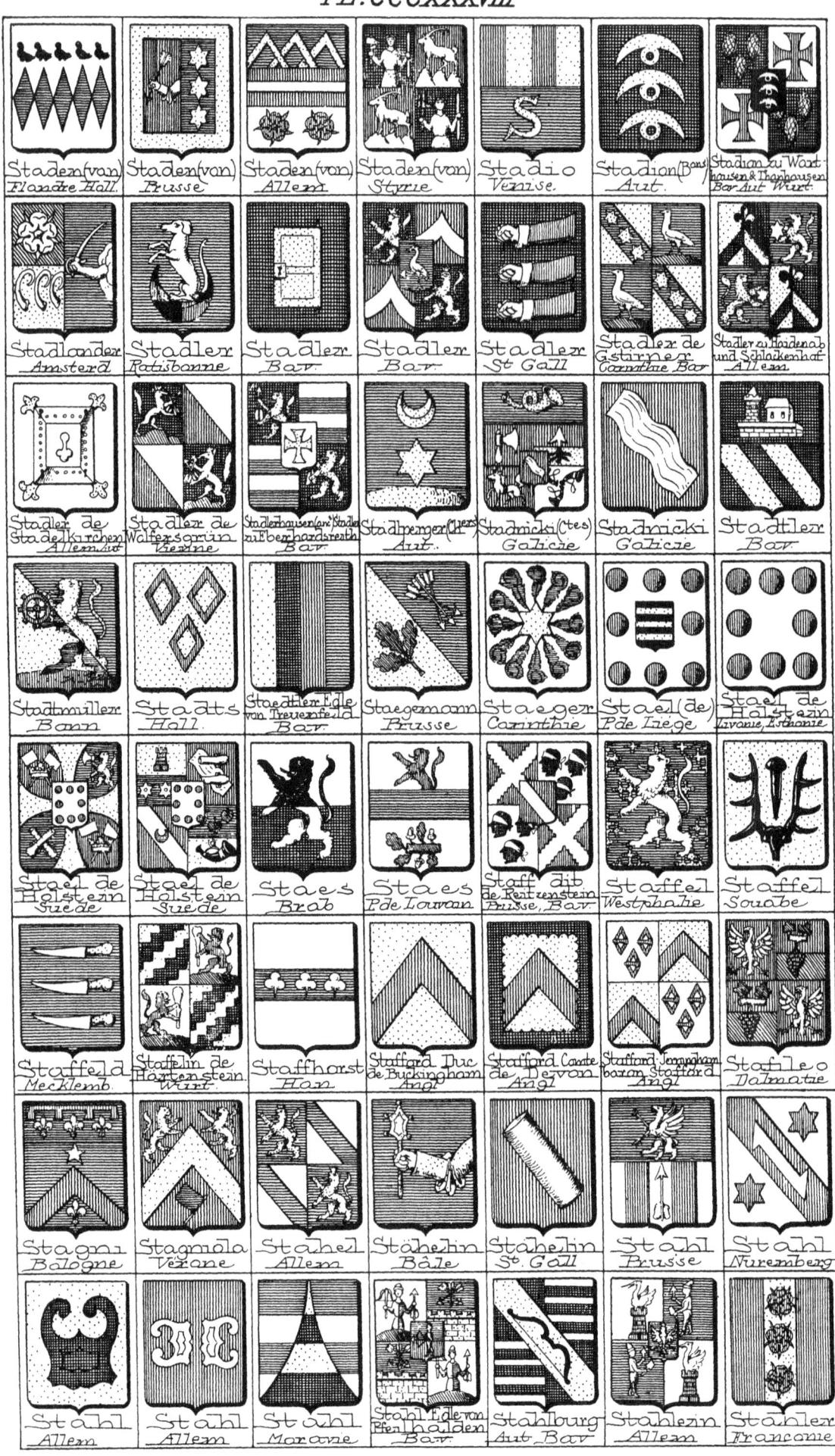

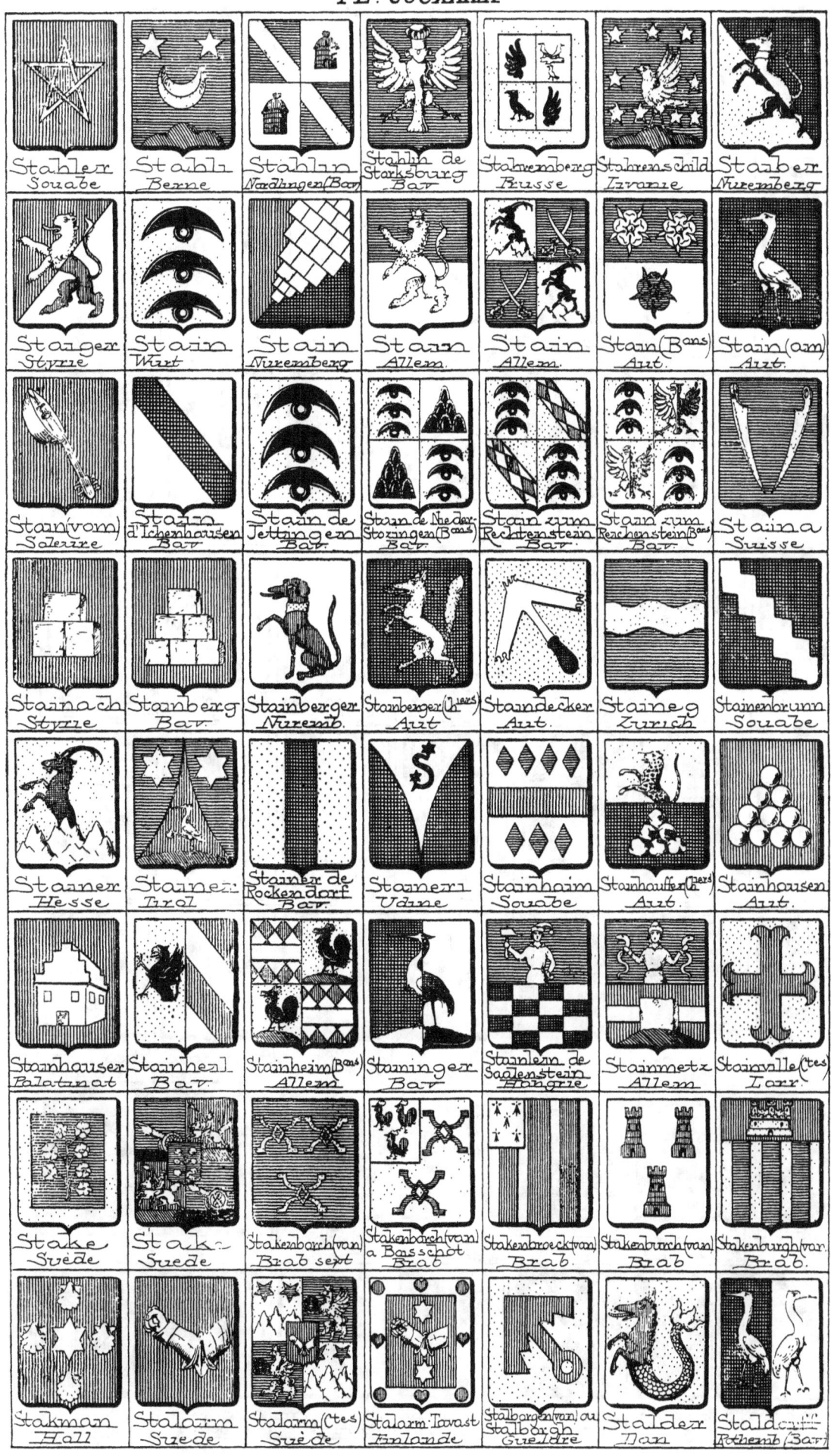

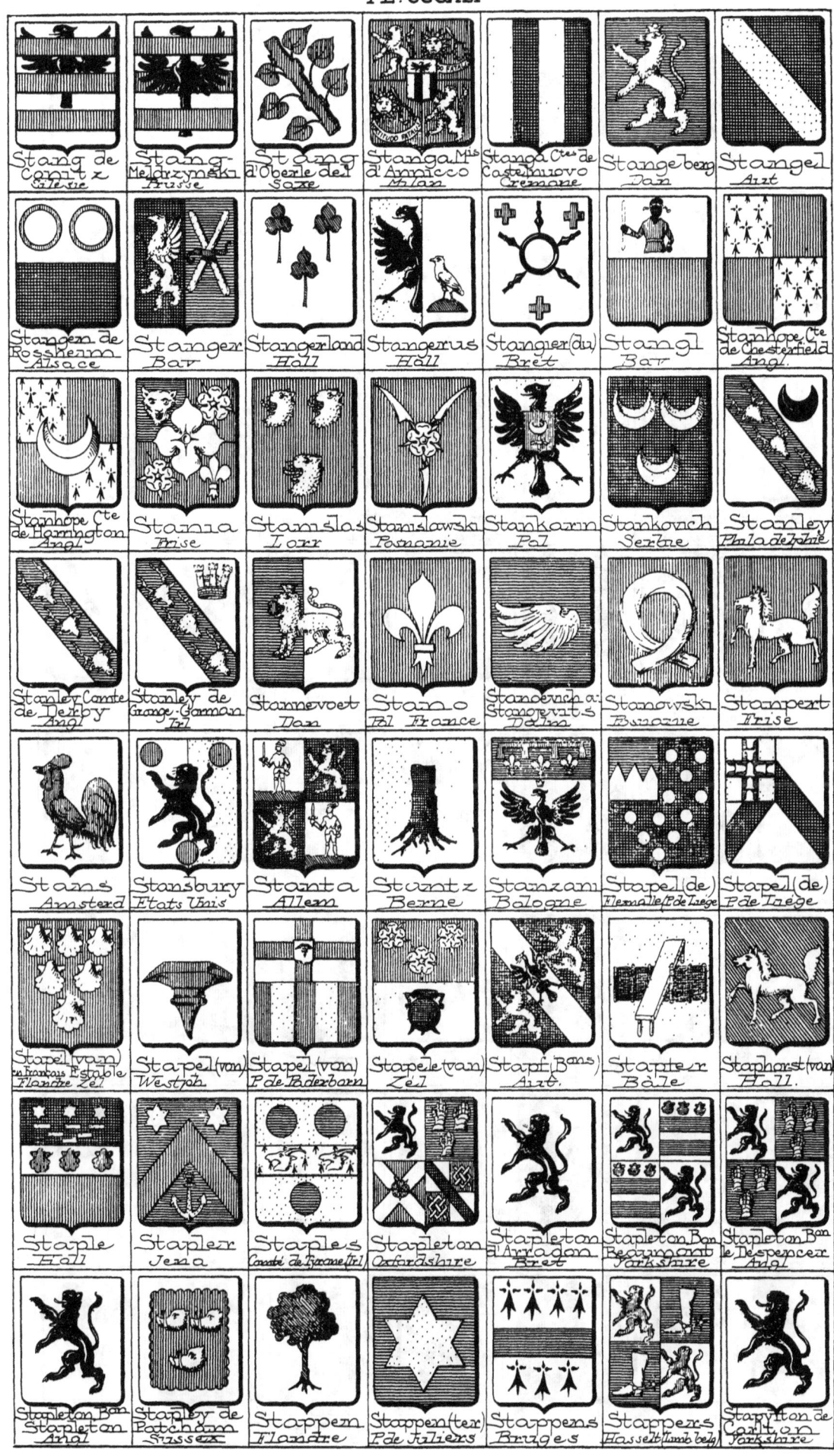

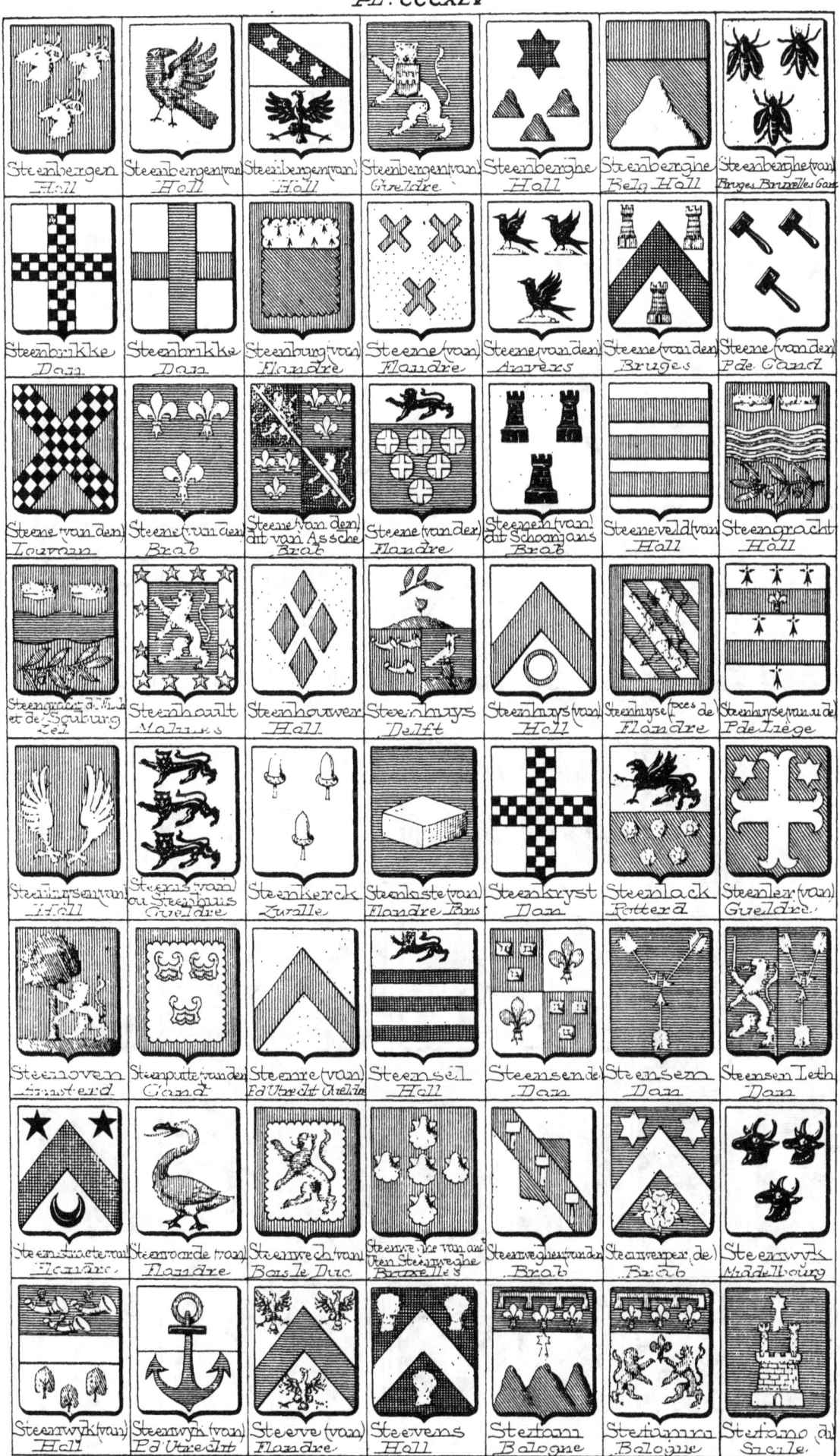

PL. CCCXLVII

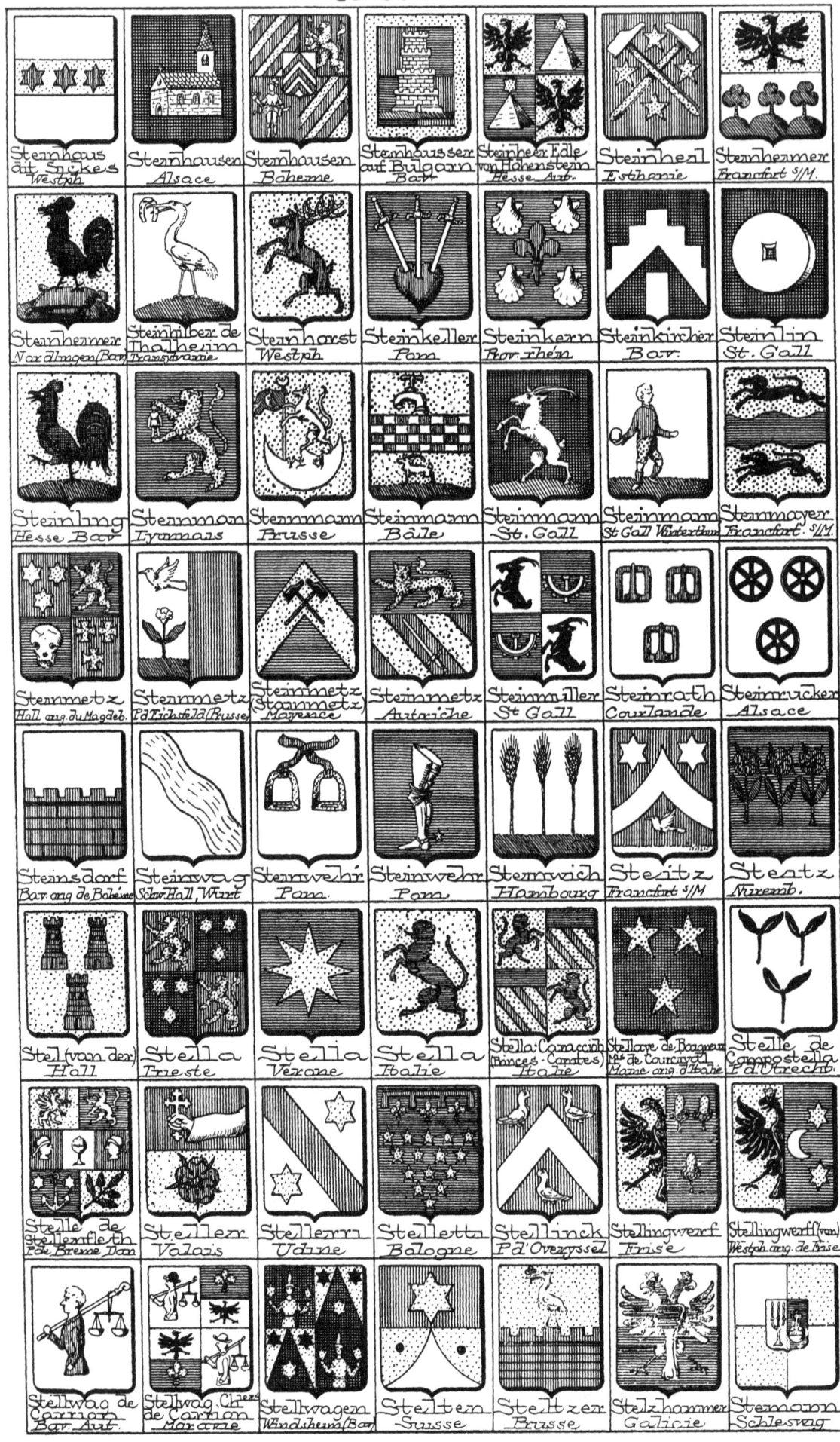

PL. CCCXLIX

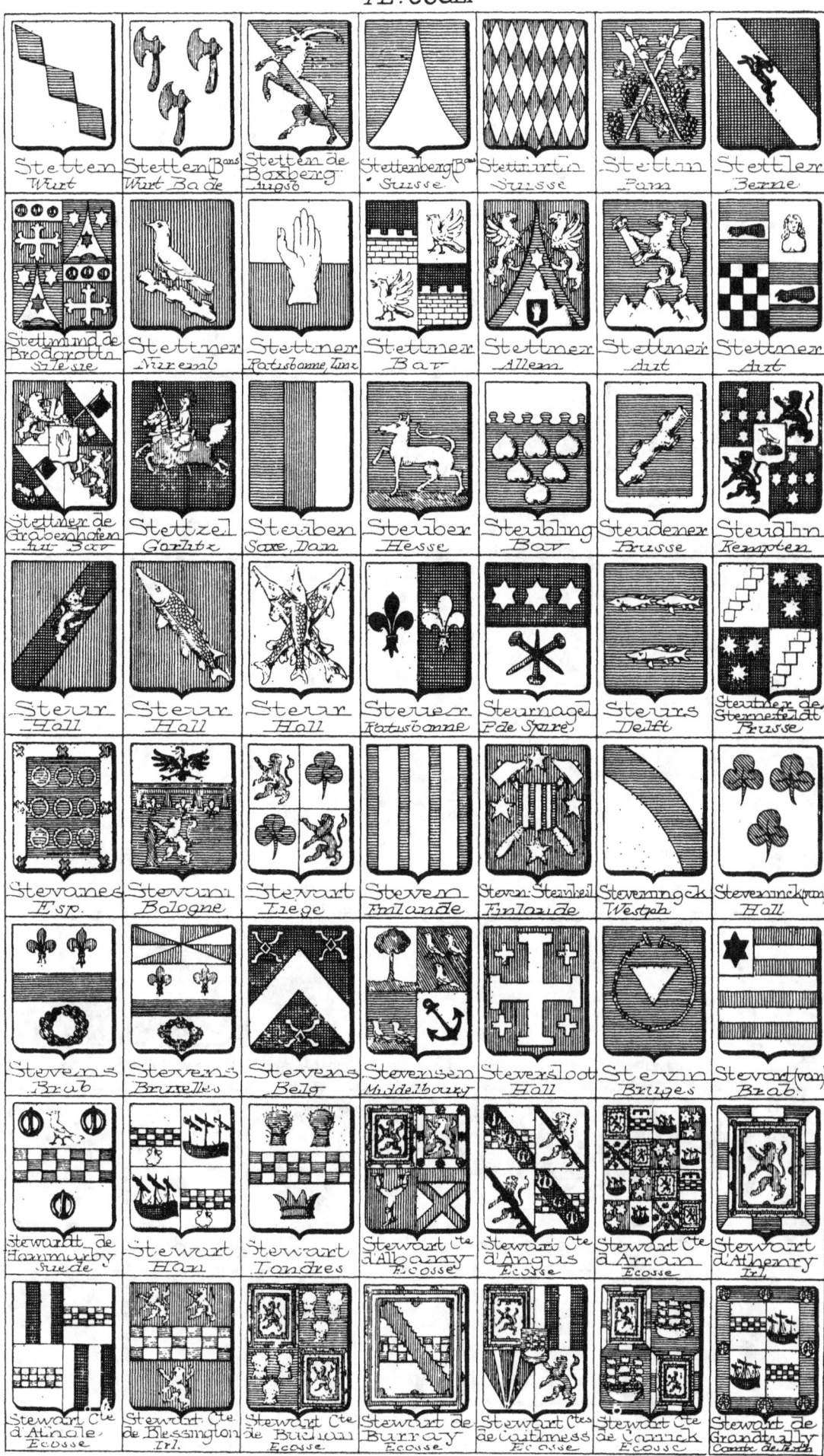

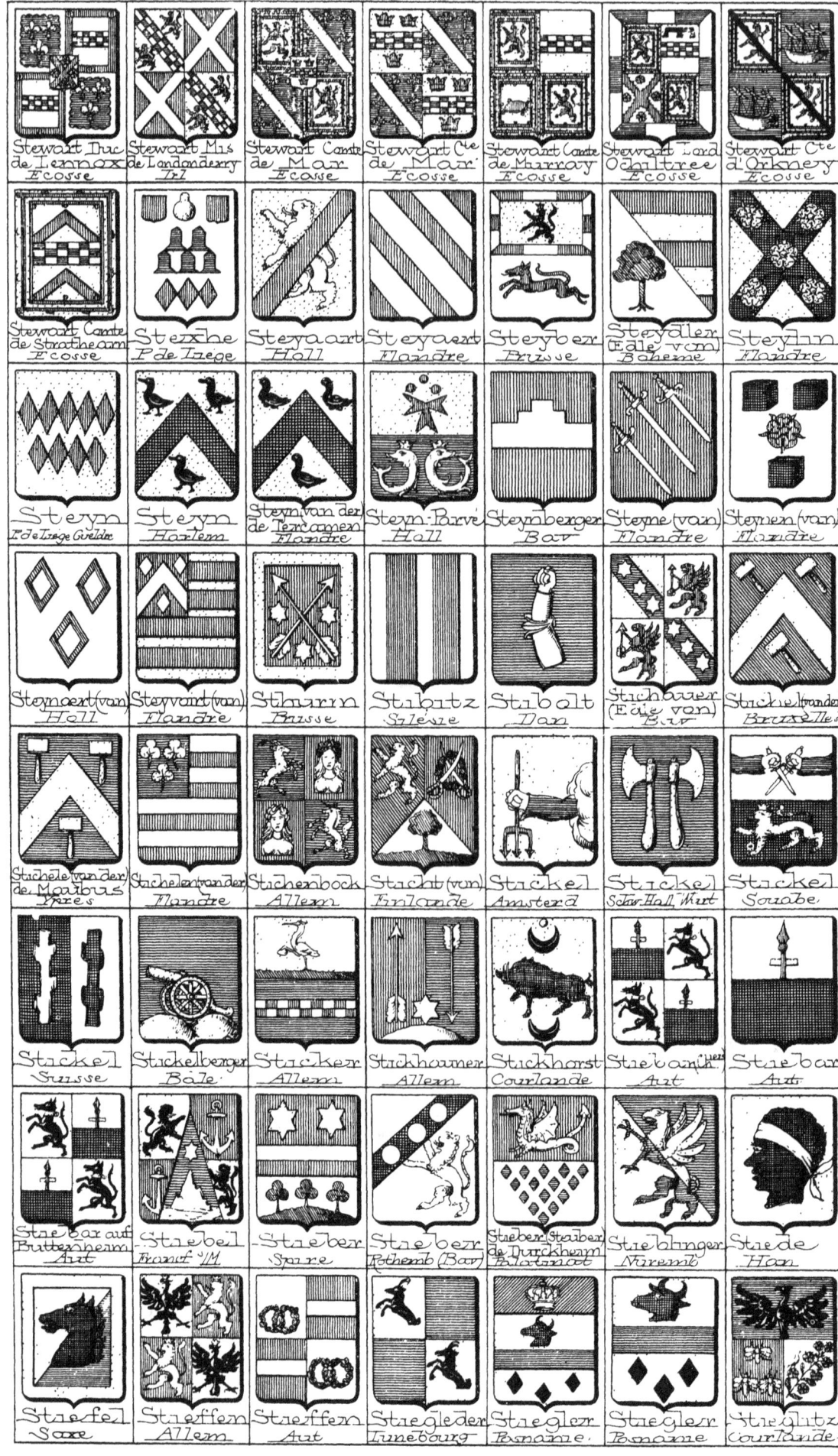

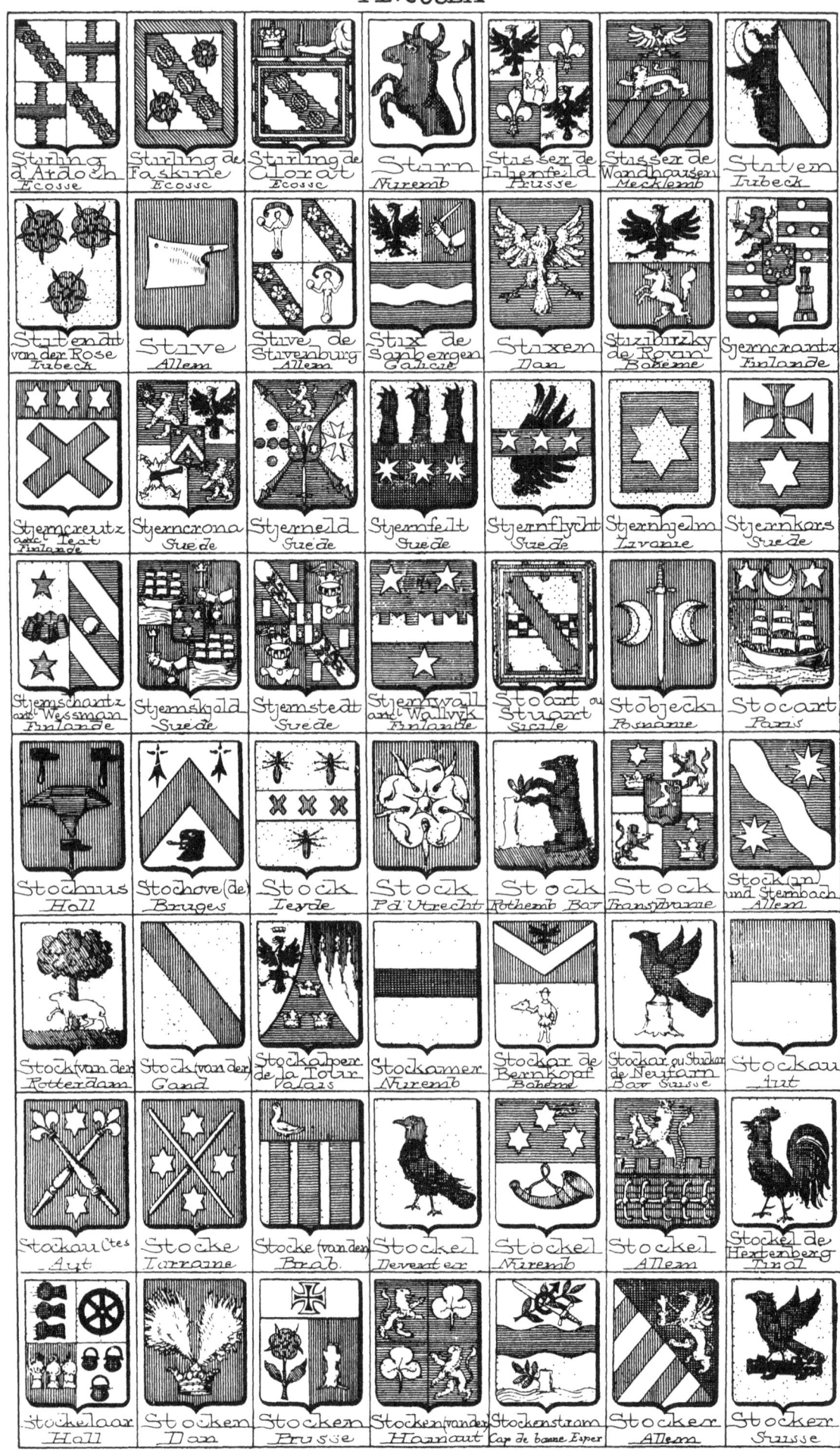

PL. CCCLVI

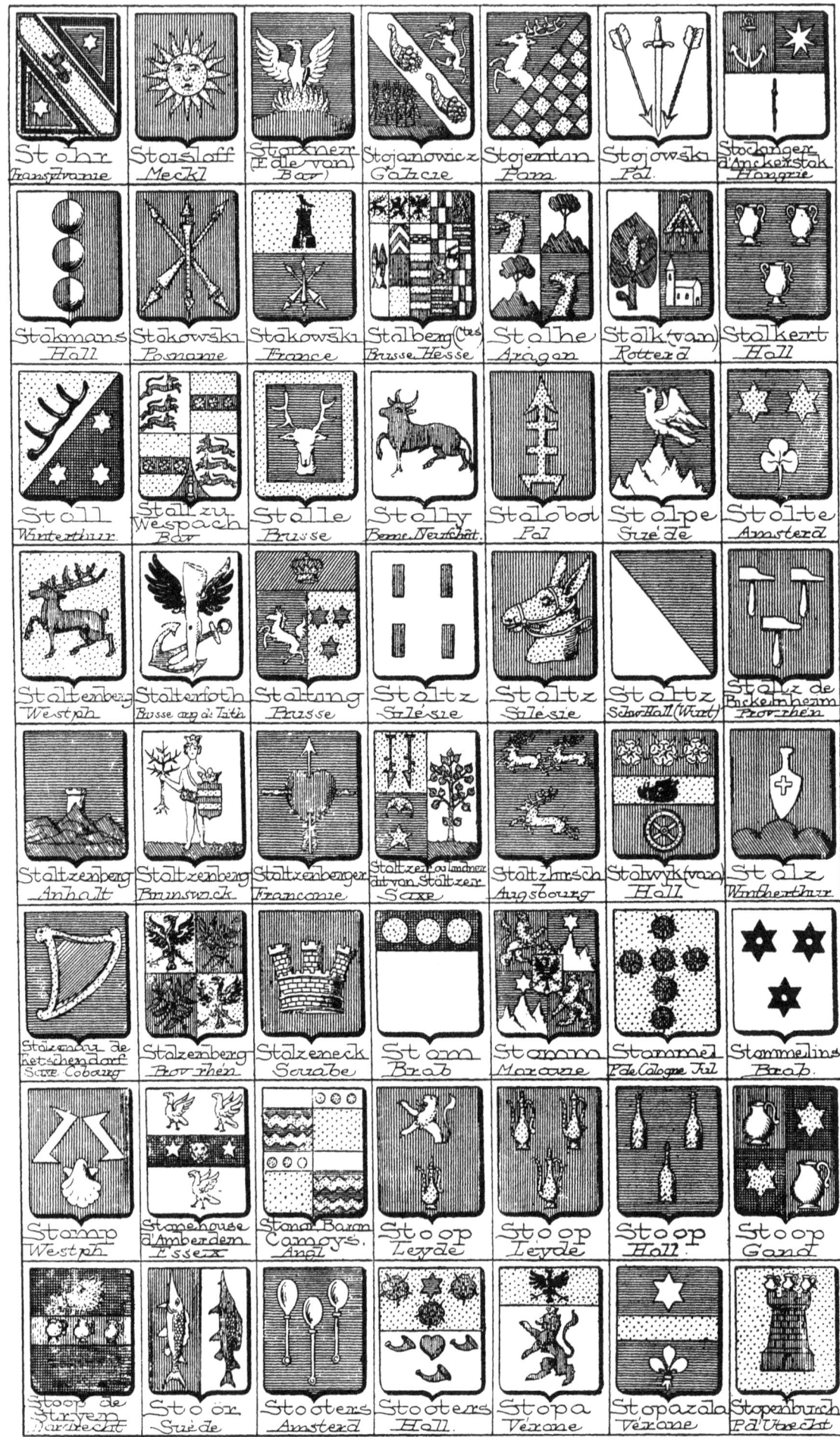

PL. CCCLVII

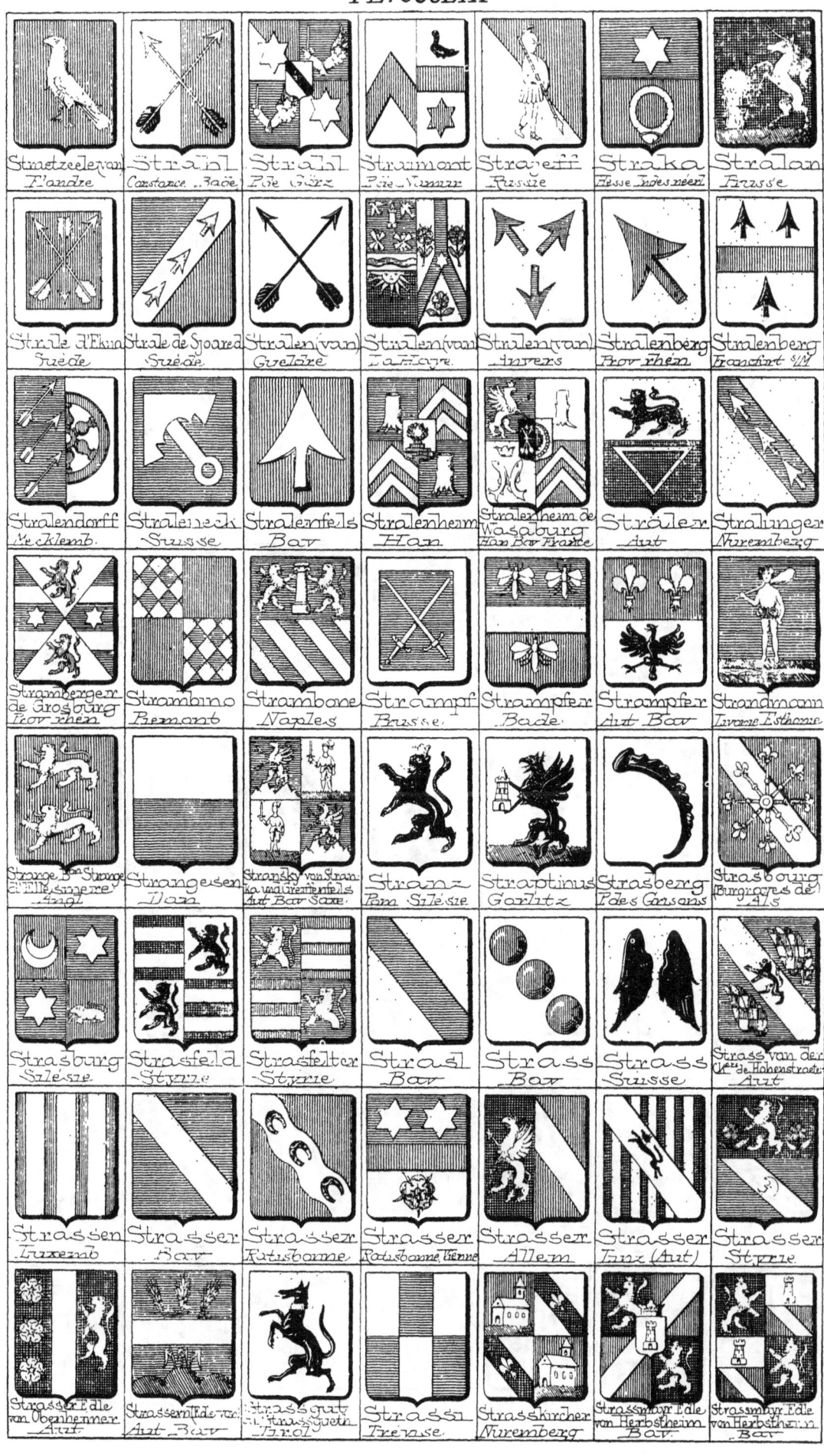

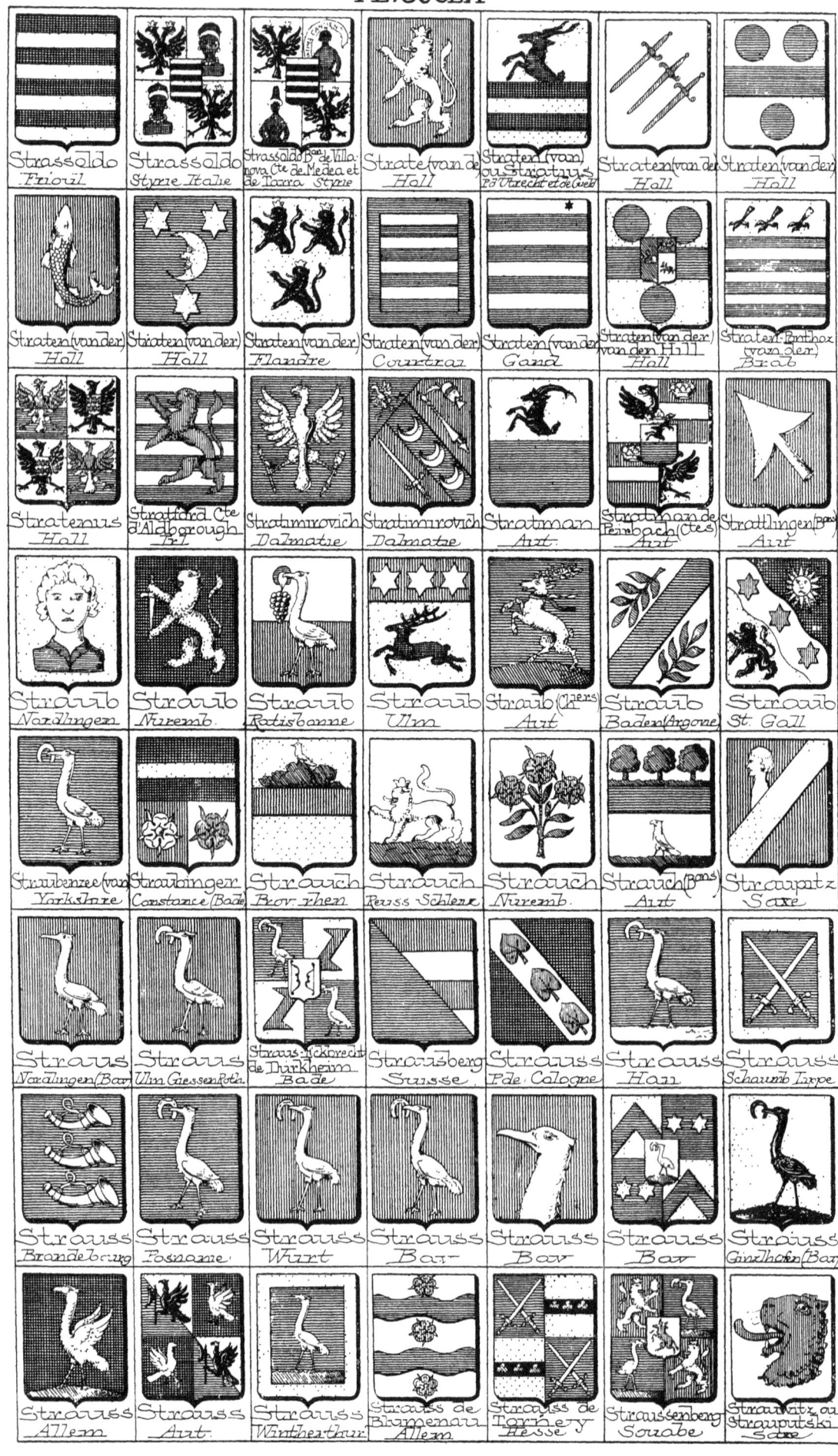

PL. CCCLXI

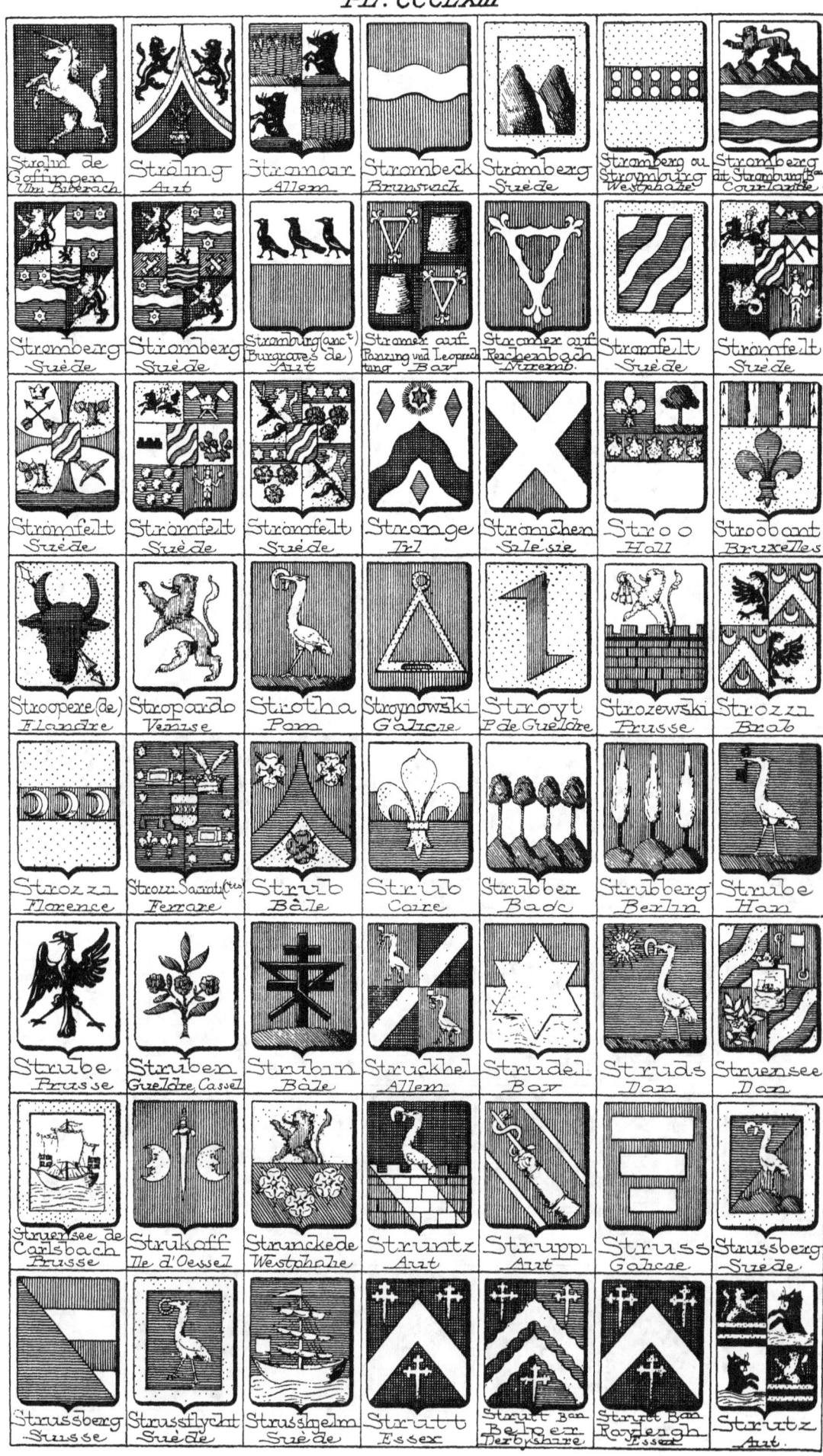

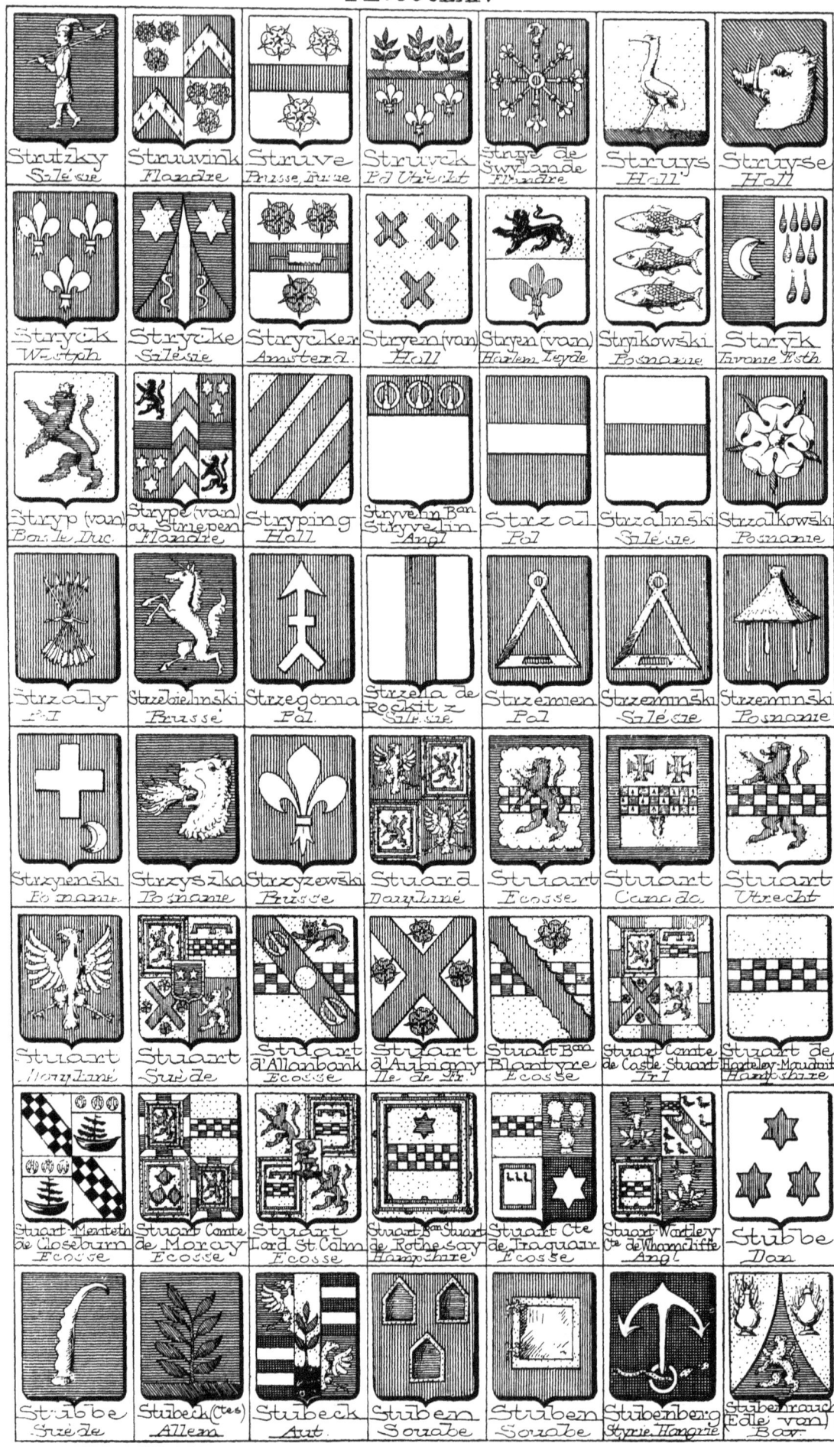

PL. CCCLXV

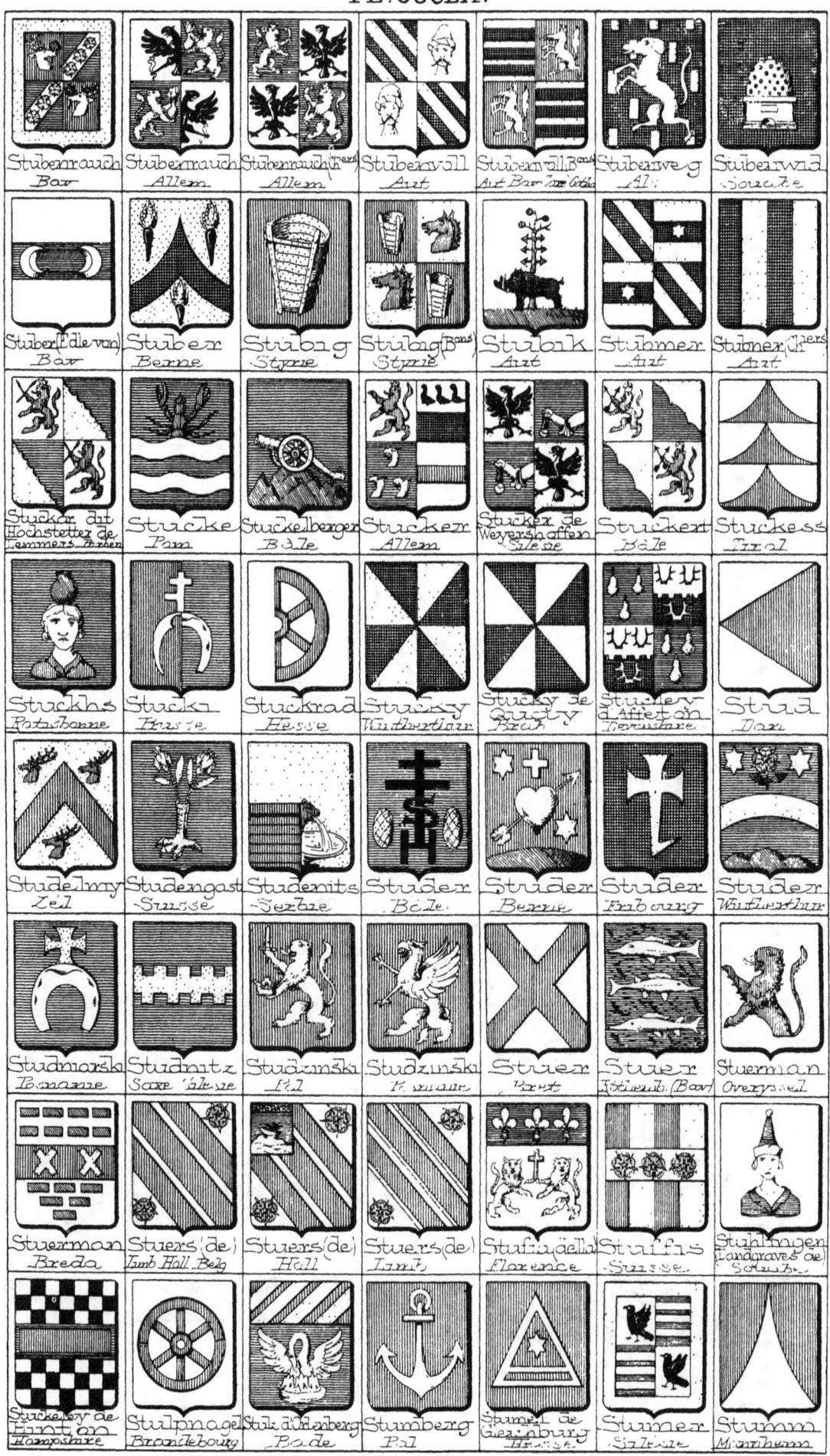

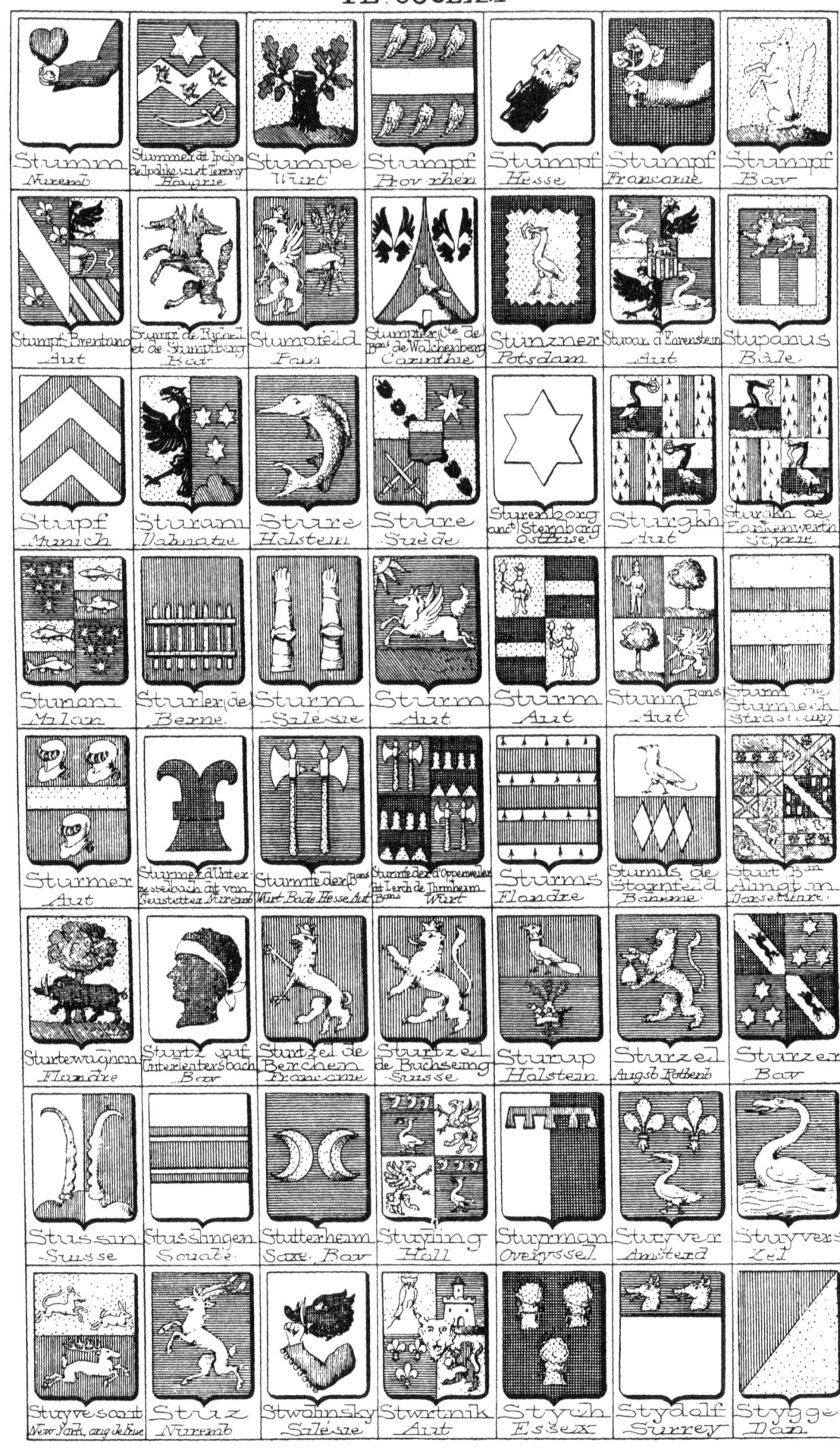

PL. CCCLXVII

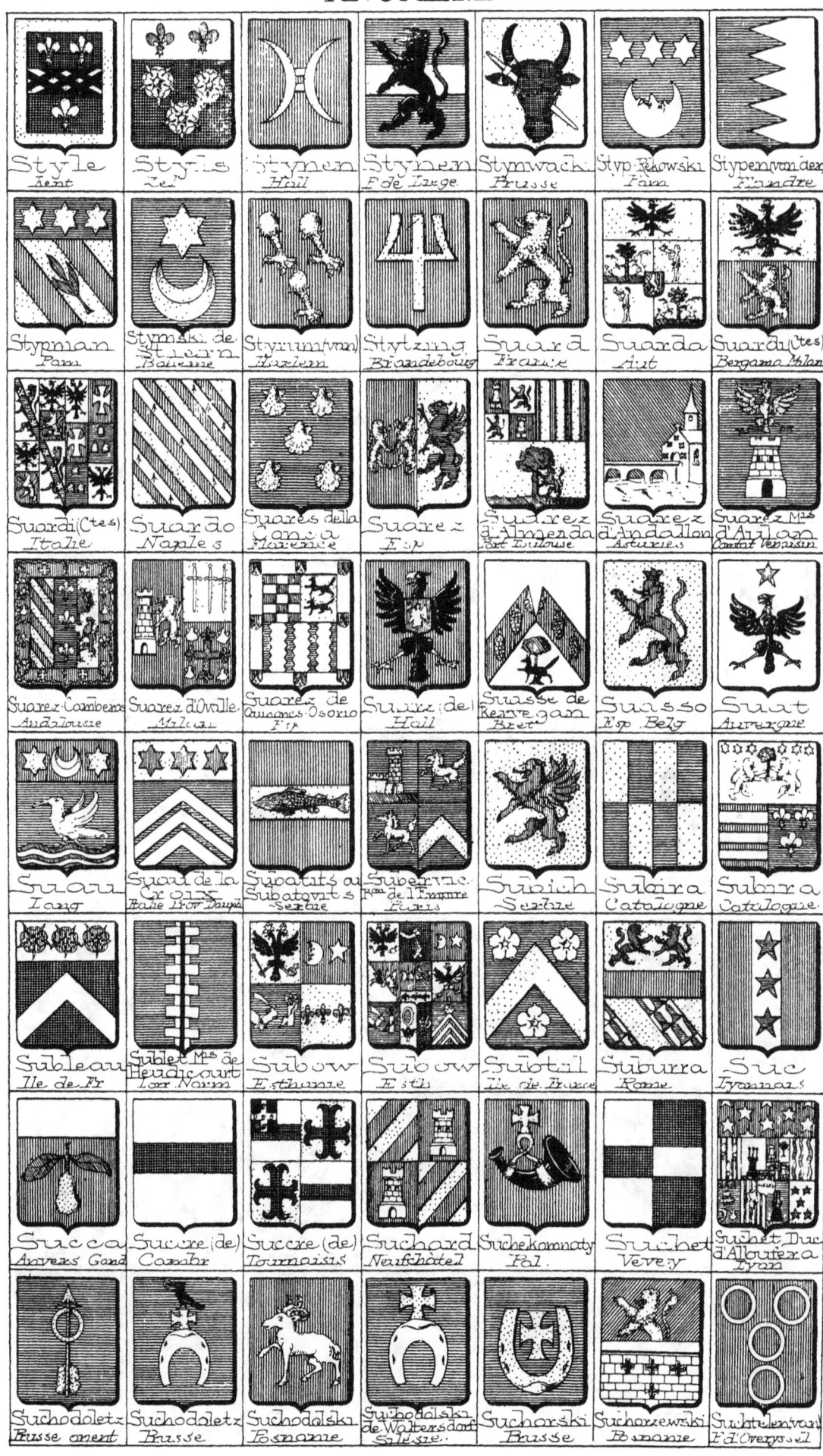

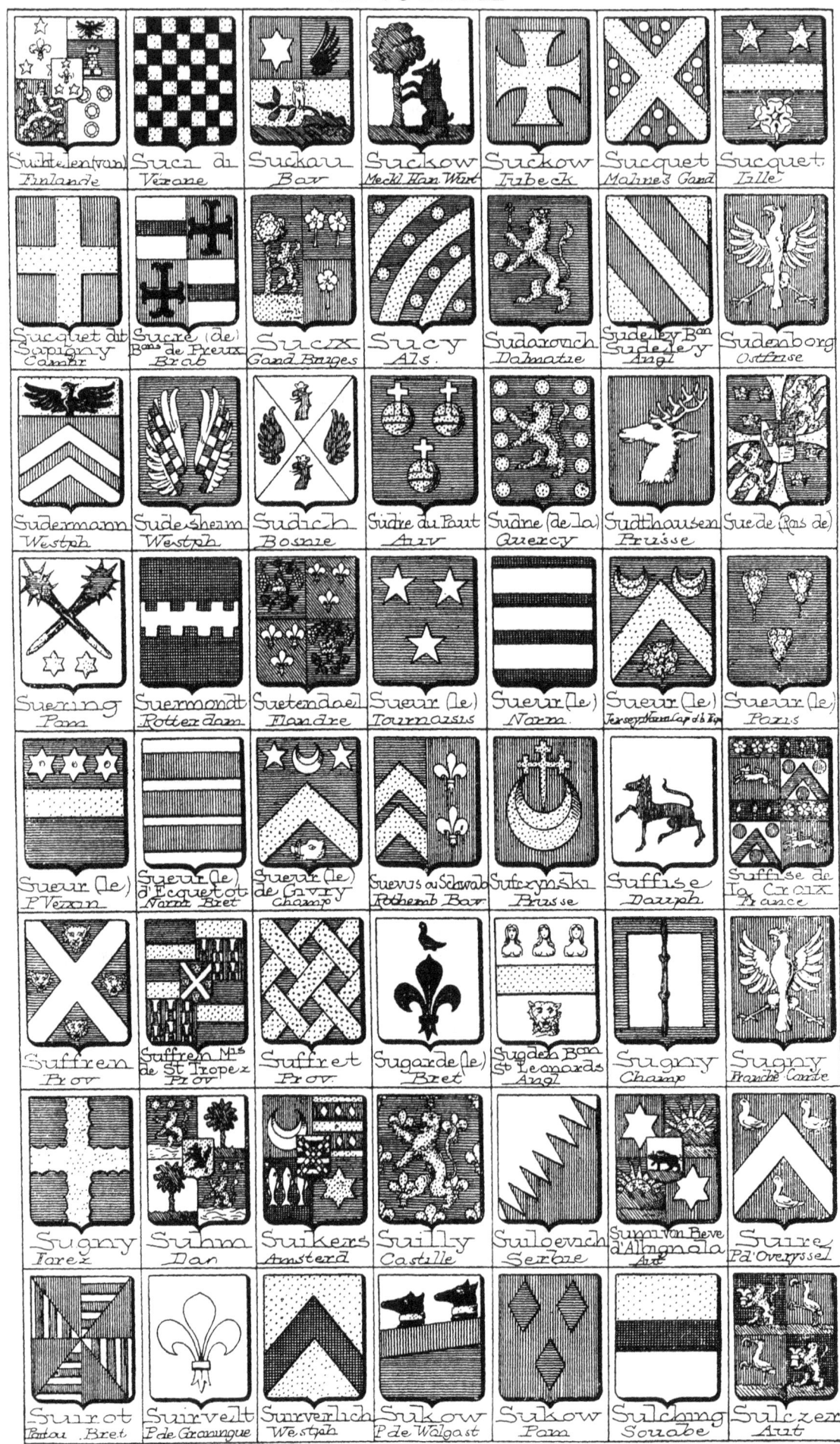

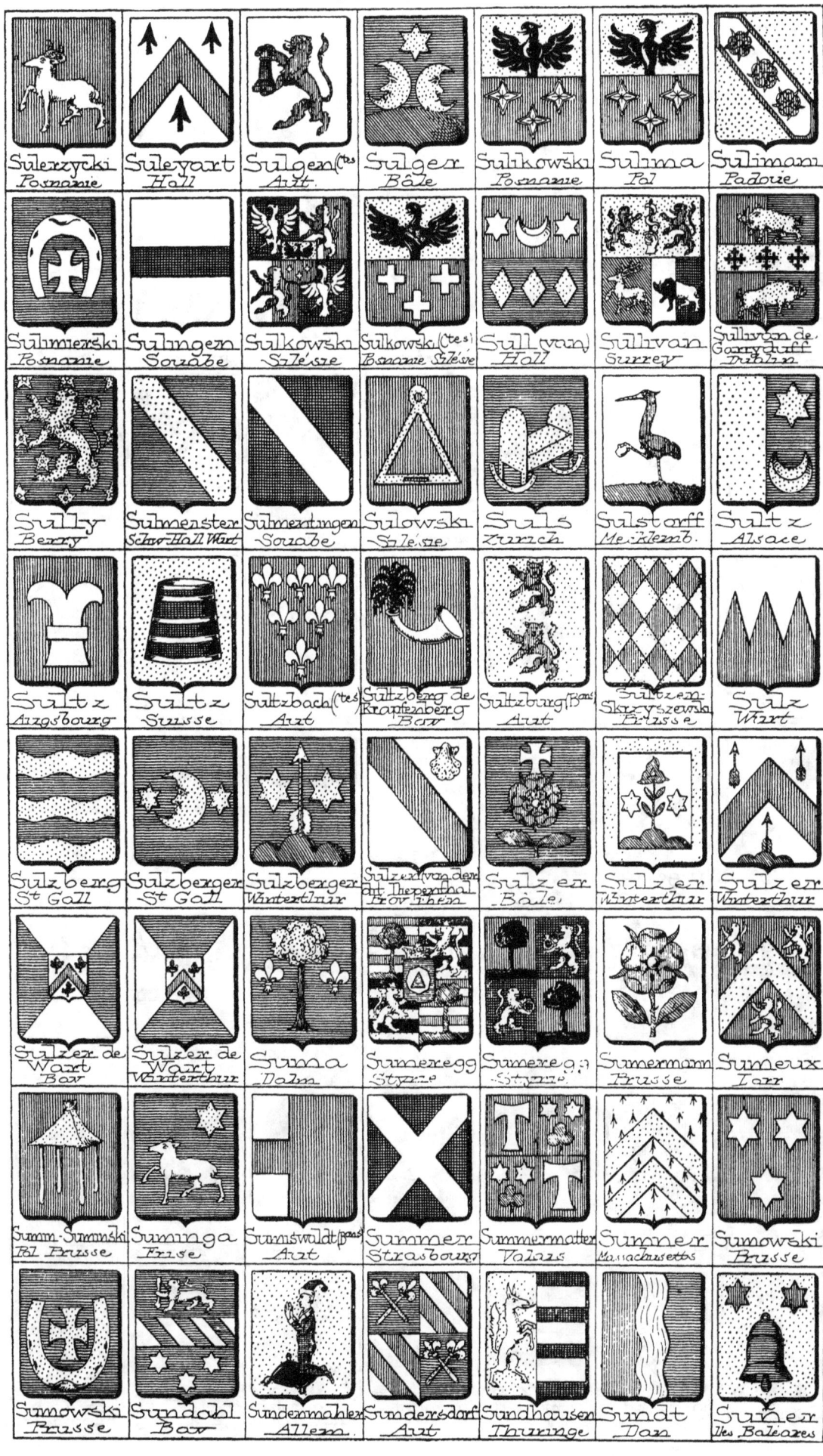

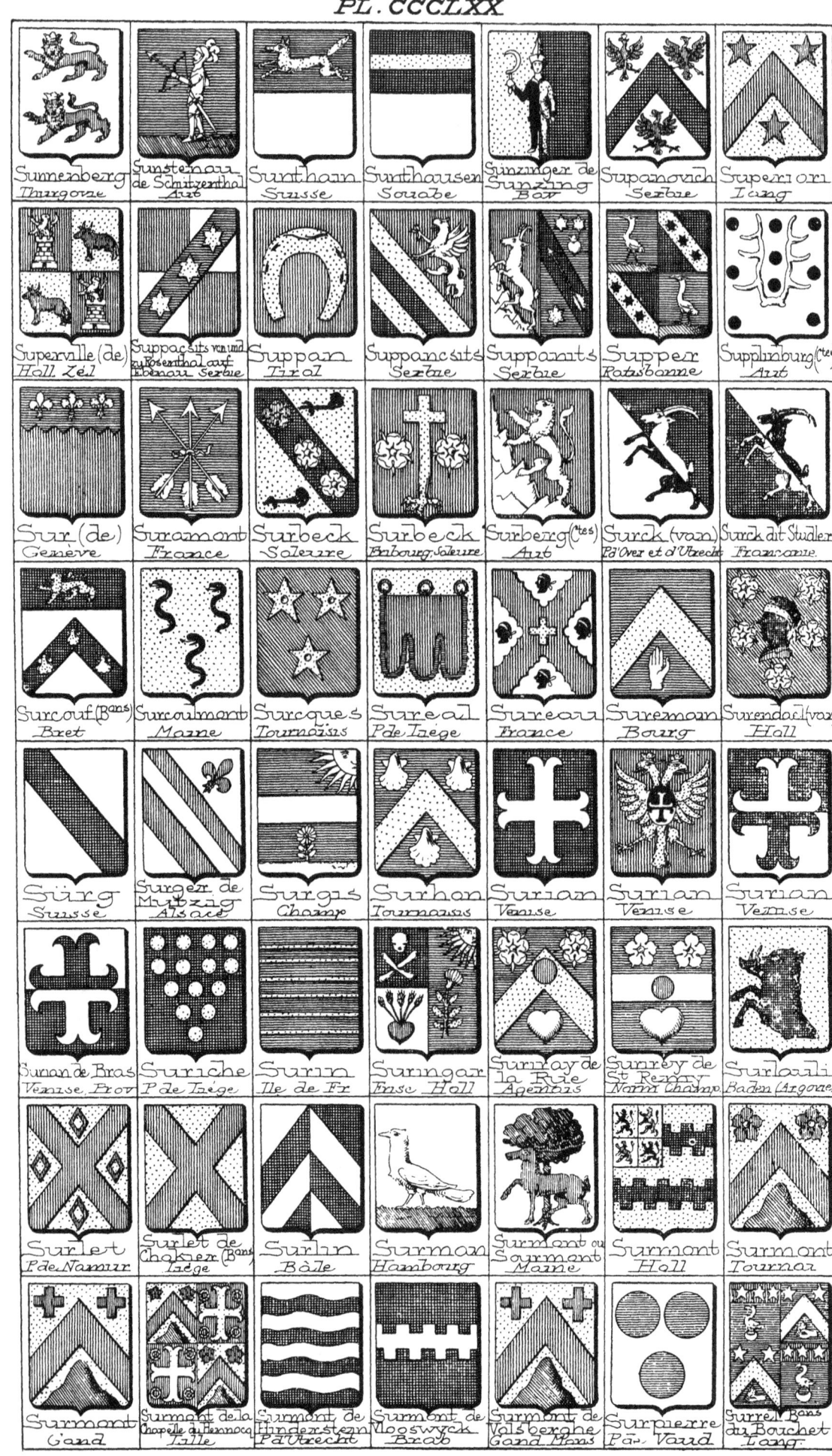

PL. CCCLXXI

PL. CCCLXXII

PL. CCCLXXIII

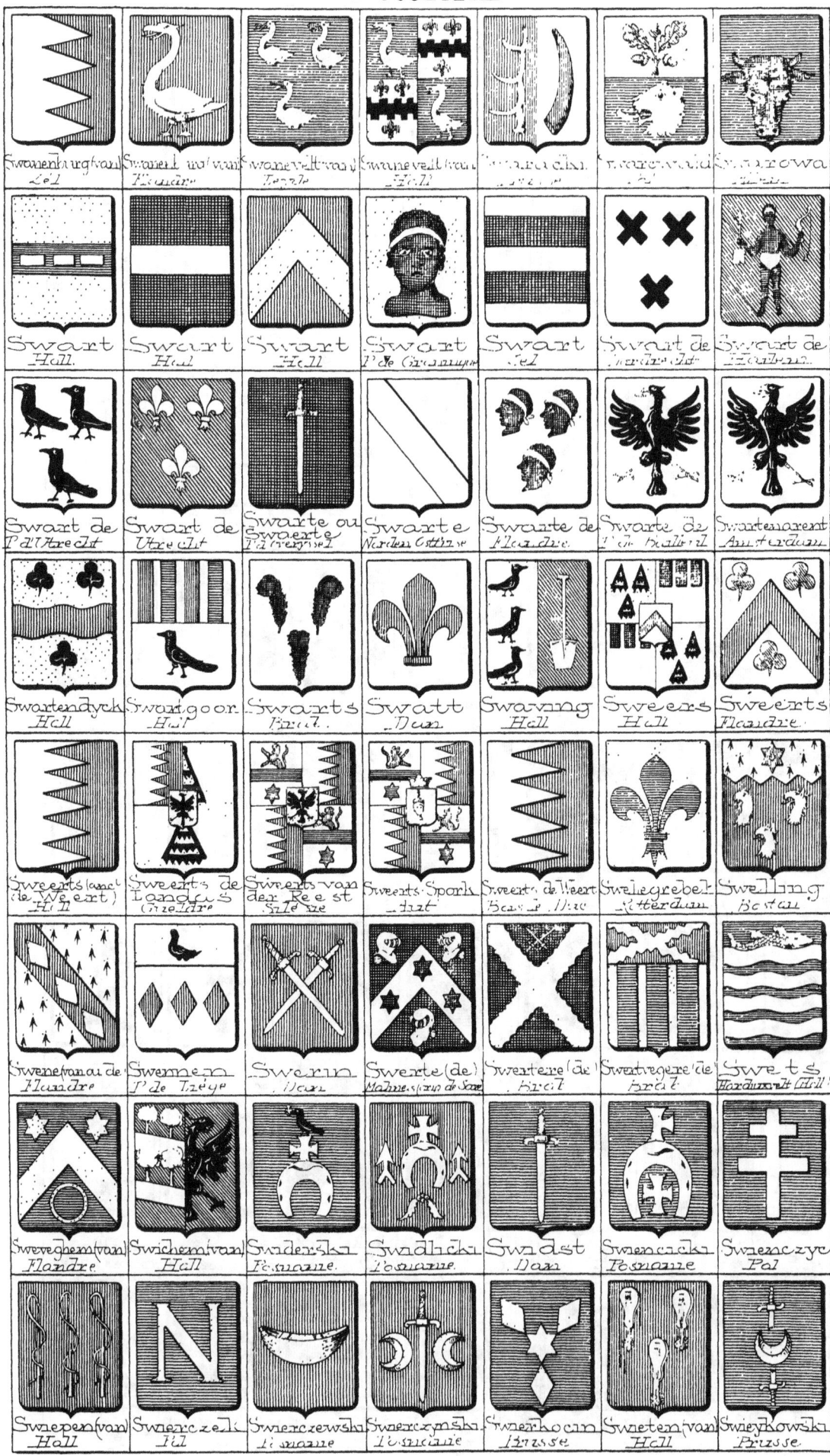

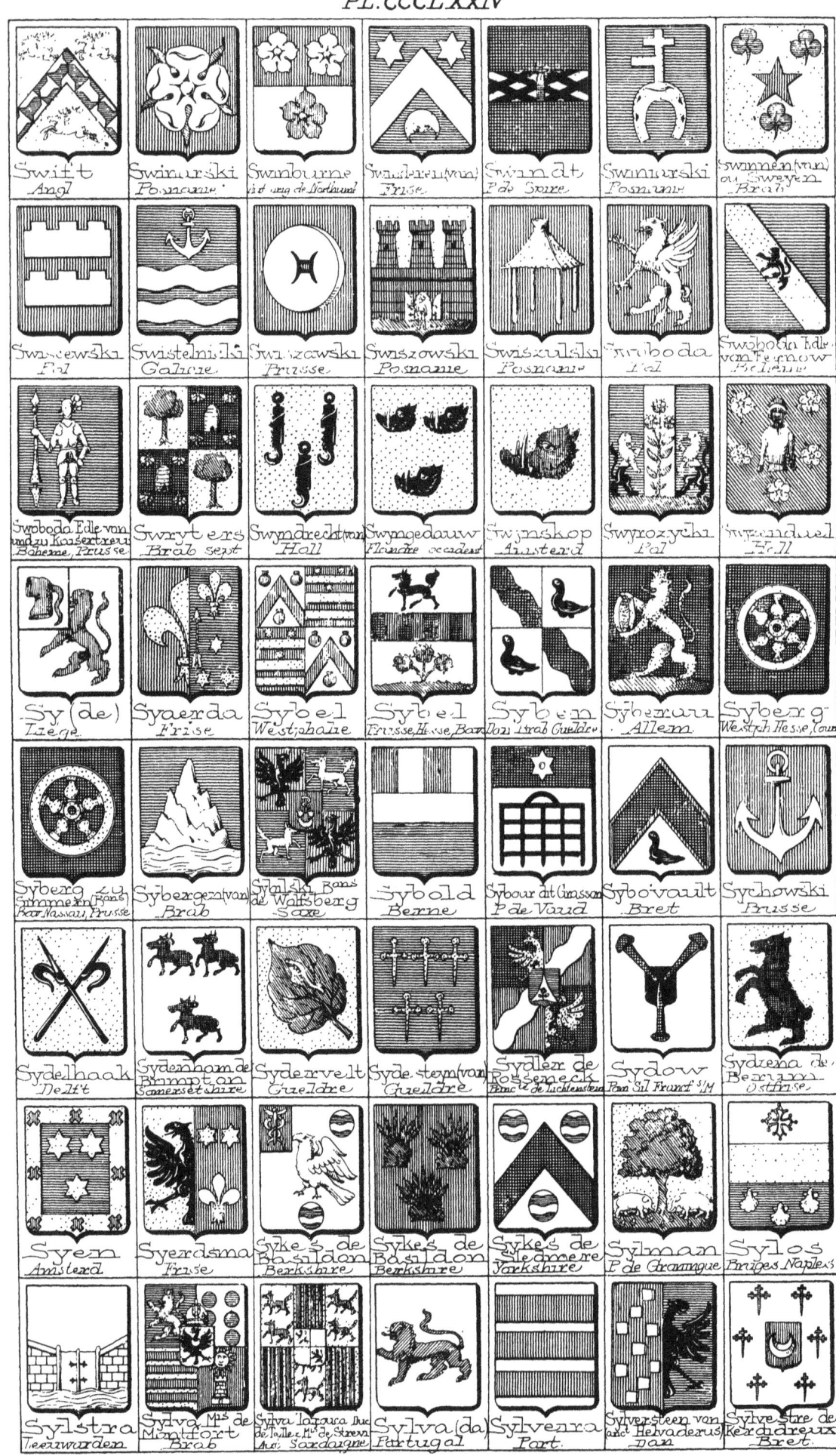

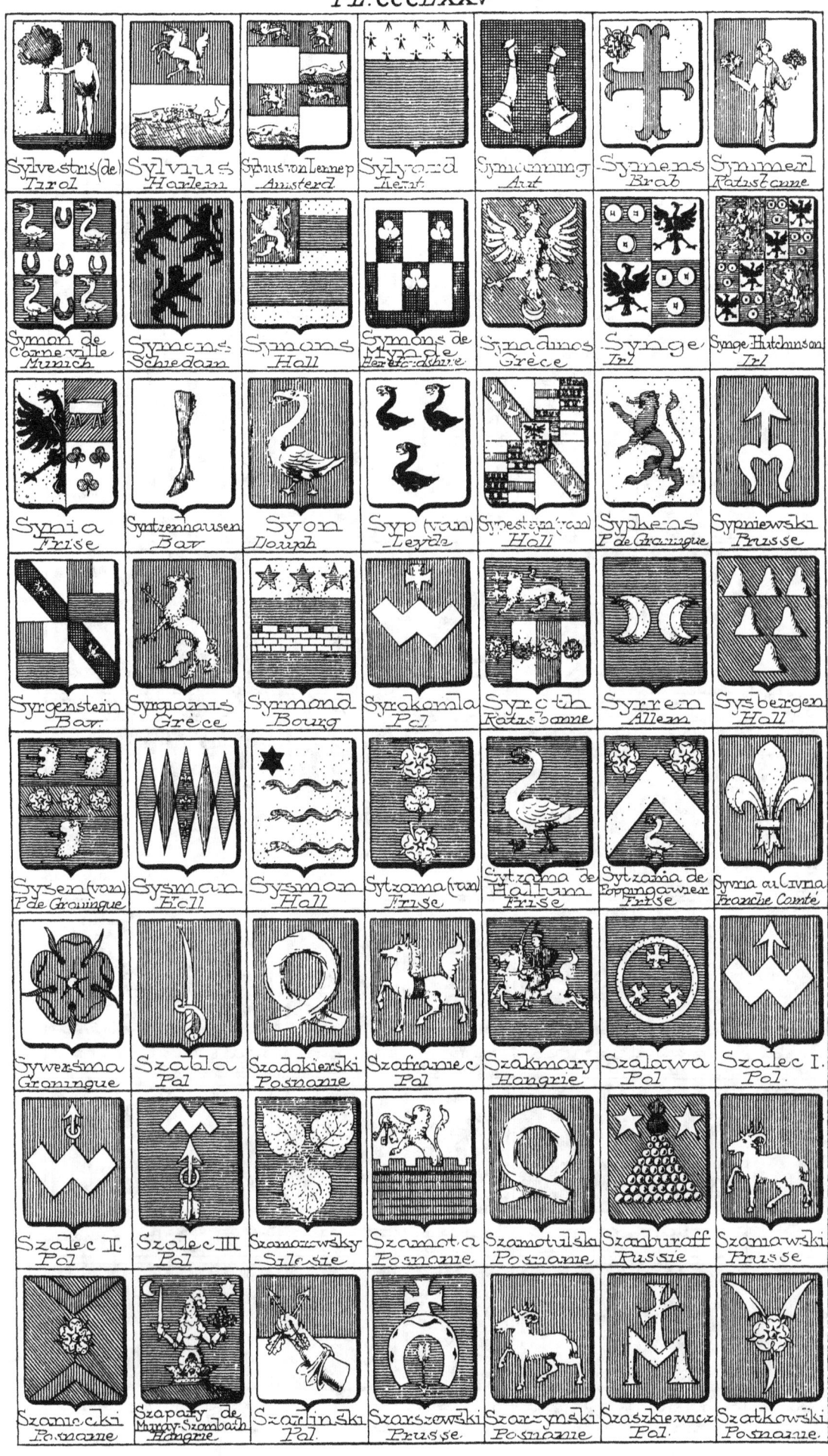

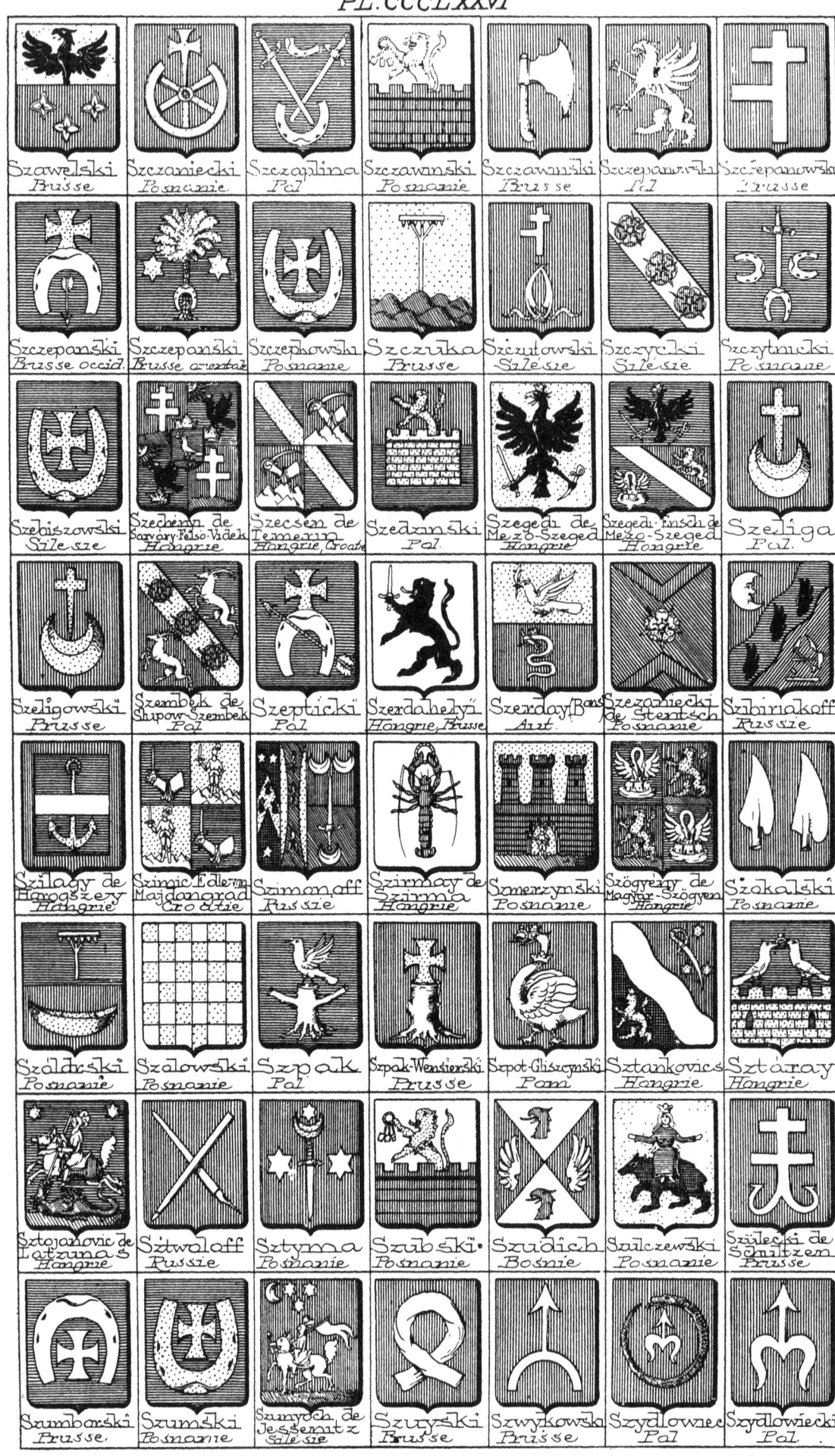

PL. CCCLXXVII

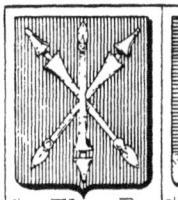    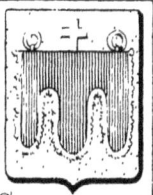 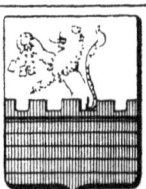 

Szydłowski — Szydłowski Posnanie — Szydłowski Prusse — Szymwocha Prusse — Szymonowicz Prusse — Szymanowski Posnanie — Szymborski Prusse

  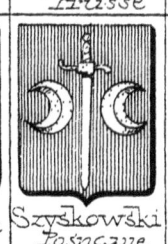

Szymońska Silesie — Szyrma Litwanie — Szyskowski Posnanie

FIN DU TOME V

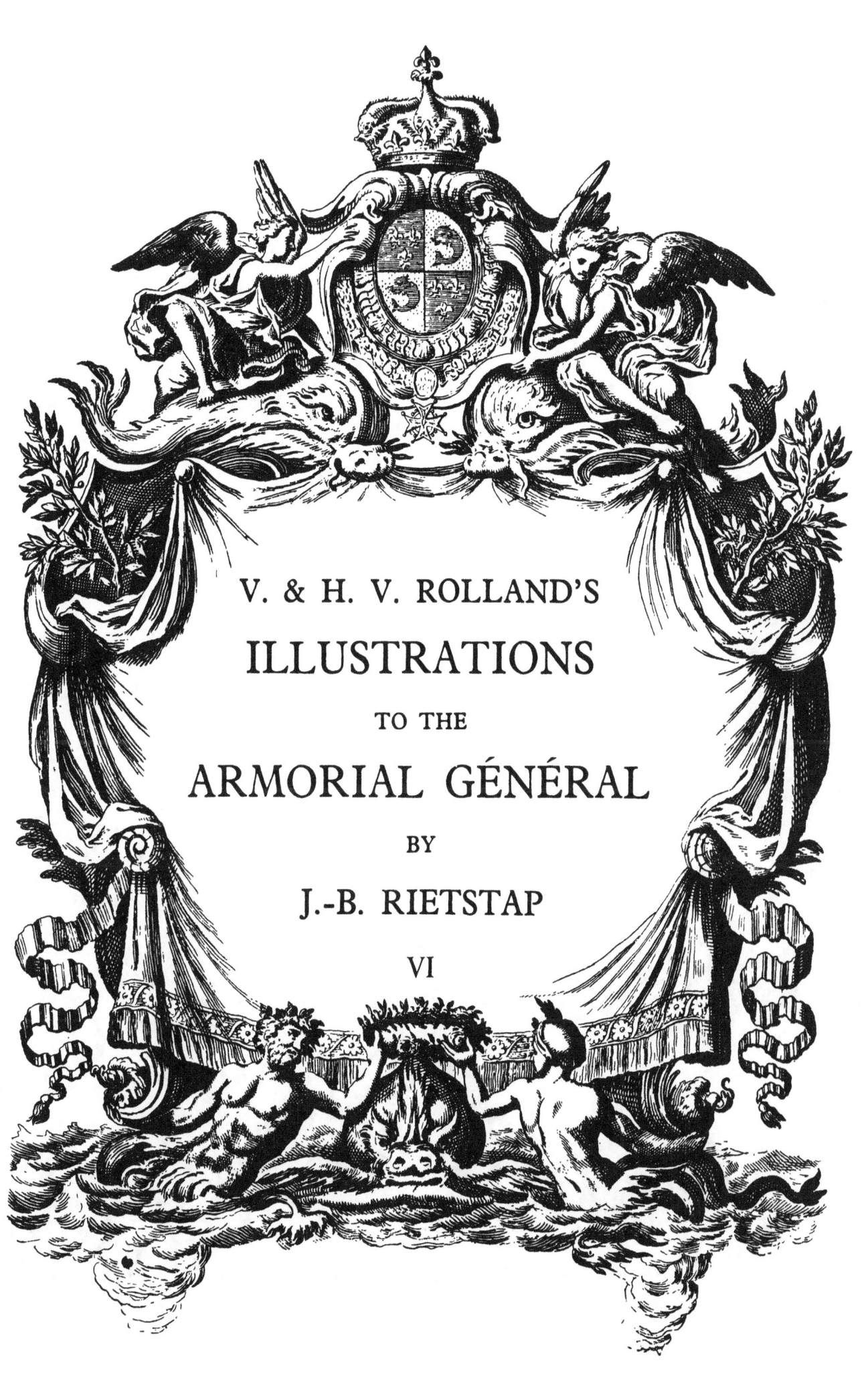

V. & H. V. ROLLAND'S

ILLUSTRATIONS

TO THE

ARMORIAL GÉNÉRAL

BY

J.-B. RIETSTAP

VI

PL. I

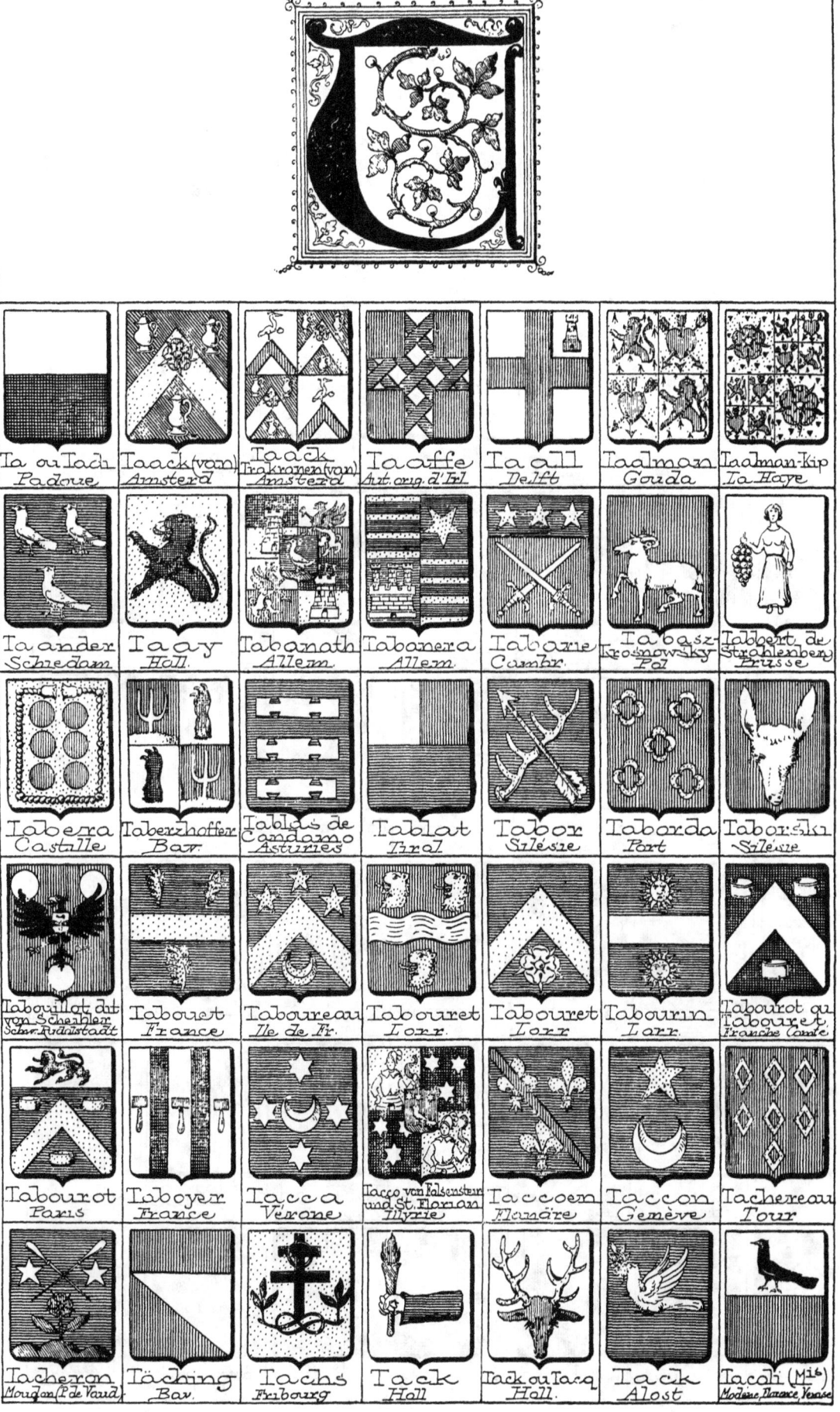

PL. IV

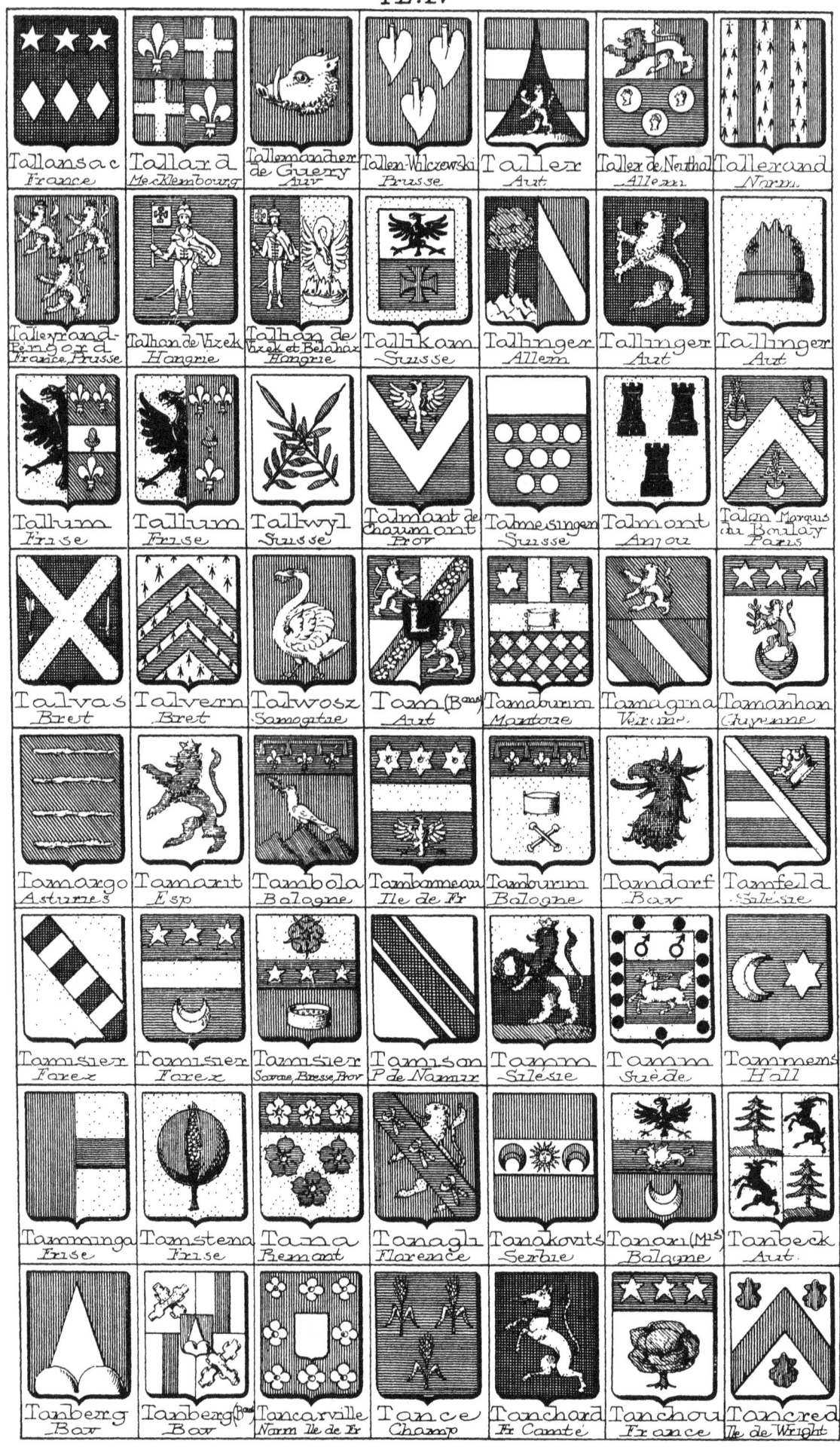

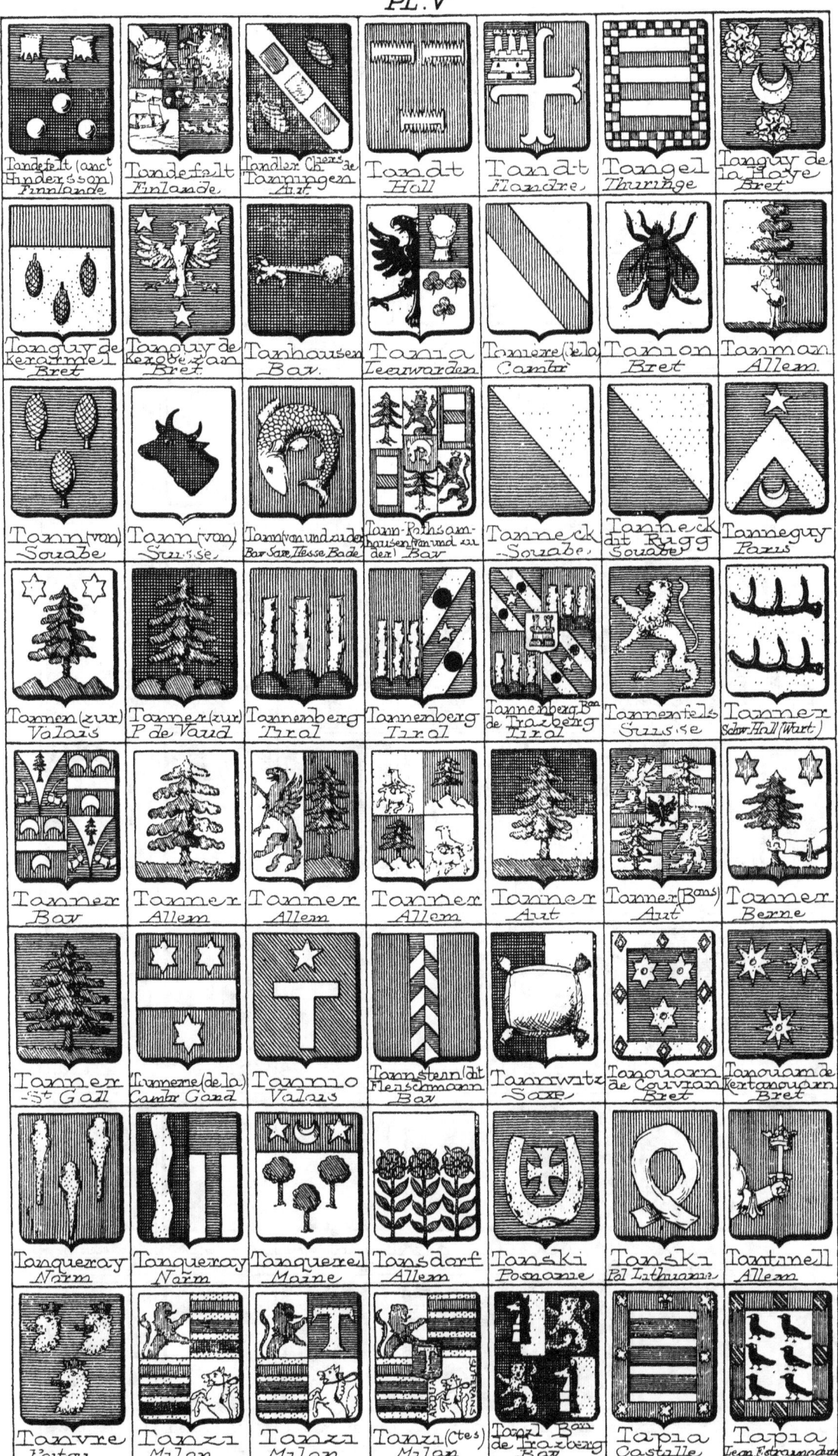

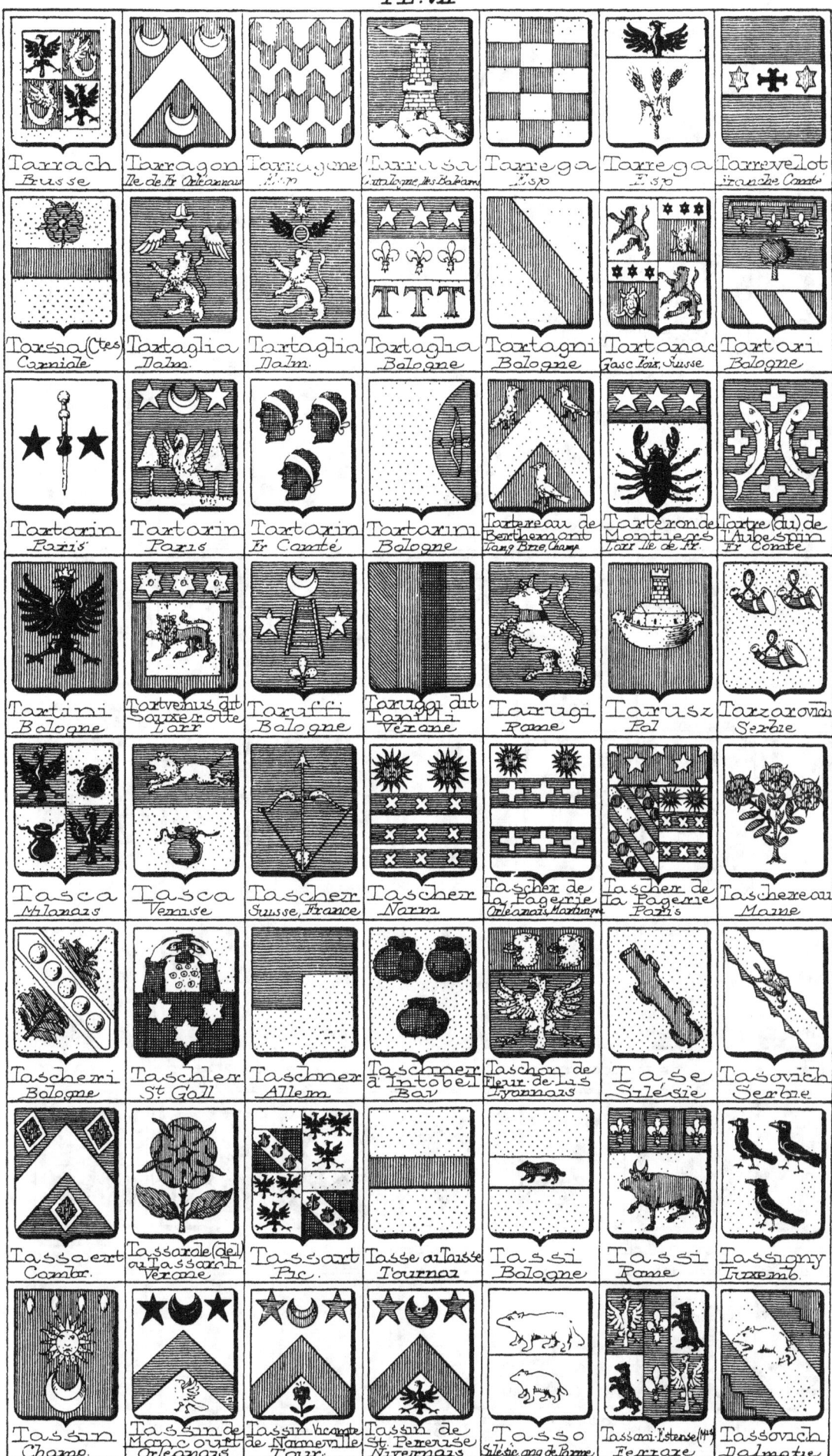

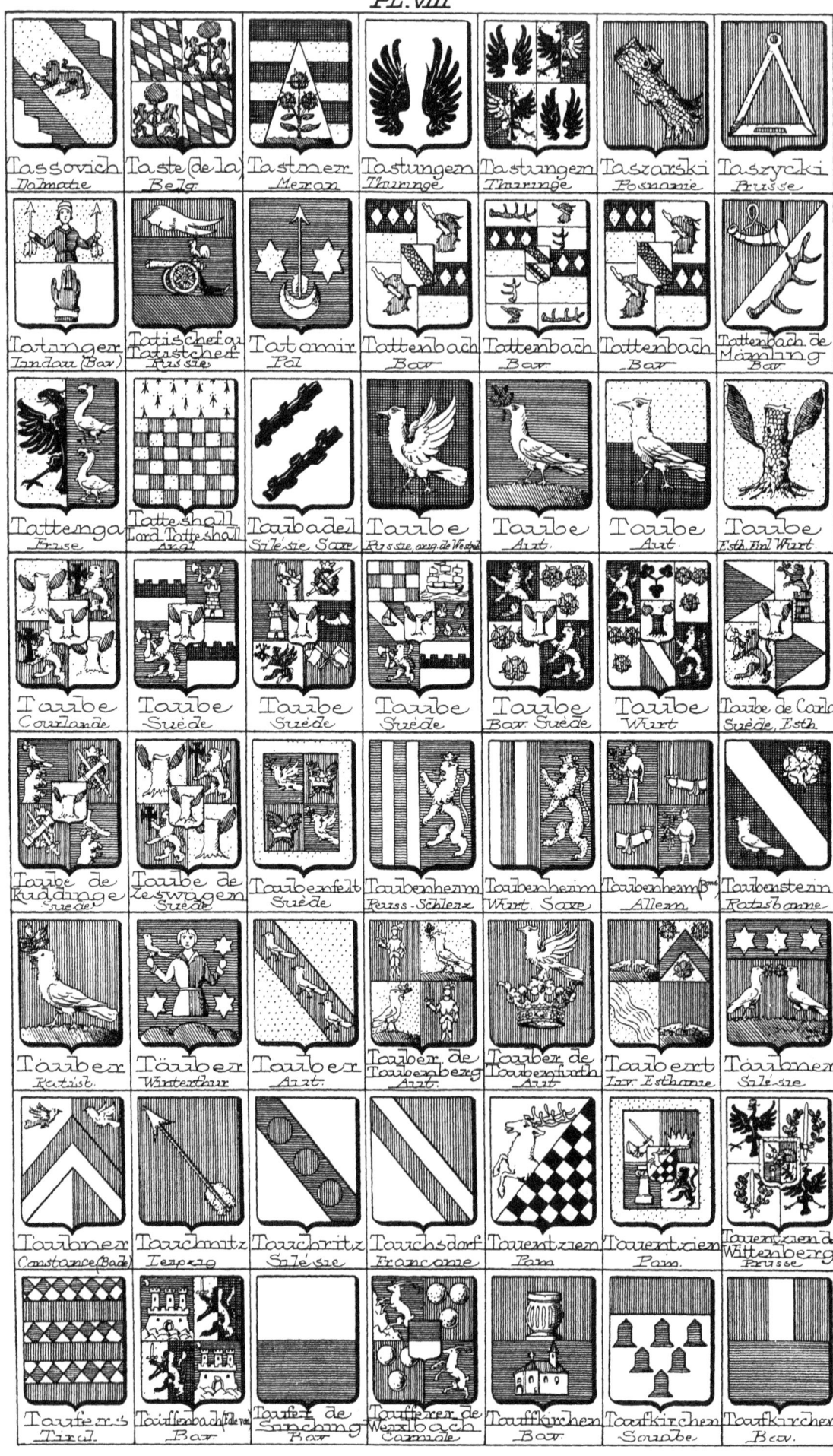

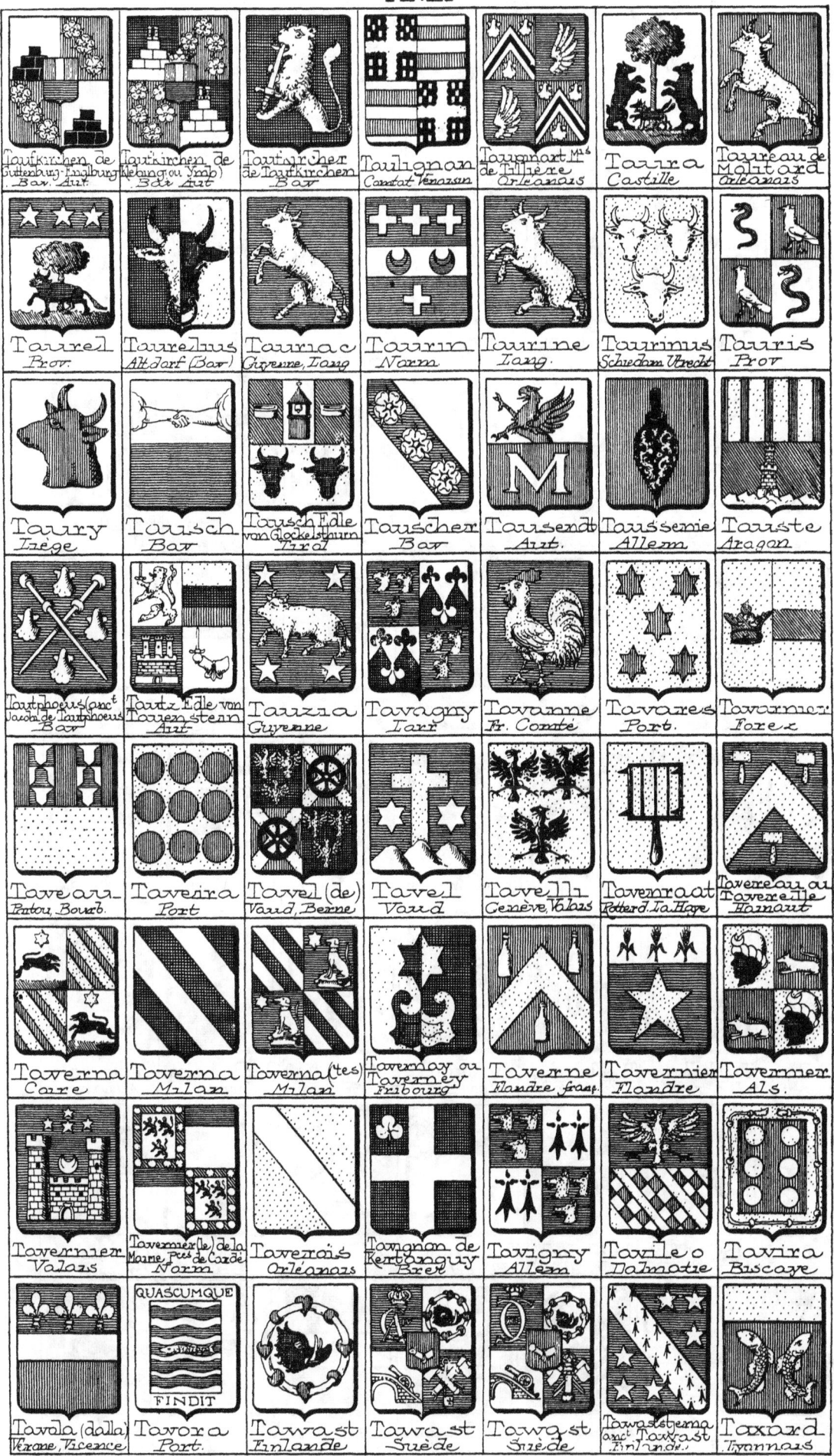

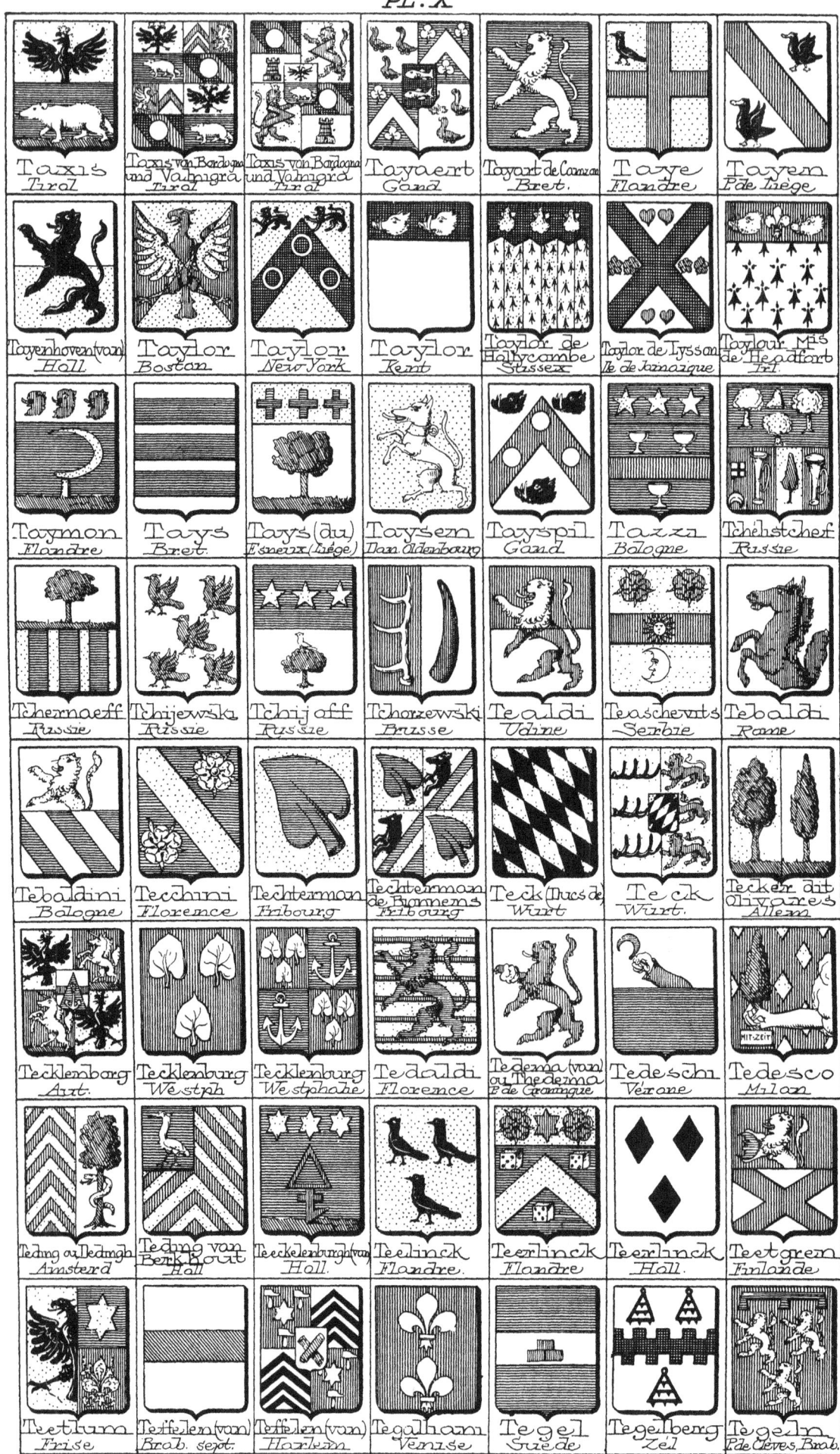

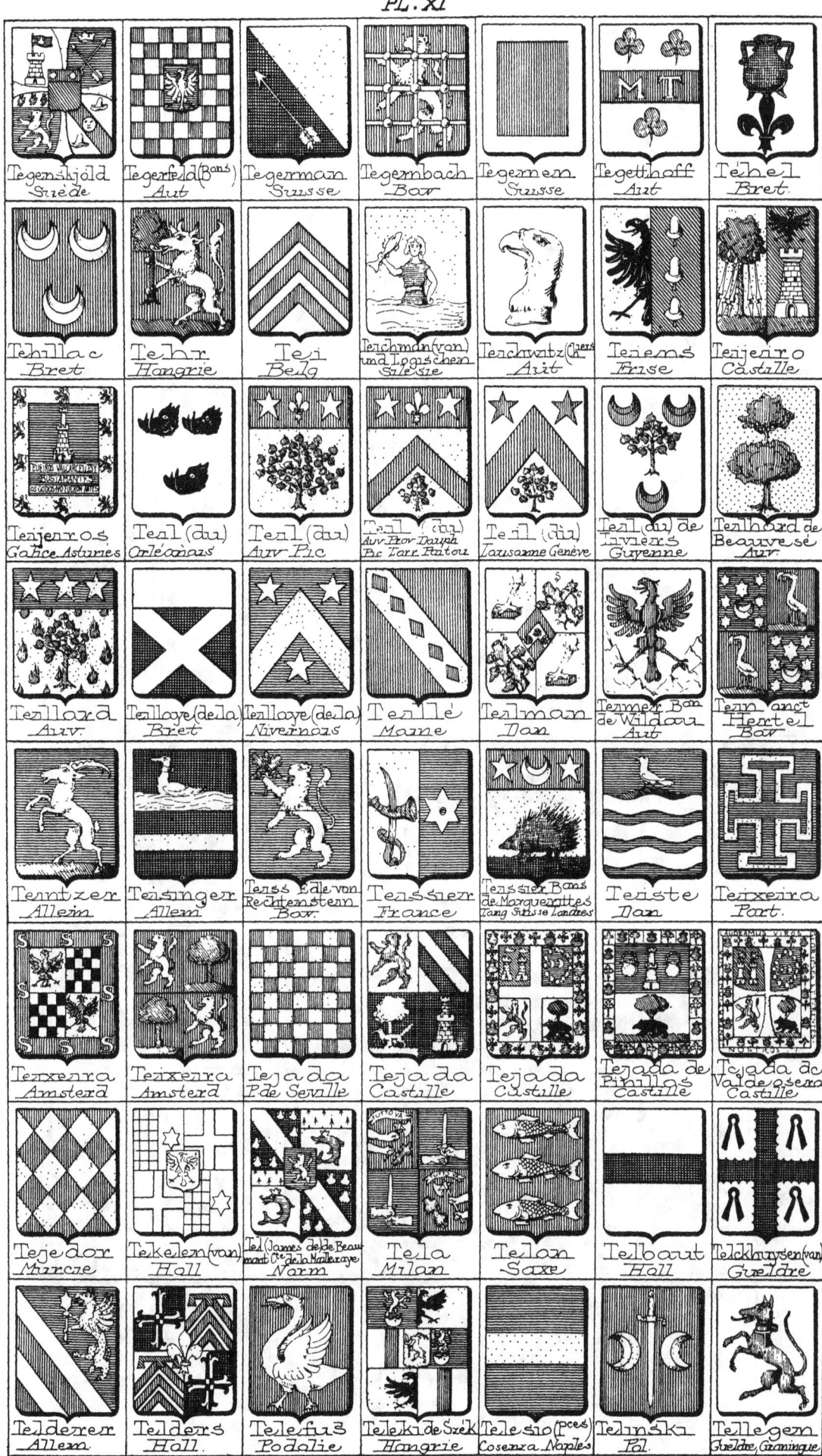

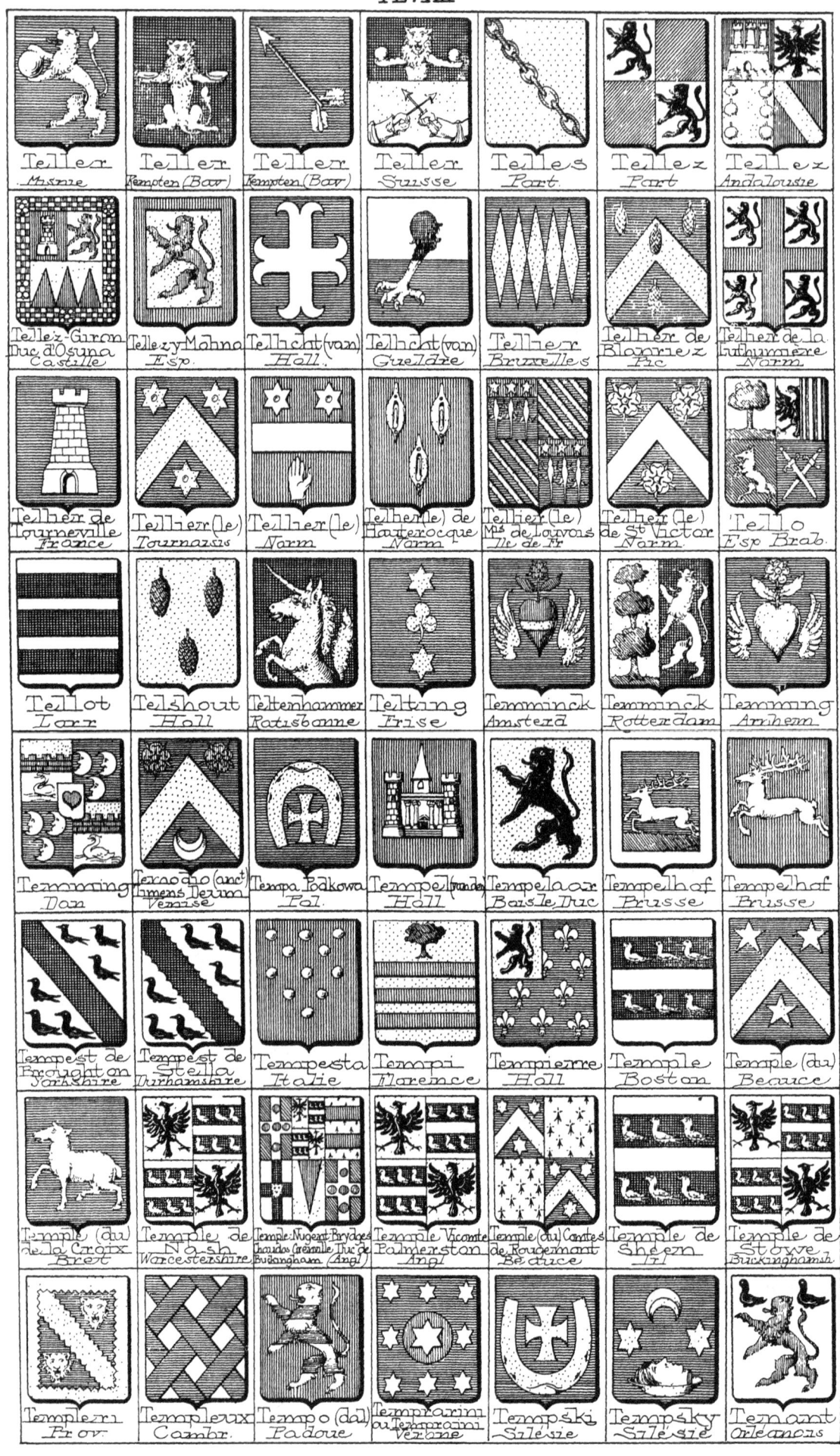
PL. XII

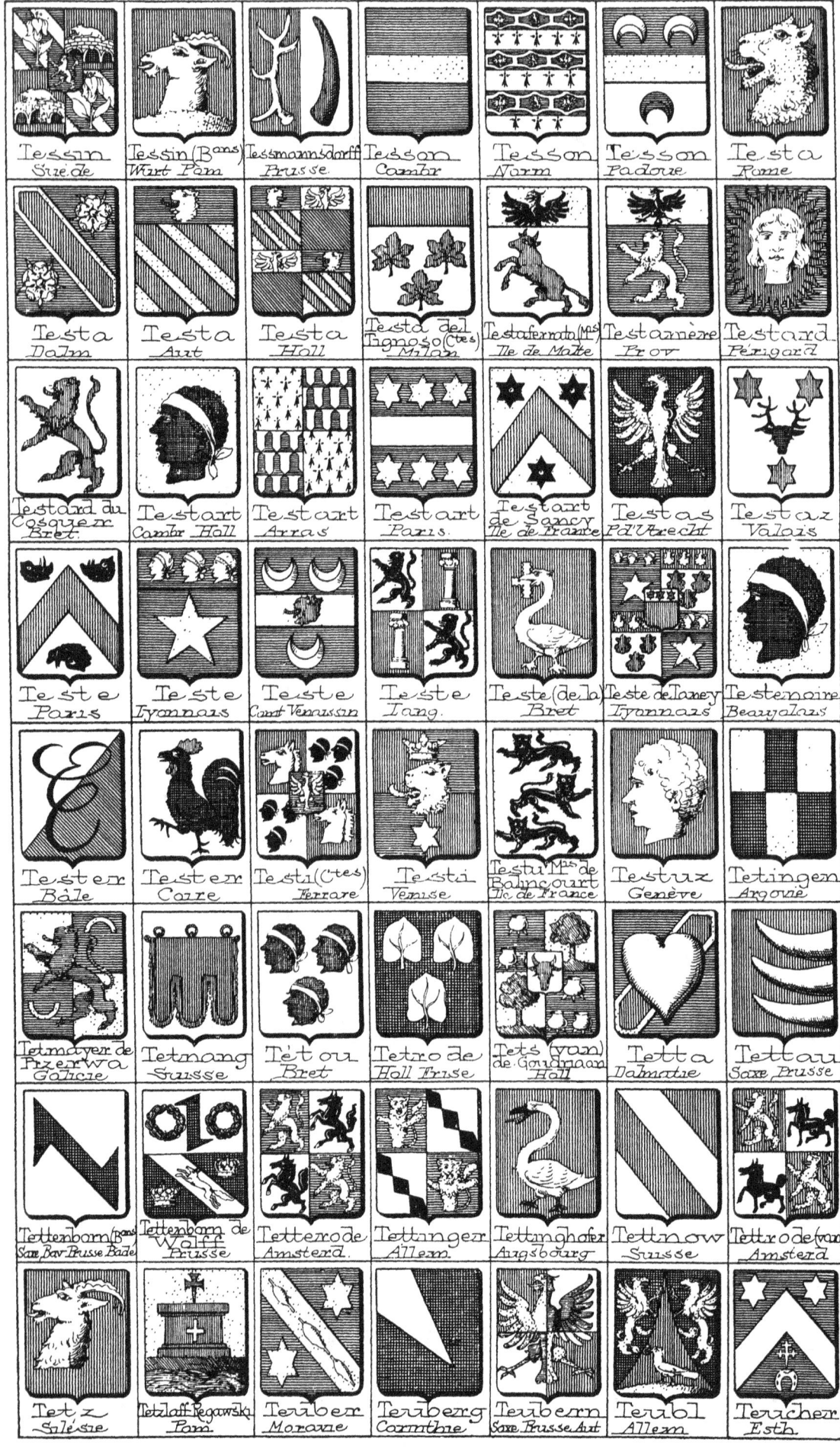

PL. XVI

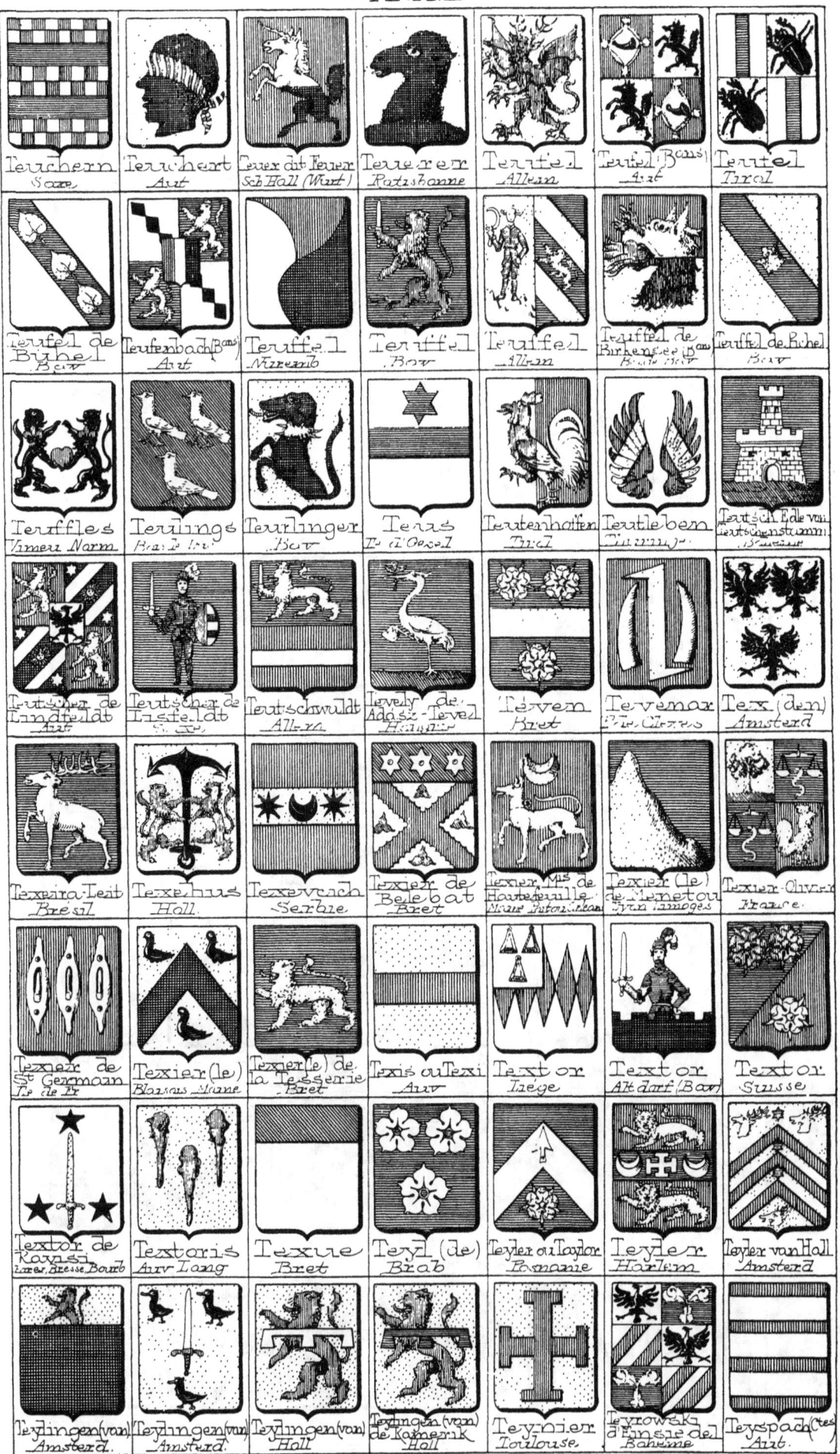

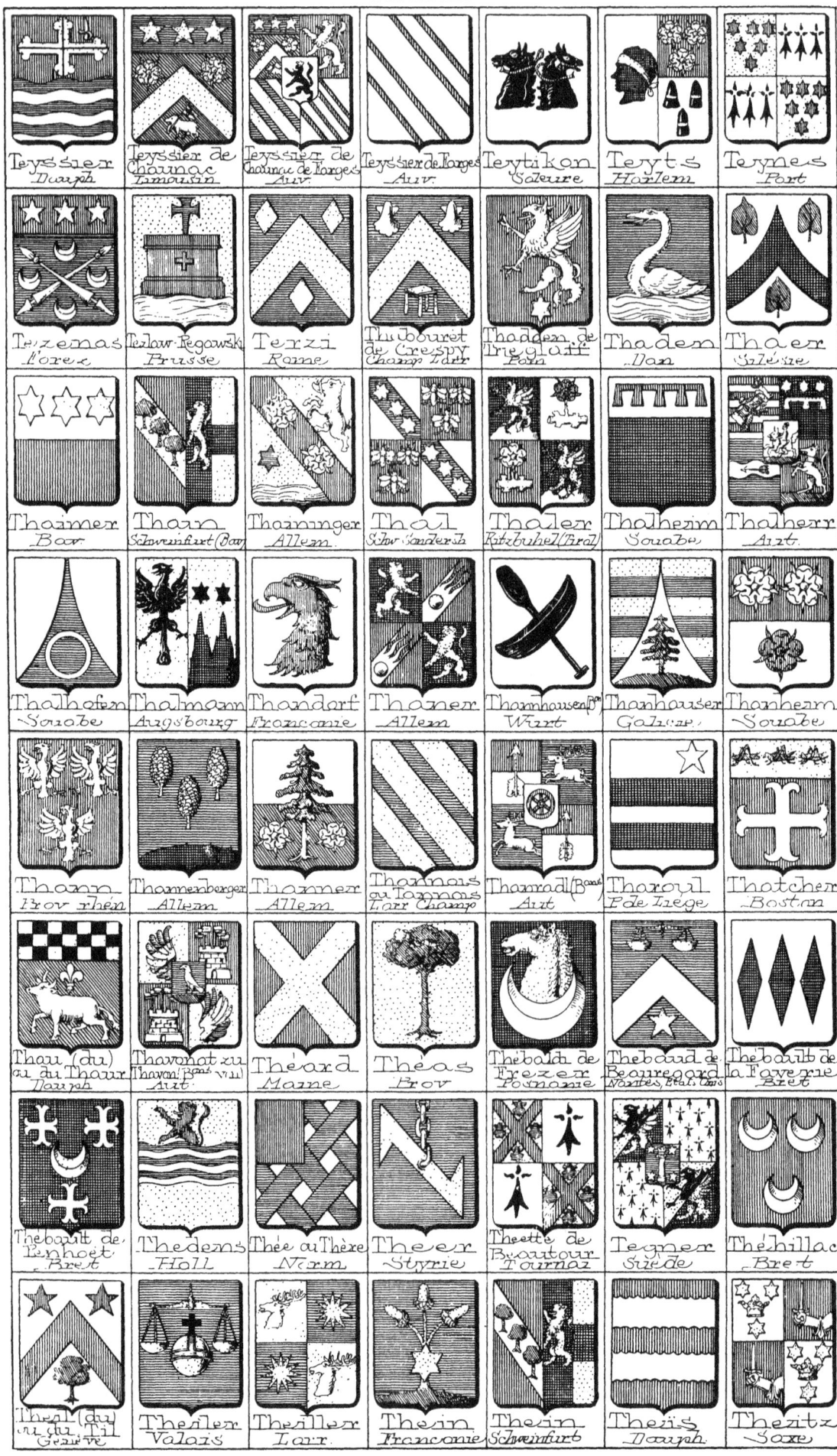

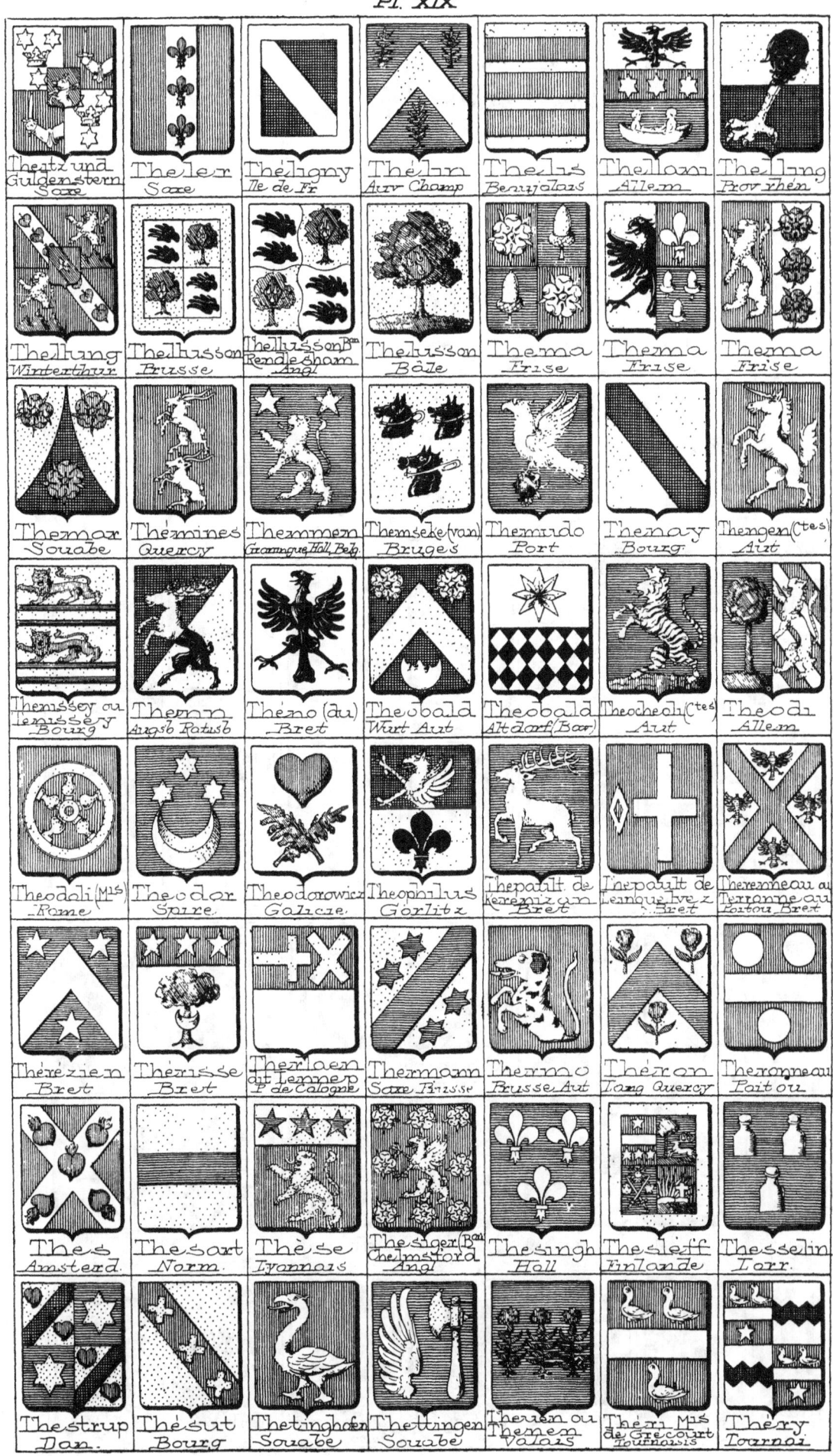

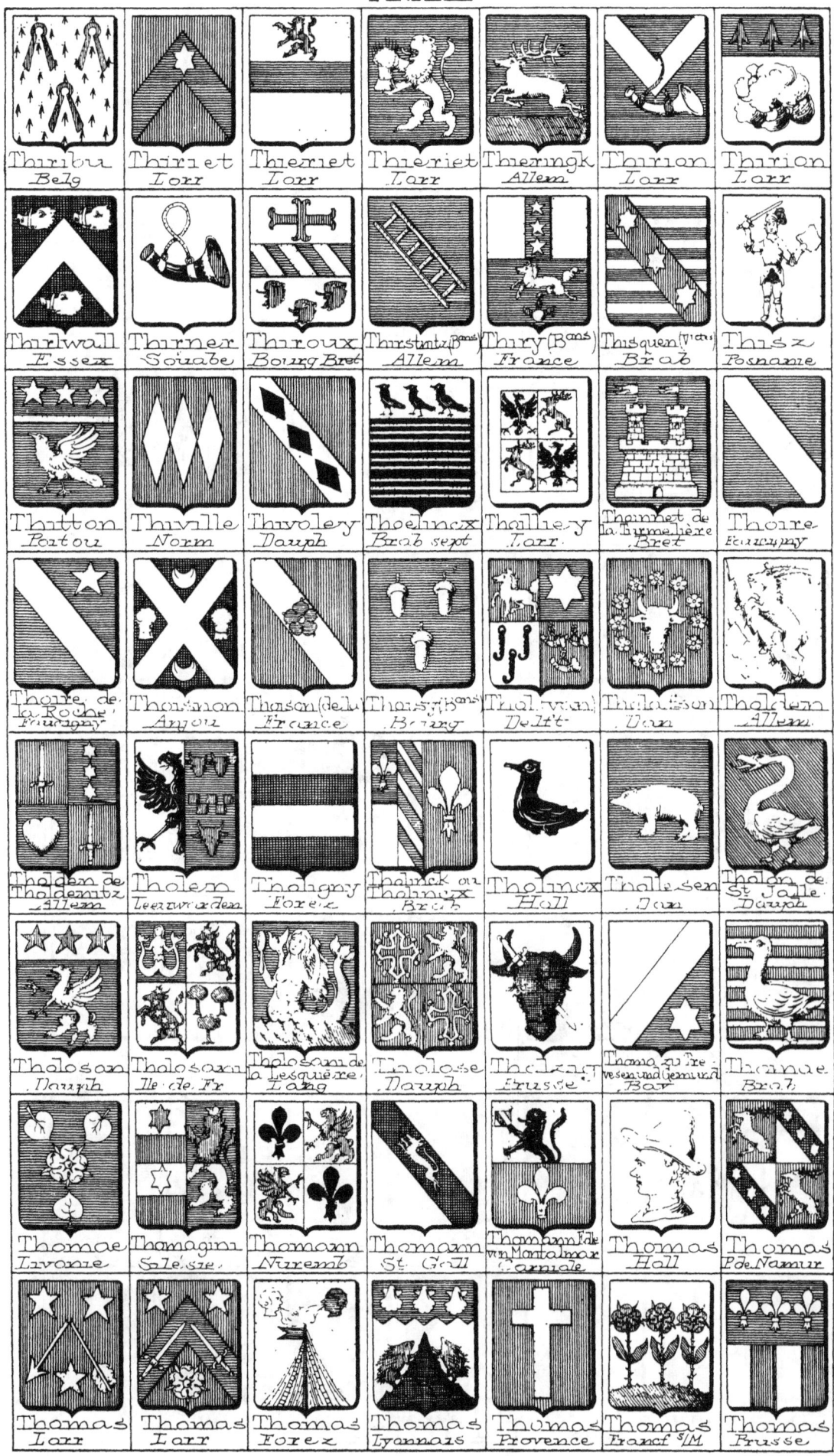

PL. XXIII

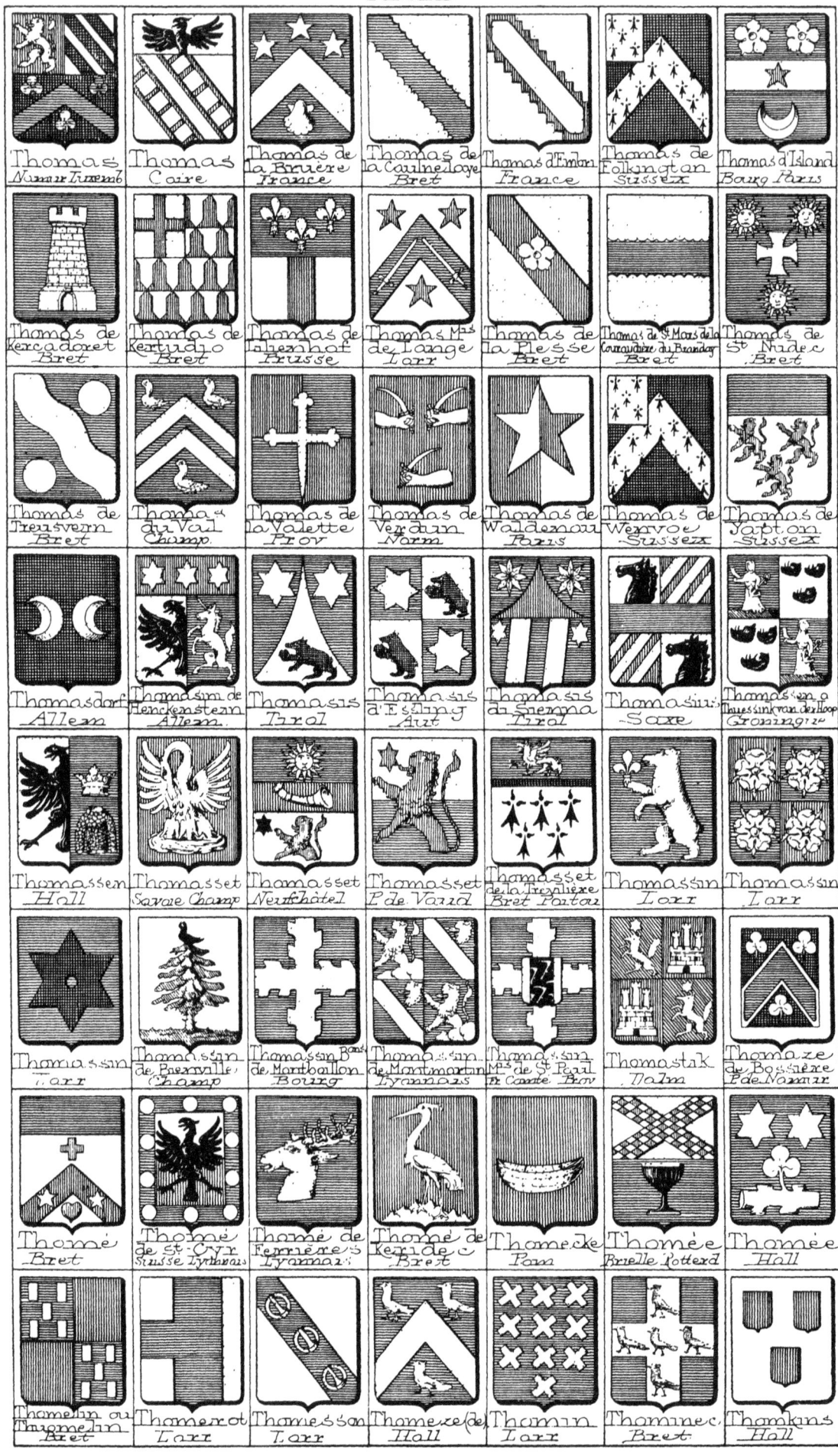

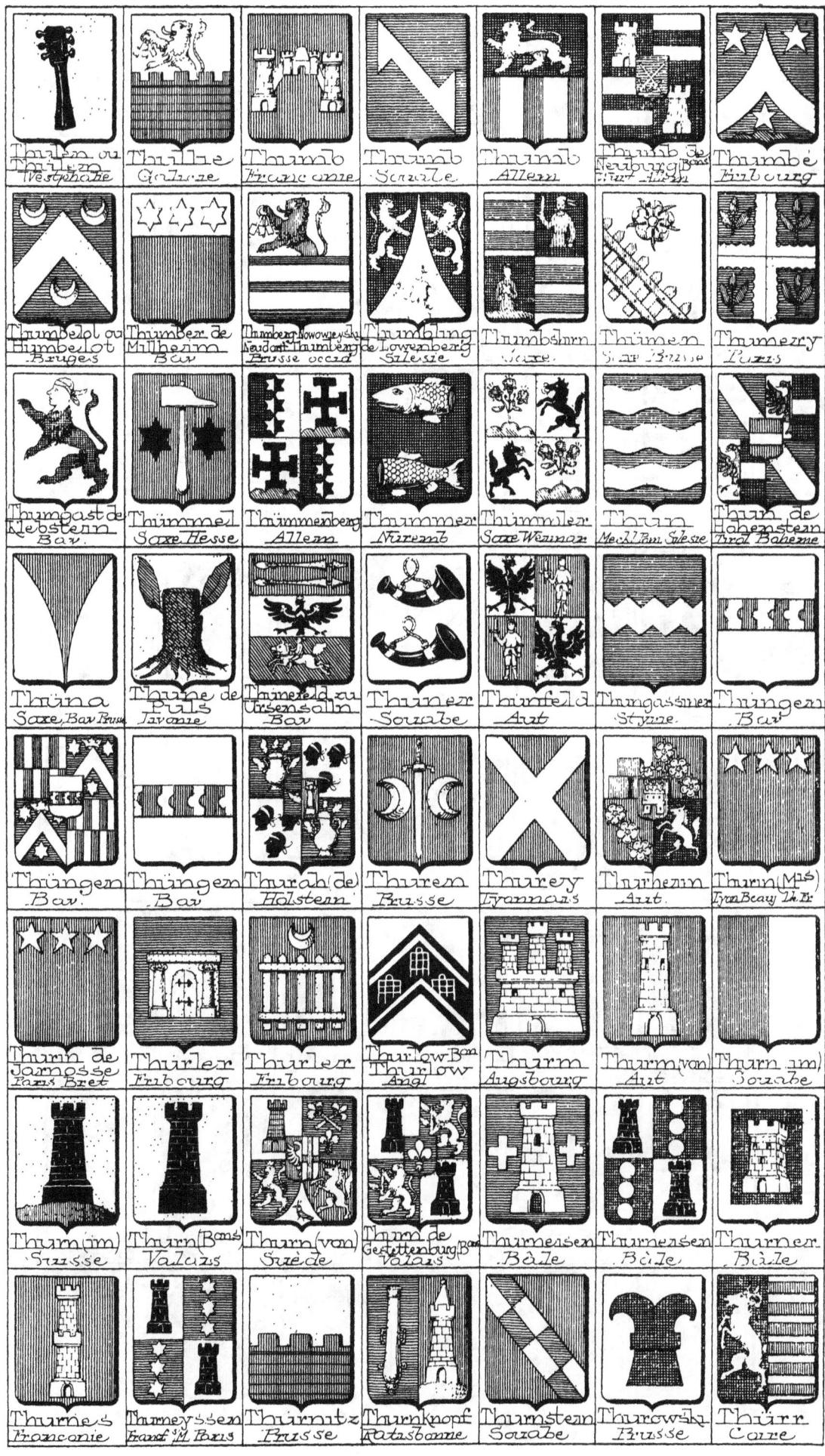

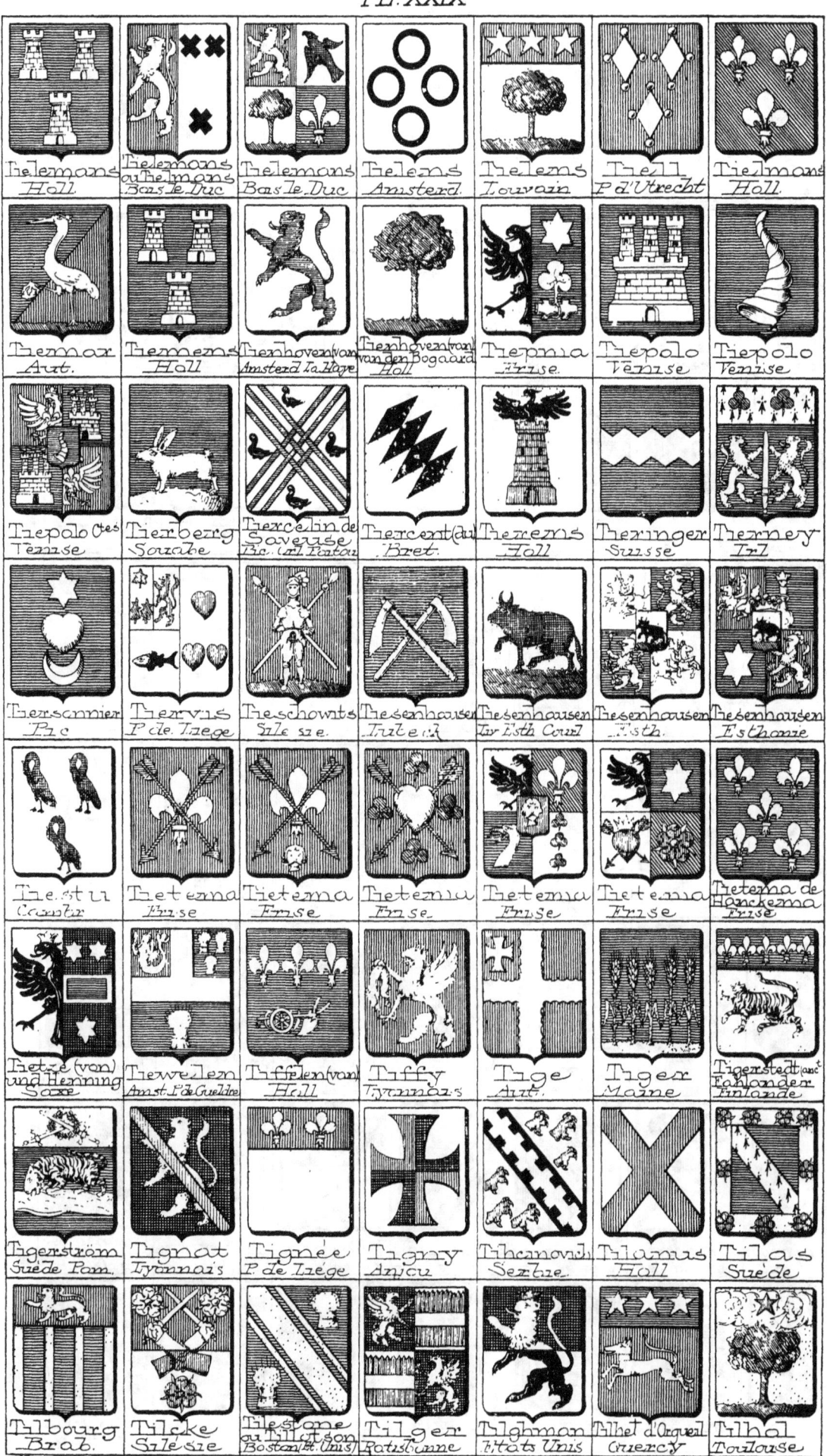

PL. XXX

PL. XXXI

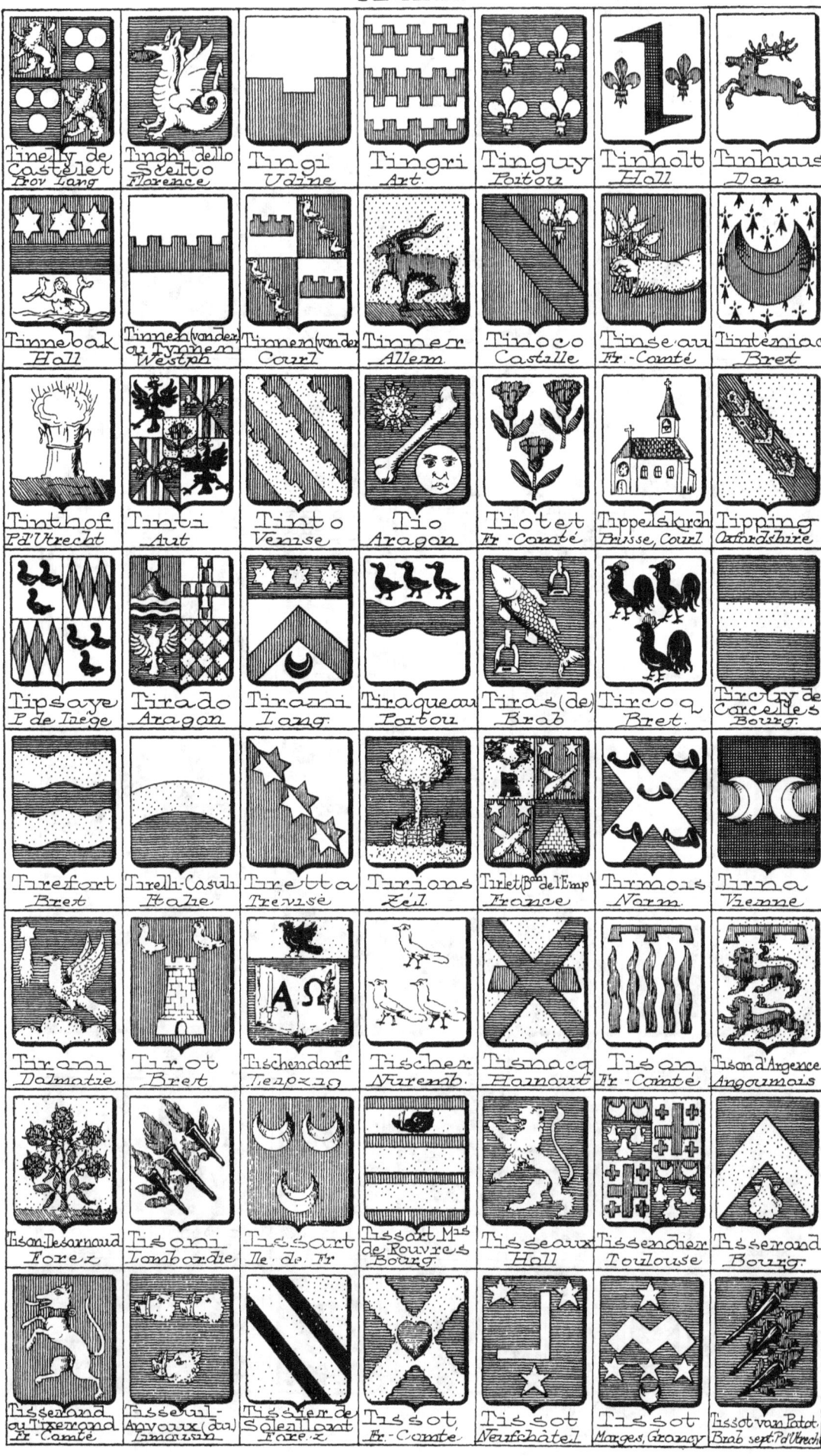

PL.XXXIII

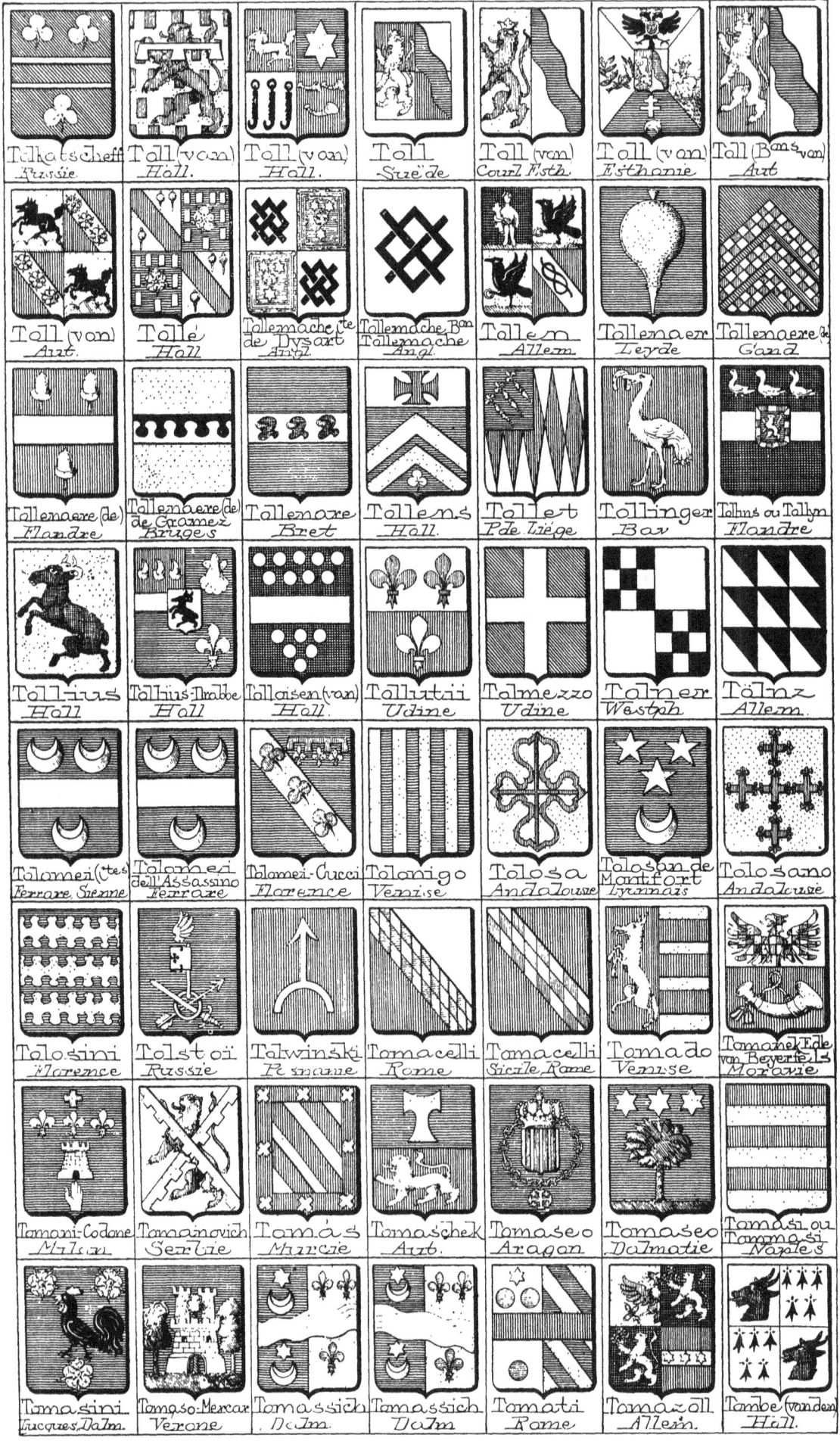

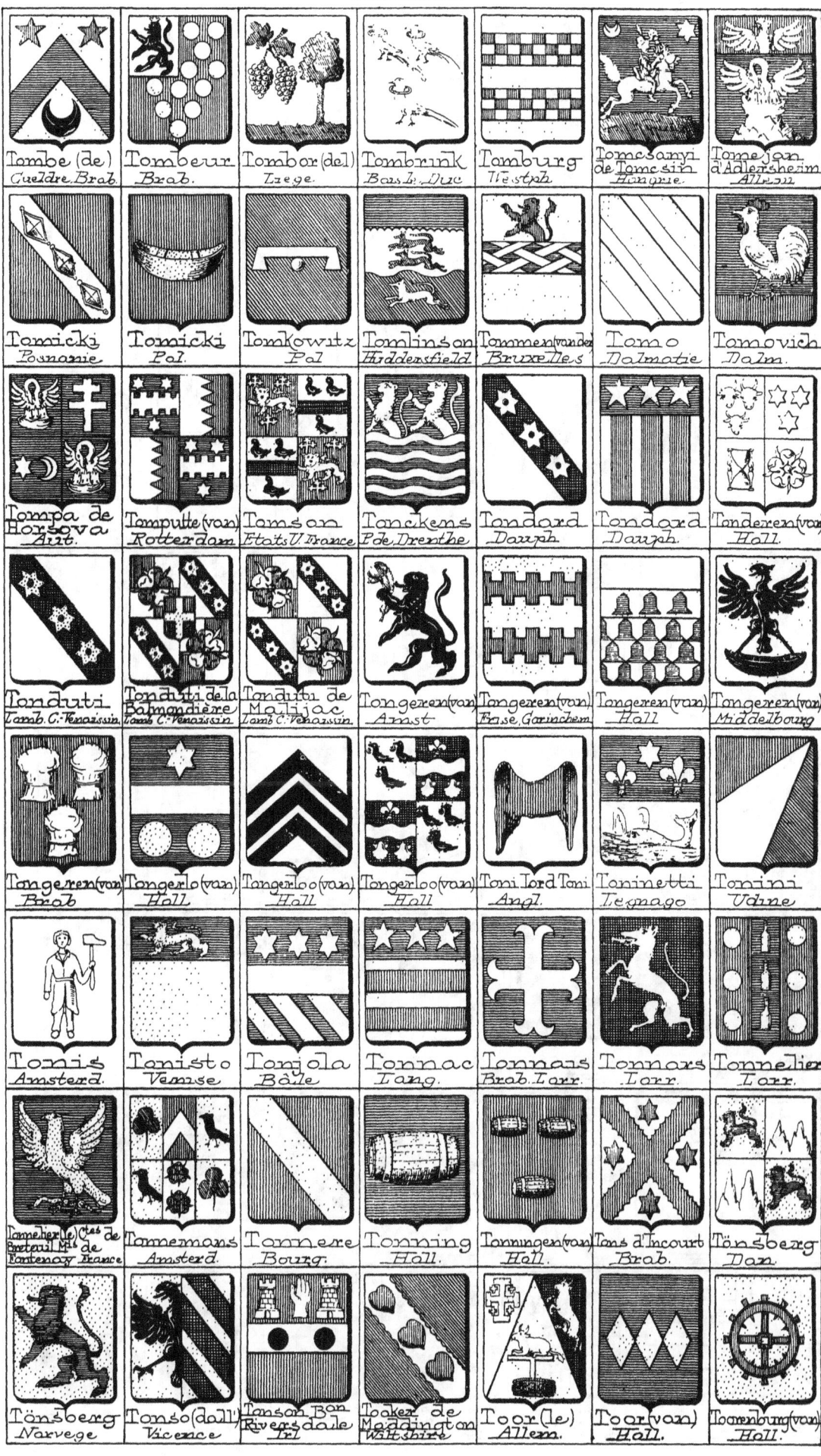

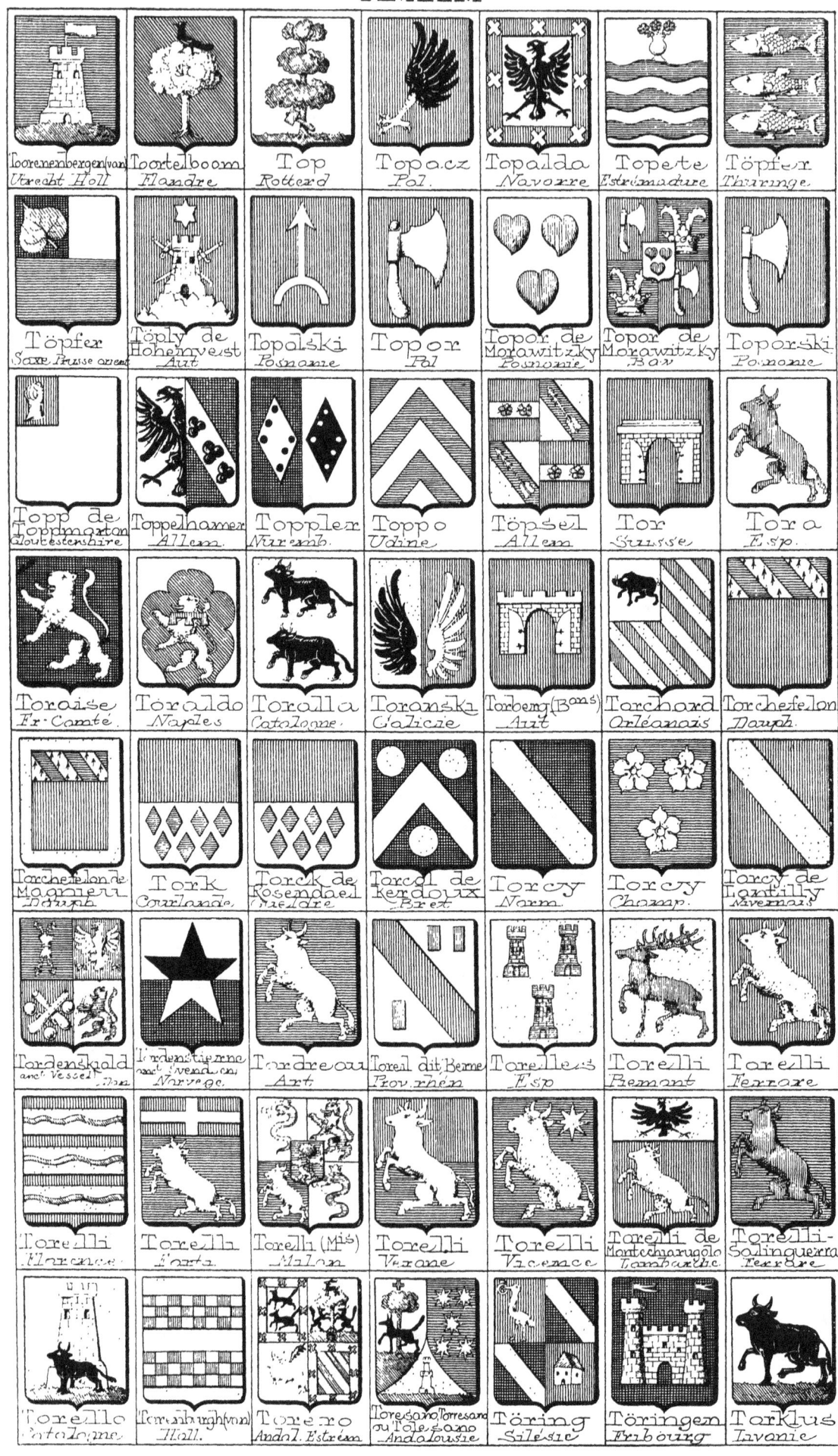

PL. XXXVII

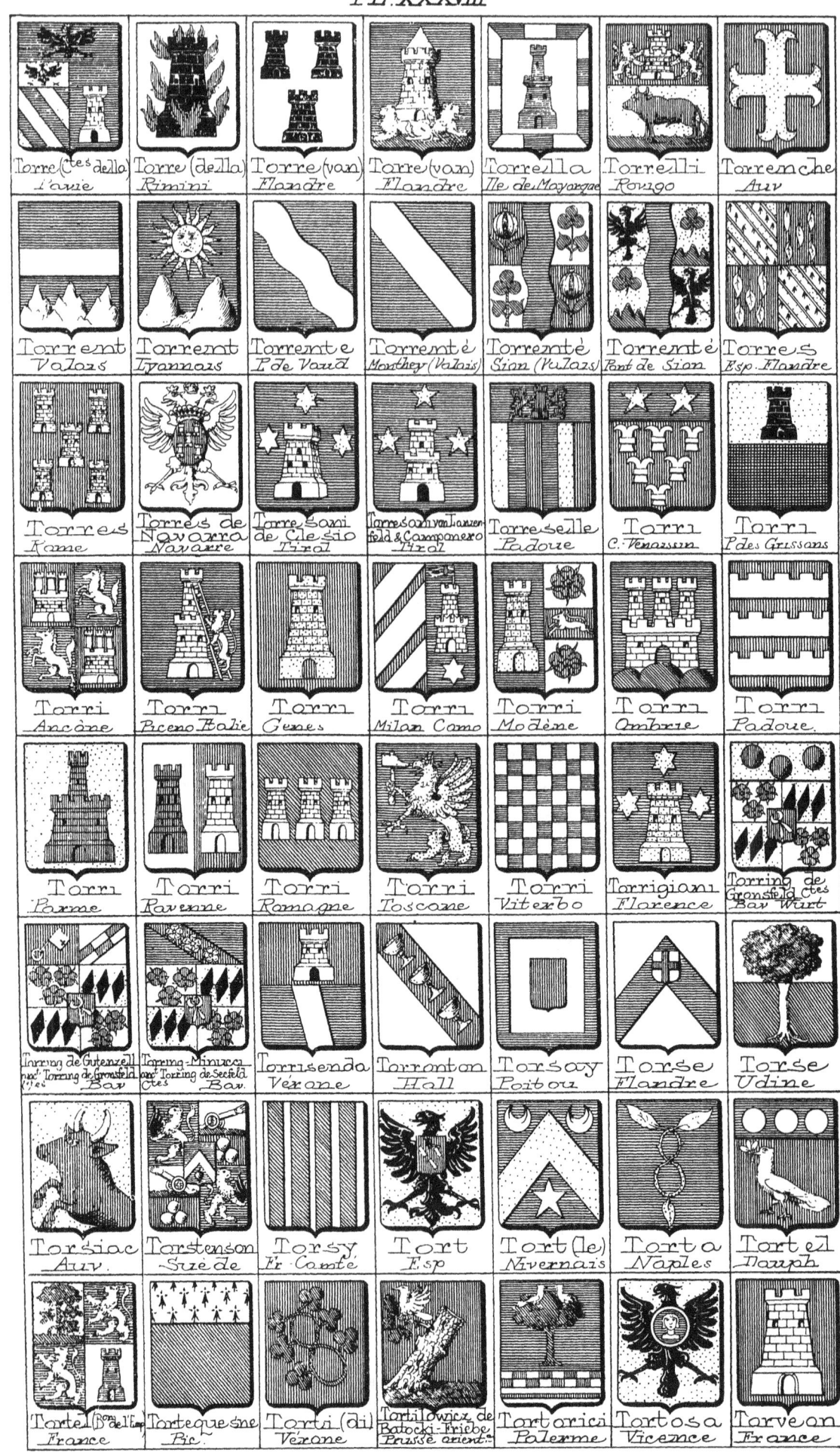

PL. XLI

PL. XLIII

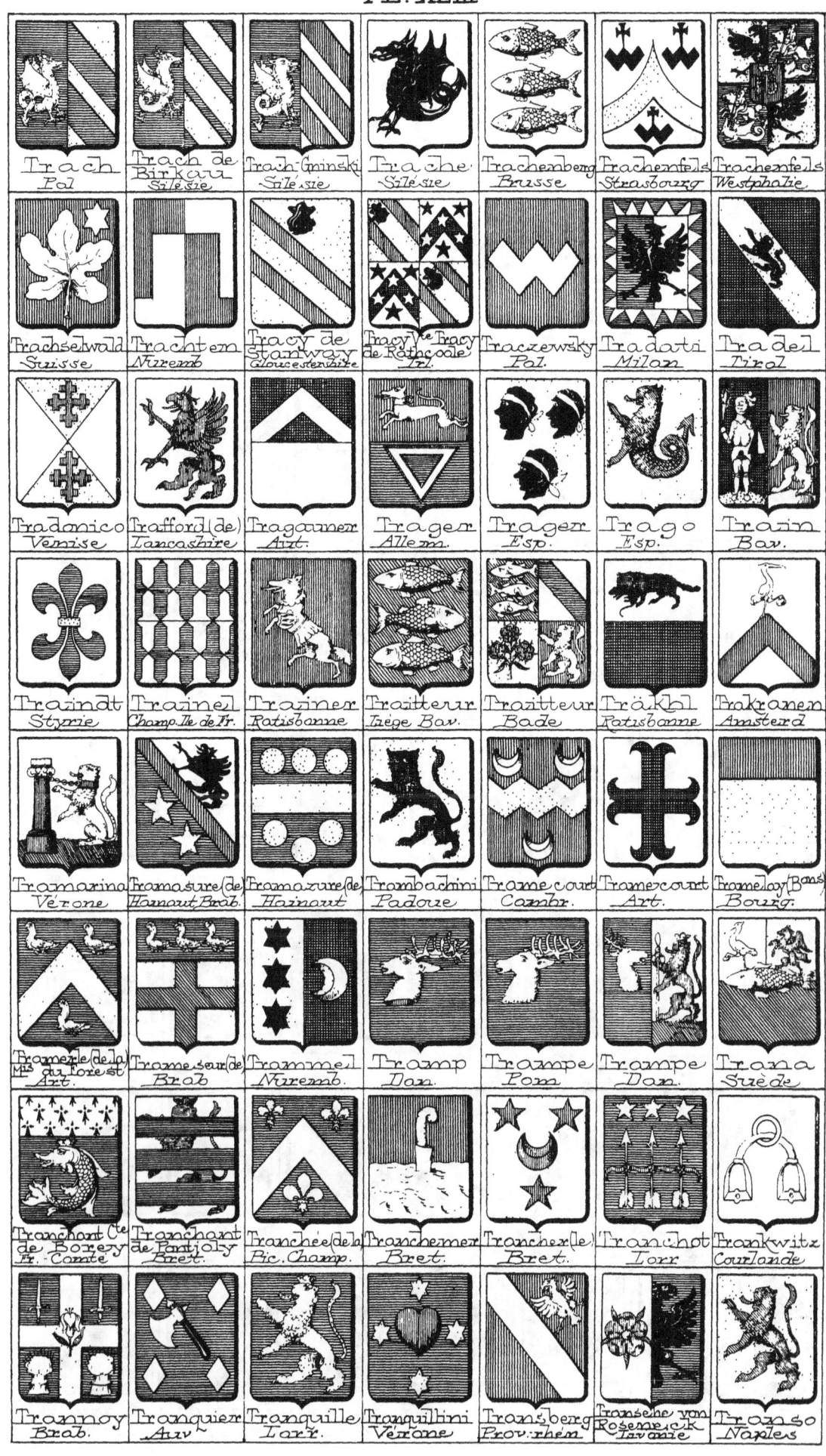

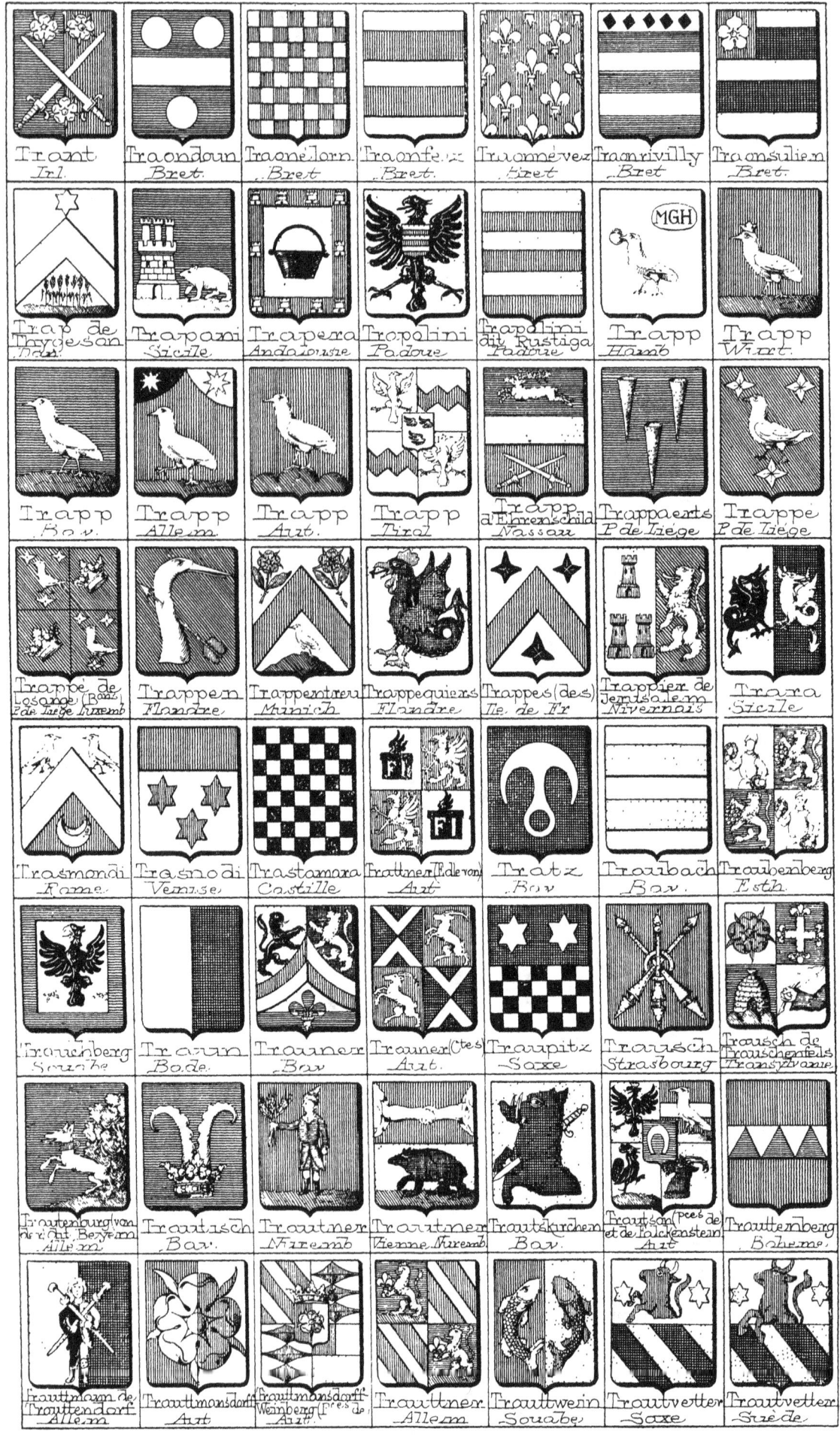

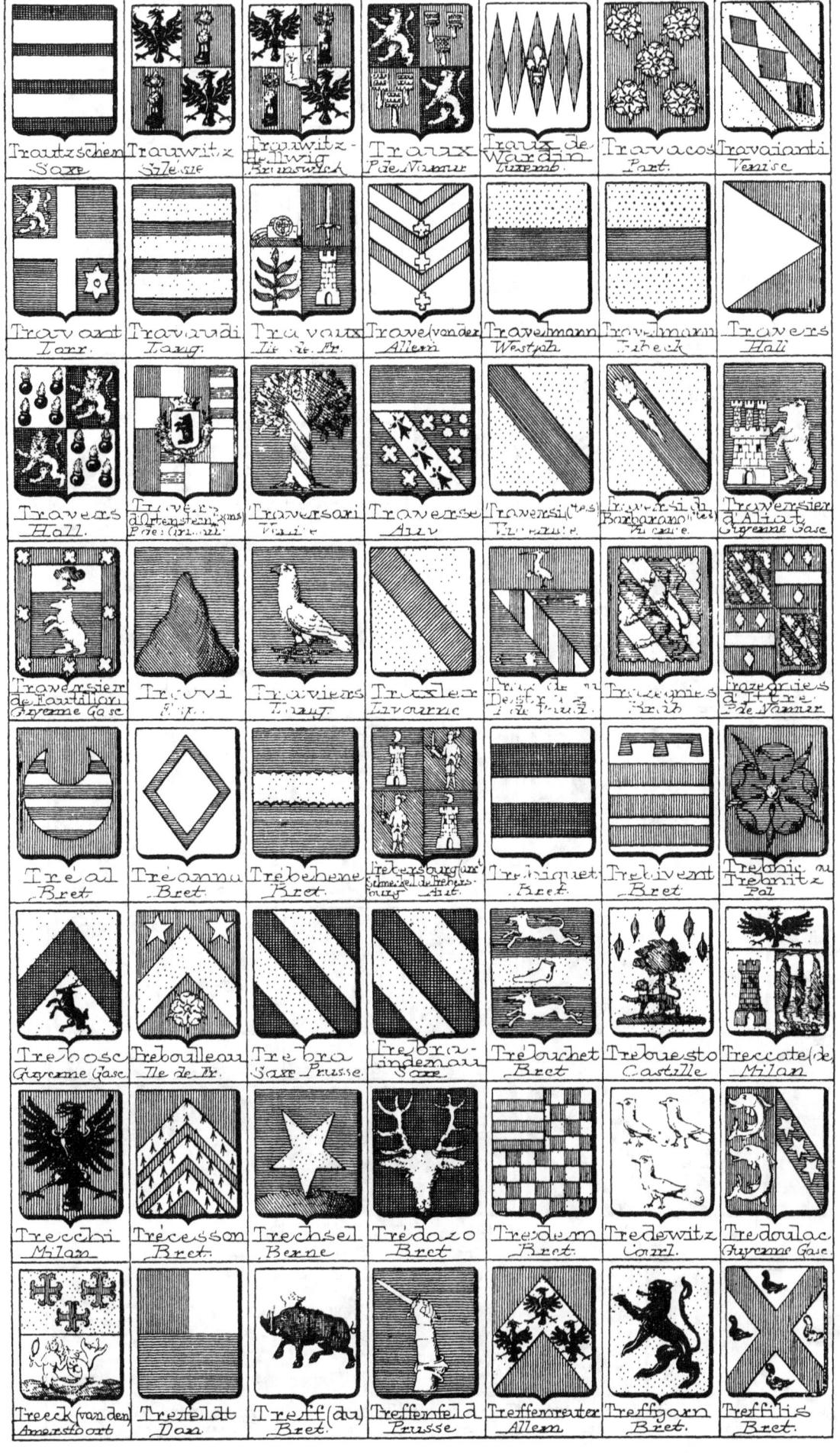

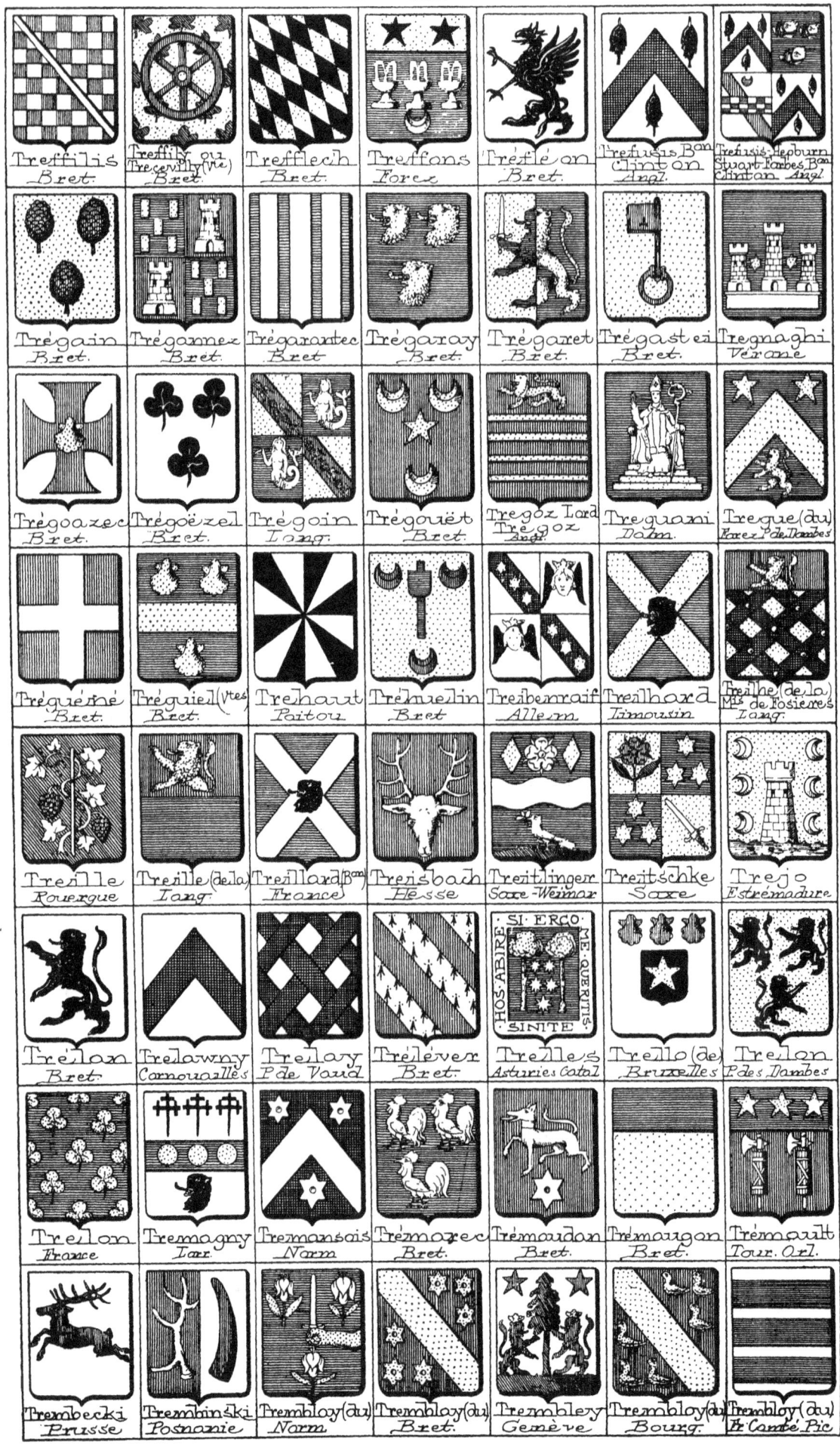

PL. XLVII

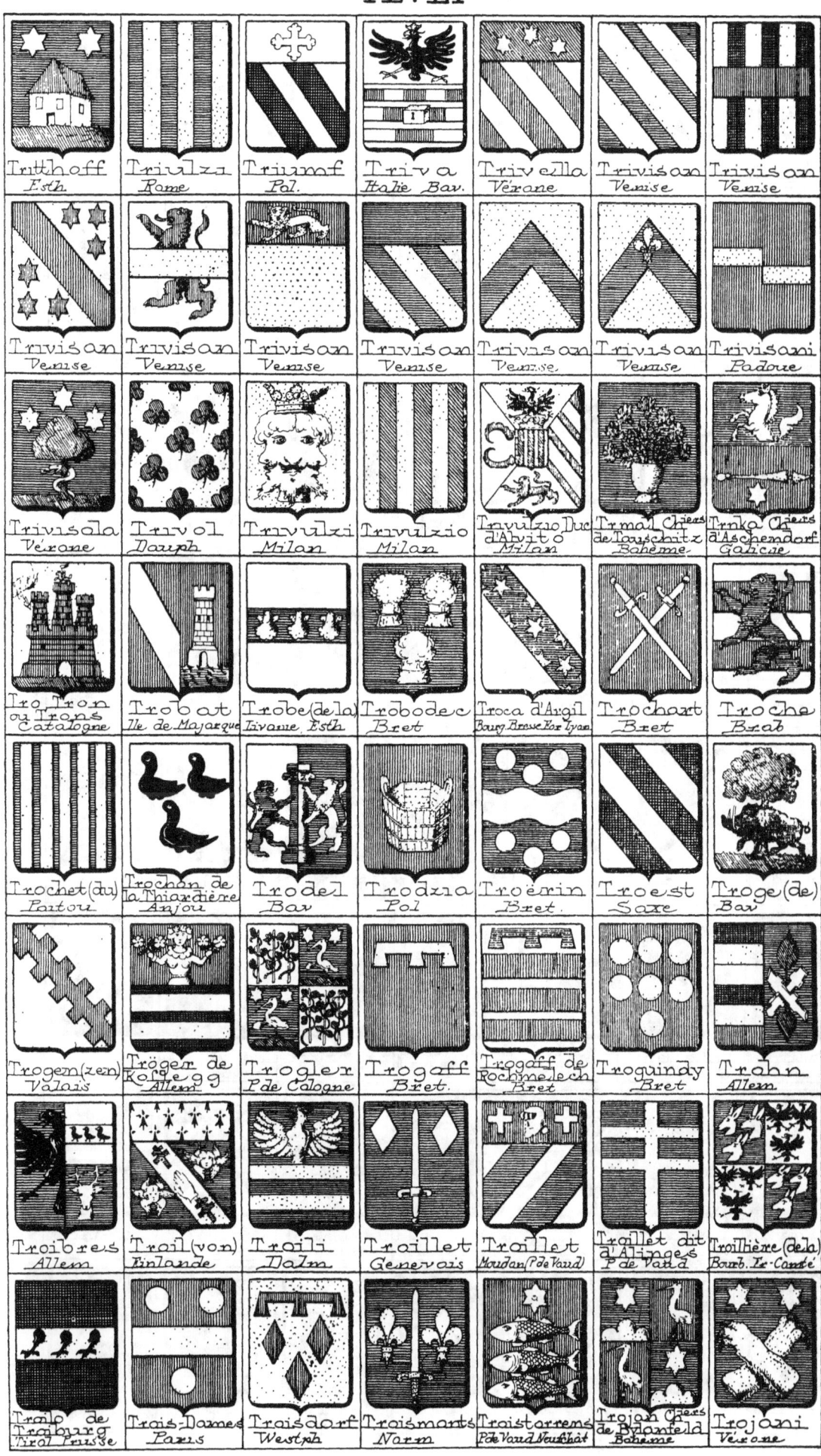

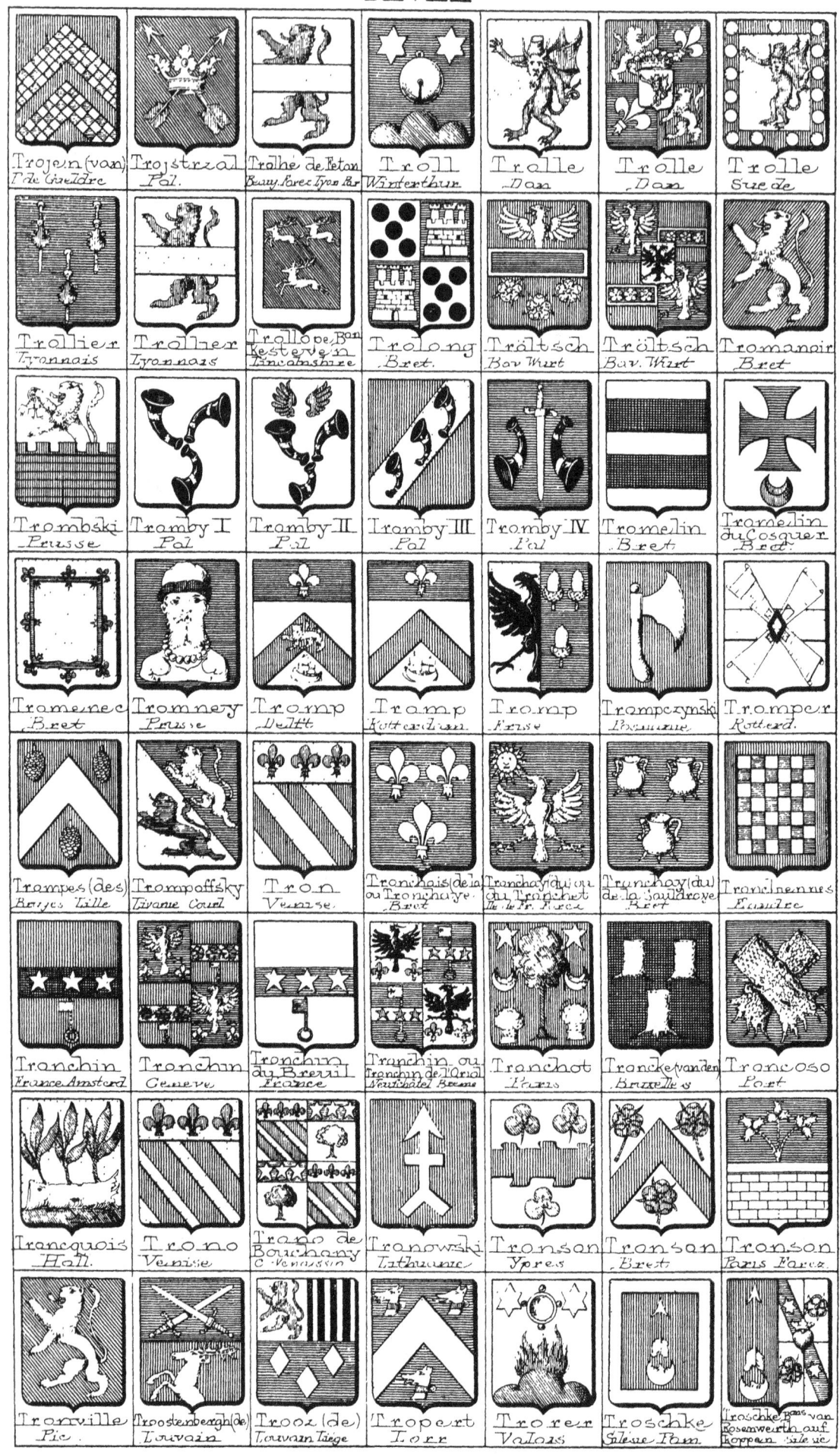

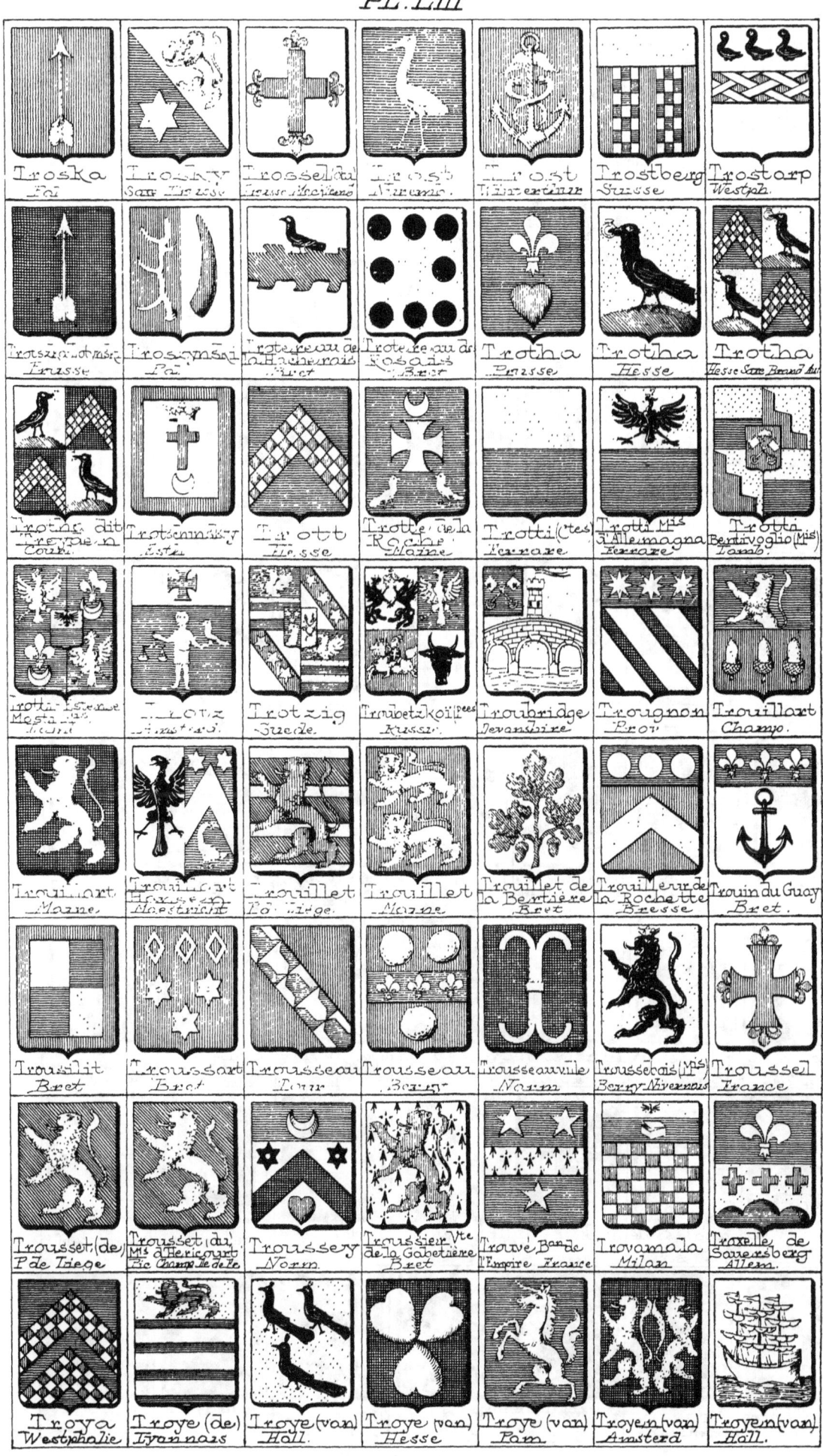
PL. LIII

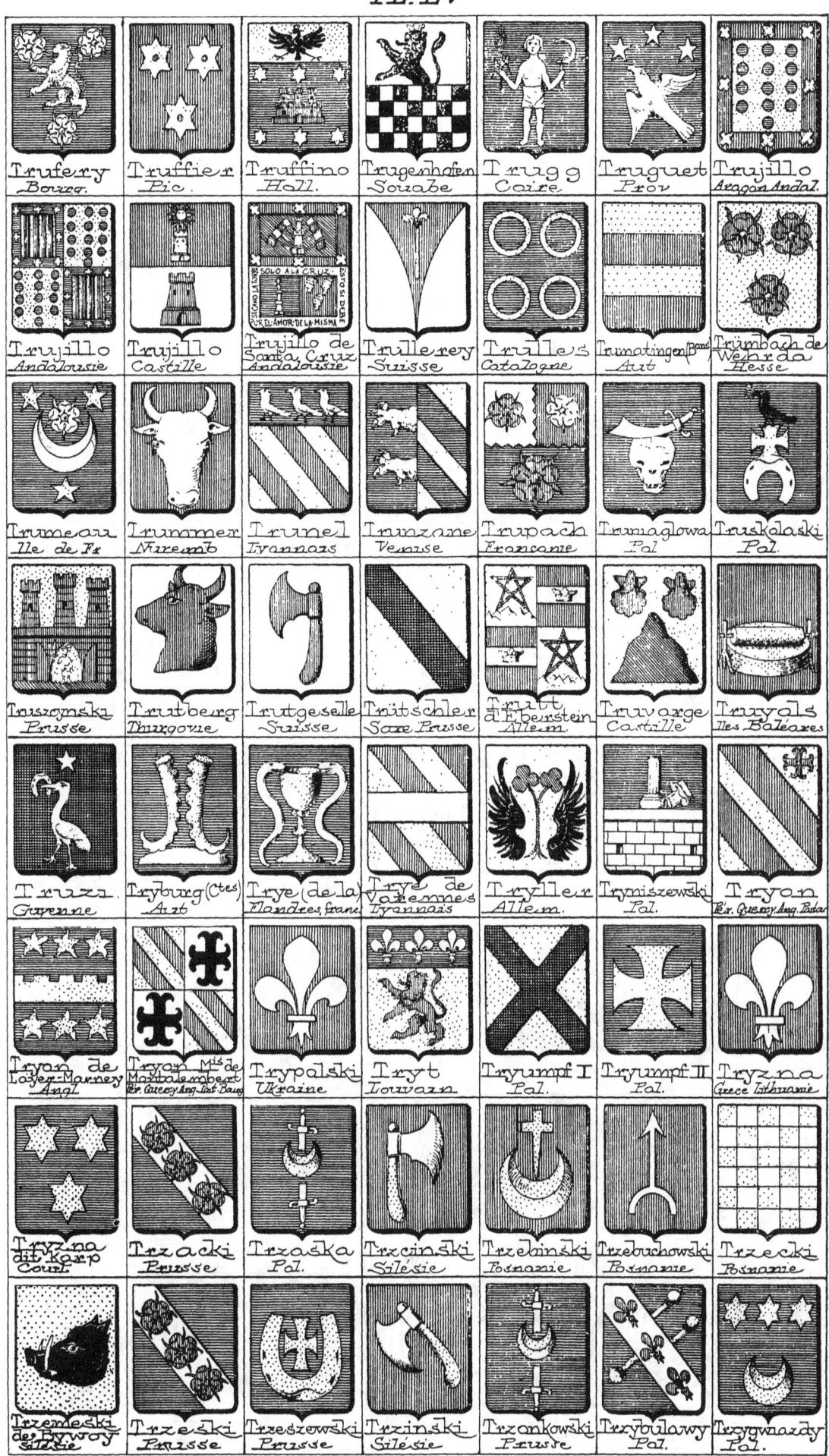

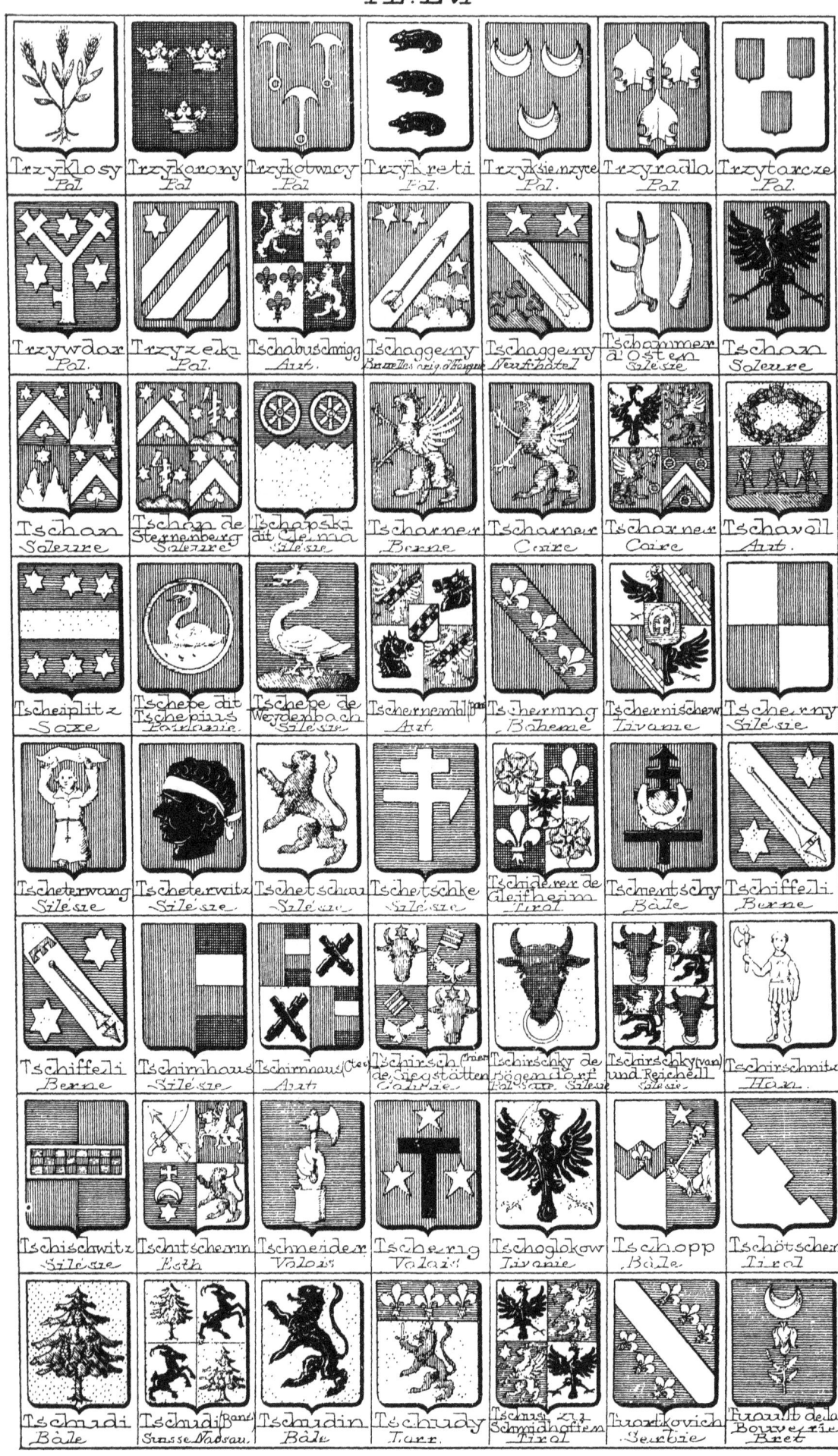

PL. LVII

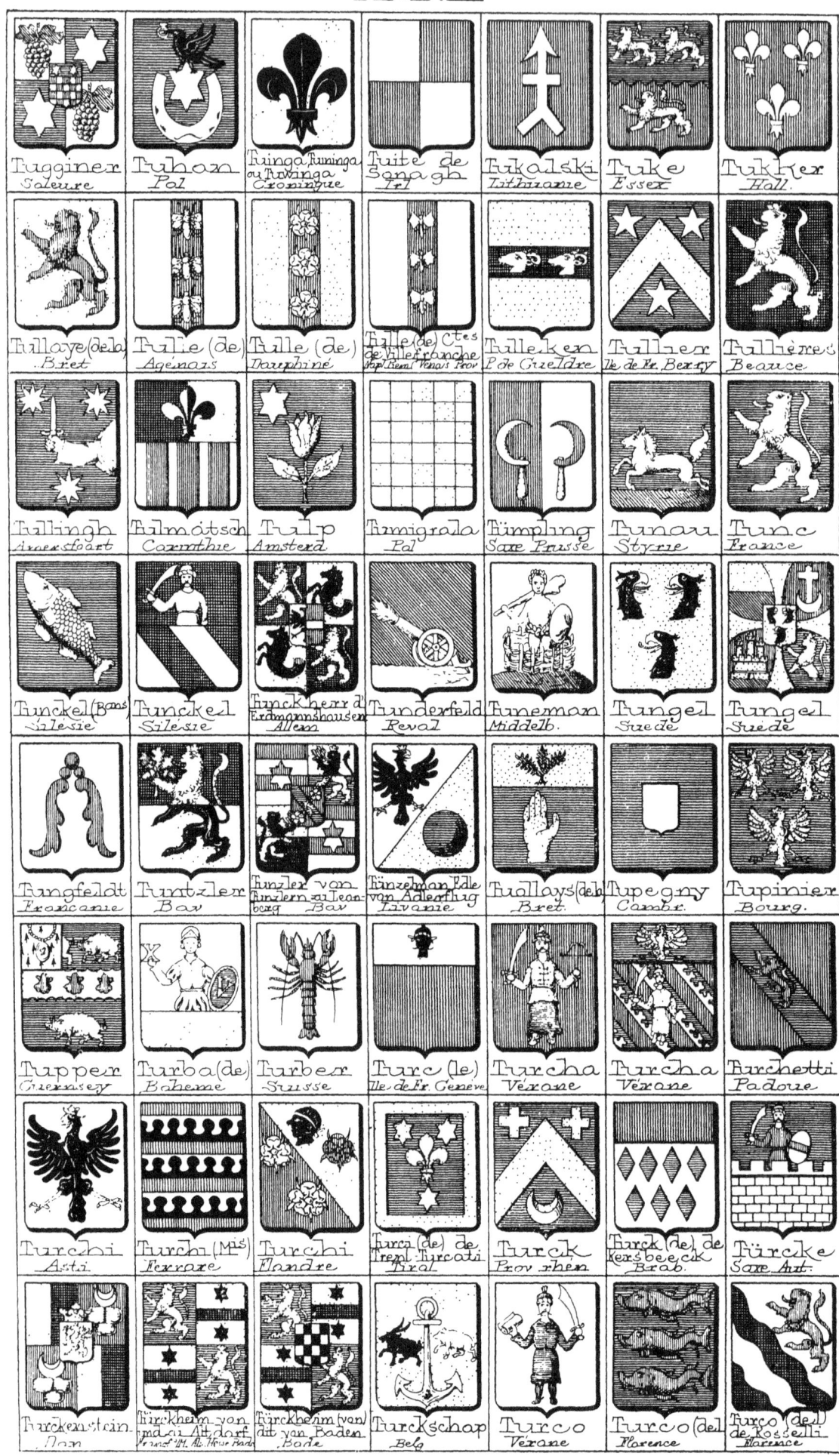

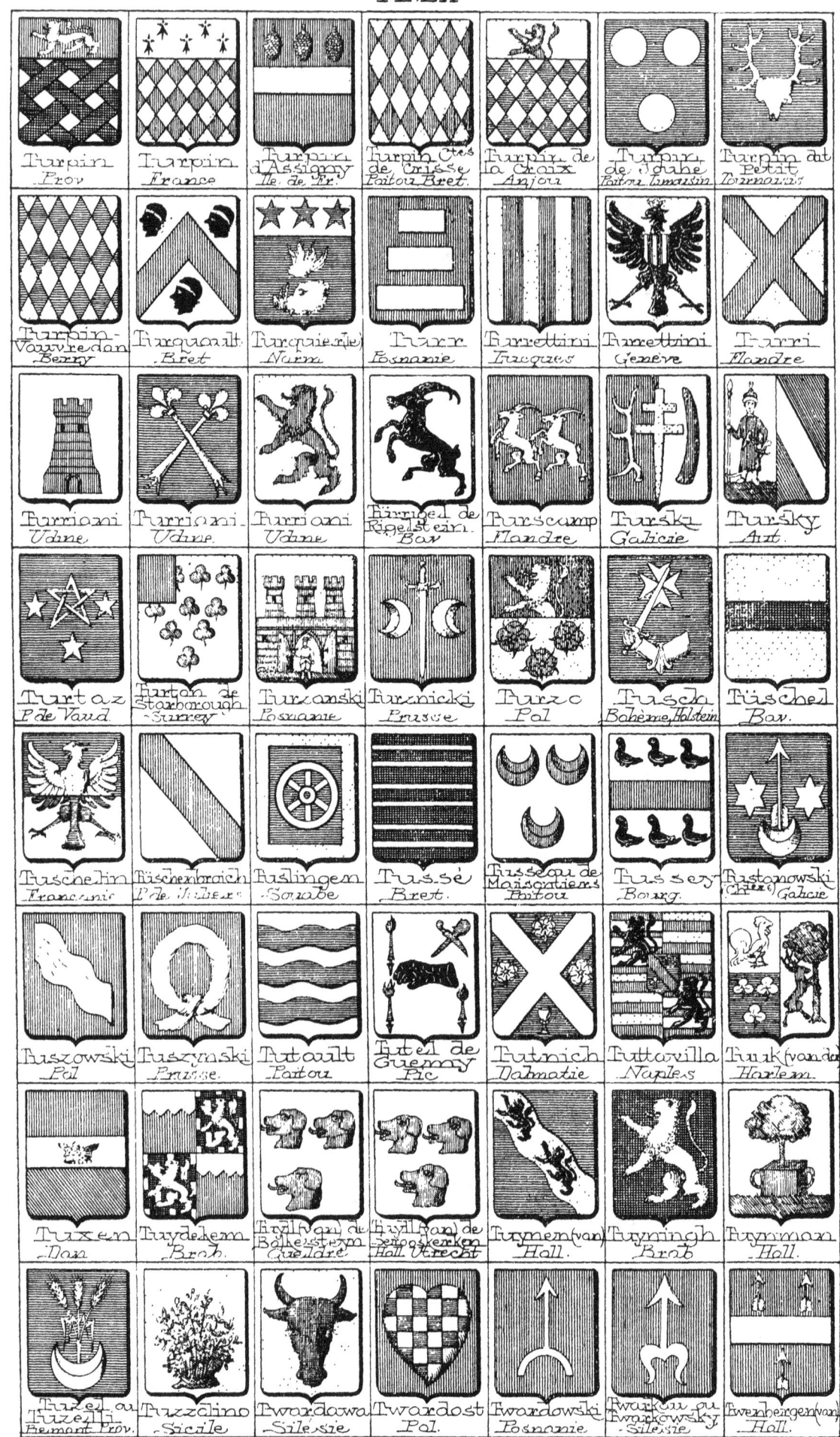

PL. LXII

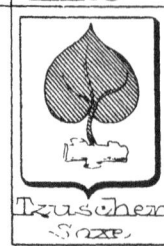

PL. LXIII

| Ubago Royaume de Léon | Ubaldi Rome | Ubaldini Florence | Ubaldini Rome | Ubbelschoten (van) P. d'Utrecht | Ubbena de Rieme des Frise | Ubbens Gronirque |
|---|---|---|---|---|---|---|
| Ubbergen (van) Gueldre | Ubbriachi Vérone | Ubbelli de Siegburg Bohême | Ubem Prov. rhen. | Uberdort Valais | Uberlingen Souabe | Uberti Vérone Vicence |
| Ubertin Ctes Toscane France | Ubertin Ctes de Chitignano Brabant | Ubertini Florence | Ubeske Pom. | Ubing Utrecht Zwolle | Ubniewski Pol. | Ubolds Milan |
| Ubaldo Chers de Villareggio Milan | Ubrichingen Souabe | Ubysz Pol. | Uccellini Florence | Uccellini Bologne | Uceta Biscaye | Uchacz Pol. |
| Uchanski Pol. | Uchelen (van) Gueldre | Uchtenhagen Brandebourg | Uchterriedt Souabe | Uchtman L. de Groningue | Uck Schleswig | Uckermann Pom. |
| Uckermann Saxe | Uckermann Saxe | Uckro Brandebourg | Uclaux Ctes de la Valette France Celeste Galicie | Udekem (d') Brab. | Udekem (d') Brab. | Udemans Zél. |

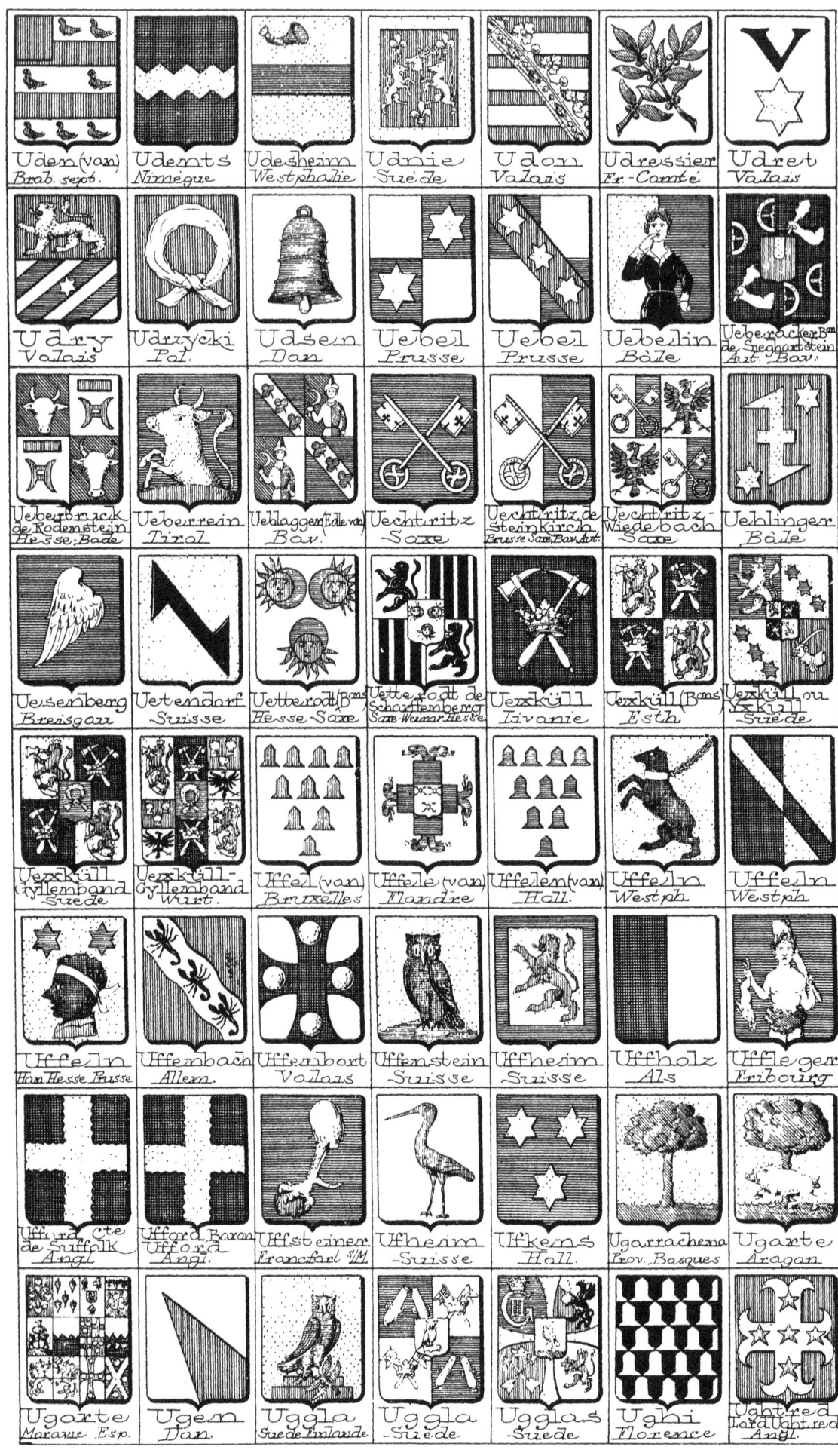

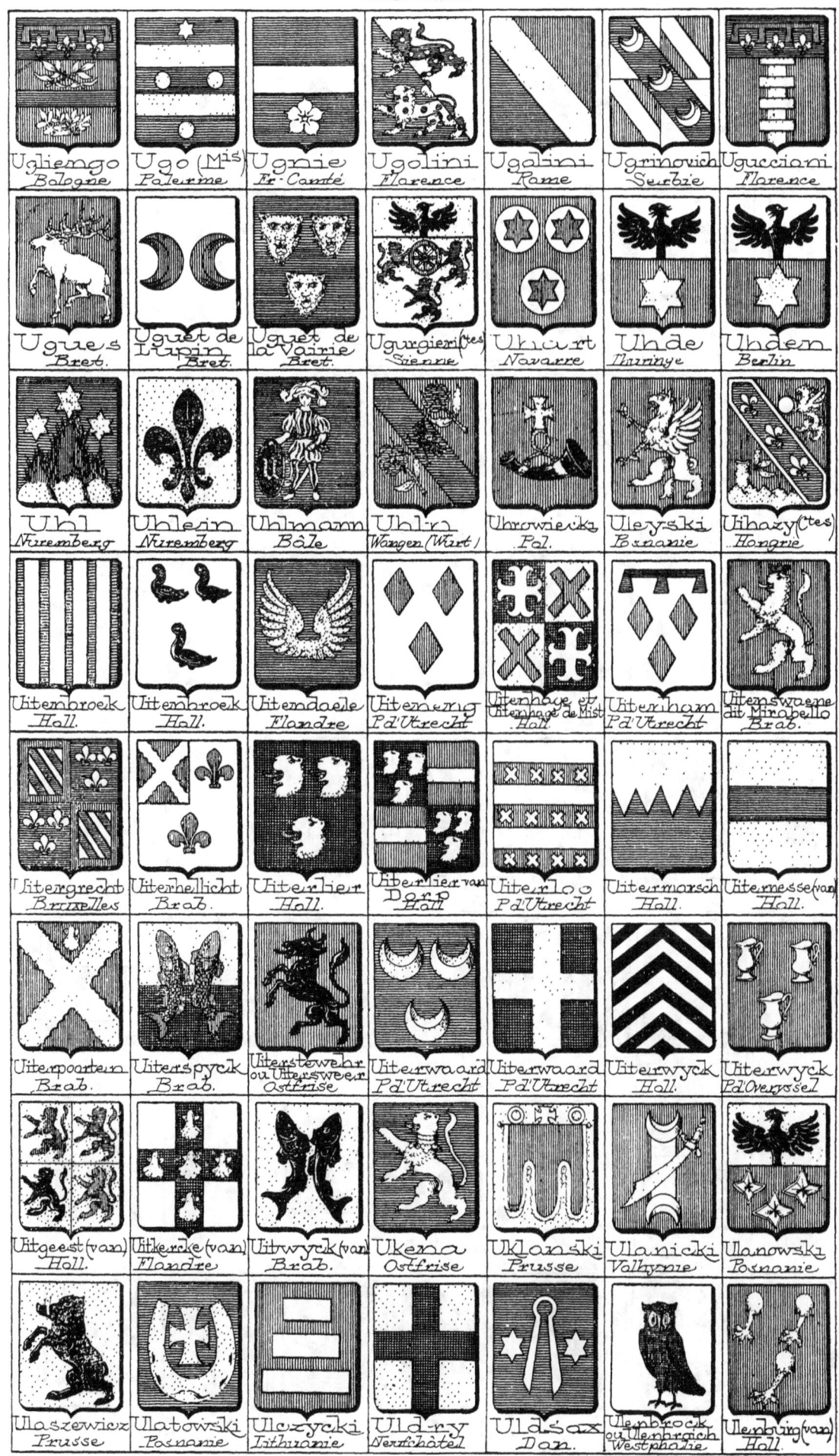

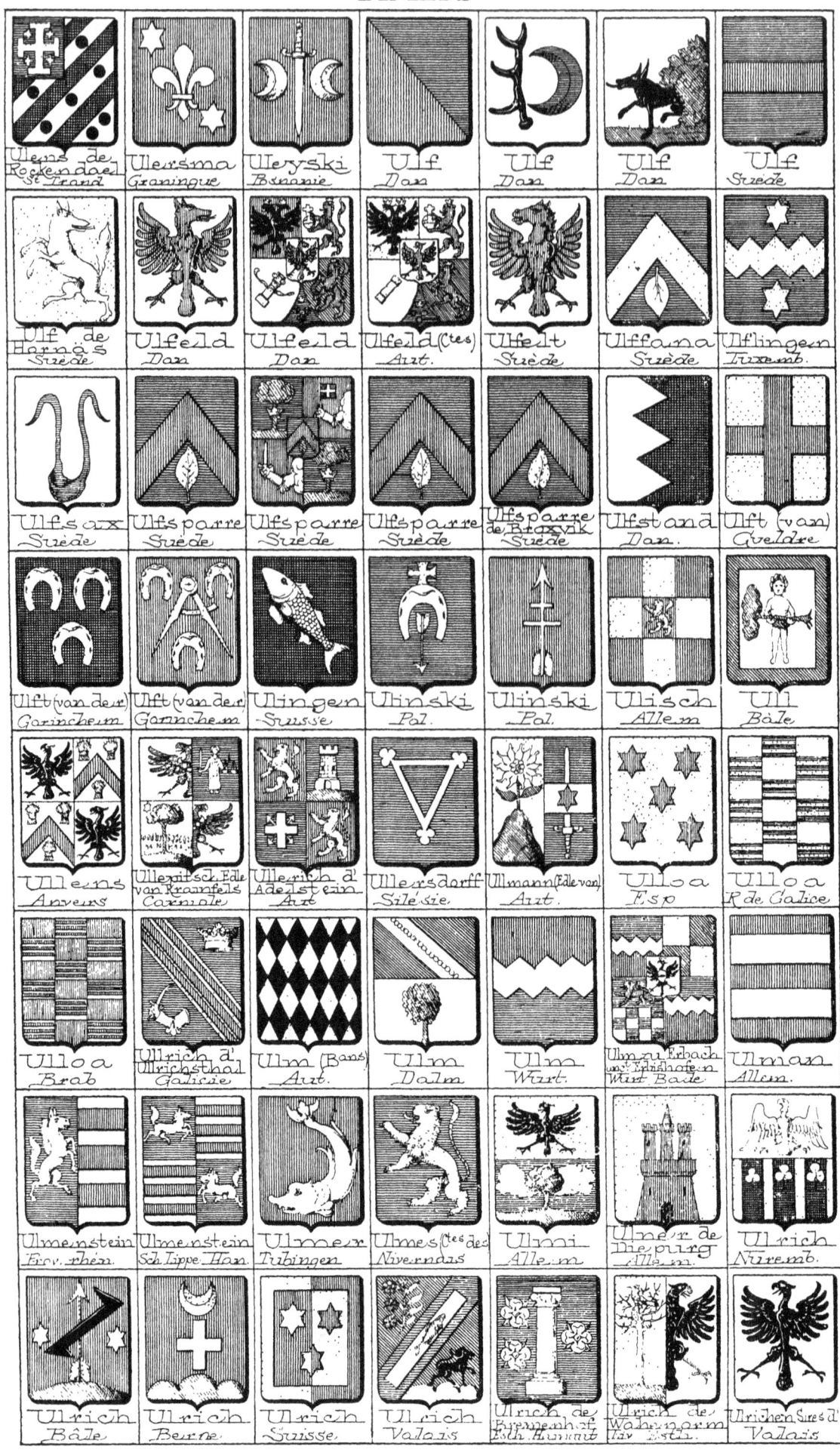

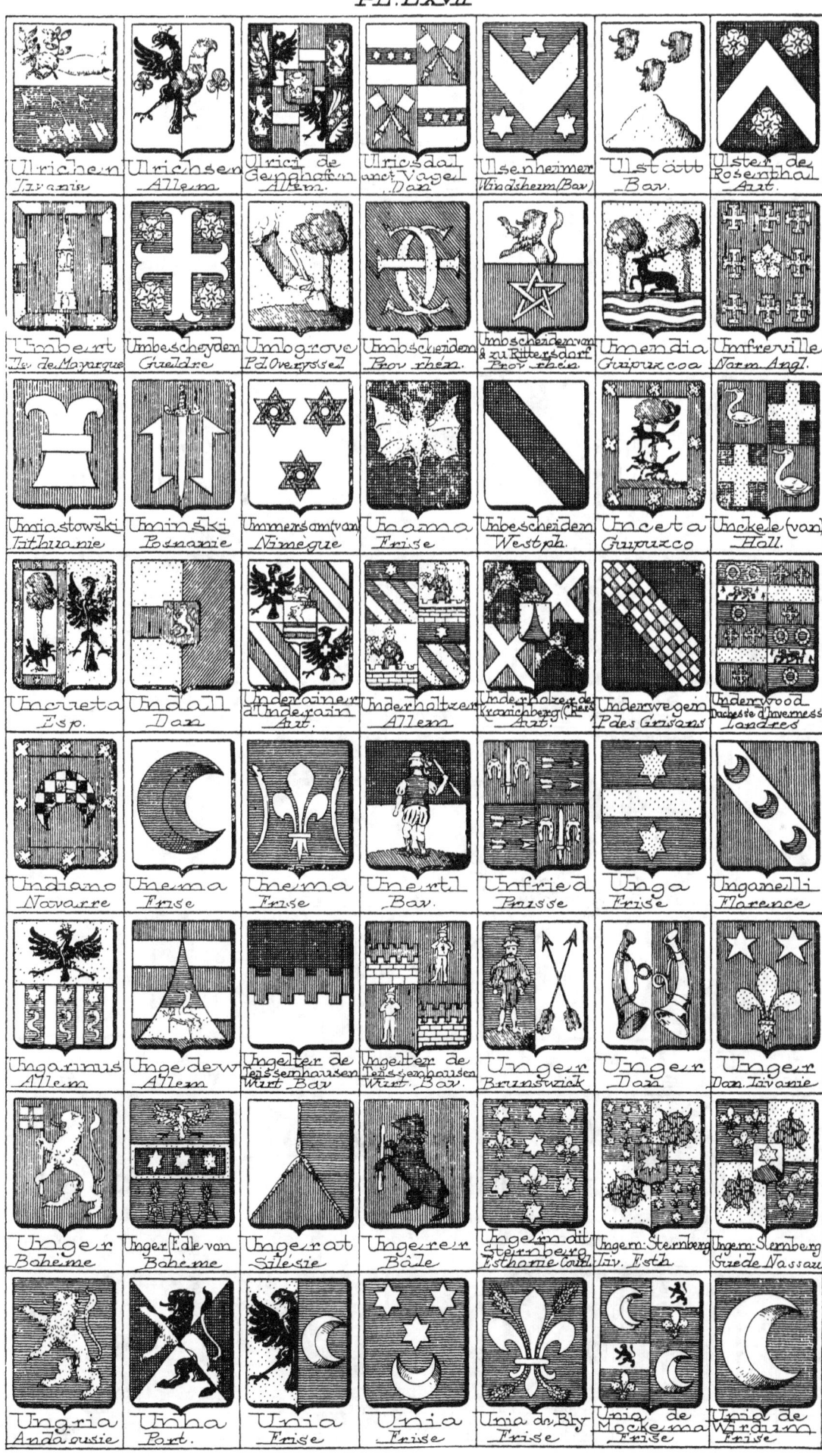

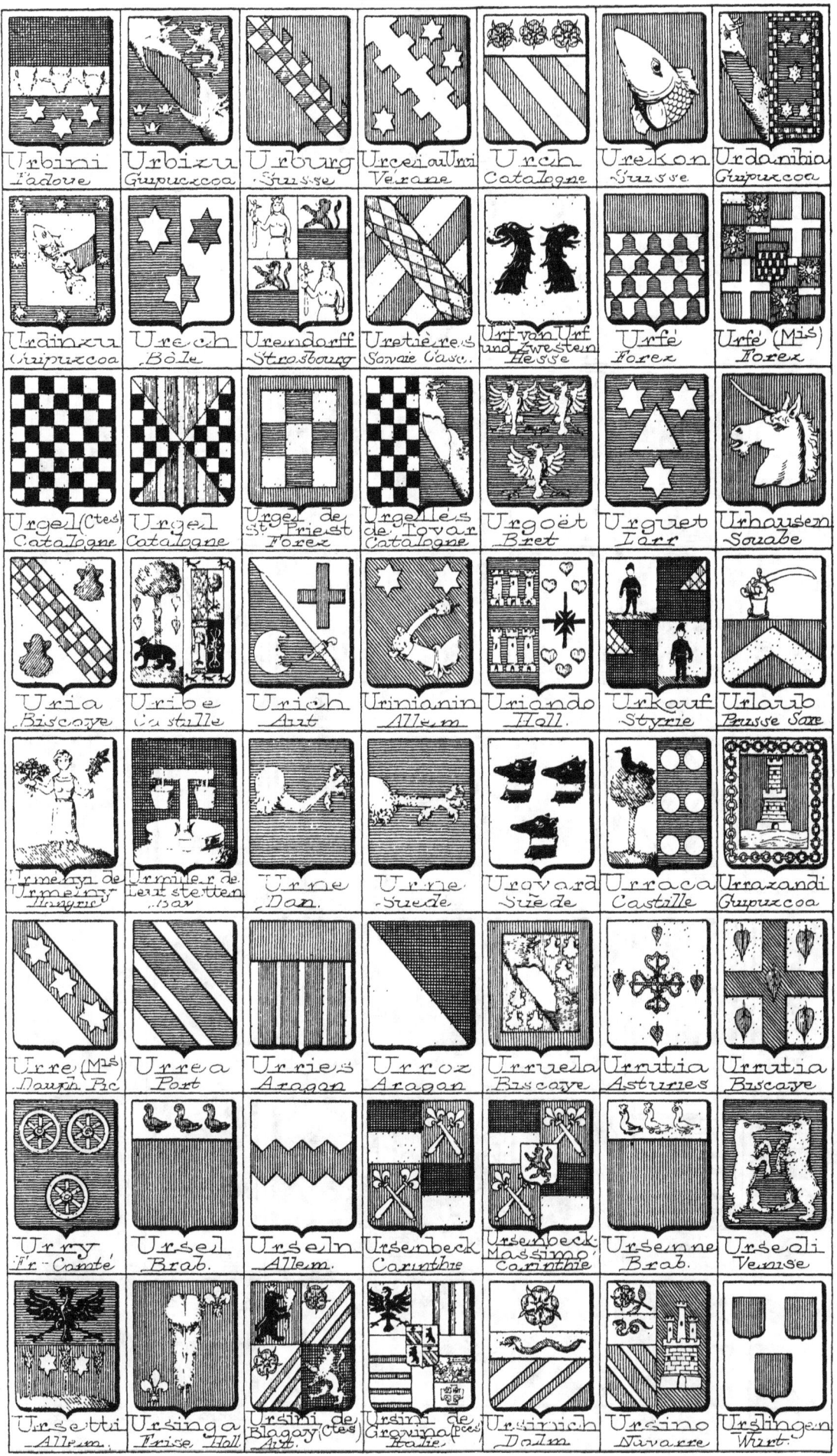

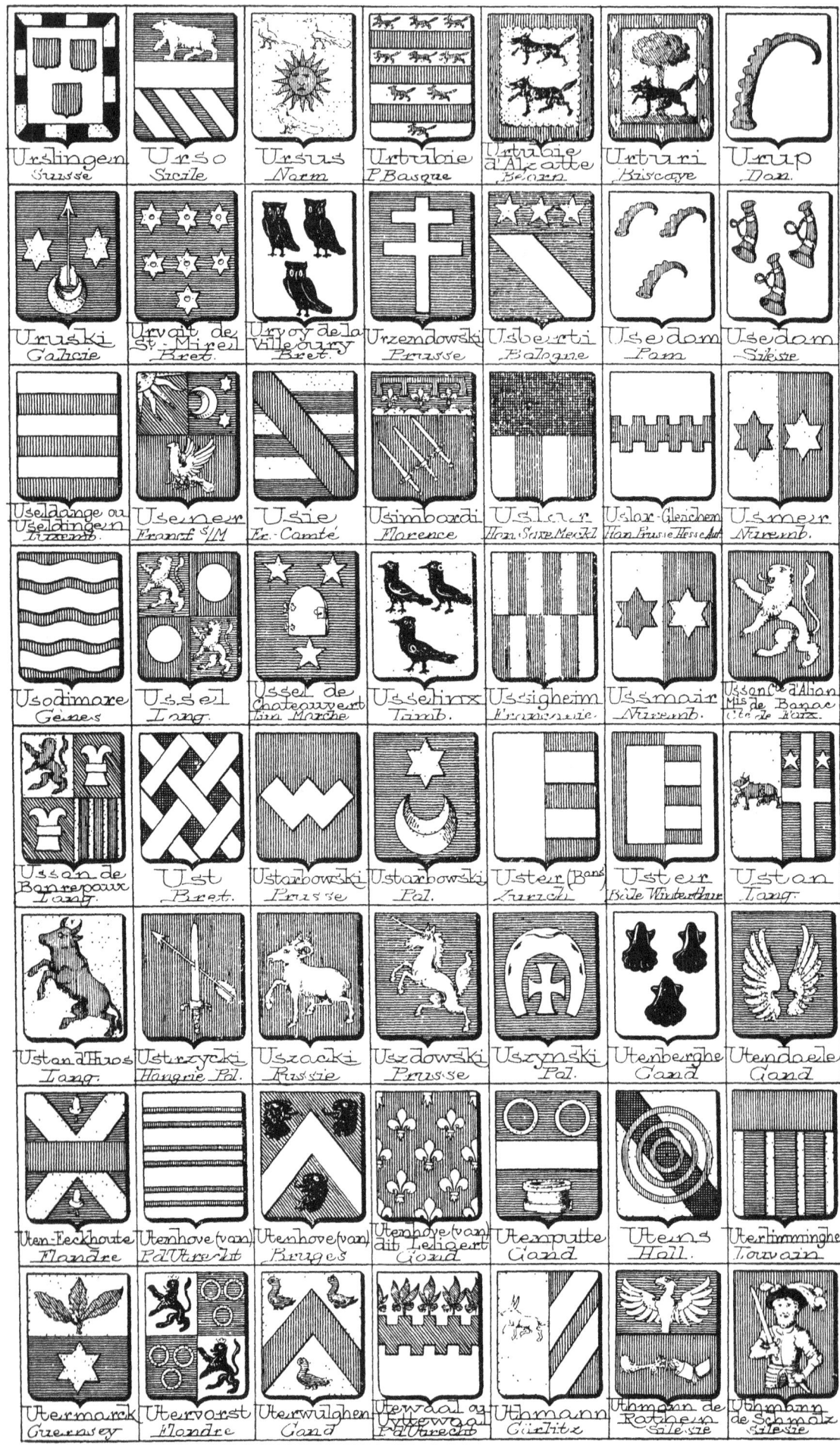

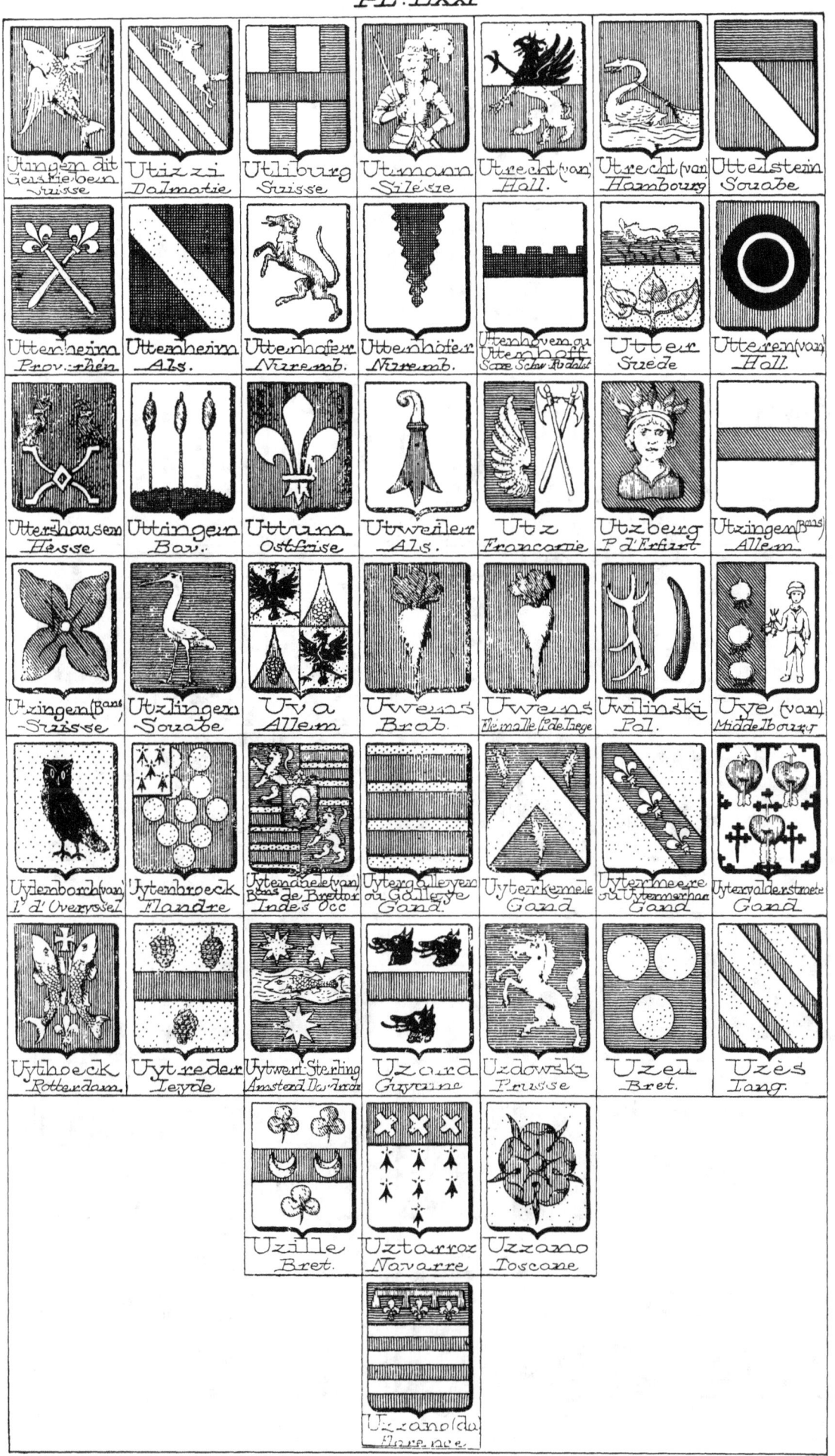

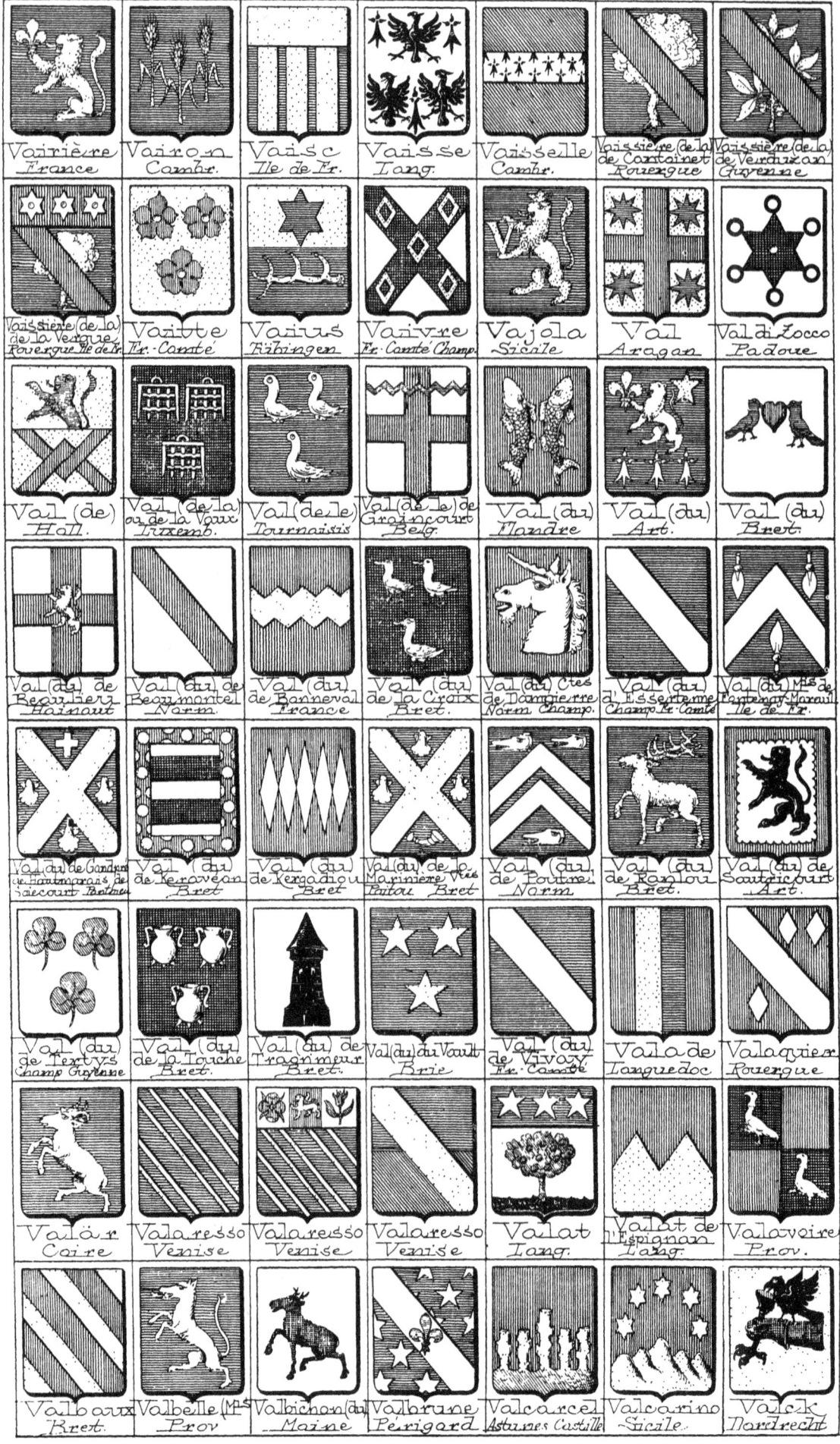

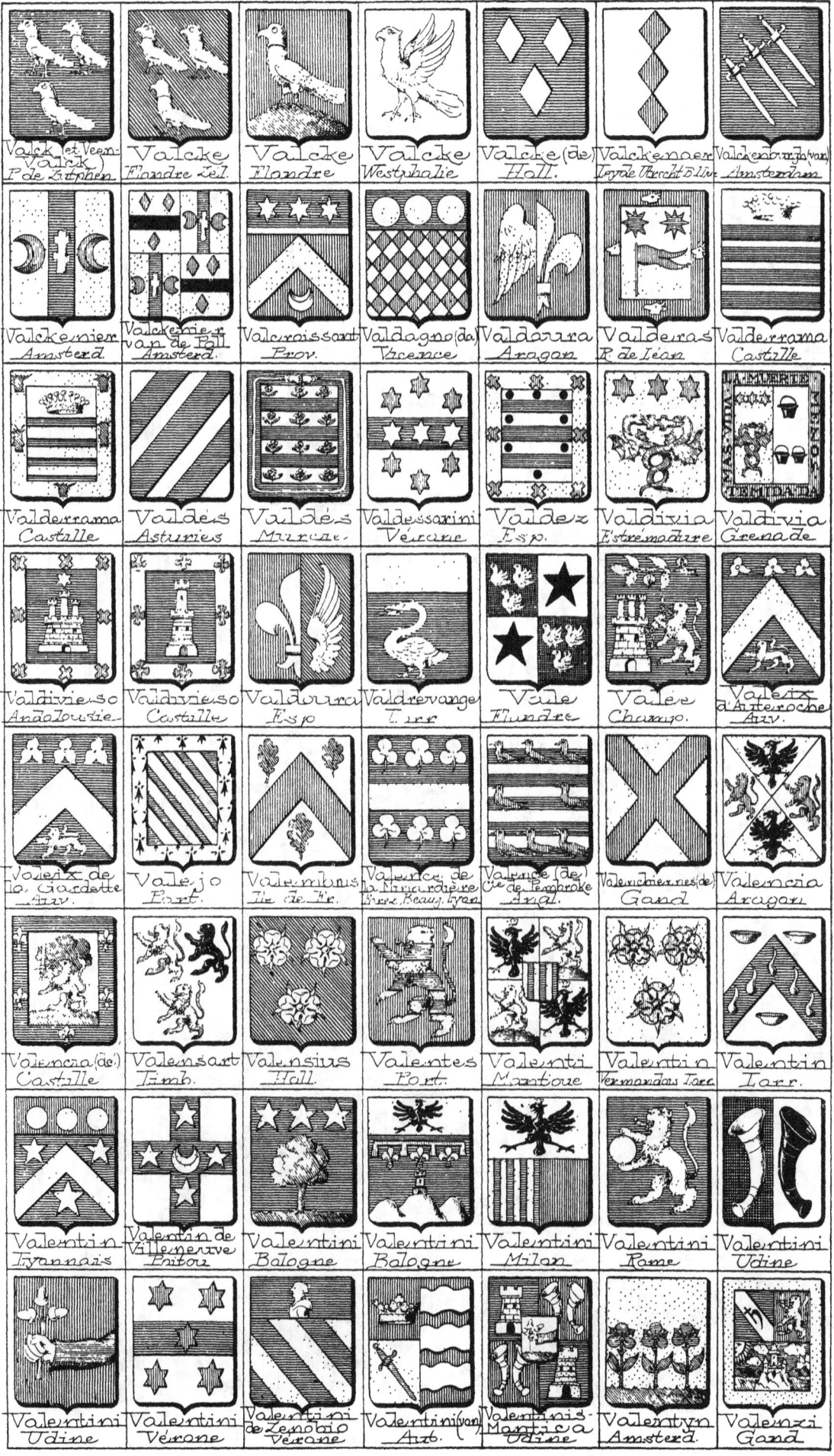

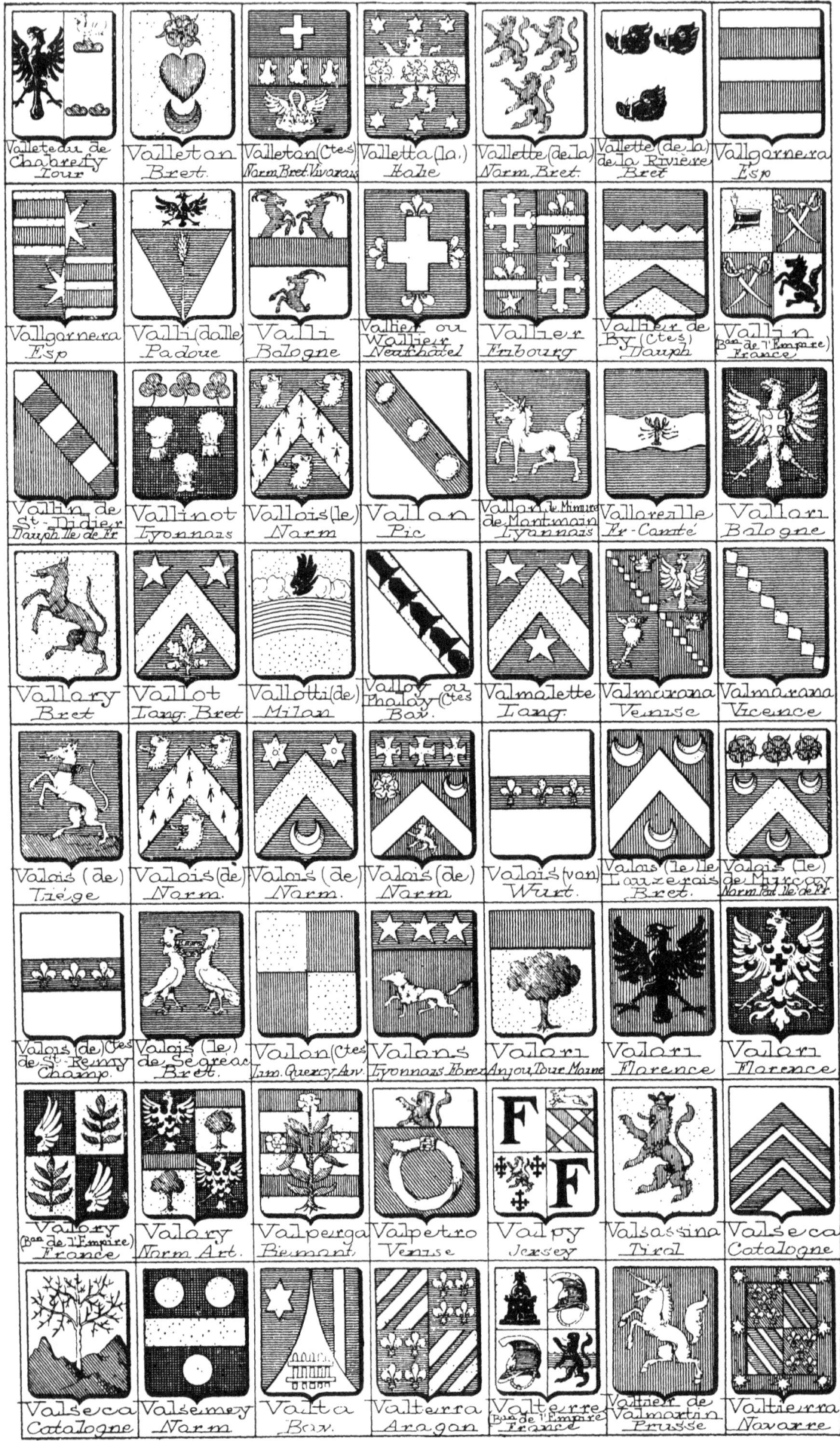

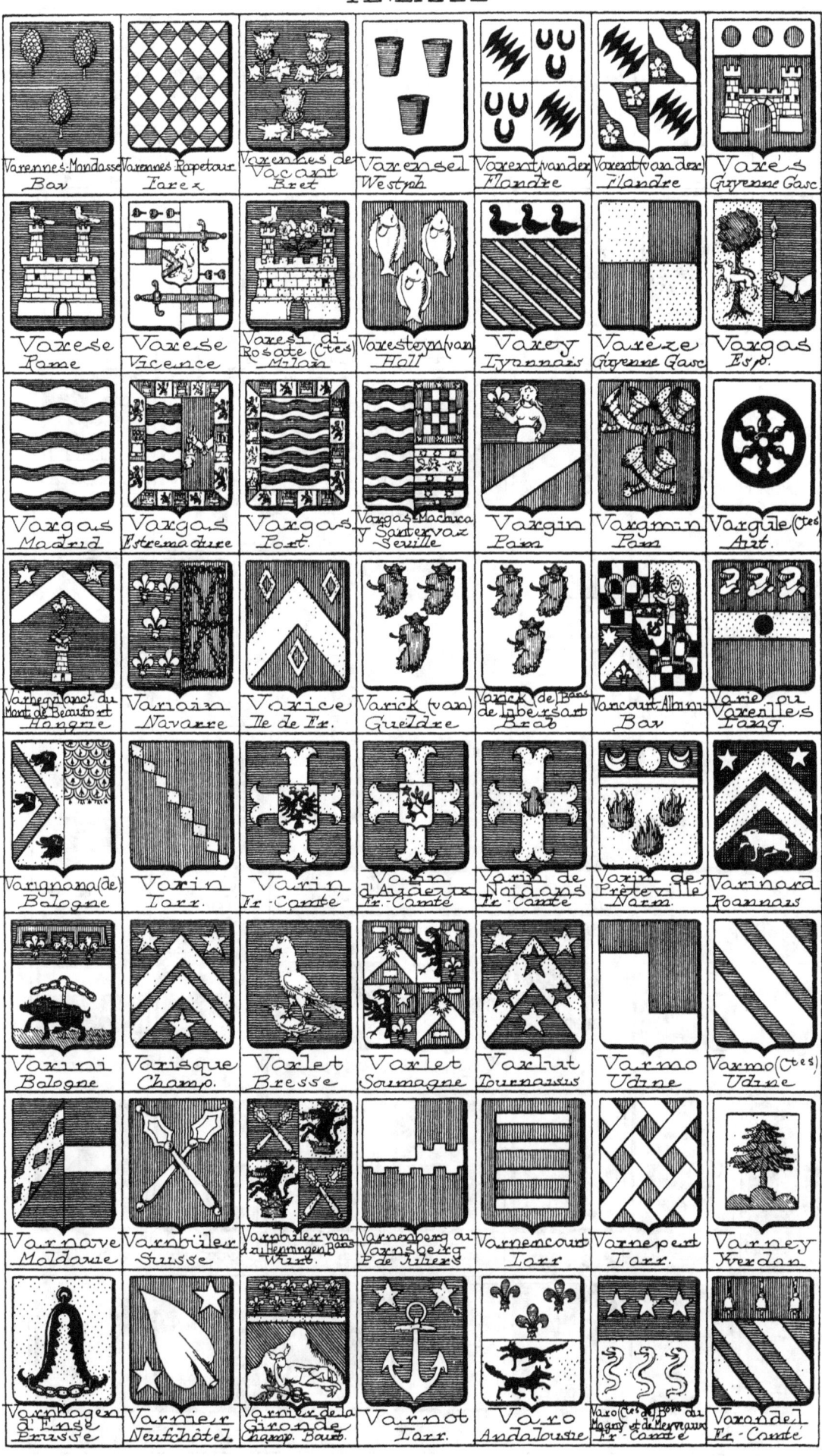

PL. LXXXV

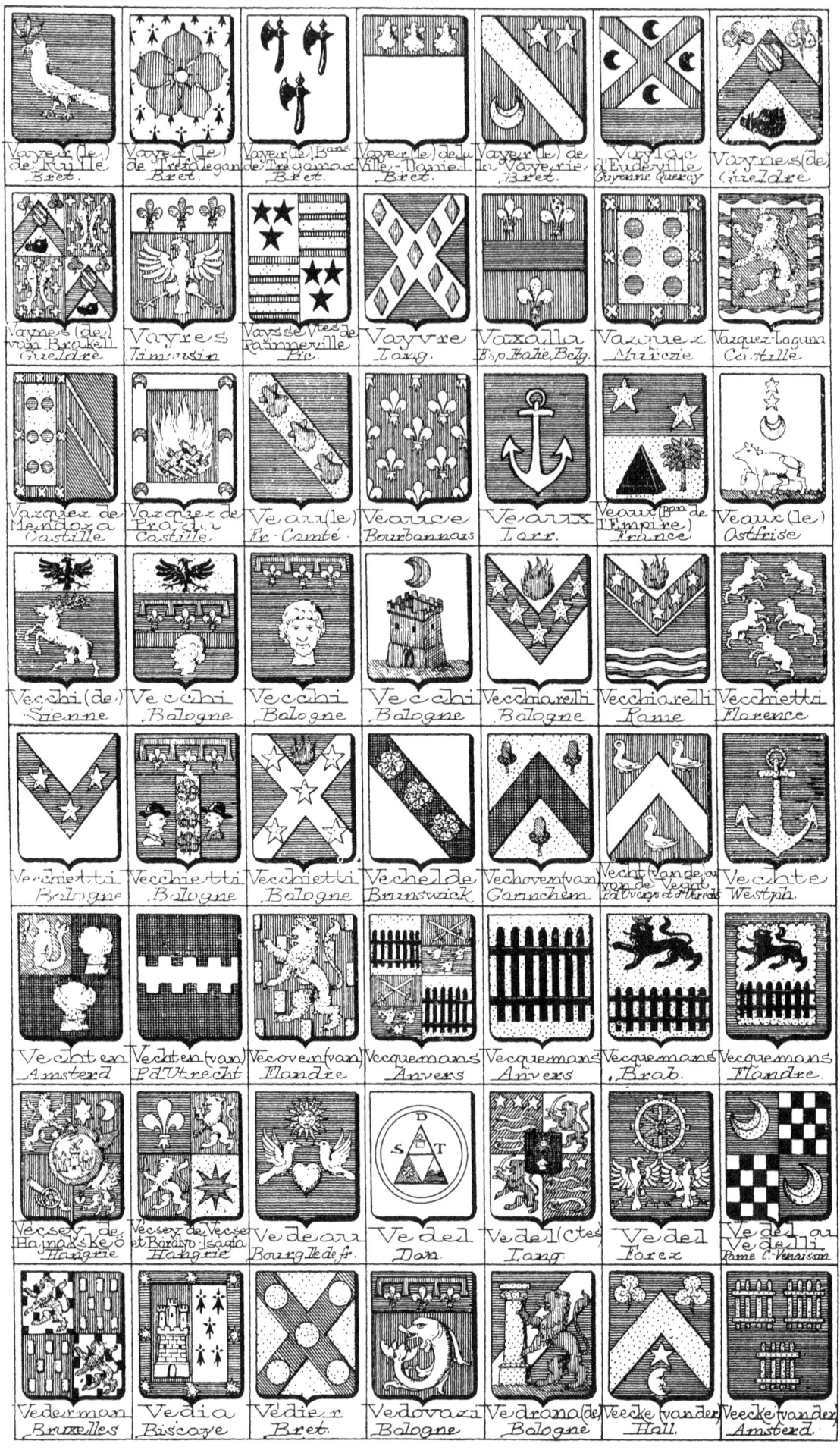

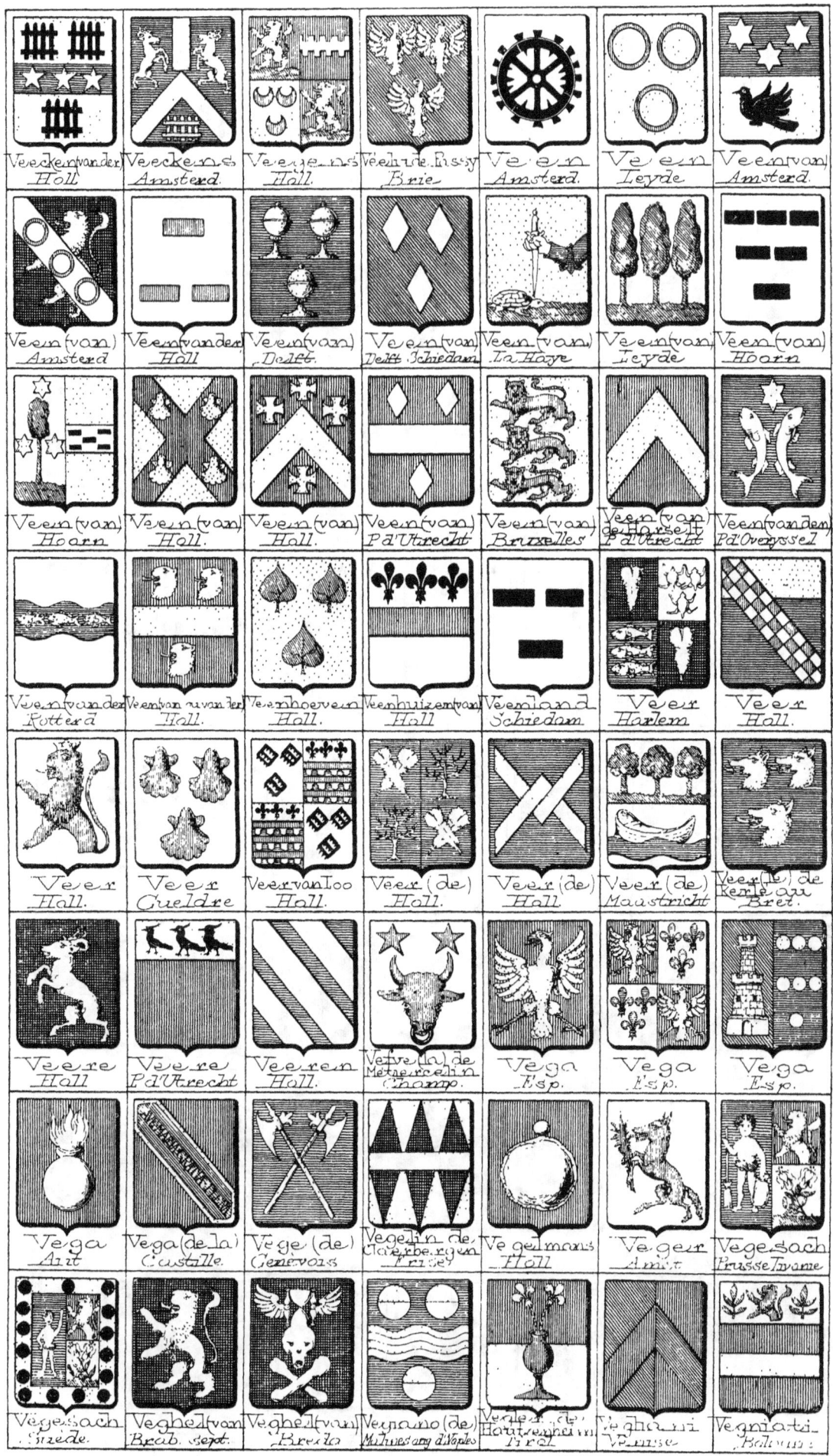

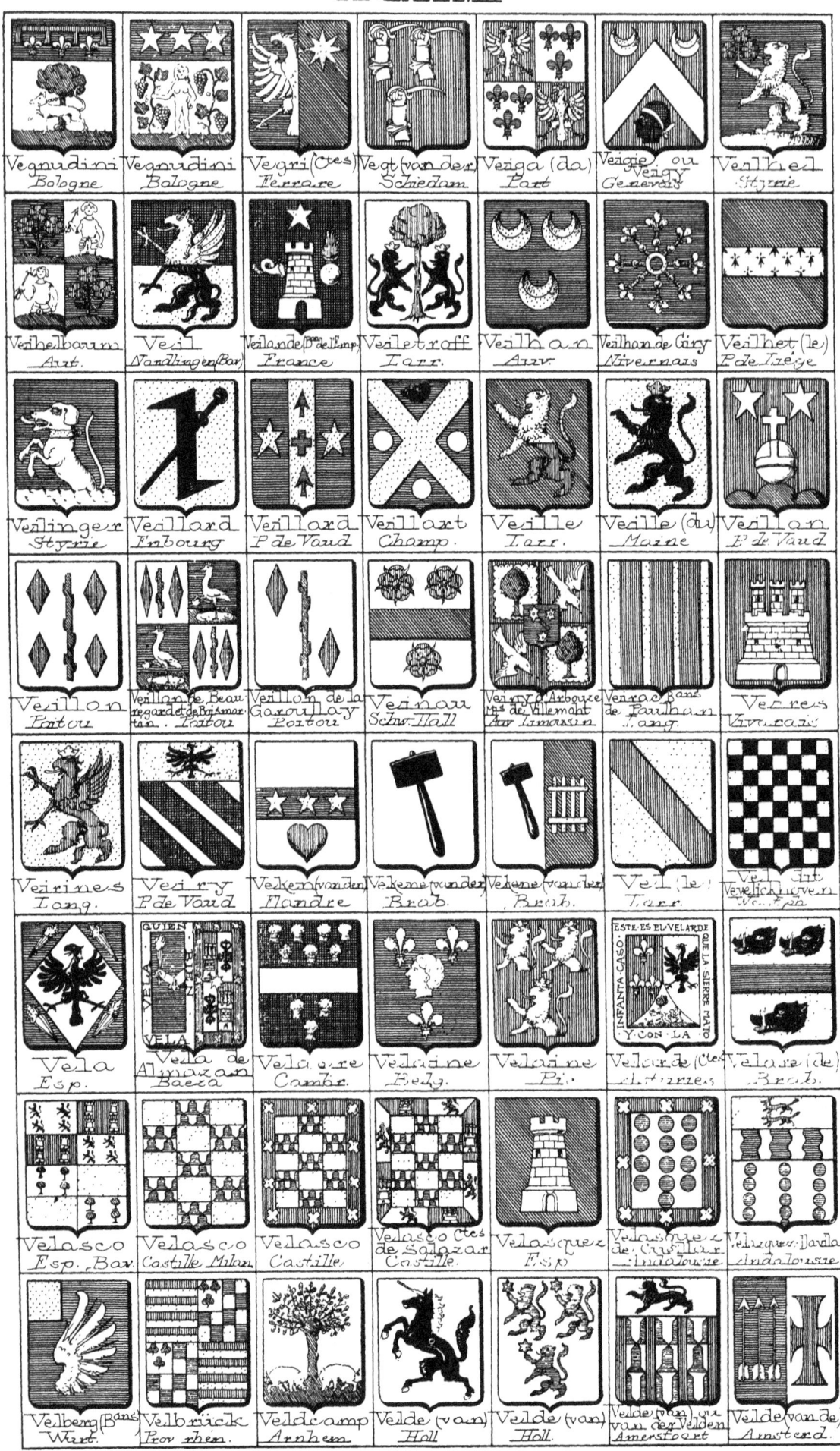

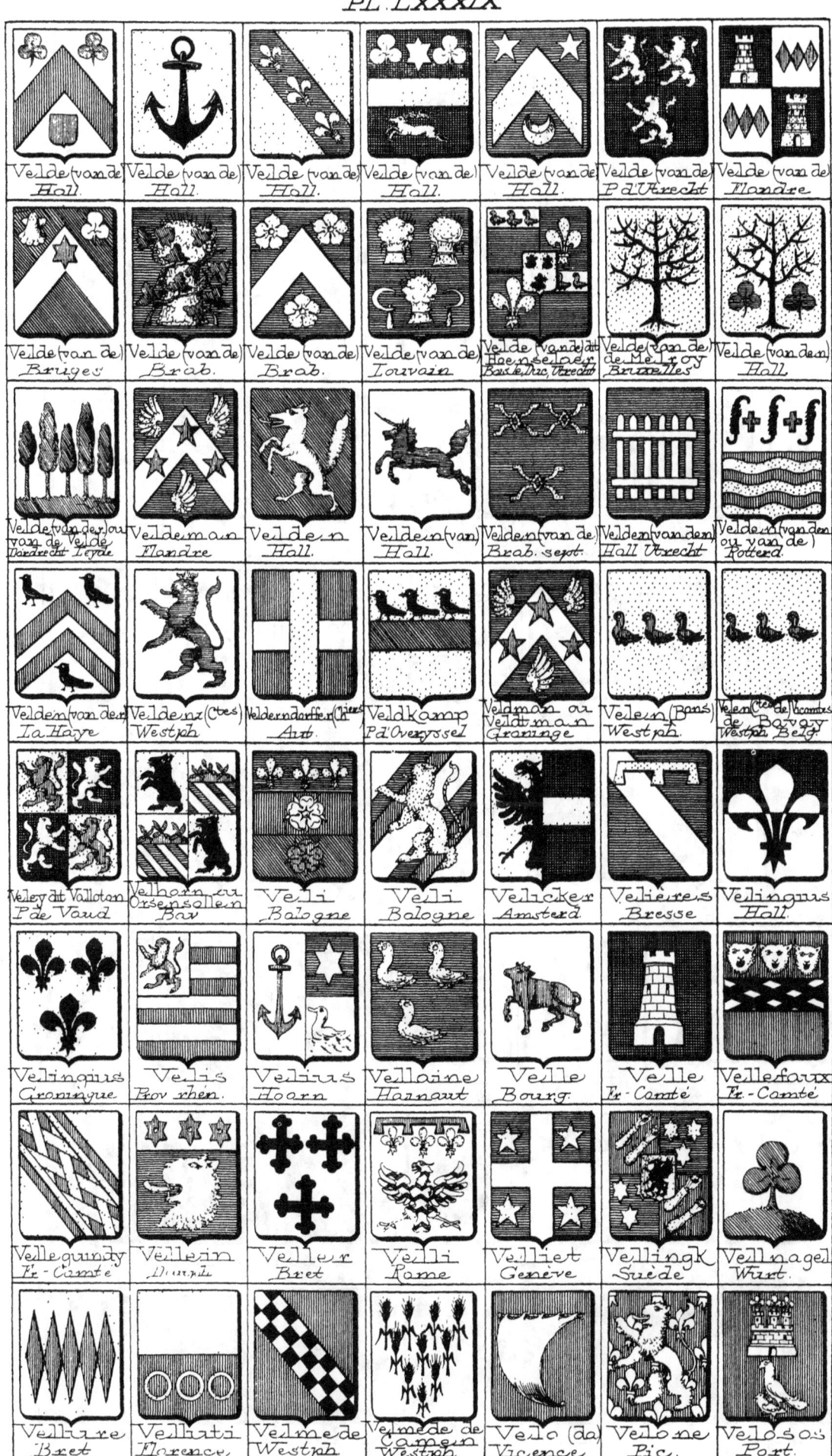

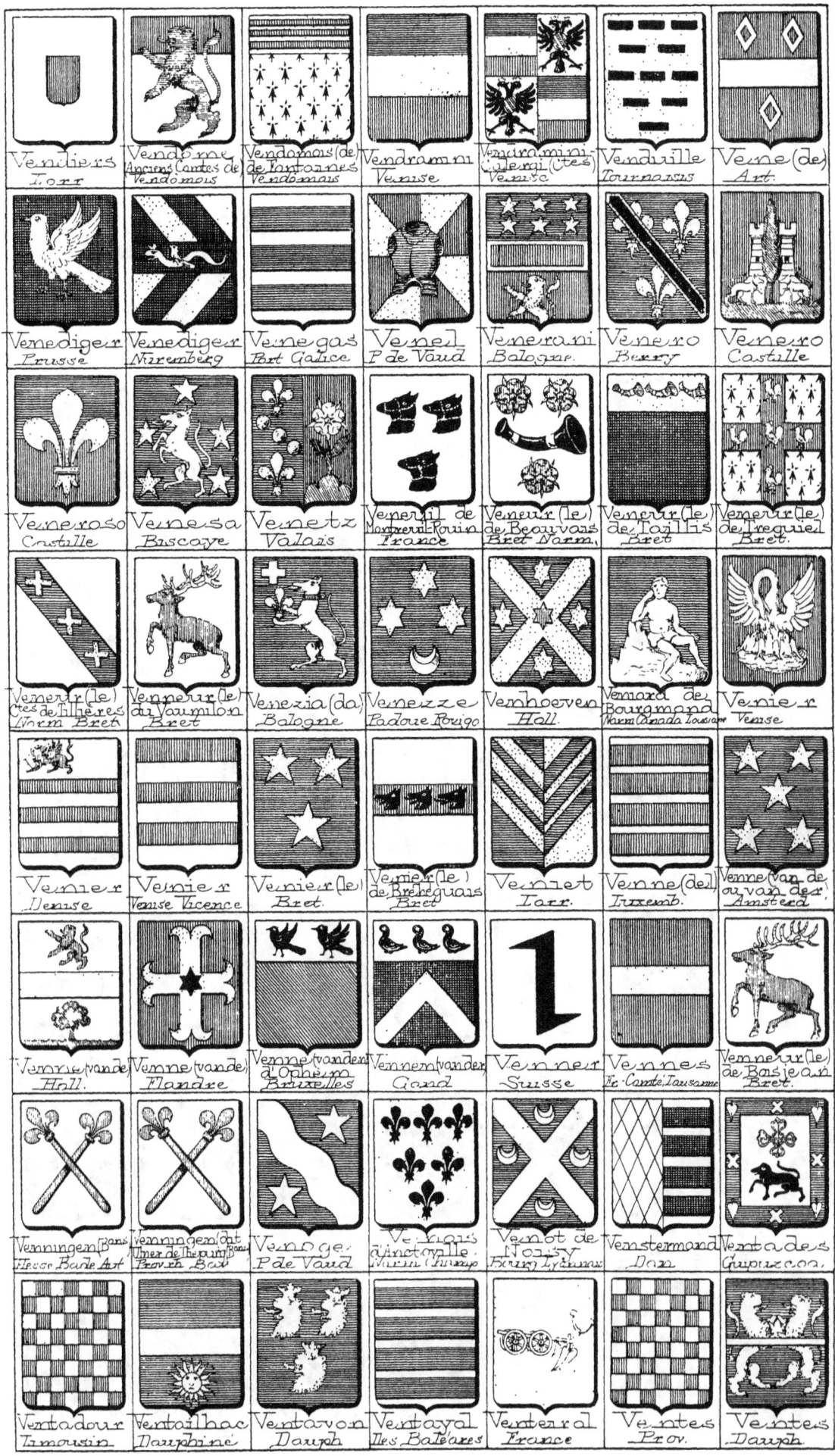

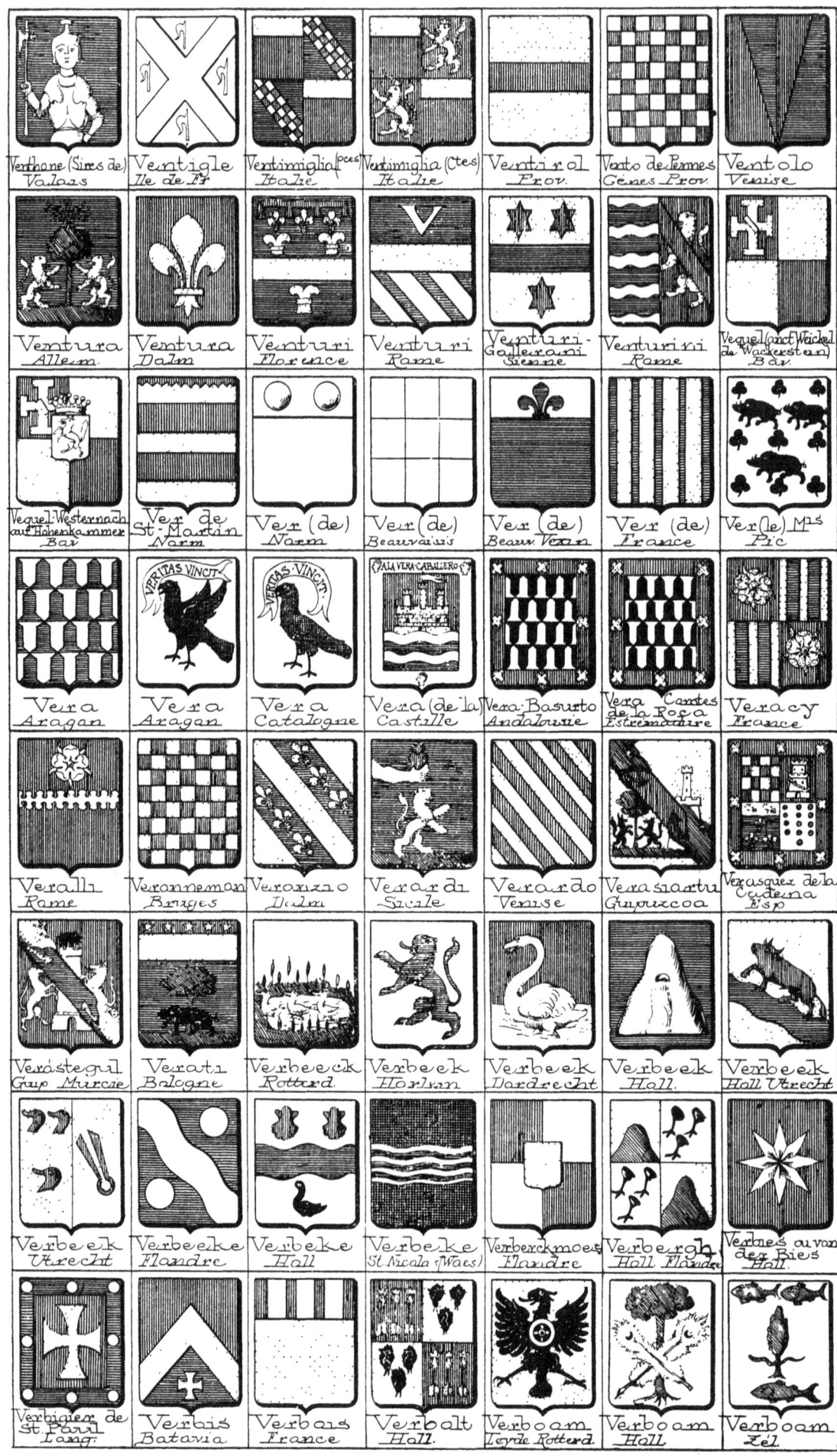

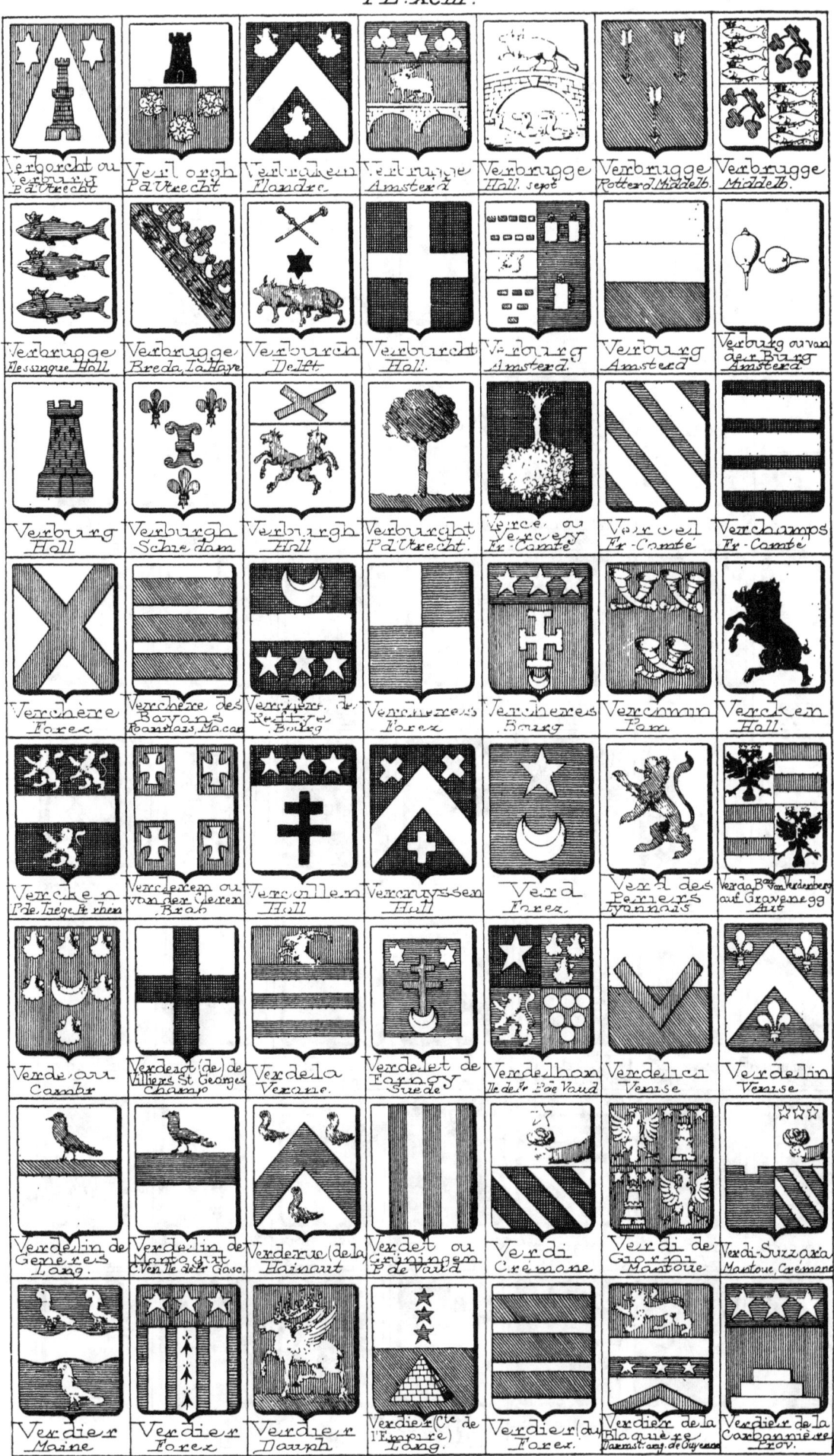

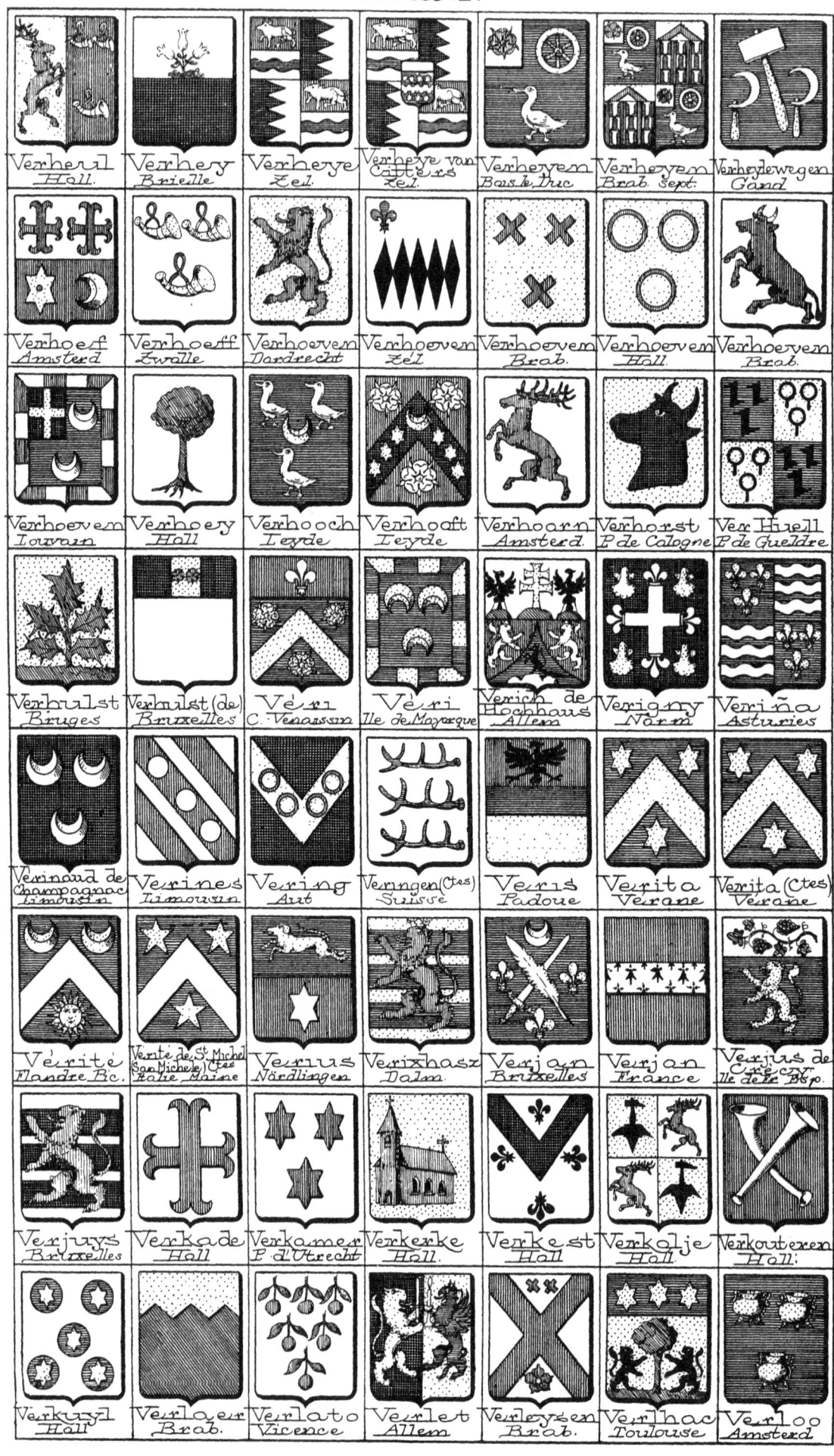

PL. XCVII.

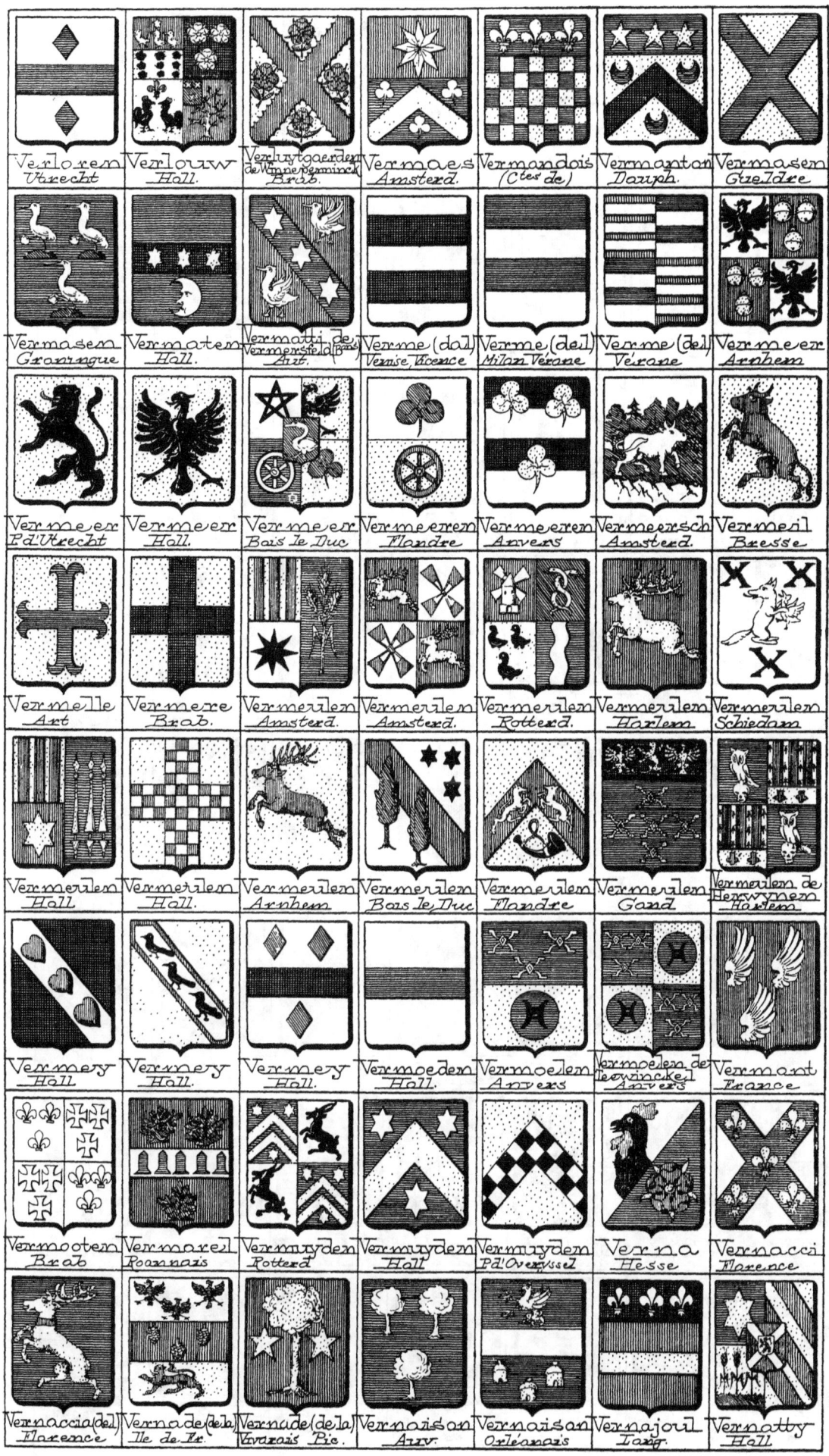

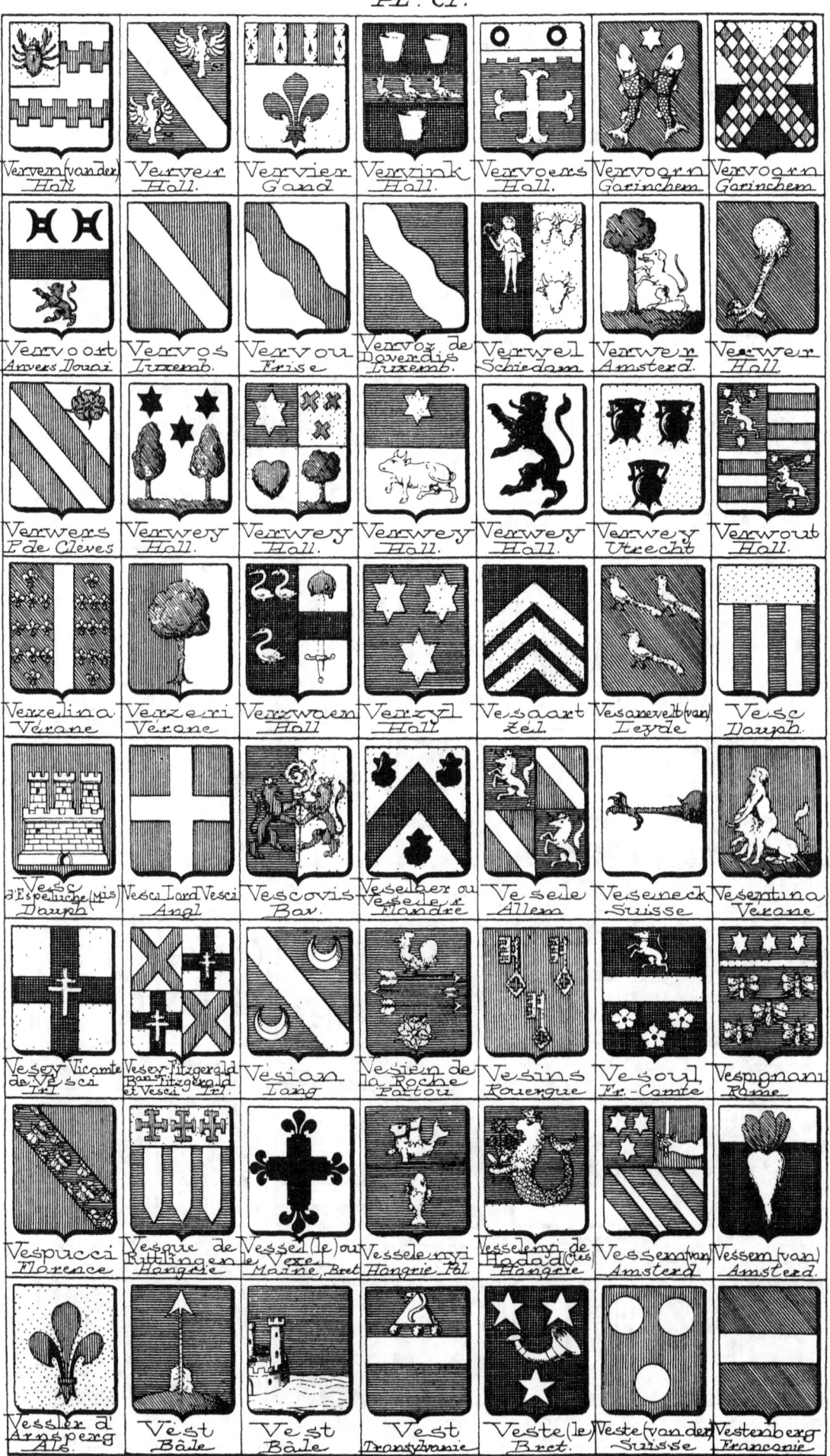

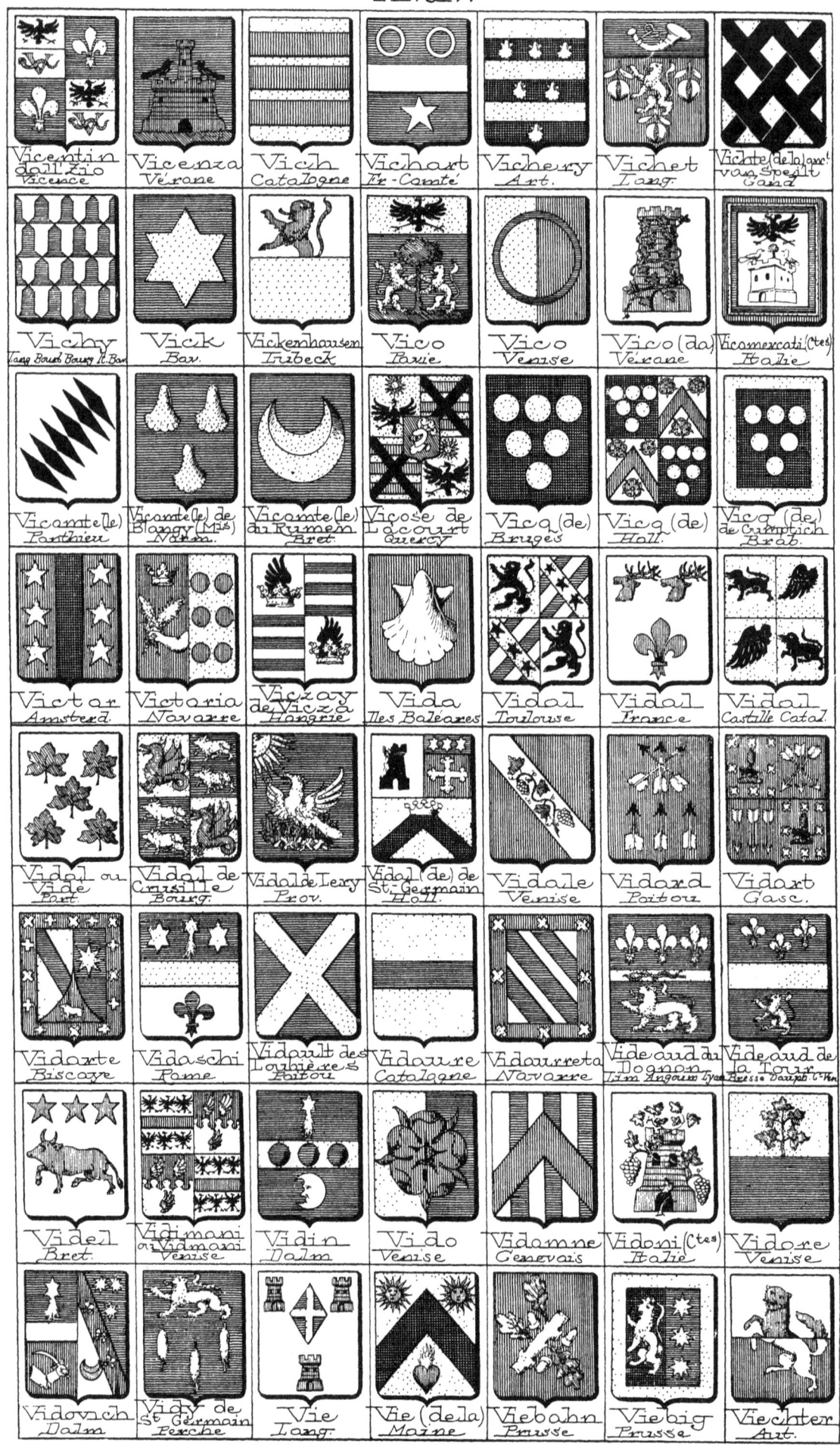

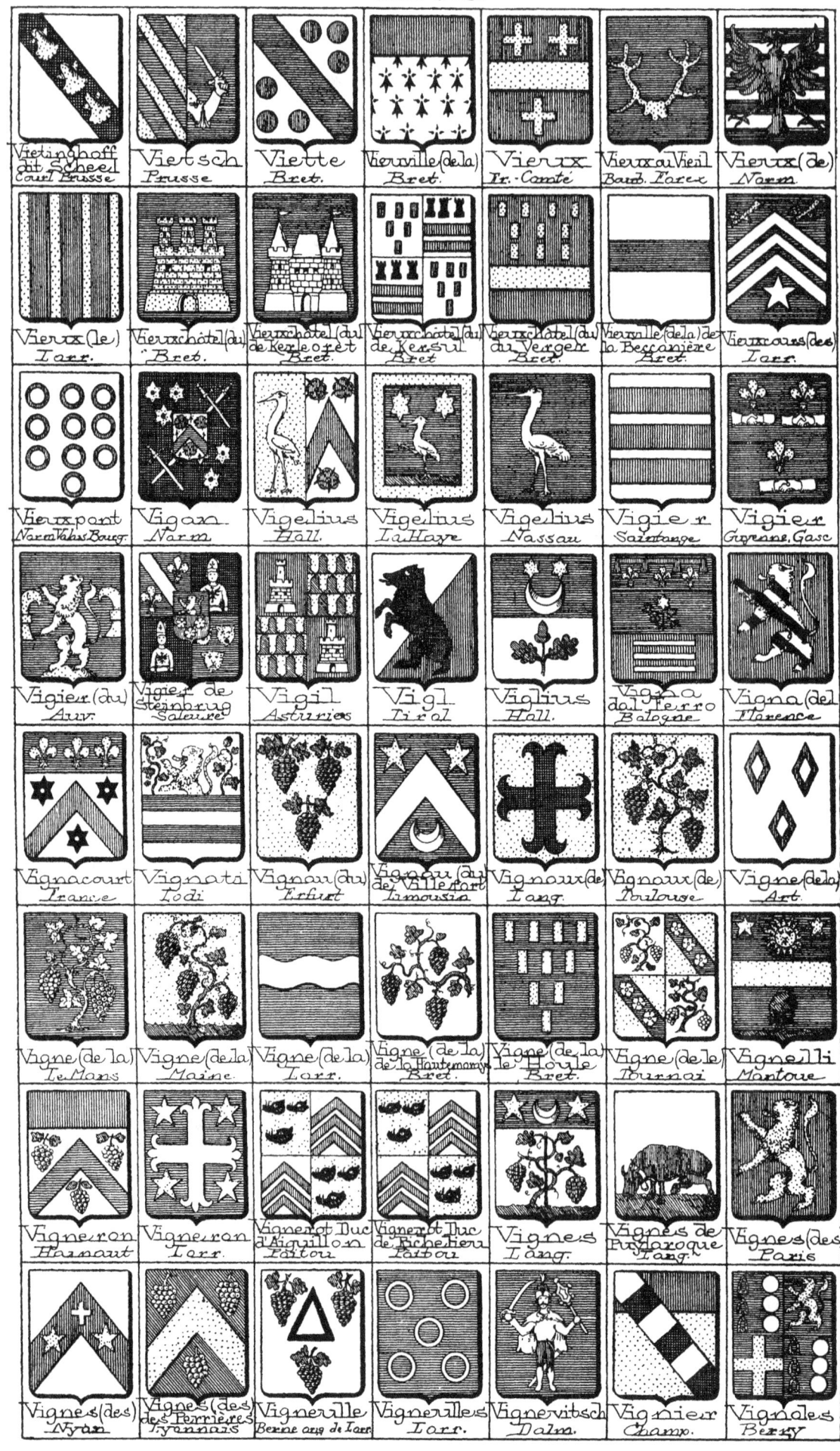

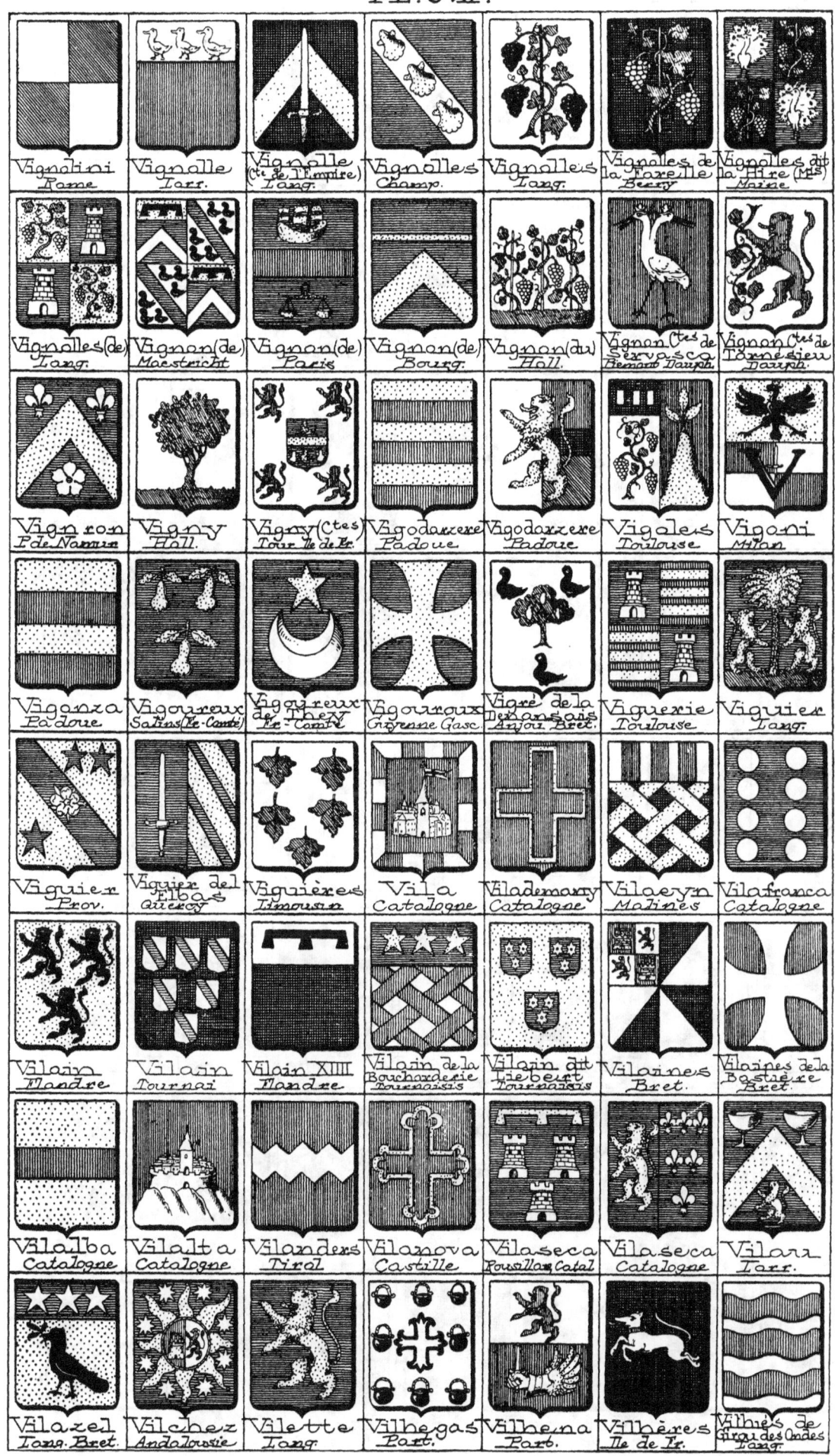

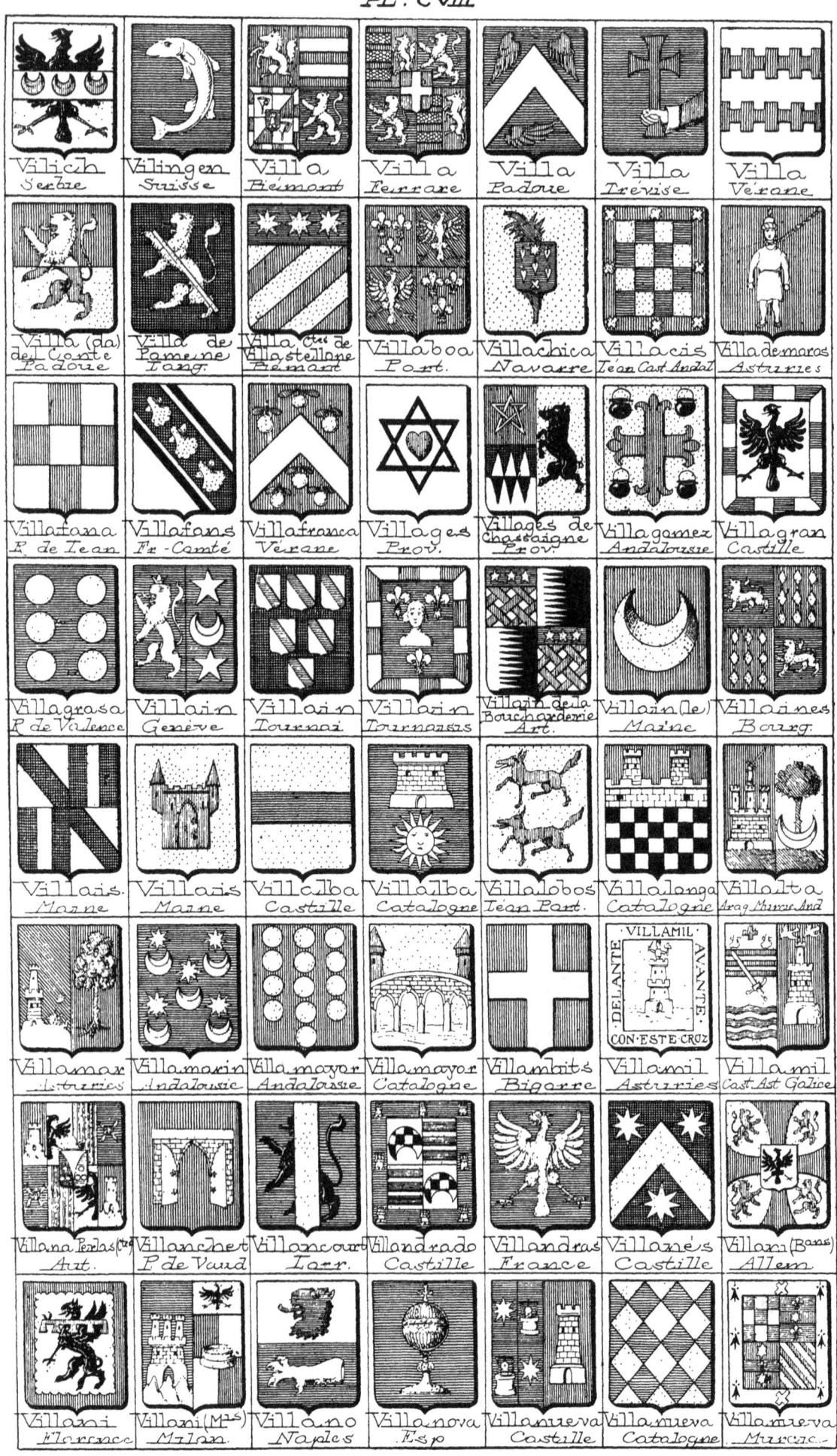

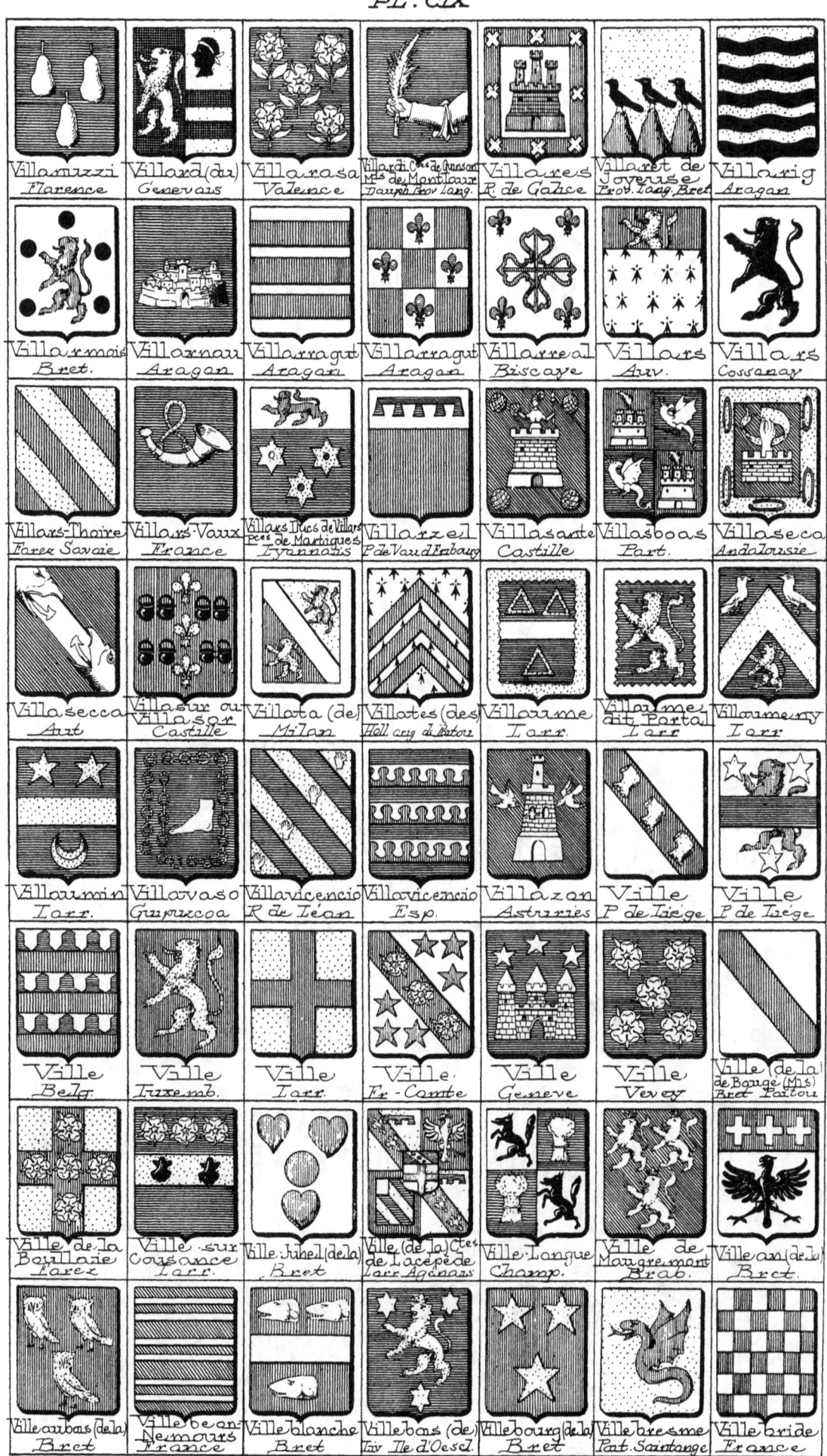

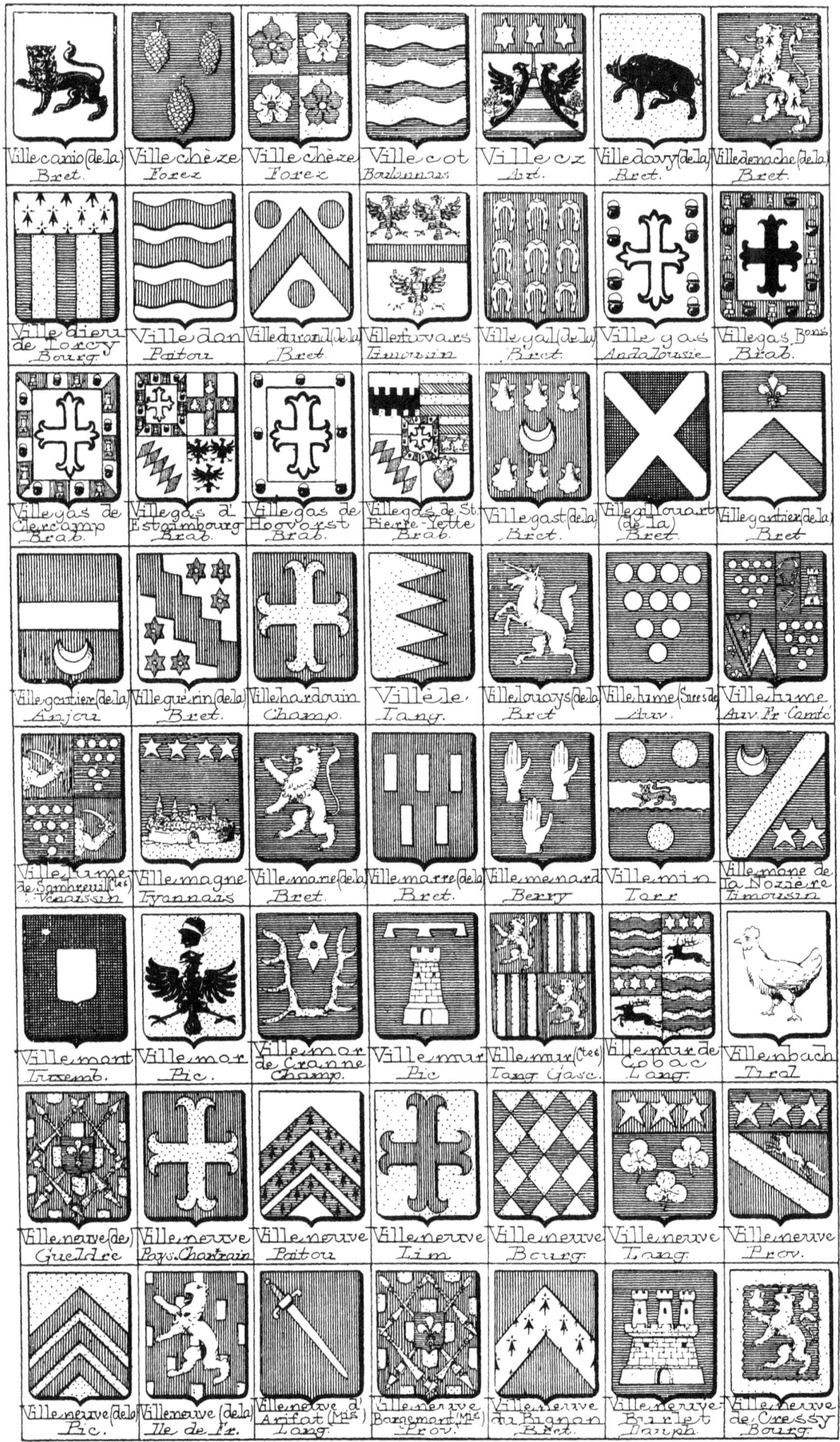

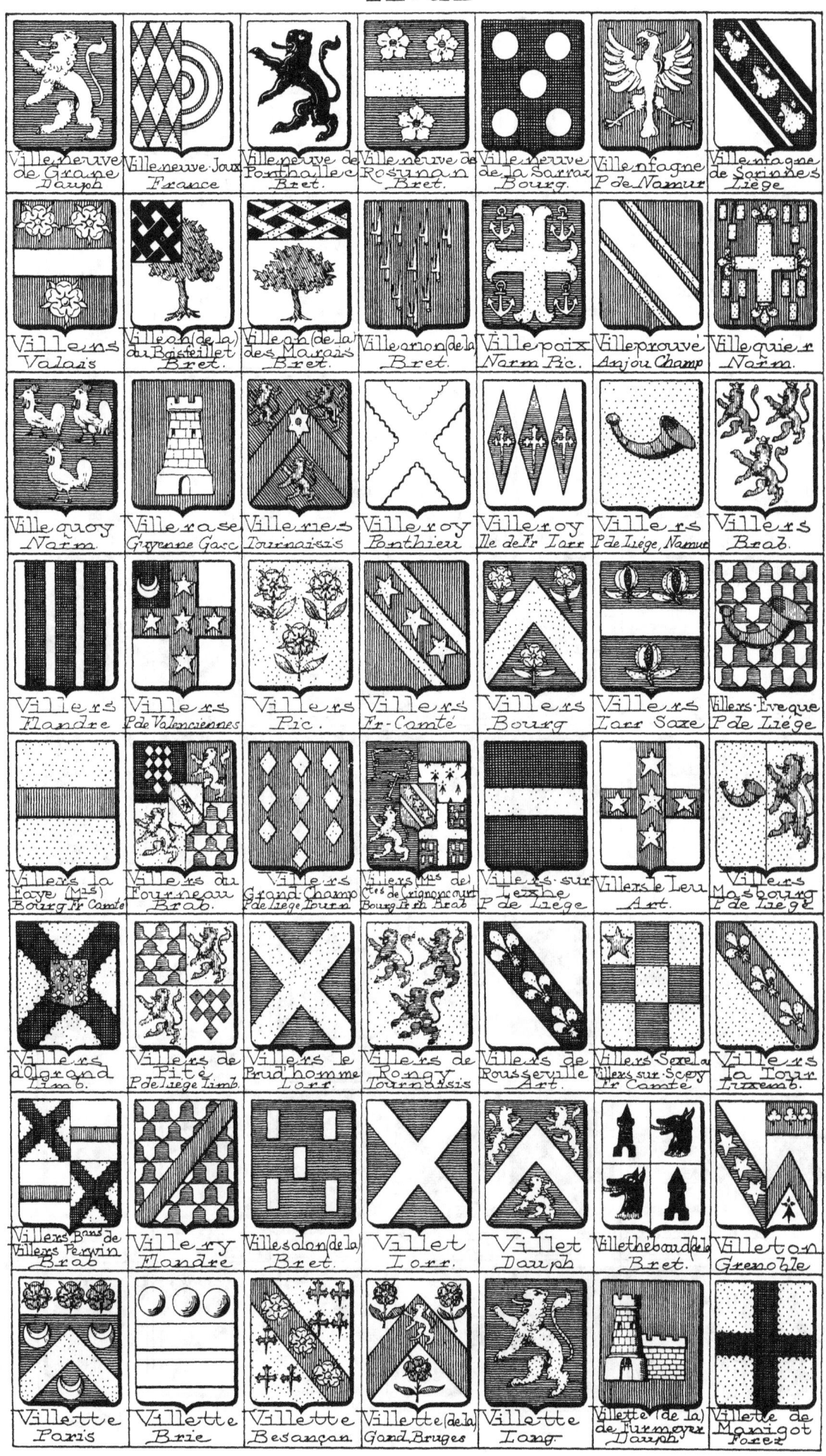

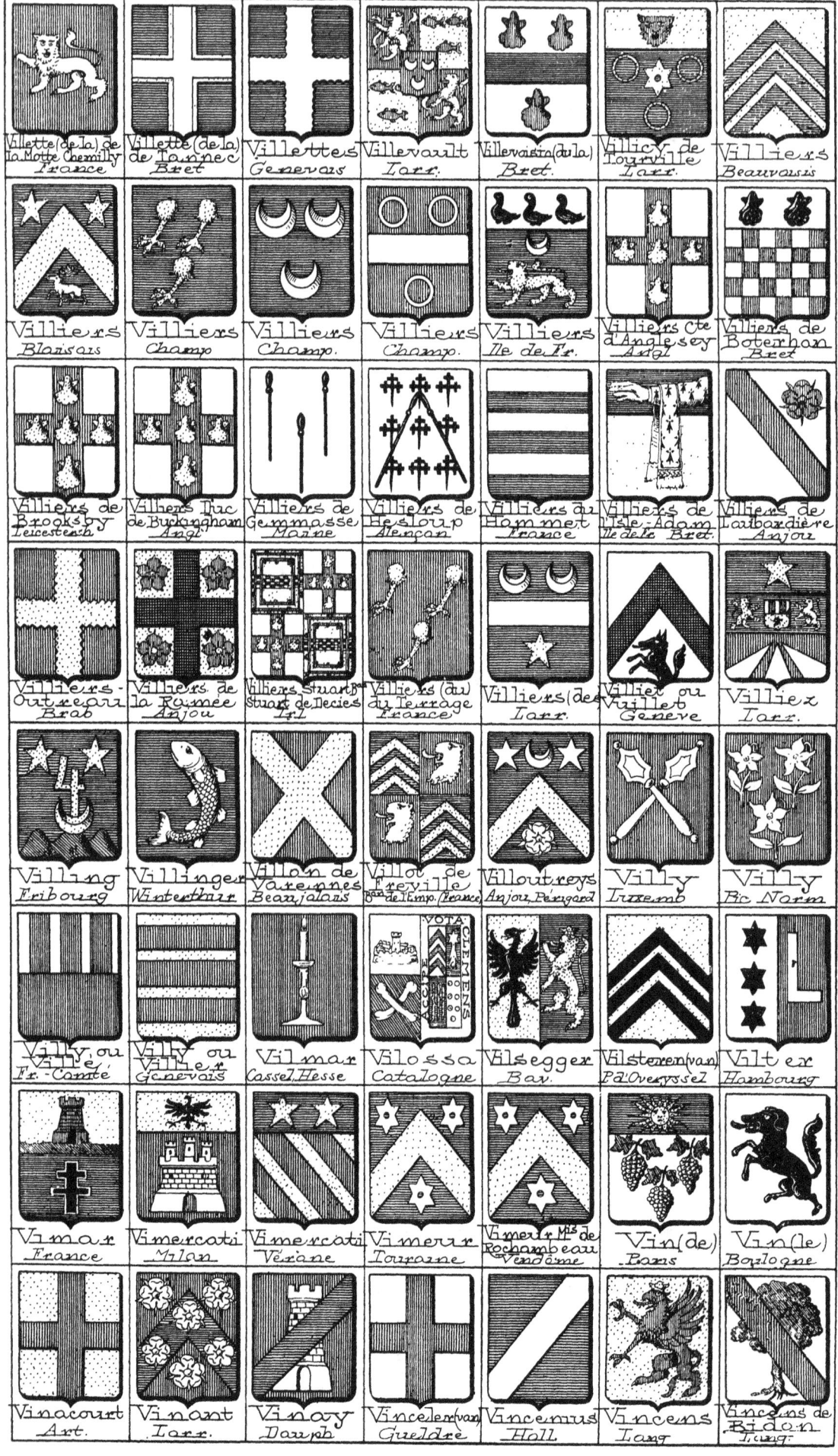

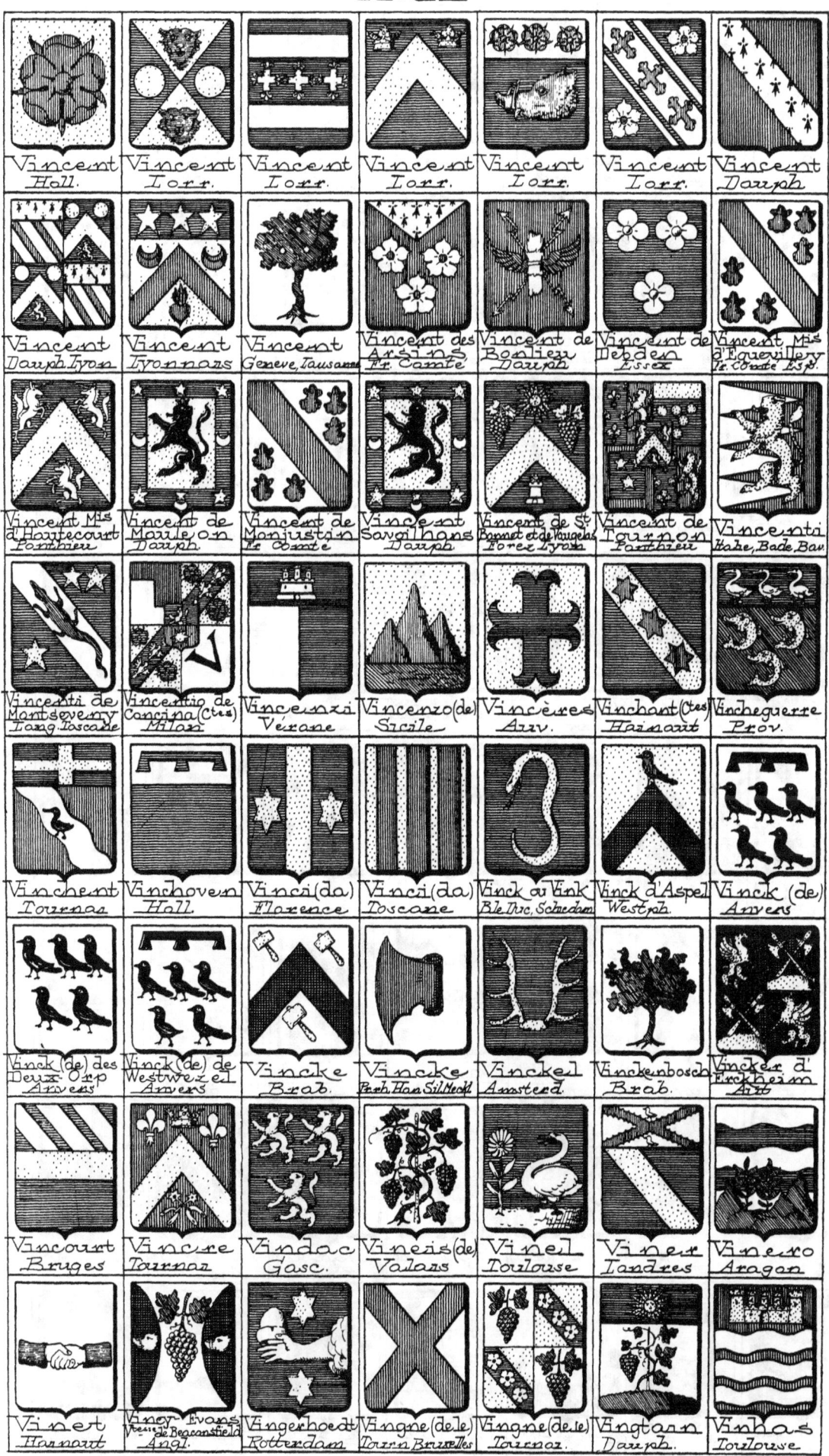

PL. CXIV

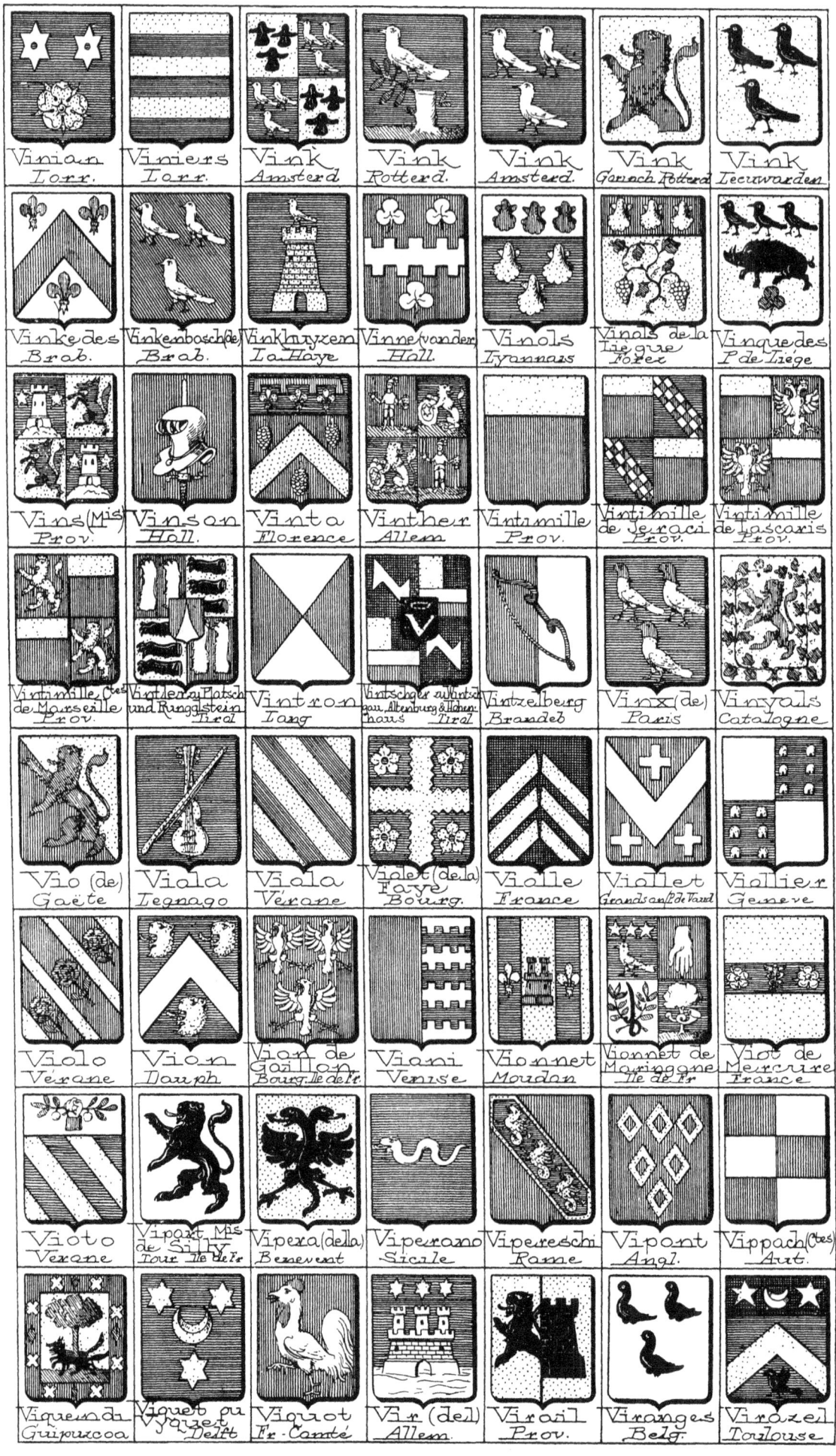

PL. CXV

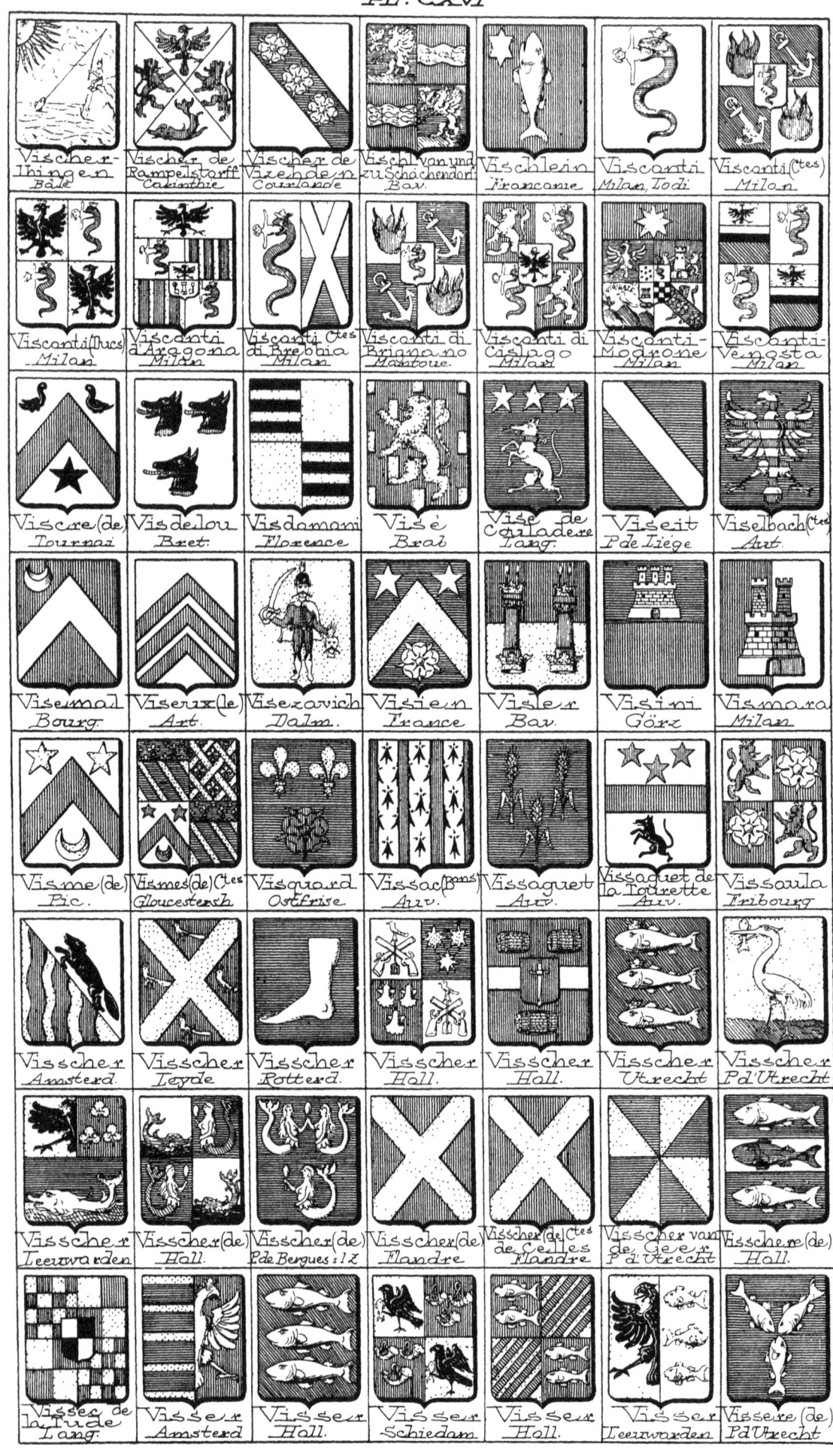

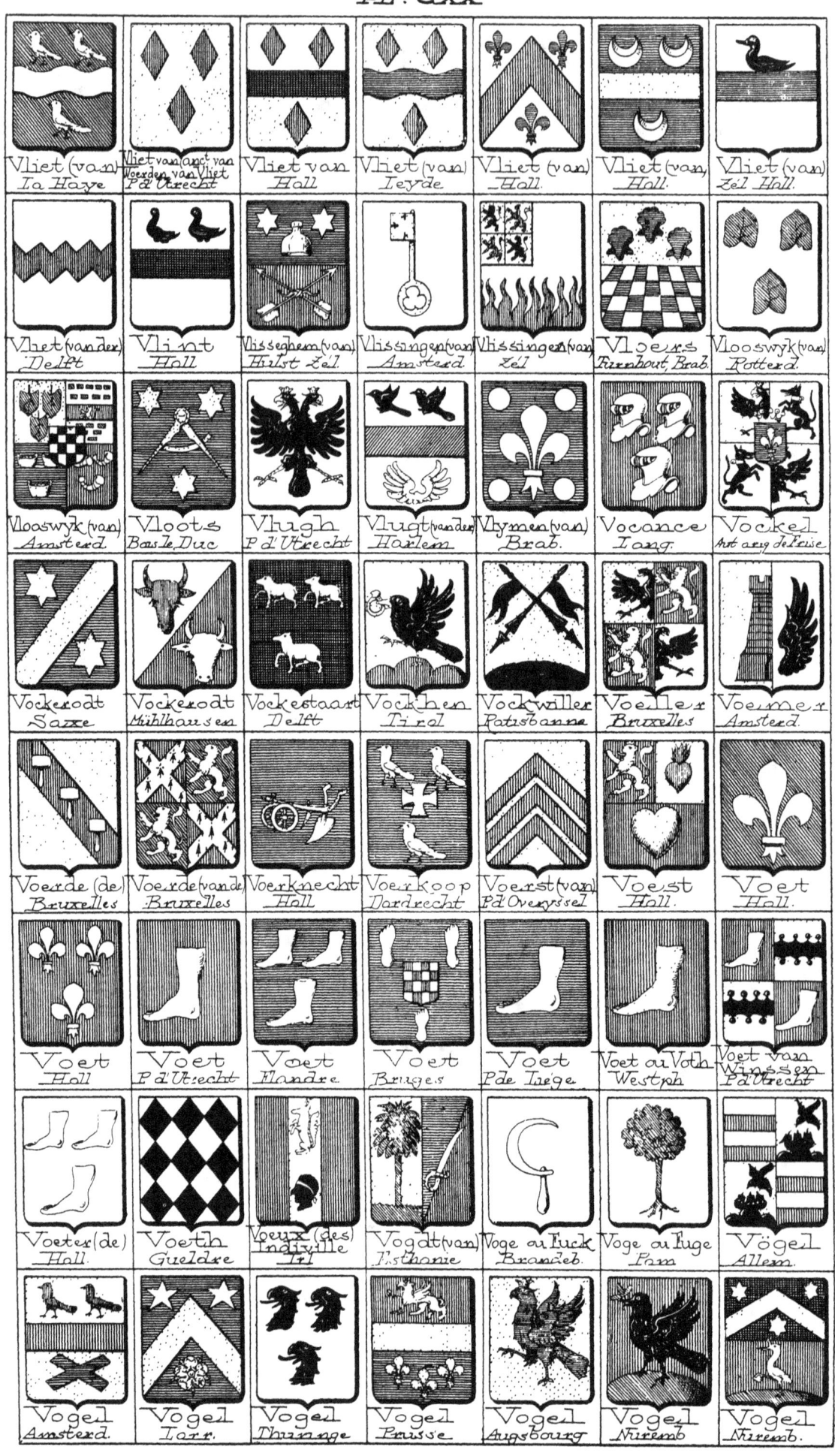

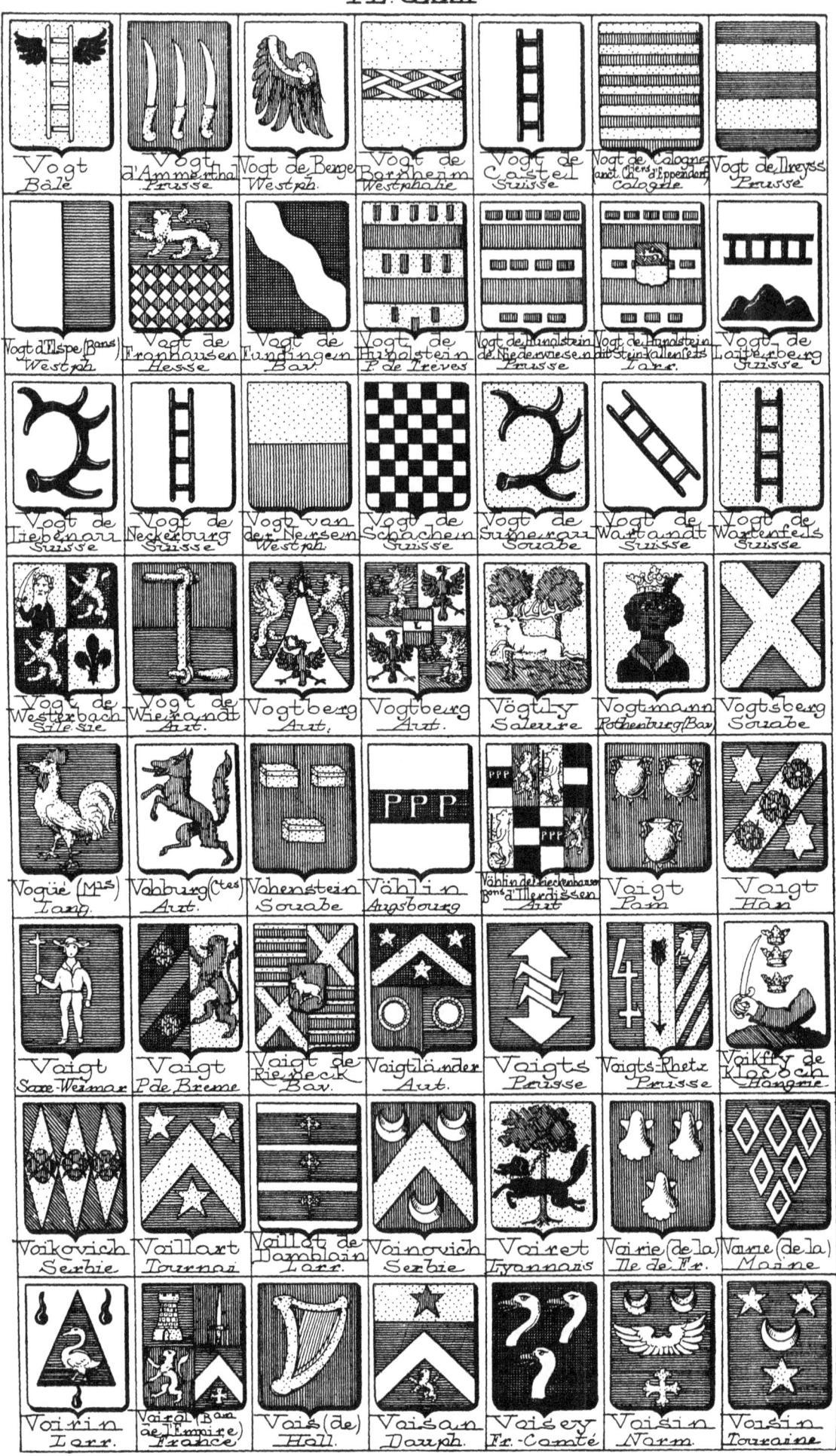

PL. CXXII

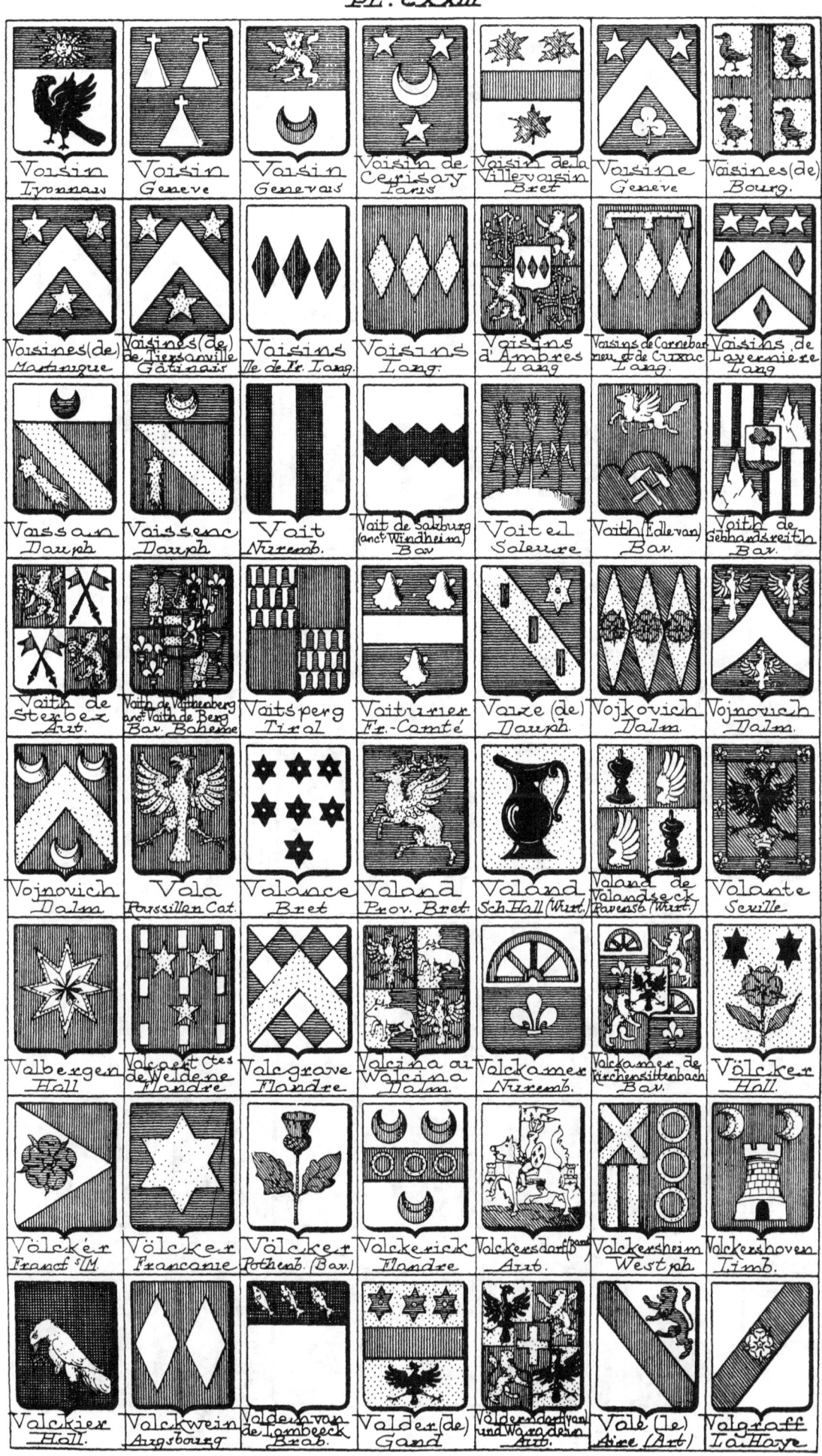

PL. CXXIV

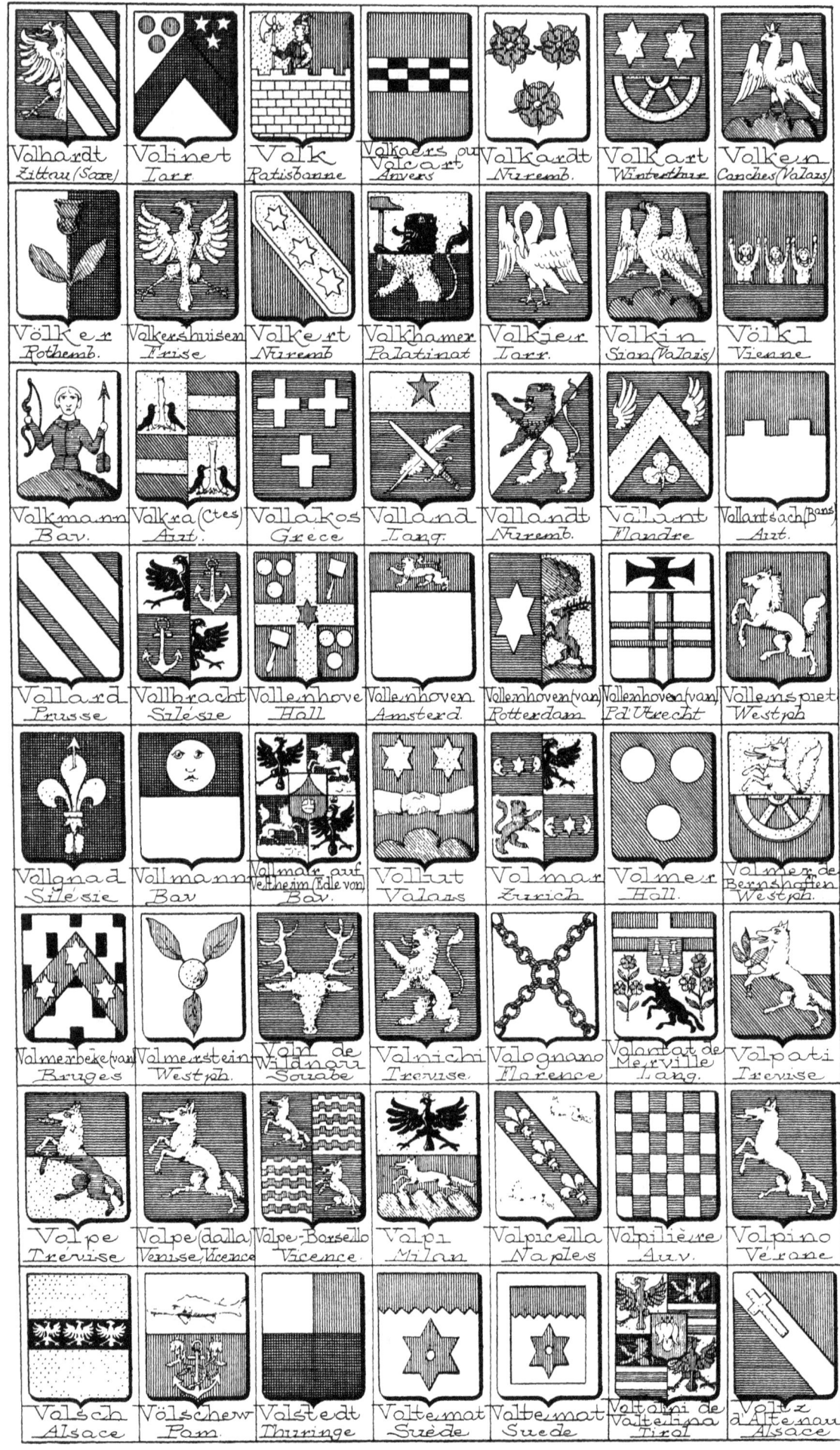

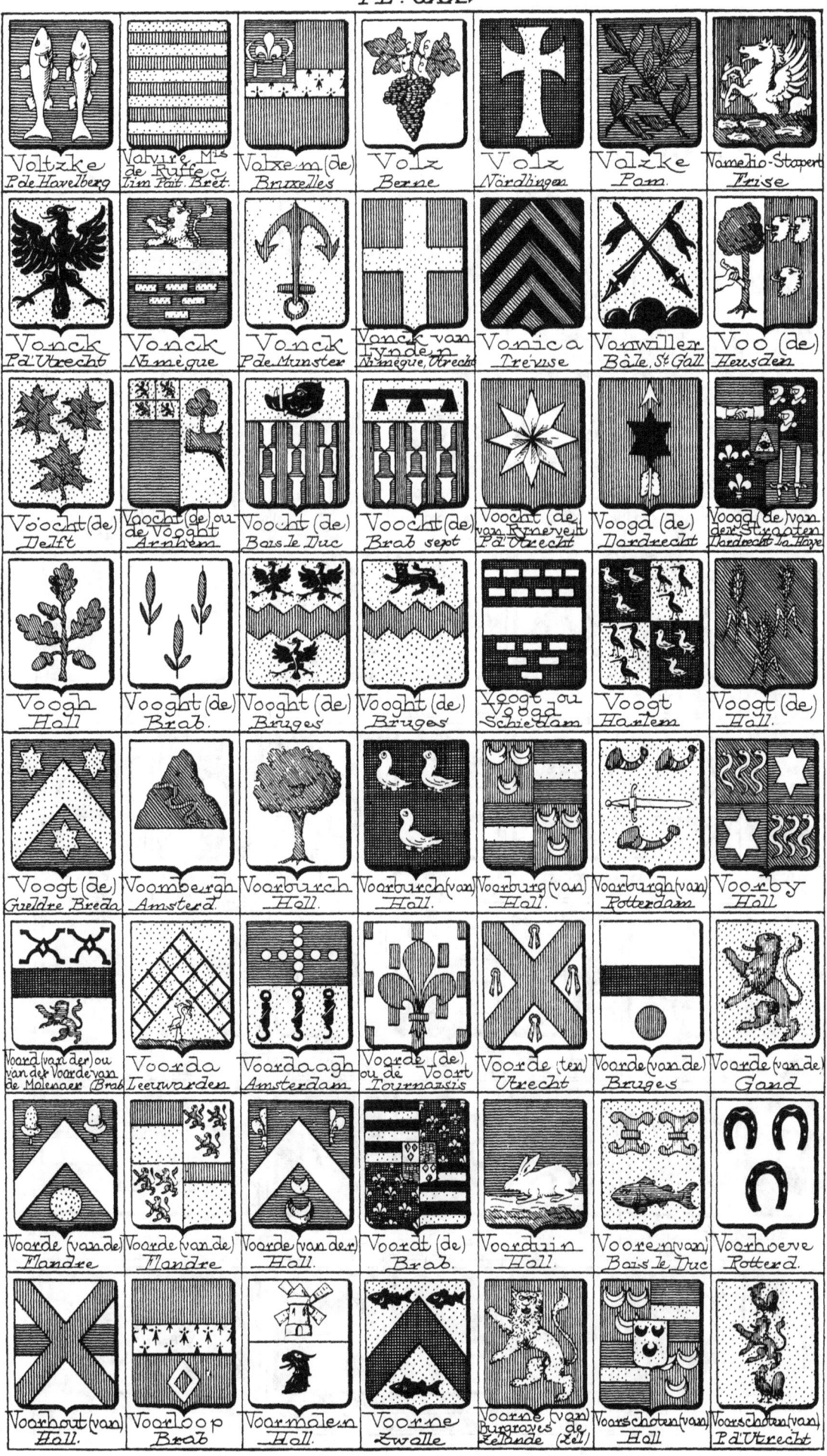

PL. CXXV

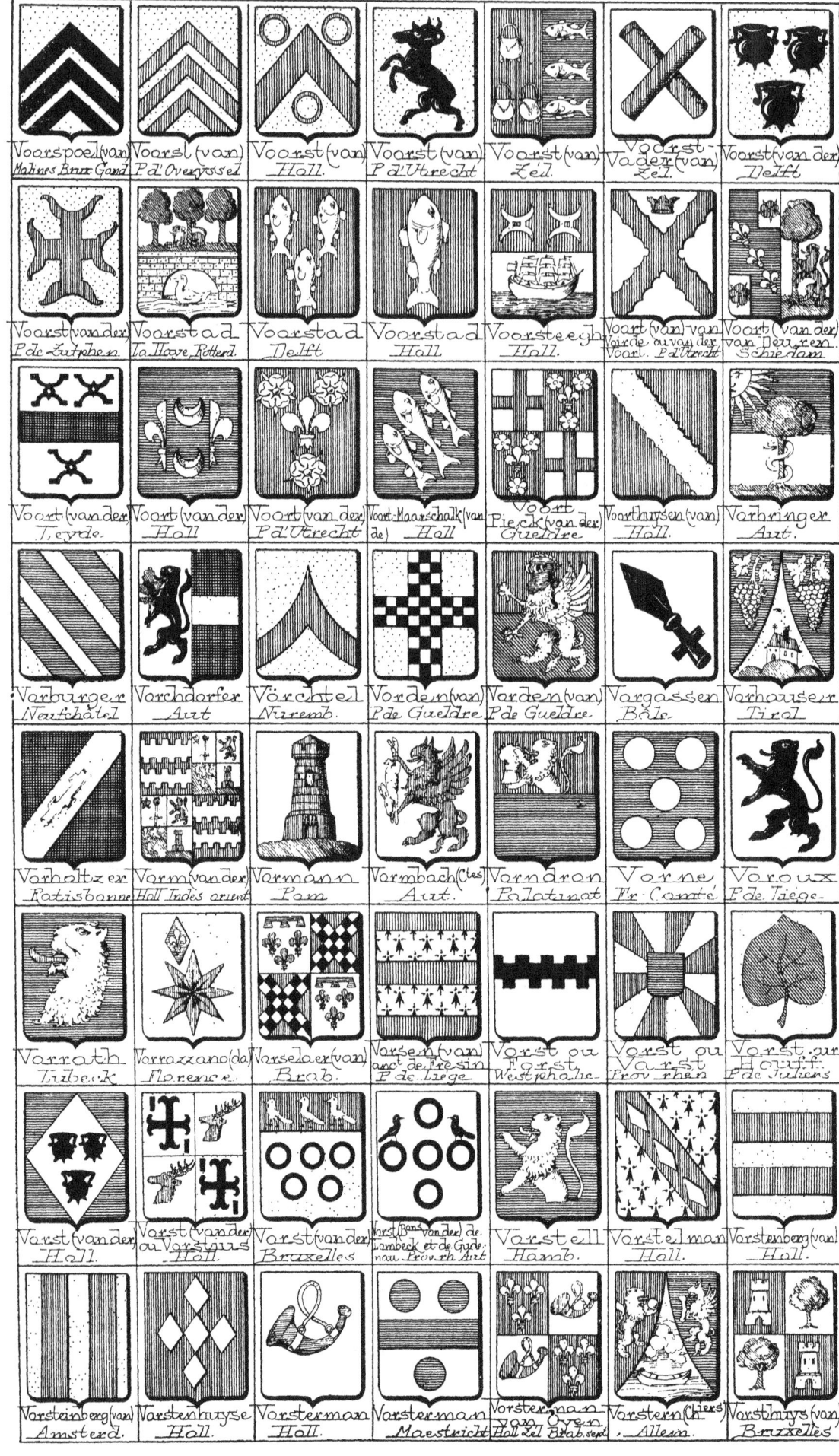

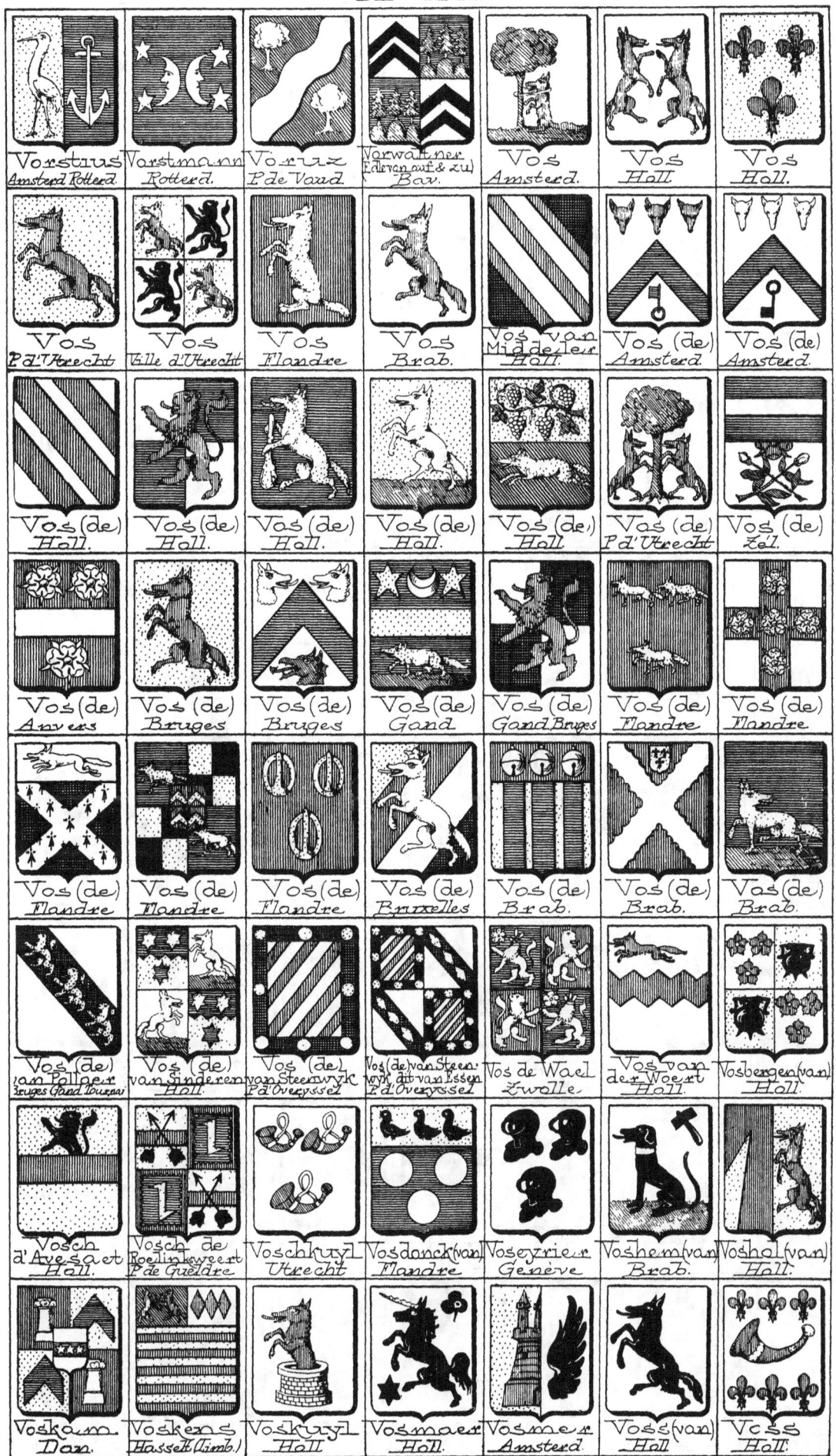

PL. CXXIX

PL. CXXX

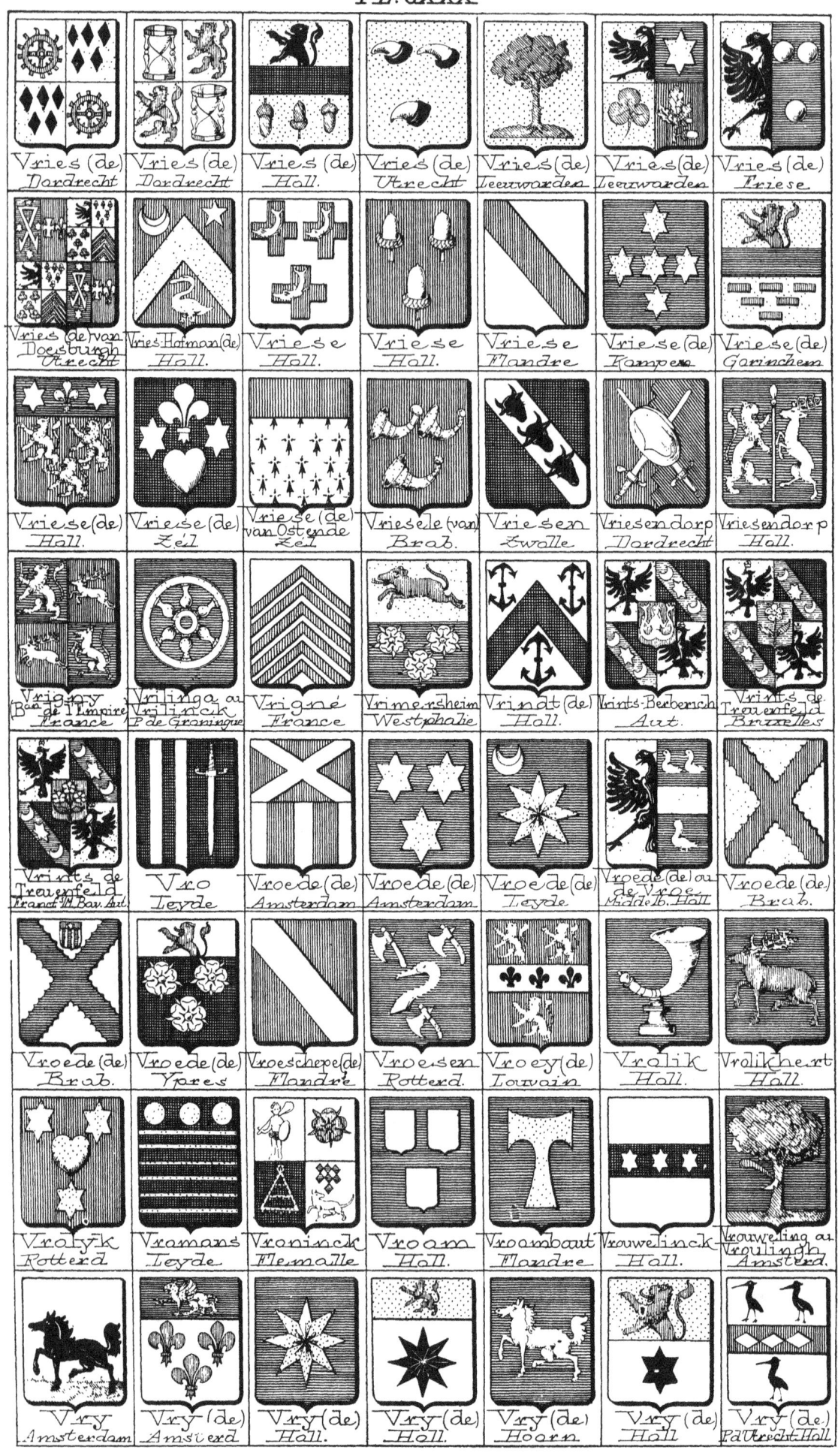

PL. CXXXII

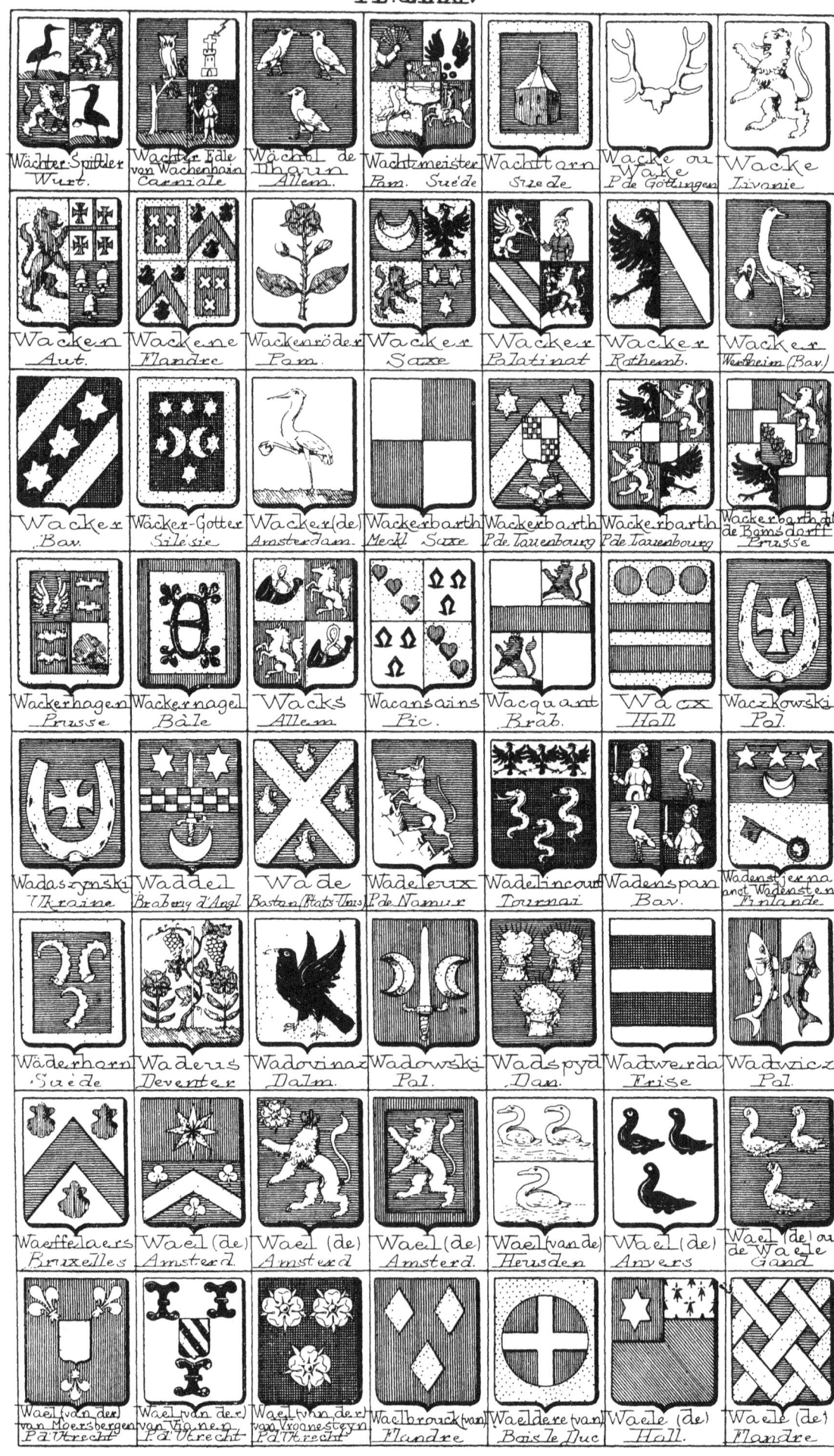

PL. CXXXV

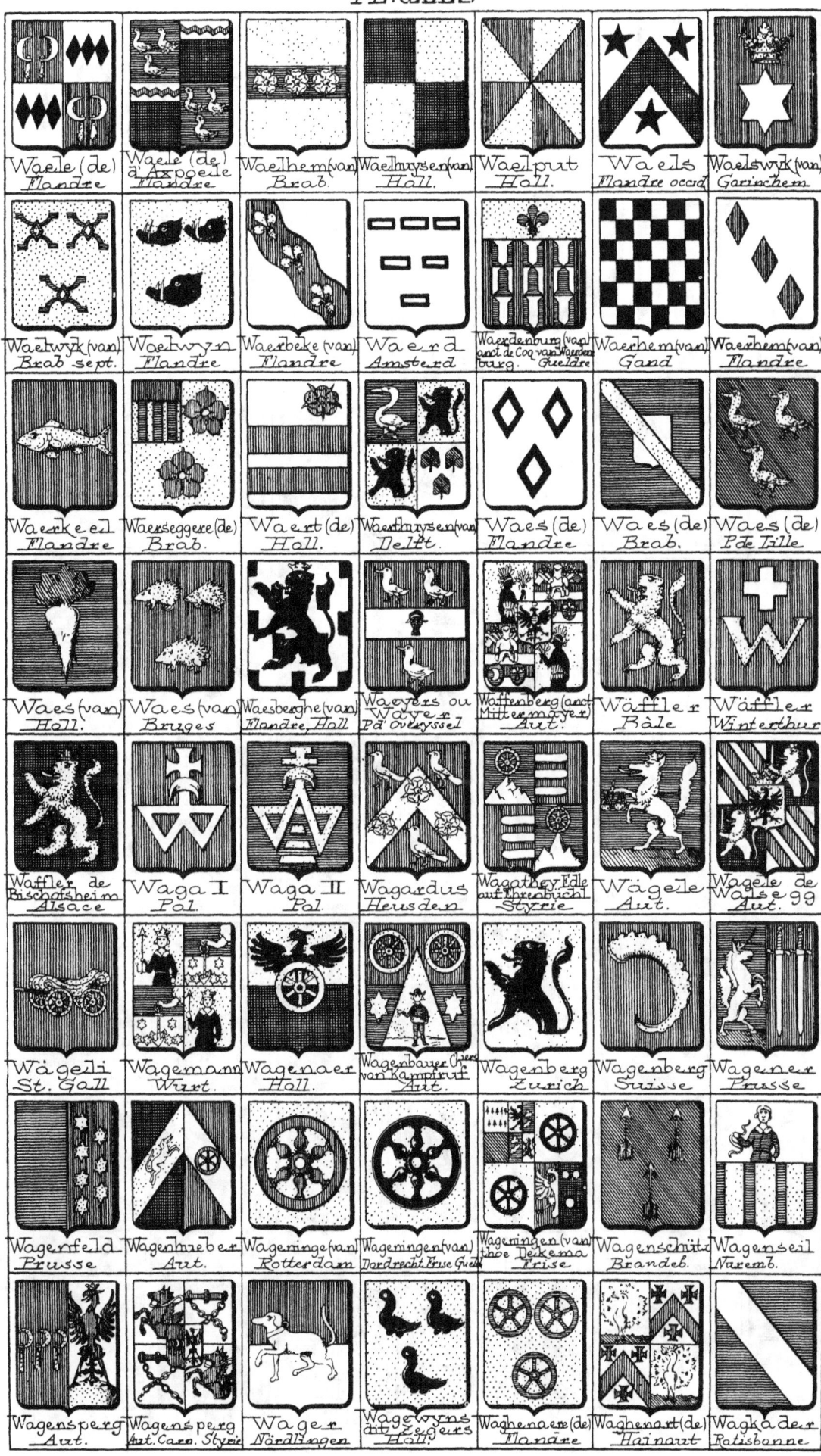

PL. CXXXVII

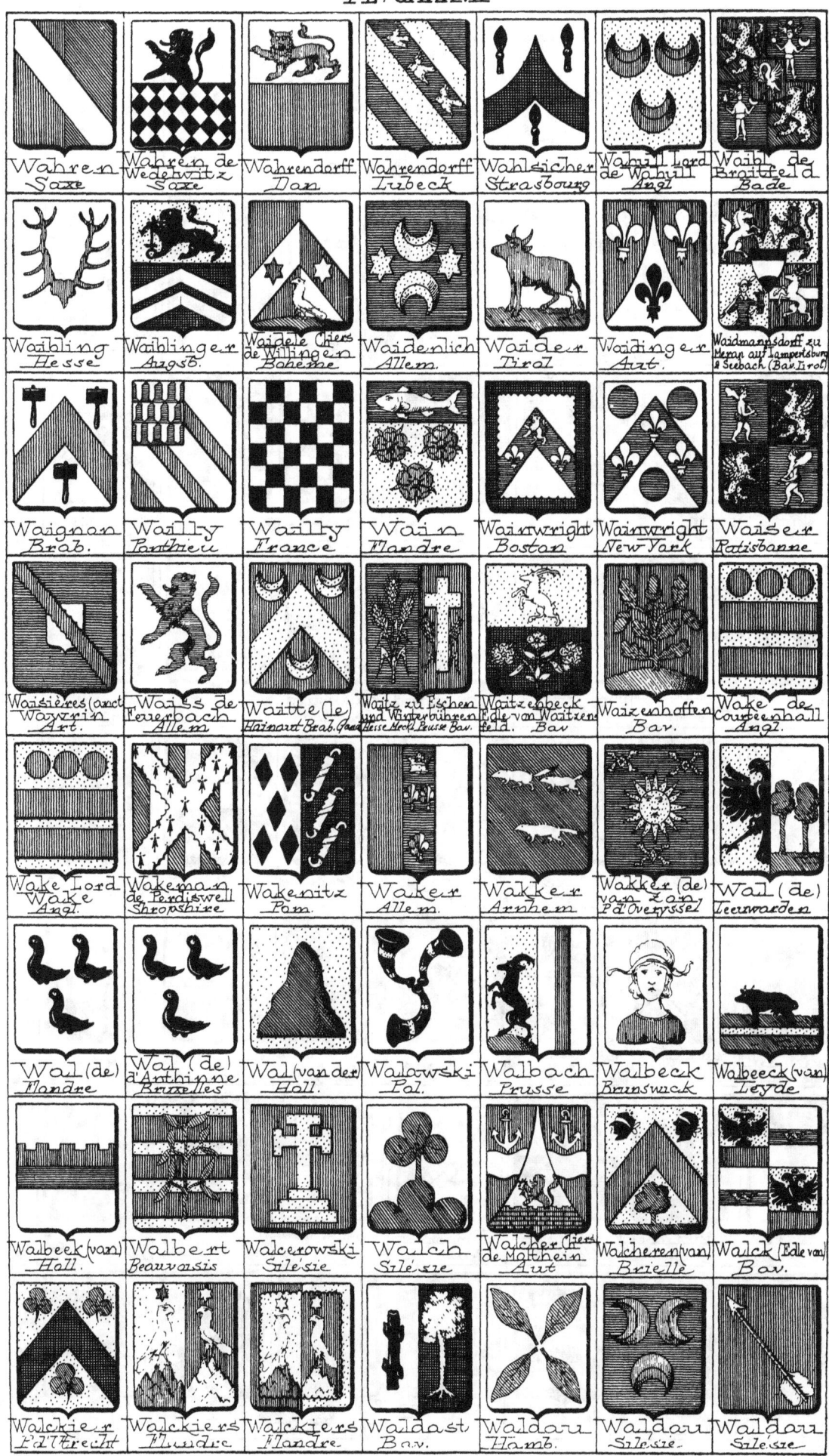

PL. CXXXVIII

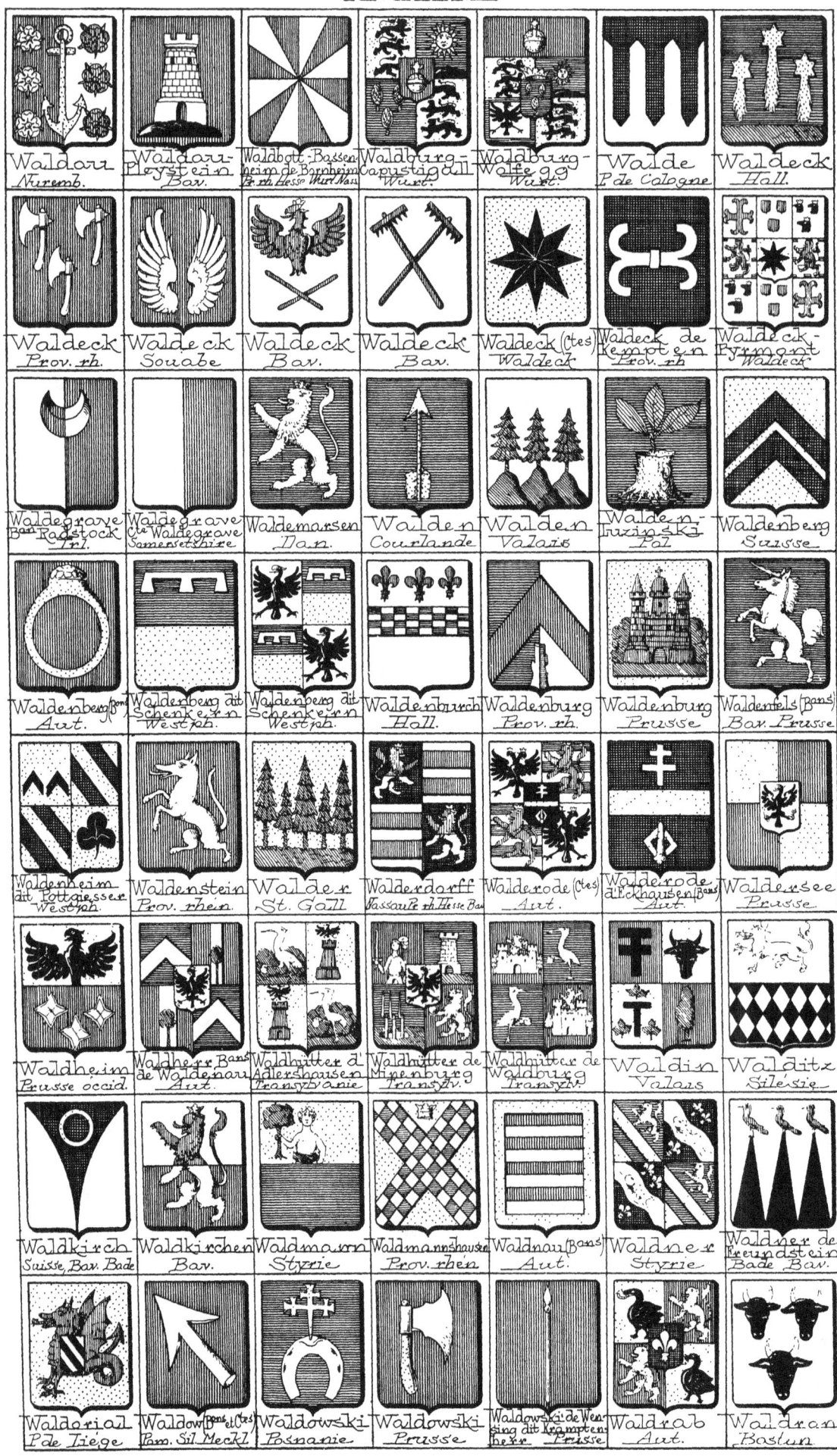

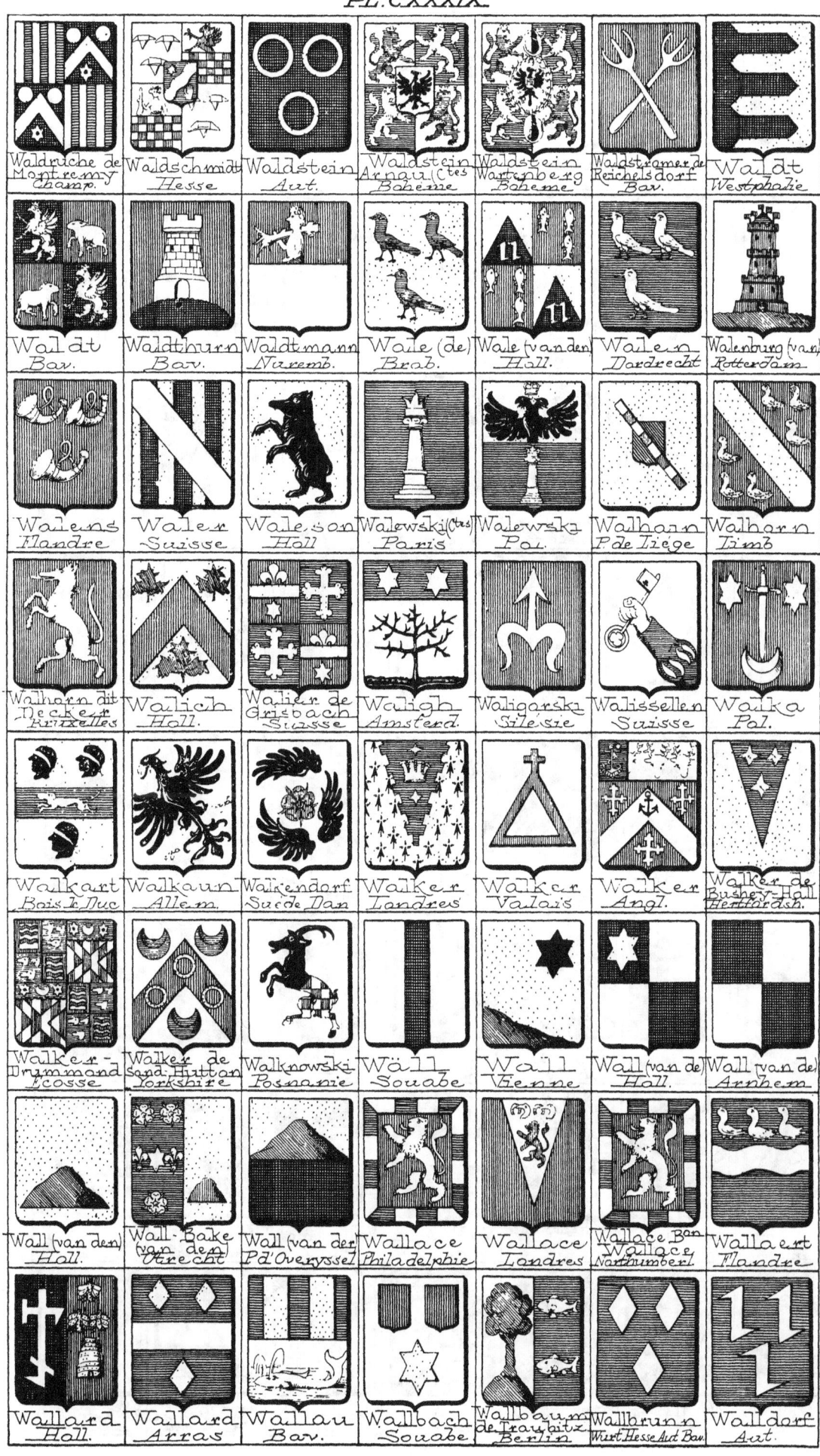

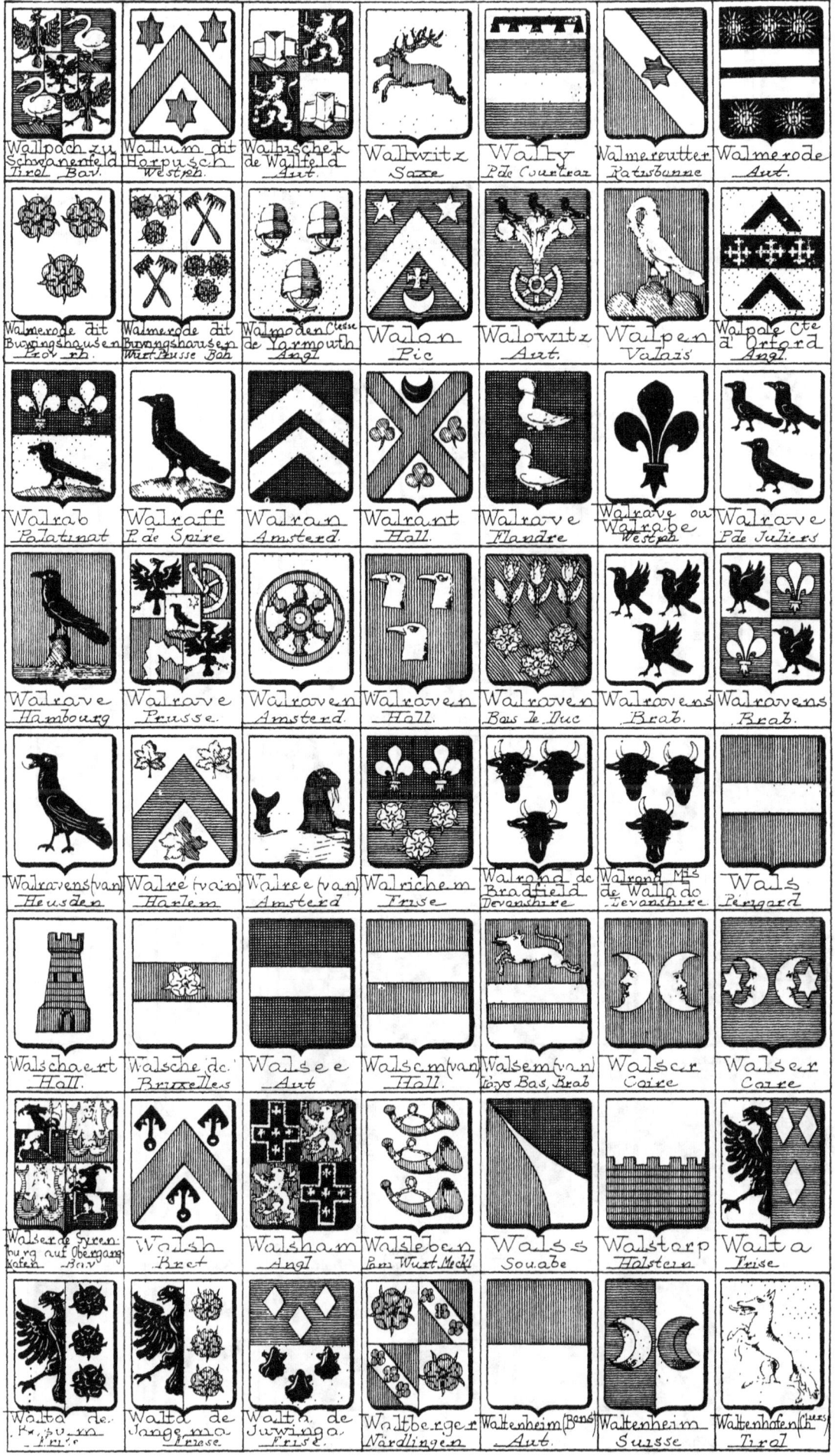

PL. CXLII

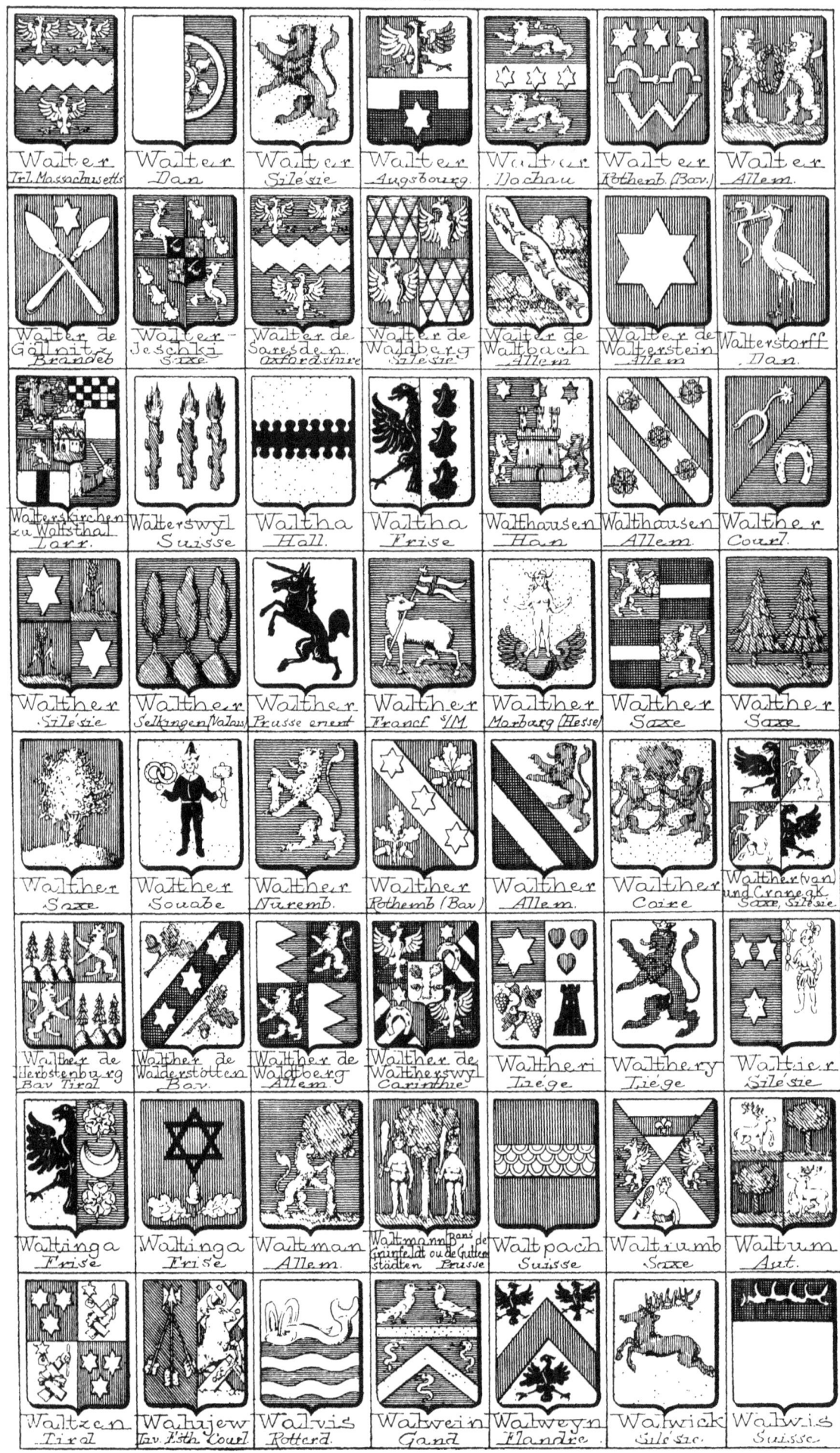

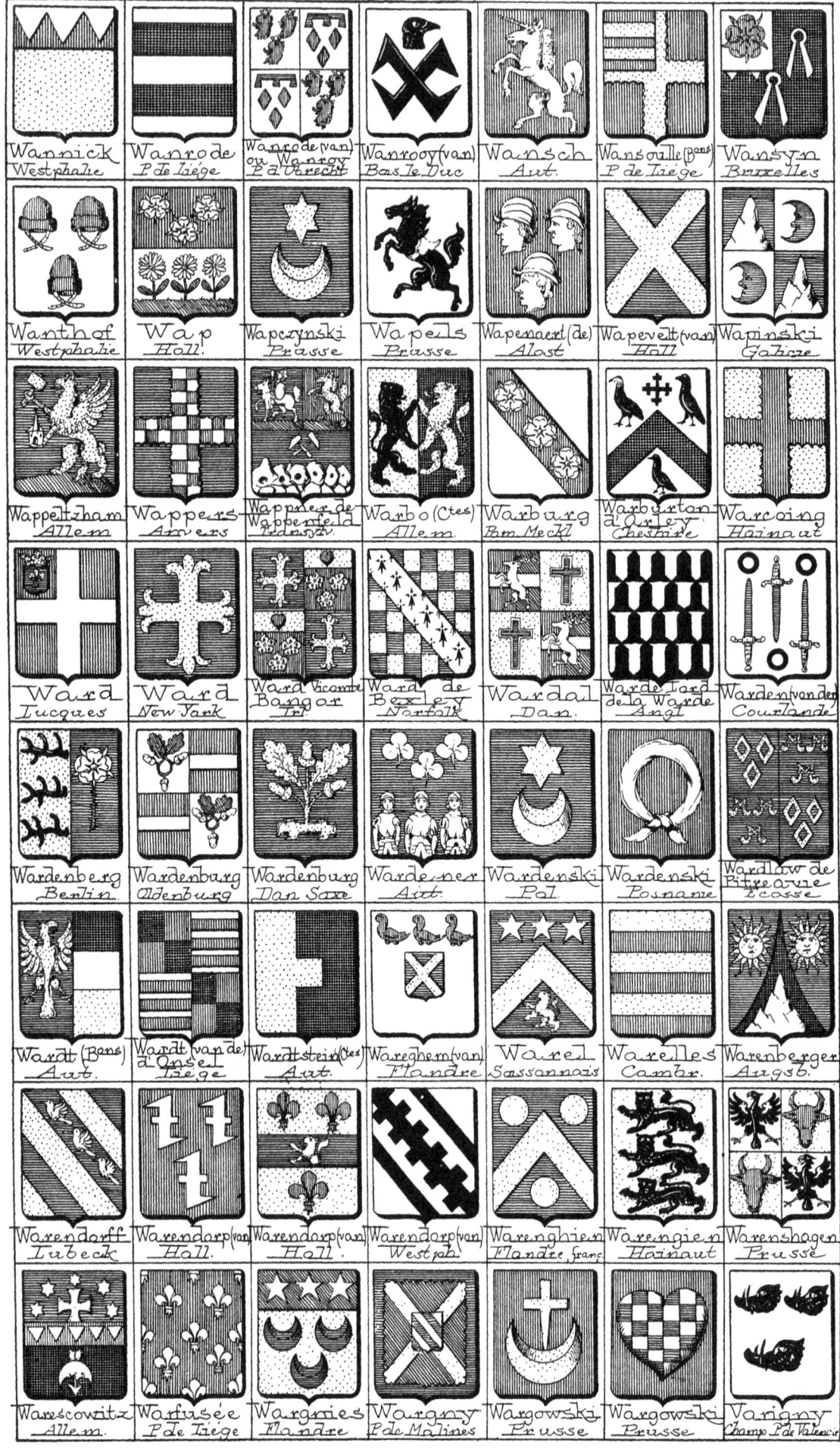

PL. CXLV

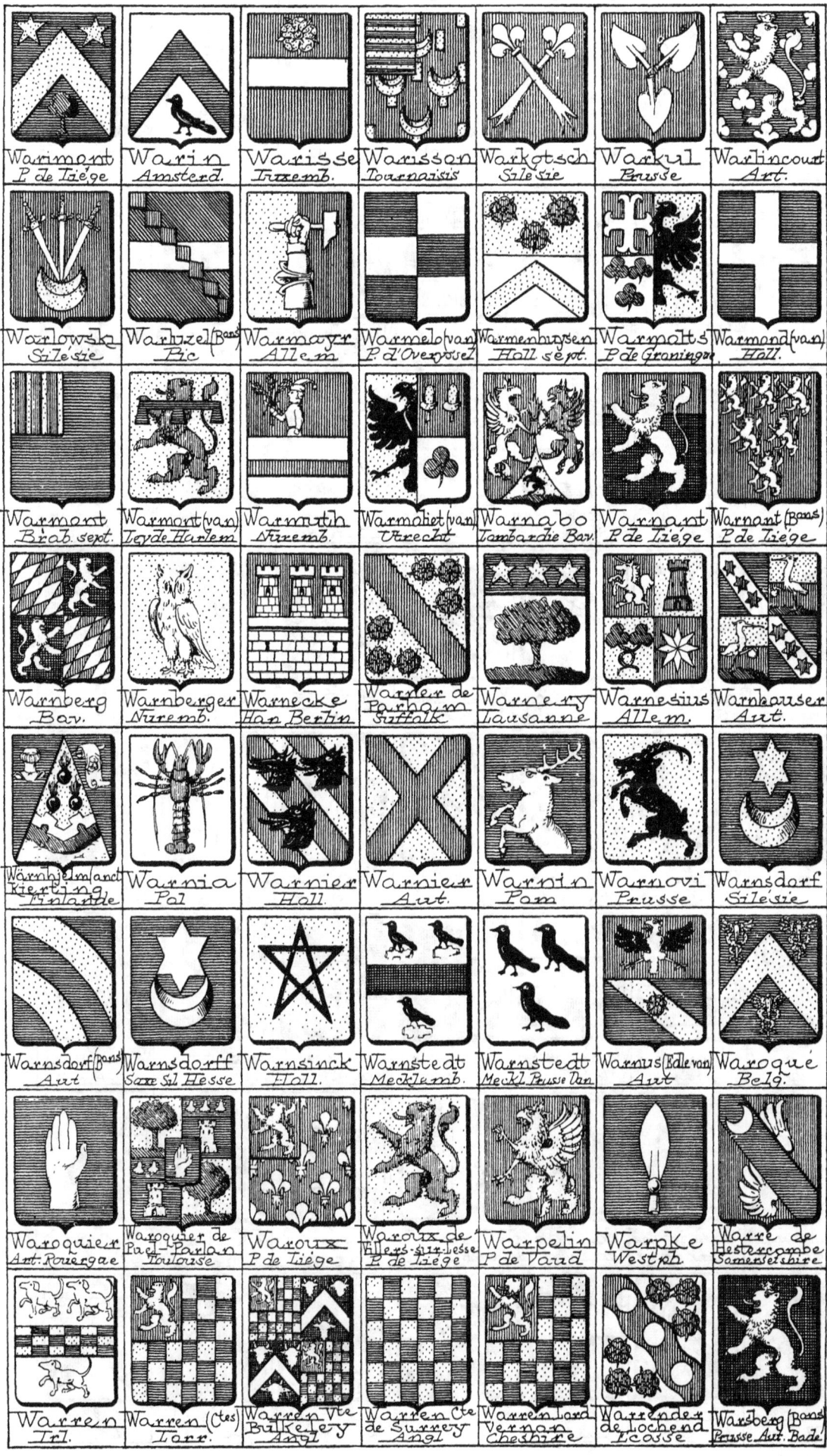

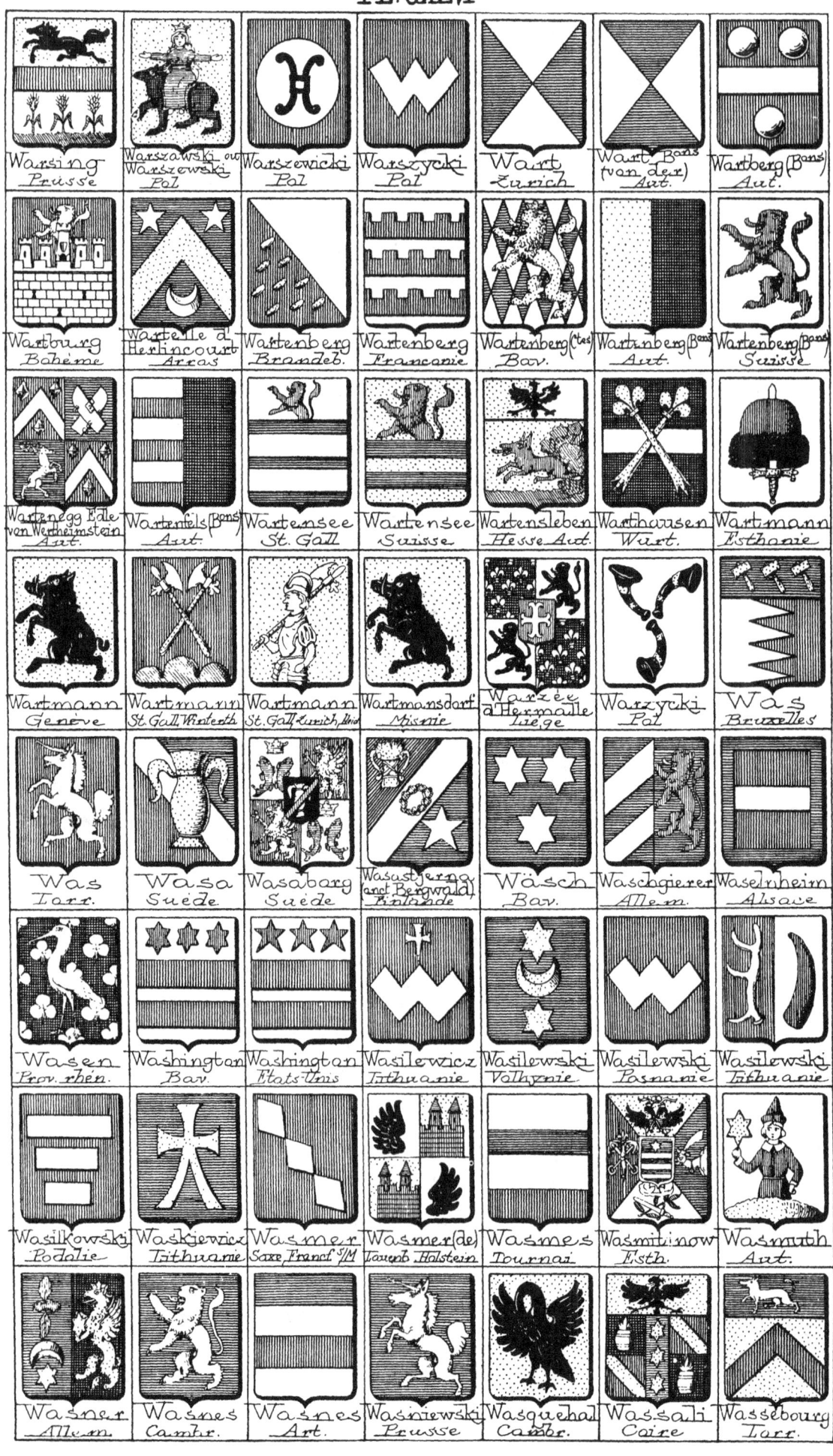

PL. CXLVIII.

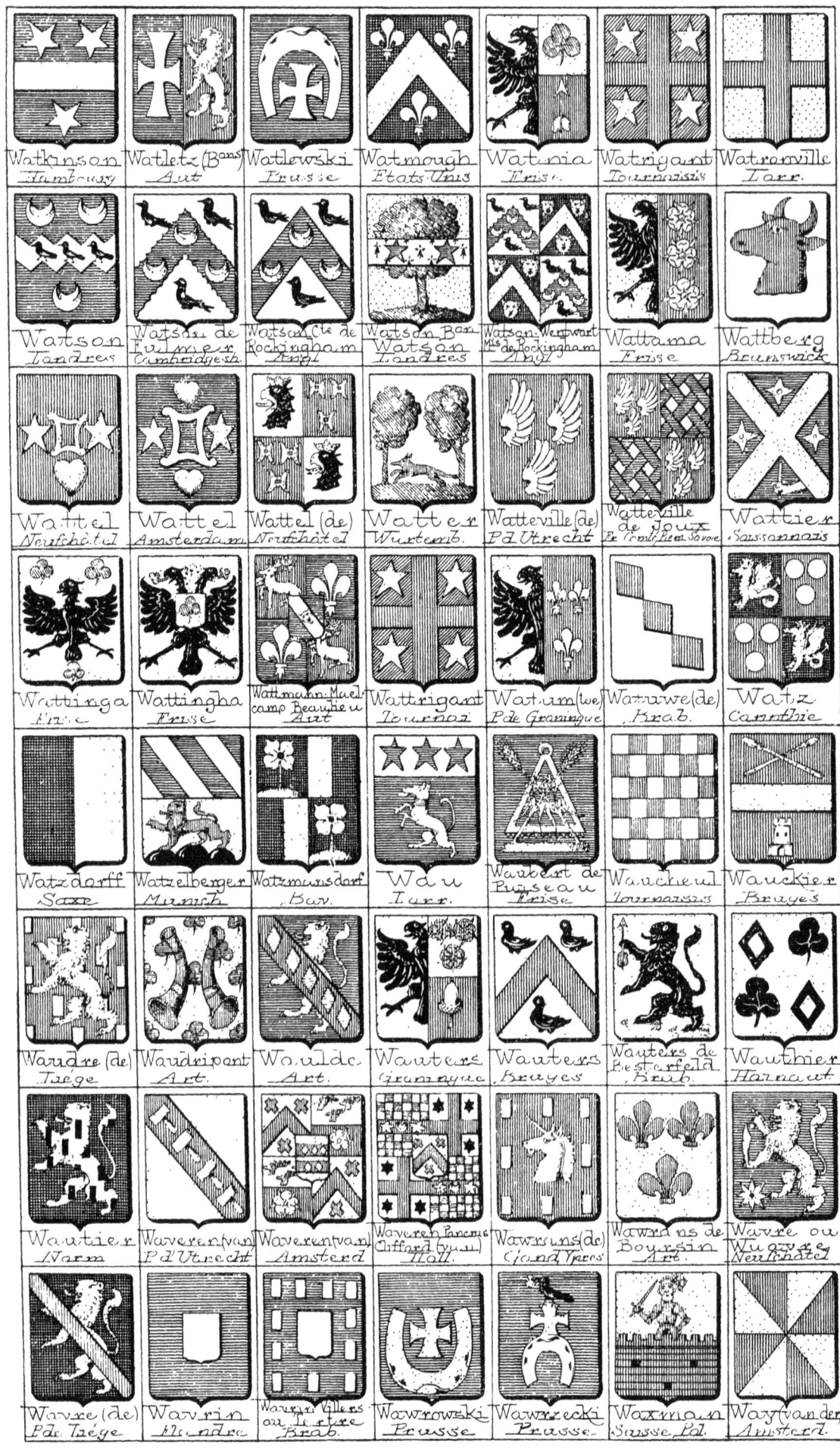

PL. CLIII

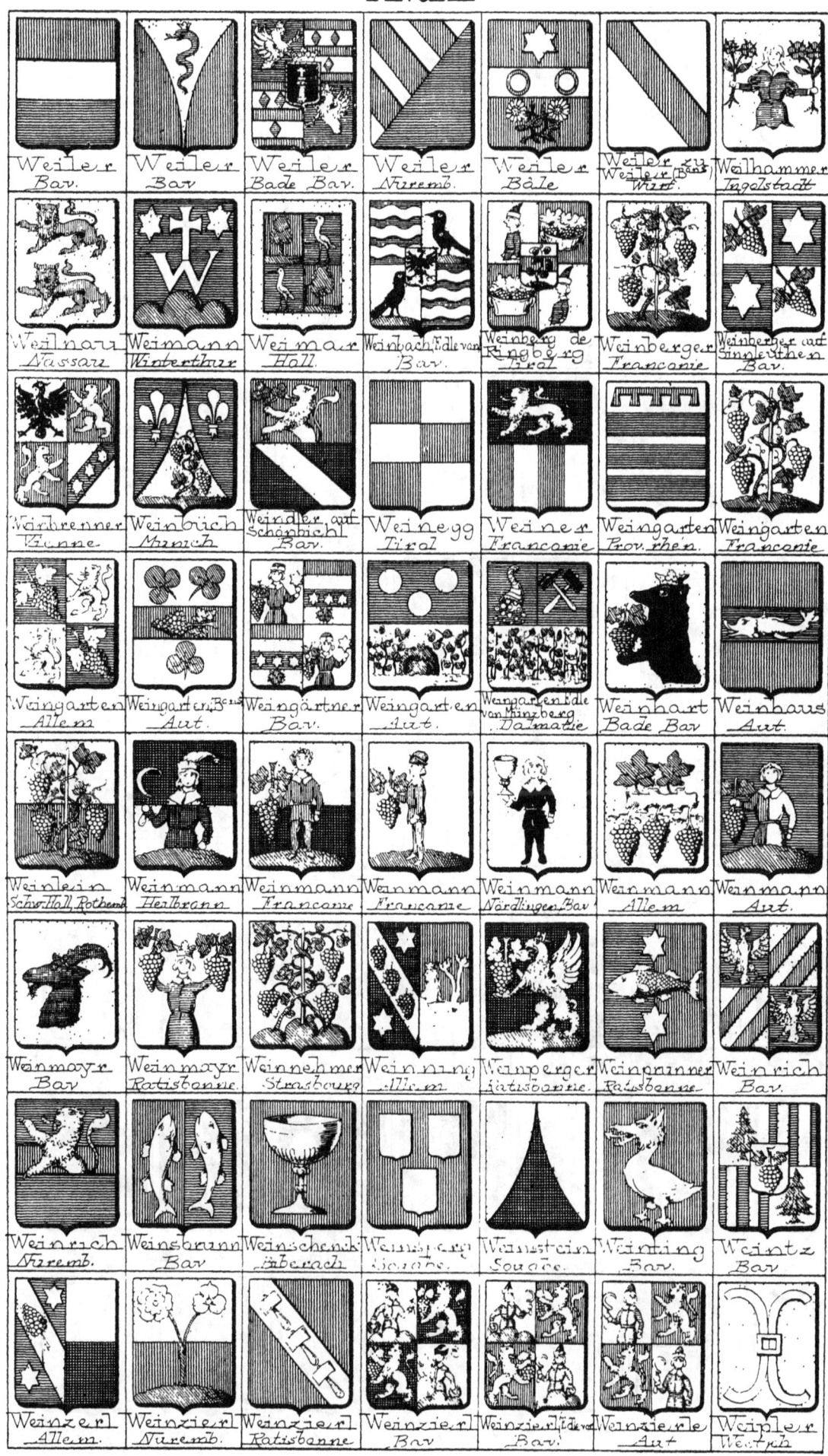

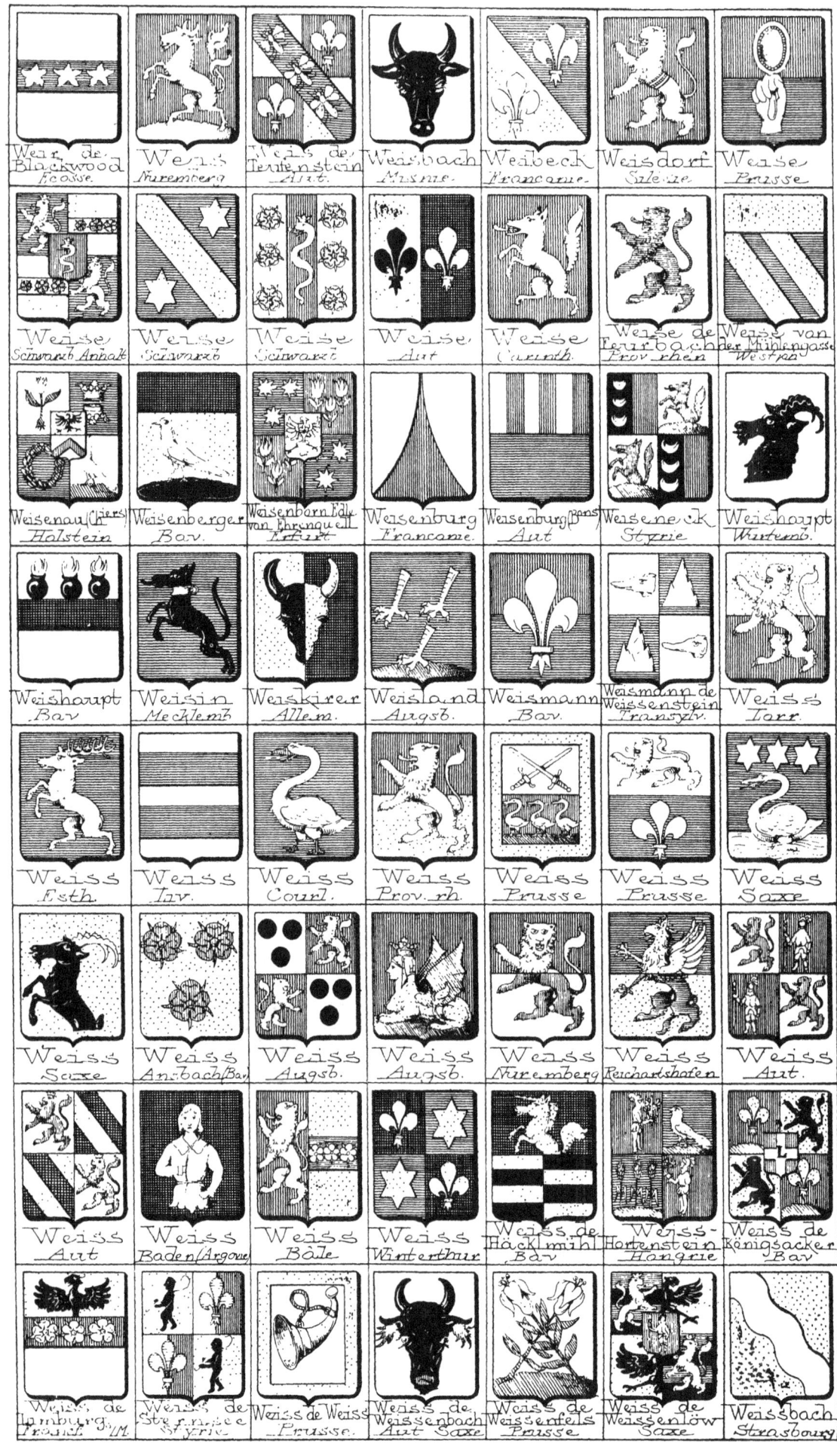

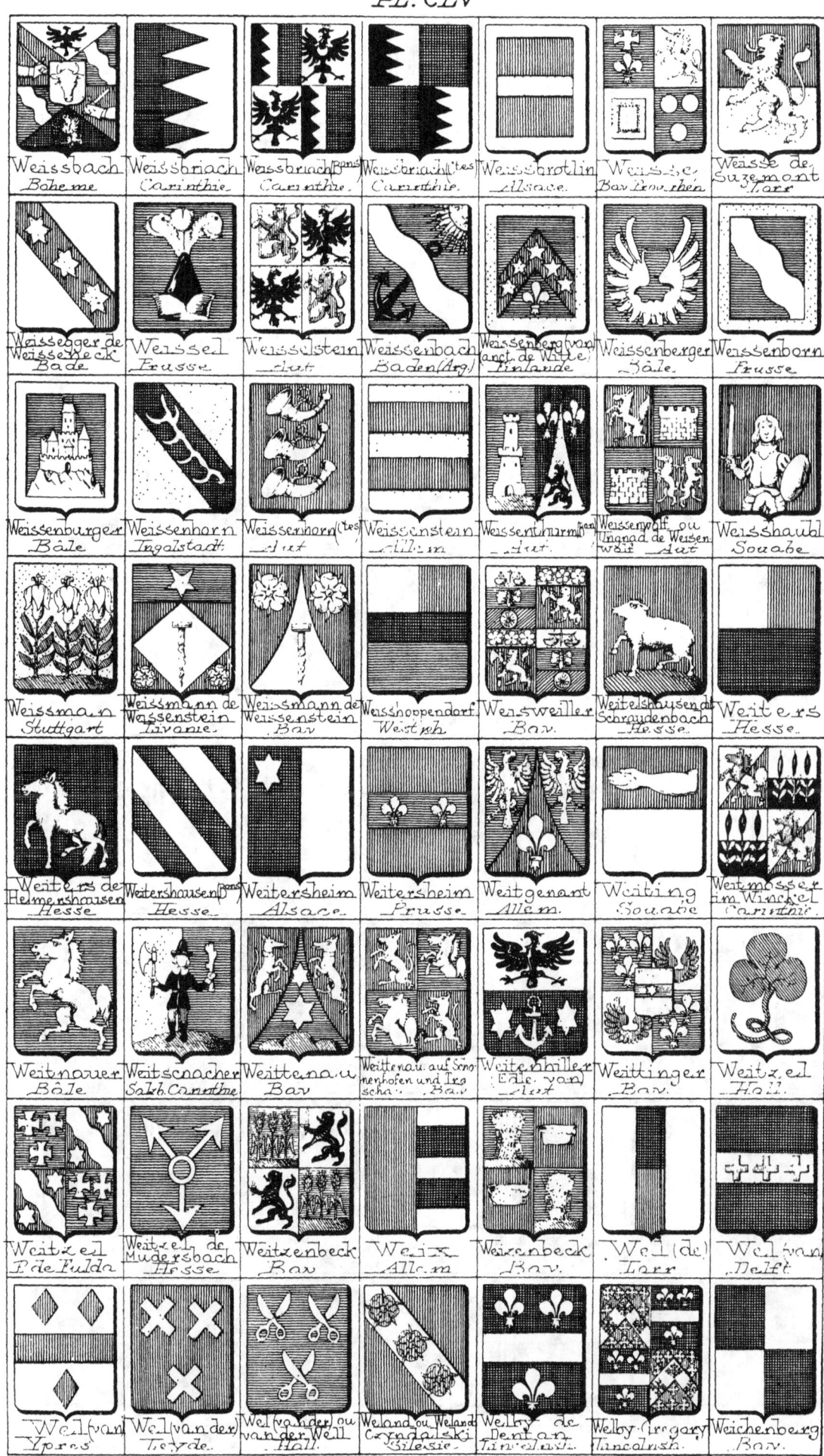

PL. CLVI

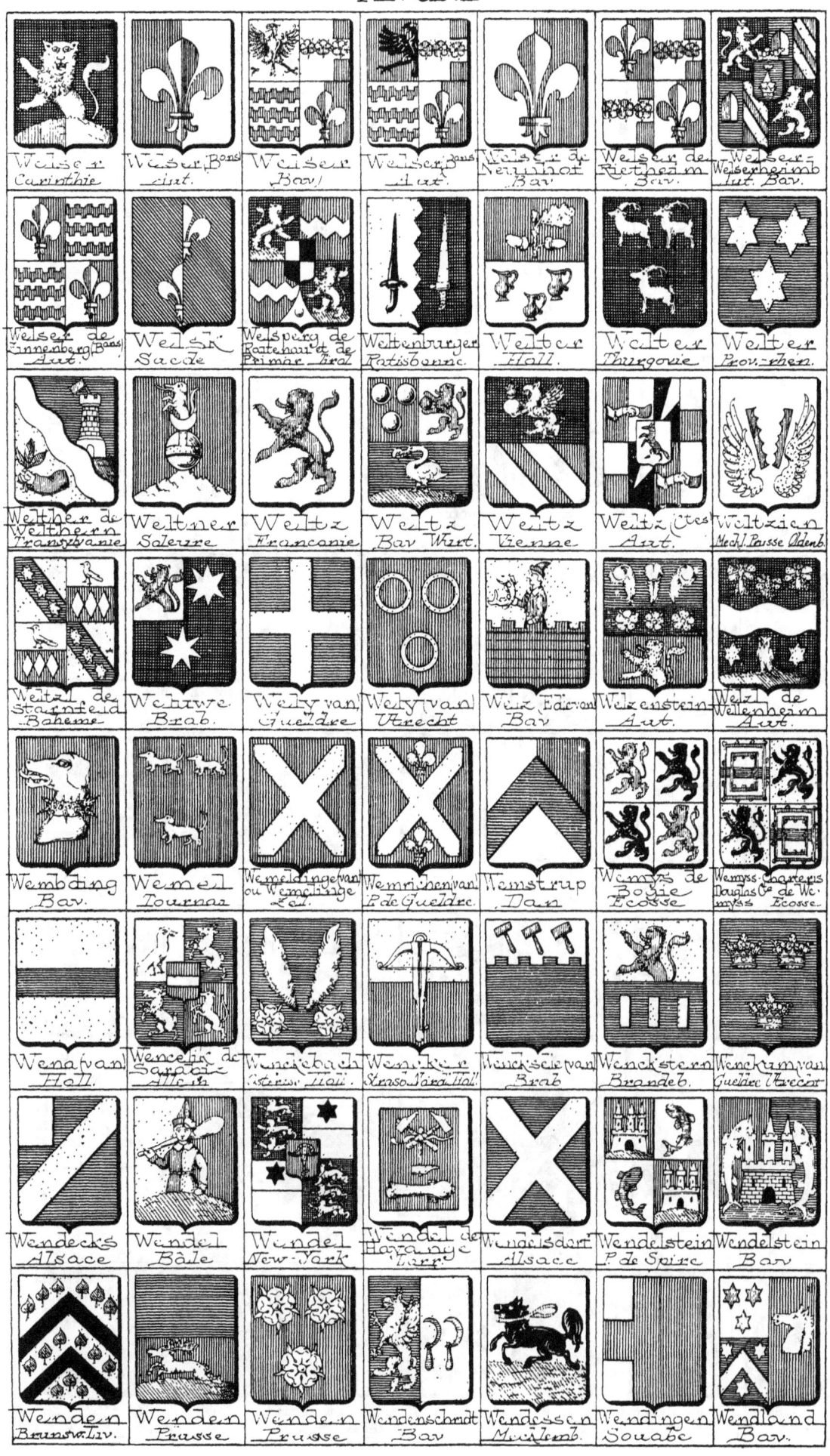

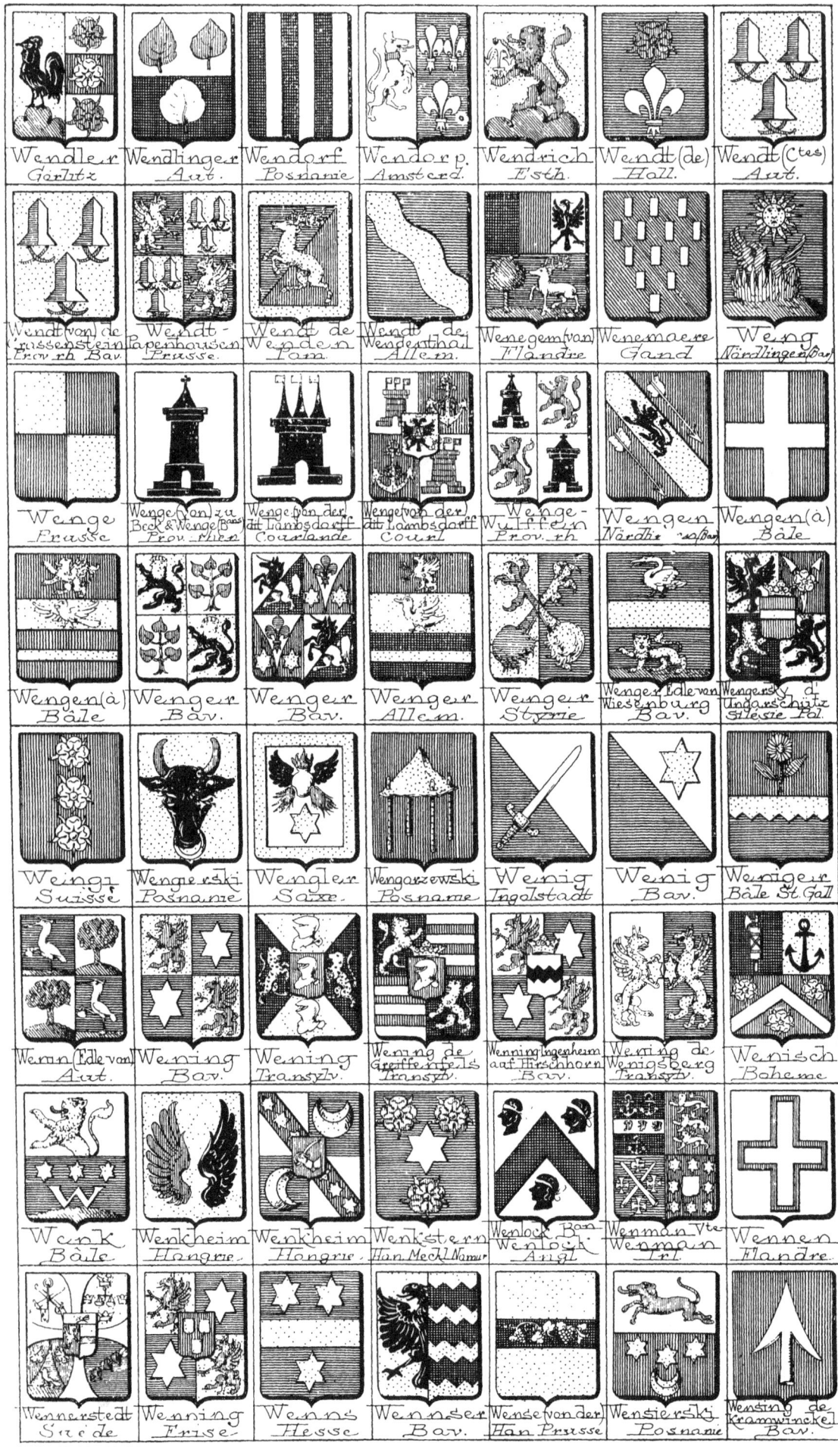

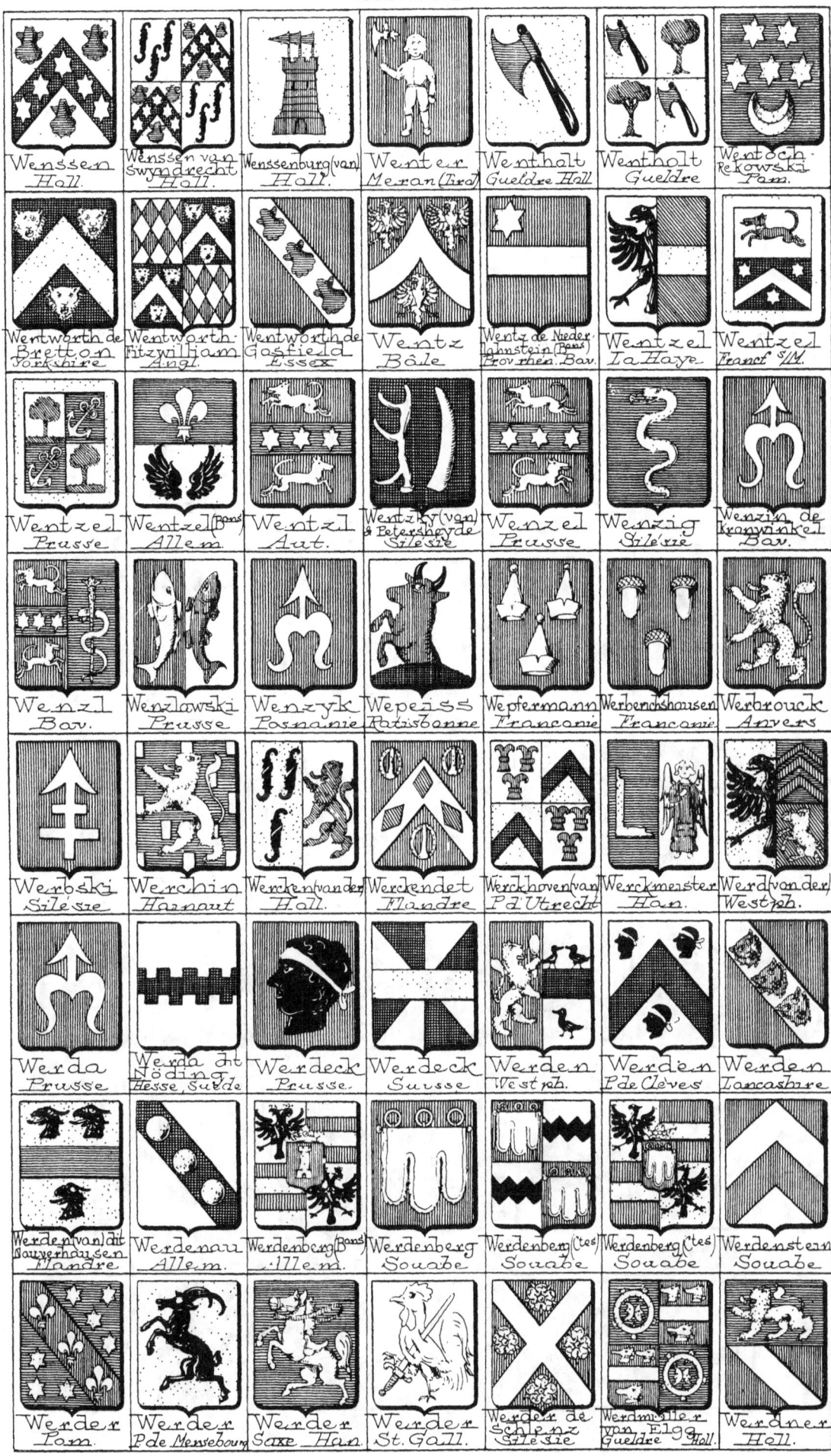

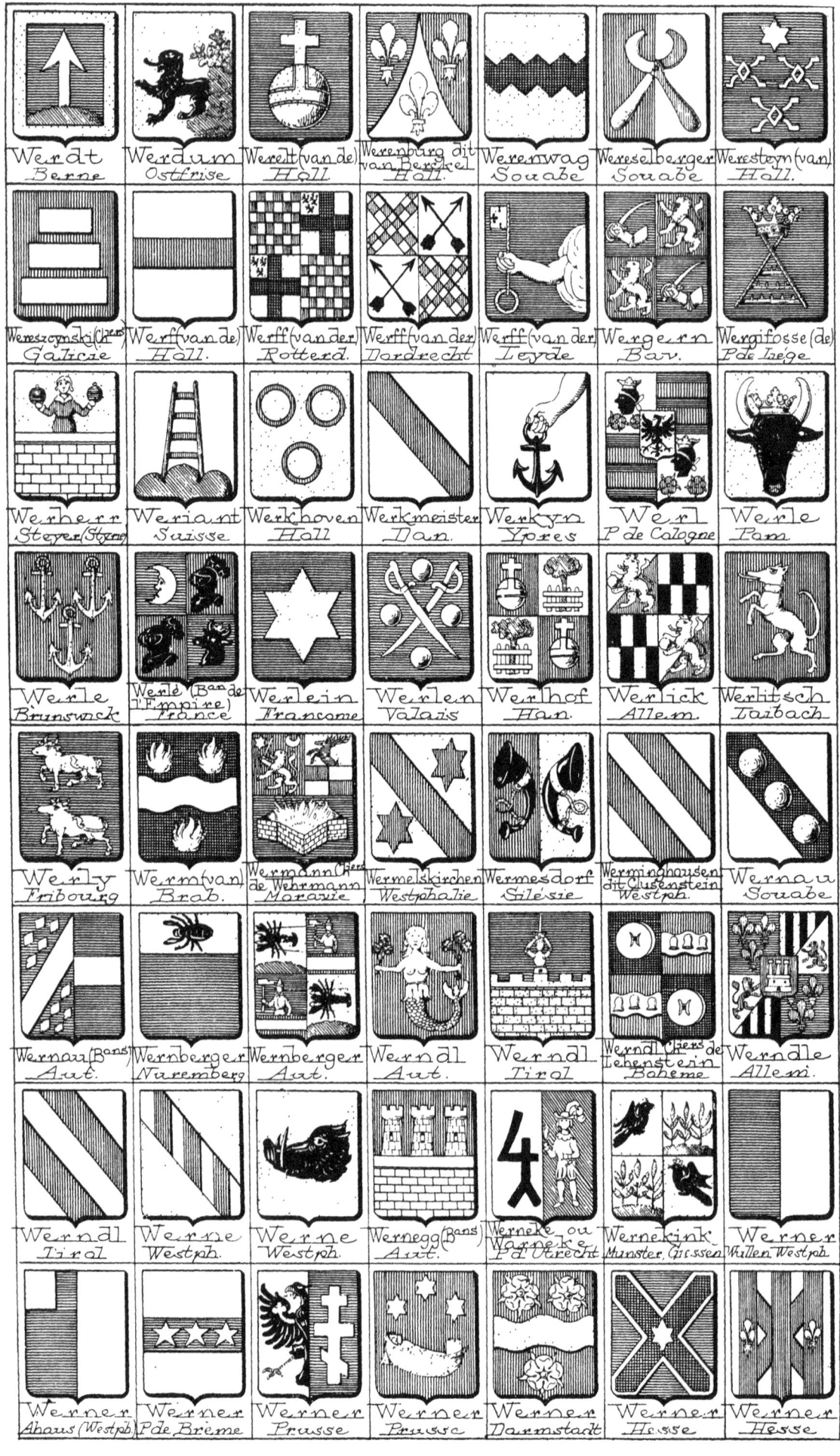

PL. CLX

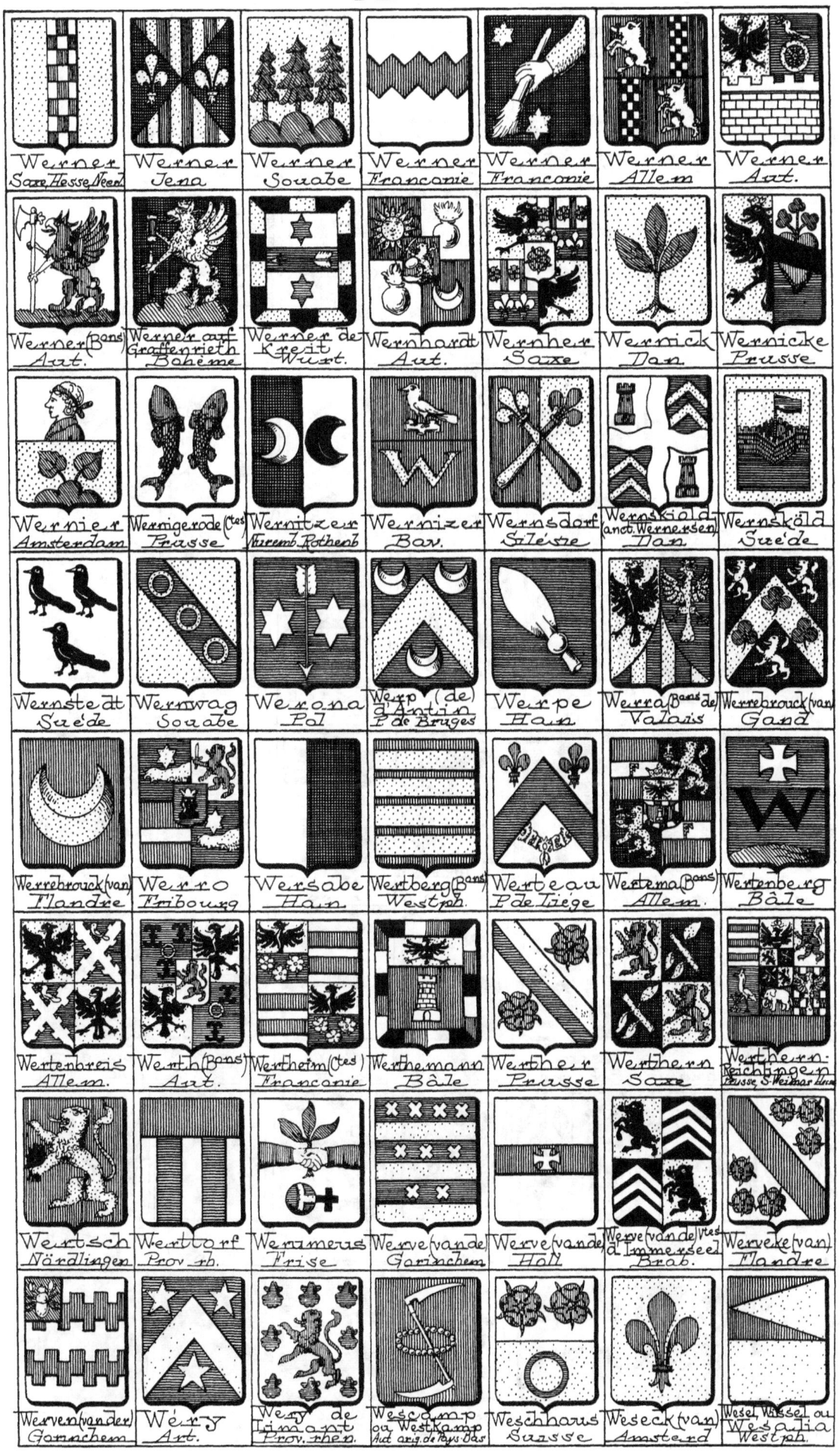

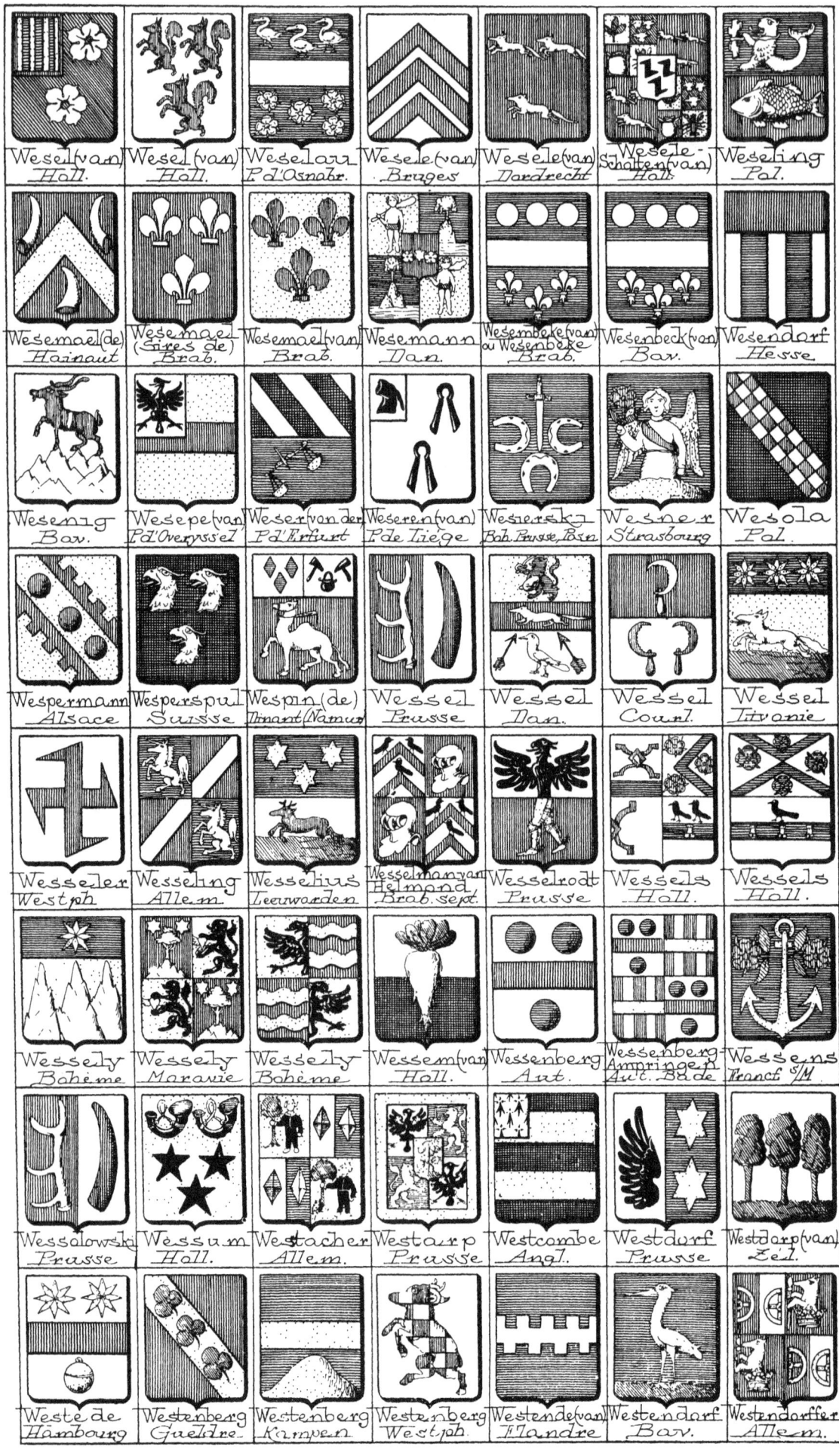

PL. CLXIII

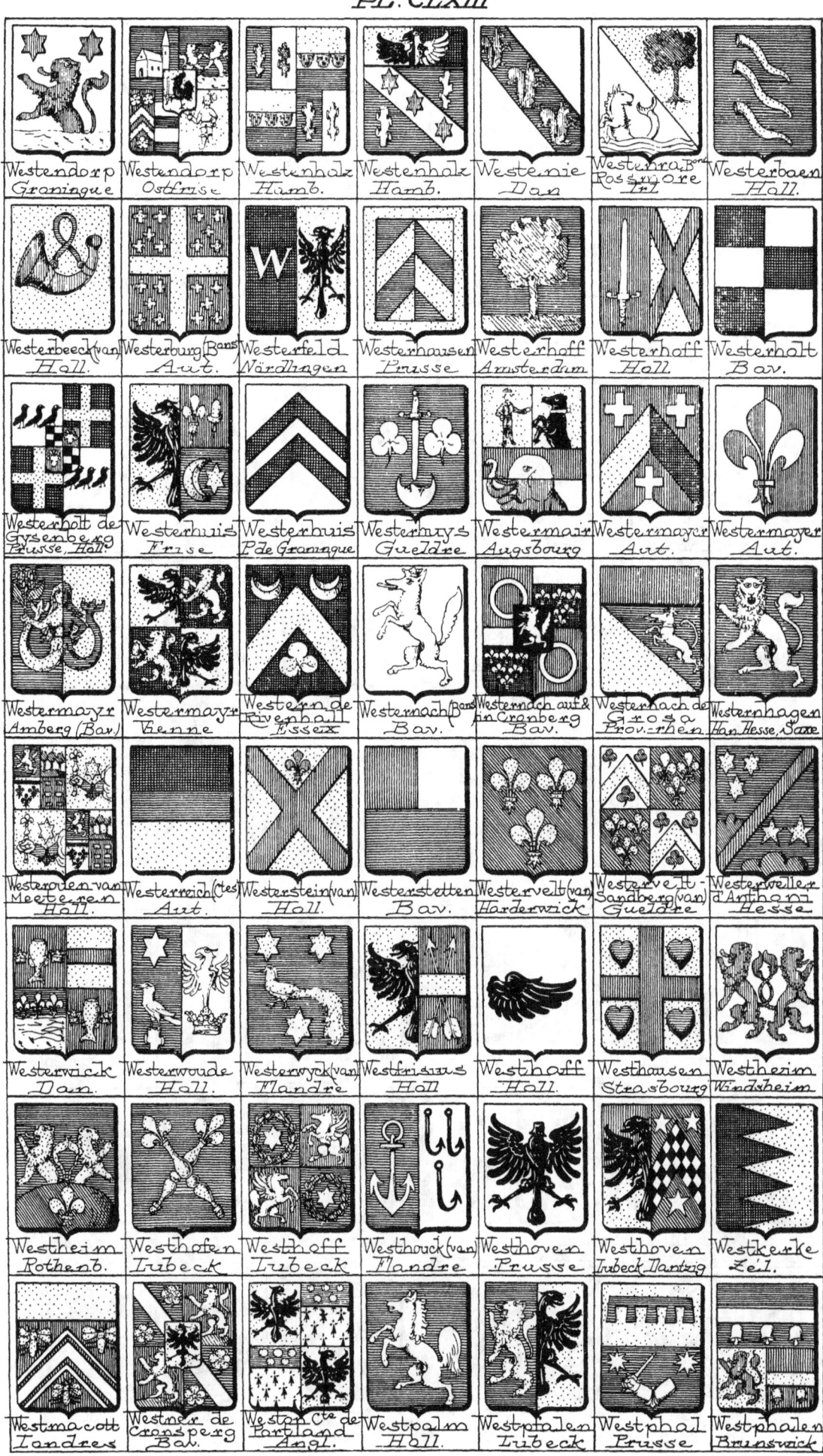

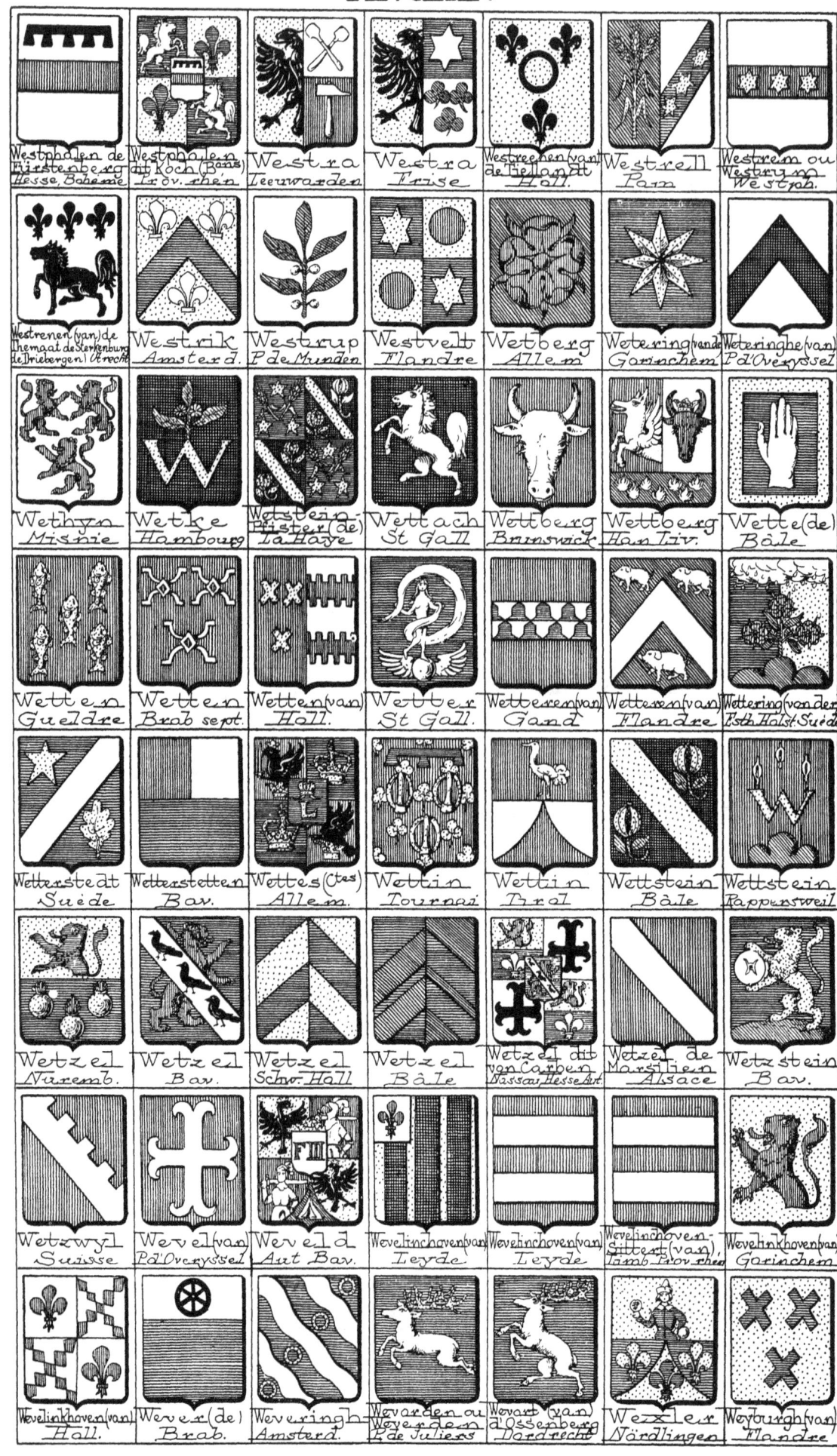

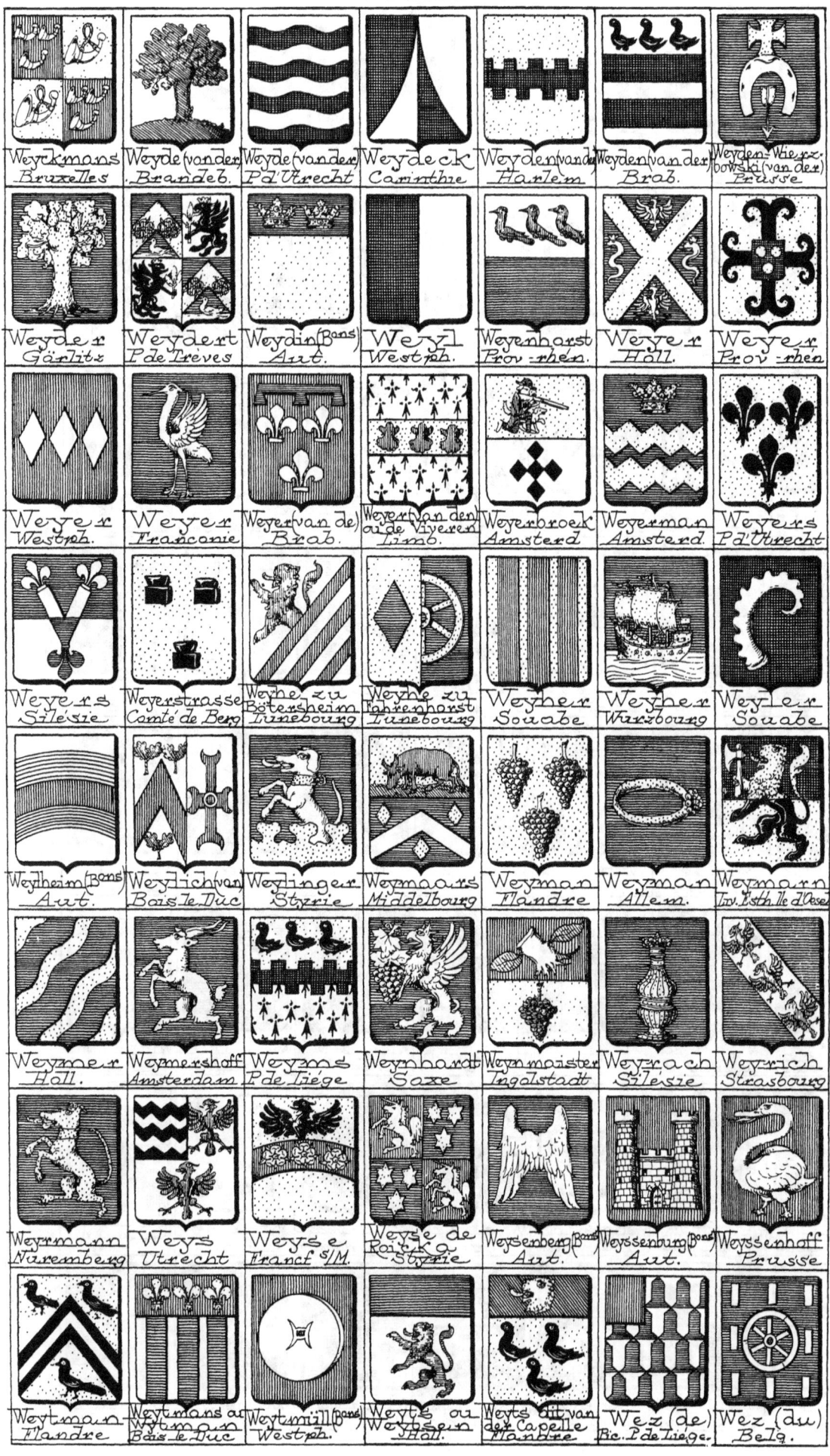

PL. CLXVI

PL. CLXVII

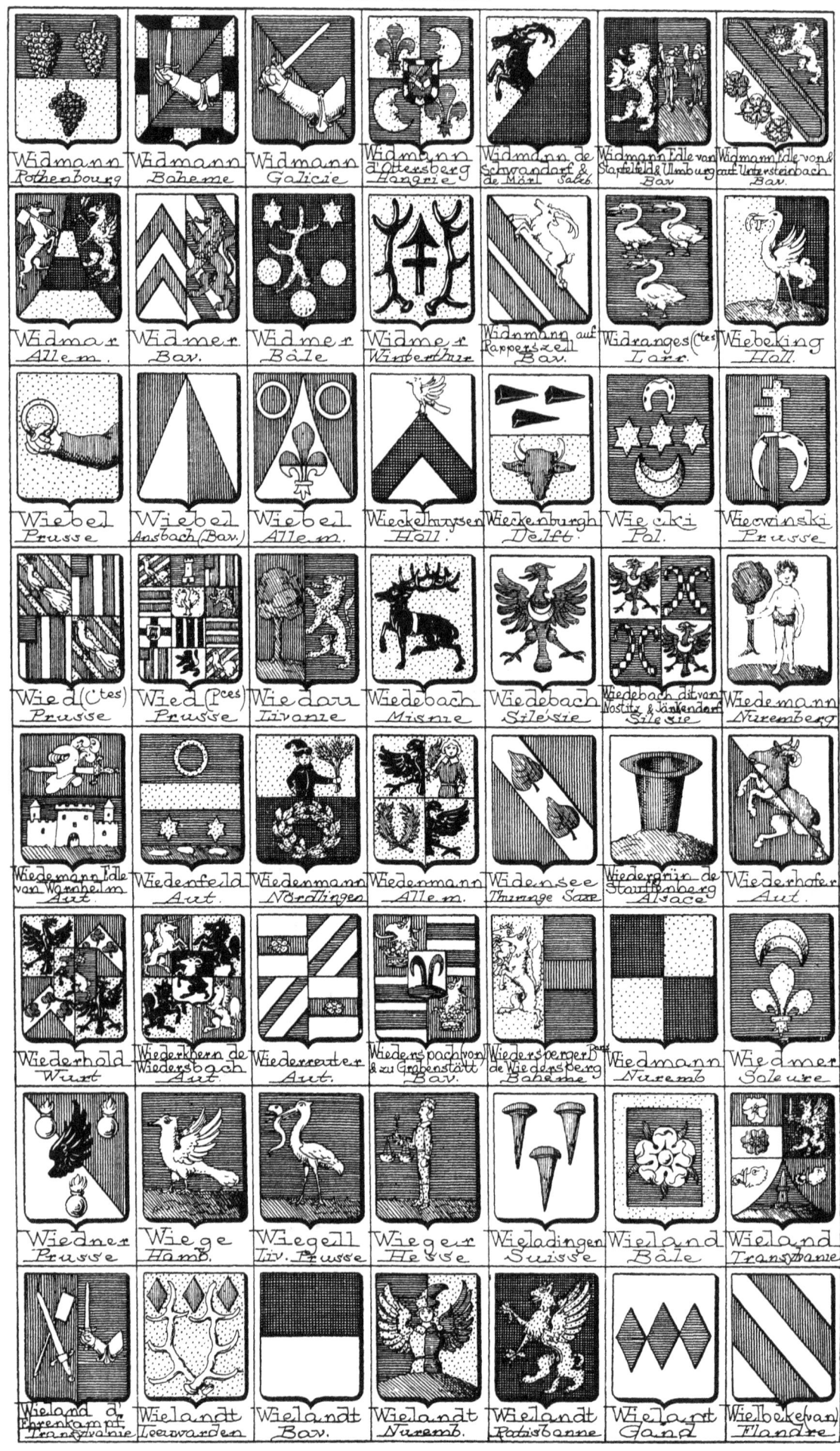

PL. CLXXI

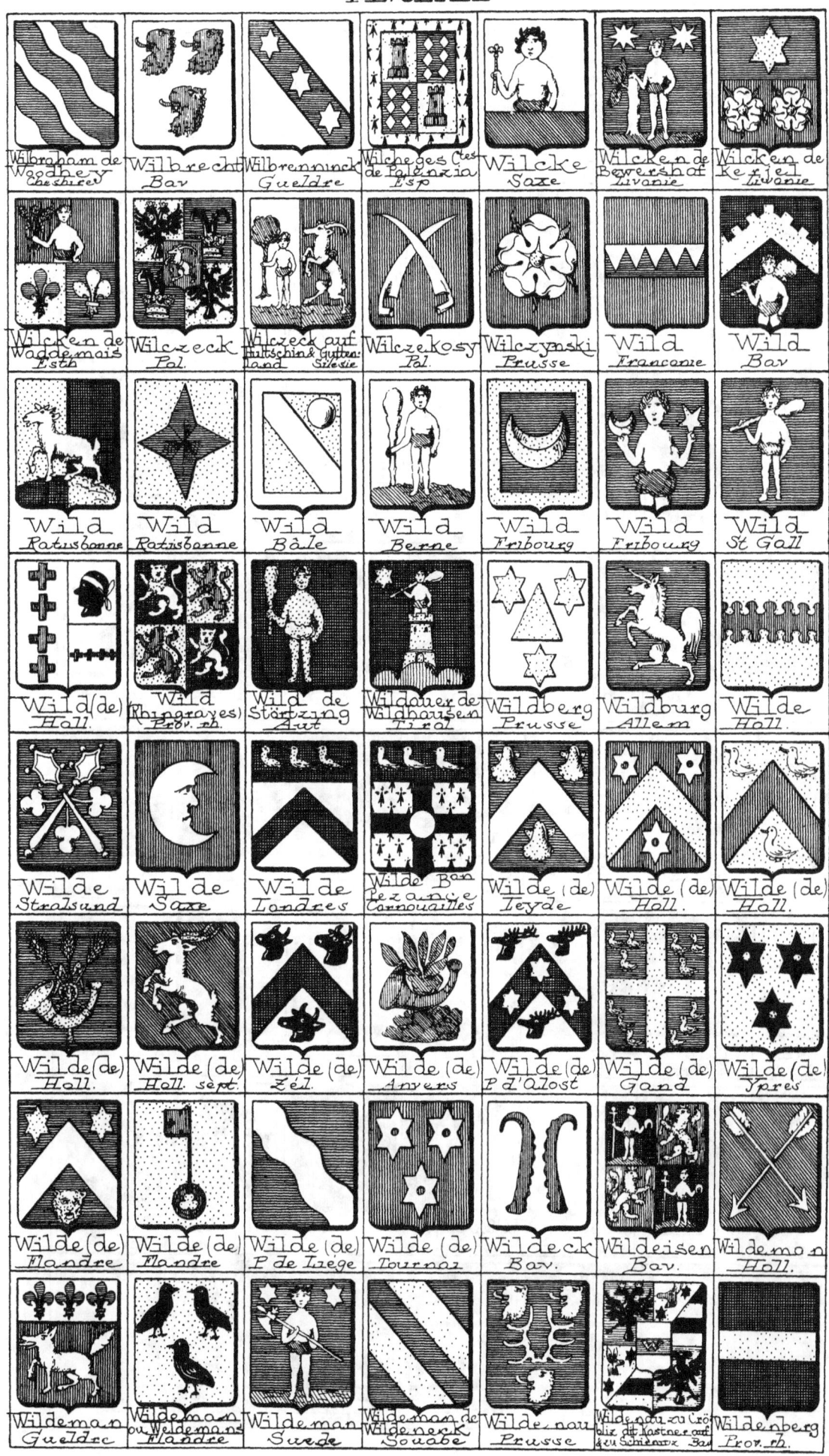

PL. CLXXIV

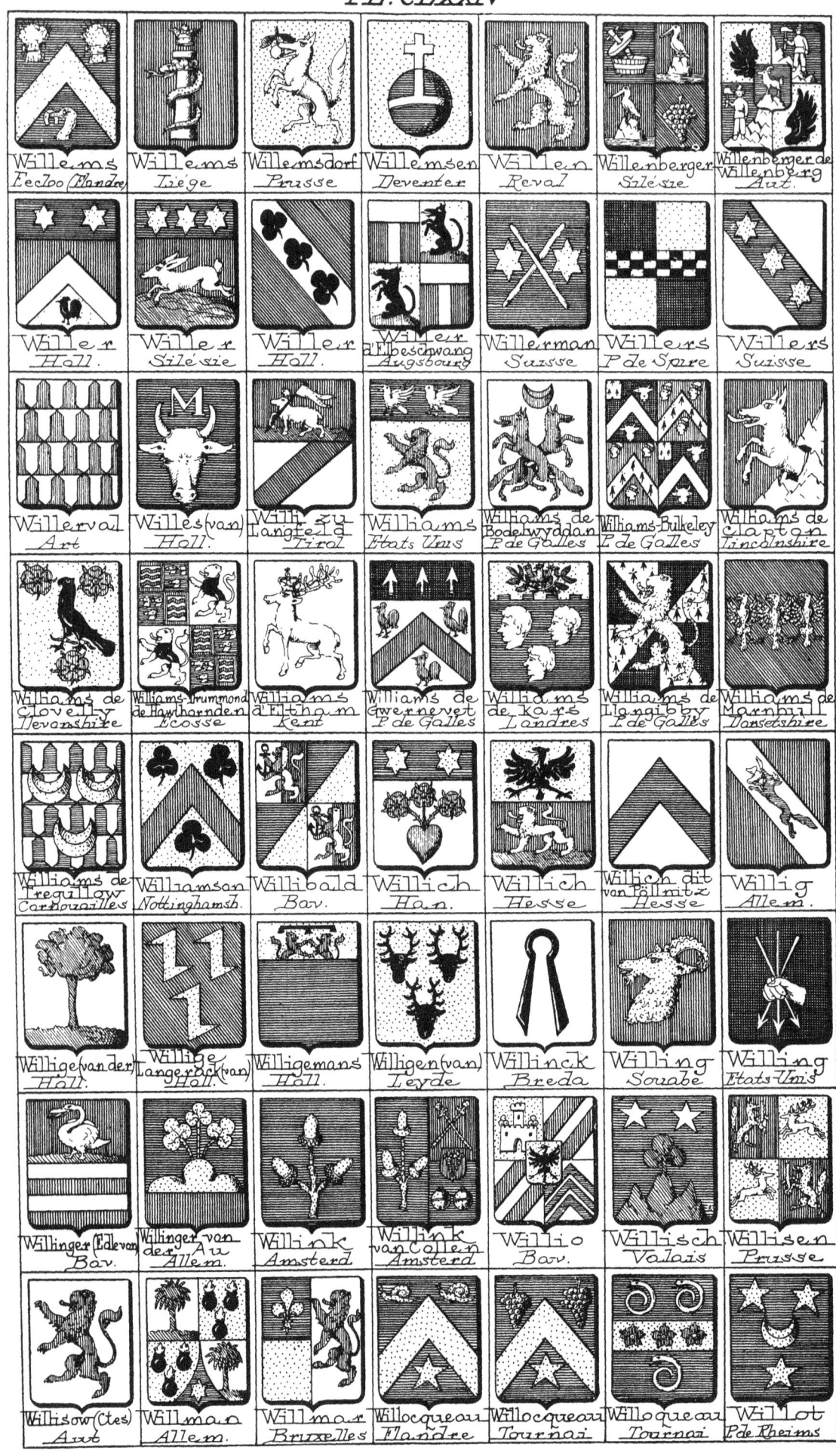

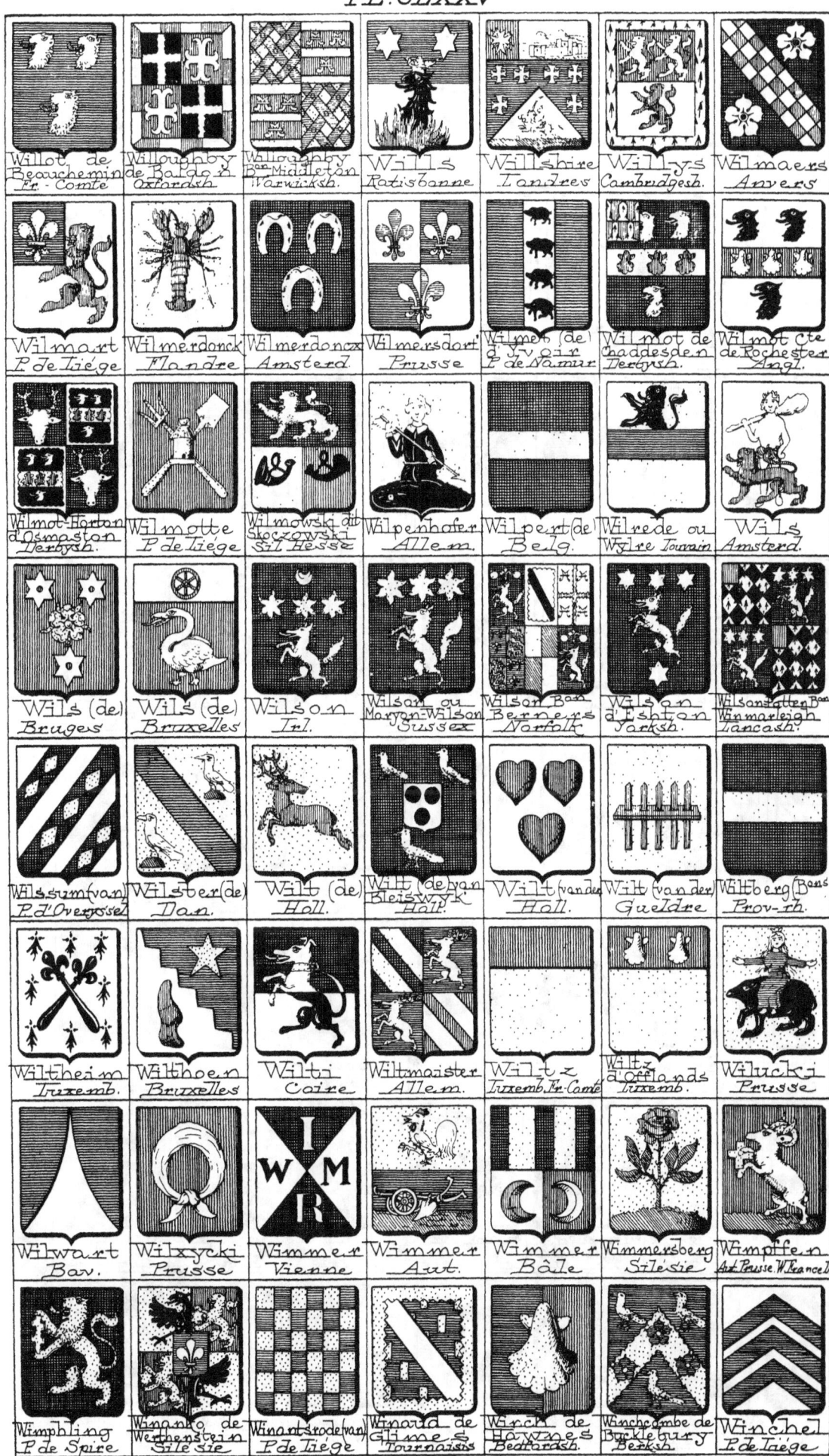
PL. CLXXV

PL. CLXXVI

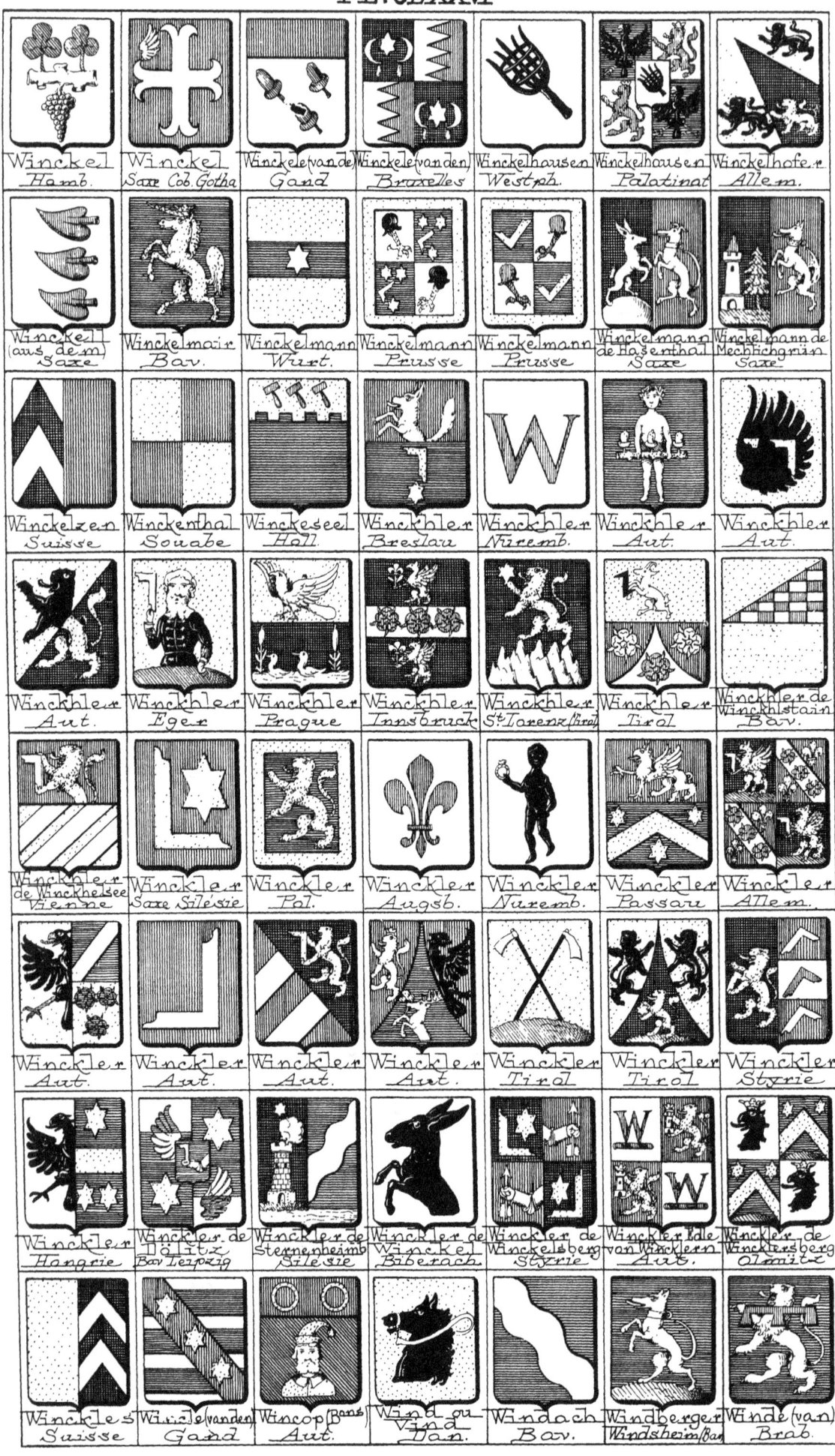

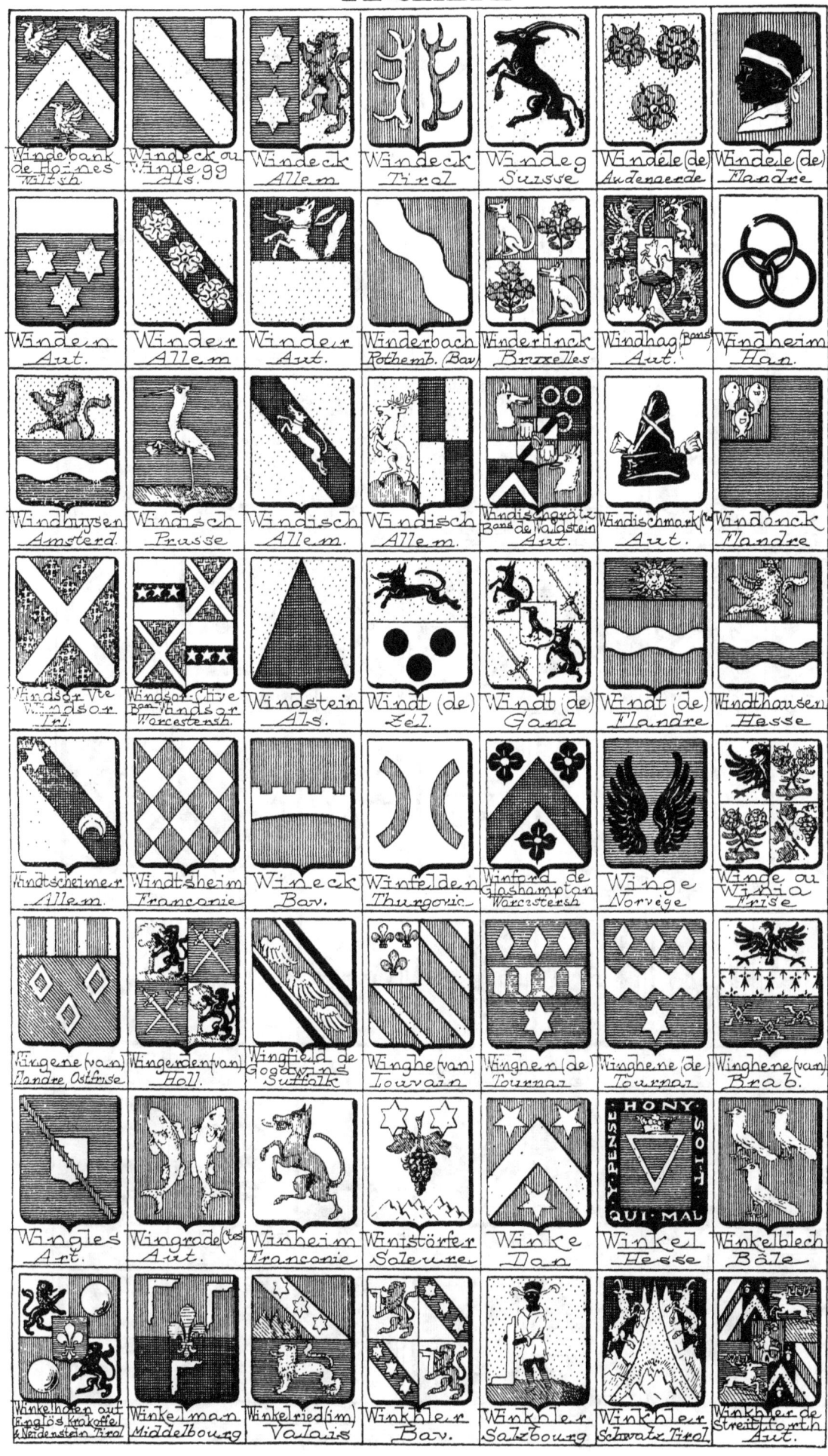

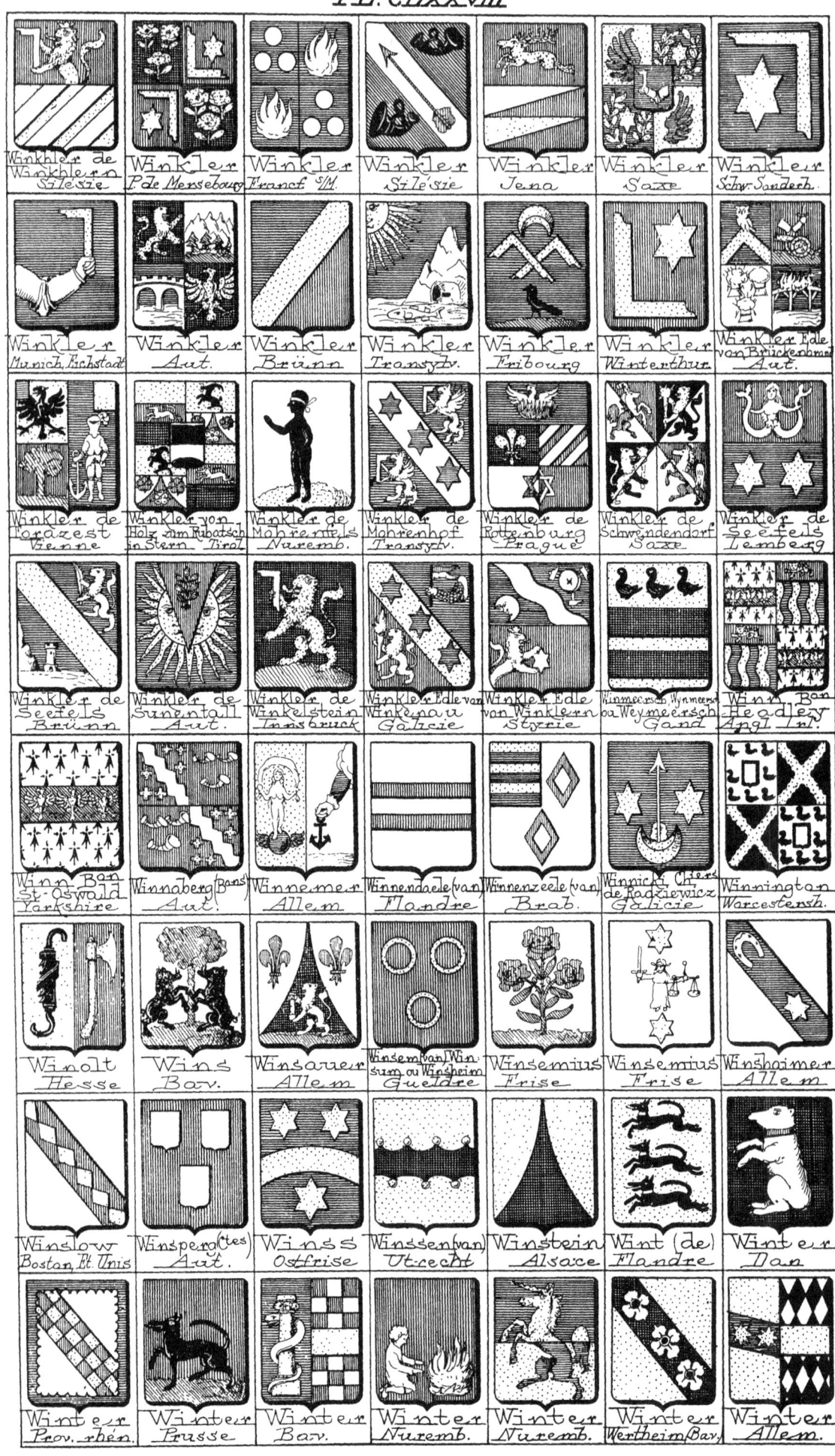

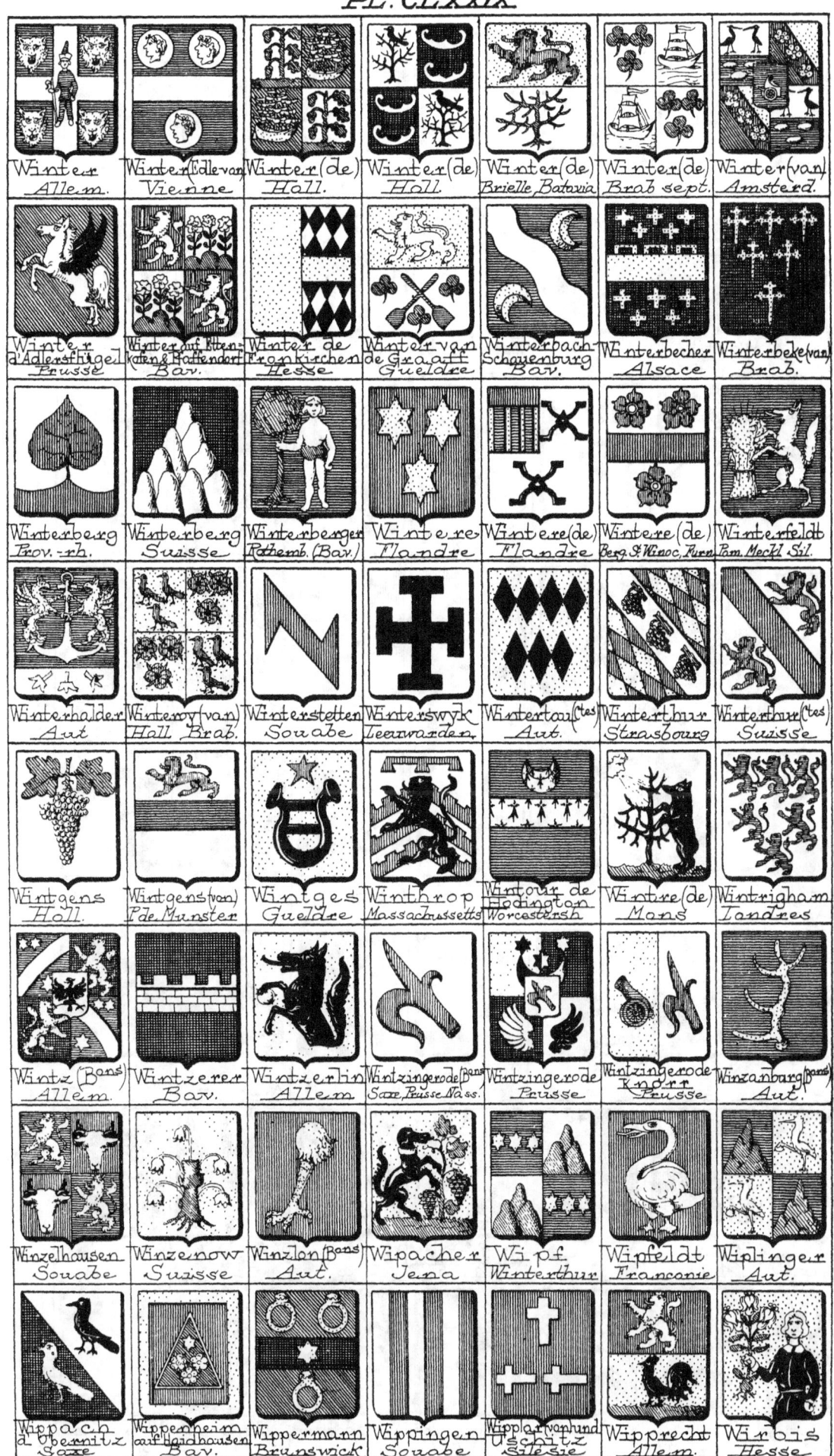

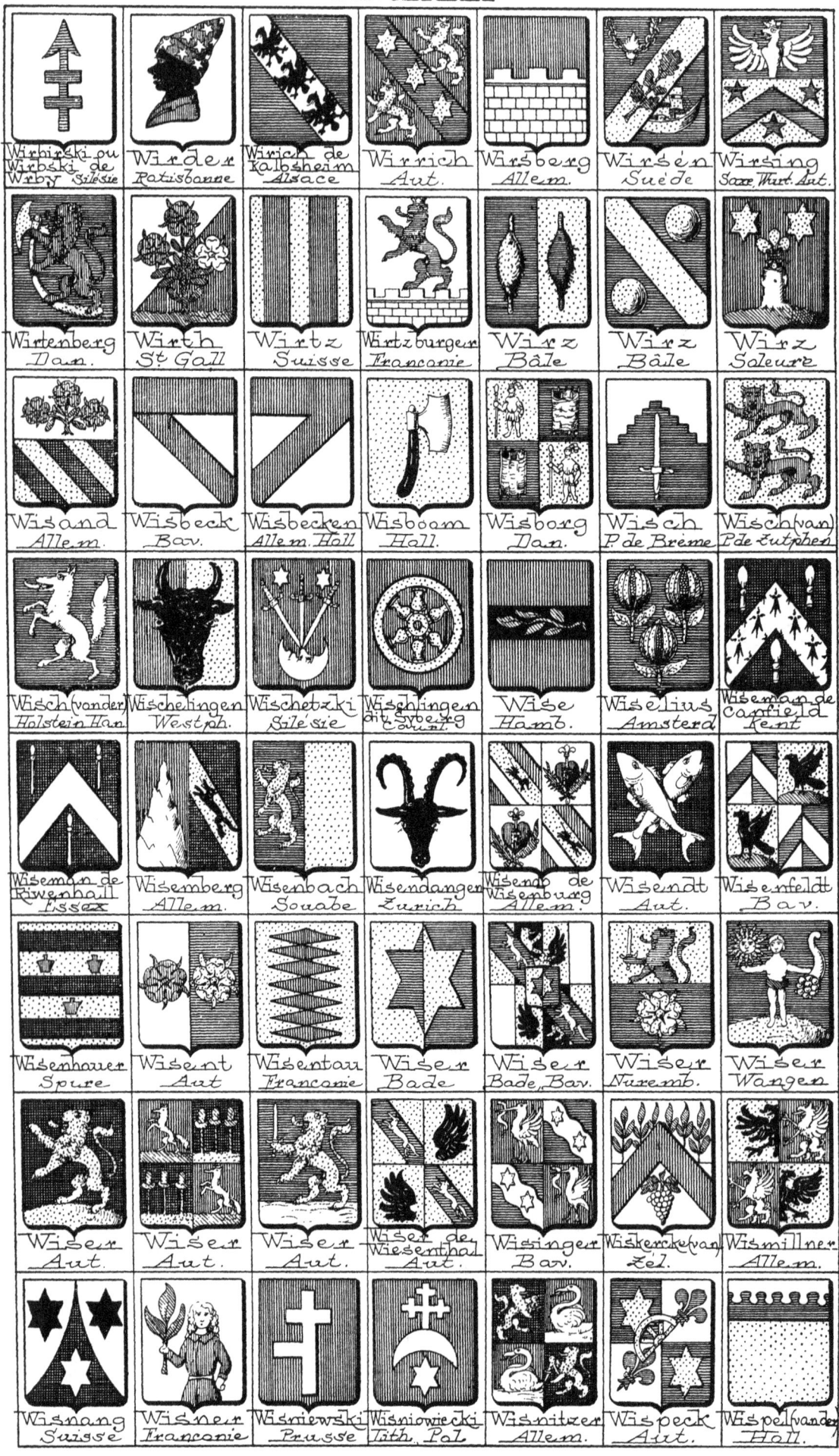

PL. CLXXXI

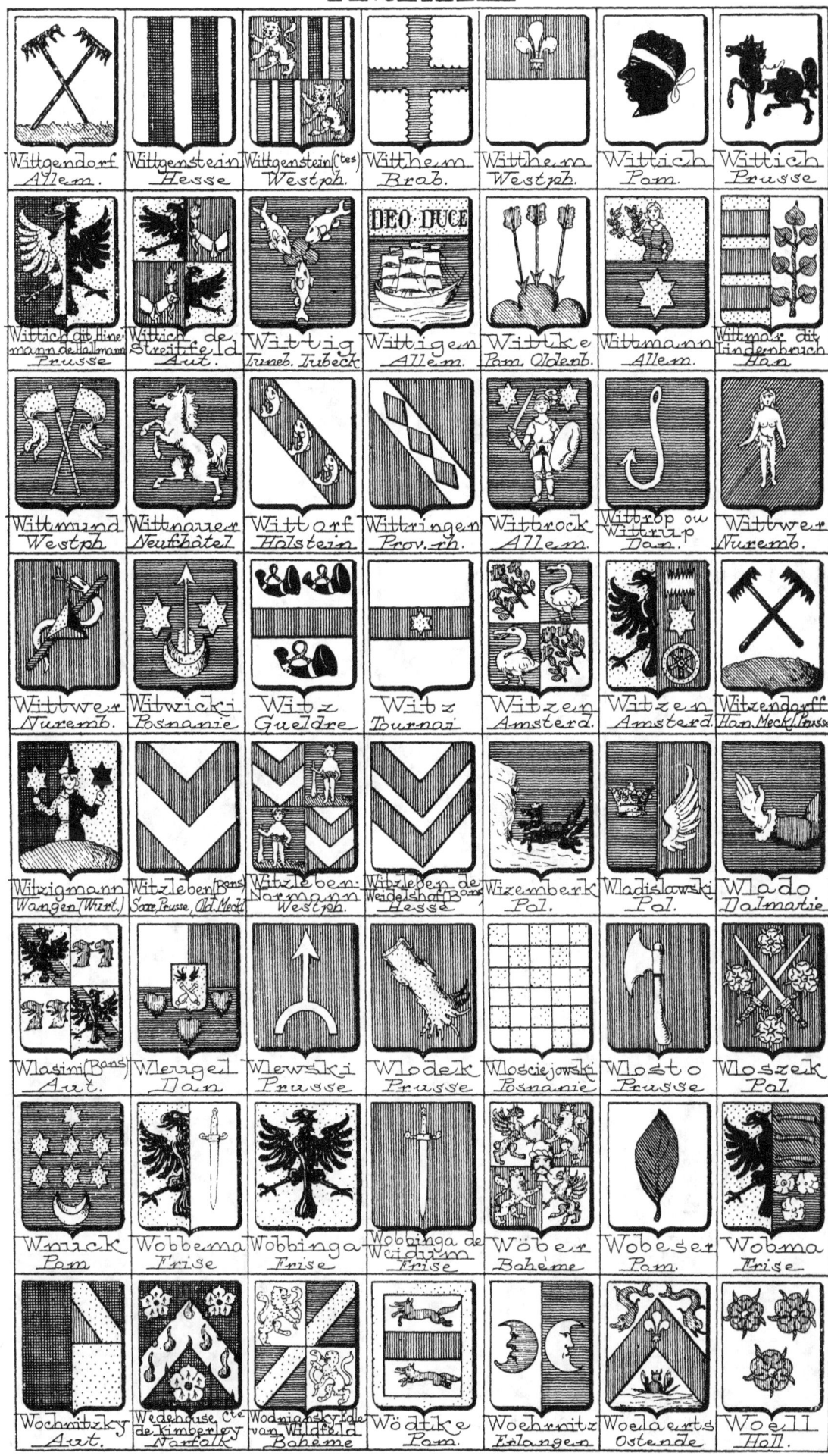

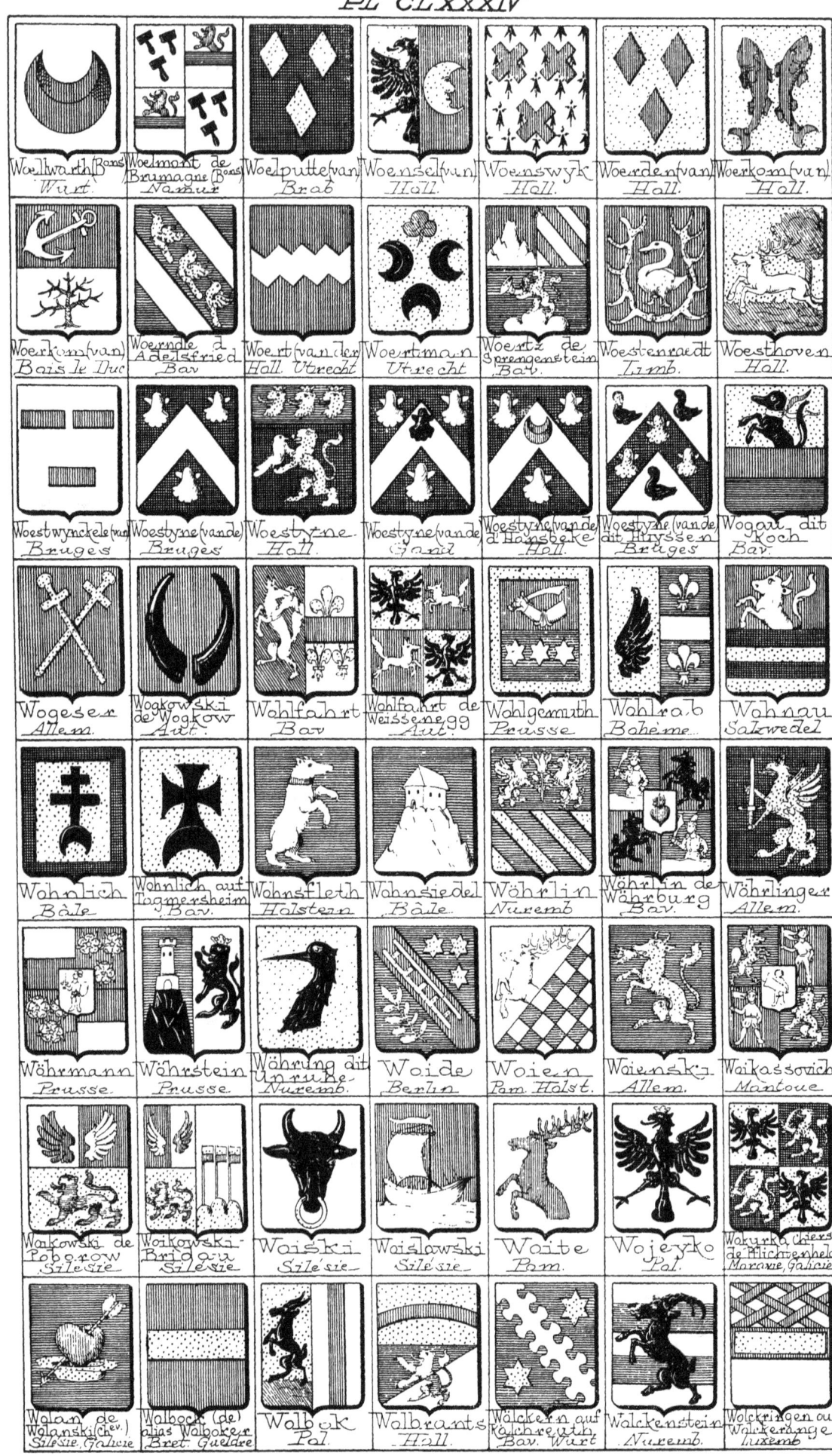

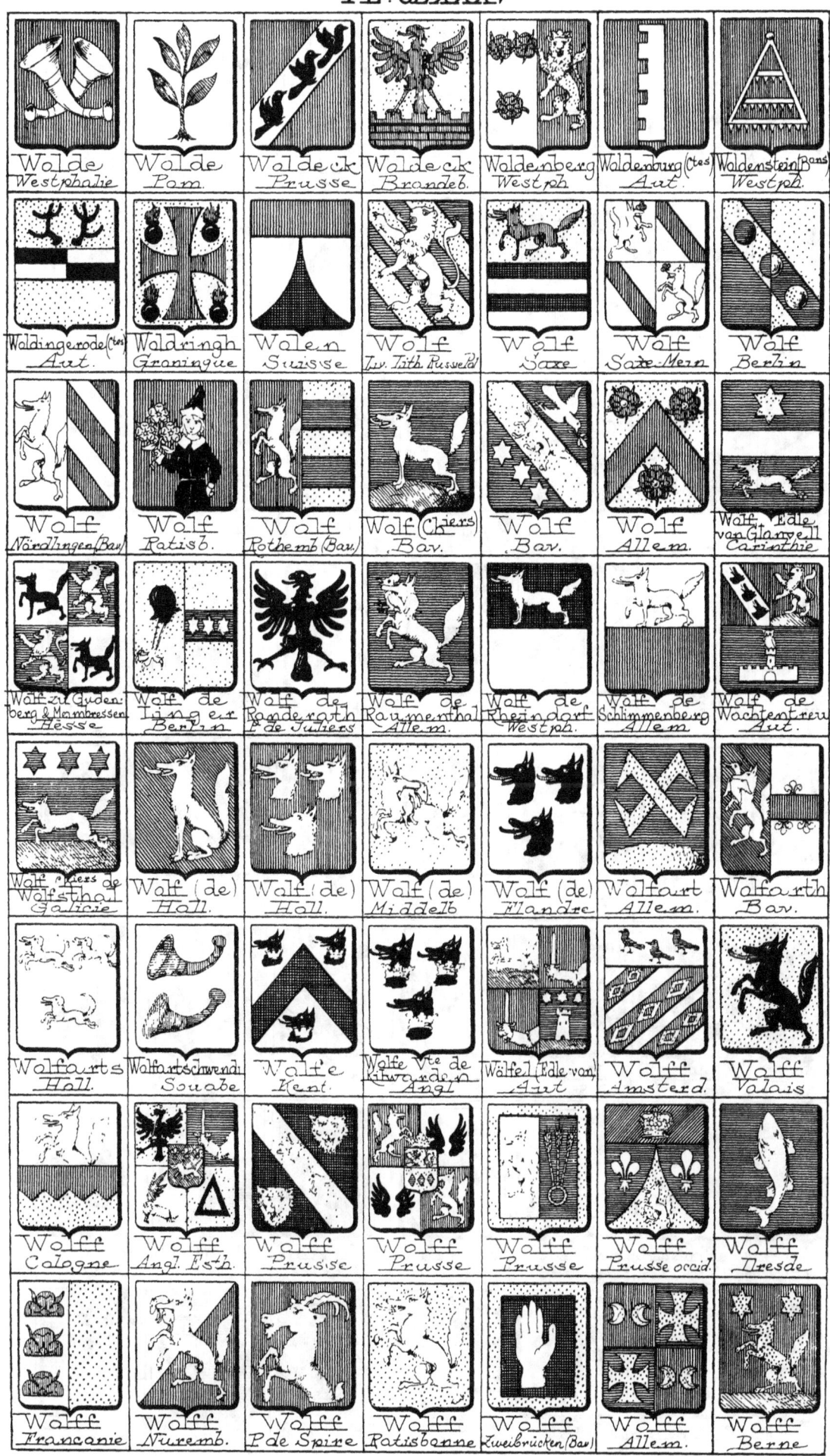

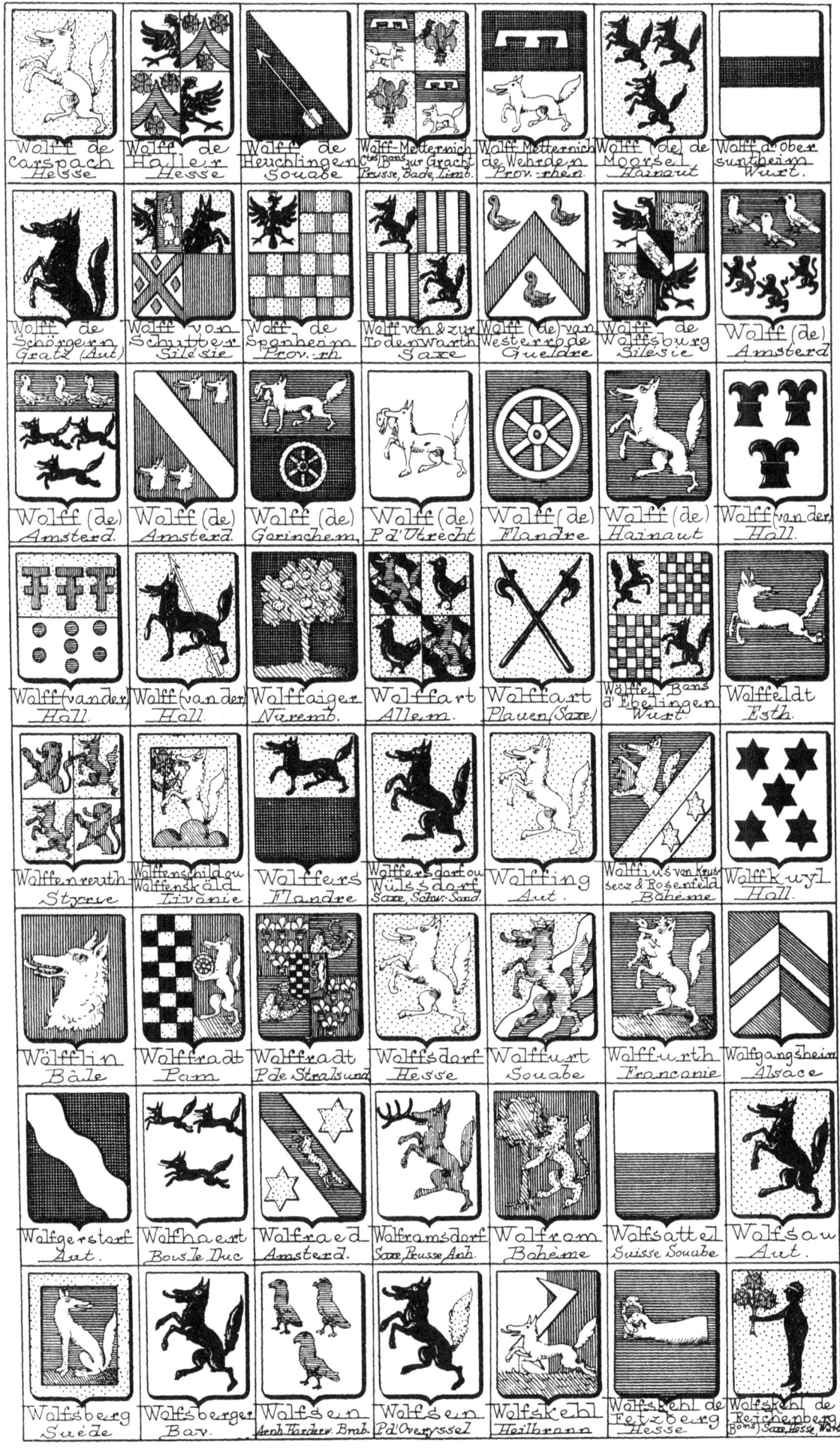

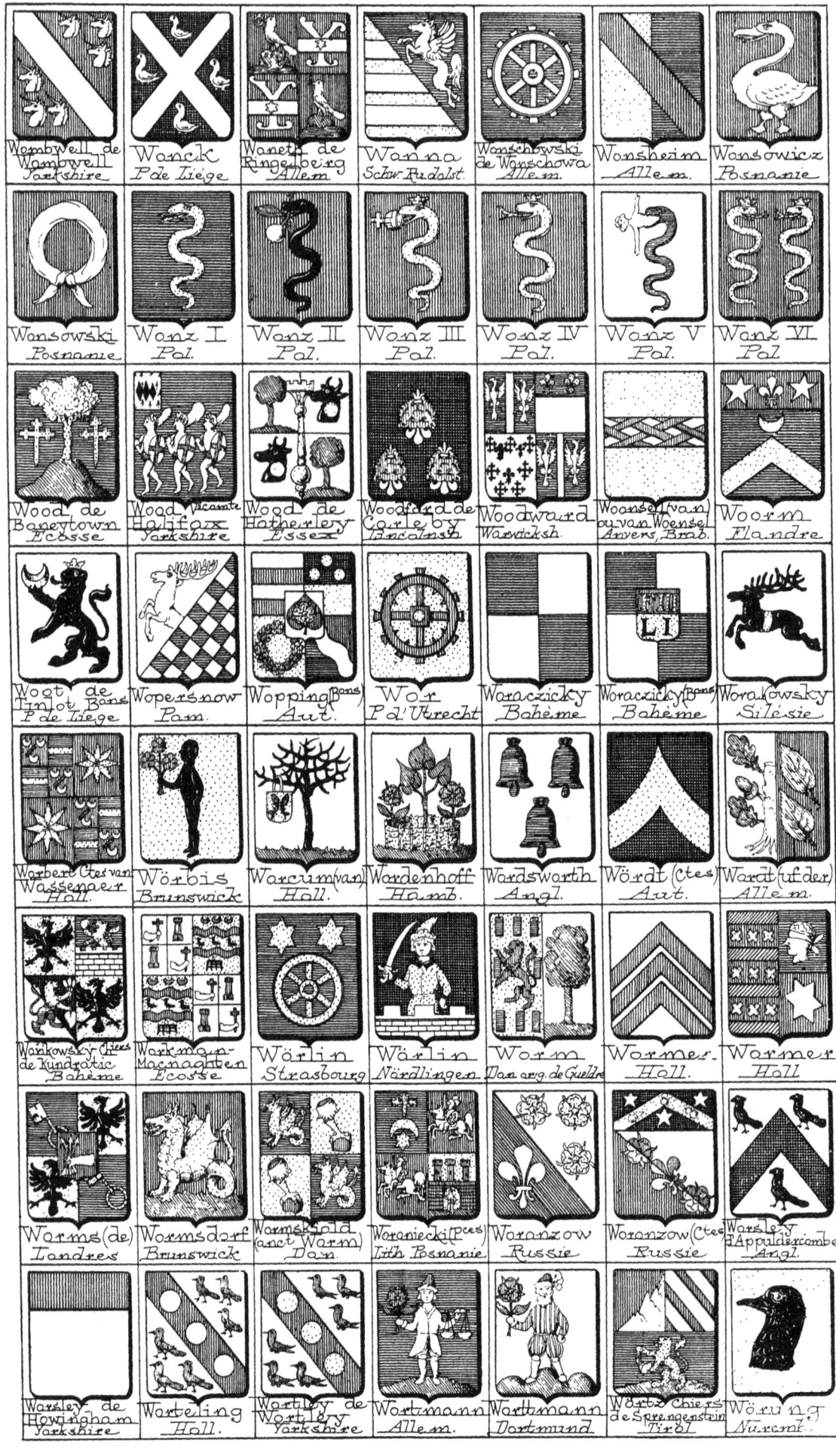

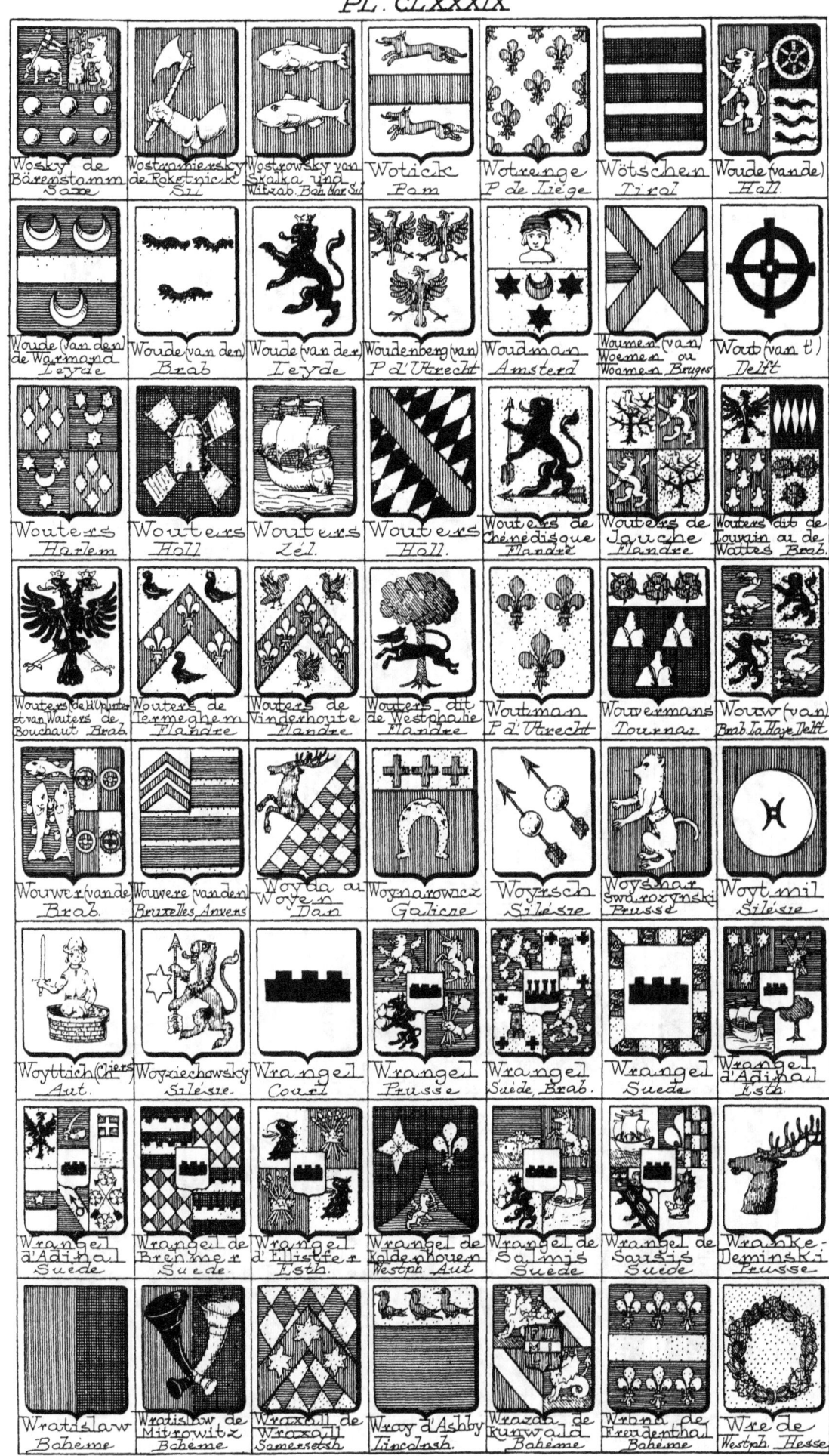

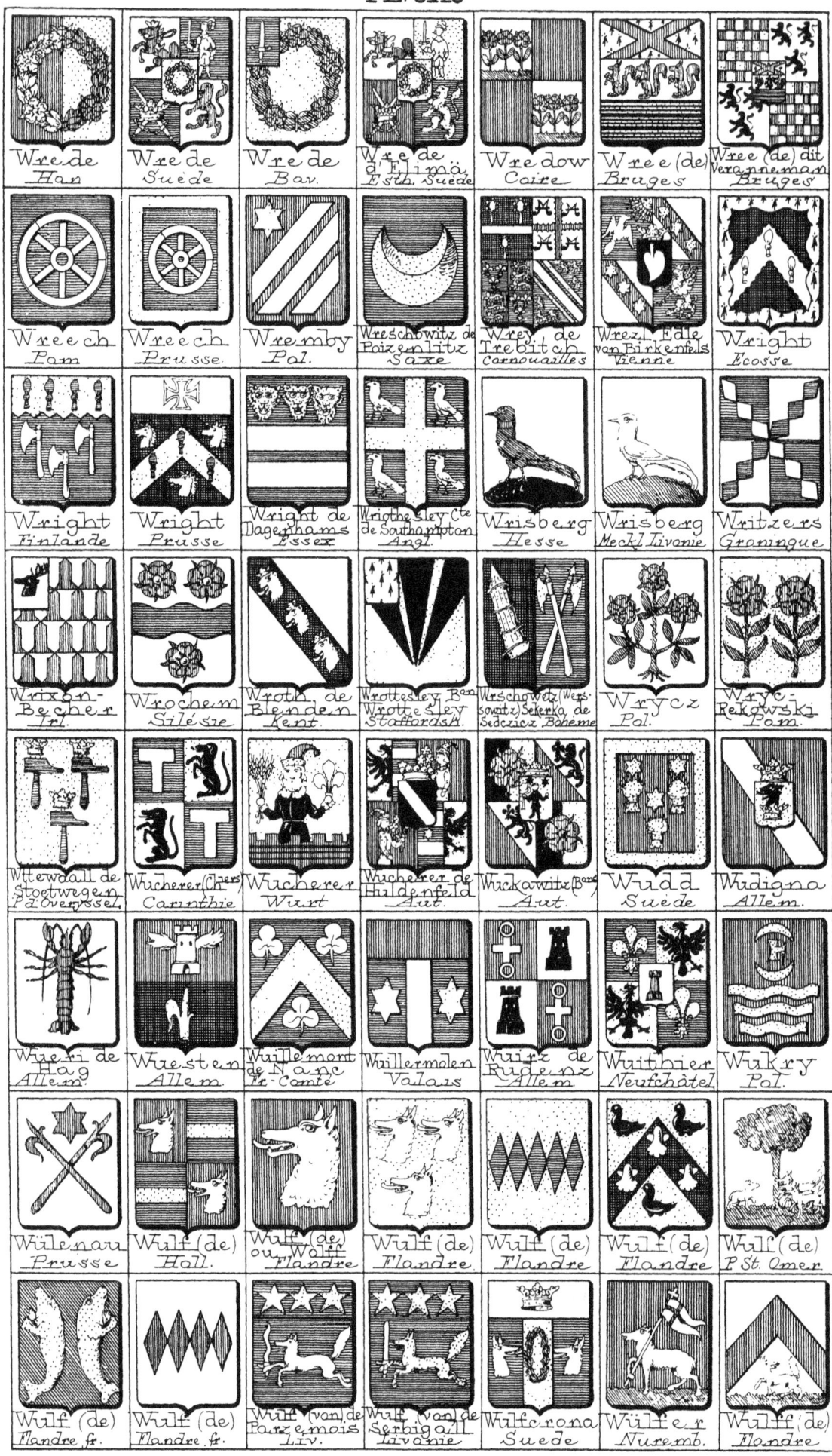

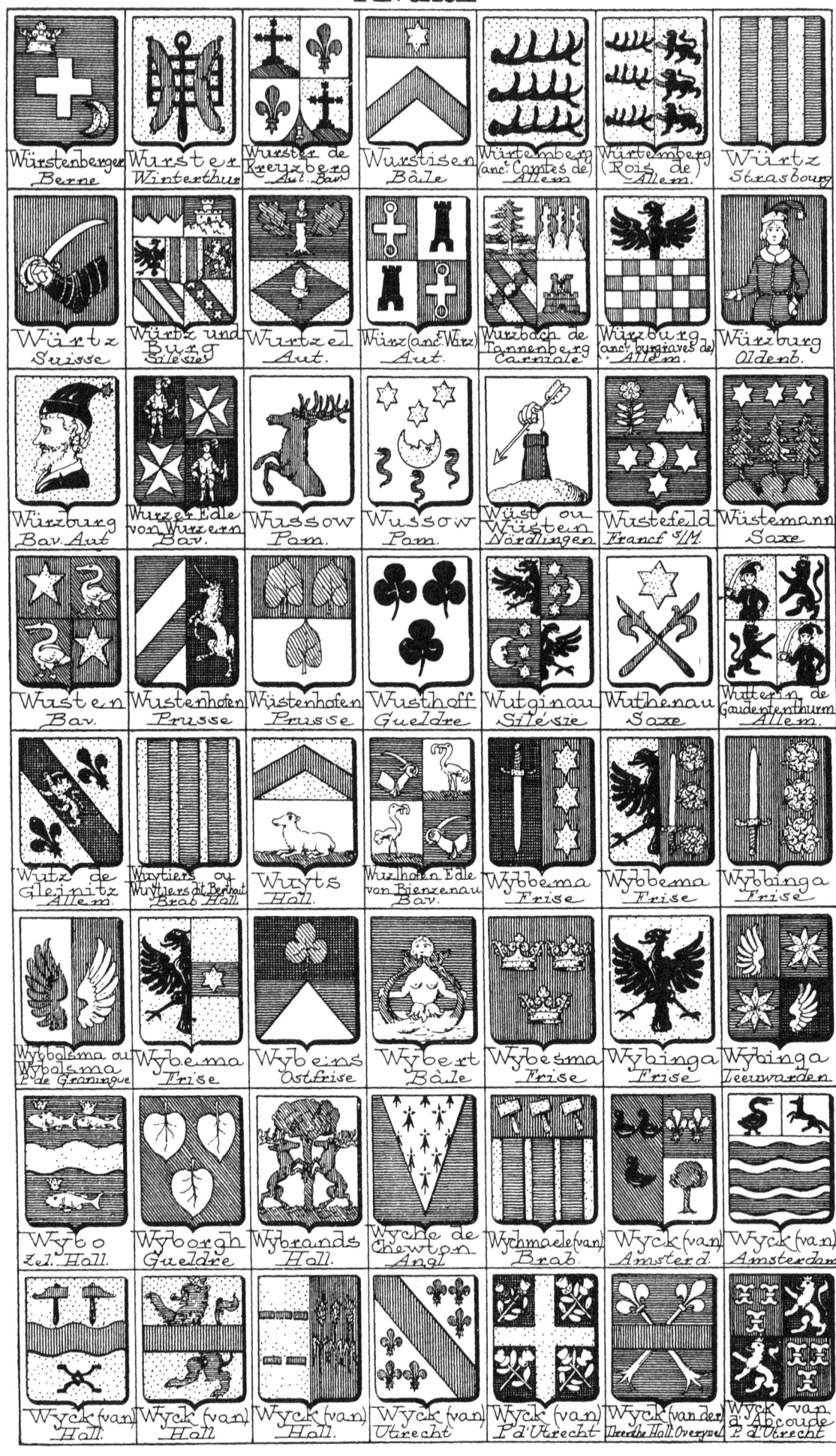

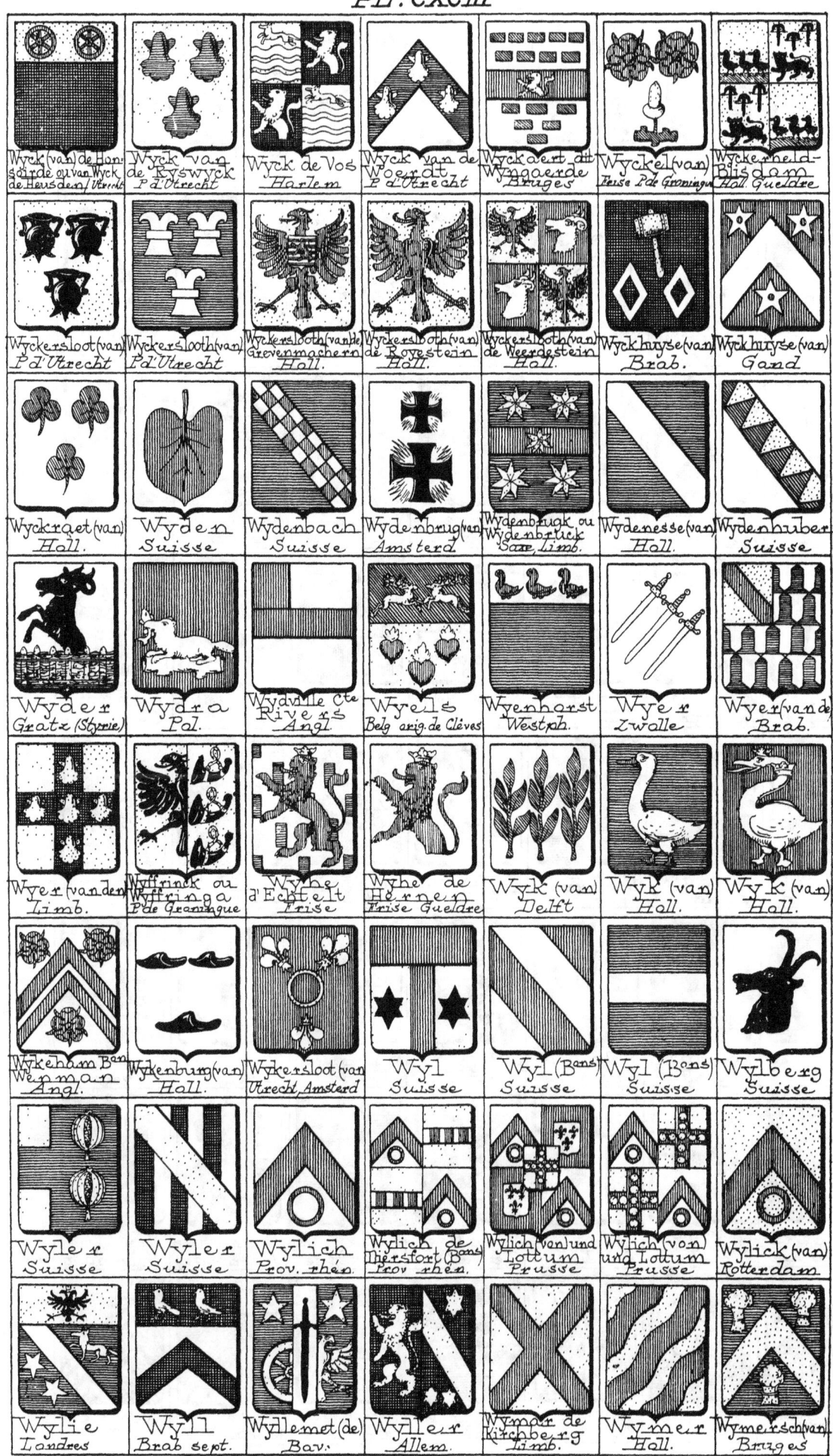

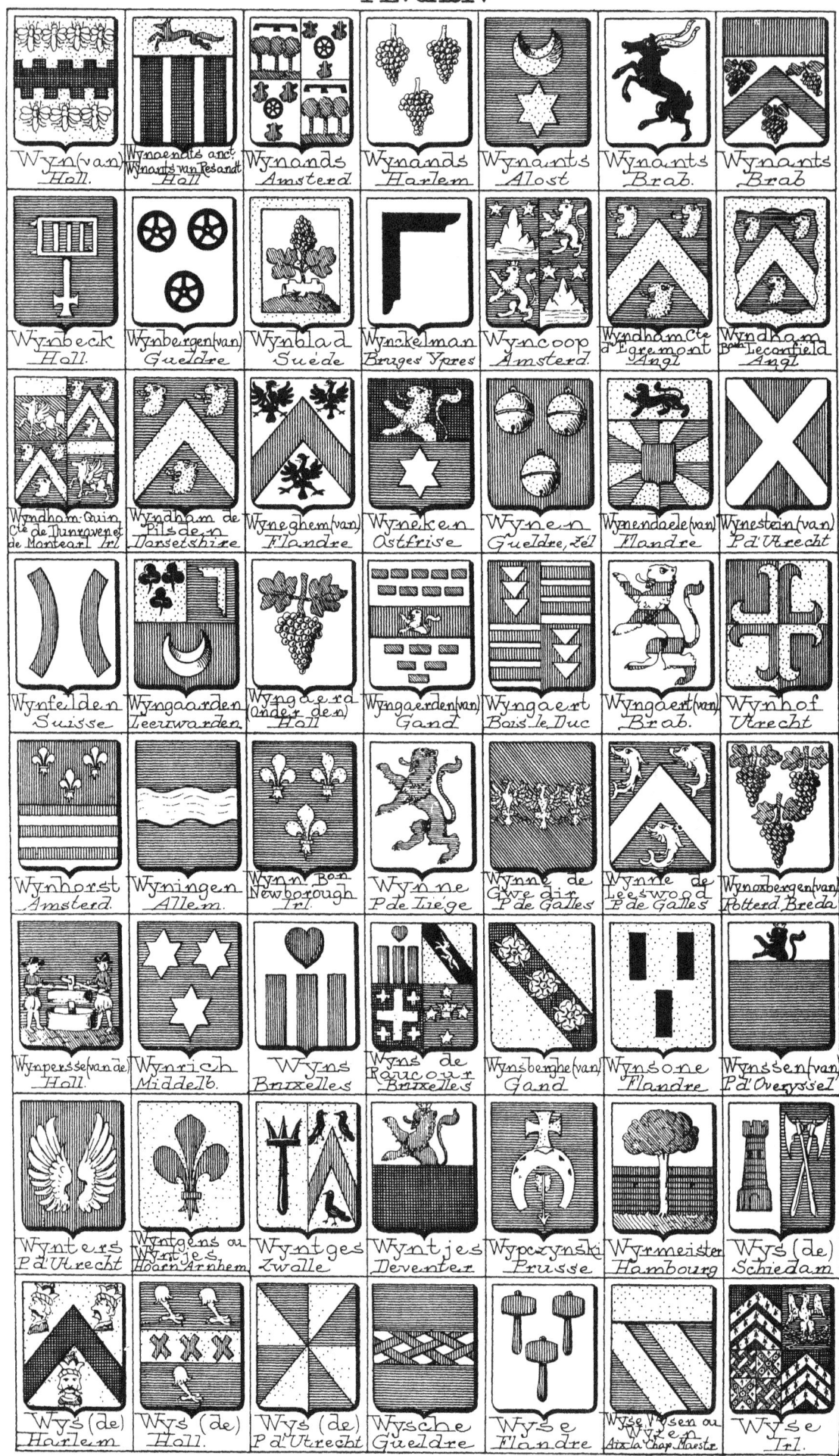

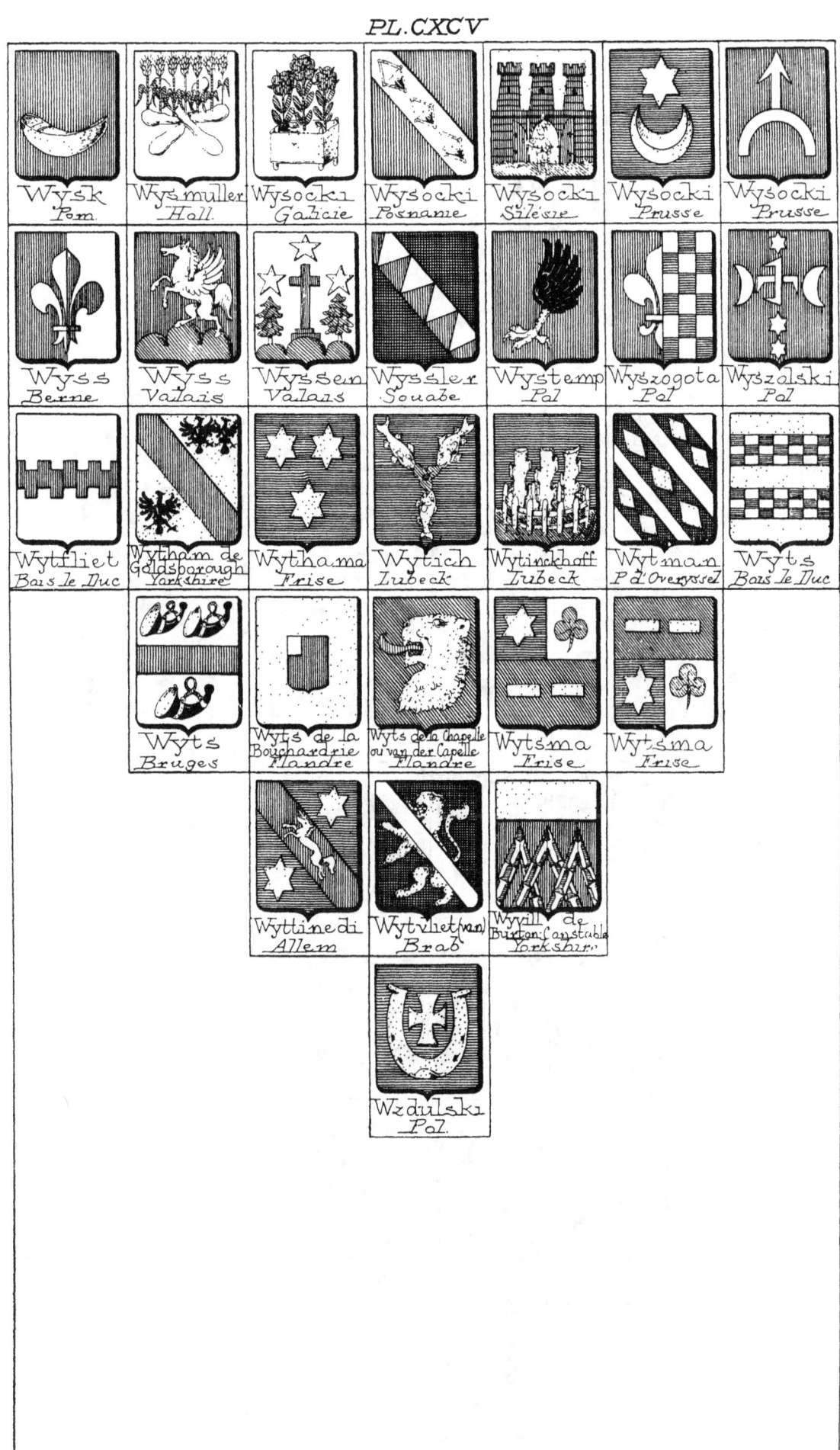

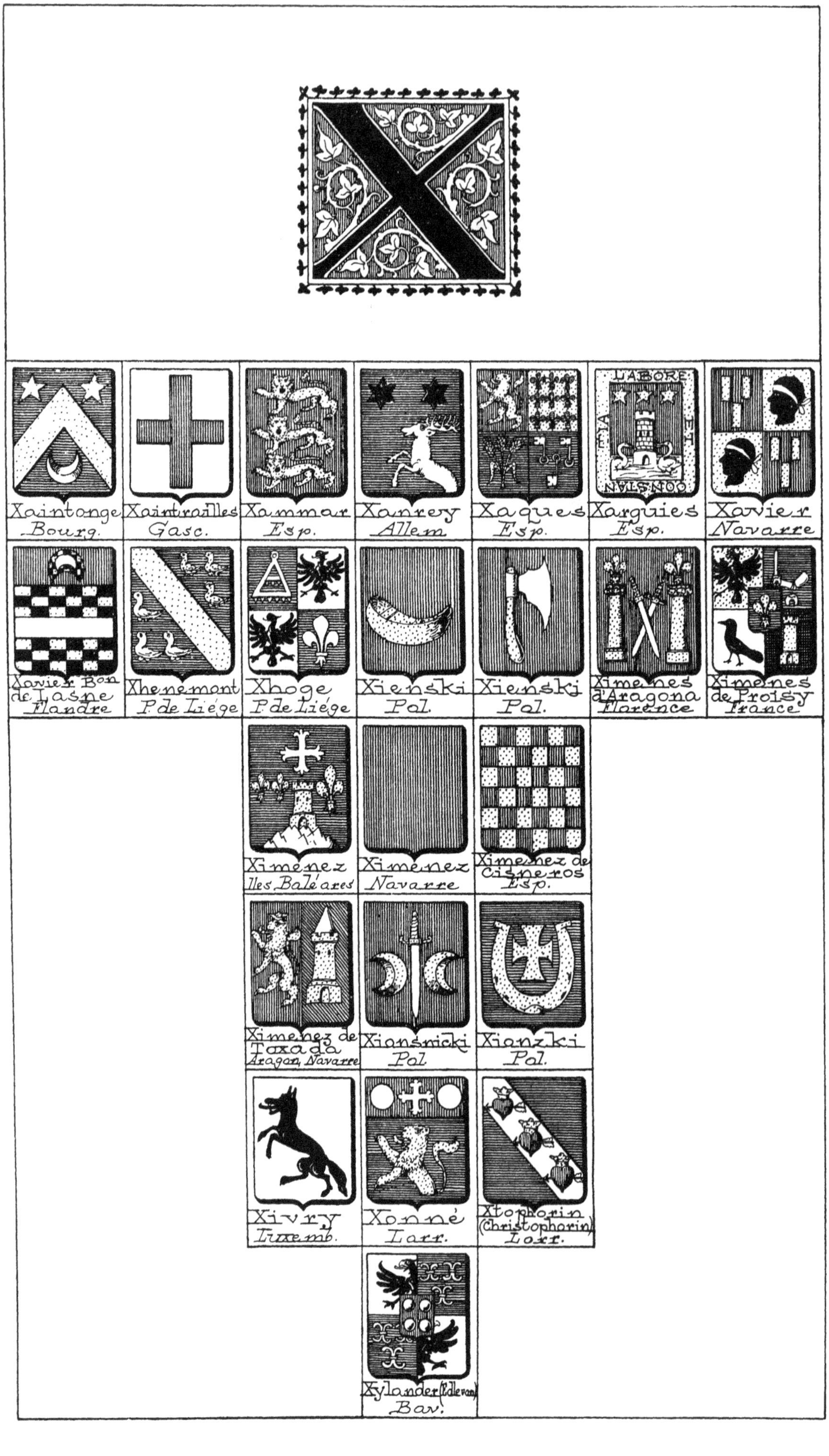
Xaintonge
Bourg.
Xaintrailles
Gasc.
Xammar
Esp.
Xanrey
Allem.
Xaques
Esp.
Xarguies
Esp.
Xavier
Navarre
Xavier Bon de Lasne
Flandre
Xhenemont
P. de Liége
Xhoge
P. de Liége
Xienski
Pol.
Xienski
Pol.
Ximenes d'Aragona
Florence
Ximenes de Proisy
France
Ximenez
Iles Baléares
Ximenez
Navarre
Ximenez de Cisneros
Esp.
Ximenez de Taxada
Aragon, Navarre
Xionsnicki
Pol.
Xionzki
Pol.
Xivry
Luxemb.
Xonné
Lorr.
Xtophorin (Christophorin)
Lorr.
Xylander (Edle von)
Bav.

PL. CXCVII

| Y de Sérucourt Champ. Pic | Yacenou Bret | Yanez Castille | Yanez de Albadalejo Murcie | Yanguas Castille | Yanguas-Velandia Castille | Yarde-Buller Bon Churston Devonshire |
|---|---|---|---|---|---|---|
| Yazza Guipuzcoa | Yate de Buckland Berckshire | Yancourt Ponthieu | Yberg (ab) St. Gall | Ybl Hongrie | Yoser Aut. | Ycard de Pérignan Lang. |
| Yck (van) Rotterd. | Yden Brab. | Ydsma Frise | Yea de Pyrland Somersetsh. | Yeamans Angl. | Ye deghem (van) Gand | Ye deghem (van) Flandre |
| Yego Bret. | Yel Lorr. | Yelin (Chiers) Bav. | Yelin de Grünholdegg Allem. | Yelverton Vte Avonmore Irl. | Yelverton Bon Grey de Ruthyn Angl. | Yemants Holl. |
| Yenni Fribourg | Yens P. de Vaud | Ypes Castille | Yeribar Guipuzcoa | Yermoloff Russie | Yernaval Pic. | Yernawe P. de Liège |
| Yeropkin Russie | Yerseke (van) Zél. | Yfan Bons Westph. | Yffendal Suisse | Yffenstein (Bons) Suisse | Ylen (van) dit van Es Holl. | Yler (van) Maestricht |

PL. CXCVIII

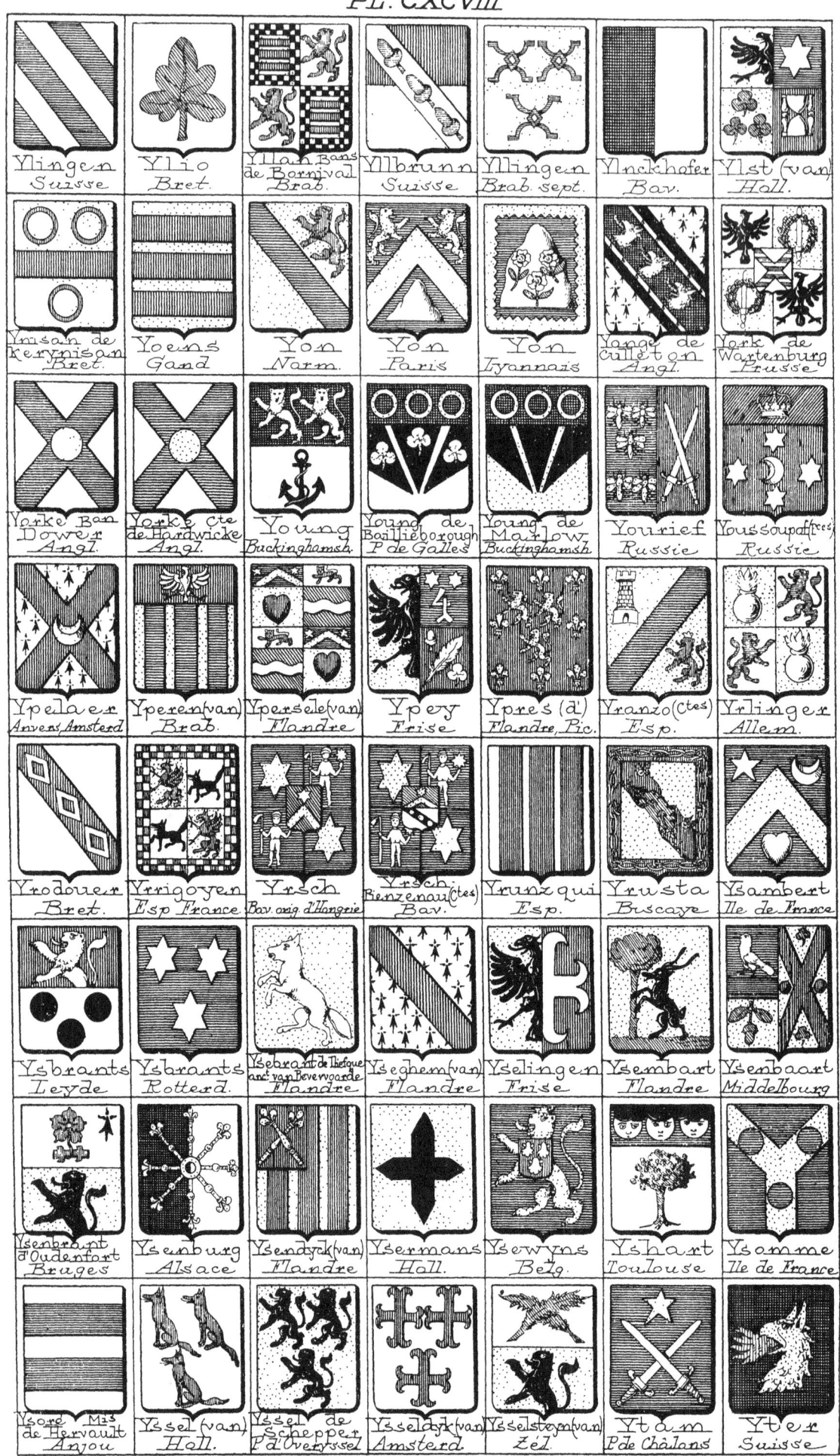

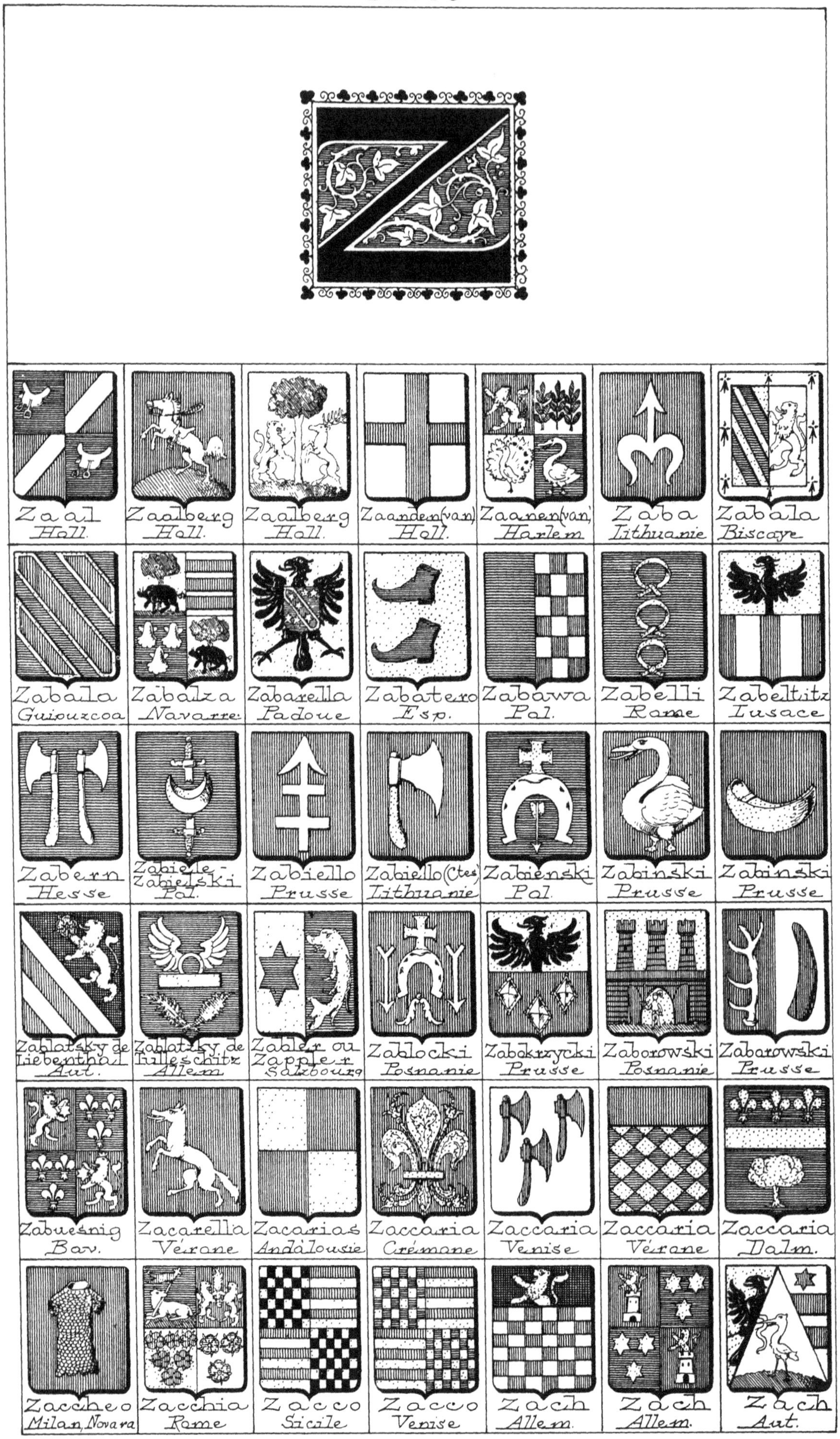

PL. CC

| Zaal Holl. | Zaalberg Holl. | Zaalberg Holl. | Zaanden (van) Holl. | Zaanen (van) Harlem | Zaba Lithuanie | Zabala Biscaye |
|---|---|---|---|---|---|---|
| Zabala Guipuzcoa | Zabalza Navarre | Zabarella Padoue | Zabatero Esp. | Zabawa Pol. | Zabelli Rome | Zabeltitz Lusace |
| Zabern Hesse | Zabielle-Zabielski Pol. | Zabiello Prusse | Zabiello (Ctes) Lithuanie | Zabienski Pol. | Zabinski Prusse | Zabinski Prusse |
| Zablatzky de Liebenthal Aut. | Zablatzky de Hilleschitz Allem. | Zabler ou Zappler Salzbourg | Zablocki Posnanie | Zabokrzycki Prusse | Zaborowski Posnanie | Zabarowski Prusse |
| Zabuesnig Bav. | Zacarella Vérone | Zacarias Andalousie | Zaccaria Crémone | Zaccaria Venise | Zaccaria Vérone | Zaccaria Dalm. |
| Zaccheo Milan, Novara | Zacchia Rome | Zacco Sicile | Zacco Venise | Zach Allem. | Zach Allem. | Zach Aut. |

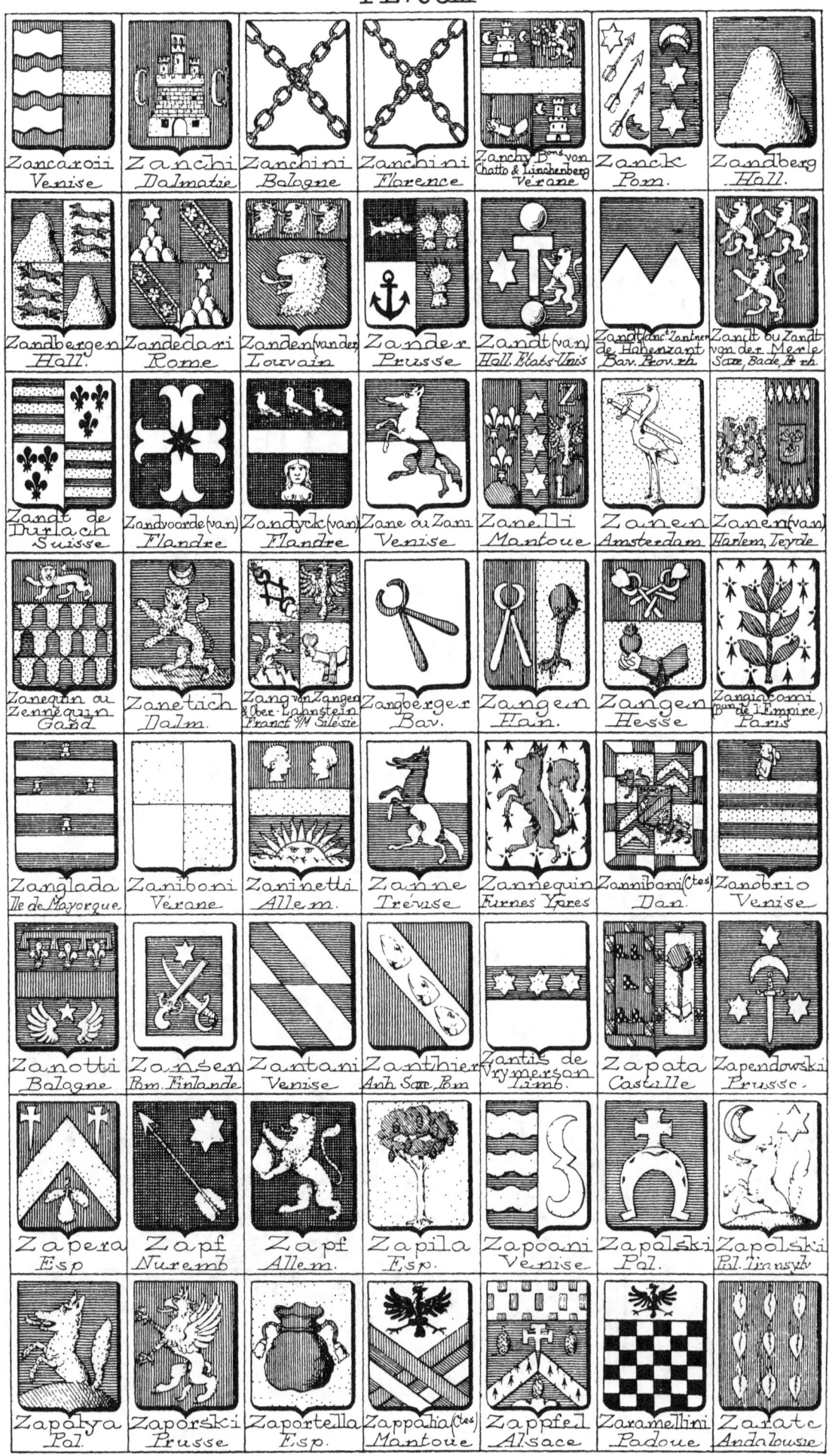

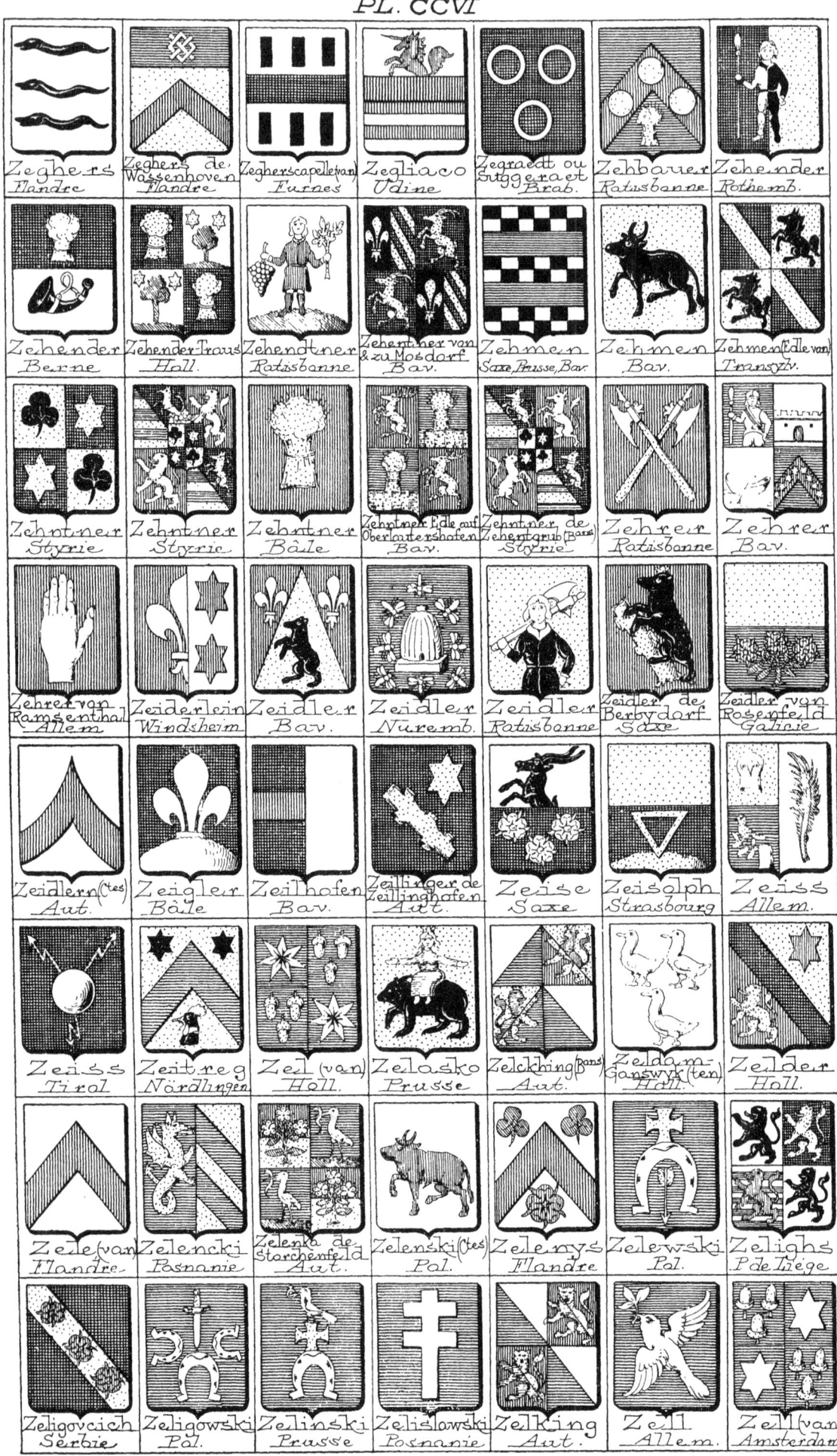

PL. CCVIII

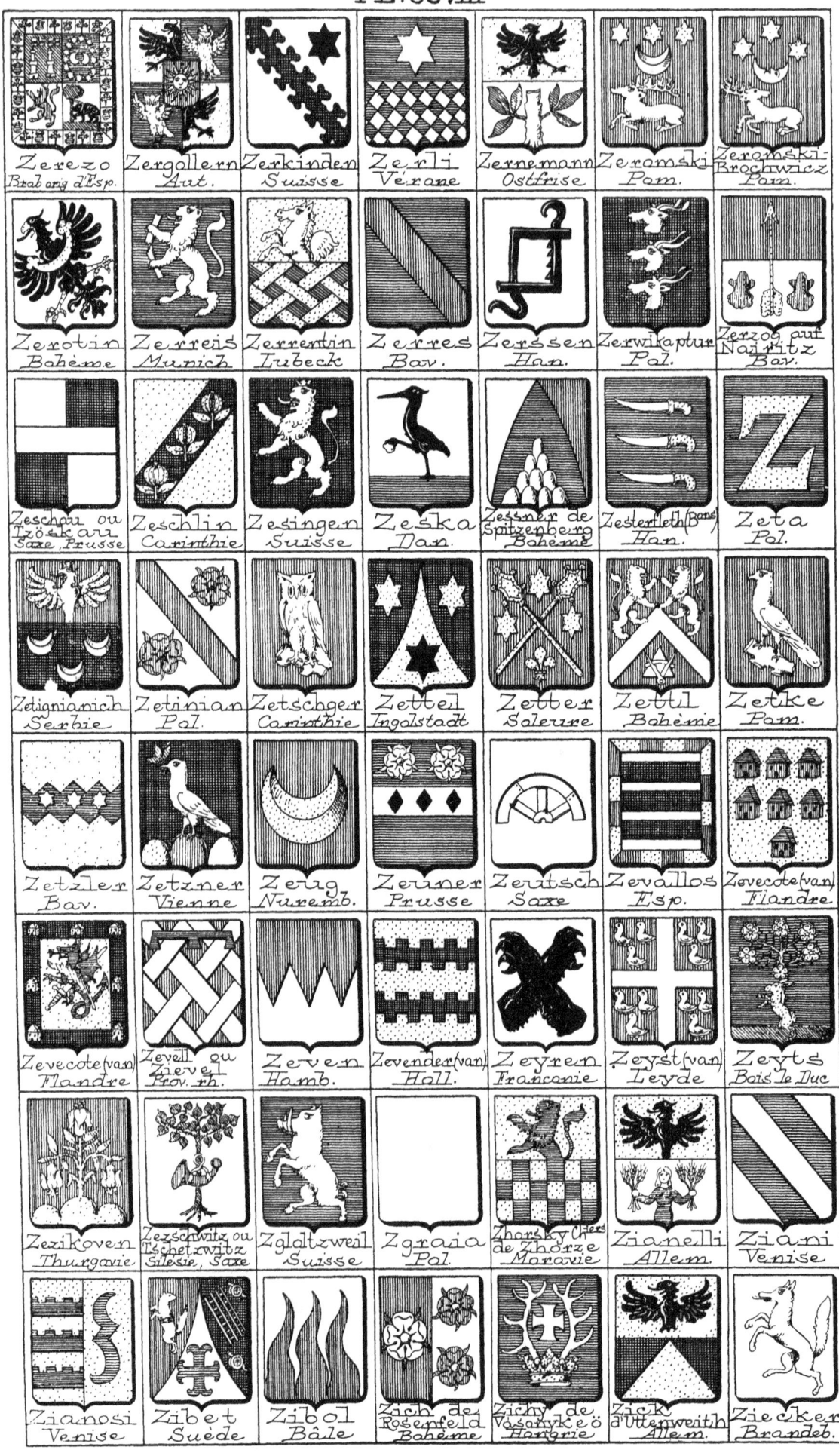

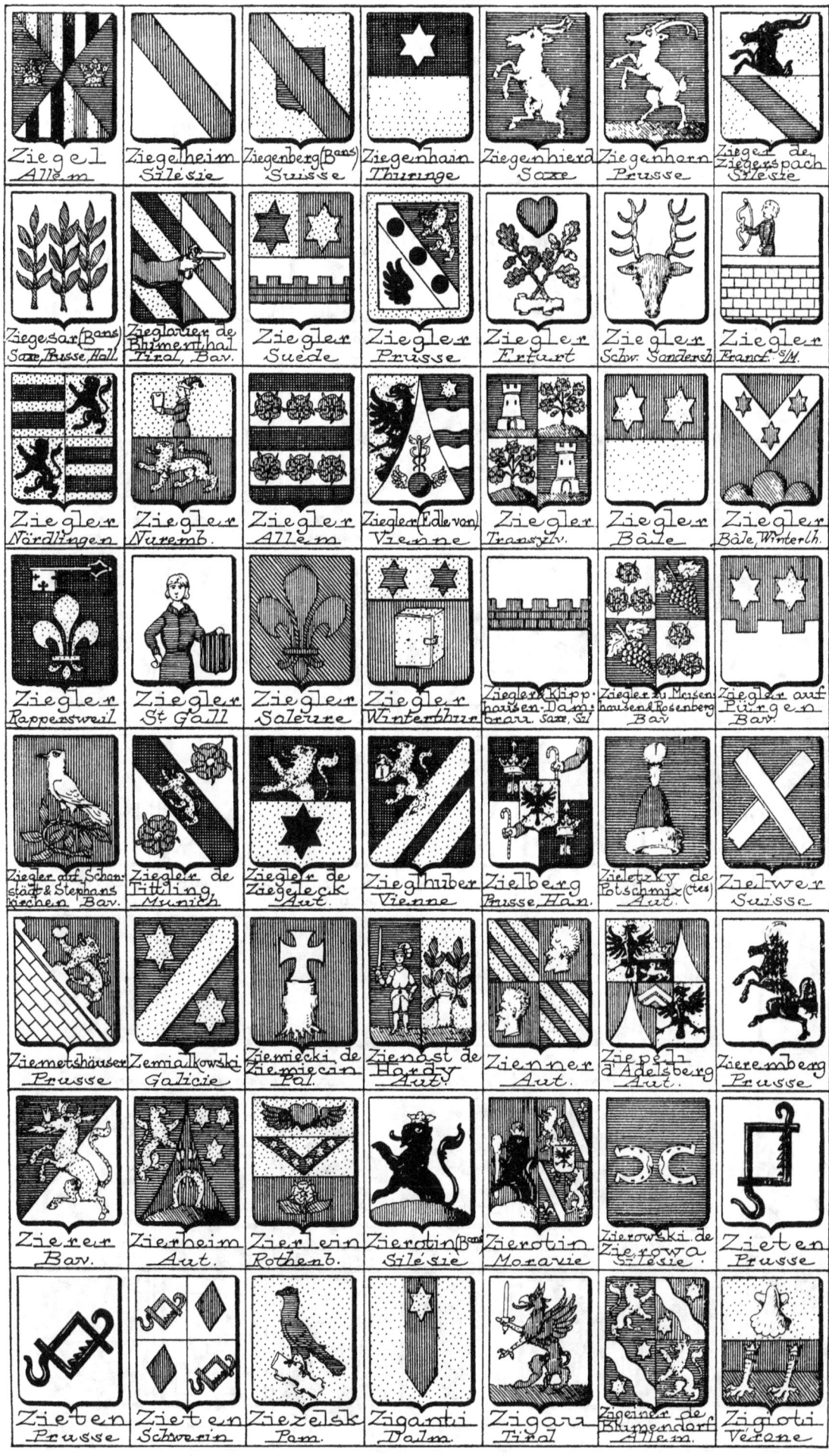

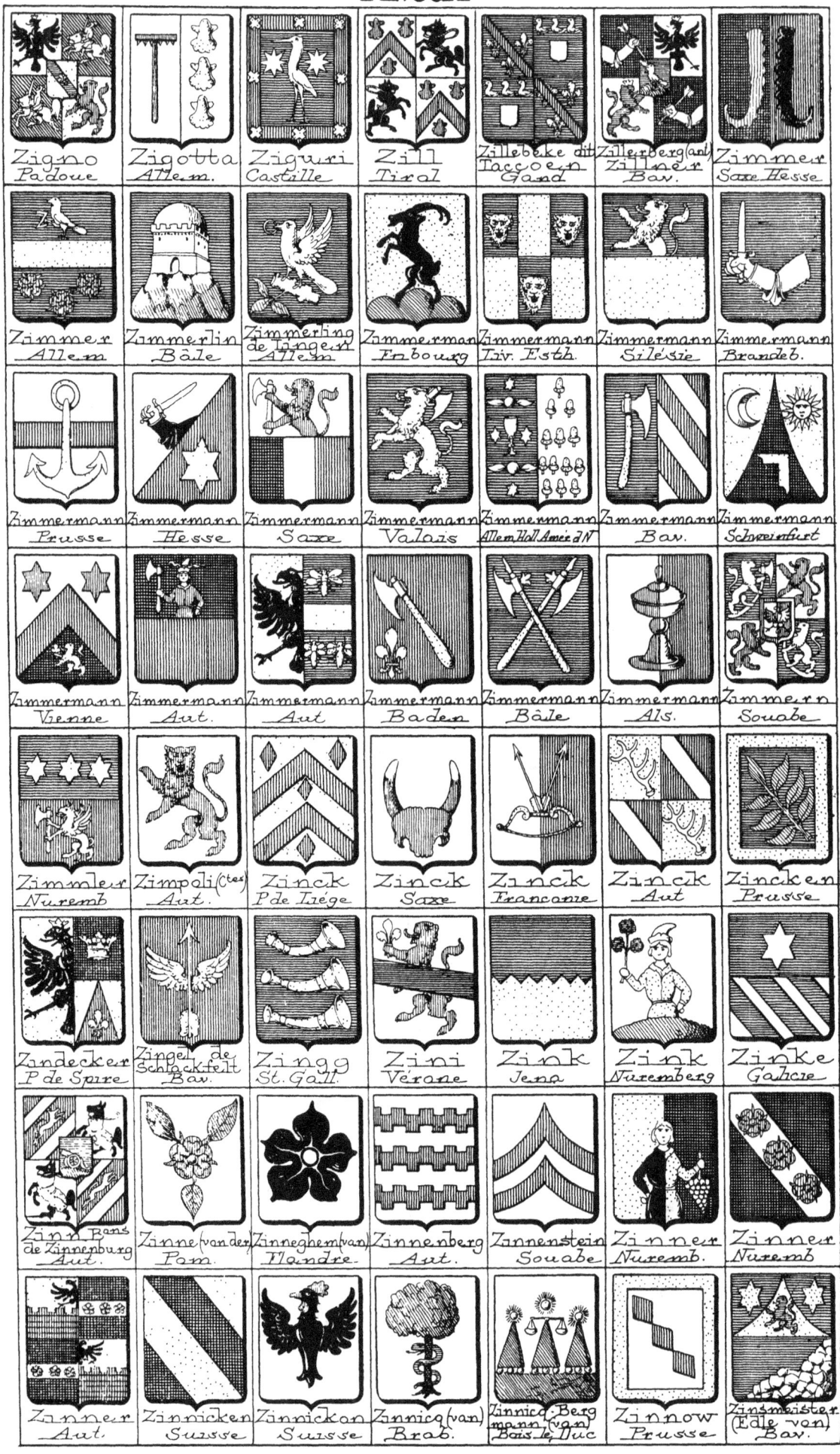

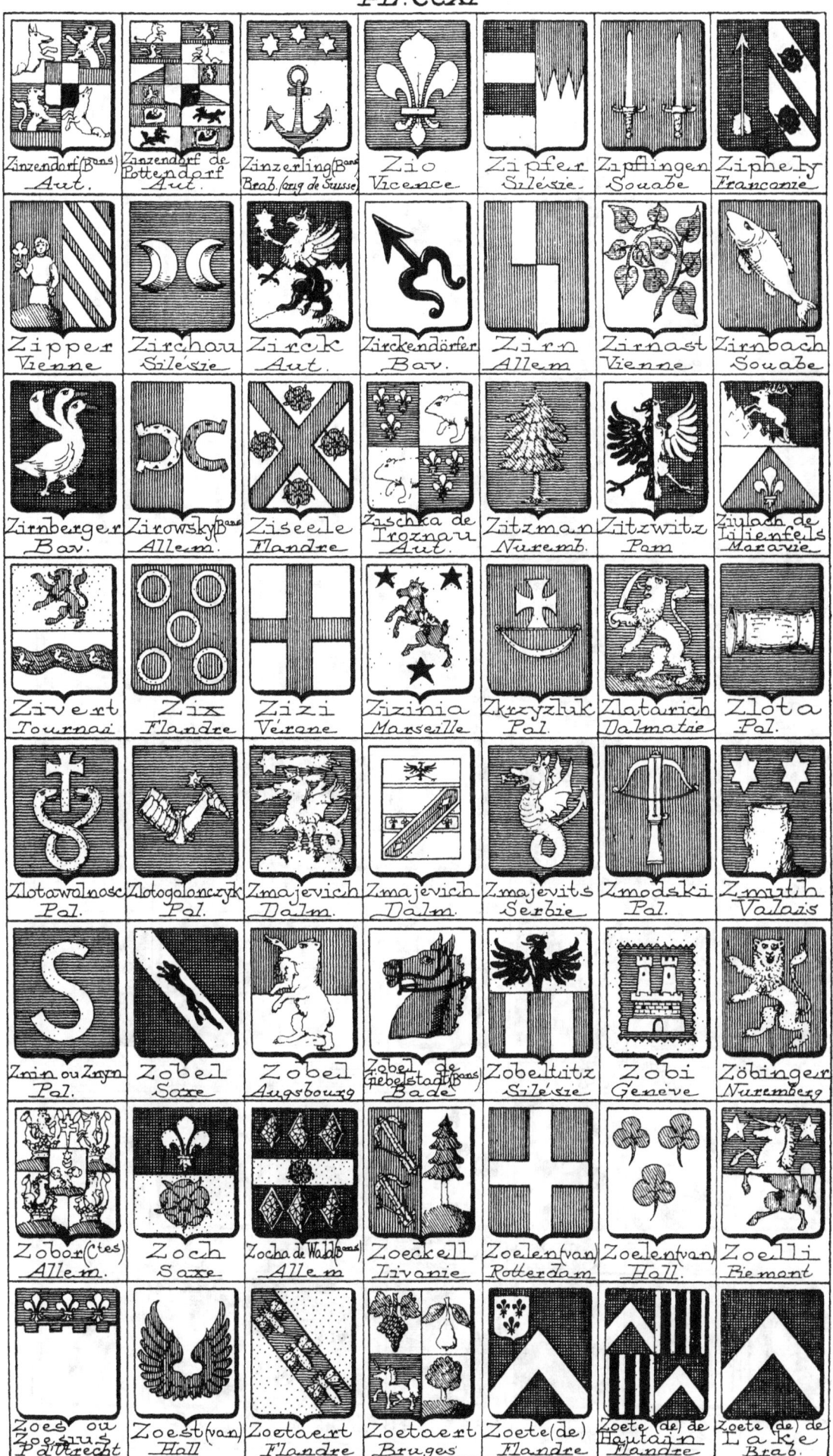

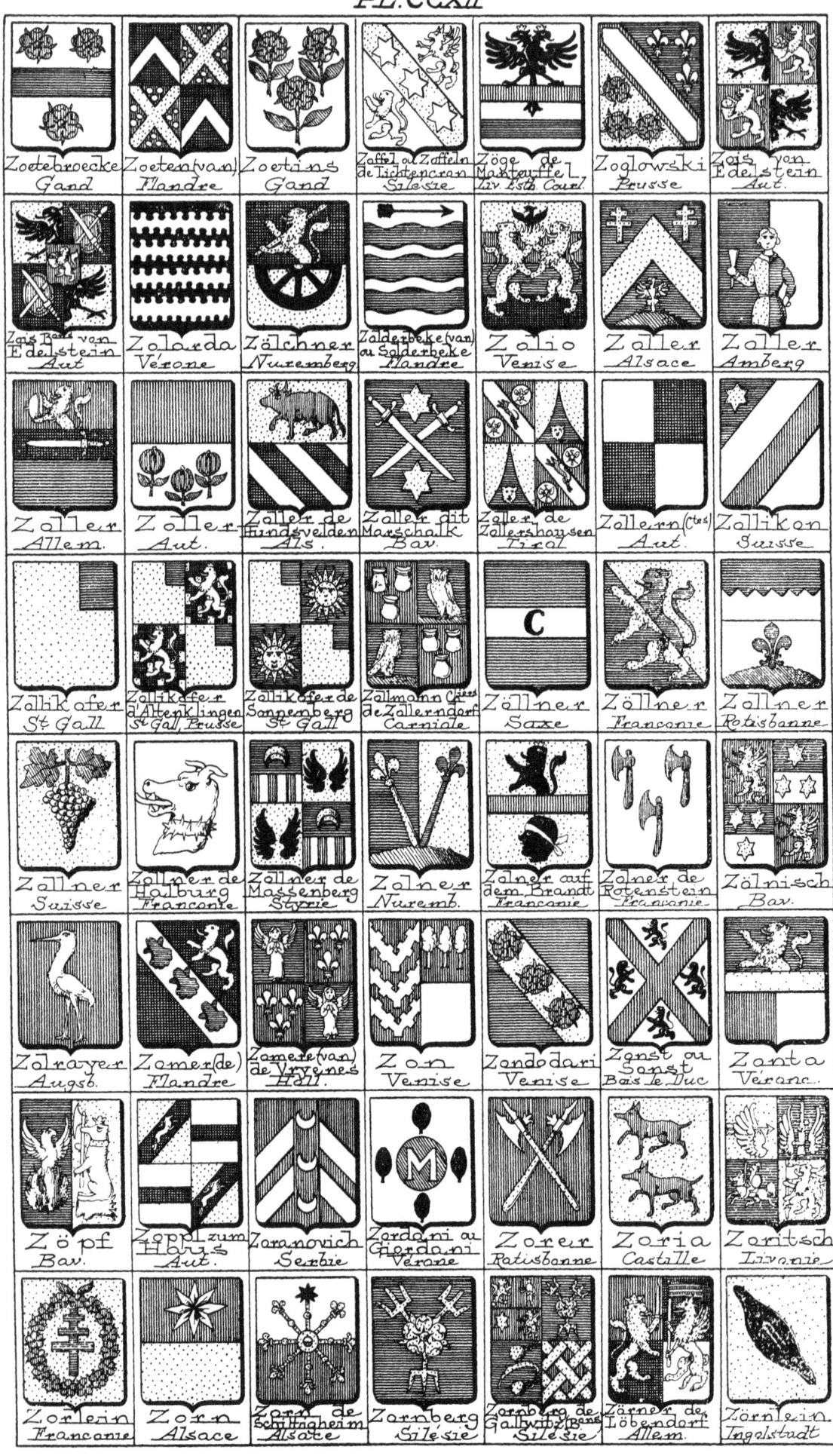

PL. CCXIII

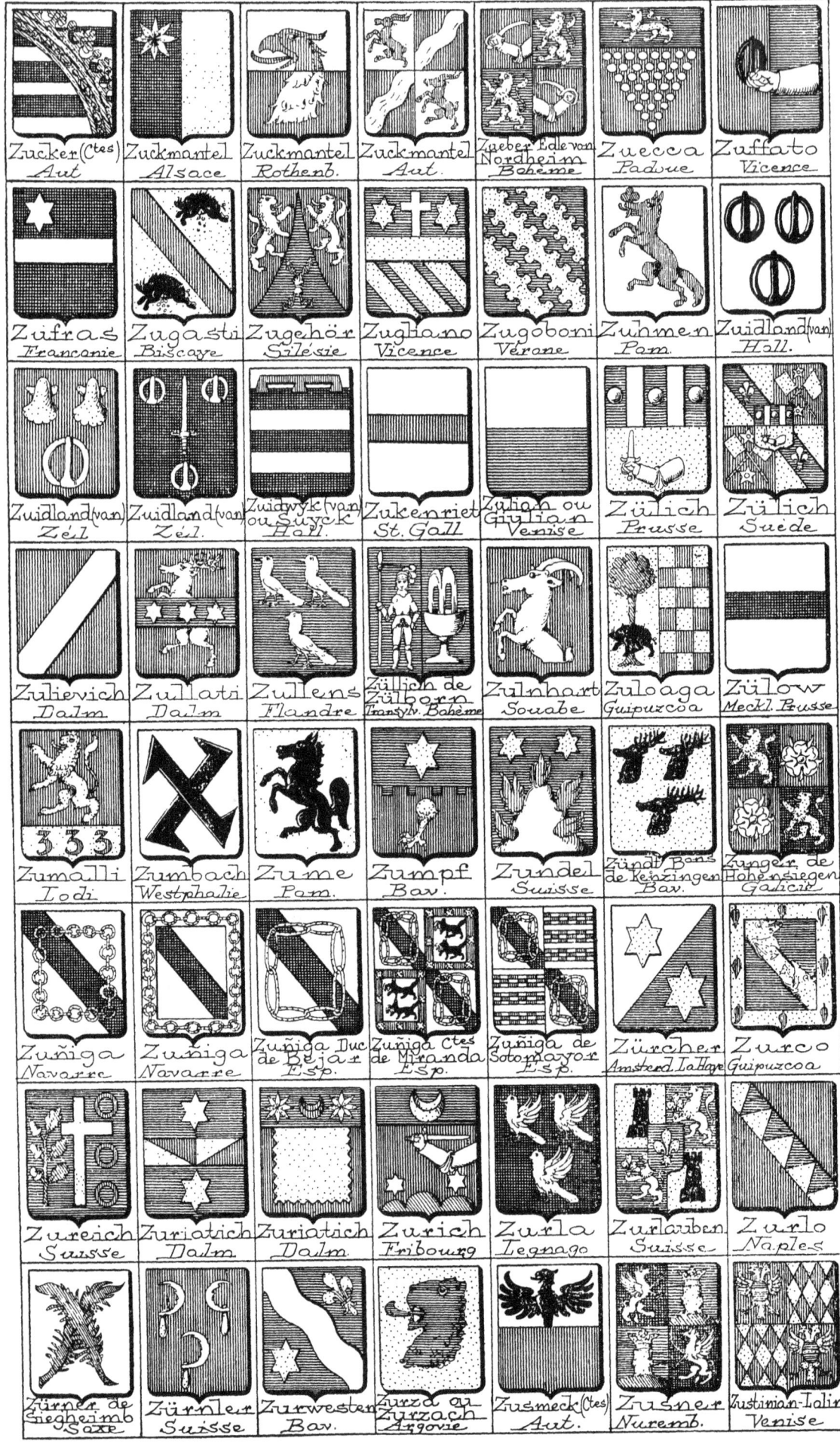

PL. CCXV

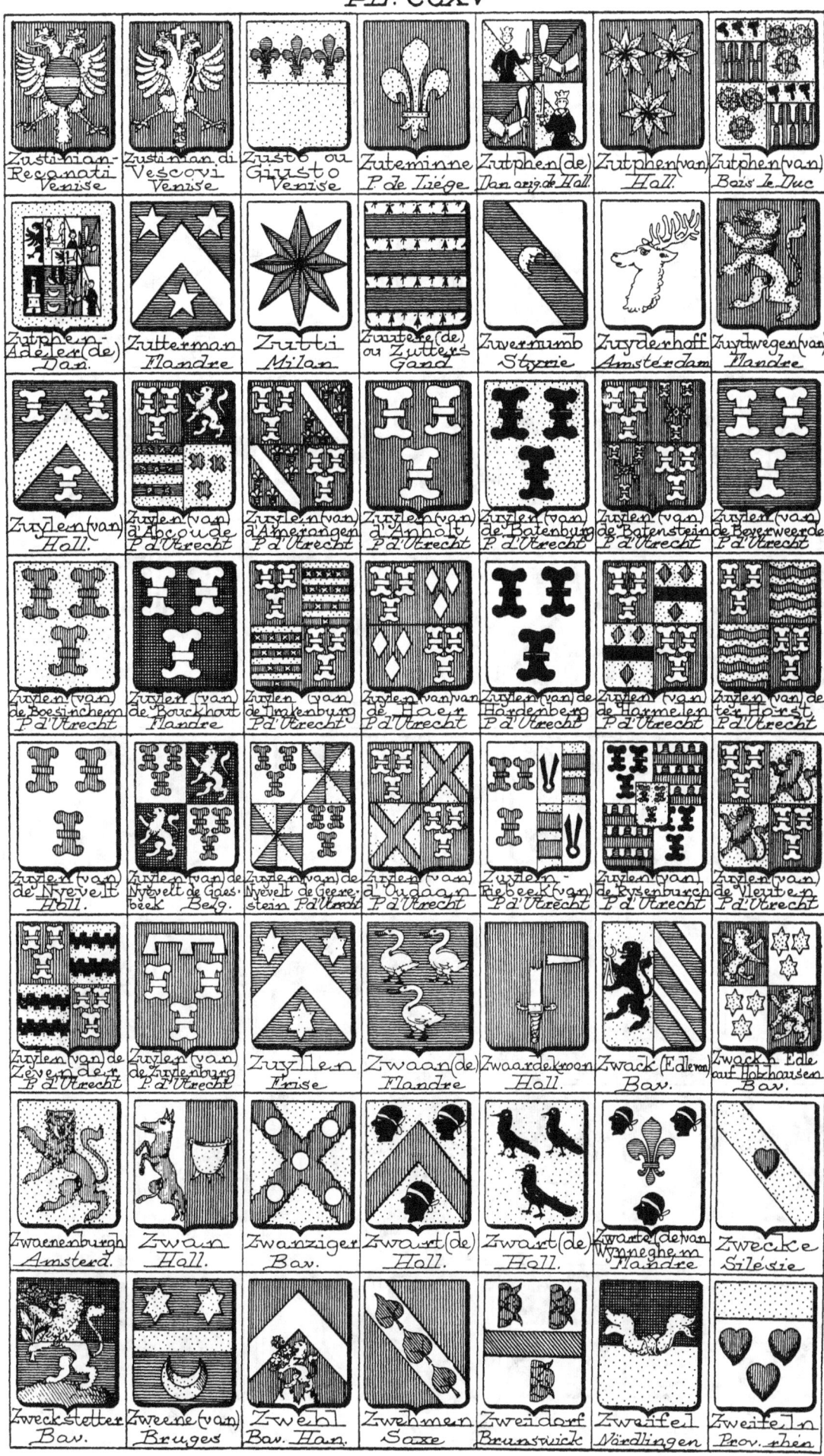

PL. CCXVI

PL. CCXVII

# FIN

OTHER PUBLICATIONS FROM

# HERALDRY TODAY

**BURKE'S GENERAL ARMORY** of England, Scotland, Ireland & Wales. 1884 (Reprint 1984). 60,000 blasons of Family & Civic Arms. cxxx + 1185pp.

**A DICTIONARY OF HERALDRY** by C. N. Elvin. Reprint of the most complete Dictionary of Heraldic Terms, each clearly illustrated, and full index. 238pp.

**ELVIN'S MOTTOES REVISED** with a Supplement and Index by R. Pinches. A new printing, 1987. 308pp. Index of Names. Invaluable in identifying or tracing a motto, choosing a new one, or translating an existing one.

**FAIRBAIRN'S BOOK OF CRESTS** of the Families of Great Britain and Ireland. 1904 (Reprint 1983). 2 vols in one. Over 4,000 illustrations of Crests.

**GALBREATH'S PAPAL HERALDRY** revised by G. R. Briggs. New edition 1972. 8 fine colour plates and 206 black and white illustrations. 256pp.

**BIBLIOTHECA HERALDICA MAGNAE BRITANNIAE** by Thomas Moule. Reprint of the only comprehensive Bibliography of heraldry, genealogy, nobility, knighthood & ceremonies, 1469-1821. 692pp

**PAPWORTH'S ORDINARY OF BRITISH ARMORIALS.** Alphabetical Dictionary of Arms arranged under charges which enables coats of arms to be identified. 1874, Reprint 1977 with a new introduction by J. Brooke-Little. xxii + 1125pp.

**THE ROYAL HERALDRY OF ENGLAND** by J. H. & R. V. Pinches Arms of all the English Royal Family lines down to grandchildren of Sovereigns. Splendidly illustrated, 9 colour plates and 258 black and white illustrations. 35 pedigrees. 352pp.

**A EUROPEAN ARMORIAL** by R. Pinches & A. Wood. An Armorial of Knights of the Golden Fleece from 15th century manuscript. Fine colour plates & illustrations. 222pp.

**NEW EXTINCT PEERAGE** by L. G. Pine. Extinct, Dormant, Abeyant & Suspended. 1884-1971. Brings Burke's work up to date. Arms & pedigrees. Illustrations. 368pp.

**SCOTTISH BURGH & COUNTY HERALDRY** by R. M. Urquhart. The Blazons and illustrations of all Burgh & County Arms and the reasons for their adoption. 296pp.

**HERALDS OF ENGLAND** by A. R. Wagner. A History of the Office & College of Arms. Royal 4to. xxvi + 609pp. Magnificent full page plates, 13 in colour. Index. 400 copies only of 1986 edition.

www.ingramcontent.com/pod-product-compliance
Lightning Source LLC
Chambersburg PA
CBHW080835010526
44114CB00017B/2310